Quantitative Sociology

International Perspectives on Mathematical
and Statistical Modeling

QUANTITATIVE STUDIES IN SOCIAL RELATIONS

Consulting Editor: Peter H. Rossi

UNIVERSITY OF MASSACHUSETTS
AMHERST, MASSACHUSETTS

Quantitative Sociology

International Perspectives on Mathematical and Statistical Modeling

Edited by

H. M. Blalock
and
A. Aganbegian
F. M. Borodkin
Raymond Boudon
Vittorio Capecchi

ACADEMIC PRESS INC., NEW YORK SAN FRANCISCO LONDON 1975
A Subsidiary of Harcourt Brace Jovanovich, Publishers

ACADEMIC PRESS RAPID MANUSCRIPT REPRODUCTION

ACADEMIC PRESS, INC.
111 Fifth Avenue, New York, New York 10003

United Kingdom Edition published by
ACADEMIC PRESS, INC. (LONDON) LTD.
24/28 Oval Road, London NW1

Library of Congress Cataloging in Publication Data
Main entry under title:

Quantitative sociology.

    (Quantitative studies in social relations)
    Bibliography: p.
    Includes index.
    1.   Sociology—Mathematical models—Addresses,
essays, lectures.   I.   Blalock, Hubert M.
HM24.Q36   301′.01′51   75-20142
ISBN 0–12–103950–1

Contents

PART I: CAUSAL ANALYSIS, STRUCTURE, AND CHANGE

PART II: DESIGN, MEASUREMENT, AND CLASSIFICATION

v

List of Editors and Contributors

A. Aganbegian, Institute of Economics and Industrial Engineering, Siberian Department of the U.S.S.R. Academy of Sciences, Novosibirsk, U.S.S.R.

H. M. Blalock, Department of Sociology, University of Washington, Seattle, Washington

Gerhard Bonelli, Institute of Sociology, University of Vienna, Vienna, Austria

F. M. Borodkin, Institute of Economics and Industrial Engineering, Siberian Department of the U.S.S.R. Academy of Sciences, Novosibirsk, U.S.S.R.

Raymond Boudon, Professor of Sociology, The Sorbonne and the Université René Descartes, Paris, France

Vittorio Capecchi, University of Bologna, Bologna, Italy

František Charvát, Deputy Director, Institute for Philosophy and Sociology, Czechoslovak Academy of Sciences, Prague, Czechoslovakia

James S. Coleman, Department of Sociology, University of Chicago, Chicago, Illinois

Otis Dudley Duncan, Department of Sociology, The University of Arizona, Tucson, Arizona

Johan Galtung, Professor, Conflict and Peace Research, University of Oslo, Oslo, Norway

Iu. N. Gavrilets, Central Economic—Mathematical Institute of the U.S.S.R. Academy of Sciences, Moscow, U.S.S.R.

Nils Petter Gleditsch, Research Fellow, International Peace Research Institute, Oslo, Norway

Tord Høivik, Research Fellow, International Peace Research Institute, Oslo, Norway

Nathan Keyfitz, Departments of Demography and Sociology, Harvard University, Cambridge, Massachusetts

Leslie Kish, Professor and Research Scientist, Survey Research Center, Institute for Social Research, The University of Michigan, Ann Arbor, Michigan

Jaroslav Kučera, Institute for Philosophy and Sociology, Czechoslovak Academy of Sciences, Prague, Czechoslovakia

Kenneth C. Land, Department of Sociology, University of Illinois at Urbana-Champaign, Urbana, Illinois

Roger Malm, Department of Human Geography, University of Göteborg, Göteborg, Sweden

B. G. Mirkin, Institute of Economics and Industrial Engineering, Siberian Department of the U.S.S.R. Academy of Sciences, Novosibirsk, U.S.S.R.

Frank Möller, University of Milan, Milan, Italy

Stefan Nowak, Department of Sociology, University of Warsaw, Warsaw, Poland

Gunnar Olsson, Department of Geography, University of Michigan, Ann Arbor, Michigan

Kullervo Rainio, Institute of Social Psychology, Helsinki University, Helsinki, Finland

Robert Reichardt, Institute of Sociology, University of Vienna, Vienna, Austria

B. Schmeikal, Stanislasgasse 2/15, Vienna, Austria (formerly, Institute of Sociology, University of Vienna)

Patrick Suppes, Institute for Mathematical Studies in the Social Sciences, Stanford University, Stanford, California

I. N. Taganov, Lensoviet Technological Institute of Leningrad, Leningrad, U.S.S.R.

Olof Wärneryd, Professor of Human Geography, University of Lund, Lund, Sweden

Herman Wold, Department of Statistics, University of Göteborg, Göteborg, Sweden

N. G. Zagoruiko, The State University of Novosibirsk, Novosibirsk, U.S.S.R.

T. I. Zaslavskaia, Institute of Economics and Industrial Engineering, Siberian Department of the U.S.S.R. Academy of Sciences, Novosibirsk, U.S.S.R.

Preface To English-Language Edition

This volume had its beginnings at the meetings of the International Sociological Association in Varna, Bulgaria during the summer of 1970. The editors, along with others who attended the sessions on methodology and mathematical modeling, recognized the serious need for increased cross-national communication in quantitative sociology and related social sciences. We therefore decided to edit a special volume that would appear in at least two languages, English and Russian, and hopefully several others.

It is, of course, impossible to select materials that are in any real sense representative or typical of work being done in any given country or region. Nor are there distinct "schools" of thought that can be delineated, a fact that may possibly distinguish methodological and mathematical research from other kinds of sociological literatures. It therefore seemed wise to set up a regional division of labor among the editors. Boudon and Capecchi took the major responsibility for locating papers written by Eastern and Western Europeans and selected a number of papers that have previously been published under their editorship in the European methodology journal, *Quality and Quantity* Aganbegian and Borodkin selected five papers from the U.S.S.R., and Blalock took the responsibility for soliciting papers by American sociologists. But, interestingly enough, it was the Russian editors who suggested that we contact Patrick Suppes, the American philosopher and mathematical psychologist, and Blalock who initially contacted Herman Wold, the Swedish statistician and econometrician.

Although this volume contains contributions from both Eastern and Western Europe, the U.S.S.R. and the United States, we cannot, of course, claim that it is truly international in flavor, since a very large portion of the countries of the world are not represented. However we hope that this initial effort will stimulate other groups to bring together works of scholars with whom the present editors are unfamiliar. The primary goal of this volume is to present a sufficiently coherent and potentially interrelated set of papers which give tangible evidence that scientific research in the social sciences, as well as the physical sciences, can profit considerably through exchanges of ideas across political and ideological boundaries.

The social sciences in general, and sociology in particular, are characterized by an extreme diversity of theoretical perspectives, foci of interest, and variables thought to be relevant in any given context. Clearly, the processes we attempt to explain are highly complex as compared with those that are often analyzed in terms of mathematical models. This implies that we must be either highly selective with respect to the processes being subjected to mathematical formulation, or we must find ways of reducing excessive quantities of data to manageable proportions. It also implies that our mathematical tools must be flexible enough to handle a wide variety of complications that need to be considered if we are to extend our models so as to approximate the real world to a reasonable degree.

In doing so, we are obviously handicapped by the absence of any high degree of consensus on reasonably precise verbal theories or paradigms that can easily be transformed into more rigorous mathematical formulations. There is, in fact, considerable disagreement among social scientists as to what the most important variables are that need to be included in these theories. Therefore there is a wide range of variables and assumptions from which to select. When we add to this the fact that many variables we would *like* to include may not be measured easily and that the necessary data are often not available for one reason or another, it becomes clear that our mathematical formulations must ideally allow for omitted variables, specification errors, and measurement errors. This implies that our mathematical models must generally be stochastic in nature, either in terms of their containing explicit assumptions about probability distributions or at least in terms of their requiring statistical tests to evaluate their goodness of fit to fallible data.

It therefore must be expected that there will be a diversity of mathematical modeling procedures involving basically different strategies of attack. Some approaches are extremely general in nature, being designed to handle a wide variety of different kinds of empirical situations, degrees of complexity, and design and data-collection strategies. Certain of these approaches are almost "meta-mathematical" models in the sense that they suggest extremely general ways of conceptualizing or expressing phenomena in mathematical or logical languages. Part I of this volume treats a number of such approaches, which are primarily programmatic in nature. These range from Galtung's discussion of diachronic process analysis, to Suppes's and Nowak's discussions of causation in terms of conditional probabilities, to Borodkin's highly general scheme for formulating causal processes. They also include a graph-theoretical formulation by Høivik and Gleditsch, an approach based on information theory by Taganov, and another highly general scheme by Gavrilets. Part I closes with a more substantively oriented discussion of social dependence by Charvat and Kučera. The common theme running through all of these chapters involves the basic question: How can we discover highly general ways of formulating our substantive problems so as to lend themselves to mathematical formulations, and what are the common properties of these formulations? The general purpose of the chapters in this section, then, is that of orienting the reader to very broad mathematical approaches within which a given concrete application can be formulated.

A second general approach involving mathematical reasoning is much more closely attached to research design, data analysis and reduction, and measurement. Chapters representing this more empirically oriented strategy appear primarily in Part II and are closely linked with conventional fields of applied statistics: experimental designs, survey sampling and panel designs, multivariate analysis, econometrics, multiple classification analysis, and other approaches to data analysis and measurement. The implicit strategy underlying this more empirical approach is that of building theories inductively by means of a continual search for variables that "work," in the sense of explaining a reasonable proportion of the variance, and models that can be demonstrated to provide a close fit between the theory and the data. There is also a concern with eliminating distortions or artifacts of various kinds, such as sampling errors or biases stemming from faulty designs, measurement errors, or incorrectly specified equations. For example, the chapter by Kish deals with the relative strengths and weaknesses of alternative designs, that by Duncan with complications arising from measurement errors in panel designs, and those by Wold and Blalock with models involving combinations of measured and unmeasured variables. The remaining four chapters by Möller and Capecchi, Zagoruiko and Zaslavskaia, Mirkin, and Reichardt and Schmeikal all deal in one way or another with complicated problems involving qualitative data and possible multidimensionality. In an important sense they are concerned with the general problem of data reduction, or that of using mathematical or statistical procedures to simplify a very complex reality.

The chapters in Part III represent still another mathematical strategy, namely that of developing specific models to account for delimited substantive problems. It is this kind of mathematical model building that most closely resembles the much less formal and rigorous processes that we generally associate with theory building in specific substantive areas. The aim is to produce a deductive or semideductive system containing axioms, definitions, and theorems that may then be examined both in terms of internal consistency (using mathematical reasoning) and their ability to explain real-world phenomena. The chapters by Land and Boudon, in this section, illustrate very well the process of moving from relatively simplistic (and unrealistic) models to more complex ones that approximate the real world more closely. Coleman's chapter presents a relatively simple explanatory model for social exchange, whereas that by Rainio involves an extremely general set of definitions and axioms that provide a potential framework for explaining choice behaviors in a variety of contexts. Keyfitz indicates how a formal theory of reproductive value can be applied to several important demographic problems. The final chapter by Malm, Olsson, and Wärneryd employs a much more inductive approach by means of simulation, illustrating the more general point that in situations where it is extremely difficult to employ strictly mathematical models to complex social processes, it is sometimes possible to use simulation techniques in ways that may ultimately lead to sufficient insights to produce more precise formulations.

It is our hope that the reader will find in this diversity of approaches to mathematical and statistical modeling an intellectual challenge to integrate them more closely, to fill in some of the missing links, and to search for new applications. If this volume helps to stimulate such an interest, the editors will have fulfilled their major purpose.

Acknowledgments

We wish to thank the publishers of *Quality and Quantity*, Società editrice il Mulino and Elsevier, for permitting us to publish revised versions of the following papers:

Stefan Nowak, "Causal Interpretations of Statistical Relationships in Social Research," Vol. 1, No. 1-2, January 1967, pp. 53-89;

Roger Malm, Gunnar Olsson, and Olof Wärneryd, "Toward a Simulation of Urban Sprawl," Vol. 3, No. 1-2, January 1969, pp. 176-200;

Johan Galtung, "Diachronic Correlation, Process Analysis and Causal Analysis," Vol. 4, No. 1, June 1970, pp. 55-94;

Tord Høivik and N. P. Gleditsch, "Structural Parameters of Graphs: A Theoretical Investigation," Vol. 4, No. 1, June 1970, pp. 193-209;

F. Charvát and J. Kučera, "On the Theory of Social Dependence," Vol. 4, No. 2, December 1970, pp. 325-353;

R. Reichardt and B. Schmeikal, "Theoretical Considerations and Simulation Models Related to the Method of Sonquist and Morgan," Vol. 7, No. 1, 1973, pp. 171-187.

We are also indebted to the North-Holland Publishing Company for permitting us to publish portions of Patrick Suppes, *A Probabilistic Theory of Causality*, *Acta Philosophica Fennica*, Fasc. XXIV, 1970; and to Gordon and Breach Science Publishers for permitting the use of James S. Coleman's paper, "Systems of Social Exchange," previously published in the *Journal of Mathematical Sociology*, Vol. 2, 1972, pp. 145-163.

Finally, we are especially appreciative of the work of Barbara L. Latimer for her patience and fortitude in typing what turned out to be a very lengthy, difficult and sometimes incomprehensible manuscript, and that of David M. Morris for drawing many of the figures.

I

Causal Analysis,
Structure, and Change

1

Diachronic Correlation, Process Analysis and Causal Analysis *

JOHAN GALTUNG
International Peace Research Institute, Oslo

1. INTRODUCTION

Time has been referred to as the forgotten dimension in contemporary social research, and a cursory perusal of social science journals seems to confirm the impression that the overwhelming majority of the articles are relatively time-free. Or to be more precise: the *data* are time-free in the sense that they refer more or less to the same point in time and usually also are collected at the same time point. *Interpretation,* however, is usually not time-free, but refers to processes and cause-effect relations. And the *findings* are not time-free either. The restriction to one point in time means that there is no replication over time, no test of whether the findings also hold true at other time-points,

*
This is a revised version of a paper delivered as a guest lecture at the Department of Statistics, University of Uppsala on 15 January 1968, at a seminar organized by Social-forskningsinstituttet, Copenhagen on 22 May 1968, at the CENTRO/UNESCO Seminar on Development Sociology in Rio de Janeiro 17 July 1968, and also discussed on other occasions. I am grateful to Professor Herman Wold, Uppsala, and Director Henning Friis, Copenhagen, for arranging excellent discussions, and to many other colleagues, particularly Nils Petter Gleditsch and Tord Høivik, for stimulating comments and criticism. The paper is published here as PRIO-publication no. M-6 from the International Peace Research Institute, Oslo.

i.e. in other contexts, *but this is often pretended.* Or, rather, there is usually no explicit effort to specify the conditions that would nail the findings down to a concrete context, and perhaps also indicate how they might change with changing contexts. Thus, there is a paradox in much of contemporary social research: from time-free data far from time-free implications are drawn, explicitly or implicitly.

This paradox can at least partly be explained by reference to the nature of what many contemporary social scientists refer to as "data." The idea is usually that they should be amenable to some kind of statistical treatment, i.e. that they should fit the form of a data matrix[1] where m units are described in terms of n variables (V) and neither m nor n (particularly not m) are small. Old research traditions with $m=1$ or $n=1$ are usually looked down upon, and there is probably a feeling that for anything to be referred to as a *project m X n* should be at least 1000, whether this means information on ten variables for each of 100 units or information on 100 variables for each of ten units.[2]

This immediately leads to three good reasons why research in this tradition usually is time-free.

First of all, if in addition to m units and n variables there should be o time-points, then the total amount of *work* needed to complete not only the data *matrix,* but the data *box* might easily be prohibitive since the relation is multiplicative, not additive. If for some reason one feels that at least five time points are needed to estimate the trajectory of a unit on one variable, then a typical project would include at least 5000 data elements. It should be pointed out that the reason for this high number is the need to *complete* data matrices and data boxes: the whole analytical tradition breaks down if there are too many empty holes. Even 10% may be too much, particularly if the holes have a tendency to cluster on certain units, certain variables and/ or certain time-point, as they usually do.

Second, if data from more time-points than *now* are wanted, then they must refer to the *past* or to the *future.* But data from the past are either not available because of

---

[1] The data matrix is introduced in Galtung, (1967b) Part I, Chapter 1.

[2] For a discussion of the relative size of m and n, see Galtung (1967b), section 1.2.

incomplete or extremely poor records that are extremely unreliable since they have been recorded for other persons, and
in other contexts, with other definitions of units, variables
and values. There are of course major exceptions to this.
For *accounting* or in general *control* purposes records are
often kept for the major units of social organization, such
as *territories* (municipalities, nations) *organizations*
(farms, firms) and *associations,* giving influx and outflux of
economic value and human beings across the borderlines of the
units. For territorial units these data are even published
as statistical yearbooks but data are also usually available
for many organizations and associations--at least in their
files. That this has stimulated the two social sciences of
economics and demography tremendously is obvious, and there
are definitely still many untapped possibilities in the
fields of micro-economics and micro-demography--focussing on
changes in the economy of organizations and the demography of
associations. But in general data tend to be unavailable far
back in time if one's search is guided by the strong requirement to fill a data box. And statistical analyses of incomplete data that are not time-free have not yet penetrated
into the "softer" social sciences.

Third, if instead of extracting data from the *past* one
wants to compensate for this by waiting for processes to unfold themselves and record the *future* at the moment when it
becomes part of the *present,* one may have to wait for a long
time. Many social processes at the macro level need time to
exhibit interesting dynamism, and the time needed may by far
exceed the requirements for rapid information diffusion or
rapid career promotion, based on publication. This may of
course lead to efforts to speed up the process (simulation,
experiments in general) or to wait for an occasion where the
system undergoes a dramatic transition.[3] But the former
strategy is dubious because of doubts about the validity and
isomorphism in general, and the latter is dubious because it
leads to an oversampling of the dramatic and discontinuous
and a corresponding underrepresentation of the statistically
normal--much like the pattern found in traditional news communication.[4]

---

[3] Methods of obtaining diachronic data are to some extent discussed in Galtung (1967b), pp. 475 ff.

[4] For an effort to systematize characteristic features of news
communications, see Galtung and Ruge, (1965).

Thus, it is difficult to extend a data matrix to a data box. Modern survey methods, content analyses, etc., not to mention computers, have enabled social scientists (1) to work with matrices with high number of units and variables, with m X n well beyond 10^6; (2) to obtain relatively complete and reliable data; and (3) not only to obtain data contained in the records mentioned above for territories, organizations and associations--but also at the level of individuals and any kind of small group consisting of individuals. Thus, the social sciences dealing with micro phenomena have been developed on the basis of synchronic data with an almost explosive growth in data collection methods. Thus, *the desire to be nomothetic has led to a restriction to be synchronic, it seems.*

In this process the type of time data usually found in historical analyses, based on highly incomplete data boxes where data elements are picked from various corners and parts of the data box, or the researcher is carried to the data by the limitations of his sources, do not lend themselves easily to nomothetic research. The data are not systematic or really complete enough. One cannot compare nations, say, because data have been collected for different units, different variables and different time-points for different nations; and one cannot compare inside nations because different variables and different time-points both in terms of chronological and social time so often are used for different units. *Hence, the desire to be diachronic has almost forced historians into an ideographic position*[5]--completing the polarization relative to sociologists, social psychologists and psychologists. And, as is well known, this has the highly undesirable consequence that the two brands of social scientists to some extent have been blocked off from each other's insights. And this is even more dangerous since the polarization is also along the micro-macro axis.

The remedy for this situation seems not to be to fight against the nomothetic/synchronic or ideographic/diachronic combinations, but rather to develop something new, to move more towards nomothetic/diachronic social science. This will probably not be a synthesis of history and sociology, since problems can be raised and even be answered within the framework presented by the nomothetic/diachronic combination

---

[5]In Galtung (1968) arguments are given why the desire to be ideographic almost forced historians into a diachronic position.

that could not easily be located in the other two. Rather, it will probably serve as *a new departure for social science,* absorbing elements of history and sociology; in other words, it will be a medium where older research tradition can meet and to some extent be absorbed. But how this can be done is by no means clear and the following is little but some efforts to draw the contours of this type of social science with an indication of the kind of problems it raises and answers it may yield to old problems.

2. SOME DIACHRONIC DESIGNS

Imagine we have a data-matrix based on m units and n variables.

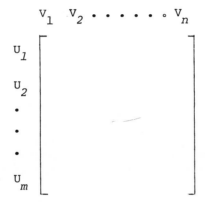

Fig. 1. THE SYNCHRONIC DATA MATRIX

As this is usually conceived, the m units are observed/ measured more or less at the same time with regard to the n characteristics, yielding the $m \times n$ values to be recorded in the matrix. If the values happen to be recorded at different points in time this is considered immaterial and due to administrative reasons mainly (one cannot ask all questions of all subjects at the same time). In more sophisticated re-search it is recognized that time may play a role even if the time interval between the first and the last observation is short (relative to the time intervals needed for the pro-cesses one is studying to unfold themselves), and efforts are made to control for this impact, for instance by randomizing the order in which subjects and/or questions are asked (if one is dealing with a survey).

But time does not enter systematically, as an independ-ent variable in the design above. Since this article has to

do with ways of including time systematically in social
science investigations, both in data-collection, data-
processing, data-analysis and theory-formation, the first
task is to look at different ways in which time can be built
into the data matrix.

There are three such designs, here compared with the
basic, synchronic design in Figure 1:

TABLE 1. A SURVEY OF DESIGNS

Design	Term	No. of units	No. of variables	No. of time-points
O	*Synchronic*	Several	Several	One
1	*Diachronic,* *one* variable	Several	One	Several
2	*Diachronic* *one unit*	One	Several	Several
3	*Complete*	Several	Several	Several

(In addition to these four combinations there are also three
combinations with only one "several" and an eighth combination with no "several" at all--but all these four designs are
so truncated that they do not belong within a nomothetic
tradition).

The representations as data matrices would look as
follows.

Design 1

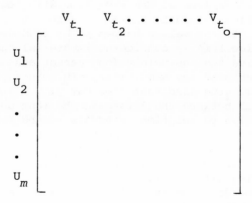

Design 2

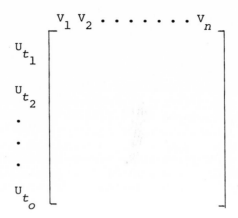

Design 3

$$\{u_i, v_j\}_{t_1}, \{u_i, v_j\}_{t_2} \cdots \cdots \{u_i, v_j\}_{t_o}$$

FIG. 2. THE THREE DIACHRONIC DESIGNS AS DATA MATRICES

Thus in design 1 the single variable is replicated through time; in design 2 the single unit is replicated through time; and in design 3 the entire synchronic matrix is replicated through time. The immediate reaction to this exercise may certainly be that this is trivial. But first of all, the three forms are different in content, and secondly: the purely formal presentation does matter psychologically since it may suggest one form of analysis to the exclusion of others.

Obviously, the complete design, no. 3, is the ideal and can be represented by a box with *m* units, *n* variables and *o* time-points. Design zero, then, is a synchronic cut of this box in the U, V-plane for a chosen value of *t*; design 1 is a diachronic cut of the box in the *t*, U plane for a chosen variable V and design 2 is a diachronic cut of the box in the *t*, V plane for a chosen unit U. Thus, design 3 may be seen as a replication not only of the synchronic design in time, but also of design 1 on the variable side and design 2 on the unit side. Since the other three designs can be derived from design 3 (but not vice-versa--for design 3 (*m.n.o*) values are needed whereas the other three together presuppose *mn+on+mo* values), why not always have data of the form 3

9

type? For the simple reason mentioned above and that any data
administrator knows: the data do not exist in ready-made form,
and to make them available requires considerable expenses in
terms of time, energy, and money. Hence, we are in general
referred to designs 1 or 2 if we want to work with time.
Whether to choose designs 1 or 2 depends, of course, on the
purpose. Design 1 is best for *nomothetic* research, since the
idea here is that several units are followed through time,
but only on one selected variable--for instance *nations* on
life expectancy, or on the diffusion of TV ownership, or
individuals on attitude, for instance party preference.
Where the latter example is concerned the design is often
referred to as a *panel* study (since the same individuals are
asked repeatedly, like a panel in a debate), and each set of
observations (for each time-point) is referred to as a *wave*.
Often $o=2$, and in that case time possibilities of analysis
are relatively limited, unless the two time-points are located before and after a crucial event.

Design 2 is correspondingly best for *ideographic* research, since the idea is that one unit is traced on several
variables through time. This is essentially what an histor-
ian (at the level of societies) or a biographer (at the
level of individuals) would do anyhow, although in general
less systematically in the sense that he might not try to
complete the entire data-matrix for design 2 in Figure 2.

In the general theory of data matrices the distinction
has been made between horizontal and vertical analyses, and
it may be worthwhile just to see where these two concepts
lead us in this connection. The results are put in tabular
form in Table 2.

TABLE 2. THE MEANING OF HORIZONTAL AND VERTICAL ANALYSIS
FOR DIACHRONIC DESIGNS

	Horizontal analysis	Vertical analysis
Design 1:		
Several units, one variable	rows called *trajectories*	columns called *distributions* with *parameters*
Design 2:		
one unit, several vari- ables	rows called *patterns* with *indices*	columns called *trajectories*

In synchronic analysis the distinction was between *distributions* and *patterns* (Galtung, 1967b, pp. 178 ff), in diachronic analysis the pattern for the same unit over time on one (or more) variable(s) is called a *trajectory*. All three are sets of comparable values.[6] If the dispersion is zero in a distribution then the units are *homogeneous;* if the dispersion is zero in a pattern then the unit is *balanced,* and if the dispersion is zero in a trajectory, then the unit is *stable*. With all three conditions satisfied at the same time the system would be highly monotonous--much like a Utopia where the assumption often is that human beings are basically *similar* (homogeneity), *consistent* (balance) and *constant* (stability).

This is also rather trivial, the point is merely that one has to make up one's mind in advance as to what one wants so as to be sure to collect the right data. Again, design 1 yields a *parameter,* typical of *nomothetic* analysis, and design 2 yields an *index,* which is a typical desideratum in an *ideographic* analysis. Both yield trajectories, which can also be expressed numerically in manners to be discussed below.

3. SAMPLING FOR DIACHRONIC ANALYSIS

The two designs with one unit, or with one variable, should only be seen as illustrations of the basic principles of diachronic analysis. For diachronic analysis, in order to be of real value, will usually have to be more comprehensive than indicated in designs 1 and 2, but not quite as extensive as design 3 indicates. In other words, *some* limitations will have to be placed on either *m, n,* or *o*. None of them shall be reduced to *one,* since that brings us back to the simpler designs already discussed. But for at least one of them "several" will have to be interpreted as "few" rather than as "many." This gives us three possibilities, all of them truncated versions of the ideal but rather expensive design 3. We arrive at these possibilities by reducing design 3, but not quite as far as down to designs 2, 1 and 0, where there is only *one* unit, *one* variable and *one* time-point respectively.

a. *Few rather than one or many units.* In this case the *units* have to be well selected, and the general methodological prescriptions in connection with comparative analysis are,

---

[6]This presupposes, of course, that the variables are measured in comparable units.

mutatis mutandis, valid.[7] Thus, the sampling will have to be systematic. The units should not only be selected because there happens to be a research institute located in one unit, data available from a second unit and so on--unless the purpose is purely exploratory. If the purpose is to generalize some of the insights gained about processes, and big random samples are excluded, then systematic samples with one or preferably two units from each cell in a factorial design spanning the most important independent variables that describe the units should be obtained. Thus, if the purpose is a study of nations "development level" might be one important variable, and a second might be "political orientation." If both are trichotomies the design would lead to a sample of at least 9, preferably 18. If this cannot be obtained, then one should rather renounce a design based on *two* variables and try to sample along *one* very well chosen and highly important dimension. In that case one should have at least four or five units well spread out on that dimension, to permit systematic testing of hypotheses about the effect of the sampling dimension.

b. *Few rather than one or many variables.* In this case the *variables* have to be well selected, and it is generally a good idea to select one on the independent side and one on the dependent side so that the interplay between them can be studied over time. A typical problem that can only be studied diachronically is the precise nature of the impact the independent variable has on the dependent variable over time. Synchronic studies can only lead to the trite conclusion "the more X, the more Y," and they may also conclude that the relation is curvilinear--e.g., that the only combination excluded by data is "X low, Y high." Such a synchronic finding would indicate that there is a lead or lag operating. Thus it may look as if there has to be a *quantitative* accumulation in X before there is a change in Y (which would then amount to a *qualitative* change in the total system), in other words some kind of *dialectical change* rather than simple *cumulative change.*[8] Diachronic studies can give us some insights into

---

[7] For an explanation of some of these problems, see Galtung (1967a), pp. 1-19.

[8] Thus, this may be one possible way of expressing aspects of one of the three dialectical principles in a langugage more familiar to researchers in the positivist tradition.

the precise nature of the lag or lead (depending on how one looks at it) and how much quantitative changes have to accumulate before there is a qualitative transition.

c. *Few rather than one or many time-points*. In this case the *time-points* have to be well selected and if they are only two they should, of course, be in accordance with the rules of the classical before-after designs.[9] This design is, actually, easily obtained simply by replication of an already existing study, for in a quickly changing world any study will always be a "before-study," and there will always be a chance of making an "after-study" if only sufficient records have been kept about the methods of the first study to give the formula for replication. On the other hand, as mentioned above, even though this would be the only rational way of using designs with $o=2$, it should be emphasized how the location of time-points on both sides of discontinuous changes will tend to over-dramatize the image presented of social reality. Equally important would be more studies of "normal" trajectories, and for this purpose at least four or five time-points would be needed, preferably much more.

Thus, we have now indicated some compromise designs, less extensive than the full fledged design 3, but more extensive than designs 1 and 2, and this extends the range of possibilities considerably. The question now is: how can diachronic data, i.e. data where $o > 2$, be processed and analyzed, and how do these possibilities feed back to the selection of design for a given problem? This can best be explored by discussing some basic forms of diachronic analysis, based on *one* variable and *two* variables, respectively.[10]

---

[9] Few people have described these designs as well as Stouffer (1962).

[10] The literature in the field of time series is not necessarily so useful since it does not, in general, deal with the problems of the softer social sciences, since it makes too many and too hard assumptions about the structure of the data, and since it is often more concerned with the solution of mathematical than substantive problems. However, Davis, (1941) contains much material of interest to the sociologist, social psychologist and psychologist. Other important works in the field are Ivakhnenko and Lapa (1964); Freeman (1965), and Hannan (1960).

4. UNIVARIATE DIACHRONIC ANALYSIS

The simplest point of departure for analysis using one variable, i.e. univariate diachronic analysis, or UDA for short, would be to detach a row from design 1 (Figure 2) or a column from design 2. This would yield a simple time series (t_i, x_i), giving for each time-point t_1, t_2, ... t_o the value of the chosen variable X, for the chosen unit U. This can then be represented in a simple two-dimensional diagram as a set of points and if X is an interval scale, each point may be meaningfully connected with the preceding and subsequent points by a straight line. For such series or trajectories a number of models are available, such as linear, logarithmic and logistic[11] growth models, and the degree of empirical confirmation can be evaluated.

The picture becomes more complicated when we want to include more of the data matrix. Since we are here concerned with one variable only, design 2 has nothing more to offer, but from design 1 there are more data to include (in principle all *m* rows). More concretely, how does one extend UDA analysis from one unit to two or more units? We assume that the variable is the same for all units, and can, of course, plot the (*t*, X) relation in the (*t*, X)-diagram separately for each unit. The result will be a set of trajectories and the interest will, of course, focus on similarities and dissimilarities between the trajectories. Thus, do the processes follow a common pattern, for instance a logistic law? Are there other important similarities between units following the same law?

There are many techniques available to answer this question, and one of them might be about as follows. The univariate analyses for each unit separately usually cannot be compared directly because the processes relate differently to the time dimension. Thus there is no reason to expect in general that the "take-off point" (however that may be

---

[11] This particular model is due to Verhulst, who studied growth phenomena under the assumption that the rate of growth was proportionate not only to the proportion that had already changed so far, but also to the proportion that could still change. For social phenomena one can imagine many other models, and it is interesting to spell them out in terms of social structure since there are obviously assumptions of a structural nature behind them. The research tradition associated with the name of James Coleman is extremely valuable in this field.

defined) should be the same point in time for each unit, nor is there any reason to expect that the same unit of time should be accompanied with the same amount of change for all units. Some units "start later" than others, some units change "more quickly" than others. In short: *social* time is not the same as *chronological time*. Hence, the first task must be to express the time series for the units relative to a comparable time dimension, to social time and not to chronological time.

This may be done by estimating the parameters of a regression curve of a given family (for instance, linear, logarithmic, logistic) in the (t, X)-diagram that best approximates the trajectory for each unit, and then transform the parameters of the idealized trajectories for each unit to a common basis. Intuitively one may perhaps require of these transformations that they should be linear in t so that they can be easily interpreted as *change of reference point* and *change of time unit,* and the whole operation would gain considerably if the relative location of the zero-points in social time on the chronological time dimension, as well as the relative size of the time units, could be related meaningfully (and with relatively high correlations) to other properties of the units.

Once the transformations have been performed a new diagram can be made showing the location of the trajectories in the (t^*, X)-diagram where t^* is social time. The empirical trajectories have now been made as similar to each other as possible using the transformations needed for the idealized trajectories to coincide. The method depends on the model; without a model of some kind no transformation would be possible--as a minimum simple linear regression must be used.[12] For this transformed scatter we would now recommend the use of correlation techniques to arrive at a measure of how closely the units follow the same posited relation between social time and X (which, for instance, is a rate in the population of the country-units). We shall refer to this correlation as $C(t^*, X)$. Ordinary interval-scale correlation techniques can often be used since the dependent variables in these analyses usually are interval scale variables (e.g., percentages expressing rates). But in general one should use

---

[12] A typical example would be the diagrams frequently encountered in the research tradition established by W. Rostow in his theory of stages of economic growth: time series for countries are superimposed on each other, but using different zero-points, and often also different units.

correlation ratios rather than correlation coefficients since
the (t^*, X)-relation is usually not linear. Thus, it may not
even be monotone, as in business cycle analyses, and this can
be studied by studying whether the derivative of the regression curve changes sign. What the correlation parameter
would do would as usual be to divide the variation in X into
two parts, that which is due to the "patterned variation" of
X with t^* and that which can--relative to the model chosen--
be referred to as "erratic variation."

The correlation parameter can also be meaningfully
calculated for the original (t, X)-diagrams for each single
unit, and for the total system of superimposed units. But
the *individual* correlation parameters will probably be less
interesting as a general expression of what one may expect
for a given unit in, say, take-off position. The correlations should be compared and be related to other properties
of the units in question, but only the correlation parameter
based on a *larger number* of units will tell us something
about how strongly we shall believe in our own model when
encountering a new unit. On the other hand, if we know more
properties of the unit it would be wise to look at the correlations for the units in the sample that are most similar
to the new unit, since they will presumably yield better
bases for predictions.

Thus, UDA analysis should, in principle, be able to
handle some of the questions we are led into if we have data
of the type given in design 1:   data about several units,
but only on one variable--through time. They lend themselves
to nomothetic analysis, but only after some transformations
have been carried out on the time dimension. And these
transformations are by no means unproblematic, since they
(1) presuppose that we have a reasonably good model, and
(2) (although this requirement would seem less mandatory to
many) presuppose that the transformations needed to compare
units can be interpreted meaningfully in terms of other
properties of the units.

5. BIVARIATE DIACHRONIC ANALYSIS

The study of relative growth rates

We now turn to the problems posed by design 2, where
there is only one unit, but more than one variable. The
simplest extension of UDA would be to time series analyses of
two variables, and the method we are developing will be referred to as *bivariate diachronic analysis,* or BDA for short.

This poses a number of problems, much more complicated than the problems in connection with UDA, and these problems are complicated further when we extend the analysis to comprise more than one unit and more than two variables.

We assume that we have, for the same unit, two time series (t_i, X_i) and (t_i, Y_i), and we are interested in "how they relate to each other." This vague expression must first be made more precise: we want to know something about the *relative growth rate*. Thus, in a given time interval, does the relative growth rate remain constant, or does it change, and if it changes, is the growth predominantly in X or in Y or is there no clear pattern? This question should not be confused with questions about causation, although it comes close, as we shall elaborate later in this chapter. The problem is simply this: from UDA analysis we know the growth (or, generally, change) pattern for X and Y separately. We now want to study the joint growth pattern in order to be able to absorb, in any theory, more complex pictures of the history of the unit. For any trajectory gives a picture of the *history* of the unit, and a richer picture the more variables are included.

To approach this problem one might superimpose the two UDA diagrams, one for each variable, on each other. The horizontal time axis would be the same for both variables, whether one prefers to use chronological time or some kind of social time, for the states of the unit on the two variables should be compared at the same point in time in order to read off the social situation of the unit at that point in time. But what about the vertical axis or axes? If we retain the variables X and Y in their original form, then the difficulty is that the diagrams will look so different depending on the relative size of the units in which X and Y are measured. To standardize them, so that different researchers working at different places at different times will easily arrive at similar diagrams, one method would be as follows. Look at the last time point for which information on all variables is available. Set the value of the variables for this time point equal to 100, and calculate the values of all other variables for all other time points relative to this, in other words as percentages of the value attained by the variables at the end of the observed process. By this device any number of variables can be handled by the vertical axis (which now runs from 0% to 100%), and if the value for the last time point is also the maximum value then all curves are kept within limits. And the curves have clear interpretations: how did the unit attain the value of 100%?

So far this would only amount to superimposed UDA analyses; the problem is how to proceed to BDA analysis. The growth rates for the UDA in their original, untransformed form are

$$\frac{dX}{dt} \text{ and } \frac{dY}{dt}, \text{ or approximated by } \frac{\Delta X}{\Delta t} \text{ and } \frac{\Delta Y}{\Delta t}$$

which may or may not be constant as a function of time. For nations statistics are often given on an annual basis reflecting the slowness with which one assumes that social processes at this macro-level usually take place, and the difference quotients are simply annual growth rates, as these are treated in development theory and statistics in general. These growth rates are, of course, dependent on the units in which X and Y are expressed; if the unit is multiplied by a constant k, so is the growth rate. With the transformation to percentages that we have undertaken, new variables have been introduced by the simple linear transformation:

$$X^* = \frac{100}{x_o} X \quad \text{or} \quad X = \frac{x_o}{100} X^*$$

$$Y^* = \frac{100}{y_o} Y \quad \text{or} \quad Y = \frac{y_o}{100} Y^*$$

where x_o and y_o are the values of X and Y for the final time point t_o. Thus, if we have the growth rates for percentage units, i.e. for X^* and Y^*, all one has to do is to divide by these factors to get the growth rates in terms of the original variables.

But we want to study the relative growth rate, R_{xy}.
This can be done by subtraction, but much better by division:

$$R_{xy} = \frac{\dfrac{\Delta Y}{\Delta t}}{\dfrac{\Delta X}{\Delta t}} = \frac{\dfrac{y_o}{100} \dfrac{\Delta Y^*}{\Delta t}}{\dfrac{x_o}{100} \dfrac{\Delta x^*}{\Delta t}} = \frac{y_o}{x_o} \frac{\Delta Y^*}{\Delta X^*}$$

Hence

$$\frac{\Delta Y}{\Delta X} = \frac{y_o}{x_o} \frac{\Delta Y^*}{\Delta X^*}$$

or
$$\frac{\Delta Y^*}{\Delta X^*} = \frac{x_o}{y_o} \frac{\Delta Y}{\Delta x}$$

The point is, of course, that the ratio between the two growth rates is equal to the growth of Y relative to X in an (X,Y)-diagram, or Y* relative to X* in an (X*, Y*)-diagram; adjusted by suitable (and very simple) multiplication constants expressing the relative magnitude of the final values of X and Y.[13]

But this means that the phenomenon we want to study, the *relative growth rate*, can be studied in an (X*,Y*)-diagram, as the derivative of the two dimensional trajectory of Figure 3.

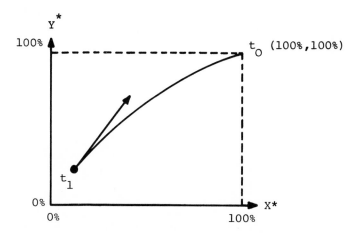

FIG. 3.   THE TYPICAL BDA DIAGRAM.

The only constraint on the two-dimensional trajectory is the point for the final time value, t_o: this point has to have the coordinates (100%, 100%).   But what about the starting point for the process studied, t_1?   One could, of course, have transformed the variables further so as to locate this point at the origin, and this is advantageous for some purposes to be developed later.   However, this transformation can also give the spurious impression that all variables develop "equally far" during the time interval studied, since they all change from 0% to 100%.

---

[13]The functional form of the trajectory in the BDA diagram can, of course, easily be found if we know the functional form of the UDA trajectories, as a function of time.

$$x = f(t) \qquad Y = g(t)$$

since we simply get

$$Y = g(t) = g(f^{-1}(X)) = gf^{-1}(X) = \phi(X)$$

Since $Y = \phi(X)$ is basic to BDA, it may be useful to know its form for the three most commonly found models in UDA, univariate growth curves:

linear $f(t) = a_1 + b_1 t; \quad g(t) = a_2 + b_2 t$

exponential $f(t) = a_1 e^{b_1 t}; \quad g(t) = a_2 e^{b_2 t}$

logistic $f(t) = c_1/(1 + a_1 e^{-b_1 t});$

$\qquad\qquad\qquad g(t) = c_2/(1 + a_2 e^{-b_2 t}).$

Assuming that $Y = qf^{-1}(X)$ the results are as follows:

g \ f	linear	exponential	logistic
linear	$(a_2 - \gamma a_1) + \gamma X$	$a_2 e^{-r} a_1 \gamma X$	$c_2/(1+a_2 e^{\gamma a_1} e^{-\gamma X})$
exponential	$e^Y = \dfrac{e^{a_2}}{a_1^{\gamma}} X^{\gamma}$	$\dfrac{a_2}{a_1^{\gamma}} X^{\gamma}$	$c_2/(1+a_2 a_1^{\gamma} X^{-\gamma})$
logistic	$e^Y = \dfrac{e^{a_2}}{\left(\dfrac{c_1}{a_1 X} - \dfrac{1}{a_1}\right)^{\gamma}}$	$a_2\left(\dfrac{c_1}{a_1 X} - \dfrac{1}{a_1}\right)^{\gamma}$	$c_2/\left[1+a_2\left(\dfrac{c_1}{a_1 X} - \dfrac{1}{a_1}\right)^{\gamma}\right]$

where $\gamma = b_2/b_1$.

The Major Types of Trajectories

To trace the trajectories in the BDA diagrams an obvious condition has to be put on the data used for superimposed UDA analyses: the values for X and Y have to refer to the same time-points, for coincidence in time is the factor used to tie the observations together in the (X,Y)-diagram. If the unit is a nation one is greatly aided in this endeavor by the circumstance that the Christian calendar is used in most countries, that decadic number systems are used and that they lend themselves to the magical concentration on information for years ending with 0 or 5—this also being reinforced by mutual international agreements. But sometimes there are holes in the system, and in order to arrive at information for missing time points the best technique is usually to use UDA diagrams for intrapolation or extrapolation, usually with a linear model, but also with a curvilinear model if it is felt that this is warranted. The degree of precision one should aim at here, as elsewhere,is not only a function of the quality of the data but also of the *need* for precision, and it is not our experience that most intra- and extra-polations of the types mentioned will upset conclusions ex-pressed in terms of the four major curve shapes to be in-dicated below.

Imagine now that we have a starting point and the ter-minal (100%, 100%) point in a BDA diagram, and then ask the question: *which are the major shapes of the bivariate trajectory with time as parameter, from t_1 to t_o?* After having scanned a great variety of such curves for the development of nations, four curve shapes seem to stand out as basic patterns, as in Figure 4. These four curve shapes are easily interpreted.

The "Straight" trajectory does of course not mean that the two growth rates are equal, nor would it be very inter-esting if this were the case. They would be equal if the straight trajectory coincided with the line $Y^* = X^*$, as it by and large does when for instance changes in life expec-tancies for males and females are compared. But again this would *only be equality in terms of the transformed variables,* so the straight line would have to coincide with the line $Y^* = \dfrac{X_o}{Y_o} X^*$ in order for the original growth rates to be

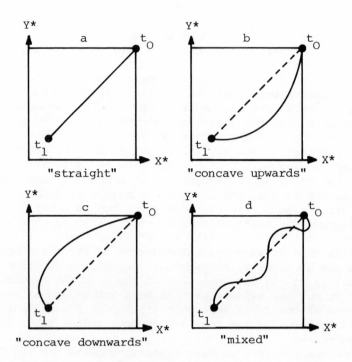

FIG. 4. THE FOUR CURVE SHAPES IN BDA ANALYSIS.

equal.[14]

However, equality is uninteresting since it depends on the units in which the *original* variables are expressed. Equality in the *transformed* variables is actually more interesting since it tells us something about the way in which the two variables concur in bringing the total system up to the t_o point of (100%, 100%); and this can, as mentioned, be read off by comparing the trajectory with the

---

[14]

For if $Y^* = \dfrac{x_o}{y_o} X^*$ then $\dfrac{\Delta Y^*}{\Delta X^*} = \dfrac{x_o}{y_o}$

and $\dfrac{\Delta Y}{\Delta X} = \dfrac{y_o}{x_o} \cdot \dfrac{\Delta Y^*}{\Delta X^*} = \dfrac{y_o}{x_o} \cdot \dfrac{x_o}{y_o} = 1.$

$Y* = X*$ line. But the correct interpretation of the straight trajectory, in general, is in terms of *constant proportion in growth rates*. What it means is simply that in the time interval studied the relative growth rate is constant, but not necessarily equal to unity, which would mean that the two underlying growth rates were equal.

This should then be contrasted with trajectories *b* and *c* in Figure 4 where the relative growth rates are *not* constant. Again, there is little sense in saying which growth rate is "higher" unless one accepts the interpretation in terms of transformed variables, in which case one only has to register whether the derivative is above or below 1, the derivative for the $Y* = X*$ line. The focus is rather on whether the derivative of the trajectories is changing: in case *b* so that the growth rate of $Y*$ becomes gradually *more* important relative to the growth rate of $X*$, in case c so that the growth rate of $Y*$ becomes gradually *less* important relative to the growth rate of $X*$. Obviously, at some point in time (and under assumptions of continuity) the trajectory is parallel to the $Y* = X*$ line, but this is of marginal interest since our focus here is on the pattern of change in the relative growth rate over time, not on how it is at one point in time.

Trajectory *d* is a mixture of *b* and *c*. It is an undulating pattern around the line connecting t_1 and t_o, the trajectory of *constant* proportions. Just as for *b* and *c* there are often pronounced turning points where the relative growth rates suddenly change. Since time is a parameter for these trajectories one can immediately read off chronological time for the turning points, and trace records in order to try to find out what happened in the total social context that may help in the exploration of the causes and consequences of the more discontinuous changes in the relative growth rates.

From what has been said so far it is obvious that the focus is not only on the relative growth rate between Y and X, or $Y*$ and $X*$, but on the *change* in the relative growth rate. The relative growth rate is expressed by the first derivative, and the change in the relative growth rate by the second derivative. But this means that the typology in Figure 4 can be expressed in simple terms in Table 3.

TABLE 3:   CURVE SHAPES EXPRESSED IN TERMS OF SECOND
          DERIVATIVE.

Trajectory	a	b	c	d
Shape	"straight"	"concave upwards"	"concave down-wards"	"mixed"
Second derivative of the trajectory	zero	positive	negative	changing sign

In other words, what we are really interested in is expressed
in the second derivative of the BDA trajectory. However,
this is not a very useful insight unless one is working with
theoretical models for which the second derivative can be
given a functional form, and not merely working inductively
on the basis of empirical data. In the latter case the
classification of a trajectory can be arrived at by simple
visual inspection.

But the expression in terms of the second derivative also
focusses the attention on the *size* of the second derivative.
The greater the magnitude of the second derivative, the more
concave the curve, in other words the greater the curvature[15]
(the smaller the radius of the circle that has the same curvature for any given point on the trajectory). The extreme
case for a monotone trajectory would be the case where the
derivative suddenly changes from zero to infinity, for instance because the trajectory is parallel to the Y* axis
after having been parallel to the X* axis. This gives us a
basis for a more precise definition of a *transition point* in

---

[15] The formula for the curvature (K) involves the use of the
second derivative. For $Y = f(t)$, $X = g(t)$ we get

$$K = \frac{X''Y' - Y''X'}{((Y')^2 + (X')^2)^{3/2}}$$

For $Y = F(X)$ we get

$$K = \frac{Y''}{((Y')^2 + 1)^{3/2}}$$

a BDA *trajectory:* it is a point (rather, a small interval)
in time where the first derivative undergoes a major change,
i.e. from prevalence in the growth of one of the variables to
prevalence in the growth of the second variable. In other
words, it is a point of rapid change in the first derivative, which means that it is a point of high values for the
second derivative. But this would direct our attention to
the *maximum* absolute value of the *second derivative,* and to
locate that point one would turn to the third derivative (to
see where it attains the value of zero) and the fourth
derivative (to study its sign). In other words, many properties of the trajectory are of interest, which again means
that conclusions based on BDA will make use of many properties of the curves.[16] However, the simple curve shape
system presented in Figure 4 and identified in terms of
second derivatives in Table 3 will generally be quite sufficient.

Trajectories *b,* *c* and *d* mean that the unit undergoes
stages or phases during the time interval studied; a first
phase where one of the growth rates prevails followed by a
second stage where the other growth rate prevails--possibly
with an intermediate stage where there is no clear pattern of
prevalence. Of course, if the trajectory starts close to the
origin and has to end up in the (100%, 100%) point without
ever crossing the straight line between t_i and t_o some conclusion of this kind will have to emerge.[17] But that does
not mean that all trajectories look the same. There are
important qualifications, and they can be expressed as
parameters of the trajectories, to which we now turn.

The Parameters of Bivariate Diachronic Analysis

First of all, not all non-linear trajectories depart
equally far from the straight *reference line* from t_1 to t_o.
In general, the farther they depart, the more pronounced are
the changes in relative growth rates during the time interval
in question. The extreme case would, as mentioned, be a
trajectory taking off from the origin, following one of the

---

[16] Or, to express it in that language: several terms of the
Taylor expansion of the trajectory are needed.

[17] This is a well-known theorem in calculus (Rolle's theorem),
and valid under relatively mild conditions (that the function
has a derivative).

coordinate axes till the 100% point is reached, then attaining the (100%, 100%) point parallel to the coordinate axis. This high level of *inconstancy* can now be measured in three ways. The first method is a simple one using the maximum distance from the straight reference line to the trajectory, and the second a more complicated one using the size of the *area* enclosed by the reference line and the trajectory:

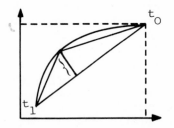 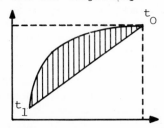

FIG. 5. THE MEASURES OF INCONSTANCY.

The second method is better, since the first method is insensitive to a great variety in trajectories. Thus, two straight lines leading up to the maximum distance point would yield the same distance parameter, but not the same area parameter, as the original trajectory. But the curved trajectory seems to exhibit more inconstancy since the relative rate is changing all the time.

And that brings us to the third method. Since we are interested in the extent to which the ratio of the growth rates changes, what would be better than a study of the first derivative, using the *range* in variation of the first derivative as the parameter? At a first glance this looks very attractive, but in practice it would not work. An empirical trajectory may make all kinds of twists and turns that would be meticulously registered in the first derivative and contribute to the range. The parameter would be too sensitive to small irregularities, whereas what we are more interested in is the gross character of the relation from t_1 to t_o. This is reflected in the area measure, or put differently: a high value of the area parameter is impossible unless there is considerable range in the variation of the first derivative. But the converse is not true: changes in the first derivative may be reflections of small oscillations around the reference line. Consequently, we stick to the area measure.

To make such parameters comparable for different pairs of variables and/or different units the reference line has to be standardized, and the simplest way of doing this would be to transform the original variables further so that the starting point t_1 is, in fact, located at the origin. In other words, this is a strong argument for that type of transformation which would not change anything in the classification of shapes of trajectories since they are invariant of such linear transformations.

Another problem has to do with trajectories of type d. In this case it is even more clear how preferable the area[18] is to the distance, for one could, as mentioned, imagine a trajectory crossing the reference line very many times and always parallel to the coordinate axes, but never departing very far from the reference line. Thus, the distance would be small, but the area might still be considerable, although not as extensive as for types b and c. On the other hand, it may be argued that this is correct. Changes lasting for only a small fraction of the total time interval should not be permitted to count as much as large-scale changes of the types contained in trajectories b and c. Incidentally, when calculating the area enclosed by the trajectory and the reference line in case d, the absolute size of the area will have to be counted; the algebraic size would only lead to mutual compensation on either side of the line.

Secondly, there is the problem of *irregularity*. There is no reason why an undular pattern of type d should be superimposed on type a only. It could just as well be superimposed on types b and c and produce highly irregular patterns where the area measure might be about the same, but the range measure much higher. The degree of irregularity can, of course, be measured by correlation techniques. An "ideal" trajectory connecting t_1 and t_o would then be calculated, for instance as a regression curve using least-squares techniques, and the degree of correspondence between the observed trajectory and the ideal trajectory could be measured as a correlation $C(X, Y)$. The higher the correlation the closer would the location of the empirical time points be to the ideal trajectory. This correlation coefficient is known as *diachronic correlation*, as opposed to or contrasted with the *synchronic correlation*, based on data from the traditional synchronic data matrix.

Thus, BDA analysis would essentially lead to two parameters: one expression of *inconstancy*, and one expression of *regularity*. Obviously the two are not related, at least not logically; for *inconstancy* is a question of how far the

---

[18] This measure, of course, is reminiscent of the Gini index in the measurement of inequality.

trajectory departs from the reference line, and *regularity* a question of how closely the time points cluster around the idealized trajectory--whether the latter is straight or curvilinear elsewhere.[19] But we shall argue in section 6 that a third parameter is also needed.

It should be noted that BDA analysis does not tell us directly *how fast* one variable grows. This information is best obtained directly from UDA analyses where time is the *independent variable.* In BDA analysis time enters as a *parameter,* which means that growth rates can be found indirectly by observing how closely or how distant to each other the time points are located on the trajectories: the more distant, the quicker the growth; the closer, the slower the growth.

Extension to Two Units

This system can now be developed further in two directions: by including more units, and by including more variables. Both extensions of the system are problematic and they will not be discussed in general, i.e. with extension to *m* units and to *n* variables. Rather, the extension to *two* units, and the extension to *three* variables will be discussed, since the principles should be clear from that.

To include one more unit raises exactly the same problems as for UDA representations. Thus, one can certainly draw separate BDA diagrams for two different units, and since the axes are identical because X* and Y* are the same for both units they can be superimposed on each other. But is this meaningful at all? The answer depends, as usual, on the purpose of the inquiry. If the purpose is some kind of synchronic comparison between the two units, then *chronological time* will obviously have to be used. But there are many problems. If transformed variables are used locating t_1 at the (0%, 0%) point and t_o at the (100%, 100%) point for both units, then curve shapes can be compared.[20] Moreover,

---

[19]This theme is developed further in a systematic application of BDA in a study of the development of Japan, currently carried out at the International Peace Research Institute, Oslo, under a contract with the UNESCO.

[20]If all trajectories are given a double transformation so that they not only are forced through the (100,100) point but also through the (0,0)-point, then the four basic curve types will appear even more clearly. All straight lines will be

28

the same time-points on the two curves can be connected by a
straight line. The longer the line the more discrepant the
units at that time-point, and the area described by these
straight lines can be calculated as a measure of the total
discrepancy between the units for the time interval chosen.
But this is artificial, for the two trajectories have been
forced, by the transformation, to pass through the same two
points even though the range covered by them on the two
variables may vary considerably and not even overlap. Consequently, this type of analysis might perhaps just as well
be carried out on completely untransformed variables.

What is clear is only that comparison of the units for
the same points in *chronological time* is the only way of
gaining information about the state of the system consisting
of those two units at that point in time, for instance, for
synchronic analysis of the international system if the units
are nations. But if the purpose is *diachronic analysis* to
gain insight in the bivariate trajectories units are likely
to allow under certain initial conditions, then some kind of
transformation to *social time* must be used.

---

transformed to the $Y^{**} = X^{**}$ line, regardless of how different the growth rates are (as long as the ratio is constant). And the *b, c* and *d* types will be readily recogniz-
able by their location relative to this line. Thus, this
transformation preserved the information we are interested
in, but the loss of information is nevertheless considerable.
For instance, the difference between these two lines is
interesting:

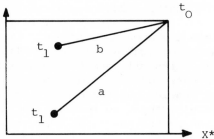

In line *a* the unit is about equally far from the terminal
point to start with, on both variables; in line *b* the unit
is close to the terminal point of variable Y^* all the time.
As a consequence, the growth rate in the t_1, t_o interval is
much higher on X^* than on Y^*, even though the relative growth
rate is constant. But this distinction is completely lost.
Nevertheless, such transformations may be highly useful, as
indicated.

This raises a number of problems. If the units show the same trajectories, only at different intervals in chronological time, then efforts can be made to express this trajectory as a model and undertake a transformation to a common standard social time—as described above for UDA. But there is also another approach: all trajectories can be traced from a common starting point defined by the value of a crucial variable, such as GNP/capita, or degree of literacy. Thus, one can decide to follow the development of nations not from a certain year but from the period when they attained a GNP/capita of $100, or a degree of literacy of 10%, or both. This would then be another way of operationalizing the hazy concept of "social time," and one ojection would be that *one* variable should not be sufficient to define the *zero point*, another that this would not define the *time unit* but leave one with the dubious assumption of equal time units across the range of units and for the total time interval. Hence, it would be more satisfactory if one could develop a good theory for developmental stages, taking into account more variables. Thus, one should at least use the covariation over time between two crucial variables, in other words, one could use BDA as a basis for transformation to social time.

But if this problem can be solved, then a much better basis exists for calculating $C(X,Y)$, the diachronic correlation between X and Y. Both BDA parameters can be calculated for superimposed trajectories, but this time idealized trajectories would have to be used, probably based on regression techniques. With only one unit the empirical trajectory could still be meaningfully used to calculate the amount of inconstancy, but an idealized trajectory was, of course, needed to calculate the amount of irregularity. This would give a better basis for evaluating the likelihood that a unit at social time zero will eventually go through the same trajectory. When based on data from a wide variety of units, subclasses can be singled out and diachronic correlations calculated separately; these correlations would then, presumably, yield even better bases for evaluating the likelihood mentioned above for any given starting unit.

This being said, it is obvious that much can still be done simply on the basis of comparing separate BDA diagrams for separate units. Thus given n variables and 2 units there are $\binom{n}{2}$ diagrams to construct for each unit. Since diagrams of type *a*, in our experience, seem to be rare, the basic distinction will be between types *b* and *c* on the one hand and type *d* on the other. Hence, if one nation

consistently shows trajectories of the first variety and the
other nation consistently shows trajectories of the second
variety then this finding is in itself interesting.[21] It
may reveal completely different internal structures in the
unit, and give some insights into the old problem of
balanced vs. unbalanced growth(Galtung and Høivik, 1967).
But one should also be careful lest one jumps too easily to
conclusions. If the social zero is different for the two
units then it may well be that differences would disappear if
a longer time interval is studied; in short that both units
would show patterns of types *b* and *c* followed by a pattern of
type *d*--only that social time and chronological time were
related in such a way that the first unit was caught in the
first phase and the second unit in the second. And this
argument also relates to the time unit: if the time unit is
changed drastically, then patterns of type *d* will appear as
a succession of patterns of types *b* and *c*. Hence, the best
procedure is probably to collect a wide variety of data,
sampling highly different units, variables and time-points,
and to be careful with interpretations.

Extension to Three Variables.

Let us then approach the problem of extension to three
variables. In principle this is unproblematic: instead of
BDA diagrams one would need TDA (trivariate diachronic analysis) *space* diagrams; we shall refer to them as *triagrams*.
With suitable material, much like what chemists use to display spatial arrangements of molecular patterns, it is possible to show a trajectory from the starting point to the
(100%, 100%, 100%) point. The projections of this trajectory
into the coordinate planes would yield three simple BDA
diagrams, but they would not add up to the complexity of a
TDA, and there would be no simple way of calculating a parameter corresponding to the measure of *inconstancy* developed
above. Of course one way of coping with this problem would
still be to measure the *maximum distance* of the trajectory
from the reference line leading from the starting point to
the (100%, 100%, 100%) point, but this is equally unsatisfactory in this context.

Hence, a better method would probably be to generalize
the *area measure*. Since the trajectory cannot be assumed

---

[21] Thus, a comparative study of development patterns in Japan
and Norway seems to indicate a certain tendency for trajectories for Japan to be more of the *b* and *c* types and for
trajectories for Norway to be more of the *d* type.

to be located in a plane the area to be measured becomes more complex. One approximation would be as follows. Imagine that both reference line and trajectory are divided into *p* equidistant intervals and that successive dividing points on the line and trajectory are connected by a straight line. Each interval could then be further subdivided and the same process could be continued. The lines between the trajectory and reference line would then form a surface, and the area of that surface would be one answer to the problem of measuring inconstancy. For BDA diagrams this method gives us our original measure.

The other parameter, of regularity, would be measured by means of standard regression-correlation techniques, using the total diachronic correlation as a measure of regularity. The partial correlations would be of less interest in this connection.

In principle the trajectory could twist itself like a coil round the reference line--but what would that mean? It might mean that X, Y and Z, the three variables spanning the space, prevail over the others where growth rate is concerned in a cyclical pattern--first most of the growth is in X, then Y takes over and twists the trajectory another way, then Z takes over, and so on. If the cycle is broken the coil will become less regular and may, in principle, spin off in any direction--but this is the general mechanism behind its twists and turns.

6. THE PROBLEMS OF MONOTONICITY

So far we have more or less implicitly assumed monotonicity, i.e. that the units either never decrease in value over time or never increase. To simplify, let us turn the value around, i.e. deal with -X instead of X, if the units never increase, so that instead they will never decrease. For instance, let us talk about "infant survival" instead of "infant mortality." Over time, then, the units either increase their values on the variables or else remain constant.

In studies of *development* it is usually understood that development variables are *monotone* variables, not only in the sense that higher values on the variable are desired, but also in the sense that empirical changes tend to be in that direction. Of course, this is a built-in assumption of development optimism that may hold true for certain periods in the lives of certain societies, but not for all societies at all times. There are *lapses* in the trends, and they may be more or less persistent until they become so persistent that they should better be referred to as *reversals*.

Let us first study monotonicity in UDA diagrams. Obviously, the definition of monotonicity would be that the first derivative of the trajectory is non-negative, since we assume that decreasing variables have been adequately reversed. The problem is only *which trajectory* to use, the *empirical* one connecting each time point to the subsequent time point, or the *idealized* one based on, say, least-squares techniques in order to find the regression curve? One approach would be to base the study on both and to define two concepts of non-monotonicity:

> *weak non-monotonicity:* the first derivative of the *empirical* trajectory changes signs;
> *strong non-monotonicity:* the first derivative of the *idealized* trajectory changes signs.

Strong non-monotonicity, of course, implies weak non-monotonicity but not vice versa. Whether a case of weak non-monotonicity is also strong depends on whether the lapses are only irregularities lowering the value of the correlation ratio, or are patterned enough to cause a downward bend of the regression curve so that its first derivative changes signs. The definition is precise, but hinges on the definition of the idealized trajectory in least-squares terms--and this principle lacks adequate theoretical rationale.[22] However, as a first approach it may still be useful until one comes up with a better way of defining the idealized trajectory--for instance relative to a deterministic model.

Let us then concentrate on strong non-monotonicity since the weak case is less interesting, for there will usually be some irregularities of that kind. How does one handle strong non-monotonicity? One approach, of course, would be to divide the process into monotone intervals, reversing the variable for every second interval, and study the processes for one interval at a time. But this is not very satisfactory since it somehow assumes that monotonicity is normal and non-monotonicity abnormal--leaving out all the interesting A-shaped, U-shaped, S-shaped or W-shaped (etc.) univariate trajectories. That these patterns cannot be covered by exponential or logistic models only point to the shortcomings of these models.

---

[22] In general, least-squares techniques are remarkably lacking in rationale, their widespread use taken into consideration. The statistical rationale is clear enough, but its connection with substantive theory is negligible.

For univariate analysis we may leave the problem there, only signalling the necessity of models and theories that can handle adequately such reversal points, defined by the first derivative being zero, and turn to the problem of non-monotonicity in connection with bivariate analysis.

First of all, since the slope of the trajectory in the X, Y diagram is given by $dy/dx = dy/dt/dx/dt$, the bivariate trajectory will be monotone as long as the two univariate trajectories are monotone (but will be indeterminate if both of them are static, have a "plateau"). *But the reverse is not true:* if both variables are decreasing, then the bivariate trajectory will still have an upward slope. And if one of them is decreasing, then the bivariate trajectory will have a downward slope. The four cases are illustrated in Figure 6. In the first diagram we have drawn two

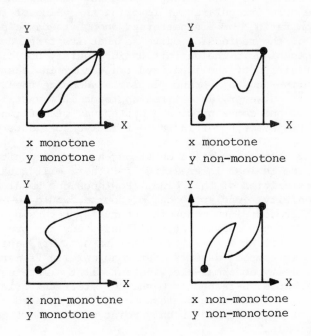

x monotone
y monotone

x monotone
y non-monotone

x non-monotone
y monotone

x non-monotone
y non-monotone

FIG. 6. THE EFFECT OF NON-MONOTONICITY ON BDA DIAGRAMS.

trajectories as a reminder that even though the two first derivatives have constant signs the second derivative may still change sign. In other words, all four diagrams may be classified as having trajectories of type d in the typology of Figure 4 and Table 3. Needless to say, we assume all trajectories in Figure 6 to be idealized trajectories.

To derive a measure of non-monotonicity one would obviously have to base oneself on the first derivatives and their change of sign. But, unlike the measure of inconstancy that we rejected based on the total range covered by the first derivative (regardless of sign), what we need here is simply information about how many times the first derivative changes signs. This can be counted relative to a given time interval, i.e. relative to chronological time, which can best be done using UDA diagrams. But it can also be done relative to social time, either by transforming chronological time or by using another variable. But the latter means using a bivariate relation, which is simple enough if one can use a monotone variable to define an interval in social time and then count the number of changes in the non-monotone variable. But what if both variables are non-monotone? This means that there is a point where the total (i.e. bivariate) trajectory relapses—even, possibly, along the same trajectory.

This case is different, and an example may illustrate how. In development theory it is commonly held that whereas the tertiary sector shows monotone growth, the secondary sector will grow in the beginning, then reach a plateau, and then decrease again. Thus, in a BDA diagram with the percentage employed in the tertiary sector on the horizontal axis (and one would generally put the monotone variable there) the trajectory would be A-shaped. But imagine a war sets in at any point, with heavy bombardment of cities and industries, destroying the modernized sectors of the economy, forcing the population into the primary sector. In that case both variables would be non-monotone, and in general this situation will probably occur as a sign of changes of the system, whereas non-monotonicity in one variable should be associated more with changes in the system (exogenous vs. endogenous changes). Thus, we shall in general discard this case, and assume that at least one of the variables is monotone

What happens to the other parameters in case of non-monotonicity. The parameter of irregularity is already taken care of since non-monotone regression-curves are permitted. As the parameter of inconstancy should not be problematic either since it is defined by the area enclosed by the trajectory and the reference line, and since both are continuous this should be well-defined enough at least for empirical approaches to the calculation problem.

Thus, a third parameter, of *non-monotonicity,* has been defined, yielding a crude indication of the magnitude of this kind of deviance from monotone development. However, it should be strongly emphasized that this indicator should only be used as a first step in empirical work and later be replaced, when more theoretical insight is obtained about why there are reversal points, why the trajectory is non-monotone.

7. CAUSE-EFFECT RELATIONS AND DIACHRONIC ANALYSIS

Let us now approach the crucial problem of causality in terms of the simple apparatus for analysis of time series developed so far. As our point of departure we shall not take any philosophical or logico-mathematical definition of causality since we are not convinced that this is likely to add much to our insight at all--but a more pragmatic conception of how we shall conceive of the cause-effect relation.

We shall conceive of the causal relation in the only way in which we are able to make real sense of it: *operatively.*[23] In other words, the relation between cause and effect is regarded like the relation between turning the steering-wheel in a car and the turning of the wheels themselves, or between pushing the button of an automat and the cigarettes/coffee/contraceptives pouring out. Thus, the cause-effect relation presupposes a change in one variable (the angular position of the steering-wheel, the position of the button) and a concomitant or subsequent (but not antecedent) change in another variable (the angular position of the wheels, the location of the cigarettes). But it is obvious that this relation presupposes something about the *context,* usually formulated in terms of all other variables, which are then referred to as *conditions.* These conditions are then divided into two kinds, the *relevant* conditions and and the *irrelevant* conditions, depending on whether or not the values of these conditions affect the relation between cause and effect.

Thus, a cause-effect relation is based on a division of the world into four parts.

---

[23]This idea is put forward in a very clear way by Herman Wold (1969, pp. 270 ff), who uses the controlled experiment as a paradigm. We have been inspired by Wold's prolific writings in this field, particularly by his papers (1956) and (1966).

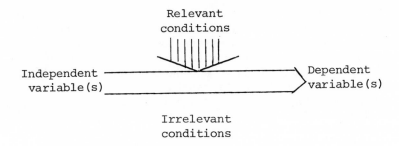

Fig. 7. THE FOUR-PARTITE DIVISION OF THE WORLD FOR CAUSAL
ANALYSIS.

This is also the paradigm for *experiments*,[24] which are
referred to as *controlled* if something is done about the
relevant conditions (the recipes can be divided into three
kinds: making the relevant conditions irrelevant through
some kind of isolation, keeping them at a constant value, or
using some process of randomization). Thus, with these
definitions the link between experiments and cause-effect
relations becomes very strong. By means of experiment one
hopes to find relations between independent and dependent
variable(s), and these relations are then often referred to
as causal under the following four conditions:
    1) that they are "immediate," i.e. that there is no
appreciable time-lag between changes on the independent and
the dependent sides,
    2) that they are "deterministic," i.e. that one can
predict with high precision the value of the dependent variable from the value of the independent variable,
    3) that they are "monotone," i.e. that for higher values
of the independent variable(s) there will at least not be
lower values on the dependent variable.
    4) that they are "invariant," i.e. that the relation be-
tween the independent and dependent variables holds regardless of the state of the rest of the world (in other words,
that all other variables are irrelevant conditions).

---

[24] This four-partite division of the world is, of course, also
a general paradigm for experimental designs, and very much in
line with the way this is discussed in Wold, (1964).

To this could be added a fifth condition to make the relation an operative relation: that the independent variable is *manipulable,* i.e. that an "operator" can change values of the independent variable so as to start the machinery. However, it may be objected that this is a pragmatic condition relating the relation between cause and effect to man, and that a relation is no less causal just because human beings cannot (here and now) manipulate the independent variables. But from the point of view of applied science the condition is, of course, crucial.

There are also other conditions that seem to be implicitly included when terms like cause and effect are used, but they are both less consensual, less obvious and less important.[25] Hence, we shall stick to these four conditions and see where they lead us, and the immediate reflection would be that such conditions are so restrictive that they at best can be said to portray a highly idealized relation.

For instance, take the automobile example. The effect on the wheels when the steering-wheel is turned is *immediate,* the relation is *deterministic* and it is *monotone*—to that turn of the steering-wheel there is immediately exactly that turn of the wheel, and with more turn of one, more turn of the other. But this is only true provided quite a few conditions are fulfilled, conditions relating to the state of the car: the nuts being tightened, the bolts being strong enough and so on. If these conditions are not fulfilled, i.e. if these variables are not kept in certain ranges, the relation will be neither immediate nor deterministic, and not even monotone. Such cars are in fact found: cars where the steering-wheel is turned and turned with no appreciable effect on the wheels (there is too much "play" in the steering mechanism) and/or with no precise relation between steering-wheel and wheels, e.g. due to loose bolts, possibly even so much that the wheels may relapse. All three phenomena are rather hazardous, and are usually taken as signs that the car is ripe for scrapping—or at least for fundamental repairs.

But the relations encountered in the social sciences seem, by and large, to be much more reminiscent of this "weakly coupled" steering mechanism than of the perfect car with the "strongly coupled" steering mechanism. As pointed out several times above the relations very often come with a *time-lag,* they are *stochastic* rather than deterministic,

---

[25] For some discussion of other conditions that seem to be implied when the term "causality" is used, see Johan Galtung, *Theory and Methods of Social Research,* cit., pp. 383 ff.

often *non-monotone,* and the set of relevant conditions is
extensive. In other words, the relations hold only under
certain specified values of the relevant conditions and may
change character completely if these conditions are changed.
Moreover, there seems to be, in general, an inverse relation
between conditions 2 and 4: the more limited the set of
relevant conditions, i.e., the fewer conditions we require
for the relation to hold, the less deterministic is the relation. Possibly, the "play" in the system may also be patterned enough to produce non-monotonicity.

The most problematic of the four conditions is the idea
of invariance of changes in all other variables, among other
reasons because "all other variables" is an unlimited set.
Some such requirements relating to "other variables" have a
special status in scientific theory, such as the requirement
that physical laws shall be time and space independent, or
that any relation between variables shall be independent of
the identity of the scientist (intersubjectivity). But the
idea that the relation should hold regardless of the value of
all third variables, singly and/or combined, in other words
that the relation should be a *universal law,* seems completely
unrealistic in the social sciences. Just to mention one such
variable: the degree of insight in the relation possessed by
the people the relation affects. This concerns their level
of consciousness, and may lead to self-fulfilling or self-
denying processes. Of course, there may be cases where the
relation is independent of the level of consciousness, where
they are *automatic* in the sense that the relation of the subjects to the relation between the variables does not affect
the latter (appreciably), but one would off-hand imagine that
these relations constitute but a small minority in the total
set of social relations. The failure to specify this condition is symptomatic, and typical of most modern social
science in the positivist tradition.

But the class of relevant conditions is much wider than
this small list indicates. Thus, one may argue that even the
most universal relation "bears in itself the seeds of its
own destruction," in the sense that the relation will contribute to the creation of the conditions that will make the
relations less universal, less invariant. The line of
reasoning is simply as follows. A relation between social
variables said to exclude, under all conditions, some combinations, means a restriction on human and social variety.
The restriction is bound to favor some individuals and groups
more than others and to disfavor some more than others.
Consequently, to posit the relationship may in itself constitute an element in a social conflict and create forces

39

that will work for the removal of that particular incompati-
bility. This will start a search for variables on whose
value the relation hinges, and since there will always be an
unlimited number of variables that have constant values for
the limited space-time region in which the invariance has
been observed and confirmed, the number of possibilities is
unlimited. From this it does not follow that one of these
variable-candidates will eventually prove to change the relation when changed itself; it does not follow that the
search will never be in vain, only that there will be plenty
of possibilities.

Let us now relate this to the theory of time series
developed in the preceding sections. The basic insight in
social affairs is that cause-effect relations tend not to be
instantaneous but to unfold themselves through time, both
since the change of the causal variable takes time and because of possible time-lag before there is any (appreciable)
change in the effect variable. *Since time* (and not, for instance, geographical and social space) *is a medium in which
these relations are found, they also have to be studied in
time, in other words diachronically.* Immediacy is an abstraction, rarely encountered in practice, if at all.

It is now easily seen how the three parameters from BDA
enter into this discussion in a fruitful way:

1. *The problem of immediacy vs. time-lag.* In BDA this
is studied by means of the parameters measuring *inconstancy*.
When inconstancy is *zero* the effect of the independent variable on the dependent variable is immediate, and stronger the
steeper the line connecting t_1 and t_o. When inconstancy is
maximum there is first a change in X (the variable that
changes first will, by definition, be referred to as the independent variable) with no change at all in Y, and then a
change in Y with no change in X. But these are only extreme
cases and often not very important in empirical practice. In
practice there will often be more change in X than in Y to
start with, and then, a reversal--if there is a time-lag in
the process, that is (in other words a curve of type *b*). It
is the gradation of the immediacy vs. time-lag dimension
that interests us here, and this gradation seems to be relatively well captured by means of the inconstancy parameter
developed above.

2. *The Problem of Deterministic vs. Stochastic
Relations.* We shall not repeat here all the reasons why
synchronic correlation between X and Y is not a sufficient
condition for inferring that there will also be a diachronic
correlation between them, but this is well substantiated in

40

practice and also theoretically.[26] Nor shall we repeat more arguments why cause-effect relations should be studied by means of diachronic and not by means of synchronic correlation.[27] But, if we accept the relevance of diachronic correlation, then its magnitude becomes a key to the *regularity* of the relation, particularly when it is based on data from several units.

3. *The Problem of Monotone vs. Non-monotone Relations.* However, the problem of "regularity" is not answered simply by *calculating* the diachronic correlation $C(X, Y)$ developed above. For this correlation to be high it is sufficient that all pairs (x_i, y_i) for all time-points t_i are located on a regression curve. It is *not* necessary that their order on the regression curve is also a time order--the correlation $C(X, Y)$ is insensitive to all kinds of permutations of the time points since time is only a parameter. Thus, even if the diachronic correlation is very high this is not sufficient if we require the relation between cause and effect to be monotone and even continuous. But if in addition both variables are monotone, then a high value of $C(X, Y)$ is tantamount to what we feel is usually referred to as a deterministic relation between cause and effect (with or without time-lag). If one or both of the variables is not monotone, then use of the relation will lead to unpleasant

---

[26] For some arguments against the use of of synchronic data in study of phenomena that take place in time, see Galtung and Høivik (1967). There is also a considerable research tradition in this field in econometrics, for instance around "the savings paradox." See Stone (1954, p. 296); Duesenberry (1949); Fuedinan, (1957)(1949).

[27] For some arguments against the use of synchronic data in the study of causation, see Galtung (1967 b, pp. 469 ff). In a sense these are arguments against the entire Lazarsfeld tradition in this field, except for the fact that Lazarsfeld himself, with his remarkable panel studies, has opened for the use of the dimension of time more than most other contemporary social scientists. But Blalock's (1964) is, in general, a typical example of sophisticated treatment of time-free data in order to infer relations in time. Moreover, the conditions, *interval scale* (as opposed to ordinal scale), *linearity* (as opposed to curvilinear relations) and *one-way relations* (as opposed to feedback relations) are very strong indeed and usually completely unrealistic.

surprises unless one limits the range of variation of X to intervals where Y changes in a monotone fashion. At any rate, the degree of non-monotonicity is at least to some extent measured by the parameter developed in the preceding section.

4. *The Problem of Invariance of Relevant Conditions.* Clearly, diachronic analysis does not solve this problem. The relations encountered are just as sensitive to the context as synchronic relations—or even more so since they are also stretched out in time. With changes in third variables, e.g. by studying socialist instead of capitalist nations, or nations that developed in the last century instead of nations that developed in today's context, diachronic relations may change completely from one shape of the trajectory to a completely different shape. But just as for synchronic relations this does not mean that relations between independent and dependent variables are uninteresting, nor that they are false or wrong or disconfirmed, only that they are *incomplete* unless some conditions are specified, and that pretenses about universal invariances are usually ridiculous.

In principle the techniques of multivariate analysis should be applicable for diachronic analysis as well as for synchronic analysis.[28] One way of doing this would be to see whether a C(X, Y) relation holds for subsets of units or for extensions of the original set of units. This type of analysis would lead to important specifications of the type of units for which a given relation is said to be valid. But these specifications are often in themselves time-dependent, for the units studied. Thus, to say that a relation looks like this for developing nations and like that for

---

[28]For a general treatment of multivariate analysis see Johan Galtung (1967b, II, 5.3). The point about this analysis is actually only that it can just as well be used for diachronic as for synchronic correlations, since there is nothing in the assumptions in this analysis that presupposes that the data are collected according to design O and not according to design 1 or 2. Another thing is that diachronic correlations perhaps are not very useful unless the condition of monotonicity is satisfied, at least for interesting intervals. But the ideal thing would be to develop a measure of correlation, a sort of process measure P(X, Y), relating variables in a transitive fashion so that if P(X, Y) and P(Y, Z), then also P(X,Z). As is well known correlation coefficients are not in general transitive, and it would be highly useful to have an operationalization of the concept of process satisfying the transitive rule. Work on this problem is in progress.

developed nations would immediately lead to the question: how was the relation for the developed countries when they still were "developing?" Such problems would lead to complete TDA approaches, just as for synchronic analyses, or at least to a division of the trajectories into two classes: for the time interval corresponding to "developing" and for the time interval corresponding to "developed."

Again, the purpose is to introduce some gradation into these massive concepts. If we refer to the set of relevant conditions for a given cause-effect relation as *Rel*, then the universal relation--or the true cause-effect relation by the classical approach--would mean that *Rel* is empty. From the circumstance that *Rel* rarely if ever is empty it does not follow that one shall glibly assume that *Irrel* is empty, but rather that it is worthwhile to try to locate some of the most important conditions in *Rel*, specify the values under which the relation holds and, preferably, even go further and try to uncover the nature of the relation when these values change, i.e. when the conditions no longer obtain. Thus, the extension of *Rel*--which is indeterminate yet significant as a conceptual tool of thought--becomes the bridge between the idealized abstraction and what one can meaningfully deal with in social reality. A better approach, however, would be to count the number of variables found to be located in *Irrel*.

The problem then is where the borderline should be drawn. A *car* has to be scrapped when the time-lag is too extensive, the stochasticity, not to mention the non-monotonicity, too pronounced and/or the relevant conditions too far from being fulfilled--but what about the *causal relation?* At which point does it cease being a causal relation and become a proposition like any other? How well do the conditions have to be fulfilled for the flattering epithet "causal relation" to be applied to a proposition? We do not know, and since the four dimensions pointed to are all non-dichotomous, and the first two are even continuous (the last two are discrete; 0, 1, 2, ... et.), there is no "objective" indication of a sharp borderline in the dimensions themselves to steer our thinking. The traditional answer has been the safe refuge in the extreme values, "immediate," "regular," "monotone" and "invariant," but this leads to a concept with (almost) no empirical referent.

Hence, the only way to answer the question seems to be by reference to the idea of causation as an *operative* relation, in other words to pragmatic criteria. The *relation is causal as long as it can be used, as long as changes in* X *do, in fact, lead to the desired changes in* Y, *within a tolerable margin of error.* In other words, a car does not cease to be a car the moment there is some "play" and some stochasticity or non-monotonicity here and there, but the moment it can no longer be usefully operated. Thus, the criterion is pragmatic. And it is difficult to see that it can be otherwise, for the causal relation is essentially a pragmatic relation, a relation extracted for the purpose of, eventually, obtaining some results--i.e. to change X so that Y takes on more desired values.

8. CONCLUSION

We have introduced three parameters of bivariate diachronic relation, *viz.*:

1) *Constancy,* measured as the area enclosed between the straight reference line and the empirical or idealized trajectory for one unit, the idealized trajectory for the case of more units. This is a measure of the over-all departure from the case of constant ratios between the rates of growth in the two variables, and the smaller the measure, the higher the constancy.

2) *Regularity,* measured as the diachronic correlation between X and Y around the idealized trajectory, whether based on one or more units. The measure will have to be based on correlation ratios if the variables are interval scale, in order to be sensitive to non-linear trajectories, in other words to low level of constancy.

3) *Monotonicity,* measured by counting the number of times the first derivative of the idealized trajectory, based on one or more units, changes signs. The higher the number, the lower the monotonicity.

In addition we have introduced a measure that relates as much to synchronic relations as to diachronic relations:

4) *Invariance,* measured by counting the number of third variables relative to which the relation has been proved to be invariant. The higher the number, the more invariant the relation, but this measure makes best sense as a set-theoretical comparison between *Irrel* for one relation and *Irrel* for another relation.

Listed like this one sees clearly how limited a concept of causal relations based on *maximum* constancy, regularity, monotonicity and invariance is. One also sees how it has at all been possible to develop this concept on the basis of synchronic correlation: simply by *assuming constancy* over time or by *failing to notice* these aspects of the relation. The focus has been on regularity, which has then been approached by means of synchronic correlation even though these correlations are often quite different from the

corresponding diachronic correlations. Most of the emphasis
has been on the condition of invariance, with completely unrealistic and hence rather uninteresting conditions for a
relation to be referred to as causal.

But if we (1) introduce diachronic analysis and (2) re-
lax these conditions, then more interesting conceptions on
how social affairs can be studied develop. One might now
construct a typology of sixteen types of relations depending
on whether the four parameters above can be classified as
high or low, but we shall not develop that scholastic exercise completely. Rather, it should be emphasized that the
four are independent of each other so that all combinations
are possible; and this can be used for a final definition:

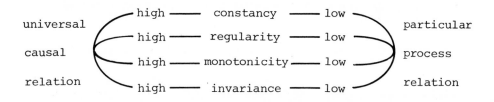

FIG. 8. A TYPOLOGY OF DIACHRONIC RELATIONS.

In other words, we shall prefer to use the term "causality" when the diachronic relation is characterized by very
high values of constancy, regularity and monotonicity and
divide them into universal and particular relations depending
on whether they hold under a very wide or very narrow variety
of conditions. The same distinction will also be used for
processes, which in general are diachronic relations characterized by lower values of constancy, regularity and monotonicity. Of course, if all of these values are very low,
then there is no relation at all to speak of.

*Thus defined, causal relations become special cases of
processes, and the latter become the more general, and much
more useful concept to be used in social science.*

REFERENCES

Blalock, H. M. 1964. *Causal Inferences In Nonexperimental Research.* Chapel Hill: University of North Carolina Press.

Davis, H. T. 1941. *The Analysis of Economic Time Series.* Bloomington, Ind.: Principia Press.

Duesenberry, J. S. 1949. *Income, Saving and the Theory of Consumer Behavior.* Cambridge, Mass.

Freeman, H. 1965. *Discrete--Time Systems.* New York: Wiley.

Fuedinan, M. 1957. *A Theory of the Consumption Function.* Princeton.

Galtung, J. 1967a. "Some Aspects of Comparative Research," *Polls,* 1-19.

Galtung, J. 1967b. *Theory and Methods of Social Research.* New York: Columbia University Press.

Galtung, J. 1968. "The Social Sciences: An Essay on Polarization and Integration," in Knorr and Rosenau (eds.), *Contending Approaches to International Relations.* Princeton: Princeton University Press.

Galtung, J. and T. Høivik. 1967. *On the Definition and Theory of Development with a View to the Application of Rank Order Indicators in the Elaboration of a Composit Index of Human Resources.* UNESCO.

Galtung, J., and M. H. Ruge. 1965. "The Structure of Foreign News," *Journal of Peace Research,* 64-91.

Hannan, E. J. 1960. *Time Series Analysis.* New York: Wiley.

Ivakhnenko, A. G. and V. G. Lapa. 1964. *Cybernetics and and Forecasting Techniques.* Cambridge: M.I.T. Press.

Modigliani, F. 1949. "Fluctuations in the Saving-Income Ratio: A Problem in Economic Forecasting," in *Studies in Income and Wealth,* XI.

Stone, R. 1954. *Measurement of Consumer's Expenditure and Behavior in U. K., 1920-38.* Vol. I. Cambridge.

Stouffer, S. A. 1962. *Social Research to Test Ideas.* Glencoe, Ill.: Free Press.

Wold, H. O. 1956. "Causal Inference from Observational Data: A Review of Ends and Means," *Journal of the Royal Statistical Society,* Series A, 119, pp. 28-61.

Wold, H. O. 1964. "On the Definition and Meaning of Causal Concepts," *Entretien de Monaco en Sciences Humaines.*

Wold, H. O. 1966. "Time as the Realm of Forecasting," University of Uppsala, Institute of Statistics (mimeo).

2

A Probabilistic Analysis of Causality *

PATRICK SUPPES
Stanford University

1. INTRODUCTION

The omission of probability considerations is perhaps the
single greatest weakness in Hume's famous analysis of
causality. As is well known, Hume said that the relation between cause and effect has three essential characteristics,
namely, contiguity, succession in time, and constant conjunction. In other words, causes and their effects are contigu-
ous in space and time, a cause precedes its effect in time,
and causes are followed by their effects in a constant fashion. I would claim that in restricting himself to the concept of constant conjunction, Hume was not fair to the use of
causal notions in ordinary language and experience. Roughly
speaking, the modification of Hume's analysis I propose is to
say that one event is the cause of another if the appearance
of the first event is followed with a high probability by the
appearance of the second, and there is no third event that
we can use to factor out the probability relationship between
the first and second events.

It is the objective of this chapter to work out the technical
details of this fundamental idea and to apply the results to
some of the typical philosophical problems that arise in discussions of causality. Section 2 develops an analysis of

A longer version of the content of this chapter is to be
found in my monograph, *A Probabilistic Theory of Causality*,
North-Holland Publishing Company, Amsterdam, 1970, quoted by
permission of the publisher.

causal relations among events within a standard probabilistic framework, and Section 3 develops a related qualitative causal algebra. Section 4 analyzes causal relations among quantitative variables or properties, and as might be expected, uses as a central concept the probabilistic concept of a random variable.

2. CAUSAL RELATIONS AMONG EVENTS

Reasons for defining causality in terms of probability have already been given. The deepest and in many ways the most substantial reason lies in the wide use of probabilistic causal concepts in ordinary talk; but after a formal theory of causality has been defined in terms of probability notions, I shall examine some scientific applications of the theory. The purpose will be to see in what way causal notions of a probabilistic sort occupy an intuitive and natural place in scientific work.

The formal theory itself is a complex and subtle matter. We must consider a number of examples and counterexamples in order to test the intuitive correctness of the definitions. It should be emphasized that the deterministic concept of cause prominent in classical physics simply occupies the place of a special case in the theory to be outlined here. Roughly speaking, we obtain the deterministic theory by letting all the probabilities in question be either 1 or 0. After working out most of the details of the definitions given here in lectures at Stanford, I discovered that a closely related analysis of causality had been given in an interesting series of articles by I. J. Good (1961, 1962), and the reader is urged to look at Good's articles for a development similar to the one given here, although worked out in rather different fashion formally and from a different viewpoint.

For the definitions and theorems of this section we assume the events referred to are all subsets of a fixed probability space, that the events are instantaneous and that their times of occurrence are included in the formal characterization of the probability space. We write $'P(A_t)'$ for the probability of event A occurring at time t, $'P(A_t/B_{t'})'$ for the probability of A occurring at time t given that event B occurred at time t', and so forth, in the standard notation of probability theory.

Prima Facie Causes

The first definition characterizes *prima facie* causes.
A number of remarks about this definition follow some illustrative examples of its application.

<u>Definition 1</u>. *The event* $B_{t'}$ *is a prima facie cause of
the event* A_t *if and only if*

(i) $t' < t$,

(ii) $P(B_{t'}) > 0$,

(iii) $P(A_t|B_{t'}) > P(A_t)$.

A familiar application of Definition 1 gives rise to
2x2-contingency tables. A classical example is the following
study of the efficacy of inoculation against cholera
(Greenwood and Yule, 1915, cited in Kendall and Stuart,
1961). The data from 818 cases studied are as follows.

	Not Attacked	Attacked	Totals
Inoculated	276	3	279
Not-inoculated	473	66	539
Totals	749	69	818

These data clearly show the efficacy of inoculation, for the
mean probability of not being attacked is 749/818 = 0.912,
whereas the conditional probability of not being attacked,
given that an individual was inoculated, is 276/279 = 0.989.
Here A_t is the event of not being attacked by cholera and $B_{t'}$
the event of being inoculated. As statisticians would put
it, these data show that inoculation is positively associated with exemption from attack; 'measures of association' is
the term commonly used in the statistical literature for
measures of the causal relationship exhibited here and required by Definition 1. In discussing measures of association, it is important to emphasize that from a causal standpoint the temporal order of the events is assumed. For example, even though measures of association are commonly
defined in such a way that the relation could be symmetric,
no one proposes that interpretation of the measure be that
attacks of cholera cause earlier inoculations. The ordinary
intuitive simple ordering of causal events is assumed and

used in any interpretation of such data.

It should be clear that within many conceptual frameworks no positive results about causality can be inferred.
A familiar example is provided by the standard coin-tossing
experiment in which past outcomes have no effect on future
ones. Let h_n be the event of a head on trial n, t_m the
event of a tail on trial m, and so forth. Then for a fair
coin used in a properly conducted experiment, for m < r

$$P(h_n) = P(t_n) = P(h_n|h_m) = P(h_n|t_m)$$

$$= P(t_n|h_m) = P(t_n|t_m) = 1/2. \qquad (1)$$

The only past events are h_m and t_m, so that for this conceptual framework there are no *prima facie* causes, as we may infer directly from the equations (1). It is important to
emphasize that the determination of a causal relationship between events or kinds of events is always relative to some
conceptual framework.

Spurious Causes

The intuitive idea of a spurious cause is that an earlier event may be found which accounts for the conditional
probability of the effect just as well. Formally we have the
following preliminary definition.

Let $B_{t'}$ be a prima facie cause of A_t. Then $B_{t'}$ is a
spurious cause of A_t if and only if there is a t" < t' and an
event $C_{t''}$ such that $P(B_{t'}, C_{t''}) > 0$ and

$$P(A_t|B_{t'}, C_{t''}) = P(A_t|C_{t''}). \qquad (2)$$

It is admitted at once that (2) defines spurious causes in
too simple a fashion. Subsequently we shall want to elaborate on this definition. Questions can be raised even about
the simplest examples of the definition. Some discussions
argue for an equation in which $\bar{B}_{t'}$, the complement of $B_{t'}$, is
included in the defining equation, so that (2) is replaced by

$$P(A_t|B_{t'}, C_{t''}) = P(A_t|\bar{B}_{t'}, C_{t''}), \qquad (3)$$

provided, of course, that $P(\bar{B}_{t'},C_{t''}) => 0$. However, under the provision just made, we may show that (2) and (3) are equivalent, simply as a consequence of elementary probability theory, and thus we do not need to bring in the complement of $B_{t'}$ in defining the spuriousness of $B_{t'}$. To show the equivalence, first let us suppose that (2) holds. Then from obvious relations for conditional probabilities, we have:

$$P(A_t|C_{t''}) = P(A_t|B_{t'},C_{t''})P(B_{t'}|C_{t''}) + P(A_t|\bar{B}_{t'},C_{t''})P(\bar{B}_{t'}|C_{t''})$$

$$(4)$$

whence, using (2), we have from (4)

$$P(A_t|B_{t'},C_{t''})(1 - P(B_{t'}|C_{t''})) = P(A_t|\bar{B}_{t'},C_{t''})P(\bar{B}_{t'}|C_{t''}) , \quad (5)$$

but of course,

$$1 - P(B_{t'}|C_{t''}) = P(\bar{B}_{t'}|C_{t''}) ,$$

and so the desired result follows from (5).

Now assume that (3) holds, then from (3) and (4) we have

$$P(A_t|C_{t''}) = P(A_t|B_{t'},C_{t''})[P(B_{t'}|C_{t''}) + P(\bar{B}_{t'}|C_{t''})]$$

$$= P(A_t|B_{t'},C_{t''}) ,$$

as claimed.

It is a temptation to make the temporal inequality in the preliminary definition weak ($t'' \leq t'$) rather than strict ($t'' < t'$) and thereby permit $B_{t'}$ and $C_{t''}$ to occur simultaneously. However, it is easy to show that without the introduction of some other restriction, this weakening will not do, because it would permit us to show that every cause is spurious. Let $t'' = t'$ and let $C_{t''} = C_{t'} = B_{t'}$. Then for any $B_{t'}$ with $P(B_{t'}) > 0$

$$P(A_t|B_{t'},C_{t'}) = P(A_t|C_{t'}) .$$

Now if we impose the natural requirement that $B_{t'} = C_{t''}$, we can still show any event is spurious if we permit the weak temporal inequality and if we can find any other event $D_{t'}$

distinct from $B_{t'}$, such that $P(B_{t'}, D_{t''}) > 0$; for we may then take

$$C_{t'} = B_{t'} \cap D_{t''},$$

and obviously (2) holds for this definition of $C_{t'}$, because

$$C_{t'} = B_{t'} \cap C_{t'}.$$

However, this last example suggests a real defect of the preliminary definition. Suppose that

$$P(A_t | B_{t'}) > P(A_t | B_{t'}, C_{t''}) .$$

It hardly seems reasonable to call $B_{t'}$ spurious when it alone predicts the occurrence of A_t with higher probability than does the joint event $B_{t'} \cap C_{t''}$. It is apparent that this inequality is consistent with the preliminary definition. In the revised definition it seem intuitively sound to require that its negation hold, i.e., to impose the weak inequality

$$P(A_t | B_{t'}, C_{t''}) \geq P(A_t | B_{t'}) .$$

Even with the inequality imposed it still seems desirable to impose the strict inequality $t'' < t'$. The reason for this is that we would make spurious any causes that are not maximal if we permitted $t'' = t'$. Thus, for example, if $B_{t'}$ were a *prima facie* cause that was not spurious in the sense being defined, but if there were an event $C_{t'}$ such that $B_{t'} \neq C_{t'}$, $P(B_{t'}, C_{t'}) > 0$ and

$$P(A_t | B_t C_{t'}) > P(A_t | B_{t'}) ,$$

then $B_{t'}$ would not be the maximal cause of A_t at time t'. It seems clearly desirable, however, to distinguish spurious from nonmaximal causes. These various remarks about spurious causes are brought together in the following definition.

Definition 2. *An event $B_{t'}$ is a spurious cause in sense one of A_t if and only if $B_{t'}$ is a prima facie cause of A_t*

and there is a $t'' < t'$ and an event $C_{t''}$ such that

(i) $P(B_{t'}, C_{t''}) > 0$,

(ii) $P(A_t | B_{t'}, C_{t''}) = P(A_t | C_{t''})$,

(iii) $P(A_t | B_{t'}, C_{t''}) \geq P(A_t | B_{t'})$.

I am still not certain that the three conditions of Definition 2 are precisely the right ones. I am particularly uneasy about (ii), because there seem to be some arguments in favor of replacing it by the inequality

$$P(A_t | B_{t'}, C_{t''}) \leq P(A_t | C_{t''}) ,$$

so that $B_{t'}$ is spurious if the other conditions are satisfied and the occurrence of $B_{t'}$ after $C_{t''}$ actually lowers the probability of A_t. When the strict inequality holds, one is inclined to call $B_{t'}$ a negative cause of A_t after the earlier occurrence of $C_{t''}$, rather than a spurious cause. My intuition is that *spurious* should mean no real influence at all, either positive or negative, and therefore I shall stand by condition (ii) for the present, but with no strong feeling of correctness about the decision.

We may define a *prima facie* cause that is not spurious as *genuine*. Familiar examples of both spurious and genuine causes are easily produced. Some simple artifical examples may be clarifying. Consider first the three-state Markov chain whose transition matrix is

n+1 \ n	0	1	2
0	0	1/2	1/2
1	1/3	0	2/3
2	1/4	3/4	0

Here every *prima facie* cause is genuine. Now consider the transition-matrix.

n+1 n	0	1	2
0	0	1/2	1/2
1	1/4	3/4	0
2	1/4	0	3/4

The process has the Markov property; but according to Definition 2, and also, I believe, according to intuition, the event of being in either state 1 or state 2 is a spurious cause of being in state 0 on the next trial, because $P(0_n)$ = .2 as $n \to \infty$ and

$$P(0_n | 1_{n-1} 0_{n-2}) = P(0_{n-2} | 2_{n-1} 0_{n-2}) = P(0_n | 0_{n-2}) = 1/4 .$$

I realize that the application of causal terminology to these simple Markov examples makes some people uneasy. For the moment I remark only that this uneasiness comes from the very strongly felt need to identify what seem to be ultimate causes and not to use causal terminology at all in dealing with processes that intentionally catch only a partial aspect of the real world.

A deeper problem may be raised about Definition 2 and its intuitive adequacy for characterizing spurious causes. Definition 2 makes a *prima facie* cause spurious if there *exists* a possible earlier event that eliminates the effectiveness of the cause when that event occurs. It is true that condition (iii) imposes a rather strong constraint on this earlier event. But an intuitively appealing alternative approach is to drop (iii) and demand a partition of the past before the spurious cause such that for every element in the partition, conditions (i) and (ii) hold. Intuitively this amounts to requiring that if we can observe a certain kind of earlier event, then knowledge of the spurious cause is predictively uninformative. The existential requirement is now moved from a demand for an event to a demand for a kind of event or property. For formal purposes we note that a partition of the sample space or universe is a collection of pairwise disjoint, nonempty sets whose union is the whole space. For our purposes we shall also require that a partition π_t consists of events that can be defined by references to times no later than t.

<u>Definition 3.</u> *An event* B_t *is a spurious cause of* A_t *in sense two if and only if* B_t *is a prima facie cause of* A_t *and there is a t" < t' and a partition* $\pi_{t"}$ *such that for all elements* $C_{t"}$ *of* $\pi_{t"}$

$$(i) \quad P(B_t, C_{t"}) > 0,$$

$$(ii) \quad P(A_t | B_t, C_{t"}) = P(A_t | C_{t"}) \ .$$

It is evident that spuriousness in sense two implies spuriousness in sense one; the simple proof is omitted.

Direct Causes

The concept of an indirect cause is of less importance but similar in structure to the concept of a spurious cause. In this case, however, it is somewhat more natural to define direct rather than indirect causes. Of course, a *prima facie* cause is indirect if it is not direct.

<u>Definition 4.</u> *An event* $B_{t'}$ *is a direct cause of* A_t *if and only if* $B_{t'}$ *is a prima facie cause of* A_t *and there is no t" and no partition* $\pi_{t"}$ *such that for every* $C_{t"}$ *in* $\pi_{t"}$

$$(i) \quad t' < t" < t \ ,$$

$$(ii) \quad P(B_t, C_{t"}) > 0 \ ,$$

$$(iii) \quad P(A_t | C_{t"} B_{t'}) = P(A_t | C_{t"}) \ .$$

The conditions of Definition 4 are almost precisely those of Definition 3 except that now time t" comes between t and t' rather than before t'.

Indeed, the symmetry of the conditions in Definitions 3 and 4 suggest that causes $B_{t'}$ and $C_{t"}$ of $A_{t'}$ with t" < t', could have the following relation. Event $B_{t'}$ is a spurious cause of A_t because of the prior partition $\{C_{t"}, \overline{C_{t"}}\}$, and concurrently $C_{t"}$ is an indirect cause of A_t because of the later partition $\{B_{t'}, \overline{B_{t'}}\}$. If this line of reasoning worked, one has the feeling we might be able to show that in many circumstances there is a natural linking of spurious and indirect causes. The following theorem shows, however, that this cannot happen.

Theorem 1. *Let* $B_{t'}$ *and* $C_{t''}$ *be prima facie causes of* $A_{t'}$ *with* t" < t'. *Then it cannot be the case that jointly* $C_{t''}$ *is an indirect cause of* A_t, *because of the partition* $\{B_{t'}, \overline{B_{t'}}\}$, *and* $B_{t'}$ *is a spurious cause (in sense two) of* A_t *because of the partition* $\{C_{t''}, \overline{C_{t''}}\}$.

Proof: To simplify notation I drop the temporal subscripts in the proof. I derive a contradiction from the hypothesis that C is an indirect cause of A because of $\{B, \overline{B}\}$ and that B is a spurious cause of A because of $\{C, \overline{C}\}$. From the hypothesis about C we have

$$P(A|BC) = P(A|B) , \qquad (6)$$

$$P(A|\overline{B}C) = P(A|\overline{B}) ; \qquad (7)$$

and from the hypothesis about B we have

$$P(A|BC) = P(A|C) , \qquad (8)$$

$$P(A|B\overline{C}) = P(A|\overline{C}). \qquad (9)$$

From (6) and (8), and the hypothesis that B and C are *prima facie* causes of A, we have

$$P(A/B) = P(A/C) > P(A) . \qquad (10)$$

From elementary probability theory

$$P(A|C) = P(A|BC)P(B|C) + P(A|\overline{B}C)P(\overline{B}|C) , \qquad (11)$$

which, using (8), we may rewrite

$$P(A|C)(1 - P(B|C)) = P(A|\overline{B}C)(1 - P(B|C)) . \qquad (12)$$

Now from the joint hypothesis about B and C, and the definitions of spurious causes and direct causes, we have

$$P(BC) , P(B\overline{C}) , P(\overline{B}C) > 0 , \qquad (13)$$

whence from (12) and (13) we infer

$$P(A|\bar{B}C) = P(A|C) , \tag{14}$$

but then from (7) and (14)

$$P(A|C) = P(A|\bar{B}) , \tag{15}$$

but since

$$P(A|B) > P(A) ,$$

we must have, in view of (13),

$$P(A|\bar{B}) < P(A) , \tag{16}$$

and so from (15) and (16)

$$P(A|C) < P(A) ,$$

which contradicts (10). Q.E.D.

Direct causes that have any degree of remoteness in time violate Hume's criterion of contiguity. The existence of such causes has been a subject of debate, dogma, theory, and experimentation in almost every branch of human thought. Within physical theories the idea of direct causes remote in time has not been as prominent as analysis of the problem of action at a distance--with the action being promulgated instantaneously. However, the theory of relativity has made any sharp separation of spatial remoteness from temporal remoteness impossible, because the concept of instantaneous action at a distance is not relativistically meaningful. It should be emphasized, however, that the concept of direct remote causes is quite consistent with relativity; and the definitions given can be modified to become relativistically invariant, although I shall not pursue this technical point here. But as Maxwell pointed out many years ago, most of us are particularly bothered by remote direct causes, once remoteness in both space and time is required by finite speeds of propagation of energy. This is what he said in the final paragraph of his *Treatise on Electricity and Magnetism* (3rd edition, 1892).

"But in all of these theories the question naturally occurs:--If something is transmitted from one particle to another at a distance, what is its condition after it has left the one particle and before it has reached the other? If this something is the potential energy of the

two particles, as in Neumann's theory, how are we
to conceive this energy as existing in a point of
space, coinciding neither with the one particle
nor with the other? In fact, whenever energy is
transmitted from one body to another in time,
there must be a medium or substance in which the
energy exists after it leaves one body and before
it reaches the other, for energy, as Torricelli
remarked, 'is a quintessence of so subtile a
nature that it cannot be contained in any vessel
except the inmost substance of material things.'
Hence all these theories lead to the conception
of a medium in which the propagation takes place,
and if we admit this medium as an hypothesis, I
think it ought to occupy a prominent place in our
investigations, and that we ought to endeavour to
construct a mental representation of all the details of its action, and this has been my constant
aim in this treatise."

The conceptual viewpoint expressed by Maxwell is so persua-
sive that most physical theories were field theories rather
than action-at-a-distance theories, once electromagnetic concepts came to the fore. Although this is true in physics, it
is profoundly not true in many other parts of science, especially any part that emphasizes historical knowledge of the
phenomena studied.

It is a widespread scientific dogma that all aspects of
historical knowledge can be replaced ultimately and in principle by a sufficiently deep structural knowledge of the current state of the phenomena in question. The depth of general conviction that this dogma asserts a fundamental truth
about the character of the real world is difficult to over-
estimate.

In terms of distinctions already drawn the matter can be
put this way. Within many theoretical or strictly experimental frameworks the existence of direct remote causes will
be affirmed with great certainty and assurance; but within
the framework of fundamental beliefs about the general character of the universe their existence will be strongly
denied.

If the assessment of the extent to which remote temporal
action is rejected is approximately correct, it is appropriate to ask why a concept of remote direct causation is
needed. The best answer perhaps can be given by looking at
the comparable status of the concept of probability in the
nineteenth century. Laplace's famous statement on the deterministic character of the universe was made in his treatise

on probability, not, as one might expect, in his treatise on
celestial mechanics. For Laplace, probability was a tool of
analysis and prediction which enabled scientists systematically to take account of their ignorance of complex causes.
The concept of remote direct causation is a tool of a similar kind and is essential for practical and scientific analysis of many sorts. Its usefulness will not disappear in the
foreseeable future in disciplines ranging from political
history to meteorology.

Supplementary Causes

Related to the notion of a direct cause is the concept
of two *prima facie* causes supplementing each other in producing a given effect.

Definition 5. *Events* $B_{t'}$ *and* $C_{t''}$ *are supplementary
causes of* A_t *if and only if* $B_{t'}$ *and* $C_{t''}$ *are prima facie
causes of* A_t *and*

(1) $P(B_{t'}, C_{t''}) > 0$,

(ii) $P(A_t | B_{t'}, C_{t''}) > \max(P(A_t | B_{t'}), P(A_t | C_{t''}))$.

Note that the definition does not require that times t' and
t" be distinct, although in many cases they will be.

Negative Causes

In the literature of causality there has been a fair
amount of discussion of negative causes. It should be clear
how *prima facie* and genuine negative causes can be defined in
purely probabilistic terms. The intuitive idea of a negative cause is that it tends to prevent an event from happen-
ing, and this concept can be expressed by little more than
the reversal of inequalities in the earlier definitions.
Formally, I consider only *prima facie* negative causes.

Definition 6. *The event* $B_{t'}$ *is a prima facie negative
cause of* A_t *if and only if*

(i) $t' < t$,

(ii) $P(B_{t'}) > 0$,

(iii) $P(A_t | B_{t'}) < P(A_t)$.

To use an example discussed earlier, inoculation is a negative cause of cholera, or, to put the matter in explicit
event-language, the event of being inoculated for cholera is
a negative cause of the event of getting cholera. To generalize on this example, the theory and practice of preventive
medicine concentrates on certain types of negative causation.

Because events form a Boolean algebra, it is easy to
give a necessary and sufficient condition on events' being
negative causes in terms of their complements' being causes.

Theorem 2. $B_{t'}$ is a *prima facie negative cause of* A_t
if and only if $\bar{B}_t$ *is a prima facie cause of* A_t.

Proof: Assume first that $B_{t'}$ is a *prima facie* negative
cause of A_t. We note first that (omitting subscripts in the
proof)

$$P(A) = P(A|B)P(B) + P(A|\bar{B})P(\bar{B}) , \qquad (17)$$

whence on the assumption that

$$P(A) > P(A|B) , \qquad (18)$$

we must have

$$P(\bar{B}) > 0 , \qquad (19)$$

for otherwise we would have $P(B) = 1$, and therefore $P(A) =$
$P(A|B)$. It then follows at once from (17), (18) and (19)
that

$$P(A) < P(A|\bar{B}) ,$$

whence $\bar{B}$ is a *prima facie* cause of A.

The argument in the other direction is analogous and
will be omitted. Q.E.D.

The causal concepts that have been introduced thus far
by no means exhaust the list of essential distinctions, nor
have the relations holding between the concepts introduced
been pursued as thoroughly as possible.

3. A CAUSAL ALGEBRA

In examining the philosophical literature on
causality I have been surprised to find no attempt to
develop the abstract algebra of causal relations in contrast to a logical calculus of causal propositions.
Perhaps the best-known calculus is that

62

of Burks (1951), and I shall compare the causal algebra of events developed here with his calculus. Further, in the present context the development of a causal algebra of events is free from the paradoxes of implication that seem to haunt most thinking about a causal logical calculus. For example, if we follow the ideas developed thus far, there is no problem of whether the algebraic relation corresponding to causal implication should exhibit a contrapositive property. From temporal considerations alone, clearly it should not.

I shall concentrate on properties of the relation of *prima facie* causality. Thus, we shall read B Π A as B is a *prima facie* cause of A. To keep the algebra as simple as possible and to permit a relatively direct contrast with causal calculi I shall omit temporal indices, but the proofs of the theorem shall be based upon the temporal assumptions made explicit in the probabilistic definitions of the preceding section. I have organized the elementary properties of Π in a sequence of seven theorems.

Theorem 3. *It is not the case A Π A.*

Proof: Trivial, since A cannot precede itself in time, and thus Definition 1 cannot be satisfied.

Theorem 4. *If B Π A then*

(i) $\bar{B} \, \Pi \, \bar{A}$

(ii) *it is not the case A Π B,*

(iii) *it is not the case $\bar{A} \, \Pi \, \bar{B}$,*

(iv) *it is not the case B Π $\bar{A}$,*

(v) *it is not the case $\bar{B} \, \Pi \, A$.*

Proof: Parts (ii) and (iii) follow from temporal considerations alone. As to (i), from the hypotheses and Definition 1, we have

$$P(A/B) \; > \; P(A) \; , \tag{20}$$

and also

$$P(B) \neq 0 \text{ and } P(\bar{B}) \neq 0 \; . \tag{21}$$

By virtue of the theorem on total probability

$$P(A) = P(A/B)P(B) + P(A/\bar{B})P(\bar{B}) \; , \tag{22}$$

whence from (20) and (22)

$$P(A) > P(A)P(B) + P(A|\bar{B})P(\bar{B}) ,$$

and thus since $P(\bar{B}) = 1 - P(B)$, we have

$$P(A)P(\bar{B}) > P(A|\bar{B})P(\bar{B}) .$$

In view of (21) we may divide both sides by $P(\bar{B})$ to obtain

$$P(A) > P(A|\bar{B}) , \tag{23}$$

which is equivalent to

$$1 - P(\bar{A}) > 1 - P(\bar{A}|\bar{B}) ,$$

and hence

$$P(\bar{A}|\bar{B}) > P(\bar{A}) ,$$

or,

$$\bar{B} \; \text{Π} \; \bar{A} ,$$

as desired.

As to (iv), from inequality (1) above, we have

$$1 - P(\bar{A}|B) > 1 - P(\bar{A}) ,$$

whence

$$P(\bar{A}) > P(\bar{A}|B) ,$$

and thus

$$\text{not } P(\bar{A}|B) > P(\bar{A}) ,$$

or

$$\text{not } B \; \text{Π} \; \bar{A}.$$

As to (v), it is a direct consequence of inequality (23) above. Q.E.D.

Part (iii) of Theorem 4 asserts that "contraposition" does not hold for Π, but the proof is not interesting, for temporal considerations only are needed. The interpretation of (i), the most significant part of the theorem, may bother some. It is natural to gloss it this way: the absence of B is a *prima facie* cause of the absence of A. In many contexts this sort of gloss seems appropriate. A child does not get measles when all of his friends do. The mother asks the doctor why, and he says, "But remember, you and your family were away at a critical time, and the absence of exposure means no measles now."

The next two theorems show how different the relation Π of *prima facie* causality is from the relation of material implication between propositions.

Theorem 5. *If* B = 0 *or* B = X *then there is no event* A *such that* B Π A.

Proof: If B = 0 the conclusion follows immediately from the requirement that $P(B) > 0$. If B = X then $P(A|B) = P(A|X) = P(A)$, and thus it cannot be the case that $P(A|B) > P(A)$. Q.E.D. Theorem 5 says that an event that is logically impossible or logically certain cannot be a *prima facie* cause. The next theorem says that such an event also cannot be the effect of a *prima facie cause*.

Theorem 6. *If* A = 0 *or* A = X *then there is no event* B such that B Π A.

Proof: If A = 0 for any B,

$$P(A|B) = P(A) = 0 ,$$

and if A = X for any B,

$$P(A|B) = P(A) = 1 ,$$

whence in neither case can the appropriate inequality hold. Q.E.D.

I have not seen the point much discussed elsewhere, but it seems intuitively desirable to have logically certain events uncaused. For example, to ask for the cause of the event of raining or not raining yesterday does not seem appropriate. A good paraphrase of Theorem 5 is that logically certain events are uncaused.

It is important to recognize that the two theorems just proved cannot be extended to the assertion that any event that is neither certain nor impossible must have a cause. Such an assertion is a very special thesis about the nature of the universe, and as has been pointed out earlier, one that is not satisfied in many theoretically and empirically important models.

Some weaker assertions must be handled with care. It might seem that the following should be a theorem: if there is an event C such that C Π A and B $\subseteq$ A then B Π A. In other words, if an event A does have a *prima facie* cause and B is a necessary consequence of A then the occurrence of B is a *prima facie* cause of the occurrence of A. The problem is that in order to have B $\amalg$ A, B must precede A in time, and this is exactly the sort of necessary connection that Hume found so mysterious and unsatisfactory. Underlying algebras of events may be constructed for stochastic processes in which necessary connections do exist between events occurring at different times, but this is unusual.[1] Temporal connections that might ordinarily be thought of as necessary are usually handled within stochastic processes by probability-one statements--a viewpoint that almost certainly would meet with Hume's approval.

To prove a theorem applicable to the unusual cases we would need to introduce explicitly temporal subscripts requiring that B_t, be before A_t, and this is against the purely algebraic spirit of this section.

There are two "addition" theorems that have a purely algebraic formulation. The first says that if A is a *prima facie* cause of C and B is also, and if A and B are mutually exclusive, then the disjunctive event A or B is a *prima facie* cause of C.

Theorem 7. *If A $\amalg$ C, B $\amalg$ C and A $\cap$ B = O, then* A $\cup$ B $\amalg$ C.

Proof: By hypothesis $P(A) > O$, $P(B) > O$, and

$$P(C|A) > P(C) , \tag{24}$$

$$P(C|B) > P(C) , \tag{25}$$

whence by virtue of the definition of conditional probability

$$P(C \cap A) > P(C)P(A)$$

$$P(C \cap B) > P(C)P(B) ,$$

and consequently, using the hypothesis that A $\cap$ B = O, we have

$$P(C \cap (A \cup B)) > P(C)P(A \cup B),$$

whence

---

[1]For an example from learning theory, see Estes and Suppes (1959). In the theory developed there, stimulus-response conditioning connections at one time have a necessary connection to such connections at another time.

$$P(C|A \cup B) > P(C) ,$$

i.e.,

$$A \cup B \amalg C .$$ Q.E.D.

It might seem that the hypothesis that $A \cap B = 0$ is unnecessary, but the following example shows that it is. Let $X = \{a_1, a_2, a_3, a_4, a_5\}$, $A = \{a_1, a_2\}$, $B = \{a_2, a_3\}$, $C = \{a_2, a_4\}$, and $P(a_1) = P(a_2) = P(a_3) = \frac{1}{4}$, $P(a_4) = \frac{5}{24}$, $P(a_5) = \frac{1}{24}$. Then $P(C|A = P(C|B) = \frac{1}{2} > \frac{11}{24} = P(C) > \frac{1}{3} = P(C|A \cup B)$.
A casual glance at Theorem 5 and Theorem 7 might suggest a contradiction, based on the idea that using Theorem 7 and showing that $A \amalg C$ and $\bar{A} \amalg C$, we could infer $A \cup \bar{A} \amalg C$, i.e., $X \amalg C$, contrary to Theorem 5. However, Theorem 4, Part (v), asserts that we cannot have both $A \amalg C$ and $\bar{A} \amalg C$, and so this special case of the hypothesis of Theorem 7 cannot be realized.

Theorem 8. *If* $A \amalg B$, $A \amalg C$ *and* $B \cap C = 0$, *then* $A \amalg B \cup C$.

Proof: By hypothesis

$$P(B|A) > P(B)$$

$$P(C|A) > P(C) ,$$

and since $B \cap C = 0$, the additivity of conditional as well as unconditional probability applies, so that we have

$$P(B \cup C|A) > P(B \cup C) ,$$

the desired result. Q.E.D.

I leave it to the reader to construct an example to show that just as in the case of Theorem 7, the hypothesis that $B \cap C = 0$ is necessary.

As a final theorem about *prima facie* causes it seems desirable to make explicit the negative fact that $\amalg$ is not transitive, still another point of formal difference from most relations of implication.

Theorem 9. *The causal relation* $\amalg$ *is not transitive.*

Proof: It is sufficient to construct an example of three events A, B and C such that $A \amalg B$, $B \amalg C$ but not $A \amalg C$. The example, although simple, illustrates clearly the general reason why transitivity can easily fail. Because temporal considerations are at the heart of the theory of causality developed here, they are explicitly introduced in the example. At time t" either A or $\bar{A}$ must occur, at t' either B or $\bar{B}$, and at t, either C or $\bar{C}$ with pairwise exclusion holding. Also let t" < t' < t. Define then the transition matrix

	C	$\bar{C}$
AB	O	1
A$\bar{B}$	O	1
$\bar{A}$B	$\frac{2}{3}$	$\frac{1}{3}$
$\bar{A}\bar{B}$	$\frac{1}{3}$	$\frac{2}{3}$

And set $P(A) = \frac{1}{4}$, $P(B|A) = \frac{2}{3}$, and $P(B|\bar{A}) = \frac{1}{3}$. Then it is easy to compute that $P(B) = \frac{5}{12}$, $P(C|B) = \frac{2}{5}$, and $P(C) = \frac{1}{3}$, which satisfies the requirement that A Π B and B Π C. On the other hand, $P(C|A) = O$, but $P(C) = \frac{1}{3}$, and so, it is not the case A π C. Q.E.D.

Unfortunately the example just constructed to show that the causal relation Π is not transitive will also suffice to show the same thing about the relations of genuine causality defined earlier (either sense one or sense two). Naive intuition argues strongly for the transitivity of causal relations, but the sort of example constructed above generalizes easily to a variety of apparently realistic examples. It seems worth investigating the structure of those stochastic processes that preserve causal transitivity.

On the other hand, sufficient or determinate causes are transitive. This follows from their definition and a simple fact of elementary probability theory: If $P(B) > O$, $P(C) > O$, $P(A|B) = 1$ and $P(B|C) = 1$, then $P(A|C) = 1$.

At the beginning of this section, I promised a comparison with Burks' (1951) causal logic. It should be clear enough by now how different is the causal algebra developed here. Few of the principles explicitly discussed by Burks hold for the relation π. Without attempting to review Burks' article in detail, I do think there are three essential features of his causal logic not possessed by the causal algebra

of this section: (i) the null event is a cause and the universal event is an effect, (ii) contraposition holds, and
(iii) his causal relation is transitive.

Naturally I think the differences between Burks' causal
calculus and the causal algebra developed here are favorable
to the algebra, but the great disparity between their formal
properties is more of a warning that our intuitions are as
yet quite superficial and undeveloped, and any proposal must
surely be wrong in several unsuspected ways.

4.   CAUSAL RELATIONS AMONG QUANTITATIVE PROPERTIES

In many scientific investigations we naturally think of
causal relations in terms of properties, especially quantitative properties, rather than events.   For example, is obesity in a baby causally related to obesity in later life?   Is
subsequent velocity a linear or nonlinear function of the
force of impact on a body; in this case we are concerned with
the exact nature of a causal relation, not its mere existence. Indeed, much of the physical sciences is primarily
concerned with the discovery and analysis of causal relationships between quantitative properties.   In the scientific
literature most such relationships have been described in
deterministic rather than probabilistic fashion.   Reasons for
adhering to the probabilistic viewpoint have been given
earlier.   It is worth noting also that much current literature in the physical sciences is probabilistic in character.
As the mathematics of probabilistic theories becomes better
developed the use of probabilistic concepts should increase.

Within the biological and social sciences a stronger
tradition of probabilistic analysis prevails, probably because of the general absence of deterministic theories with
any serious pretense of accuracy of prediction.   The classical statistical techniques of correlation and regression
analysis have been the primary tools for the investigation
of causal relations.   Although correlation and regression
are discussed later, I shall mainly draw on a more general
and abstract theory of dependence for random variables (or
quantitative properties) developed by Lehmann (1966).

I use the standard notion of a random variable as the
basic formal tool of analysis.   Each quantitative property
will be represented by a random variable, and any finite
family of random variables considered will be assumed to
have a joint probability distribution.

The form of definitions in this section will be similar
to the corresponding definitions in Section 2.   However,
only weak inequalities will be used, because of the

mathematical awkwardness of strong inequalities, and the verbal form of the definitions of this section reflect this fact.

Definition 7. *The property* $Y_{t'}$ *is a (weak) prima facie quadrant cause of the property* X_t *if and only if*

   (i) $t' < t$,

   (ii) *For all x and y if* $P(Y_{t'} \geq y) > 0$ *then*
$$P(X_t \geq x \mid Y_{t'} \geq y) \geq P(X_t \geq x) .$$

The term *quadrant* is used because (ii) may be rewritten

$$P(X_t \geq x, Y_{t'} \geq y) \geq P(X_t \geq x) P(Y_{t'} \geq y) ,$$

which expresses a comparison between the probability of any quadrant $X_t \geq x, Y_{t'} \geq y$ under the given distribution and the probability of this quadrant in the case of independence.

In the literature of applied statistics the most common notion of dependence between random variables or quantitative properties is that of correlation. Following the methods of Lehmann (1966) we may prove the following theorem to show that the notion of *prima facie* cause defined here implies that of nonnegative correlation. Some standard probabilistic concepts are needed.

In many ways the most theoretically important measure of dependence of random variables is their covariance, which we define together with their correlation.

Definition 8. *Let X and Y be two random variables. The covariance of X and Y is defined as:*

$$\mathrm{cov}(X,Y) = \int_{-\infty}^{\infty} \int_{-\infty}^{\infty} (x - E(X))(y - E(Y)) f(x,y)\,dx\,dy ,$$

and the correlation coefficient $\rho(X,Y)$ *as:*

$$\rho(X,Y) = \frac{\mathrm{cov}(X,Y)}{\sigma_X \sigma_Y} .$$

It is important to note that if X and Y are independent then the covariance and correlation coefficient equal zero, but the converse is not always true.

The concept of partial correlation is also important for the analysis of spurious causes. The usual discussion of these matters is restricted to a multivariate normal distribution. Such normal distributions have many special attractive features, and it is not possible to develop a correspondingly attractive theory for arbitrary multivariate distributions.

For the general case it is natural to use the conditional correlation as the measure of correlation in the presence of a third variable.

Definition 9. *Let X, Y and Z be three random variables. The conditional correlation of X and Y with Z held constant is defined as*

$$\rho(X,Y \mid Z = z) = \frac{\text{cov}(X,Y \mid Z = z)}{\sigma(X \mid Z = z)\sigma(Y \mid Z = z)} .$$

In other words, the conditional correlation is defined in terms of the conditional covariance of X and Y and conditional variances of X and Y. If $\rho(X,Y) \neq 0$, but for every z $\rho(X,Y \mid Z = z) = 0$, we say that the correlation between X and Y is *spurious*. An important and surprising fact about a multivariate normal distribution is that the value of $\rho(X,Y \mid Z = z)$ is independent of z, as are the conditional covariance and the conditional variances. The idea of correlation is that of a linear dependence between two variables, and in the multivariate normal case this is the only kind of dependence.

The classical notion of a partial correlation coefficient may be founded on this notion of linearity.

Definition 10. *Let X and Y be two random variables with finite means and variances, and with variances not zero. Then the equation*

$$Y = \mu_Y + \rho_{XY} \frac{\sigma_Y}{\sigma_X} (X - \mu_X)$$

is the least squares regression line of Y on X.

We next define the partial correlation coefficient in the form proposed by Wilks (1962, p. 94).

Definition 11. *Let X, Y and Z be three random variables with finite covariances and variances, and with variances not zero. Let U be defined as the difference of X and the least squares regression line of X on Z, i.e.,*

$$U = X - \mu_X - \rho_{XZ} \frac{\sigma_X}{\sigma_Z} (Z - \mu_Z) \ ,$$

and let V be defined similarly as the difference of Y and the least squares regression line of Y on Z. Then the correlation of U and V, $\rho(U,V)$, is called the partial correlation of X and Y with Z held constant, and is written $\rho(XY.Z)$.

We then have the following theorem, which expresses the partial correlation in the standard form.

Theorem 10. Under the hypothesis of Definition 11,

$$\rho(XY.Z) = \frac{\rho_{XY} - \rho_{XZ}\rho_{YZ}}{\sqrt{1 - \rho_{XZ}^2} \cdot \sqrt{1 - \rho_{YZ}^2}} \ .$$

Proof: Using the relevant linear regression definitions of U and V given above, we have

$$\mathrm{cov}(U,V) = E(UV) - E(U)E(V)$$

$$= E(XY) - \mu_X\mu_Y - \rho_{YZ} \frac{\sigma_Y}{\sigma_Z} (E(XZ) - \mu_X\mu_Z) - \mu_X\mu_Y + \mu_X\mu_Y$$

$$+ \rho_{YZ} \frac{\sigma_Y}{\sigma_Z} (\mu_X\mu_Z - \mu_X\mu_Z - \rho_{XZ} \frac{\sigma_X}{\sigma_Z} (E(YZ) - \mu_Y\mu_Z)$$

$$- \rho_{XZ} \frac{\sigma_X}{\sigma_Z} (\mu_Y\mu_Z) - \mu_Y\mu_Z) + \rho_{XZ}\rho_{YZ} \frac{\sigma_X\sigma_Y}{\sigma_Z} (E(Z^2) - \mu_Z^2)$$

$$- E(U)E(V) \ .$$

Noting that $E(U = E(V) = 0$ and cancelling, we obtain

$$\mathrm{cov}(U,V) = \mathrm{cov}(X,Y) - \rho_{YZ} \frac{\sigma_Y}{\sigma_Z} \mathrm{cov}(X,Z) - \rho_{XZ} \frac{\sigma_X}{\sigma_Y} \mathrm{cov}(Y,Z)$$

$$+ \rho_{XZ}\rho_{YZ}\sigma_X\sigma_Y \ .$$

By similar methods, we obtain

$$\sigma_U^2 = \sigma_X^2(1 - \rho_{XZ}^2)$$

$$\sigma_V^2 = \sigma_Y^2(1 - \rho_{YZ}^2) \ .$$

So that, after simplifying, we have

$$\rho(U,V) = \rho(XY.Z) = \frac{\sigma_X \sigma_Y \rho_{XY} - \sigma_X \sigma_Y \rho_{XZ} \rho_{YZ}}{\sigma_X \sqrt{1 - \rho_{XZ}^2} \cdot \sigma_Y \sqrt{1 - \rho_{YZ}^2}}$$

$$= \frac{\rho_{XY} - \rho_{XZ} \rho_{YZ}}{\sqrt{1 - \rho_{XZ}^2} \cdot \sqrt{1 - \rho_{YZ}^2}} \quad ,$$

as desired.   Q.E.D.

In the case of a multivariate normal distribution, $\rho(XY \mid Z = z) = 0$ for all z if and only if $\rho(XY.Z) = 0$, and so there is just one notion of spurious correlation for normal distributions. As has already been suggested, for nonnormal distributions the partial correlation coefficient is not as meaningful. The following is a simple example for which $\rho(XY \mid Z = z) = 0$ for all z, but $\rho(XY.Z) \neq 0$, and it seems intuitively clear that the meaningful relationship is the zero conditional correlation of X and Y for all values of Z.

Example. Let X, Y and Z take only the values 0 and 1, and let the joint probability of each possible triple be a function of a single parameter b between 0 and 1.

X	Y	Z	p
1	1	0	b/9
1	0	0	2b/9
0	1	0	2b/9
0	0	0	4b/9
1	1	1	4(1 - b)/9
1	0	1	2(1 - b)/9
0	1	1	2(1 - b)/9
0	0	1	(1 - b)/9

Then the reader may easily check that $\rho\,(XY) \neq 0$, $\rho\,(XY\,|\,Z = z)$ $= 0$ for all z and if b $\neq 1/2$, $\rho\,(XY.Z) \neq 0$.

Theorem 11. *If* $Y_{t'}$ *is a prima facie quadrant cause of* X_t *and if the variances of* $Y_{t'}$ *and* X_t *exist as well as their covariance, and if neither variance is zero, then the correlation of* X_t *and* $Y_{t'}$ *is nonnegative.*

Proof: By hypothesis of the theorem the correlation coefficient $\rho\,(X,Y)$ is well defined. From the definition of covariance, we may derive at once

$$cov(X,Y) = E(XY) - E(X)E(Y) \ .$$

The following lemma is due to Höffding (1940).

If F_X *and* F_Y *are the marginal distributions of* X *and* Y, *then*

$$E(XY) - E(X)E(Y) = \int_{-\infty}^{\infty} \int_{-\infty}^{\infty} [F(x,y) - F_X(x)F_Y(y)]\,dx\,dy$$

provided the expectations exist.
Now from clause (ii) of Definition 7, it follows from the lemma that

$$cov(X,Y) \geq 0 \ ,$$

and thus $\rho\,(X,Y) \geq 0$.   Q.E.D.

Some closely related remarks on regression are included below.
I turn next to spurious causes and restrict the considerations to sense two as used in Definition 3. The partition required in that definition is not needed in the numerical case and thereby some simplification is perhaps obtained by the demand for a prior random variable $Z_{t''}$ at the same logical level X_t and $Y_{t'}$.

Definition 12. *A property* $Y_{t'}$ *is a spurious quadrant cause of* X_t *in sense two if and only if there is a* t" < t' *and a property* $Z_{t''}$ *such that*

(i) $Y_{t'}$ *is a prima facie quadrant cause of* $X_{t'}$,

(ii)   *For all x, y and z if* $P(Y_{t'} \geq y, Z_{t''} \geq z) > 0$ *then*

74

$$P(X_t \geq x | Y_{t'} \geq y, Z_{t''} \geq z) = P(X_t \geq x | Z_{t''} \geq z) .$$

In the literature of applied statistics, the notion most closely corresponding to that of spurious quadrant causality is that of spurious correlation. Roughly speaking, two random variables are said to be spuriously correlated if the correlation between them can be shown to vanish when a third variable is introduced and "held constant." The necessity of investigating the possibility of spurious correlation before using the existence of a correlation to make an inference about causal relations has long been recognized in statistics. A good detailed discussion of the causal significance of spurious correlations is to be found in Simon (1954).

However, the relation between correlations and causal inferences is still confused in much of the statistical literature. When a third variable is considered and a correlation is still found between the original two variables, this correlation is called *partial*. In discussing these matters, Kendall and Stuart, in their well-known treatise on statistics, say (1961, vol. 2, p. 317), "As with ordinary product-moment correlations, so with partial correlations: the presumption of causality must always be extra-statistical." The only sense in which the viewpoint developed here is consistent with this statement is that the choice of conceptual framework or theory is extra-statistical. In making a claim of genuine causality we must relativize the claim to some conceptual framework. The quantifier embedded in the definition must be understood to range just over the events, or, in the present case, the random variables or properties of the given framework. That there are additional extra-statistical methods of causal inference beyond this fixing of the framework is denied. I take it that the position being defended here remains close to Hume's. The two steps taking us beyond Hume are the probabilistic considerations and the relativization of an explicit causal inference to a given conceptual framework.

Corresponding to the preceding theorem about correlations, we may prove the following theorem about spurious correlations.

Theorem 12. *Spurious quadrant causality implies spurious correlation.*

Proof: Let $Y_{t'}$ be a *prima facie* cause X_t and let $Z_{t''}$, with $t'' < t'$, be the property that renders $Y_{t''}$ spurious. In what follows, for simplicity of notation I shall drop the temporal subscripts.

Now from (ii) of Definition 12 we have

$$P(X \geq x \mid Y \geq y, \ Z \geq z) = P(X \geq x \mid Z \geq z)$$

for all x, y and z, whence by elementary probability theory we may infer the conditional independence of X and Y given Z:

$$P(X \geq x, \ Y \geq y \mid Z \geq z) = P(X \geq x \mid Z \geq z) P(Y \geq y \mid Z \geq z) \ ,$$

and thus

$$\mathrm{cov}(X,Y \mid Z = z) = 0$$

for all z and so also

$$\rho(X,Y \mid Z = z) = 0 \ . \qquad\qquad \text{Q.E.D.}$$

The extension of the concept of direct cause to random variables is completely straightforward and will be omitted. The analysis of dependence and thereby of putative causality is a very large topic in statistics, and a great deal more could be said about the standard methods of analysis running from multiple correlation and the analysis of variance to regression models, but I shall terminate the technical developments at this point.

It is important to emphasize that the causal concepts defined in this section lead out into a large and sophisticated statistical literature that is relevant to well-designed empirical investigations in all branches of science.

There is a large list of important problems that must be dealt with in any complete analysis of causality. Even if it were possible to give such an analysis within the confines of this article, I am sure that there are many problems whose solution I do not understand properly. Those that I have some feeling for I have dealt with in some detail in the monograph mentioned at the beginning of the chapter in the first footnote. This monograph contains a number of examples as well as a fairly extensive discussion of some of the most important philosophical issues concerning causality.

REFERENCES

Burks, A. W. 1951. "The Logic of Causal Propositions," *Mind*, 60, pp. 363-382.

Estes, W. K. and P. Suppes. 1959. "Foundation of Statistical Learning Theory, II. The Stimulus Sampling Model," Technical Report No. 26, Stanford University, Intitute for Mathematical Studies in the Social Sciences.

Good, I. J. 1961. "A Causal Calculus (I)," *The British Journal for the Philosophy of Science,* 11, pp. 305-318.

Good, I. J. 1962. "A Causal Calculus (II), "*The British Journal for the Philosophy of Science,* 12, pp. 43-51.

Greenwood, M. and G. U. Yule. 1915. "The Statistics of Anti-typhoid and Anti-cholera Inoculations, and the Interpretation of Such Statistics in General," *Proceedings of the Royal Society of Medicine,* 8, pp. 113-190.

Höffding, W. 1940. "Maszstabinvariante Korrelationstheorie," *Schriften des Mathematischen Instituts und des Instituts für Angewandte Mathematik der Universität Berlin,* 5, pp. 181-233.

Kendall, M. G. and A. Stuart. 1961. *The Advanced Theory of Statistics. Vol.* 2. Inference and Relationship, London: Griffin.

Lehmann, E. L. 1966. "Some Concepts of Dependence," *The Annals of Mathematical Statistics,* 37, pp. 1137-1153.

Maxwell, J. C. 1892. *A Treatise on Electricity and Magnetism,* London: Oxford University Press. (3rd ed.)

Simon, H. A. 1954. "Spurious Correlations: A Causal Interpretation," *Journal of American Statistical Association,* 49, pp. 467-492.

Wilks, S. 1962. *Mathematical Statistics,* New York: Wiley.

3

Causal Interpretations of Statistical Relationships in Social Research *

STEFAN NOWAK
Warsaw University

1. THE PROBLEM OF CAUSALITY

The scientist, who has observed in his research that the event S was followed by the event B or that the class of events S was (or usually is) followed by the events belonging to the class B (when both classes may be finite or infinite in their number), may formulate on the basis of such findings two different types of conclusions:

(a) he may simply assert that in his population or on a much larger scale (if he makes an inductive generalization from his findings) *S is followed by B;* or

(b) he may also say that in his population or on a much broader scale (if not on a universal scale) *S is the cause of B,* or--in other terms--B is the effect of S.

As we know, philosophers differ strongly in their opinions as to whether the propositions of the last category are acceptable at all in the body of science. Moreover, if they accept the notion of causal relations as a special category of connections between the observable events or variables, they have different ideas of the notion of causality. (See Blalock, 1964.) It is not the aim of my chapter to analyze these differences of definition of causal relations. I would rather like to stress here one very important similarity

---

*
The following chapter is a continuation of ideas presented in Nowak (1960b) and (1965a). In some sections the text has been basically changed as compared with the text which appeared in *Quality and Quantity.*

between all these notions. Both philosophers and research
workers seem to agree on the *operational definition of causal
relation,* namely that the causal connections between the
events are those connections which under conditions of a
controlled experiment lead (or would lead) to the observable
sequences of events S and B prescribed by the given design of
the experiment.[1]

The words in parentheses: "would lead" stress that the
above definition is a conditional operational definition of a
causal connection. It distinguishes in a literal sense as
causal connections only those which have been submitted to
experimental control and "behaved" in those conditions in the
"prescribed" way, but it permits us to characterize as causal
all other connections for which we have other (i.e., nonexperimental) premises permitting us to predict that, if
taken under experimental control, these relationships would
also lead to the sequence of events conforming to the rules
of the experiment.

As we know, the experimental manipulations of variables
preceding in time a given effect B permit us to obtain such
combinations of variables characterizing the initial conditions for the given effect B, which are hardly obtainable
and observable in natural situations. Thus if the experiment
delivers us the instances of "only agreement" or of "only
difference" prescribed by the rules of inductive analysis, we
are able to say whether after the occurrence of "S only" B
always occurred or after the disappearance of "S only" B also
disappeared. Then we are able to say whether the occurrence
of B was or was not dependent on the occurrence of S.

But the experimental manipulation of antecedent variables of a certain effect B has another very important implication for our conclusions, usually underestimated in methodological analyses of experimental research. By producing (or
changing) the necessary values of the independent variables
of a given effect B in different time and space coordinates,
in different situations, we also prove (usually unconsciously)
that all other variables which were not taken under experimental control, but which have different values for different
experimental situations, are irrelevant for the occurrence of
B.

---

[1] For convenience we may take as an example of the class S a
"stimulus" and as an example of the class B a "behavior," but
we should keep in mind that the following analysis does not
refer only to these two classes of variables. S means "any
cause" and B "any effect."

This is true both for the variables which are occurring at the same time as S occurs and for those which are prior to S. Anticipating what will be said below, we may say that the other (uncontrolled and different in different instances) events occurring together with S cannot be the supplementary factors for S. It also proves that the relation between S and B cannot be a spurious one, i.e. caused by a prior factor.[2]

The last conclusion is true only when we accept one assumption, namely that the time-space coordinates for the given experimental control of the relation between S and B were not (consciously[3] or unconsciously) correlated with some events essential for the occurrence of B and prior to S or occurring at the time of S.

This assumption seems to be valid for most rigorously conducted experiments and its fulfillment is even included in some experimental schemes (e.g., in the form of the random selection of the experimental sample) but it is not necessarily true for natural situations. Let us look a little closer at the uncontrolled conditions antecedent to S. It is often true that a certain S occurs in nature mostly or only as the effect of a certain A. When we then observe that S is followed by B we do not know and we are not able to say whether S is only an intermediary link in the causal chain of events A ---> S ---> B, or the relation BS is spurious, caused by the common cause A. In other words we are not able

---

[2] I am using the traditional meaning of the term spurious correlation, as introduced by P. F. Lazarsfeld (1955 and other works). A correlation is spurious when the sequence of the two classes of events S and B is produced by the fact that they have a common cause A, which must be prior in time to S. But we should stress that the correlation of S and B is also spurious in the situation where A occurs jointly with S (being its constant correlate) and where A is causally related to B and S is not. Thus, e.g., in the famous Hawthorne experiment the presence of the experimenter (A) would be located in the same time period as all other experimental stimuli (S), but it was the only factor producing all changes in the workers' behavior (B) and also producing a spurious correlation SB.

[3] A man who would like to "produce" the flute of a river at the time when he knows that it will occur anyway would be the simplest example of this category.

to say whether S would also be followed by B in the case
where S would follow after non-A.[4]

The notion of a causal connection is sometimes defined
or better presented in the form: "S produces B," (Blalock,
1964) because some authors seem to assume that the term "to
produce" has a more understandable intuitive meaning for the
reader. The equivalence of these two terms seems to be based
on the same definition of causality which was presented above
and which I would like to state now in a little different
form.

*To say that S is the cause of B means that: wherever
and whenever within the limits of validity of the given
causal generalization S occurs (or would occur) it is (or it
would be) followed by B, independently of whether S occurs
(or would occur) "spontaneously" or was (or would be) brought
into existence by some "voluntary" action of any "actor" or
"producer."*

2. TYPOLOGY OF CAUSAL RELATIONS

In the first section of this chapter we have analyzed
the situation in which a certain S, exemplified for the purpose of convenience as the "stimulus," was causally connected
with a certain B, "behavior," in a special way--S was a sufficient condition for B. But the causal relationship between
S and B may also be of a different type--for example S may
produce B only when some other conditions are fulfilled:
e.g., when a certain D occurs.[5] In other terms: S and D
jointly are the sufficient condition for B, being simultaneously necessary components of this condition.

We see that the term "causal connection" may have different meanings. Let us analyze some different possible
meanings of the statement; "S is the cause of B" under the
assumption that both S and B are defined in such a way that
they are "dichotomous attributes," i.e., they may either occur

---

[4]This is the reason why it is so difficult to make causal inferences concerning, e.g., natural developmental sequences of
biological phenomena "in vivo" until they are controlled "in
vitro."

[5]For convenience D may be exemplified here as a "disposition"
to behave in the manner B when "stimulus" S occurs.

or not occur.[6]

When we say "S is a cause of B," we may think either of *unconditional* or of a *conditional* type of *causal relation*. By an unconditional type of causal relation I mean the type of relationship between variables which is usually characterized in general terms by "always" or "never." By a conditional type of causal relation I mean the type of relationship between attributes which is characterized by statements like "unless," "provided that," "when some additional conditions hold," etc.

When we say that there is an unconditional causal relation between S and B it may mean:

(a) that S is a *sufficient condition* for B. This means that B always occurs when S occurs;

(b) that S is a *necessary condition* for B. This means that B never occurs when S does not occur;

(c) that S is both a *necessary and a sufficient* condition for B. This means that B never occurs if S does not occur and that B always occurs when S occurs.

When we say that A is a necessary but not a sufficient condition for B, this implies:

(d) that there exists at least one *supplementary factor* (D) such that D together with S is the sufficient condition for B.

When we say that S is a sufficient but not a necessary condition for B, this implies:

(e) that there exists at least one *alternative cause* (A) such that B always occurs when A occurs.

Let us return to the case where S is a necessary but not a sufficient condition. Statements of this type are *unconditional in their negative form* (because non-S is never followed by B) but they are *conditional in their positive form*. Only under the condition that D occurs is S always followed by B. We could write this in the following implicational form:

$$D \longrightarrow (S \longrightarrow B) \text{ and } (S' \longrightarrow B')$$

In the case where S is a sufficient but not a necessary condition we have an *unconditional positive causal relation, but a conditional negative one*. Suppose that A and S are the

---

[6] Some problems connected with the typology of causal relations for "continuous" variables will be analyzed in the final sections of this chapter.

only possible alternative sufficient conditions for B; we may say that S is always followed by B, but non-S will always be followed by non-B only under the condition that A does not occur. Or symbolically:

$$A' \longrightarrow (S' \longrightarrow B') \text{ and } (S \longrightarrow B)$$

It is often true that there is no unconditional causal relation between S and B either in its positive or in its negative form, but we are inclined to say that under some specific conditions S is causally related to B. This means that S is an essential component of one sufficient condition (DS), but in reality (or in the population of events being analyzed) there exists at least one alternative sufficient condition for B. Let us designate it by A. In the case mentioned above the *relation is conditional both in the negative and in the positive forms*. S always will be followed by B only if D occurs or another alternative cause A occurs. And non-S will be followed by non-B only when another alternative cause does not occur. Or symbolically:

$$(A \text{ or } D) \longrightarrow (S \longrightarrow B); \quad A' \longrightarrow (S' \longrightarrow B')$$

Thus we see that the causal relations between variables may be:
   (a)   unconditional both in the positive and in the negative forms (S is a necessary and sufficient condition for B);
   (b)   unconditional in the positive but conditional in the negative form (S is a sufficient but not a necessary condition for B);
   (c)   unconditional in the negative but conditional in the positive form (S is a necessary but not a sufficient condition for B); or
   (d)   conditional both in the positive and in the negative forms (S is an essential component of one alternative sufficient condition for B).

3.   STATISTICAL LAWS AND HISTORICAL GENERALIZATIONS

The existence of conditional causal relations between classes of events has some interesting implications for the nature of the theoretical conclusions which we may draw from the analysis of empirical data. Let us assume that we are analyzing the situation in which in reality the necessary and sufficient condition for a certain B is composed of two classes of events (or traits)--S and D--but we only know about the importance of S for B, and the existence of D or its role in producing B is unknown to us. The analysis of the empirical relationships between the variables S and B may lead us to the conclusion that S and B are somehow interrelated, but *the nature of our generalizations is here strongly dependent on the way in which the unknown factor D exists in empirical reality.*

Let us analyze some possible ways in which the factor D may exist and their implications for the theoretical conclusions based on the empirical analysis of the relationship between S and B:

1. D may exist "practically everywhere" so that every S will act under the conditions of a certain D. If this is the case we will be able, without discovering the importance of D, to formulate a universal law saying that "S is a sufficient condition for B" and this law will not be falsified by empirical research even though for an "adequate" law of science there should be two components of a sufficient condition for B (S and D).[7]

2. D may exist practically everywhere but in such a way that its occurrence may be characterized as a relatively even random distribution for S. This means that only some S's will act under condition D, but for every sufficiently large sample of S's the proportion of those occurring together with D to all S's will be relatively constant and approximately equal to p.[8] If this is the case, we will be able, without discovering the role of D in affecting B, to formulate a *universal probabilistic law* stating that there is a constant probability (p) that S will be followed by B.

3. D may exist in such a way that it characterizes all S's in a certain population defined in terms of some time-space coordinates, but outside of these coordinates D either

---

[7]In some cases we may be able to discover the importance of D for B by means of theoretical analysis, e.g., trying to deduce the relationship S $\longrightarrow$ B from a more general theory.

[8]We may take as an example of D some personality trait for which we assumed this relatively even random distribution (it should be rather strongly connected with the genetic determination of human dispositions) and take an example of behavior for which this D is an essential factor.

occurs irregularly or not at all.[9] If this is the case then we will be able to formulate, without discovering the importance of D for B, a "*historical generalization*" saying that within the time-space limits h, S is always followed by B.[10]

Thus we see that there is an interesting analogy between the two categories of statements which till now usually have been classified in quite different methodological categories--namely between universal statistical laws and historical generalizations valid only for one given population. *Both types of propositions refer to conditional causal connections in which some essential factor is unknown to the scientist.*[11] *They differ only in the way this unknown factor exists.* In the case of historical generalizations this factor characterizes all events within the limits of one "historical population," whereas in the case of universal statistical laws it occurs regularly with a constant probability "practically everywhere."

4. D may exist in such a way that it is relatively evenly distributed (and its probability of occurrence together with S is equal to p) but only within some time and space limits h. If this is the case we will be able to formulate, without discovering the importance of D for S, a *probabilistic historical proposition* saying that "within the time-space limits h the probability that S will be followed by B is equal to p."[12]

---

[9] An "internalized" pattern of behavior characteristic of the culture of a given historically defined population may be a good example of this category of "dispositional traits."

[10] These space-time coordinates in this case play a special role: they are substitutes for the unknown factor D and their coverage should be equivalent to those areas of reality in which the factor D exists practically everywhere. See Nowak (1965b).

[11] At least some of them refer to the conditional causal connections, because some historical or statistical relations between S and B may involve so-called "spurious relationships between variables" that will be analyzed below.

[12] All insurance companies base their predictions on this type of relationship, i.e., probabilistic propositions with validity limited for one population only.

5. But it may happen that the sufficient condition for B is composed of, let us say, the three factors S, D_1, and D_2, and at the same time:

D_1 is characteristic for all events in one historical population h;

D_2 is characterized by a relatively even random distribution and occurs practically everywhere (with probability p).

If this is the case, then we will be able to formulate, as in case 4, a historical probabilistic statement, but the situation will be quite different if we later discover the importance of one of the two supplementary factors for B, namely:

(a) if we discover the importance of D_1, we will be able to formulate a universal statistical law saying that the probability that SD_1 will be followed by B is equal to p;

(b) if we discover the importance of D_2, we will be able to formulate a historical generalization saying that in the population h all SD_2 are followed by B.

Only if we discover the importance of both previously unknown factors (D_1 and D_2) will be able to transform our generalization into a universal law of science of the type SD_1D_2 is always followed by B.

4. STATISTICAL RELATIONSHIPS IN UNCONDITIONAL AND CONDITIONAL CAUSAL PATTERNS

In section 2 we distinguished unconditional and conditional causal relations between "dichotomous" variables. It should be noted here that such relations may have a universal or a historical character. When I mean that a relation between S and B is unconditional in its positive form, it may mean:

(a) either that S is always followed by B practically everywhere because it is a sufficient condition for B (a universal law); or

(b) that S is always followed by B in one population h, because in this population all events (persons) are under the influence of all other supplementary factors, which implies that the occurrence of S is a practically sufficient (in this population) condition for B (a historical generalization).

When we say that the causal relation between S and B is an unconditional one in a negative form, it may mean:

(a)   that S is always and everywhere a necessary condition for B (a universal law); or

(b)   that in the population h,S is a necessary condition for B,e.g., for the reason that all other theoretically possible alternative causes of B do not occur in the population h (a historical generalization).

All that will be said below about statistical relationships between different classes of events treated as functions of the causal connection between these events refers to both types of situations, i.e., both to the situation where a relation of the given type has a historical and universal character.[13]

Now suppose that we are interested in the question, "What is the conditional probability of the occurrence of B when S occurs, under the assumption that S is a sufficient condition for B?" The question seems to be rather simple, and *the answer may easily be derived from the notion of the concept of a sufficient condition.* Instead of saying, "S is always followed by B," we may say, "The conditional probability of the occurrence of B when S occurs is equal to 1." Or symbolically:

$$p(B|S) = 1 \text{ [14]} \quad \text{or graphically: } S \longrightarrow B . \quad (1)$$

If we assume that S is a necessary condition for B we may say that the conditional probability of the occurrence of B when S does not occur is equal to 0. Or symbolically:

$$p(B|S') = 0. \text{ [15]} \quad (2)$$

When S is both a necessary and a sufficient condition for B we may say that the conditional probability of the occurrence of B when S occurs is equal to the conditional probability of the occurrence of S when B occurs, and both are equal to 1:

---

[13] Although in practical analyses of empirical social data we shall usually encounter instances in which the given general relation between S and B is usually limited to some "historical coordinates."

[14] Or the equivalent: $p(S'|B') = 1.$ We use the symbol S here to indicate "the occurrence of S" and symbol S' to indicate "the occurrence of non-S." The same notation will be used with other "attributes" or "events" such as D and A.

[15] Or $p(S|B) = 1.$

$$p(B|S) = p(S|B) = 1 .^{16} \tag{3}$$

In the case where S is a necessary but not a sufficient condition for B, we may say that the conditional probability of the occurrence of non-B when non-S occurs is equal to 1, but that the conditional probability of the occurrence of B when S occurs is less than 1 and greater than 0.

$$p(B'|S') = 1 \qquad \text{and } 0 < p(B|S) < 1 .^{17} \tag{4}$$

If S is a sufficient but not a necessary condition for B, we may say that the conditional probability of the occurrence of B when S occurs is equal to 1, but the conditional probability of B being preceded by S is less than 1 and greater than 0.

$$p(B|S) = 1 \qquad \text{and } 0 < p(S|B) < 1 . \tag{5}$$

Now suppose that D is a supplementary factor which together with S forms a necessary and sufficient condition for B,

or graphically:
$$\begin{array}{c} S \\ |\!\!\longrightarrow\!\! B \\ D \end{array}$$

In this case we may say that the conditional probability of the occurrence of B when S occurs is equal to the conditional probability of the occurrence of D when S occurs:

$$p(B|S = p(D|S) . \tag{6}$$

Between the two supplementary factors D and S there may be, in different populations, quite different statistical associations. They may be associated positively or negatively or they may also be statistically independent.

---

[16] Or $p(B|S') = p(S|B') = 0$.

[17] We omit, from here on, other equivalent formulas. Moreover we must here introduce another limitation, i.e., that they are valid only for those causal relations between variables which are really acting to produce B in the population under analysis. If, for example, S is a necessary condition for B, but the supplementary factor D forming together with S a sufficient condition for B does not occur at least with some S's, then $p(B|S) = 0$. The same is true for equation (5), under the additional assumption that $p(S|A) < 1$.

In the case where the two supplementary factors are statistically independent, the conditional probability of the occurrence of effect B when one factor (S) occurs is equal to the relative frequency of another factor (D) in the population:[18]

$$p(B|S) = p(D) .$$

Let us now analyze an interesting case where S is either a sufficient but not a necessary condition, or an essential component of such a sufficient but not necessary condition. In the language proposed in this chapter we will say that in reality (or at least in the population that is the object of analysis) B may be the effect of two or more alternative causes (e.g., S and A).

When S and A are two different alternative sufficient conditions for B, the situation may be presented graphically as follows:[19]

If this is the case, the following equation must be true:

$$p(B|S) = p(B|A) = 1 \text{ and } p(S|B) = 1 - p(A|B) + p(AS|B). \tag{8}$$

And if S and A are mutually exclusive we have:

$$p(B|S) = p(B|A) = 1 \qquad \text{and } p(S|B) = 1 - P(A|B) \tag{9}$$

Now let us suppose that S is an essential component of one alternative cause for B (let us designate this cause by SD) but that there exists another alternative cause for B, namely A (where A is a sufficient condition for B). Graphically we may present this case as follows:

S
D ──→ B
A ──→

---

[18] When previously analyzed the situation in which the unknown factor D had a relatively even random distribution, S and D were statistically independent. The other possible situation is when S and D are not independent but D has a relatively even probability of occurrence when S occurs, namely $P(D|S) = p$.

[19] The assumption is being made that in the given population, or on a universal scale, these are the only existing sufficient conditions, i.e., that (S´ and A´) is followed by B´.

If this is the case the following equation must be true:

$$p(B|S) = p(D|S) + p(A|S) - p(DA|S) \text{ and } p(B|S') = p(A|S') .$$

(10)

And if A and D are mutually exclusive:

$$p(B|S) = p(D|S) + p(A|S) \qquad \text{and } p(B|S') = p(A|S') . \quad (11)$$

This means that in the situation where a certain S has a probability greater than O and less than 1 of being followed by a certain B, and the probability of the occurrence of non-B when non-S has occurred is also greater than O and less than 1, S may be at most the essential component of one alternative sufficient condition. It should be noted that this is the kind of relation we usually discover in empirical social research. It means that *in social research we usually discover causal relations which are conditional both in their positive and in their negative forms*. The statistical values of our relations are substitutes for the other unknown causes, i.e., both for the other components of the same sufficient conditions and for the other alternative sufficient conditions of our effect. If we discover them, we may formulate a general unconditional causal law with its antecedents composed of many elements jointly, e.g.,

$$(A \text{ or } SD) \longrightarrow B$$

Thus the notion of conditional causal relations permits us to apply the idea of causality to the situations in which we do not observe general, necessary relations between S and B, but where we discover statistical relations only.

Moreover if we compare this with equation (6), we see that the conditional probability of occurrence of B when S occurs is greater than in a non-alternative scheme of causal relations.

In this situation *p(A|S) may be called the noncausal or spurious component* of the overall observed probability p(B|S), where p(D|S) may be called its *causal component*. Since the existence of alternative sufficient conditions of the same effect is a rather general phenomenon, at least in the social sciences, we may say that in all probabilistic relations between social phenomena which we interpret in causal terms we should try to distinguish and to evaluate the relative strengths of their spurious and causal components and to systematize them in different theoretical propositions, relating different sufficient conditions to the same effect.[20] This can be done by means of "multivariate analysis" and especially in multivariate experimental designs, the analysis of which would go beyond the scope of this chapter.

Now suppose that D is a necessary condition for B but that it may form two different sufficient conditions with two different supplementary factors, S_1 and S_2. Graphically we may present it as follows:

If this is the case, then we have, of course:[21]

---

[20] To give a trivial example, we may say that the probability of death of a tubercular patient is usually higher than is determined by the "pure mechanisms" of tuberculosis. It is also determined, e.g., by the probability of a tubercular patient's dying in a traffic accident. And when the "alternativeness" of causal relations is a rather general phenomenon, this means that we rather rarely have "pure one-cause" statistical relationships. It should also be noted here that we are speaking about the spurious component of a probabilistic relation and not about a spurious correlation which was discussed by many methodologists of social sciences. See, e.g., Lazarsfeld (1955). A probabilistic relation might be called completely spurious, if S does not produce B at all but has some probability of occurrence jointly with A, being in this case the only cause of B. It might be called completely causal if the probability B|S is due only to the probabilities of the joint occurrence of other components of the same sufficient condition to which S belongs.

[21] We assumed here for simplicity's sake that S_1 and S_2 are mutually exclusive. We assume the same in equation (13) for S_1, S_2 and A. Otherwise, for equation (12) we will have:

$$p(B|D) = p(S_1|D) + p(S_2|D) - p(S_1S_2|D)$$

For equation (13) we will have:

$$p(B|D) = p(S_1|D) + p(S_2|D) + p(A|D) - p(S_1S_2|D) - p(S_1A|D)$$

$$- p(S_2A|D) - p(S_1S_2A|D)$$

$$p(B|D) = p(S_1|D) + p(S_2|D) .$$ (12)

Thus we might think that there are no differences between the case described here and the case described in the
equation (10). But in the case described in equation (10) we
have $p(B|S') > 0$, while here we have $p(B|D') = 0$. Finally,
let us take the case where D has two different supplementary
factors S_1 and S_2 but where there exists in our population
another alternative cause of B, namely A.

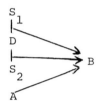

Then we have the following equations:

$$p(B|D) = p(S_1|D) + p(S_2|D) + p(A|D), \text{ and } p(B|A) = 1 .$$
(13)

5. STATISTICAL RELATIONSHIPS IN MULTISTAGE CAUSAL CHAINS

On the previous pages we analyzed the cases in which two
different variables that were causally related to effect B
were either different components of the same sufficient condition (different supplementary factors) or components of two
different alternative causes (or two alternative causes themselves). But two different variables may both be causally
connected with effect B and causally connected with each
other because they are *elements of different links in the
same causal chain.* Suppose that we analyze variables C, S
and B, and that t_1, t_2 and t_3 indicate three consecutive
cross-cuts of time. The most simple case will be:

t_1 $\qquad t_2$ $\qquad t_3$

C ———> S ———> B

This means that C is a sufficient condition for S, and S is a sufficient condition for B. Let us call the causal relation SB the *direct causal relation*, and the relation CB the *indirect causal relations*.[22] But the case where the indirect cause is the sufficient condition of the direct cause is only one of many possible patterns of causal relations.[23] Let us analyze some other patterns.

Suppose that both C and S are essential components of two successive necessary and sufficient conditions of B. Graphically this may be presented as follows:

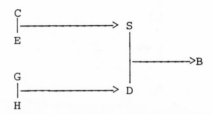

If this is the case, then the following equation is true:

$$p(B|C) = p(S|C) \cdot p(D|S). \qquad (14)$$

Let us now assume that the pattern of causal relations is both multistage and alternative, according to the following graphical scheme:

---

[22] It would be more correct to say that the relation SB is more direct than CB instead of introducing a dichotomous classification. It is obvious that for any causal relation we may find one which is more direct than it.

[23] This is a rather rare case which might be called "an isolated chain of causal transformations" which is the fulfillment of Laplace's deterministic ideas (even when limited in time and space).

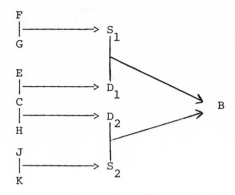

If this is the case, the following equation is true:

$$p(B|C) = p(D_1|C) \cdot p(S_1|D_1) + p(D_2|C) \cdot p(S_2|D_2) \tag{15}$$

or $p(B|C) = p(FGE|C) + p(HJK|C)$.[24]

Suppose now that two different supplementary factors, D and S, have one common cause C when their other causes are different. Or graphically:

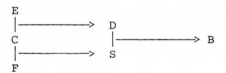

The following equation must be true:

$$p(B|C) = p(DS|C) = p(EF|C) \text{ or } p(B|C) = P(D|C) \cdot p(S|D). \tag{16}$$

Lastly let us analyze the case where factor C (being equivalent either to C_1 or to C_2 for different cross-cuts of

---

[24] The equation applies only to situations in which S_1D_1 and and S_2D_2, or FGE and HJK, are mutually exclusive. If they are not mutually exclusive, $p(B|C) = p(FEG|C) + p(HJK|C) - p(FEGHJK|C)$.

time) is the component of some consecutive sufficient conditions which form the necessary elements of several links in the causal chain. For example:[25]

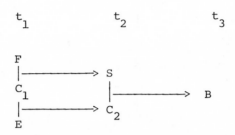

If this is the case then the following equations are true:

$$p(B|C_1) = p(S|C_1) \cdot p(C_2|S) \text{ or } p(B|C_1) = p(FE{\downarrow}C_1). \tag{17}$$

6. CAUSALITY, CORRELATION AND SPURIOUS INDEPENDENCE

In the last two sections we have analyzed the probabilistic relations between the variables viewed as functions of causal connections between those variables. But, as we know, statements about relative frequencies or probabilities of some events, when other events have occurred, are not the only category of statistical descriptions of relationships between the classes of events. We are often interested not only in what the probability of B is when S occurs, but also in their interdependencies, or in other words whether the occurrence of S *increases the probability of the occurrence of B*. Put still another way, we may ask whether the

_____

[25] Let us give an example to clarify this scheme. Suppose that in order to fulfill a difficult combat task (B) at time t_3 it is necessary for a soldier at time t_2 to have both courage (C_2) and a favorable orientation to the situation (D). But in order to be courageous at time t_2 it was necessary to be both courageous (C_1) and not shocked by the enemy's artillery (E) at time t_1. And in order to be favorably oriented to the situation (D) it was necessary to be both courageous enough (C_1) to look for information and to be in a favorable place where this information might be found (F) at time t_1.

knowledge of the fact that S has occurred increases the accuracy of our predictions concerning the occurrence of S. In brief, we are often interested in whether S and B are statistically independent or--if they are "correlated"-- whether their correlation is positive or negative.[26]

As we know, two classes of traits or events, S and B, are statistically independent when the following equation is true:

$$p(SB) = p(S) \cdot p(B). \tag{18}$$

But the situation of statistical independence may also be described in another way. The two classes of events, S and B, are statistically independent if the following equation is true:

$$p(B|S) = p(B|S'). \tag{19}$$

To say it in other words: two classes of events are statistically independent when the occurrence of one event does not increase (or decrease) the probability of occurrence of the other event.

If the occurrence of one event increases the probability of occurrence of the other one--then they are positively correlated according to the formula:[27]

$$p(B|S) > p(B|S'). \tag{20}$$

Finally, S and B are negatively correlated when the occurrence of S decreases the probability of occurrence of B according to the formula:[28]

---

[26] It would be more proper to use the term "association" than "correlation," because we are dealing here with "dichotomous attributes" and not with "continuous variables." But the term "correlation" often has a broader meaning which also denotes the case of association between dichotomous attributes, and in this broader meaning it is used here.

[27] This is of course equivalent to the well-known formula of positive correlation: $p(SB) > p(S) \cdot p(B)$.

[28] This is equivalent to $p(SB) < p(S) \cdot p(B)$.

$$p(B|S) < p(B|S'), \tag{21}$$

Thus we see that the correlation between S and B is here a function of the probabilities $p(B|S)$ and $p(B|S')$. Let us consider on what these two probabilities depend.

As we remember from section 4, the probability of B when S does occur depends on two factors:

(a) the relative probability of occurrence of the supplementary factor D, when S has occurred i.e., $p(D|S)$:

(b) on the relative probability of occurrence of the alternative cause A, when S has occurred i.e., $p(A|S)$ constituting its "spurious component" (equations (10) and (11)).

But on the other hand both $p(D|S)$ and $p(A|S)$ are functions of the relative frequency of D and A in our population ($p(D)$ and $p(A)$) and their correlation with S.

To put it briefly:

the more frequent the supplementary factors D in our population;

the more frequent the alternative causes A in our population; and

the more highly correlated both A and D are with S;

the greater the probability that S will be followed by B.

Let us now look at the other side of equation (19) and analyze which factors contribute to the probability that non-S will be followed by B. Here of course the supplementary factor D is irrelevant (Because it may produce B only when it occurs with S), and the relative frequency of B when non-S occurs is a simple function of the relative frequency of the alternative cause A, when non-S occurs. But $p(A|S')$ is a function of the relative frequency of A in our population and of the correlation between S and A. To put it briefly:

the more frequent A is in our population; and

the stronger its negative correlation with S

the greater will be the probability that non-S will be followed by B.

Thus we see that the frequency of the alternative cause A[29] and the sign and strength of its association with our "predictor" S has an important role in determining what will be the predictive value of the variable S for the variable B. If A is positively associated with S it increases its

---

[29] Or, as often happens, the sum of frequencies of all different alternative causes of B, e.g., A_1, A_2, A_3 and the pattern of their associations with S.

predictive value. If S and A are statistically independent
the existence of A in the population does not eliminate the
prognostic value of S for B. (See below.) If they are
negatively correlated it decreases, more or less, the prognostic value of S for B. Let me stress two special cases
for which the existence of A diminishes the prognostic value
of S for B.

The situation may be graphically presented as follows:

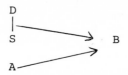

Let us suppose for simplicity's sake that there is a
perfect negative correlation between S and A (i.e., that they
are mutually exclusive).

If in this situation

$$p(D|S) \;=\; p(A|S')$$

we then have

$$p(B|S) \;=\; p(B|S') \tag{22}$$

This is the situation which may be called *spurious independence,* because the two variables S and B are statistically independent in a situation in which they are causally
connected.

If it happens that $p(A|S')$ is greater than $p(D|S)$ we
would have:

$$p(B|S) \;<\; p(B|S') \tag{23}$$

This means that B and S are negatively correlated in a
situation where they are connected causally. This situation
may be called *spurious negative correlation.*

Thus we see that the relation between the fact that the
variables are causally connected and the prognostic value of
one variable for the other is highly conditional. The prognostic value of a cause for its effect is diminished by the
existence of alternative causes of our effect in the studied
population if they are negatively correlated with our predictor. In some cases--as we have seen--it diminished the
prognostic value of S for B to 0 or even changes its sign to
a negative one.

In all these cases we again obtain the positive correlation between S and B when we take the alternative cause A as a constant factor in multivariate analysis.[30]

Let us now look more systematically at this problem, studying the statistical relationships between S and B for the four kinds of causal relations between S and B distinguished above.

1. If S is a necessary and sufficient condition for B, then according to what was said above, $p(B|S) = 1$ and $p(BS') = 0$. In such a situation the correlation between S and B will be positive and equal to $+ 1.0$.

2. If S is a necessary but not a sufficient condition for B, then $0 < p(B|S) < 1$, but $p(B|S') = 0$. In this case there will be a positive correlation between S and B.

3. If S is a sufficient but not a necessary condition for B, then $p(B|S) = 1$, whereas $0 < p(B|S') < 1$. Here again there will be a positive correlation between S and B.[31]

Thus we may say that *if the causal relation between S and B is unconditional, either in its positive aspect or in its negative aspect or in both, there must be a positive correlation between S and B.*

4. If S is a necessary component of only one of the alternative sufficient conditions, then S may be either positively or negatively correlated with B or independent of B.

Therefore *if the causal relation between S and B is conditional both in the positive and in the negative senses such a situation does not imply a positive correlation between S and B.*

Nevertheless there is a class of situations in which there will be always a positive association between S and B, even if S is not a sufficient condition for B and if there

---

[30]The problem of interpretation of partial relationships with the application of a test factor was introduced into the methodology of social research by P. F. Lazarsfeld (1955). See also Herbert Hyman (1955) and Herbert Simon (1957).

[31]One should remember the additional assumptions made here. In situation 2 we assume that the supplementary factor D occurs in our population at least with a certain proportion of S's; otherwise $p(B|S) = 0$. In situation 3 we assume that the alternative sufficient condition A does not always occur when non-S occurs; otherwise $p(B|S')$ would be equal to one. If these assumptions are not valid (as they usualy are) there is no correlation between S and B in situations 2 or 3.

are some alternative causes A of our B, whatever the relative frequency of A in our population and whatever the probability of $D|S$ (provided that $p(D|S) > 0$). *This will always happen when these alternative causes A are statistically independent of S.*[32] Let us first consider the situation where D and A are mutually exclusive and S and A are statistically independent.

Here we will have:

$$p(B|S) = p(D|S) + p(A|S) \qquad (24)$$

but, because S and A are statistically independent, we may write:

$$p(B|S) = p(D|S) + p(A) .$$

On the other side

$$p(B|S') = p(A) .$$

As a result of this we have:

$$p(B|S) > p(B|S') .$$

If D and A are not mutually exclusive, but S, A, and D are mutually statistically independent we will also have a positive association between S and B, because here:

$$p(B|S) = p(D) + p(A) - p(D) . p(A) \qquad (25)$$

$$p(B|S') = p(A)$$

and because

$$p(D) - p(D) . p(A) > 0$$

then

$$p(D) + p(A) - p(D) . p(A) > p(A);$$

therefore in this case we will always have

---

[32] We assume that the sum of probabilities of occurrence of these alternative causes of B in our population is less than 1.0, because if it is equal to one, then $p(B|S) = p(B|S') = 1$, i.e., S and B are statistically independent.

$$p(B|S) > p(B|S').$$

We can summarize by saying that *if all components of all alternative sufficient conditions of our effect are mutually statistically independent, this will result in a positive association between any of the essential components of any of the sufficient conditions and their effect.* This seems to be a necessary assumption in everyday research practice, which takes for granted that the causal relations between variables can be assessed by the observation of positive associations and correlations between them. But this assumption should be clearly formulated in any inference from statistical to causal relations, especially because it is by no means universally valid, as we saw above.

Sometimes we can make a weaker assumption, namely that one of the causes--the variable S--that is a necessary component of one of several sufficient conditions of B is statistically independent both from all its supplementary factors D_1, D_2,... D_n and from all alternative sufficient conditions A_1, A_2,... A_n, whatever the mutual statistical relationships between these variables A_1, A_2 ... A_n, D_1, D_2 ... D_n. It is obvious that in this situation there will always be a positive relationship between S and B, although not necessarily between B and any of its other causes.

It should be noted that there is a fairly common research situation in which we may assume that the variable S is statistically independent of all other variables involved in producing B, i.e. both from all supplementary factors D_1, D_2 ... D_n and also from all alternative sufficient conditions A_1, A_2 ... A_n. Therefore it will always be positively associated with B. *This is the situation of random experiments,* in which we randomly assign the subject to either the "experimental" or the "control" group. Randomization makes the distributions of all relevant variables approximately equal in both groups. If we then apply the "stimulus" S to the experimental group only, S will be statistically independent of all its supplementary factors as well as all other alternative causes of B. Then, according to the above reasoning the causal connection between S and B must be revealed by comparison of the frequencies of B in the two groups with $p(B|S) > p(B|S')$. *It seems that the basic logical foundations for the validity of random experiments in revealing causal connections consist of the fact that its procedures guarantee us that the assumption of independence discussed above is fulfilled.*

7. SPURIOUS CORRELATIONS

In the previous section of this chapter we mentioned that a positive association of the alternative cause of B with our "predictor" S increases the prognostic value of S for B, contributing, more or less, to the positive correlation between S and B. This correlation is in general a function of the two factors:

(a) the relative probability of the occurrence of supplementary factor D, when S occurs, and
(b) the relative frequency of the other cause of B (let us designate it here by C) and the association between C and B, which constitutes the spurious component of this relation.
The relative size of the "contribution" of these two factors to the total strength of the correlation between S and B may vary; the one extreme of this variation is the situation where the correlation with our predictor S is completely determined by the factor C and its association with S. This means that in our population (or on a universal scale) B is not the effect of S. This may happen either when:
(a) S is not causally related to B or
(b) S may be a conditional cause of B but does not "meet" in this population its supplementary factor D together with which it forms a sufficient condition for B.
This situation where S is positively correlated with B but is not connected causally with S for any of these reasons is called "spurious correlation."
Let us analyze different types of spurious correlations.
By a spurious correlation we often mean the correlation which is produced by the fact that two variables that are causally unrelated have one or more causes in common. If this is not a "perfect" (i.e., 1.0) correlation this means that the common cause of S and B (or in our terminology, common essential component of two different sufficient conditions of S and B), in connection with different supplementary factors, forms two sufficient conditions for the two original variables. Or, graphically, the correlation SB is spurious when, for example:

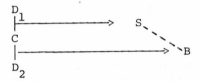

Here we have of course:

$$p(S|C) = p(D_1|C)$$

$$p(B|C) = p(D_2|C) \ .$$

(26)

It should be stressed that the fact that two variables S and B have one cause (C) in common does not yet imply that they have to be positively associated. The association (correlation) between S and B is here primarily a function of the correlation between D_1 and D_2, and we can well imagine a situation where there will be a perfect negative correlation between S and B even though they have one common cause C. This happens when D_1 and D_2 are mutually exclusive. Then of course S and B are also mutually exclusive.

Even when D_1 and D_2 are not completely mutually exclusive but are strongly negatively associated, it may result in a negative correlation between S and B, or (if their negative association is not too strong) it may result in statistical independence between S and B.

Let us now analyze our favorite situation in which C, D_1 and D_2 are statistically independent. In this case we will have:

$$p(B|S) = p(D_2C)/p(D_1C) \ .$$

(27)

But, since all variables are independent and S and B have the same variable C in common, it turns out that

$$p(B|S) = p(D_2) \ .$$

On the other hand

$$p(B|S') = p(CD_2)/p(D_1C)'$$

But now we have another situation, namely, that due to the independence of (CD_2) from $(D_1C)'$:

$$p(B|S') = p(CD_2) = p(C) \cdot p(D_2) \quad \bullet$$

And since

$p(D_2) > p(C) \cdot p(D_2)$, therefore $p(B|S) > p(B|S') \quad \bullet$

Let us now see what will happen if we apply Lazarsfeld's (1955) multivariate analysis, keeping C constant and looking for partial relationships between S and B both for C and for non-C.

For C:
$$p(B|S) = p(D_2)$$
$$p(B|S') = p(D_2)$$
(28)

For non-C: $p(B|S)$ cannot be computed because

S is absent for non-C

$$p(B|S') = 0$$

We see here that in the case *where C, D_1 and D_2 are statistically independent, the relationship between S and B must be positive in the whole population, and it must disappear when C is held constant as the "test variable" in multivariate analysis.*

The same will happen when C is not a necessary condition for B, but when B has in this population another alternative sufficient condition, namely A, if we assume that A is statistically independent of CD_1 and CD_2 (which are also mutually independent, as above). Graphically we may present this as follows:

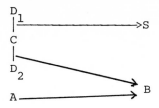

Here we will have:

$$p(B|S) = p(D_2) + p(A) - p(D_2) \cdot p(A)$$
(29)

on the other side:

$$p(B|S') = p(D_2) \cdot p(C) + p(A) - p(D_2) \cdot p(C) \cdot p(A)$$

and since

$$p(D_2) - p(D_2) \cdot p(A) > p(D_2) \cdot p(C) - p(D_2) \cdot p(C) \cdot p(A)$$

therefore

$$p(B|S) > p(B|S').$$

We see that in this case also there will be a positive association between S and B. When we take C as constant the partial relationships will look as follows:

For C:
$$p(B|S) = p(D_2) + p(A) - p(D_2) \cdot p(A)$$
$$p(B|S') = p(D_2) + p(A) - p(D_2) \cdot p(A)$$

(30)

For non-C: $p(B|S)$ cannot be computed because S is absent in this situation

$$p(B|S') = p(A) .$$

Finally if we assume that S and B may in addition have some alternative causes A_1 and A_2 to which C does not belong, e.g.:

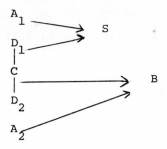

and all five variables (A_1, A_2, C, D_1, D_2) are statistically independent in all possible combinations, we will obtain the typical results as described by Lazarsfeld (1955), in which the relationship between S and B is positive in the total population and disappears both for C and for non-C. But

$p(B|S) > 0$ in groups of the test variable, namely:

For C: $p(B|S) = p(D_2) + p(A_2) - p(D_2) \cdot p(A_2)$

$p(B|S') = p(D_2) + p(A_2) - p(D_2) \cdot p(A_2)$

For non-C: $p(B|S) = p(A_2)$

$p(B|S') = p(A_2)$ (31)

But now suppose that we have our previous most simple situation in which:

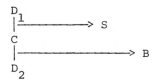

But D_1 and D_2 are positively associated, so that $p(D_1|D_2) > p(D_1|D_2')$. If they are in addition either independent of or related to C in the same way, it is obvious that the correlation between S and B will not disappear for the group C. It will still be positive and will "disappear" only for the group non-C, where both S and B are absent. The same conclusion can be extended to all of the more complicated situations analyzed above.

Let us again consider the situation described above in formula (31), but under the assumption that A_2 is positively associated with CD_1, with all the other variables being mutually independent. Without further analysis we can see that the relationship between S and B will not disappear in the group C if we keep C constant; it will only decrease, due to the "contribution" of the variable A_2 to the relationship between S and B in group C, since $p(B|S) = p(B|S')$ is equal to $p(A_2)$ for this group.

Thus we may say that *if S and B have one cause C in common, their relationship will disappear after making C constant only under the condition that all other variables responsible for the occurrence of S and B in this population are statistically independent in all possible combinations.*

And lastly, let us analyze the scheme where the spuriousness is caused by the fact that S and B have more than one

cause in common. Graphically this may be presented as follows:

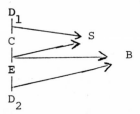

If this is the case, it is quite obvious that under all
assumptions mentioned above the spurious relationship will
never disappear in the partial correlation when we take as
the test variable either C or E. It can disappear only in a
more complicated four-variable scheme of analysis in which
we keep both C and E constant.

This means that *the definition of the "causal" statistical correlation as a correlation which never disappears after
introducing a third test variable* (e.g., Lazarsfeld, 1955)[33]
*is too broad because it also denotes all types of spurious
correlation analyzed above, and also many others omitted here.*

In all cases analyzed above the spurious correlation between S and B was produced by the fact that both S and B
have a common cause C. But it may happen that there is no
causal connection between C and S (and C is causally connected only with B), but there is nevertheless a positive
correlation between S and C resulting in a spurious correlation between S and B. We can imagine, for example, the
situation in which we have a pattern of causal connections
between the variables as follows:

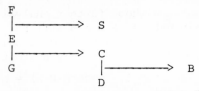

If in this situation we obtain a positive correlation
between CD and S, it will result in a spurious correlation
between S and B although:

---

[33]See Lazarsfeld (1955). According to the author, the correlation is spurious when, after introducing a "test variable" (C) antecedent in time to the independent variable (S),
we obtain independence in the partial relationship between SB
when C is held constant.

(a) S is not causally connected with B;

(b) S is not causally connected with C.

In this situation the spurious correlation between S and B will disappear when we take C as a test factor in multivariate analysis.[34] But C does not necessarily precede S in time.[35] It may precede it, it may occur at the same time, or, in some cases, it may even occur after S and, nevertheless, the correlation between S and B will be spurious.

The situation where S and C occur at the same time seems to be especially worth mentioning. This is the situation where both C and S are elements of a composed syndrome of variables, e.g., a syndrome of dispositional traits, or of stimuli. It is well known that in many psychological researches the effects (B) first attributed to variables of the S type were later interpreted as the results of some other elements (C) of the same syndrome to which S belonged. If the correlation between S and C is not a perfect one, the "spuriousness" of the connection between S and C might easily be discovered if we took C as a test factor in a multivariate scheme of analysis.

8. THE TEST VARIABLE AS A SUPPLEMENTARY FACTOR AND AS AN ALTERNATIVE CAUSE OF B.

In the previous section of this chapter we have analyzed hidden assumptions behind usually applied methods of discovering whether a certain correlation is a spurious or causal one. But it should be remembered that proof of causality or of spuriousness is not the only possible result of multivariate analyses. The other possible results may constitute the evidence that the "test variable" introduced in order to interpret the initial relationship SB is either a supplementary factor (D) or an alternative cause of B(A), or a necessary component of such an alternative cause A_1. Let us designate the alternative sufficient condition for B as $A_1 A_2$.

---

[34]This assumes we make some additional assumptions which were analyzed above for the "classical" type of spurious correlation.

[35]In the definition of spurious correlation by Lazarsfeld (1955) it was formulated that the real cause of B precedes the "spurious independent variable" S in time.

Let us assume that:

(a) SD is a sufficient condition for B, and
(b) there is no alternative cause of B in this situation.

Then we have the following pattern of relationships between S and B, when we take D as constant:

for D :

$$p(B|S) = 1$$

$$p(B|S') = 0$$

for non-D :

$$p(B|S) = p(B|S') = 0 .$$

In other words, we have a positive (1.0) correlation between S and B for subgroup D and no correlation for non-D.

In the situation where the relation between S and B is conditional upon the occurrence of D (or the relation between D and B is conditional upon S), when S and D are necessary components of the same sufficient condition, we may say that we have the case of *interaction* between S and D in producing the effect B.

In the situation where S and A are either two alternative sufficient conditions of B or are necessary components of two alternative sufficient conditions, we may say that S and A (or D and A) are *additive causes* of the effect B.

In the above case we assumed that there are no additive causes of B in our population, that all B's are the effects of the interaction between S and D only.

Let us now assume that there is another alternative cause (A) of B in our situation but all factors, S, B and A, are statistically independent and the relative frequency of A is equal to p_1.

Here we will have:

for D :

$$p(B|S) = 1$$

$$p(B|S') = p_1$$

for non-D :

$$p(B|S) = p_1$$

$$p(B|S') = p_1$$

If the sufficient condition for B is more complex, namely SD_1D_2, but we control only D_1 (assuming that the alternative cause is here A with relative frequency p_1 and all

110

variables are statistically independent), we will have:

for D_1 :
$$p(B|S) = p(D_2) + p_1 - p(D_2) \cdot p_1$$

$$p(B|S') = p_1$$

for non-D_1 :
$$p(B|S) = p_1$$

$$p(B|S') = p_1 .$$

In general it may be said that:

(a) if D_1 and S are components of the same sufficient condition;

(b) if the probability of the joint of occurrence of all unknown components (D_n) of the same sufficient condition to which S and D_1 belong is equal to p_1;

(c) if the probability of the occurrence of all alternative causes (A_n) of B is equal to p_2; and

(d) if all the variables involved in producing B in this population are statistically independent; then

(e) the pattern of probabilities for B may be presented in the following fourfold table with two independent variables:

	D_1	D_1'
S	$p_1 + p_2 - p_1 \cdot p_2$	p_2
S'	p_2	p_2

If S, D_1, D_2 and A are not independent the pattern of relationships may be a little different, but we will usually still have the situation in which we have a visible positive correlation between S and B for one value of the test variable (for D_1) and a lack of relationship between S and B for non-D.[36]

The situation will be different if the test variable A is an alternative *additive sufficient condition of B* or, what is more interesting, when it is a necessary component of another alternative sufficient condition of B.

Now suppose that we have a situation in which B may be produced in our population by two alternative sufficient conditions, (S and D_1) or (A and D_2). Suppose additionally that all four variables are statistically independent and the relative frequencies of the unknown supplementary factors D_1 and D_2 are respectively:

$$p(D_1) = P_1$$

$$p(D_2) = P_2$$

If we then control for S and A in a multivariate analysis, we obtain the following frequencies for the effect of B.

	S	S´
A	$P_1 + P_2 - P_1 \cdot P_2$	P_2
A´	P_1	O

If we denote p(B) in the four cells of our table as follows:

	S	S´
A	P_I	P_{II}
A´	P_{III}	P_{IV}

we will of course have:

$$P_I > P_{II} \quad \text{and} \quad P_{III} > P_{IV}$$

---

[36] Unless A is negatively associated with S and D_1.

but also
$$P_I > P_{III} \text{ and } P_{II} > P_{IV} .$$

Now suppose that in addition to the causes SD_1 and AD_2, B has another alternative cause C in our population, completely unknown to us, independent of the partially controlled causes S and A and having a relative frequency equal to p_3. If we then control for S and A as above, the multivariate frequencies of B will be as follows:

	S	S´
A	$p_1 + p_2 + p_3 - p_1 \cdot p_2 - p_1 \cdot p_3$ $- p_2 \cdot p_3 - p_1 \cdot p_2 \cdot p_3$	$p_2 + p_3 - p_2 \cdot p_3$
A´	$p_1 + p_3 - p_1 \cdot p_3$	p_3

Also if we denote the frequencies of B in our table by:

	S	S´
A	P_I	P_{II}
A´	P_{III}	P_{IV}

we will have: $P_I > P_{II} \text{ and } P_{III} > P_{IV}$

and also $P_I > P_{III} \text{ and } P_{II} > P_{IV} .$

I think that this represents a case which is *typical of that we obtain from multivariate analysis in which we control for two additive causes.* It should be noted that *this situation is only partly additive.* In each case when we are adding the probabilistic values with which any of two or three different causes produces the given effect in the absence of all other causes, this sum has to be diminished by the combinatorial product of the probabilities, relating to all causes involved in the given situation.

The fact that the additive causes are only "partly additive" in their probabilistic effects deserves special attention in statistical analyses of social data.

9. SOME OTHER FUNCTIONS OF THE TEST VARIABLE

Lazarsfeld (1955) describes a certain situation in which:
(a) there is a positive correlation between the test variable and the independent variable;
(b) the independent variable precedes in time the test variable; and
(c) the initial correlation between independent and dependent variables disappears when we keep the test variable constant.

In this situation the initial total correlation is by no means a spurious one; it is only less direct than the causal relation between the test variable and the dependent variable. If we designate the test variable as M in order to exemplify it (e.g., as "motive") we may present this situation as follows:

$$S \longrightarrow M \longrightarrow B$$

If we assume that between the variables belonging to different links of a causal chain there exist probabilistic relationships, we might present them as follows:

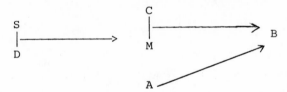

The statistical associations between S and B are here quite obviously functions of the causal connections between S and B and of the statistical association between M and the alternative cause A of the variable B. The reader may easily formulate the assumptions on which the patterns of simple and partial relationships described by Lazarsfeld for this case will hold true. Accepting for simplicity's sake these assumptions, I would like to present some other more complicated patterns of causal connections between S and B, on the one hand, and a test variable designated as T (the test variable), on the other.

The first pattern may be presented as follows:

In this situation S is both an indirect cause of B (by producing its other cause T) and a direct one, because S and T are interacting causes of B, belonging to the same sufficient condition of B.[37] Here the relationship between T and B is partly spurious and partly causal. In this situation we have the following patterns of relationships between the three variables:

(a) S precedes T in time;

(b) there is a positive correlation between S and T;

(c) after holding T constant the relationship between S and B increases for T and disappears for non-T.

A different case is the situation in which the relationship between S and B does not disappear for both subgroups of the variable T (all other relationships being the same as in the previous case).[38] If this occurs we may say that S produces B both directly and indirectly by the mediating factor T, and T and S are (or belong to) two alternative additive causes of B. Graphically we may present this as follows:[39]

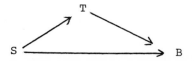

In both these cases the relationship between S and B is by no means a spurious one; moreover it is indirect for only one group of B, whereas for the other group of B it is as direct as the relationship between T and B.

---

[37] A more adequate pattern of relations would be as follows:

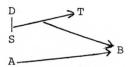

[38] This relationship usually decreases in both subgroups of T, and the amount of decrease is a function of the strength of the correlation between S and T.

[39] Or more adequately:

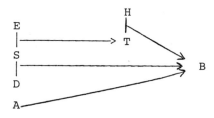

115

Another type of situation is the case where the correlation SB is partially spurious and partially causal. In this situation the pattern of relationships between the three variables is as follows:

(a)   T precedes S in time and
(b)   T is correlated with S.

There are three possible categories of situations in which S produces B both directly and indirectly by producing T.

If after holding T constant the relationships SB decrease in both subgroups of T but are still positive and approximately equal, this means that T and S belong to alternative causes of B according to the following scheme:

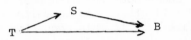

If the partial relationship SB is much stronger for T and disappears for non-T, this means that T and S are necessary components of the same cause according to the scheme:

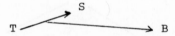

Let me give two examples illustrating the two situations presented above. In a study of social attitudes of Warsaw students I found that a student's egalitarianism (B) is related both to his parents' income (S) and to his parents' occupational group (T). T and S were strongly correlated.[40] When we held either of these variables constant there was a visible correlation between egalitarianism and the other variable in all subgroups of the test variable. This means that we had the following pattern of causal relations between these three variables:

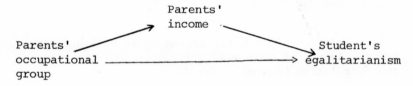

---

[40] Nowak, (1960), where the figures for these two examples are presented.

In other words, occupational group and income (although causally connected to each other) were in this population components of alternative additive causes of students' egalitarian attitudes.

Another example may be the relationship between egalitarianism, parents' occupational group and the place of the student's habitation. The last two variables were also strongly correlated; the dormitories were inhabited mostly by students coming from lower social strata. When we held the place of living constant we found that the correlation between family background and a student's egalitarianism increased visibly for students living with families and disappeared for those who lived in dormitories. This pattern of causal connections may be presented as follows:

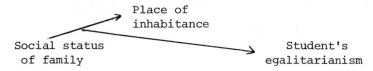

Place of inhabitance

Social status of family

Student's egalitarianism

10. A TYPOLOGY OF THREE-VARIABLE ANALYSES

In an earlier section of this chapter I analyzed the probabilistic and correlational relationships between an independent variable x and a dependent variable y under different patterns of causal relationships between x and y, and in different patterns of statistical associations between x and a set of alternative causes of y in the given population.[41] Then we analyzed the results of the introduction of test variables (t) into these patterns of relationships, taking into account the time order of the variables x and t, their statistical association and the partial relations between x and y when t was held constant. The results of the above analyses may be briefly summarized in a table in which we have the following criteria of classification:
1. the time order of t and x:
   a) t precedes x;
   b) x precedes t;
   c) time order of x and t irrelevant;

----

[41] The reader should note that I am changing the symbols for the variables in order to apply the symbols which were proposed for multivariate analysis by Lazarsfeld (1955). The typology of elaborations used here is different from that proposed by Lazarsfeld.

2. statistical association between x and t:
    a) t and x statistically independent;
    b) t and x positively associated;
3. the partial relationship between x and y when test
variable t is constant:
    a) xy disappears in both groups of the test
variable t;
    b) xy positively associated in both groups of the
test variable t;
    c) xy disappears for non-t and increases for t.
The results of the above analyses may be presented as in
Table 1.

11. ADDITIVITY AND INTERACTION BETWEEN THE QUANTITATIVE
     VARIABLES

In the earlier sections of this chapter I analyzed the
statistical relationships between dichotomous attributes as
functions of the causal relations among them. The typology
of possible causal connections was based on the idea that we
are looking for either conditional or unconditional causal
relations (in both the positive and the negative senses of
this term) of a certain class of dichotomously defined events
B. We also wish to discover all other (dichotomously defined) supplementary factors of the given conditional cause
and also all alternative causes of B existing in the given
population.
This type of reasoning seems to be useful both for discovering the existing causal connections between a set of
variables in a given population and for analyzing hidden
assumptions and limitations of methods of statistical analysis usually encountered in empirical research. The fact that
the models presented above are only valid for dichotomous
events or attributes is nevertheless a serious limitation
with respect to their applicability. It may also be, as some
authors have already indicated, a source of more basic
methodological difficulties because a dichotomous classification is usually based on more or less artificial cutpoints in
some quantitative variable.[42]
It seems that a way of reasoning similiar to that we
applied for dichotomous attributes may also be applied to

---

[42]For an analysis of this type of problem connected with
artificial cuts in continuous variables, see Blalock (1964).

		Partial relationship between x and y when t is held constant		
Statistical relationships between the independent and the test variables (x, t)	time order between independent variable x and test variable t	xy disappears in both groups of the variable t	xy increases for t and disappears for non-t	xy is positive and equal approximately for t and for non-t
x and t statistically independent	time order of x and t irrelevant	introduction of another test variable (e.g.,z) explaining this inconsistent pattern necessary	t and x belong to the same sufficient condition for y x |————————> y t both xy and ty causal relations	t and x belong to different alternative causes of y x ————>y t both xy and ty are causal relations
x and t positively associated	t precedes x	original relationship xy spurious x t————> y relationships tx and ty causal	t produces y both directly and indirectly by producing x x t————> y x and t belong to the same sufficient condition of y. Relationship xy partially spurious, partially causal. Relationship ty causal	t produces y both directly and indirectly by producing x x t————> y x and t belong to different alternative causes of y. xy partially spurious, tx causal
	x precedes t	t is a mediating variable between x and y x————> t————>y x is an indirect cause of y when t is a direct cause of y. All relationships, xt, ty, xy are causal	t is a mediating variable between x and y and a supplementary factor for x t x————> y Relationship xy is causal, when ty is partially spurious and partially causal	t is a mediating variable between x and y and belongs to alternative cause of y t x————> y Relationship xy is causal, when ty is partially spurious and partially causal

Table 1: TYPOLOGY OF THREE-VARIABLE ANALYSES

quantitative variables, where we can interpret the statistical correlation as a function of the given type of causal connection between the quantitative variables. Let us present some premises for this type of analysis.

Let us assume that we have four quantitative variables S, D, A, B, which for simplicity's sake have been given some measurable values:

the variable S may have as its values S_0, S_1, S_2;

the variable D may have as its values D_0, D_1, D_2;

the variable B may have different values depending on the functional relationship between D, S, A and B.

It seems that, looking for different patterns of causal relations among these quantitative variables and taking, for simplicity's sake, only monotonic "rectilinear" functional relations between them, we might distinguish quite a few different causal patterns. These patterns can be classified into two large groups depending on whether S,A and D act additively or interact with each other in determining B's value.

1. Before we do that we should distinguish the simplest pattern of causal connection between S and B: the situation in which the relation B = f(S) is an *unconditional or completely functional causal relation*. This means that in all possible conditions (including all possible values of D) the value of B is completely determined by the value of S and the values of D are irrelevant. This may be presented as follows:

	S_0	S_1	S_2
D_0	B_0	B_1	B_2
D_1	B_0	B_1	B_2
D_2	B_0	B_1	B_2

Looking for an analogy to this type among the types of causal connections between dichotomous attributes, this situation corresponds to the case where S is a necessary and sufficient condition for B because we have a complete correspondence of values of the two variables S and B according to the formula:

$$s_0 = B_0$$

$$s_1 = B_1$$

$$s_2 = B_2 .$$

For a sociologist a much more realistic situation is when the given D does not change the strength of the statistical relationship between S and B (i.e., R_{SB}) according to the formula.[43]

$$R_{SB}(D_0) = R_{SB}(D_1) = R_{SB}(D_2) .$$

It should be noted, moreover, that if D and S are statistically independent, we shall have $R_{DB} = 0$ in the total population. If they are correlated positively there will be a positive correlation between D and B in the total population which will disappear after holding S constant (e.g., in a partial correlation of the type $R_{BD.S}$) thus showing the spurious character of the relationship R_{DB} in the total population.

2. Then we have a class of *additive situations* in which

$$B = f_1(A) \pm f_2(S)$$

Remember that additivity means that A and S are independent alternative causes due to a functional relation B = f(A) and B = f(S), or to essential components of two such different alternative causes.

(2a) A deterministic pattern of additive relations between SA and B might be presented as follows when the sign of the above formula is positive.

	S_0	S_1	S_2
A_0	B_0	B_1	B_2
A_1	B_1	B_2	B_3
A_2	B_2	B_3	B_4

---

[43] Let us read $R_{SB}(D_0)$ as "The correlation between S and B for the subgroup of the population characterized by the value D_0 of the variable D and consequently also for the other groups."

(2b) It may also happen that $B = f_1(A) - f_2(S)$ when there are two factors which *counteract* each other in determining the value of B. If we also introduce for B some negative values, the result of two (negatively additive) counteracting factors could be presented for deterministic situations as follows:

	S_0	S_1	S_2
A_0	B_0	B_1	B_2
A_1	B_{-1}	B_0	B_1
A_2	B_{-2}	B_{-1}	B_0

It should be remembered that for two (positively or negatively) additive factors the following formulas are true

$$A_{const} \longrightarrow B = f(S)$$

$$S_{const} \longrightarrow B = f'(A).$$

This means that when the values of one independent variable are kept constant, we obtain a functional relationship between the other variable and the effect, and vice versa. But in both cases the relationship between one independent variable and the dependent variable will be slightly different for different values of the test variable. We know that a general formula for a linear functional relation is as follows:

$$y = ax + b$$

In our case (for the situation 2a) when holding constant the variable A, the relation between S and B will be as follows:

for A_o : $\quad\quad$ B = S

for A_1 : $\quad\quad$ B = S + 1

for A_2 : $\quad\quad$ B = S + 2 .

If we take S as the test variable, we will have

for S_o : $\quad\quad$ B = A

for S_1 : $\quad\quad$ B = A + 1

for S_2 : $\quad\quad$ B = A + 2 .

We can observe this when we control both additive variables at the same time. But now suppose that we observe in the total population only the overall relation between S and B. In this case it is very likely that for any given value of S we will observe a certain range of values of B, but not lower (if S and A are positively additive) than the pure effect of the given value of S upon B, and not higher than the sum of the impact of this value of S upon B and of the impact of the highest possible value of A. Thus, the range of values of B

for S_o $\quad\quad$ will be $\quad\quad$ B_o, B_1, B_2

for S_1 $\quad\quad$ " $\quad$ " $\quad\quad$ B_1, B_2, B_3

for S_2 $\quad\quad$ " $\quad$ " $\quad\quad$ B_2, B_3, B_4

as can be seen from Table 3.

We therefore see that the range of variation of the values of the dependent variable for the given value of the independent variable is a significant indicator of the range of variation of the dependent variable due to alternative, additive causes of this dependent variable in the given population.

It is interesting to study what the observed mean value of B will be for given values of S. This of course depends upon the correlation between S and A in our population. We can distinguish some different situations:

(a) S and A are positively correlated and their correlation is equal to 1.0.

In this case we will have

$$\text{for } S_0 : \quad B_0$$

$$\text{for } S_1 : \quad B_2$$

$$\text{for } S_2 : \quad B_4$$

or in other words the observed functional relation between S and B corresponds to a theoretical relation of the type B = 2S.

(b) If the correlation between S and A is positive but not perfect in the total population we will observe a certain relation between S and the mean values of B, the regression line of which has a steeper slope than unity. The correlation between S and B is here partly spurious.

(c) We can also assume that there is a perfect negative correlation between S and A. In this situation there will be no correlation between S and B in the total population because there will be a constant value of B for all values of A. This will be a clear case of spurious independence for quantitative variables.

(d) We can also assume that S and A are correlated negatively but $R_{SA} > - 1.0$. In this case the mean values of B for S will indicate a regression line with a slope which is less than their "genuine" functional relation. In this case their observed relations should be regarded as having a component of a spurious independence.

(e) Finally, we can assume that S and A are statistically independent. In such a case for a given value of S we obtain the mean value of B which is the sum of two components:

α: the value of B which is produced by the given value of S due to their functional relation; and

β: the mean value of B which is due to the action of the other alternative cause A in our population.

Suppose, for example, that in our population A has such an impact upon the dependent variable B--due to the given functional relation B = f(A) and the given distribution of values of (A)--that as a result of the action of A alone (i.e., for S_0),B has in our population the mean value = 1.8. Then the relationship between S and B in this population corresponds to the formula (if S and A are independent):

$$B = S + 1.8$$

or for specific values of S we will have:

$$\text{for } S_o : \quad B = 1.8$$

$$\text{for } S_1 : \quad B = 2.8$$

$$\text{for } S_2 : \quad B = 3.8 \text{ etc.}$$

All this refers to situations in which we observe the total relation between S and B in our population, which is here a function of its "genuine" and "spurious" component. This is similar to the case of dichotomous attributes. When we observe the impact of the two variables S and A in a multivariate design, the nature of the "disguised" functional relation behind the statistical relations among any of them and their effect can be clearly established--under assumption, of course, that no other causes of B are acting in this population.

If there are some other additive causes involved in determining the values of B in this population we will observe in our multivariate design similar effects in terms of variations of mean values of B for two independent variables jointly, to those we discussed above for the situation where we observed only one independent variable and B was a function of two additive causes. Needless to say, this is what we usually have in sociological data, even if we can believe that all variables involved have additive effects.

3. When we say that S and D are *interacting* in producing B (here changing the symbol for the other variable) this means that the existence, shape, direction, or strength of the causal (functional or statistical) relation between S and B depends upon the value of the variable D.[44] It may be the case that:

(3a) The functional relations between S and B exist only for some specific values of D (e.g., when D_1 occurs) according to the formula $D_1 \longrightarrow (B = f(S))$ whereas

$$D_1' \longrightarrow [B \neq f(S)] .$$

Here (see below) D_1 is the *determiner of the existence of the relation* between S and B.

---

[44]The role of interaction as an obstacle in causal interpretations of multivariate statistical relationships between quantitative variables was strongly stressed by Blalock (1964).

	S_0	S_1	S_2
D_0	B_0	B_0	B_0
D_1	B_0	B_1	B_2
D_2	B_0	B_0	B_0

This seems to be only one of an infinite number of interaction situations which correspond to the case analyzed above for dichotomous attributes, where the two variables were supplementary factors for each other. We may say that D_1, together with different values of the variable S, creates sufficient conditions of different values of the variable B according to the formula:

$$D_1S_1 = B_1$$

$$D_1S_2 = B_2$$

$$D_1S_3 = B_3 \text{ etc.}$$

when for the other values of the variable D there is no relation between S and B.

This causal pattern has very clear probabilistic implications for situations in which we observe only one independent variable, namely S. What we must take into account is the relative frequency of D_1 among the different values of S. Suppose that the frequency of D_1 among all possible values of D is equal to .5 and its occurrence is relatively evenly distributed for all values of S (i.e., that S and D_1 are independent). In this case the mean value of B for S will be:

for S_0 :   B = 0

for S_1 :   B = .5

for S_2 :   B = 1

But D_1 does not necessarily have to be independent of S, and different values of S may have different probabilities of joint occurrences with D_1. This may have an impact upon the shape or strength of the relationship between the values of S and the mean values of B. If $p(D_1)$ increases regularly with increases in S, then our linear relation between S and the mean values of B will be much "steeper" than in a conditional scheme of analysis with D_1 held constant. If $p(D_1)$ decreases with the values of S, it may eliminate any linear relation at all. We can also imagine such a pattern for the distribution of $p(D_1)$ for different values of S that will result in a u-shape curvilinear relation between S and mean values of B. As in the case of multivariate determination for dichotomous attributes, everything is possible for the situation where the variables involved are not independent.

(3b) In some cases the values of the variable D may determine the strength of the functional relation between S and B, according to the formula:

$$D_1 \longrightarrow (B = f_1(S)) \quad \text{e.g.,} \quad D_1 \longrightarrow (B = S)$$

$$D_2 \longrightarrow (B = f_2(S)) \qquad\qquad D_2 \longrightarrow (B = 2S)$$

$$D_3 \longrightarrow (B = f_3(S)) \qquad\qquad D_3 \longrightarrow (B = 3S)$$

Let us call the variable D the *modifier of the strength* of the relation between S and B. Its role can be observed in the following table:

	S_1	S_2	S_3
D_1	B_1	B_2	B_3
D_2	B_2	B_4	B_6
D_3	B_3	B_6	B_9

Here again the observable statistical relation between
S and B is additionally a function of the correlation between
S and the variable D, which is the modifier of the strength
of $B = f(S)$. If S and D are perfectly correlated we have a
case of the function $B = S^2$. If they are correlated negatively, with $R = - 1.0$, the observation will show in this example no relationship between S and B. Finally, if S and D
are independent we will observe the effect of the mean impact
of the modifier D upon the strength of the correlation between S and B in the given population for specific values of
S.

(3c)   The values of the variable D may also *determine
the direction* of the functional relation between S and B,
according to the scheme:

	S_0	S_1	S_2
D_0	B_0	B_1	B_2
D_1	B_2	B_1	B_0
D_2	B_2	B_1	B_0

Here D will be a *modifier of the direction* of the relation
between S and B.

(3d)   B may be functionally related to S only when the
values of the other variable D covary in a certain way.   S
and D are here *necessary covariates for B* according to the
following scheme: $(D = S) \longrightarrow [B = f(S)]$ or $(D = S) \longrightarrow$
$[B = f(D)]$.

	S_0	S_1	S_2
D_0	B_0	B_0	B_0
D_1	B_0	B_1	B_0
D_2	B_0	B_0	B_2

We have here:

$$D_o S_o = B_o$$

$$D_1 S_1 = B_1$$

$$D_2 S_2 = B_2 \, .$$

(3e) It may also happen that the value of B is a function of whichever independent variable, in any given case, takes on the greater (or smaller) value. We can say that in this case B is a function of the more (less) intensive variable, according to the schemes:

	S_o	S_1	S_2		S_o	S_1	S_2
D_o	B_o	B_1	B_2	D_o	B_o	B_o	B_o
D_1	B_1	B_1	B_2	D_1	B_o	B_1	B_1
D_2	B_2	B_2	B_2	D_2	B_o	B_1	B_2

Here again, for all these situations one could present the relation between the mean values of B and the values of S as a function of the distribution of the values of the interacting variable D or the correlation between the interacting variable D and our predictor S. For reasons of brevity we will not discuss all these details, assuming that the main ideas of this type of reasoning have been sufficiently illustrated above.

These are mere examples of different categories of nonadditive, interactive causal relations. It is obvious that an infinite number of other situations could be defined if we were to depart from the linear character of our functional relations between S and B and also to take into account other patterns of determination of this relation by different values of the variable D. It is equally clear that with an increase in the number of interacting variables the patterns of their possible interaction become more and more complicated.

There is one important thing about all these situations involving interaction between S and D that distinguishes them from the additive patterns, namely that *in these cases we cannot expect that the relationship between S and B will hold if we keep D constant*. It is equally important to know the level at which the value of D has been established. Suppose, for example, that the pattern of interaction between S and D corresponds to type (3a) according to which:

$$D_1 \longrightarrow (B = f(S))$$

$$D_1' \longrightarrow (B \neq f(S))$$

In this case it is not enough to know that the value of D is constant (e.g., by controlling it in experimental conditions) in order to expect that there will be in our situation, characterized by the given constant value of D, a functional (or probabilistic) relation between S and B. If it happens that we "stabilize" the value of D on the level D_1, then we will observe the relation between S and B which is codetermined by this value of D. But if we stabilize the value of D on the level D_2 (or D_o), there will be no relationship between S and B in those conditions.

It may also happen that the variable D has only one constant value D_1 in natural conditions (or in our population). Then we may come to the conclusion that there is an unconditional causal relation of the form $B = f(S)$. Attempts to verify this relation in other populations where the (constant) value of D is different will show us that this relation is conditional. If on the other hand the constant value of D has been naturally stabilized in our population on the level D_2 or D_o, then we may come to the conclusion that S and B are not causally related to each other.

The same is true for all other patterns of interaction mentioned above. Suppose that we have a situation of type (3b) in which

$$D_1 \longrightarrow B = S$$

$$D_2 \longrightarrow B = 2S$$

$$D_3 \longrightarrow B = 3S$$

Suppose that it happens that the value of D is kept constant on the level D_2. Then we observe a functional relation $B = 2S$. But it would be incorrect to say here, "other things equal, $B = 2S$," because this is only true if the interacting D has the value D_2 but not the values D_1 or D_3.

In the formulation of hypotheses (especially in the behavioral sciences) we often encounter the following type of statement: "Other things equal, $B = f(S)$." It is clear from the above analysis that this formula can be applied only in such situations where these "other things" refer to additive (alternative) causes A_1, A_2, ... A_n of B, because on whatever levels A_1, A_2 ... A_n have been stabilized (held constant), there will always be the same definite pattern of observed relationships between S and B plus (minus) the total effect of all additive causes upon the mean value of B in our population. The situation is quite different for interacting causes D_1, D_2, ... D_n, because here it is not enough to assume that their values are held constant. We have to assume that they are held constant on just that level which determines the given direction or strength of the relation between S and B, which is necessary for the truth of the formula $B = f(S)$.

We can omit all additive causes in the formulation of a law describing the given relation between S and B and substitute for them the formula, "Other additive factors being equal, $B = f(S)$." But we cannot do this with non-additive causes. They have to be specified in the formulation of our law as the necessary components of its antecedent.

And a final comment: until now we have been discussing some statistical effects of functional relations between one dependent and several independent variables, separately for additive and for interacting independent variables. It is obvious that one could also present the statistical relationships between the quantitative variables for situations in which some of the independent variables are additive, whereas others are interacting with them according to the different possible patterns of interaction, just as we did for the dichotomous attributes.

REFERENCES

Blalock, H. M. 1964. *Causal Inferences in Nonexperimental Research.* Chapel Hill: University of North Carolina Press.

Hyman, H. 1955. *Survey Design and Analysis.* Glencoe, Ill.: The Free Press.

Lazarsfeld, P. F. 1955. "Interpretation of Statistical Relations as a Research Operation," in P. F. Lazarsfeld and M. Rosenberg (eds.), *The Language of Social Research.* Glencoe, Ill.: The Free Press.

Nowak, S. 1960a. "Egalitarian Attitudes of Warsaw Students," *American Sociological Review, XXV,* pp. 219-231.

Nowak, S. 1960b. "Some Problems of Causal Interpretation of Statistical Relationships, *Philosophy of Science, XXVII,* pp. 23-38.

Nowak, S. 1965a. "Causal Interpretation of Statistical Relationships in Social Research," in S. Nowak, *Studies in the Methodology of the Social Sciences.* Warsaw.

Nowak, S. 1965b. "General Laws and Historical Generalizations in the Social Sciences," in S. Nowak, *Studies in the Methodology of the Social Sciences.* Warsaw.

Simon, H. A. 1957. *Models of Man.* New York: John Wiley.

4

On a General Scheme of Causal Analysis *

F.M. BORODKIN

Institute of Economics and Industrial Engineering, Novosibirsk

In this chapter an attempt is made:

1. To state some principles for the analysis of causal
    scheme structures.

2. To define (to formulate), on a heuristic basis, some
    indices of dependencies between variables under a
    given causal structure (the so-called influence co-
    efficient).

3. To formulate an hypothesis concerning correlations
    between the variables in systems having a goal.

1. ANALYSIS OF THE CAUSAL SCHEME STRUCTURE

Functional causality has been well defined by Suppes
(1970, p. 67):
   "In a deterministic setting, we say, that $y_{t'}$ is
the functional cause of x_t if $t' < t$ and there is
a function f such that

$$x_t = f(y_{t'})$$

Once errors are introduced, this equation becomes

---
*
This work has been carried out at the Institute of Economics
& Industrial Engineering, Siberian Department of the USSR
Academy of Sciences, Novosibirsk.

$$x_t = f(y_{t'})$$

and, now reverting to our explicit random variable notation, assumptions about the distribution of errors are made so that the function f holds for the conditional expectation of x_t given a value of $y_{t'}$. Explicitly, we then have the following definition.

The property $y_{t'}$ is the functional cause of x_t if and only if

(i) $t' < t$

(ii) there is a function f such that for all real numbers

$$E(x_t | y_{t'} = y) = f(y)."$$

Later in my discussion I will not use time as a property of causality in order to simplify our reasoning, on the one hand, and because there is no sufficiently sophisticated mathematical tool for devising the necessary theory, on the other.

Usually, the causal relations are formulated for some definite set of variables beforehand on the basis of professional experience (see, for instance, Simon, 1957; Ashby, 1960; Boudon, 1968). I shall formalize the statement about the structure of causal relations by means of graph theory. The structure of causal relations stated on a definite set of variables can be represented by a graph in the following way.

Suppose that a definite set of variables is given and variables are numbered by integers i = 1,2,..., k. Each variable i associates with one and only one vertex.[1] In our case we have a directed graph G, which can be represented by its incidence vertex matrix $A = [a_{ij}]$ where

$$a_{ij} = \begin{cases} 1, & \text{if an arrow (directed edge) goes out from the } i\text{-th vertex and comes to the } j\text{-th vertex} \\ 0, & \text{otherwise} \end{cases}$$

---

[1] The terminology of graph theory has been borrowed from Ore (1962).

In our further analysis two special types of graphs will be useful--minimal and maximal.[2] Now let us define these graphs.

Let some graph G with its incidence matrix $\underset{\sim}{A}$ be given. I shall call this graph initial or IG. The set of paths from the i-th vertex will be designated by μ_{ij} and can be assiated with every pair of vertices (i,j). Now consider two graphs $G = (X, \Gamma)$ and $G^* = (X, \Gamma^*)$ where X represents the vertex set, Γ a binary relation on the elements of this set and $\Gamma^* \subset \Gamma$. In the graph G^* every pair of vertices can be associated with μ^*_{ij}, the set of paths from the i-th vertex to the j-th vertex. Then the graph G^* is a permissible graph for G iff $\mu_{ij} \neq \emptyset$ implies $\mu^*_{ij} \neq \emptyset$ for every i,j = 1,2,..., k. Let F be a set of permissible graphs for some fixed I G and $\underset{\sim}{A^*}$ the incidence matrix of some permissible graph G^*. Then let

$$\max_{F} \; \Sigma_i \; \Sigma_j \; a_{ij} = a_o \; .$$

The *minimal graph* for some fixed IG is such a permissible graph $\underset{\sim}{G}$ for whose incidence matrix $\underset{\sim}{A} = [\underset{\sim}{a}_{ij}]$ the following condition holds:

$$\underset{ij}{\Sigma\Sigma} \; a_{ij} = a_o, \quad i,j = 1,2,...,k \; .$$

If IG has no circles, the minimal graph for such IG can be found in a very simple way, namely,

$$\underset{\sim}{A} = \underset{\sim}{A} - \underset{\sim}{A} \; \underset{\lambda}{\dot{x} \Sigma} \; A^\lambda, \; \lambda = 2,...,k \; .$$

where the symbol $\dot{x}$ designates the following operation. Let

$$[c_{ij}] = [a_{ij}] \; \dot{x} \; [b_{ij}], \; i,j = 1,2,...,k$$

Then $c_{ij} = a_{ij} \, b_{ij}$ for every i,j. All the operations of summation and multiplication are Boolean.

The minimal graph has a remarkable property. If some linkage in IG can be either direct or indirect,[3] every arrow in the minimal graph represents only a direct linkage (in the

---

[2]These graphs in Ore's (1962) terminology correspond to the basic graph and transitive closure graph, respectively.

[3]Direct means that the given two variables are linked through some variables which are not included in this causal scheme. Indirect means that the given two variables are linked through some variables included in the causal scheme under study.

causality sense). The binary relation of the minimal graph is the necessary condition for the existence of a fixed IG.

Consider an illustration by Blalock (1961). The causal scheme includes five variables: x_1 = urbanization, x_2 = percentage of nonwhite population, x_3 = whites' income, x_4 = nonwhites' level of education, x_5 = nonwhites' income. The incidence matrix of IG for this scheme is the following:

$$\underset{\sim}{A} = \begin{bmatrix} 0 & 1 & 1 & 0 & 1 \\ 0 & 0 & 1 & 1 & 1 \\ 0 & 0 & 0 & 0 & 0 \\ 0 & 0 & 0 & 0 & 1 \\ 0 & 0 & 0 & 0 & 0 \end{bmatrix}$$

The minimal graph for this IG has the following incidence matrix:

$$\overset{\sim}{\underset{\sim}{A}} \begin{bmatrix} 0 & 1 & 0 & 0 & 0 \\ 0 & 0 & 1 & 1 & 0 \\ 0 & 0 & 0 & 0 & 0 \\ 0 & 0 & 0 & 0 & 1 \\ 0 & 0 & 0 & 0 & 0 \end{bmatrix}$$

Thus, for instance, the direct linkage between x_1 and x_5 is not obligatory. It is enough that direct linkages between x_1 and x_2, x_3 and x_4, x_4 and x_5 exist. But the existence of these direct linkages is necessary if IG is correct.

It is necessary to comment on another property of the minimal graph, discovered in numerous experiments. Obviously, the causal scheme can be constructed only by experts. Usually, the graphs formulated by experts are very diverse, but the differences among minimal graphs for the given IG are very minor.

Now let us define the maximal graph for IG. Consider some initial graph G. Graph G´ is an absorbing graph for G iff the graph G is permissible for G'. Designate the set of absorbing graphs for the fixed IG as T, and the incidence matrix of some absorbing graph as $\underset{\sim}{B} = [b_{ij}]$ (i,j = 1,2,...,k).

Then let

$$\max_{\substack{G \in T}} \Sigma\Sigma_{ij} b_{ij} = b_o \quad (i,j = 1,2,\ldots,k).$$

The *maximal graph* for the fixed IG is a certain absorbing graph $\hat{G}$, for which the incidence matrix $\hat{\underset{\sim}{B}} = [\hat{b}_{ij}]$ satisfies the following condition

$$\Sigma\Sigma_{ij} \hat{b}_{ij} = b_o \quad (i,j = 1,2,\ldots,k).$$

The interpretation of the maximal graph is obvious: some new arrows appearing in the maximal graph duplicate paths which exist in the IG. The incidence matrix of the maximal graph can be determined by the following formula:

$$\hat{\underset{\sim}{B}} = \sum_{\lambda} A^{\lambda}, \quad (\lambda = 1,2,\ldots,k).$$

In this formula all the operations are Boolean. For instance, the maximal graph for Blalock's scheme has the following incidence matrix:

$$\hat{\underset{\sim}{B}} = \begin{bmatrix} 0 & 1 & 1 & 1 & 1 \\ 0 & 0 & 1 & 1 & 1 \\ 0 & 0 & 0 & 0 & 0 \\ 0 & 0 & 0 & 0 & 1 \\ 0 & 0 & 0 & 0 & 0 \end{bmatrix}$$

Obviously, the minimal graph for the given IG is unique if the IG has no circuits and the maximal graph is unique for any graph. The graph can be used to check on the causal scheme's identifiability. If the causal scheme can be identified, the matrix $\hat{\underset{\sim}{B}}$ is triangulable.

We cannot be certain that the fixed IG maps only a direct linkage. Any graph between minimal and maximal graphs, that is, any graph which is permissible for the maximal graph, proves to be a graph which has only direct linkages. It is easy to show that the number of such graphs

$$h(F) = 2^{\theta}$$

where

$$\theta = \Sigma\Sigma_{ij} r_{ij}$$

and

$$[r_{ij}] = \hat{\underset{\sim}{B}} - \tilde{\underset{\sim}{A}}$$

Under these circumstances the analysis of the minimal and maximal graphs is simpler and more definite.

Now let us define two other structures which are connected with the analysis of causal schemes: automatons and simple structures. Let some IG be given. An *automaton* is a subgraph of IG such that for every pair of its vertices at least one path from one vertex to the other exists. Thus, an automaton is a strongly connected graph. If we deal with an IG that has a large number of vertices and arrows, usually it is very difficult to assess the identifiability of the causal scheme before its numerical evaluation. Moreover, in some cases automatons, if they exist, can be excluded from the scheme and the rest of the scheme can be evaluated. A connected but not strongly connected graph is called a *simple structure*. A very simple algorithm for discovering the automaton can be constructed on the basis of the following statement. Let us have for some IG the maximal graph $\hat{G}$ with incidence matrix $\hat{\underset{\sim}{B}} = [\hat{b}_{ij}]$, $i,j = 1,2...,k$. A vertex set R together with incident arrows is an automaton if $\hat{b}_{ij} \, \hat{b}_{ji} = 1$ for every $i,j \varepsilon R$. The algorithm for discovering the automaton is as follows.

1. The maximal graph $\hat{G}$ with incidence matrix $\hat{\underset{\sim}{B}} = [\hat{b}_{ij}]$, $i,j = 1,2, ..., k$ is obtained.

2. In the matrix $\hat{\underset{\sim}{B}}$ an arbitrary row i_1 and a column $j_1 = i_1$ are fixed. Thus we have two vectors:

$$\hat{\underset{\sim}{b}}_{i_1 \cdot} = (\hat{b}_{i_1 1}, ..., \hat{b}_{i_1 k}) \quad \text{and} \quad \underset{\sim}{b}_{\cdot j_1} = (\hat{b}_{1 j_1}, ..., \hat{b}_{k j_1}).$$

Then we find the product of the two vectors on the basis of the following rule: the product of two vectors

$$\underset{\sim}{x} = (x_1, x_2, ..., x_i, ..., x_k) \quad \text{and} \quad y = (y_1, y_2, ..., y_i, ..., y_k)$$

is a vector $\underset{\sim}{z} = (z_1, z_2, ..., z_i, ..., z_k)$ for which $z_i = x_i y_i$ for every $i = 1,2,...,k$. Hence, we shall find the vector

$\hat{\underset{\sim}{b}}_{i_1} = (b_1, b_2, \ldots, b_k)$ in which $b_r = \hat{b}_{i_1 r} \hat{b}_{ri_1}$, $r = 1, 2,$

..., k. Suppose the numbers of the nonzero components of the vector $\underset{\sim}{b}_{i_1}$ form the set R_1. Then all the vertices with numbers $i = R_1$ and incident arrows form one automaton.

3. Exclude from the matrix $\hat{B}$ all the rows and columns with numbers $i = R_1$. As a result, we shall have the matrix $\hat{\underset{\sim}{B}}_1$.
4. The 2nd and 3rd steps are applied to the matrix $\hat{\underset{\sim}{B}}_1$. The procedure is continued until all the rows and columns of the matrix $\underset{\sim}{B}$ are checked.

But we cannot be satisfied with merely excluding the automatons. Indeed, if we only remove automatons from the IG we can lose some causal ties. For instance, suppose we have the following graph

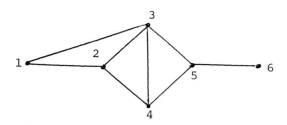

Merely removing the automaton consisting of the 2nd, 3rd and 4th vertices and incident arrows will yield the following graph

1.
                5
                •————————>• 6

But in the IG we had a path, for example, 1 ——> 3 ——> 5 from which it is clear that the 1st variable has an influence on the 5th variable. It is logical to keep such ties. A similar necessity may also arise in the case of removing some variables from the initial causal scheme.
        Now let us state an algorithm and the necessary definitions for the correct reduction of a graph. Let some initial graph $G = (X, \Gamma)$ with the incidence matrix $\underset{\sim}{A} = [a_{ij}]$, $i, j = 1, \ldots, k$ be given. The vertices i and j are incident if $a_{ij} + a_{ji} > 0$. Suppose some set β of variables with incident

arrows must be removed from the graph. As a result we shall have a graph $G^* = (X^*, \Gamma^*)$ and $X^* = X \setminus \beta$ (where "$X \setminus \beta$" means "X excluding β"), $\Gamma^* \subset \Gamma$ with incidence matrix $A^* = [a^*_{ij}]$ $i, j \in X^*$. Let the vertices from the β set be incident to the vertices from some subset $S \subset (X \setminus \beta)$. We designate the set of paths connecting vertices $r, t \in S$ and passing through vertices $j \in \beta$ by μ_{rjt}. We shall call some graph

$G^* = (X^*, \Gamma^*)$, $X^* \subset X$, $\Gamma^* \subset \Gamma$ a *reduced graph* for graph

$G = (X, \Gamma)$, if $\mu_{rjt} \neq \emptyset$ involves $a^*_{rt} = 1$ for every $r, t \in S$

and $j \in \beta$. The set of arrows connecting vertices from S with vertices from β will be designated by U, and an arrow directed from vertex i to vertex j will be designated by u_{ij}.

The problem of causal scheme reduction is solved by the following algorithm.

1. The matrix $A = [a_{ij}]$ $(i, j = 1, 2, \ldots, k)$ associates with the matrix $P = [p_{ij}]$ in which

$$p_{ij} = \begin{cases} 1, \text{ if } a_{ij} = 1, \ i, j \in \beta \quad \text{or } u_{ij} \in U \\ 0, \text{ otherwise} \end{cases}$$

2. Let the number of vertices in set S be equal to n. Consider the set of matrices $D_m = [d^{(m)}_{ij}]$ $(m = 1, 2, \ldots, n+2)$.

$$D_{m+1} = D_m Q_m \qquad \text{where} \qquad Q_m = [q^{(m)}_{ij}],$$

$$q^{(m)}_{ij} = \begin{cases} 1, \text{ if } d^{(m)}_{ij} > 0, \ i, j \in \beta \text{ or } u_{ij} \in U \\ 0, \text{ otherwise} \end{cases}$$

and $D_1 = P$.

3. Let

$$\tilde{\mathcal{B}} = [\tilde{b}_{ij}] = \sum_{m=1}^{n+2} \tilde{D}_m$$

Then in matrix $\tilde{A}^*$

$$a_{ij}^* = \begin{cases} 1, & \text{if } a_{ij} + \tilde{b}_{ij} > 0, \ i,j \ \varepsilon \ (X \setminus \beta) \\ 0, & \text{if } a_{ij} + \tilde{b}_{ij} = 0, \ \text{or } i,j \ \varepsilon \ \beta \ . \end{cases}$$

Now we must answer at least one more question: can we always reduce the initial causal scheme, and if not always, what reduction rule (or rules) can be stated?

From Simon (1957), Boudon (1968) and Blalock (1961) we can get some conditions for reduction. Indeed, in accordance with Boudon's terminology, for every causal scheme, there exist some implicit factors "that act on the explicit variables of the causal scheme without being stated explicitly" (Boudon, 1968, p. 200). These factors must not be correlated if we want to get the correct causal numerical evaluation. We know nothing about the correlation among implicit factors, but we can at least require that the following condition be satisfied: any variable which is subject to removal from the initial scheme must not influence (directly or indirectly, through variables which are subject to removal) more than one variable from the variable set which is kept under consideration.

This rule is realized in the incidence matrix in a simple way.
1. The matrix $\tilde{A} = [a_{ij}]$ associates with matrix $\tilde{T} = [t_{ij}]$ in which

$$t_{ij} = \begin{cases} 1, & \text{if } a_{ij}=1, \ i,j \ \varepsilon \ \beta \ \text{or } i \ \varepsilon \ \beta \ \text{and } j \ \varepsilon \ (X \setminus \beta) \\ 0, & \text{otherwise} \ . \end{cases}$$

2. Let the number of elements in the β set be equal to n. Find the matrix

$$\tilde{\mathcal{B}} = [b_{ij}] = \sum_{\lambda=1}^{m} \tilde{T}^{\lambda} \ .$$

Now we can state our rule. Some vertex $i \in \beta$ can be removed from the scheme iff

$$\sum_{j \in (X \setminus \beta)} b_{ij} = 0$$

For example, in the above-mentioned Blalock's structure we cannot remove variables x_1 and x_2 and can remove variables x_3, x_4 and x_5.

In Section 3 I shall state an hypothesis from which it follows that for the correct numerical evaluation of the causal connection between two variables it is necessary to take into consideration not only their common cause but their common effect too. If this hypothesis is correct, we cannot remove from the scheme variables which are the effects of more than one variable contained in the rest of the scheme (from the set $X \setminus \beta$). In order to satisfy this condition we must consider the transpose of the matrix A in the previous algorithm. Suppose in this case we have as a result the matrix $D = [d_{ij}]$ instead of matrix B. Then some vertex $i \in \beta$ can be removed from the scheme iff

$$\sum_{j \in (X \setminus \beta)} b_{ij} = 0 \text{ and } \sum_{j \in (X \setminus \beta)} d_{ij} = 0.$$

I have another remark to make which seems to me very important. As can be seen from the reduction rules, when reducing the causal scheme we must satisfy the following two conditions:

1. It is necessary to retain causal connections which are realized through removed variables.

2. Not all variables can be removed from the given scheme.

From all the above remarks it follows that when constructing a causal scheme for anlysis and evaluation, we must observe at least the following rules.

1. In the first step the causal scheme must include the maximum possible number of variables independently of their measurability and character. Any variable which is supposed to be causally connected with others under consideration must be included in the initial causal scheme.

2. In accordance with reduction rules some variables (unmeasurable or others) are removed from the initial scheme.

3. If the student intends to evaluate the causal scheme numerically, it is necessary to discover all the automatons and to remove them from the scheme.

4. The minimum and maximum graphs are defined on the basis of the new scheme. These graphs are analyzed. They both can then be numerically evaluated in addition to the initial scheme.

2. NUMERICAL EVALUATION OF CAUSAL CONNECTIONS[4]

There are several different methods for numerical evaluations of causal connections. These methods are widely discussed in the literature and I shall not describe them. I should only like to note that they do not give us any measure of influence that is familiar and convenient for interpretation such as the correlation coefficient. Later on I shall state the measure of the causal connection for a pair of variables which will be similar to the correlation coefficient; it will be the mathematical expectation of a product of two normalized random variables. Our method can be used for any causal scheme without automatons, for minimum, maximum or initial graphs.

I shall suppose that:

1. The causal scheme with incidence matrix $\underset{\sim}{A} = [a_{ij}]$, $i,j = 1,2,\ldots,k$ is given. This scheme has no automaton.

2. Every vertex i of graph G associates with a vector of realization of the random variable $\underset{\sim}{x}_i = (x_{i1},\ldots, x_{in})$

and

$$\sum_{\nu=1}^{n} x_{i\nu} = 0 , \quad \sum_{\nu=1}^{n} x_{i\nu}^2 = n .$$

3. For every pair of vertices i and j, for which $a_{ij} = 1$ a form of regression function $\hat{x}_j = \phi_{ij} (x_i)$ is given. This function is linear with regard to unknown parameters.

The problem is to evaluate the influence of the i-th variable on the j-th one if $a_{ij} = 1$ provided the influence of all variables for which $a_{si} = 1$ (s = 1,2,..., k; s ≠ i) and $a_{sj} = 1$ (s = 1,2,...,k; s ≠ j) has been eliminated. Such values must be in the interval (-1,1) and be equal to -1 or 1

---

[4]The main result which will be discussed in this section is stated in Borodkin and Lukatskaia (1966).

only in the case of a linear functional connection between the variables. This value I shall call the causal co-efficient and designate it by P_{ij}.

Now we can begin to solve the problem. At first, the graph is divided into layers. The first layer is formed by the vertices of the graph entries, that is, by vertices for which in the incidence matrix a_{ij} = o for every i=1,2...,k. Within the first layer, vertices are numbered from 1 to ℓ_1. If we now remove from the graph all vertices of the first layer together with arrows incident to them we shall have a subgraph. In this subgraph there are some vertices forming its entries and these vertices are included in the second layer. In this layer vertices are numbered from ℓ_1+1 to ℓ_2. Continuing with this procedure we shall divide the initial graph into some number of layers. It is clear that every vertex will be included within some layer and that the number of layers must not exceed the number of graph vertices. Later we shall consider numbers of vertices as numbers defined in the procedure of dividing a graph into layers. Thus, for any causal coefficient P_{ij} we will always have j > i, i,j = 1,2,..., k. The coefficient P_{ij} is defined by the following general formula:

$$P_{ij} = a_{ij} \frac{\Delta_i \Delta_j^{(i)}}{n\sigma_i \sigma_j^{(i)}}$$

where Δ_i is the row vector x_i orthogonalized in relation to all other vectors x_λ for $\lambda < i$; $\Delta_j^{(i)}$ is the column vector x_j orthogonalized in relation to all other vectors except vector x_i; and σ_i and $\sigma_j^{(i)}$ are the standard deviations of vectors Δ_i and $\Delta_j^{(i)}$, respectively. To obtain vector Δ_i by the least-squares method, we solve for the parameters of the following regression function x_i on vectors x_λ (for $\lambda < i$)

$$\hat{x}_i = \sum_{\lambda < i} a_{\lambda i} \emptyset_{\lambda i} (x_\lambda)$$

Then

$$\Delta_i = x_i - \hat{x}_i$$

For the orthogonalization of vector $\underset{\sim}{x}_j$ in relation to all vectors except the i-th one, it is first necessary to substitute vectors $\underset{\sim}{x}_\nu^{(i)} = \underset{\sim}{x}_\nu - \underset{\sim}{\hat{x}}_\nu$ for vectors $\underset{\sim}{x}_\nu$ ($i < \nu < j$) where $\underset{\sim}{\hat{x}}_\nu = a_{i\nu}\ \phi_{i\nu}\ (\underset{\sim}{x}_i)$, and where $\phi_{i\nu}$ is a regression

function whose parameters are found by the least-squares method. Further, the approximation of vector $\underset{\sim}{x}_j$ by vectors $\underset{\sim}{x}_\nu^{(i)}$ is obtained by the least-squares method. Then $\underset{\sim}{\Delta}_j^{(i)} = \underset{\sim}{x}_j - \underset{\sim}{x}_j^{(i)}$, where $\underset{\sim}{x}_j^{(i)}$ is the above-mentioned approximation. Thus we have two vectors $\underset{\sim}{\Delta}_i$ and $\underset{\sim}{\Delta}_j^{(i)}$ on the bases of which the coefficient P_{ij} is defined.

We will show the causal coefficients for schemes with three variables for the case of linear regression. The following designations will be used:

$$\underset{\sim}{t}_1 = (t_{11},\ t_{12},\ \ldots,\ t_{1n})$$

$$\underset{\sim}{t}_2 = (t_{21},\ t_{22},\ \ldots,\ t_{2n})$$

$$\underset{\sim}{t}_3 = (t_{31},\ t_{32},\ \ldots,\ t_{3n})$$

observation vectors for which

$$\sum_{j=1}^{n} t_{ij} = 0;\quad \sum_{j=1}^{n} t_{ij}^2 = n;\quad i=1,2,3;$$

$r_{i\ell}$: correlation coefficient, $\ell, i = 1,2,3$;

$$r_{i\ell} = \frac{1}{n} \sum_{j=1}^{n} t_{ij} t_{\ell j};$$

$\underset{\sim}{t}_{\ell i} = r_{i\ell}\underset{\sim}{t}_\ell$: linear approximation of vector $\underset{\sim}{t}_i$ by vector $\underset{\sim}{t}_\ell$ ($\ell \neq i$) obtained by the least-squares method;

$\underset{\sim}{\Delta}_i = \underset{\sim}{t}_i - \underset{\sim}{t}_{\ell i}$; $\sigma^2(x)$: dispersion of variable x.

It is clear that $\sigma^2(t_i) = 1$ for any i, and the vector $\underset{\sim}{\Delta}_i$ is orthogonal with respect to vector $\underset{\sim}{t}_\ell$.

By the definition for the graph shown in Fig. 1

$$P_{12} = r_{12}$$

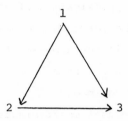

Fig. 1

The causal coefficient P_{23} is obtained on the basis of the following vectors:

$$\underset{\sim}{\Delta}_2 = \underset{\sim}{t}_2 - r_{12}\underset{\sim}{t}_1;$$

$$\underset{\sim}{\Delta}_3 = \underset{\sim}{t}_3 - r_{13}\underset{\sim}{t}_1$$

for which $\sigma^2(\Delta_2) = 1 - r_{12}^2$; $\sigma^2(\Delta_3) = 1 - r_{13}^2$.

According to the algorithm

$$P_{23} = \frac{r_{23} - r_{12}\, r_{13}}{\sqrt{(1 - r_{12}^2)(1 - r_{13}^2)}}.$$

Now find P_{13}. First, we must get the vector $\underset{\sim}{\Delta}_2$ orthogonalized with respect to vector $\underset{\sim}{t}_1$:

$$\underset{\sim}{\Delta}_2 = \underset{\sim}{t}_2 - \underset{\sim}{r}_{12}\underset{\sim}{t}_1.$$

Then we shall get vector $\underset{\sim}{\Delta}_3^{(2)}$ which is orthogonal in relation to $\underset{\sim}{\Delta}_2$. The linear approximation of the vector $\underset{\sim}{t}_3$ by vector $\underset{\sim}{\Delta}_2$ is

$$\hat{\underset{\sim}{t}}_3 = \frac{r_{23} - r_{12}r_{13}}{\sqrt{1 - r^2_{12}}} \quad \frac{\underset{\sim}{t}_2 - r_{12}\underset{\sim}{t}_1}{\sqrt{1 - r^2_{12}}}$$

and

$$\underset{\sim}{\Delta}_3^{(2)} = \underset{\sim}{t}_3 - \hat{\underset{\sim}{t}}_3$$

$$\sigma^2(\Delta_3^{(2)}) = 1 - \frac{(r_{23} - r_{12}r_{13})^2}{1 - r^2_{12}} \quad .$$

Thus
$$P_{13} = \frac{r_{13}\sqrt{1 - r^2_{12}}}{\sqrt{1 - r^2_{12} - (r_{23} - r_{12}r_{13})^2}} \quad .$$

For the graph in Fig. 2 it is necessary to get P_{13} and P_{23}.
By definition

$$P_{13} = \frac{r_{13} - r_{23}r_{12}}{\sqrt{1 - r^2_{23}}}$$

$$P_{23} = \frac{r_{23} - r_{12}r_{13}}{\sqrt{1 - r^2_{13}}}$$

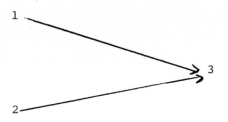

Fig. 2

It is not difficult to show that the causal coefficient is insensitive to the reorientation of some arrows in the scheme. For instance, in the scheme of Fig. 1 we can re-orient the arrow between x_2 and x_3, but P_{23} will not change.

In conclusion I would like to emphasize the following point. This causal coefficient has no profound theoretical basis. Thus far it only has heuristic value.

It is impossible, however, to use the partial and multiple correlation coefficients (which have good mathematical bases in the general case) for the evaluation of influence in causal schemes. This prohibition, as a formal result, has been proved in Borodkin, Dontcheva, Penkov (1970).

3. SOME CONSIDERATIONS IN USING THE ENTROPY FUNCTION IN CAUSAL ANALYSIS

The entropy function is very useful in causal probability analysis. It provides us with certain numerical values and gives an opportunity to interpret causal relations in the very familiar terms of information theory. Indeed in every kind of analysis of experimental results we always deal only with information about events and/or values. Equivalences between an approach based on information (or entropy) and the probabilistic approach can easily be demonstrated. At present we are working on a formulation of this approach, and in the near future some papers on this subject will appear.

Now I wish to remind the reader of some well-known facts about the entropy function. The entropy function for some random variable V is

$$H(V) = -\int_{-\infty}^{\infty} f(V) \log f(V) dV$$

where $f(V)$ is a density function.

Let us take two random variables X and Y. Then

$$H(X,Y) = H(X) + H(Y|X) = H(Y) + H(X|Y) \tag{1}$$

where $H(Y|X)$ is a conditional entropy

$$H(Y|X) = -\int_{-\infty}^{\infty} \int f(x,y) \log f(y|x) dx dy$$

where $f(y|x)$ is a conditional density function.
For the normal distribution with parameters $(0, \sigma_i^2)$

$$H(X_1, \ldots, X_n) = \log(2\pi e)^{n/2} \sqrt{\text{Det } [a_{ij}]}, \quad i, j = 1, 2, \ldots, n \quad (2)$$

where $[a_{ij}]$ is a correlation matrix,

$$a_{ij} = \sigma_i \sigma_j r_{ij}, \quad i, j = 1, 2, \ldots, n,$$

and r_{ij} is a correlation coefficient. Now we need some definitions. For one thing, there is Suppes' definition (1970), p. 61:

"Definition 15. The property $Y_{t'}$ is a (weak) prima facie quadrant cause of the property X_t if and only if

(i) $t' \leqslant t$

(ii) For all X and Y if $P(Y_{t'} \leqslant y) > 0$

then $P(X_t \geqslant X | Y_{t'} \geqslant y) \geqslant P(X_t \geqslant x)$

The term *quadrant* is used because (ii) may be rewritten

$$P(X_t \geqslant x, Y_{t'} \geqslant y) \geqslant P(X_t \geqslant x) P(Y_{t'} \geqslant y),$$

which expresses a comparison between the probability of any quadrant $X_t \geqslant x$, $Y_{t'} \geqslant y$ under the given distribution and the probability of this quadrant in the case of interdependence."

Now let us state one further definition. Consider the finite set of continuous random variables $X_1, \ldots, X_n$ about which it is known that the property X_n is related to a subordinate system (in the sense of time) and the ordering of the rest of the variables is unknown.

Definition. The system of properties $X_1, \ldots, X_{n-1}$ is a generalized prima facie cause of the property if and only if
(i) X_n is a subordinate property (in the sense of time) with respect to the system $X_1, \ldots, X_{n-1}$;
(ii) $P(X_n \geqslant x_n | X_1 \geqslant x_1, \ldots, X_{n-1} \geqslant x_{n-1}) \neq P(X_n \geqslant x_n)$.
This is a usual condition for dependent systems. But the relations among properties under these conditions seem to be of great interest.

The condition (ii) of the above definition is equivalent to the following:

$$H(X_n) - H(X_n|X_1, \ldots, X_{n-1}) > 0.$$

But another condition is more interesting:

$$H(X_n) - H(X_n|X_1, \ldots, X_{n-1}) > c, \quad c > 0. \tag{3}$$

The term c may be considered as a threshold for the process of receiving causal information. In some fields, such as psychology, this threshold can be measured experimentally. In other, non-experimental sciences it may be taken as an evaluation of the discriminating power of one's research methods. Suppose that $X_1 \ldots, X_n$ are normally distributed with parameters $(0,\sigma_i)$. From (3) it follows that

$$\log_b \sqrt{\frac{Det[a_{pq}]}{Det[a_{ij}]}} > \log_b b^c, \quad p, q = 1, 2, \ldots, n - 1$$
$$i, j = 1, 2, \ldots, n.$$

But $b > 0$, $c > 0$. Therefore

$$\frac{Det[a_{pq}]}{Det[a_{ij}]} > b^{2c}.$$

Remembering the multiple correlation coefficient

$$R^2 = 1 - \frac{Det[a_{ij}]}{Det[a_{pg}]}$$

we get the inequality

$$R^2 > 1 - \frac{1}{b^{2c}} \tag{4}$$

The meaning of this inequality is very simple. For the given conditions the ability to identify causal relations depends on measurability. For instance, if $b = 2$ and $c = 1$ $R^2 > 0.75$. This means that for $R^2 \leqslant 0.75$ we cannot state that the causal relation exists because the measurement error is too great. If we have only two properties X and Y under the indicated conditions then

$$r^2_{XY} > 1 - \frac{1}{b^{2c}} \text{ is obvious.}$$

Consider the case of three properties X, Y, Z where Z is a subordinate property. For this system

$$1 - r^2_{XY} > b^{2c}(1 + 2r_{XZ}r_{XY}r_{YZ} - r^2_{XZ} - r^2_{YZ} - r^2_{XY}).$$

(5)

The inequality

$$r^2_{XZ} + r^2_{YZ} > 1 - \frac{1}{b^{2c}}$$

is a necessary condition for the independence of X and Y. Indeed, suppose that

$$r^2_{XZ} + r^2_{YZ} \leqslant 1 - \frac{1}{b^{2c}} \qquad (6)$$

Then, from (5)

$$r^2_{XY} (b^{2c} - 1) > 2b^{2c} r_{XY}r_{XZ}r_{YZ} - b^{2c}r^2_{XY}$$

If $r_{XY} = 0$, we have the contradictory $0 > 0$.

If (6) is true, $r_{XY} \neq 0$ and

$$|r_{XY}| > \frac{2b^{2c}}{2b^{2c} - 1}|r_{XZ}r_{YZ}|.$$

The necessary condition stated above can be easily generalized for the case of an arbitrary finite number of variables. Let us have a set of normally distributed variables $X_1, \ldots, X_n$ where the variable X_n is subordinate. Then the necessary condition for mutual independence of variables $X_1, \ldots, X_{n-1}$ is the following inequality:

$$\sum_{i=1}^{n-1} r^2_{in} > 1 - \frac{1}{b^{2c}}$$

On the basis of this analysis the following hypothesis seems to be of theoretical and empirical interest.

Hypothesis. The nonzero correlation of two random variables can be not only because of a common cause, but because of a common effect too. The truth of this hypothesis is obvious for a case where the researcher deals with goal systems. In this case the whole system (or its parts) is oriented to the achievement of the set goal (or goals inherent to this system), and a need arises to coordinate the behavior of its elements. Of course, I do not mean to imply time reversibility since the goal stands out as a factor related to the past for each given effect. If, however, some special goal has already been achieved or is being continuously achieved "in part" and the researcher has at hand only a set of observed values of all variables, then it appears as though the future values of some variables determined the past values of other variables, since the values of some variables are dependent on the need to plan the future states. In an artificially constructed system it is often easy to relate the goal in the past to one of the causes for the change in the values of variables. In natural as well as poorly known structures which, moreover, have a system of goals, this representation may be difficult or even impossible. From the above statements a still more rigid hypothesis follows: the correlation between variables may be the higher, the more strict the requirement to achieve some goals and the weaker the association between certain variables and characteristics of the goal the higher the correlations between these variables may be. The possibility of this situation should make the sociologist think over the correlation between variables, not only in terms of the past but also of the future states of the system. If a goal (in the form of a system of variables describing it) can be singled out explicitly and if the correlation between planned and actual states is sufficient, then, in the study, time can be reversed, and, as a consequence, we may deal with recursive systems. Otherwise, the use of the causal analysis technique is unjustifiable, and it is necessary to use a simultaneous-system approach.

4. CONCLUSION

1. Before numerically evaluating all kinds of indices in causal systems, it is necessary to analyze the structure of relationships. First, it may turn out that the researcher cannot state a single hypothesis concerning the structure of relationships, and it becomes necessary to test

several hypotheses. Second, in systems involving large
numbers of variables, the researcher may not be able to distinguish and eliminate automats without using formal techniques. Third, the analysis of systems having goals is to
be conducted with specialized methods.

2. In suitable causal structures the influence in each
pair of variables can be evaluated with a special index,
i.e., an influence coefficient.

REFERENCES

Ashby, W. Ross. 1960. *Design for a Brain: The Origin of
Adaptive Behavior*. New York: Wiley.

Blalock, H. M. 1961. "Correlation and Causality: The
Multivariate Case." *Social Forces* 39 (March): 246-251.

Borodkin, F. 1968. *The Statistical Evaluation of Association Between Economic Variables*. (Russian). Moscow:
Statistika.

Borodkin, F., S. Doncheva, and M. Penkov. 1970. "About
Measuring Influence in a System of Parameters." Paper
submitted at 7th World Congress of Sociology.

Borodkin, F., and M. Lukatskaia. 1966. "On Statistical
Evaluation of Causal Influence." (Russian). *Nauchn.
trudy Nov. gos. univ*. Novosibirsk.

Boudon, R. A. 1968. "A New Look at Correlation Analysis."
In H. M. Blalock and A. B. Blalock (eds.) *Methodology
in Social Research*. New York: McGraw-Hill.

Ore, O. 1962. *Theory of Graphs*. American Mathematical
Society Colloquium Publications XXXVIII.

Simon, H. A. 1957. *Models of Man*. New York: Wiley.

Suppes, P. 1970. *A Probabilistic Theory of Causality*.
Acta Philosophica Fennica, Fasc. XXIV. Amsterdam:
North-Holland Publishing Company.

5

Informational Measures of Causal Influence

I.N. TAGANOV

Lensoviet Technological Institute of Leningrad

1. THE GENERAL PROBLEM

The analysis and interpretation of empirical sociological data, in most cases, are undertaken for finding qualitative and quantitative relations between the elements within a certain group of factors or attributes allowing the interpretation in terms of main categories, concepts and inferences of general sociological theory. After substantive definitions of considered factors have been stated and the empirical study carried out, the sociologist obtains some estimates of the values of gradations of factors for the surveyed social population.

The simplest task is the establishment of some quantitative measures between the factors considered. This task can be solved by means of correlation analysis. But correlation analysis techniques allow one to obtain only a set of measures of symmetrical association between the factors, but in no way do they take account of the structure of actual interrelationships among the sociological concepts and categories specific for a particular social study. For a broad class of tasks, the structure of interrelationships among sociological concepts and categories may be represented by a system of cause-and-effect relations between the factors or attributes studied, and in many cases such a system may be established a priori on the basis of general sociological theory. Once the structure of cause-and-effect relations has been established there follows a task of defining quantitative measures for the intensity of causal influences in the considered group of factors on the basis of an analysis of empirical findings.

At present, the qualitative analysis of causal relations is carried out in sociology largely by path-analysis (p-analysis) techniques. The main ideas of p-analysis as stated by S. Wright (1934) have been actively developed by various researchers, and now it is one of the most popular quantitative techniques in mathematical sociology.

P-analysis as well as a number of its modifications are based on the use of linear (sometimes quasi-linear) functional relations between variables amenable to quantitative measurement. The use of linear relationships between the variables makes p-analysis a special case of regression analysis where regression coefficients are interpreted in terms of cause and effect. The application of p-analysis in sociology is connected with quite a number of difficulties. First, one must not think that linear or any other fixed functional relation between variables can satisfactorily represent all the diversity of cause-and-effect relations in real sociological structures. Second, the necessity of quantitative measurement of variables in p-analysis imposes very rigid constraints on the class of solvable sociological tasks since the overwhelming majority of sociological factors are of a qualitative character, and the arithmetization is always somewhat arbitrary. These difficulties are caused by the fact that p-analysis uses the functional model of cause-and-effect relations, and they are not expected to be overcome by further development of this method.

2. FROM ENTROPY TO A CAUSAL MEASURE

The functional model of cause-and-effect relations represents the determination of the states of object-effect by the states of object-cause. But the objective relations between the events determine not only the correlation between the states of objects which are in a cause-and-effect relation, but they also determine the contingency among the measures of statistical uncertainty of the states of objects. Therefore, the area of conceivable states of object-cause not only determines the area of conceivable states of object-effect, but the statistical uncertainty of the states of object-cause also determines the measure of statistical uncertainty of the states of object-effect. With some or other quantitative measures of statistical uncertainty of variables it is possible to build a model of a cause-and-effect relation in the form of a functional relation between these measures. This model is then invariant with regard to the functional model of the relation between the states of objects.

A quantitative measure for statistical uncertainty of the states of a certain object is the entropy functional.[1] It should be noted that the entropy functional, apart from its quality of uniqueness (see Khinchin, 1953, 1956), is invariant with respect to single-valued functional transformations of the states of object, which eliminates the problem of the quantitative measurement of qualitative factors when building the model of cause-and-effect relations.

Let us consider two objects A and B which are characterized by finite or infinite sets of states $\{a\}$ and $\{b\}$. It is possible, e.g. empirically, to obtain probability distributions for these sets and for a set of various pairs of states $\{ab\}$. Let B be the effect of A. According to the approach being developed, instead of the functional model of the cause-and-effect relation $b = f(a, ...)$, it is possible to postulate a more universal correlation between the entropies $H(A)$ and $H(B)$

$$H(B) = F[H(A), ...].\tag{1}$$

As we are going to confine ourselves to a linear approximation in our subsequent discussion, let us expand (1) into a series near

$$H(B) = F\Big|_{H(A) = 0} + \frac{d(F)}{dH(A)}\Big|_{H(A) = 0} H(A) + ...\tag{2}$$

According to (1) the variable $F\big|_{H(A) = 0}$ is the entropy of the object B under the assumption that the object A has no statistical variance of states and is equal to the conditional entropy $H_A(B)$. Noticing then that the difference $H(B) - H_A(B)$ determines the information functional $I(A,B)$, it is possible to obtain from (2) as a linear approximation the following model of the cause-and-effect relations between the objects A and B:

---

[1]In our further discussion the terms "entropy" and "information" are used in the theoretical probabilistic sense as the functionals from the probability densities (see Khinchin, 1953, 1956).

$$I(A,B) = \Gamma_{BA} \, H(A) \, . \tag{3}$$

In interpreting (3) one can understand the cause-and-effect relation as an information channel between the object-cause and object-effect. From this viewpoint, (3) is the formalization of an assumption that with the same statistical uncertainty of the effect the greater the statistical uncertainty of the cause, the greater the information coming from the cause must be. The coefficient Γ_{BA} serves as the coefficient of information transmission in the informational channel $A \rightarrow B$. It should also be noted that the relation (3) may be obtained as the expansion of the definition of the simplest cause (prima facie cause) suggested by Suppes (1970) if one proceeds from absolute and conditional probabilities used by Suppes to the corresponding functionals of entropy.

The factor of proportionality Γ_{BA} in (3) is interpreted as a *general coefficient of causal influence* in the isolated cause-and-effect relation $A \rightarrow B$. As it follows from the analysis of (3), $\Gamma_{BA} = 0$ if there is statistical independence of the objects A and B. In the case where the state of object B is uniquely determined by the state of object A (rigid functional determination) $\Gamma_{BA} = 1$.

Thus

$$0 \leq \Gamma_{BA} \leq 1 \, . \tag{4}$$

The expression (3) may be seen as the phenomenological relation that holds for binary cause-and-effect relations between the objects regardless of the concrete nature of these objects. Phenomenological relations of this kind, because of their universal character, must permit their thermodynamic interpretation. The neg-entropy principle of information of Carno-Brillouin is the most interesting in this respect as it connects the entropy and informational characteristics of physical systems in the process of their evolution. The relation (3) must be true for arbitrary time moments. In particular, for two successive time moments t_1 and t_2

$$I_{t_1}(A,B) = \Gamma_{BA} H_{t_1}(A)$$

(5)

$$I_{t_2}(A,B) = \Gamma_{BA} H_{t_2}(A)$$

can be written. By subtracting the second equality from the first and by omitting irrelevant indices we obtain

$$\Delta I = \Gamma_{BA} \Delta H .$$

(6)

Taking into account the inequalities (4), the relation (6) can be rewritten in a form equivalent to the neg-entropy principle of Carno-Brillouin

$$\Delta(H - I) \geq 0$$

(7)

Thus, the formal relation (3) and neg-entropy principle of information of Carno-Brillouin are at least consistent.

Heretofore the cause-and-effect relation between two isolated objects has been considered. For the analysis of complex multifactor systems, the generalization of the relation (3) for the case of a set $\{A\}$ of mutually complementing causes A_i is of interest:

$$I(B,\{A\}) = \sum_{\{A\}} \gamma_{BA_i} H(A_i) .$$

(8)

According to (8), the information contained in the effect B with regard to the set $\{A\}$ of mutually complementing causes is a linear function of the entropies of object-causes A_i. The coefficients γ_{BA_i} serve as *partial coefficients of causal influence* and in the general case $\gamma_{BA_i} \neq \Gamma_{BA_i}$. The total and partial coefficients of causal influence are equal only in the case of statistical independence of mutually complementing causes. The difference $\Gamma_{BA_i} - \gamma_{BA_i}$ may serve as an evaluation of the indirect causal influence of the object A_i on the object B.

In order to calculate the partial coefficients of causal influence for any more or less complicated system, it is necessary to develop a procedure which would give a closed system of linear equations of type (8). This procedure seems to have to be built as a result of successive consideration of pairs of objects which are in a cause-and-effect relation. It is more convenient to set forth our further discussion in terms of graph theory (using the terminology of Ore, 1962).

A group of n factors A_1, A_2,..., A_i, ..., A_n between which cause-and-effect relations have been established may be presented by a directed graph G with n vertices. Each vertex is associated with some factor. The directed edge of the graph incident to some two vertices A_i and A_j corresponds to the cause-and-effect relation between the factors A_i and A_j. The maximum number of directed edges in such a graph is $k = \frac{1}{2} n(n-1)$. Each vertex of the graph is associated with two local vertex degrees p_i and p_i^*. The local degree p_i is determined by the number of factors of which the factor A_i is the immediate cause, i.e. by the number of directed graph edges going from the vertex A_i. The local degree p_i^* is determined by the number of factors of which the factor A_i is the immediate effect, i.e. by the number of directed graph edges going to the vertex A_i.

The pair of states a_i, a_j of the objects A_i and A_j between which the cause-and-effect relation has been established may be regarded as a state a_{ij} of some complicated object A_{ij}, which is a combination of the factors A_i and A_j, i.e. $A_{ij} = A_i \cup A_j$. The join of factors corresponds to a structural procedure having the properties of idempotency, commutativity and associativity. Such a structural procedure brings about the structural transformation G_{ij} of the original graph G. The graph G_{ij} is a graph G in which the pair of vertices A_i and A_j is replaced by a new vertex corresponding to the complex factor A_{ij}. The local degrees of the vertex A_{ij} will be

160

$$P_{ij} = P_i + P_j - 1$$

and

$$P^*_{ij} = P^*_i + P^*_j - 1.$$

The number of conceivable structural transformations of the original graph G equals the number of its edges.

If, for each of the factors A_{ij} generating the structural transformation G_{ij}, a relation of type (8) is constructed, then we shall get a closed system of k linear algebraic equalities with k unknown partial coefficients of causal influence. To each factor A_{ij} an equality of type (8) corresponds with P^*_{ij} unknown partial coefficients of causal influence. If for a certain factor $P^*_{ij} = 0$, then such a factor in the considered system of relations is the absolute cause, and a pair A_i, A_j can be used for defining $\gamma_{ij} = \Gamma_{ij}$ from a relation of type (3).

Thus, for each consistent system of attributes or factors, a system of linear algebraic equalities may be obtained whose matrix of coefficients is made up of entropies of states or of gradations of factors, and the vector of free terms is made up of informational functionals of different orders. The solutions to such a system of equalities will be partial coefficients of causal influence in the causal network under consideration. To define total coefficients of causal influence, it is possible to use a set of relations of type (3) for all causally connected pairs of factors.

3. AN ILLUSTRATION

It would be reasonable to illustrate the suggested approach by a concrete example.

Consider a causal network presented by 4-vertex graph G with 5 directed edges

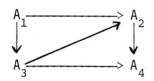

This graph permits five structural transformations: G_{24}, G_{34}, G_{32}, G_{13}, and G_{12}. The structural transformation G_{24} has the following form

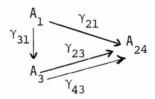

Since $\overset{*}{p}_2 = 2$ and $\overset{*}{p}_4 = 2$, the number of unknown coefficients in the equality for the vertex A_{24} must be $\overset{*}{p}_{24} = 3$. The relation (8) for the vertex A_{24} has the form

$$I(A_{24}, A_1, A_3) = \gamma_{21}H(A_1) + (\gamma_{23} + \gamma_{43})H(A_3) . \qquad (9)$$

In a similar way the rest of the equalities corresponding to permissible structural transformations can be obtained:

$$G_{34} : \quad I(A_{34}, A_1, A_2) = \gamma_{31}H(A_1) + \gamma_{42}H(A_2) \qquad (10)$$

$$G_{32} : \quad I(A_{32}, A_1) = (\gamma_{21} + \gamma_{31})H(A_1) \qquad (11)$$

$$G_{12} : \quad I(A_{12}, A_3) = \gamma_{23}H(A_3) . \qquad (12)$$

For the structural transformation G_{13} , $\overset{*}{p}_{13} =$ holds. In this connection the factor A_{13} may be used for defining $\gamma_{31} = \Gamma_{31}$ from a relation of type (3):

$$I(A_3, A_1) = \Gamma_{31}H(A_1) . \qquad (13)$$

After solving the equalities (9)-(13) we can get the entire set of partial coefficients of causal influence. For defining general coefficients of causal influence the relations of type (3) must be used:

$$I(A_2, A_1) = \Gamma_{21} H(A_1)$$

$$I(A_2, A_3) = \Gamma_{23} H(A_3)$$

$$I(A_4, A_2) = \Gamma_{42} H(A_2)$$

$$I(A_4, A_3) = \Gamma_{43} H(A_3)$$

The evaluation of indirect causal influences in the network considered is made using the differences of type $\Gamma_{ij} - \gamma_{ij}$.

In defining the coefficients of causal influence from empirical data, it is most difficult to calculate the functionals of information for the joined factors, since this requires using empirical evaluations of multidimensional distributions. But in most cases of statistical analyses of complex systems the use of multidimensional distributions is inevitable.

4. SUMMARY

This chapter suggests a model of cause-and-effect relations between two objects in the form of the relations between the measures of statistical uncertainty of the states of objects. In the case of the linear approximation this model leads to the proportionality of the functionals of information and entropy, given by eq. (3). A generalization of the model for the case of a set of mutually complementary causes has been suggested by eq. (8). For the purpose of analysis and interpretation of sociological data we have suggested a method for evaluation of the coefficients of causal influence which uses the proposed model of cause-and-effect relations and does not require any assumptions about the nature of functional relations between the variables.

REFERENCES

Brillouin, L. 1956. *Science and Information Theory.* New York: Academic Press, Inc.

Khinchin, A. Y. 1953. *Uspekhi Mat. Nauk* 3 (55): 3-20 (Russian).

Khinchin, A. Y. 1956. *Uspekhi Mat. Nauk* 1 (67): 17-75 (Russian).

Ore, O. 1962. *Theory of Graphs.* New York: American Mathematical Society.

Suppes, P. 1970. *A Probabilistic Theory of Causality.* Amsterdam-Helsinki: North Holland Publishing Company.

Wright, S. 1934. "The Method of Path Coefficients," *Annals of Mathematical Statistics* 5 (3): 161-215.

6

The Structure of Multidimensional Random Variables and Its Utilization in Social Research *

Iu. N. GAVRILETS

Central Economic—Mathematical Institute, Moscow

1. INTRODUCTION

A social individual is usually characterized by a set of a large number of different attributes. These attributes are closely interconnected, so that a change in some of them implies a change in the others. The relations between the attributes are as a rule of a stochastic nature; according to this, statistical methods of analysis of such relations are very important in mathematical sociology.

These methods are especially important in studying mass behavior of individuals acting as members of certain social groups. Some sociologists hold as the most important task in their field of knowledge an answer to the question: With what probabilities will particular social groups behave in this or in that manner under certain definite fixed conditions?" If x is the index of a social group, a the index of the conditions, and y the behavior of the group, then it is necessary to find a function of the conditional probability $p(y|x,a)$; where the variables can be expressed on an arbitrary scale.

If the variable representing the j-th attribute of a typical individual taken at some fixed time is denoted by

---

*
This chapter deals with the first results of the theory for a structure of random variables. This theory is now being developed by the author; for more details see Yu N. Gavrilets (1974).

x_j $(j = 1,2,...,n)$, then the most comprehensive model for the whole population of individuals considered could be obtained from the function representing the distribution of individuals on all possible sets of variables $f(x_1, x_2,...,x_n)$. Here the function f has, for example, the meaning of a density function. But the task of constructing the function $f(x)$ (where $x = (x_1, x_2, ..., x_n)$) on the basis of statistical information (for example, in the form of ordinary sociological questionnaires) proves to be extremely complicated, since the number of possible combinations of attribute levels and variables is tremendously large. Thus, for the case where the j-th attribute has r_j different levels, it equals $R = r_1 \cdot r_2 \cdot \ldots \cdot r_n$. If $r_j = 4$, $n = 20$, then $R = 4^{20} \simeq 10^{12}$. It is clear for this situation it is physically impossible to have a table with 10^{12} cells, though it would be very desirable to be able to find the probability of any combination. Equally complicated is the task of finding conditional probabilities $p(y|x)$, and the difficulties in predicting the distribution $f(x)$ are boundless, as for example, by means of transitional probabilities of Markov chains.

Besides the above-mentioned tasks, the problem of the analysis of the structure of relations among the variables describing the statistical individual is of great interest. What variables are most important in influencing the data? How is an indirect influence realized? What variables can be treated as causes and what ones as effects? These are only some of the questions which are to be answered. The analysis of the structure of relations is dealt with in quite a number of works, in particular Borodkin (1968), Suppes (1970), and Blalock and Blalock (1968).

The present chapter is devoted to building the elements of a theory of random variables having a structure, so to speak, the elements of "structural-functional analysis." The main findings are formulated in the language of discrete random variables though they can easily be extended to the more general case as well.

2. FORMALIZATION OF THE CONCEPT OF DIRECT CONNECTION

A discrete multidimensional random variable $\xi = (\xi_1, \xi_2,...,\xi_n)$ with values $= (X_1, X_2,..., X_n)$ from some space $(\psi_1,..., \psi_n)$ containing a finite number of points is considered. Let $P(X) = P(X_1,..., X_n)$ be the probability density of the variable ξ, i.e., this means the probability of a certain combination of values X_j. Denote the set of indices of its components by $I = \{1,2,\ldots,n\}$. If a set of (unordered) components X_j ($j \in A \subseteq I$) is denoted by X_A, then

$$P(X_A) = \sum_{j \notin A} P(X_1,\ldots,X_n), \text{ and } P(X_A|X_B) = \frac{P(X_A, X_B)}{P(X_B)} \text{ will de-}$$

note absolute and conditional probability densities. The order of the elements $i,j,\ldots,k$ in sets A,B is irrelevant, and the symbol P will be the probability function of corresponding combinations of values of variables. (It would be more correct to write $P(X_A)$ and $P(X_A|X_B)$ as, for example, $P_A(X_A)$ and $P_{AB}(X_A|X_B)$, but to simplify the notation the subscripts are omitted). Obviously true are the familiar relations:

$$P(X_i, X_j, \ldots, X_n) \geqslant 0;$$

$$\sum_{i,j,k} P(X_i,X_j,\ldots,X_k) = 1;$$

$$P(X_1,X_2,\ldots,X_n) = P(X_1|X_2\ldots X_n)\ldots P(X_r|X_{r+1}\ldots X_n)P(X_{r+1}\ldots X_n)$$

where $P(X_2,X_3,\ldots,X_n) \neq 0$.

Let $A,B,C,D \subseteq I$. Sometimes we shall write X_A, X_B instead of $X_{A \cup B}$ if the sets A and B do not intersect. The two following lemmas hold (the appropriate proofs are omitted).

Lemma 1.

For some components X_A, X_B, X_C, let $P(X_A,X_C) \neq 0$ and $P(X_A,X_B) \neq 0$. Then the equality $P(X_C|X_A, X_B) = P(X_C|X_A) \forall X_B$ implies the equality $(P(X_B|X_A,X_C) = P(X_B|X_A) \forall X_C$.

Lemma 2.

For some values of X_A and X_D and for all X_B for which $P(X_A, X_B) \neq 0$, let the following hold: $P(X_D|X_A,X_B) = P(X_D|X_A) \forall X_B$. Then the relation $P(X_D|X_A,X_C) = P(X_D|X_A) \forall X_C$ holds, where $P(X_A,X_C) \neq 0$ and where $C \subseteq B$.

Case 1. Let $P(X)$ be such that for each $i \in I$ there exists some set (not containing i and perhaps empty) $\Delta(i) \subseteq I$ such that the following equalities are satisfied:

$$P(X_i | X_{I - \{i\}}) = P(X_i | X_{I-\{i,k\}}) \forall k \in \Delta(i), P(X_{I-\{i\}}) \neq 0$$

Given this, suppose that all numbers $k \in I$ of X_k variables which can be removed one by one in (3) from the condition $X_{I-\{i\}}$ with respect to X_i are included in $\Delta(i)$. By Lemma 1 the relations (3) imply the relations $P(X_k | X_{I-\{k\}}) = P(X_k | X_{I-\{k;i\}})$. Thus the mapping $\Delta(i)$ on the set I is symmetrical. It may be regarded as some symmetrical graph without loops $\Delta(i)$, indicating for each $i \in I$ those variables which are not directly connected with this one. The relation (3) is a formalization of Ashby's (1962) concept for a stochastic situation.

Case II. Let $P(X)$ be such that for all $i \in I$ a certain set $\Gamma(i) \subseteq I$ (not containing i and possibly empty) is given, so that the following relations are satisfied:

$$P(X_i | X_{I-\{i\}}) = P(X_i | X_{\Gamma(i)}), \quad i \in I, \quad P(X_{I-\{i\}}) \neq 0 \qquad (4)$$

and no element of X_k, $k \in I$ variables can any longer be excluded. We can assume that this graph indicates for each variable X_i, $i \in I$ those variables which are directly connected with it. With some additional assumptions, and with the help of (3) or (4), it is possible to establish the equivalence of the definitions for direct connections.

3. GENERAL DEFINITIONS AND THEOREMS

Definition 1.

The set Y of points $(X_i, X_j, \ldots, X_k)$ is called irreducible if for each pair of its points $(X_i^o, X_j^o, \ldots, X_k^o)$ and $(\bar{X}_i, \bar{X}_j, \ldots, \bar{X}_k)$ there exists a sequence of points

$\{(X_i^m, X_j^m, \ldots, X_k^m)\}_{m=1}^{m=M} \in Y$ and numbers $\{\alpha(m)\}_{m=2}^{m=M}$ from the set

$\{i, j, \ldots, k\}$ such that

$$(X_i^1, X_j^1, \ldots, X_k^1) = (X_i^o, X_j^o, \ldots, X_k^o),$$

$$(X_i^M, X_j^M, \ldots, X_k^M) = (\bar{X}_i, \bar{X}_j, \ldots, \bar{X}_k),$$

$$X_i^{m-1} = X_i^m ; X_j^{m-1} = X_j^m ; \ldots , X_k^{m-1} = X_k^m ; \text{ but } X_{\alpha(m)}^{m-1} \neq X_{\alpha(m)}^m \cdot \quad (5)$$

Otherwise the set Y is called reducible.

Definition 2.
We shall say that the random variable ξ and density $P(X)$ satisfy the requirement for irreducibility if for any values of the components $\bar{X}_A$ ($A \subset I, \bar{X}_A \in \psi_A$) the set Ω ($\bar{X}_A$) of those points X_{I-A} for which $P(\bar{X}_A, \bar{X}_{I-A}) \neq 0$ is irreducible.

Theorem 1.
(a) Let ξ, a random variable satisfying the requirement for irreducibility, have the property that a graph $\Delta(i)$ of it exists such that the conditions (3) hold. Then it is possible to construct a mapping $\Gamma(i) = I - \{i\} - \Delta(i) = I \smallsetminus \{i, \Delta(i)\}$ (where the symbol "$\smallsetminus$" denotes exclusion) such that conditions (4) will hold.
(b) Conversely, if for some graph $\Gamma(i)$ (4) is true, then for the graph $\Delta(i) = I - \{i\} - \Gamma(i)$ the conditions (3) will also hold.

Proof.
(a) Let (3) be correct. Then for all i equalities of the following type are satisfied.

$$P(X_i | X_{I \smallsetminus \{i, \Delta(i)\}}, X_k, X_\ell, \ldots, X_p, X_r)$$

$$\equiv P(X_i | X_{I \smallsetminus \{i, \Delta(i)\}}, X_k, X_\ell, \ldots, X_p) \forall X_r ,$$

$$P(X_i | X_{I \smallsetminus \{i, \Delta(i)\}}, X_k, X_\ell, \ldots, X_p, X_r) \quad (6)$$

$$\equiv P(X_i | X_{I \smallsetminus \{i, \Delta(i)\}}, X_k, X_\ell, \ldots, X_r) \forall X_p ,$$

$$\ldots \ldots \ldots \ldots \ldots \ldots \ldots \circ \ldots \ldots \ldots$$

$$P(X_i | X_{I \smallsetminus \{i, \Delta(i)\}}, X_k, X_\ell, \ldots, X_p, X_r)$$

$$\equiv P(X_i | X_{I \smallsetminus \{i, \Delta(i)\}}, X_\ell, \ldots, X_p, X_r) \forall X_k ,$$

where $k, \ell, \ldots, p, r$ are related to the given $\Delta(i)$ so that $\Delta(i) = \{k, \ell, \ldots, p, r\}$. To meet the requirement for irreducibility, for each fixed value

$$\bar{X}_{I-\{i\}-\Delta(i)} \quad \text{the set } \Omega(\bar{X}_{I-\{i\}-\Delta(i)})$$

$$= \{(X_k, x_\ell, \ldots, X_p, X_r) : P(\bar{X}_{I-\{i\}-\Delta(i)}, \ldots, X_r) \neq 0\}$$

will be irreducible. Therefore, for any two values

$$(\bar{X}_{I-\{i\}-\Delta(i)}, X_k^o, X_\ell^o, \ldots, X_p^o, X_r^o) \text{ and}$$

$$(\bar{X}_{I-\{i\}-\Delta(i)}, X_k^*, X_\ell^*, \ldots, X_p^*, X_r^*)$$

such that the corresponding densities are non-zero, there exists a sequence of numbers $\alpha(m)$ from $\Delta(i)$ and values

$$(\bar{X}_{I-\{i\}-\Delta(i)}, X_k^m, X_\ell^m, \ldots, X_p^m, X_r^m) \quad (m = 1, 2, \ldots, M) \text{ for which}$$

the relations (5) hold. We shall show that the density on these two values is the same. Denote the density on the first value by Z:

$$P(X_i | \bar{X}_{I \smallsetminus \{i, \Delta(i)\}}, X_k^o, X_\ell^o, \ldots, X_p^o, X_r^o) = Z. \qquad (7)$$

By that relation from (6) where in the right-hand side the variable $X_\alpha(1)$ is absent, and by equality (7)

$$Z = P(X_i | \bar{X}_{I \smallsetminus \{i, \Delta(i)\}}, \ldots, X_p^1, X_r^1)$$

$$= P(X_i | \bar{X}_{I \smallsetminus \{i, \Delta(i)\}}, X_k^o, \ldots, X_{\alpha(1)}^1, \ldots, X_r^o)$$

$$= P(X_i | \bar{X}_{I \smallsetminus \{i, \Delta(i)\}}, X_k^1, X_\ell^1, \ldots, X_p^1, X_r^1)$$

takes place. By the equality in (6) corresponding to the number $\alpha(2)$, the previous equality may be extended:

$$Z = P(X_i | \bar{X}_{I \smallsetminus \{i, \Delta(i)\}}, X_k^1, \ldots, X_{\alpha(2)}^2, \ldots, X_r^1)$$

$$= P(X_i | \bar{X}_{I \smallsetminus \{i, \Delta(i)\}}, X_k^2, \ldots, X_\ell^2, \ldots, X_p^2, X_r^2).$$

Continuing our reasoning we can obtain

$$Z = P(X_i | \bar{X}_{I \smallsetminus \{i, \Delta(i)\}}, X_k^{M-1} \ldots, X_{2(M)}^M, \ldots, X_r^{M-1})$$

$$= P(X_i | \bar{X}_{I \smallsetminus \{i, \Delta(i)\}}, X_k^M, \ldots, X_r^M)$$

$$= P(X_i | \bar{X}_{I \smallsetminus \{i, \Delta(i)\}}, X_k^*, X_\ell^*, \ldots, X_p^*, X_r^*)$$

Thus, for all variables from $\Omega(\bar{X}_{I \smallsetminus \{i, \Delta(i)\}})$ the value of the corresponding density is the same. Therefore, we can write

$$P(X_i | \bar{X}_{I \smallsetminus \{i, \Delta(i)\}}, X_k, \ldots, X_r)$$

$$= f_i(X_i, \bar{X}_{I \smallsetminus \{i, \Delta(i)\}}) \forall (X_k, \ldots, X_r) \varepsilon \ \Omega(X_{I \smallsetminus \{i, \Delta(i)\}})$$

From the last relation it follows that

$$P(X) = f_i(X_i, X_{I \smallsetminus \{i, \Delta(i)\}}) P(X_{I \smallsetminus \{i, \Delta(i)\}}, X_k, \ldots, X_r). \tag{8}$$

By the definition of conditional density

$$P(X_i | X_{I \smallsetminus \{i, \Delta(i)\}}) = \frac{P(X_i, X_{I \smallsetminus \{i, \Delta(i)\}})}{P(X_{I \smallsetminus \{i, \Delta(i)\}})} \tag{9}$$

$$= \frac{\sum_{X_k, \ldots, X_r} P(X)}{P(X_{I \smallsetminus \{i, \Delta(i)\}})} \ .$$

Substituting in the numerator of (9) the value $P(X)$ from (8) and performing addition we have

$$P(X_i | X_{I \smallsetminus \{i, \Delta(i)\}}) = \frac{f_i(X_i, X_{I \smallsetminus \{i, \Delta(i)\}}) \ P(X_{I \smallsetminus \{i, \Delta(i)\}})}{P(X_{I \smallsetminus \{i, \Delta(i)\}})}$$

Cancelling out the non-zero factor, we obtain:

$$P(X_i | X_{I \smallsetminus \{i, \Delta(i)\}}) = f_i(X_i, X_{I \smallsetminus \{i, \Delta(i)\}}).$$ Therefore

$$P(X_i | X_{I \smallsetminus \{i, \Delta(i)\}}, X_k, \ldots, X_r) = P(X_i | X_{I \smallsetminus \{i, \Delta(i)\}})^{\forall}$$

$$(X_k, X_\ell, \ldots, X_r): \quad P(X_{I \smallsetminus \{i, \Delta(i)\}}, X_k, \ldots, X_r) \neq 0$$

(b) for every $i \in I$ let some subsets $\Gamma(i) \subseteq I$ be given such that for each of them the relations (4) are satisfied.

Prior to this, we shall show that under the conditions of irreducibility for each i, instead of all $\Gamma(i)$ it is possible to use only their intersection. For definiteness let $\Gamma(i) = A \cup B$, $\Gamma'(i) = A \cup C$ and $A \cap B = \emptyset$, $A \cap C = \emptyset$, $B \cap C = \emptyset$, $I = \{i, A, B, C, D\}$. In this case the equality of type (4) will take the form of

$$P(X_i | X_A, X_B, X_C, X_D) = P(X_i | X_A, X_B) \forall (X_C, X_D) , \quad P(X_A, X_B, X_C, X_D) \neq 0$$

$$(10)$$

$$P(X_i | X_A, X_B, X_C, X_D) = P(X_i | X_A, X_C) \forall (X_B, X_D) , \quad P(X_A, X_B, X_C, X_D) \neq 0$$

We shall show that for any combination X_A, X_B, X_C, X_D such that $P(X_A, X_B, X_C, X_D) \neq 0$ the value of the conditional density $P(X_i | X_A, X_B, X_C, X_D)$ will be independent of X_B, X_C, and X_D. Then by analogy with the previous proof we shall have the equality $P(X_i | X_A, X_B, X_C) = P(X_i | X_A)$. In fact, for any combinations of non-zero probability

$$(\bar{X}_A, \ X_B^o, X_C^o, X_D^o) \text{ and } (\bar{X}_A, X_B^*, X_C^*, X_D^*)$$

there exists a sequence of combinations $(\bar{X}_A, X_B^m, X_C^m, X_D^m)$

$(m = 1, 2, \ldots, M)$ whose probabilities are also non-zero and such that

$$(\bar{X}_A, X_B', X_C', X_D') = (\bar{X}_A, X_B^o, X_C^o, X_D^o)$$

$$(\bar{X}_A, X_B^M, X_C^M, X_D^M) = (\bar{X}_A, X_B^*, \ X_C^*, X_D^*) ,$$

and $(\bar{X}_A, X_B^{m+1}, X_C^{m+1}, X_D^{m+1})$ is expressed through

$(\bar{X}_A, X_B^m, X_D^m)$ by replacing one of the components in X_B or X_C or X_D according to a certain function $\alpha(m) \in B \cup C \cup D$, $(m = 1, 2, \ldots, M)$. For definiteness, suppose that $\alpha(m)$ first runs through the values from $B \cup D$, $(m = 1, 2, \ldots, M_1)$, then the values from $C \cup D$ $(m = M_1+1, \ldots, M_2)$, then again from $B \cup D$, and so forth. For clarity, we shall write out a sequence of combinations and numbers m, $\alpha(m)$ corresponding to them.

$$\left.\begin{array}{l} \bar{X}_A, X_B^1, X_C^1, X_D^1 \\[4pt] \cdots \cdots \cdots \cdots \\[4pt] \bar{X}_A, X_B^{M_1}, X_C^{M_1}, X_D^{M_1} \end{array}\right\} \quad \alpha(1) \in B, \;\; \alpha(m) \in B \cup D, \;\; m = 2, \ldots, M_1$$

$$\left.\begin{array}{l} \bar{X}_A, X_B^{M_1+1}, X_C^{M_1+1}, X_D^{M+1} \\[4pt] \cdots \cdots \cdots \cdots \\[4pt] \bar{X}_A, X_B^{M_2}, X_C^{M_2}, X_D^{M_2} \end{array}\right\} \quad \alpha(M_1+1) \in C, \;\; \alpha(m) \in C \cup D, m = M_1+2, \ldots, M_2$$

$$\left.\begin{array}{l} \bar{X}_A, X_B^{M_2+1}, X_C^{M_2+1}, X_D^{M_2+1} \\[4pt] \cdots \cdots \cdots \cdots \\[4pt] \bar{X}_A, X_B^{M_3}, X_C^{M_3}, X_D^{M_3} \end{array}\right\} \quad \alpha(M_2+1) \in B, \;\; \alpha(m) \in B \cup D, \;\; m = M_2+2, \ldots, M_3$$

$$\cdots \cdots \cdots \cdots \cdots \cdots \cdots \cdots \cdots$$

$$\left.\begin{array}{l} \bar{X}_A, X_B^{M-1}, X_C^{M-1}, X_D^{M-1} \\[4pt] \bar{X}_A, X_B^M, X_C^M, X_D^M \end{array}\right\} \quad \alpha(m) \in C \cup D, \;\; m = , \ldots, M-1, M \qquad (11)$$

Let $P(X_i | \bar{X}_A, X_B^o, X_C^o, X_D^o) = Z$. From the equalities (10) and the first group of combinations (11) we can write:

$$Z = P(X_i | \bar{X}_A, X_B^{M_1}, X_C^{M_1}, X_D^{M_1}) = P(X_i | \bar{X}_A, X_B^{M_1})$$

Passing to the second group of combinations (11) we have:

$$Z = P(X_i | \bar{X}_A, X_B^{M_2}, X_C^{M_2}, X_D^{M_2}).$$

Continuing our reasoning we eventually have

$Z = P(X_i \diagdown \bar{X}_A, X_B^*, X_C^*, X_D^*)$. Thus we can assert that in satisfying the requirement for irreducibility, the graph $\Gamma(i)$ is given uniquely.

We now show that the graph $\Gamma(i)$ is symmetrical. Let the relations

$$P(X_i | X_{I \diagdown \{i\}}) = P(X_i | X_{\Gamma(i)}), \ P(X_{I \diagdown \{i\}}) \neq 0 \qquad (12)$$

$$P(X_k | X_{I \diagdown \{k\}}) = P(X_k | X_i, X_A), \ P(X_{I \diagdown \{k\}}) \neq 0 \qquad (13)$$

hold. Let $I \diagdown \{i\} = \Gamma(i) \cup \{k\} \cup B$ so that $X_{I \diagdown \{i\}}$

$= (X_{\Gamma(i)}, X_k, X_B)$. From (12) by Lemma 2 we have:

$$P(X_i | X_{\Gamma(i)}, X_k, X_B) = P(X_i | X_{\Gamma(i)}, X_B) .$$

Hence, by Lemma 1: $P(X_k | X_i, X_{\Gamma(i)}, X_A) = P(X_k | X_{\Gamma(i)}, X_B)$,

$$P(X_i, X_{\Gamma(i)}, X_B) \neq 0.$$

Comparing the last relation with (13) and remembering that

$\{\Gamma(i), B\} \cap \{i, A\} \supseteq A$, we have:

$$P(X_k | X_i, X_A) = P(X_k | X_A)$$

i.e. from the condition (X_i, X_A) for X_k it is possible to exclude X_i. Therefore the graph $\Gamma(i)$ is symmetrical.

After establishing the fact of symmetry for the graph $\Gamma(i)$, by Lemma 2 we obtain:

$$P(X_i | X_{I \diagdown \{i\}}) = P(X_i | X_{\Gamma(i)}) = P(X_i | X_{I \diagdown \{i,k\}}) \forall X_k, k \varepsilon I \diagdown \{i, \Gamma(i)\} .$$

$$(14)$$

Thus, if $I \diagdown \{i, \Gamma(i)\}$ is denoted by $\Delta(i)$, then we can regard the second statement of the theorem to be proved.

Definition 3.

The graph $\Gamma(i)$ is called a graph of immediate connections of the variable ξ if (4) holds. Let

174

$i,j\epsilon I, A \subset I, \; i,j \notin A$. A set $_iL_j = \{i,k_1,k_2,\ldots,k_r,j\}, k_1\epsilon\Gamma(i)$, $k_2\epsilon\Gamma(k_1),\ldots,j\epsilon\Gamma(k_r)$ in the graph $F(i)$ from junction i to junction j we shall call a chain.

Definition 4.

An order triple of non-intersecting elements i,j and the set A from I is called Markov and is denoted by $\{i,A,j\}_\Gamma$ if $_iL_j \cap A \neq \emptyset \; \forall \; _iL_j$.

Definition 5.

We shall say that multidimensional random variable $\xi = (\xi_1, \xi_2,\ldots,\xi_n)$ has a structure if there exists such a symmetrical graph without loops $\Gamma(i)$, $i\epsilon I$ that the following relations hold:

$$P(X_i|X_A,X_j) = P(X_i|X_A) \; \forall \; X_j, \; \{i,A,j\} = \{i,A,j\}_\Gamma$$

Lemma 3.

For a random variable satisfying the requirement for irreducibility, with density $P(X)$, let the following relations hold:

$$P(X_i|X_{I\smallsetminus\{i\}}) = P(X_i|X_{\Gamma(i)}) \; \forall X_{I\smallsetminus\{i\}};$$

$$P(X_{I\smallsetminus\{i\}}) \neq 0, \; \Gamma(i) \subseteq I\smallsetminus\{i\}$$

for all $i \in A \subset I = \{1,2,\ldots n\}$. Then

$$P(X_A|X_{I\smallsetminus A}) = P(X_A|X_{\Gamma(A)}) \; \forall \; X_{I\smallsetminus A} : P(X_{I\smallsetminus A}) \neq 0, \quad (16)$$

takes place where $\Gamma(A) = \underset{i=A}{U} \; \Gamma(i) \smallsetminus A$.

First consider a case where the set A consists of two elements $A = \{i,j\}$. In this case $\Gamma(A) = \Gamma(i,j) = \Gamma(i) U \Gamma(j) \smallsetminus \{i,j\}$. The relation

$$P(X_i,X_j|X_{I\smallsetminus\{i,j\}}) = P(X_j|X_{I\smallsetminus\{i,j\}}) \cdot P(X_i|X_{I\smallsetminus\{i\}}). \quad (17)$$

must hold.

Denote by the letter Z that part of the set I which does not contain the elements i, j and $\Gamma(i,j)$, i.e. $I = \{i,j\} U \Gamma(i,j) U Z$. Then according to equation (15), equation (15), equation (17) may be rewritten as

$$P(X_i, X_j | X_{I-\{i,j\}}) = P(X_j | X_z, X_{\Gamma(i,j)}) P(X_i | X_{\Gamma(i)}) \tag{18}$$

For $\Gamma(i)$ and $\Gamma(j)$ the inclusions

$$\Gamma(i) \subset \Gamma(i,j) \cup \{j\} \subset \Gamma(i,j) \cup \{j\} \cup z$$

$$\Gamma(j) \subset \Gamma(i,j) \cup \{i\} \subset \Gamma(i,j) \cup \{i\} \cup z \tag{19}$$

are true.

On the basis of these inclusions, according to Lemma 2,

$$P(X_i | X_{\Gamma(i,j)}, X_j, X_z) = P(X_i | X_{\Gamma(i,j)}, X_j),$$

$$P(X_{\Gamma(i,j)}, X_j, X_z) \neq 0$$

$$P(X_j | X_{\Gamma(i,j)}, X_i, X_z) = P(X_j | X_{\Gamma(i,j)}, X_i),$$

$$P(X_{\Gamma(i,j)}, X_i, X_z) \neq 0$$

must be satisfied.

By Lemma 1, it follows from the last equalities that

$$P(X_z | X_{I-z}) = P(X_z | X_{\Gamma(i,j)}, X_j)$$

$$P(X_z | X_{\Gamma(i,j)}, X_i) \neq 0, \qquad P(X_{I-\{i\}}) \neq 0.$$

From the last relations, because we must satisfy the requirement for irreducibility, similarly to the previous case, we have:

$$P(X_z | X_{\Gamma(i,j)}, X_j) = P(X_z | X_{\Gamma(i,j)}) \text{ if } P(X_{I-z}) \neq 0.$$

For $P(X_z, X_{\Gamma(i,j)}) \neq 0$ we have:

$$P(x_j | x_z, x_{\Gamma(i,j)}) = P(x_j | x_{\Gamma(i,j)}).$$ (20)

Now return to formula (18). From (20) and the first of the inclusions (19) we can write:

$$P(x_i, x_j | x_{I \smallsetminus \{i,j\}}) = P(x_j | x_{\Gamma(i,j)}) \cdot P(x_i | x_{\Gamma(i,j)}, x_j)$$

$$= P(x_i, x_j | x_{\Gamma(i,j)}).$$

By induction it is easy to check upon the validity of the Lemma for the case of an arbitrary set A as well.

Theorem 2.

In order that the graph $\Gamma(i)$ be a graph of direct connections of the random variable $\xi = (\xi_1, \xi_2, \ldots, \xi_n)$ satisfying the requirement for irreducibility, it is necessary and sufficient to satisfy the conditions:

$$P(x_i | x_A, x_j) = P(x_i | x_A) \; \forall \{i, A, j\}_\Gamma .$$ (21)

In other words in a situation of irreducibility the graph of direct connections coincides with the structure of the variable.

Proof. Sufficiency is proved rather trivially since (4) follows from (21) directly. Let us prove necessity. Consider a Markov triple $\{i, A, j\}_\Gamma$. Let $k \in \Gamma(i)$. Take those of the elements k which are not contained in A:

$$\{k_1, k_2, \ldots, k_r\} = \Gamma(i) \smallsetminus A.$$

Then consider $\Gamma(i, k_1, \ldots, k_r) \smallsetminus A = \{q_1, q_2, \ldots, q_m\}$. Evidently $q_1, q_2, \ldots, q_m$ are connected with i by a chain not passing through A. Next form a set $\{i, k_1, \ldots, k_r, q_1, \ldots, q_m\}$ and consider

$$\{p_1, p_2, \ldots, p_s\} = \Gamma(i, k_1, \ldots, k_r, q_1, \ldots, q_m) \smallsetminus A .$$

These $p_1, p_2, \ldots, p_s$ are also connected with i by a chain not passing through A. As the graph is finite we can, by iterating the process, get at some stage:

$$\Gamma(i,k_1,\ldots,k_r,q_1,\ldots,q_m,\ldots,t_1,\ldots,t_\ell) \neq \emptyset \qquad (22)$$

or

$$\Gamma(i,k_1,\ldots,k_r,q_1,\ldots,q_m,\ldots,t_1,\ldots,t_\ell) \subset A, \qquad (23)$$

$t_1,t_2,\ldots,t_\ell$ being connected with i by a chain not passing through A, and $j \notin \{i,k_1,\ldots,k_r,\ldots,t_\ell\}$ since there otherwise would exist a sequence $\{i,a,b,\ldots,c,j\}$ such that $i \varepsilon \Gamma(a), a \varepsilon \Gamma(b),\ldots,c \varepsilon \Gamma(j)$ and $A \cap \{i,a,\ldots,c,j\} \neq \emptyset$. But this is impossible since the triple $\{i,A,j\}_\Gamma$ is Markov.

According to Lemma 3

$$P(X_i,X_{k_1},\ldots,X_{t_\ell}|X_{I \setminus \{i,k_1,\ldots,t_\ell\}})$$

$$= P(X_i,X_{k_1},\ldots,X_{t_\ell}|X_{\Gamma(i,k_1,\ldots,t_\ell)})$$

must be satisfied. From (22) and (23)

$$P(X_i,X_{k_1},\ldots,X_{t_\ell}|X_{I \setminus \{i,k,\ldots,t_\ell\}}) = P(X_i,X_{k_1},\ldots,X_{t_\ell}|X_A)$$

$= P(X_i,X_{k_1},\ldots,X_{t_\ell}|X_A,X_j)$ must be satisfied. By folding the last equality on all $k_1,k_2,\ldots,t_\ell$ we have

$$P(X_i|X_A) = P(X_i|X_A,X_j) \; \forall \; \{i,A,j\}_\Gamma \; .$$

So the theorem is proved.

Evidently, the existence of a structure presupposes more interesting properties of the variable ξ than does the existence of a graph of direct connection.

Moreover, it is easy to show that the graph $\Gamma(i)$ is a graph structure of the connection of the variable ξ with the density $P(X)$ if and only if the equality

$$P(X_A|X_B,X_C) = P(X_A|X_B) \; \forall \; X_C$$

is satisfied for all non-intersecting subsets A, B, C of the set I for which all chains between the elements of the sets A and C pass through B. (Such triples of sets we shall also call Markov and denote by $\{A, B, C\}_\Gamma$).

4. FOLDING AND EXPANDING THE STRUCTURE OF A RANDOM VARIABLE

Let the random variable $\xi = (\xi_1,\xi_2,\ldots,\xi_n)$ have a structure given by the graph $\Gamma(i)$. Consider the variable

$\xi^{\prime} = (\xi_1, \ldots, \xi_{i-1}, \xi_{i+1}, \ldots, \xi_n)$. We may ask whether the variable $\xi^{\prime}$ will have a structure and what graph of connections Γ^i given on the set of indices $I^i = \{1, 2, \ldots, i-1, i+1, \ldots, n\}$ will hold for it.

Theorem 3 (about Folding).

Let $\Gamma(i)$ ($i \in I$) be a density structure $P(X) = P(X_1, X_2, \ldots, X_n)$. Let $D \subseteq I$, $C \subseteq I$ form the partition of the set I so that $D \cup C = I$, $D \cap C = \emptyset$. Let $P(X_D)$ be the density folding $P(X)$ on all X_i such that $i \in C$. Then the density $P(X_D)$ will have the structure given by the graph $\Gamma^C(i)$ ($i \in D$):

$$\Gamma^C(i) = (\Gamma(i) \cap D) \cap E_i \qquad (24)$$

where E_i is a set of all such elements $k \in D \setminus \{i\}$ for which there exists at least one chain $_k L_i$ connecting elements k and i relating to the set C without its ends k and i.

Proof. Let $i \in D$. Present $D \setminus \{i\}$ in the form of two non-intersecting subsets $C_i \cup E_i = D \setminus \{i\}$, where C_i is a set of such elements $j \in D \setminus \{i\}$, for which any chain $_i L_j$ without its ends passes through $D \setminus \{i, j\}$, i.e., $_i L_j \cap (D \setminus \{i, j\}) \neq \emptyset$

$$\forall \, _i L_j, \; j \in C_i \qquad (25)$$

Let $i \in I$, $j \in D \setminus \{i\}$, $j \notin (\Gamma(i) \cap D) \cup E_i$.
Consider the triple $\{i, (\Gamma(i) \cap D) \cup E_i, j\}$. Since $j \notin E_i$, $j \in C_i$, and therefore by (25) and the relation

$(\Gamma(i) \cap D) \cup E_i \subseteq D \setminus \{i\}$ the condition

$$_i L_j \cap [(\Gamma(i) \cap D) \cup E_i] \neq \emptyset \; \forall \, _i L_j, \; j \in C_i \qquad (26)$$

must be satisfied. The latter means that the triple $\{i, (\Gamma(i) \cap D) \cup E_i, j\}$ is Markov. Hence

$$P(X_i | X_{(\Gamma(i) \cap D) \cup E_i}, X_j) = P(X_i | X_{(\Gamma(i) \cap D) \cup E_i}) \, \forall j \in C_i$$

The Rigid Structure and Pseudo-Connections.

Let the graph Γ be a graph of connections of the variable ξ. Consider a graph $\Gamma^{\prime}$ given on the same set I and such that $\Gamma \subseteq \Gamma^{\prime}$. In other words, in the graph $\Gamma^{\prime}$ compared with the graph Γ some pairs of vertices $(i,j),\ldots,(k,\ell)$ are additionally connected with each other. It is easy to see that the graph Γ' will also be a graph of direct connections of the variable ξ. If for the variable ξ with the structure Γ, $P(X_i|X_{I\setminus\{i\}}) = P(X_i|X_{\Gamma(i)})$ held true, then the relation $P(X_i|X_{I\setminus\{i\}}) = P(X_i|X_{\Gamma(i)}, X_{j_1},\ldots,X_{j_k})$ by Lemma 2 will also be satisfied, and $j_1, j_2,\ldots,j_k$ denote those vertices with which the vertex i is additionally connected.

Thus, exploring the variable ξ with the help of only the graph Γ' we cannot reveal some of the relations of type $P(X_C|X_A,X_B) = P(X_C|X_A)$, while the triple $\{C,A,B\}$ is not Markov in the sense of the graph Γ' being such for the graph Γ. This is why the structure Γ is better than the structure Γ'. The best of all the structures will be denoted as an essential one.

Definition 6.

A structure Γ will be called an essential structure if eliminating one or more links gives a graph that is not a structure.

Definition 7.

Let us call the structure of the variable ξ generated by the graph of connections $\Gamma(i)$ a rigid structure if the equality $P(X_C|X_A,X_B) = P(X_C|X_A)$ is a necessary and sufficient condition for the triple $\{C,A,B\}$ to be Markov. In Rodionov (1972) the conditions for the existence of a rigid structure are considered in detail. If the equalities $P(X_C|X_A,X_B) = P(X_C|X_A)$ are also satisfied for the case where the triple $\{C,A,B\}$ is not Markov (i.e. there exists a chain from C to B not passing through A), then it is natural to call some of these connections (expressed by the above-mentioned chain) pseudo-connections. Pseudo-connections may arise, for example, when we consider a complex of random variables some of which are functions of the others.

The following theorem is true:

Theorem 4.

Let $X_I = (X_1, X_2,\ldots,X_n)$ be a set of values of the random variable $\xi_I = (\xi_1,\xi_2,\ldots,\xi_n)$ with the density $P(X)$

having the structure $\Gamma(i)$, $i\varepsilon I = \{1,2,\ldots,m\}$.

Let $R(X_I,X_J)$ (with $X_J = (X_{m+1}, X_{m+2},\ldots,X_{m+n}))$ be the density of the variable $\xi = (\xi_I,\xi_J)$ (with

$\xi_J = (\xi_{m+1}, \xi_{m+2},\ldots,\xi_{m+n})$ satisfying the requirement for irreducibility, so that

$$R(X_I,X_J) = R(X_I)R(X_J|X_I), \text{ where } R(X_J|X_I)$$

is the conditional density of the variable ξ_J relative to ξ_I. Finally, let the conditional distribution $R(X_J|X_I)$ possess a "conditional structure," i.e. satisfy the relation

$$R(X_{m+k}|X_1,\ldots,X_m,X_{m+1},\ldots,X_{m+k-1},X_{m+k+1},\ldots,X_{m+n})$$

$$= R(X_{m+k}|X_{\phi(m+k)}, X_{\Delta(m+k)})\,\forall\, k = 1,\ldots,n \tag{27}$$

where $\phi(j) \subset I$ is a mapping of the elements of the set $J = \{m+1,m+2,m+3,\ldots,m+n\}$ into the elements of the set I, and $\Delta(i)$ is a symmetrical mapping of the set J into itself. Then the variable $\xi = (\xi_I,\xi_J)$ will have the structure given by the graph $\hat{\Gamma}$ on the set $\{1,2,\ldots,m+n\}$:

$$\hat{\Gamma}(k) = \phi(k) \cup \Delta(k) \qquad\qquad \forall\, k\varepsilon J$$

$$\hat{\Gamma}(k) = \Gamma(k) \qquad\qquad \forall\, k\varepsilon I, k \not\subset \phi(J) \tag{28}$$

$$\hat{\Gamma}(k) = \Gamma(k) \cup \phi^{-1}(k) \cup [\phi(J)\diagdown\{k\}] \qquad \forall\, k\varepsilon\phi(J) .$$

Here $\phi(J) = \cup \phi(j)$, and $\phi^{-1}(k)$ denotes a set of such elements ℓ from $\{m+1\ m+2,\ldots,m+n)$ for which $k\varepsilon\phi(\ell)$.

<u>Proof.</u> Consider $R(X_1,X_2,\ldots,X_{m+n})$. According to the conditions of the theorem for the density R, the relations (27) hold. As is easy to see, they directly correspond to the first relations from (28) for the graph $\hat{\Gamma}$. Let $k\varepsilon I$, $k \not\subset \phi(J)$. By Lemma 3, $R(X_J|X_I) = R(X_J|X_{\phi(J)})$ and then, by Lemma 2, $R(X_J|X_{\phi(J)}) = R(X_J|X_{I\diagdown\{k\}})$.

From this it follows that

$$R(X_k|X_{I\diagdown\{k\}}, X_J) = R(X_k|X_{\phi(J)}) = R(X_k|X_J) = R(X_k|X_{\Gamma(k)}) .$$

Thus, the second of the relations from (28) prove to be true.

Now let $k \varepsilon \phi(J)$. We have

$$R(X_k \big| X_{I \diagdown \{k\}}, X_J) = \frac{R(X_I, X_J)}{R(X_{I \diagdown \{k\}}, X_J)} = \frac{R(X_{\phi(J) \cup \Gamma(k)}, X_J)}{R(X_{[\phi(J) \diagdown \{k\}] \cup \Gamma(k)}, X_J)} \cdot$$

$$\tag{29}$$

$$\cdot \frac{R(X_{I \diagdown \phi(J) \cup \Gamma(k)} \big| X_{\phi(J) \cup \Gamma(k)}, X_J)}{R(X_{I \diagdown \phi(J) \cup \Gamma(k)} \big| X_{[\phi(J) \diagdown \{k\}] \cup \Gamma(k)}, X_J)}$$

Consider the numerator of the second factor in the expression (29). Evidently,

$$\Gamma[I \diagdown \phi(J) \cup \Gamma(k)] = \cup \Gamma(j) \subseteq \Gamma(k) \cup \phi(J) \diagdown \{k\}, \tag{30}$$

$$j \varepsilon I \diagdown \phi(J) \cup \Gamma(k) .$$

Indeed, for any $j \varepsilon I \diagdown \phi(J) \cup \Gamma(k)$ the set $\Gamma(j)$ either intersects with $\phi(J) \cup \Gamma(k)$, or not. Since we examine all elements j from $I \diagdown \phi(J) \cup \Gamma(k)$, $\Gamma(I \diagdown \phi(J) \cup \Gamma(k)) \subset \phi(J) \cup \Gamma(k)$. The element k cannot belong to any $\Gamma(j)$ (otherwise $j \varepsilon \Gamma(k)$ would be satisfied). Therefore instead of the last inclusion it is possible to write (30). Since by what has been proved above for all j (with $j \varepsilon I, j \notin \phi(J)$), $R(X_j \big| X_{I \diagdown \{j\}}, X_J) = R(X_j \big| X_{\Gamma(j)})$ holds, then $R(X_{I \diagdown \phi(J) \cup \Gamma(k)} \big| X_{\phi(J) \cup \Gamma(k)}, X_J)$

$$= R(X_{I \diagdown \phi(J) \cup \Gamma(k)} \big| X_{\Gamma[I \diagdown \phi(J) \cup \Gamma(k)]}) \cdot \tag{31}$$

By the inclusion (30) and Lemma 2 the numerator of the second factor (29) will equal the expression

$$R(X_{I \diagdown \phi(J) \cup \Gamma(k)} \big| X_{\Gamma(k) \cup \phi(J) \diagdown \{k\}})$$

Using Lemma 2 again, we can proceed from this expression to the expression

$$R(X_{I \diagdown \phi(J) \cup \Gamma(k)} \big| X_{\Gamma(k) \cup \phi(J) \diagdown \{k\}}, X_J)$$

which is the denominator of the same fraction. Thus, the fraction equals unity. So from formula (29) we can pass to the formula:

$$R(X_k \big| X_{I \diagdown \{k\}}, X_J) = R(X_k \big| X_{\phi(J) \cup \Gamma(k) \diagdown \{k\}}, X_J) \tag{32}$$

We can eliminate some of the components of the set X_J in the condition of density (32), for the relation (27) only binds the components X_k with the components $X_{\phi^{-1}(k)}$. So instead of (32) we can write

$$R(X_k | X_{I \smallsetminus \{k\}}, X_J) = R(X_k | X_{\phi(J) \cup \Gamma(k) \smallsetminus \{k\}}, X_{\phi^{-1}(k)})$$

which is the proof of the third relation of (28). Q.E.D.

Corollary.

In addition to the conditions of the theorem suppose that the graph $\Delta(j), j \in J = \{m+1, m+2, \ldots, m+n\}$ consists of several unconnected subgraphs so that the set J is broken into non-intersecting subsets: $A_1, A_2, \ldots, A_N$;

$$\bigcup A_r = J, \qquad A_r \cap A_k = \emptyset, \ \Delta(i) \cap \Delta(j) = \emptyset,$$

$$\forall i, j, k, r; \ i \in A_k, \ j \in A_r, \ k \neq r .$$

In this case the graph $\hat{\Gamma}$ can be simplified, i.e. some of the connections can be excluded. In order to find the form of the graph $\hat{\Gamma}$ we shall successively add the sets $A_1, A_2, \ldots, A_N$ to the set I.

Thus, first consider the variable (ξ_I, ξ_{A_1}) with the density

$$R(X_I, X_{A_1}) = P(X_I) R(X_{A_1} | X_I) = P(X_I) \sum_{k \notin A_1} R(X_J | X_I) .$$

Since for all $i \in A_1$, $\Delta(i) \subseteq A_1$ then from (27), by Lemmas 2 and 3, we can write:

$$R(X_i | X_I, X_{A_1} \smallsetminus \{i\}) = R(X_i | X_{\phi(i)}, X_{\Delta(i)}) \quad i \in A_1 . \tag{34}$$

Hence, using the theorem we can construct the graph Γ_1 on the set $I \cup A$, which will be the structure of the variable (ξ_I, ξ_{A_1}). Further, we can consider the variable $(\xi_I, \xi_{A_1}, \xi_{A_2})$ with the density $R(X_I, X_{A_1}, X_{A_2})$
$= R(X_I, X_{A_1}) R(X_{A_2} | X_I, X_{A_1}) = R(X_I, X_{A_1}) R(X_{A_2} | X_I) .$
It is possible to construct a graph of connection Γ_2 on

$I \cup A_1 \cup A_2$ in the same way as in the preceding case, and so on. As a result, a final graph $\hat{\Gamma} = \Gamma_N$ will be constructed on $I \cup J$. In this case it may turn out that not all the elements are from $\phi(J)$ since, according to the rules of construction, elements p,q are connected only when there exists such a set A_k (k = 1,2,...,N) that $q, p \varepsilon \phi(A_k)$. This very circumstance enables us to get a "better" graph than that obtained on the basis of the direct application of theorem 5.

The Structure of Some Discrete Random Processes.

The concept of structure may also be employed in studying discrete stochastic processes. Consider a uniform Markov chain $\{\xi^o, \xi^1, \xi^2, ..., \xi^t, \xi^{t+1}, ...\}$ with the initial density $P^o(x^o)$ and the transition probability density $P(x^{t+1}|x^t)$ so that

$$P^T(x^o, x^1, x^2, ..., x^T) = P^o(x^o) P(x^1|x^o) P(x^2|x^1) ... P(x^T|x^{T-1}).$$

Let the initial density $P^o(x^o)$ possess a structure Γ^o on the set $I = \{1,2,...,n\}$ and let the transition probability $P(x^{t+1}|x^t)$ possess a "conditional structure," i.e.,

$$P(x_i^{t+1}|x_{I \smallsetminus \{i\}}^{t+1}, x_J^t) = P(x_i^{t+1}|x_i^t, x_{\phi(i)}^{t+1}, x_{\Delta(i)}^{t+1}) \forall t = 1,2,...,$$

where $\phi(i) \subseteq I$, $\Delta(i) \subseteq J$ and $\Delta(i)$ is symmetric. According to theorem 5, we can find the structure of the density $P^1(x^o, x^1)$, then of the density $P^2(x^o, x^1, x^2)$, and so forth.

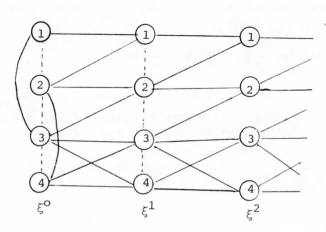

Figure 1.

184

The dotted lines in Figure 1 show the connections which have arisen after the variables ξ^1 were added to the variables ξ^0, and so forth. It is clear that in a similar sense it is possible to construct a structure for a non-uniform Markov chain as well, when the "conditional structure" of the density $p^t(x^t|x^{t-1})$ depends on the time t. The meaning of the process structure remains the same.

5. THE APPLICATION OF STRUCTURE TO THE ANALYSIS OF COMPLEX STATISTICAL POPULATIONS

Let $P(X) = P(X_1,X_2,...,X_n)$ be the density of a random variable having the structure $\Gamma(i)$, $i\epsilon I = \{1,2,...,n\}$.

The relation

$$P(X) = P(X_1|X_2,X_3,...,X_n)P(X_2|X_3,...,X_n)...P(X_{n-1}|X_n)P(X_n) \quad (35)$$

holds for it. The presence of the structure allows us to partition the sets of indices from all conditions (35):

$\{2,3,...,n\},\{3,4,...,n\},...,\{n-1,n\},\{n\}$ into two subsets $\{A_1,B_1\},\{A_2,B_2\},...,\{A_{n-1},B_{n-1}\}$, (with $A_i,B_i \subset J$), so that the triples $\{1,A_1,B_1\}_\Gamma$, $\{2,A_2,B_2\}_\Gamma,...,\{n-1,A_{n-1},B_{n-1}\}_\Gamma$ will be Markov (though some of the subsets may prove to be empty). As a result, instead of expansion (35) we shall obtain a formula in which the factors have, generally speaking, a smaller number of variables:

$$P(X) = P(X_1|X_{A_1})P(X_2|X_{A_2})...P(X_{n-1}|X_{A_{n-1}})P(X_n) . \quad (36)$$

Here a property (known in theoretical cybernetics) of complicated systems having a "structure," namely "organization" is revealed. This allows us to analyze them "by parts," "decomposing" them into interacting subsystems. In our case the knowledge of some number of conditional and absolute densities from a small number of variables allows us to find the absolute density for the whole multidimensional random variable. Here the presence of the structure gives additional informational gain.

Consider an example. Let it be known that the density $P = P(X_1,X_2,X_3,X_4,X_5)$ has a structure given by the graph $\Gamma(i)$ as in Figure 2. Then we can write

$$P(X) = P(X_5|X_1,X_2, X_3,X_4)P(X_4|X_1,X_2,X_3)P(X_1,X_2,X_3)$$

or
$$P(X) = P(X_5|X_4)P(X_4|X_2,X_3)P(X_1,X_2,X_3) .$$

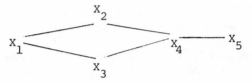

Figure 2

The conditions (X_1,X_2,X_3) and (X_1) have been excluded from the first two factors, since the triples $\{(5),(4),(1,2,3,)\}_\Gamma$, $\{(4),(2,3),(1)\}_\Gamma$ are Markov. We write the expansion in the form of:

$$P = P_4^5 \cdot P_{2,3}^4 \cdot P^{1,2,3}$$

where P_B^A denotes the conditional probability $P(X_A|X_B)$. Though we know only three of the probability values, we can determine any of them. Let it be necessary to find some probability (conditional or absolute). This can be done by turning to the last formula. Suppose it is necessary to find the conditional probability of the value X_4, when the values of X_1 are known. So:

$$P_1^4 = \frac{P^{1,4}}{P^1} = \frac{\sum_{(2,3,5)}P^{1,2,3,4,5}}{\sum_{(2,3,4,5)}P^{1,2,3,4,5}} .$$

must be satisfied.
The numerator of the last fraction will be presented as

$$P^{1,4} = \sum_{(2,3)}P_{2,3}^4 P^{1,2,3} \sum_{(5)} P_4^5 = \sum_{(2,3)} P_{2,3}^4 P^{1,2,3} .$$

The sum over X_5 gives 1 since it is the total (conditional) probability of X_5. The denominator will be:

$$P^1 = \sum_{(2,3)}P^{1,2,3} \sum_{(4)}P_{2,3}^4 \sum_{(5)}P_4^5 = \sum_{(2,3)}P^{1,2,3}$$

since after folding on X_5 the sum over X_4 also gives unity. As a result we shall have the formula:

$$P_1^4 = \frac{\sum_{(2,3)} P_{2,3}^4 \cdot P^{1,2,3}}{\sum_{(2,3)} P^{1,2,3}}$$

This expansion of type (36) can be optimized from the viewpoint of the number of variables included in the factors. First, the partitioning of the conditions into subsets A_i, B_i can be done in such a way that A_i will be minimal with respect to the number of elements. Secondly, the sequence of sets of the indices of conditions may be obtained in different ways; their total number will be of the order of n!. For this reason some optimization problems arise, but we shall not consider them here.

6. CONCERNING THE PHYSICAL MEANING OF A RANDOM SET STRUCTURE

The concept of a graph for describing the connection between the elements in a system of variables has been used for over 10 years now rather widely. We shall not consider any results of this usage, but we will note that Ashby (1962) introduces the concept of "a scheme of direct interactions," which indicates the presence (or absence) of direct connections between X- and Y- variables when, having fixed the values of all other variables and changed the value of one variable from a pair, the value of the other variable is also changed. This is just the way Borodkin (1968) interprets the intuitive meaning of the directed graph of connection using this concept for the calculation of the coefficients of connection between variables.

The concept of random variable and its use in the expansion of a probability distribution function was introduced in 1967-1968 and used in experimental calculations at the Laboratory for Sociological Models (Central Economic Mathematical Institute of the Soviet Academy of Sciences). The concept of structure has been mainly used to facilitate the representation of the structure of the labor supply and consumption groups in society for optimal planning models (Gavrilets, 1970a).

Some findings involving a tentative testing of the hypothesis concerning the existence of a graph of connections have been published in Gavrilets (1969).

It should be noted that in the above two works, as well as in the paper (Gavrilets (1970b)) submitted at the 7th World Congress of Sociology, the structure Γ of the random set ξ was determined with the help of Markov triples $\{i,A,B\}_\Gamma$ which were absolutely necessary for the expansion of the distribution function. Later it was shown that for certain assumptions this definition follows from the simpler equalities (3) and (4). Incidentally, Ashby's definition of the "scheme of direct interactions" coincides, in a certain sense, with the definition of the formula (3).

Physically and substantively, the concept of a random set structure has several theoretical and applied aspects. We shall merely list some of them: the statistical analysis of the system of interconnected attributes; factor analysis, using structures of a certain type; the concept of set structure can be applied to mathematical methods for diagnosis in medicine; the random set structure can also be used as a means of revealing and predicting the sociodemographic structure of society.

Of the above-mentioned aspects, the first is the most general. Let us consider some statistical population at a definite time. Suppose this population can be described by a distribution function $F(X_1,X_2,\ldots,X_n)$. We may be interested in direct or immediate, as well as indirect, connections between the variables. How are they to be revealed and what is their substantive meaning in general, if the population is being considered "regardless of time" in statics? Obviously, if the function $F(X)$ has the structure $\Gamma(i)$, $i \varepsilon I$, then the concepts of direct and indirect connections in statics have a distinct meaning. That is, the indirect connection differs from the direct one in that the former may be negligible, if the direct (or "less indirect") connection is known.

There is, however, one fundamental complication because we refer to "connections" when the system is being considered at one and the same time. This term is used in the analysis of correlational or functional connections, for example, when there is no dynamics. Note that a random variable with a structure is, in a certain sense, a generalization of a complex of mutually independent variables. Independence requires that all the equalities of type

$P(X_C|X_A,X_B) = P(X_C|X_A) = P(X_C)$ should be satisfied, while the structure requires that only part of these equalities for some subsets A,B,C from the set I should be satisfied.

The problem of defining cause-and-effect connections by means of statistics is very important. It seem that the question, "Can mathematical-statistical methods reveal causes and effects?" has the same meaning as the question, "Is it possible to prove mathematically that the planets are revolving around the sun in ellipses?" Formal methods, though they represent real processes, need experimental data to confirm jointly (or refute) theoretical inferences. According to this, if mathematics has "proved" that the planets are revolving in ellipses, then statistics can "separate" cause from effect—provided the necessary empirical data are available.

The negative answer to this question concerning this possible use of statistics which is sometimes given may perhaps be attributed to the fact that the empirical data being processed usually relate to one and the same point in time. In this case, obviously, no causes and effects can be revealed (without adding some other information). It is another matter, however, when empirical data are available for all points in time, i.e., when there is information about the process. Then we can try to determine statistically which variables characterize the cause and which variables relate to the effects.

Now let us clarify what is meant by cause and effect. A statistical system is being considered at times $t = 0,1,2,\ldots$. At each time t the state of the system is characterized by a set X, and we assume that the influence of the environment is either absent or constant, i.e., the system is comparatively isolated. The main hypothesis is that the state of the system at time t_1 determines (in a probabilistic sense) its states at the moment t_2 (with $t_2 > t_1$). By the hypothesis concerning determination, the process under consideration is to be regarded as Markov (the relationship between the Markov property and causality has been pointed out by Bellman (1959)), since it would otherwise be impossible to explain the state of the system at subsequent times.

Now suppose that the process under consideration has a structure. For instance, let the graph of connection for (X^t, X^{t+1}) have the shape shown in Figure 3. Now define the

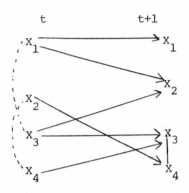

Figure 3

immediate cause of variable X_i^{t+1} as any of the variables $X_{\phi(i)}^t$, where $\phi(i)$ is a mapping in the sense of theorem 5 indicating the numbers of those variables of the set X^t which are directly connected with the number i on the graph of connection. In Figure 3 the variable X_1^{t+1} has one cause X_1^t; the variables X_2^{t+1}, X_3^{t+1} and X_4^{t+1} have as causes, respectively, (X_1^t, X_3^t), (X_3^t, X_4^t) and, (X_2^t). Notice the connection between the variables X_3^{t+1} and X_4^{t+1}. Both variables relate to the same time; hence, one cannot regard this connection as causal. At the same time, one must not disregard it since, by definition of a process with a structure, we have:

$$P(X_3^{t+1}|X^t, X_1^{t+1}, X_2^{t+1}, X_4^{t+1}) = P(X_3^{t+1}|X_3^t, X_4^t, X_4^{t+1}),$$

and $P(X_4^{t+1}|X^t, X_1^{t+1}, X_2^{t+1}, X_3^{t+1}) = P(X_4^{t+1}|X_2^t, X_3^{t+1}),$

where, of the remaining conditions, neither X_4^{t+1} nor X_3^{t+1} can be excluded. Thus, in analogy with the construction of a process with a structure, we assume a "simultaneous interaction" of the connection type between X_3^{t+1} and X_4^{t+1}. It may be regarded as a "functional connection" in its pure form. At the same time, its emergence can be explained in two ways (if it is not regarded as a manifestation of the immanent properties of the process). Either both variables represent two different aspects of the same phenomenon or

190

this connection has been produced as a result of aggregation or folding, because our chosen time interval is too large, but with smaller time periods indirect connections would correspond to it. At any rate, a knowledge of the process structure allows us to state categorically that some variables are the direct causes of the others. It is natural that we shall call a variable an indirect cause when it relates to an earlier time if it is possible to draw a path from the index connecting it with the index of the given variable.

Therefore we must conclude that, in the analysis of a system of interconnected variables, the notion of the structure of a random set or random process not only aids the conceptualization process but it also contributes a deeper insight into the actual interdependencies between the phenomena, as well as forecasting the values of some variables on the basis of the others.

Apart from the generally known processes with a structure to which Markov chains belong, there is a field in contemporary mathematical statistics in which random variables with a structure of a certain type are studied. This field is factor analysis, which has been developed in order to explain correlations in one set of variables (X) on the basis of their connections with another set (f). In factor analysis it is assumed that each component of vector X is a linear function of several factors:

$$X_i = \sum_{k=1}^{m} \ell_{ik} f_k + U_i, \quad i = 1, 2, \ldots, n .$$

The factors f_k may or may not be mutually independent. Evidently, this case is equivalent to the presence of a structure in the variable of form (X, f) shown in Figure 4. There is no direct connection between variables X_i and X_j, but there is a connection through variables f_k which manifests itself, for example, in the value of the correlation

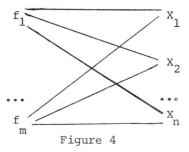

Figure 4

191

coefficient $\rho(X_i, X_j)$. As for the structure of the connection between factors f_k, it is usually assumed that the factors are independent (a subgraph from isolated vertices).

A very interesting fact to be explained with the help of the random set structure has been conveyed to this author by Iu. N. Tiurin. This concerns an attempt to use probabilistic methods for diagnoses of diseases in medicine. Formally, the problem is described in the following way. There are N hypothetical diseases H_1, H_2,...,H_N. Moreover, there exist M symptoms S_1, S_2,...,S_M, which may be observed during the disease or be absent. It is necessary, by means of the observed number of present and absent symptoms S_m, to determine (with a certain probability of being correct) the disease H_n. It is assumed that the necessary statistical data can be obtained. Obviously, the estimation of the probability of disease H_{n*}, for given values of the symptoms $\bar{S}_1,...,\bar{S}_M$, can be made by the Bayesian formula:

$$P(H_n|\bar{S}_1,...,\bar{S}_M) = \frac{P(H_{n*}) \cdot P(\bar{S}_1,\bar{S}_2,...,\bar{S}_M|H_{n*})}{\sum\limits_{n=1}^{N} P(H_n)\cdot P(\bar{S}_1,\bar{S}_2,...,\bar{S}_M|H_n)} .$$

$P(H_n)$ here is the absolute probability of the disease estimated from the statistical data. Unfortunately, the conditional probability functions of specific manifestations (or non-manifestations) of symptoms $S_1, S_2,...,S_M$, if the disease is known, are very difficult to represent in tabular form because of its high dimensionality ($M \simeq 200$). But the estimates based on the assumption of equality:

$$P(S_1,S_2,...,S_M|H_n) = P(S_1|H_n)P(S_2|H_n)...P(S_M|H_n) \qquad (37)$$

give a satisfactory result (in the sense of the diagnosis). How is this fact to be explained? It can be explained very simply if we assume that the structure of the set $(H,S_1,S_2,...,S_M)$ has the form shown in Figure 5. In fact, in this case $P(S_m|H,S_1,...,S_{m-1},S_{m+1},...,S_M) = P(S_m|H)$, i.e. symptom S_r is "connected" with symptom S_m only through the disease H. Note that a generalization of

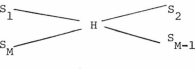

Figure 5

formula (37) is suggested here. Indeed, very often a complex of symptoms associated with some or other disease is
observed, i.e., syndromes. One can assume that in the graph
of connections of the value $(H,S_1,S_2,\ldots,S_M)$ symptoms form
groups $(S_{k_1},S_{k_2},\ldots,S_{k_r})$ in which they must in addition be
connected with each other. Then instead of formula (37) a
formula of type

$$P(S_1,\ldots,S_M|H) = P(S_{A_1}|H)\ldots P(S_{A_q}|H)$$

must be used where $A_1,\ldots,A_q$ are groups of symbols relating
to one syndrome. But even this formula can be made more precise if the sets $A_1,\ldots,A_q$ intersect with each other.

Finally, let us turn to a fourth example where the concept of a distribution function structure helps to elucidate
the problem and ways of achieving its solution. The problem
is to find the social structure of a society when it is considered as a statistical system, as an aggregation of individuals described by a set of indices: sex, age, level of
education, residence, job, family type, and so forth. How
should one gain an understanding in this extremely complex
situation of every possible dependent and independent index,
and how should he select the most important and exclude the
unimportant? Of what real groups is the society formed?
Membership in what groups affects the behavior of individuals,
and what groups may exist only in the mind of an inexperi-
enced investigator? It is generally known that workers and
employees and retired people have some level of education,
read some books, go to the cinema, and so forth. But perhaps workers read different books than the retired. Moreover, all people, young, old and middle-aged, go to the
cinema and read books. Men, women, persons with small
families, urbanites and rural people--all of them form
groups, and members of all these groups can participate in
some similar or dissimilar activities, and so on. One can
assume that this situation is not too complex, since all

young people have mostly the same level of education, differing from that of old people, and the workers probably will
prove to be devoted to some definite leisure activity, and so
forth. As a result, this diversity of groups may be reduced
to some smaller number. One can assume that of all the factors included in the set by which individuals are compared
and distinguished there may exist one factor underlying all
others, for instance, a factor expressing the kind of work
activity. But all these assumptions are unfounded until the
structure of connections is actually revealed. Thus, we are
implying the necessity of revealing the set structure as a
graph of connections among the attributes. Then, for example, the hypothesis concerning the primary meaning of a
single factor assumes the form of equalities:

$$P(X_i | X_j, X_k, \ldots, X_r, f) = P(X_i | f)$$

for all $i, j, \ldots, r$ where X_i is the value of the i-th attri-
bute, f the primary factor, and $P(X|Y)$ the conditional dis-
tribution of attribute X for a fixed value of the attribute
Y. The graph of connections will in this case have the form:
the f-factor will be in the center and other factors will go
out from it as "rays." But, obviously, a real society will
have a structure of its own, and the number of such "central"
attributes may be more than one, and "secondary" attributes
may also be connected with each other. In general, the type
of graph of connection depends, first of all, on the aggregation being employed. And as was shown above, the static
graph of connection depends on the dynamic one. Thus if we
are to represent the problem of social structure in the form
of a set of non-intersecting subsets, then we must study the
structure of the process and its changes, and only later find
its attributes at a fixed time.

7. THE PROBLEM OF FINDING THE RANDOM VARIABLE STRUCTURE

As has been shown on the previous pages, information
about the structure (if such exists) of a random set representing a statistical system under study may be extremely
useful since it decreases the dimensionality of variables being considered simultaneously and simplifies the necessary
analysis. But to do this we must know not only that the
given random set has a structure, but also its form. Unfortunately, thus far no general algorithmic techniques have
been developed for establishing the existence of a non-
trivial structure, and for its best representation in the

form of a graph of connection ("best" means a graph with the smallest numbers of edges). But in some cases, while satisfying certain assumptions, the structure of a statistical system can be determined not only by heuristic methods but by regular methods as well.

The most tempting assumption is that paired connections give a full characterization of the structure. It turns out that this is exactly the case for the normal distribution of $P(X_1, X_2, \ldots, X_n)$. This is not surprising since in the case of normality the whole distribution in general can be described on the basis of paired distributions. But since a knowledge of the structure is not yet a knowledge of the distribution, we can hope that in cases other than normality it is also possible to find a structure by paired connections that are more easily and reliably established (and this is very important) than any others. At any rate we shall first consider a case where $P(X)$ has the normal density.[1] We shall need the following:

Theorem 5.

The necessary and sufficient conditions for a normal random variable $\xi = (\xi_1, \xi_2, \ldots, \xi_n)$ with its center at the origin of the coordinates to have the structure $\Gamma(i), i \varepsilon I = \{1, 2, \ldots, n\}$ are the relations:

$$\rho_{i,j} = \sum_{k, r \varepsilon A} \rho_{ik} \rho_{rj} \rho^{kr} \; \forall \{i, A, j\}_\Gamma \qquad (38)$$

where ρ_{ij} are correlation coefficients and ρ^{kr} are matrix coefficients such that $[\rho^{kr}] = [\rho_{kr}]^{-1}$, $k, r \varepsilon A$.

Proof. Let $P(X) = R \exp \{-\frac{1}{2} X^T Q X\}$ be the normal density of variable ξ, where $Q = [q_{ij}]$ is of dimensionality (nxn). We can show (see, for example, Feller (1966)) that the non-degenerate transformation

$$Y_1 = X_1, \; Y_2 = X_2, \ldots, Y_{n-1} = X_{n-1}, Y_n = \sum_{k=1}^{n} q_{kn} X_k \qquad (39)$$

---

[1] The fact that a continuous variable is now being considered is altogether unimportant. All the results obtained for discrete densities are also wholly transferred to this situation.

transforms $Q(X) = X^T Q X$ to:

$$Q(X) = \frac{1}{q_{nn}} Y_n^2 + Q'(Y_1, Y_2, \ldots, Y_{n-1}) \tag{40}$$

where Q' is the quadratic form of the other variables. As the last formula shows, the random variable $\xi = (\xi_1, \xi_2, \ldots, \xi_n)$ obtained from $\tilde{\xi}$ by the transformation of (39) has a property that its nth component does not depend on the other $\xi_1, \xi_2, \ldots, \xi_{n-1}$. Its conditional density will be the one-dimensional normal distribution with variance $\frac{1}{q_{nn}}$ and mathematical expectation $-\frac{q_{1n}}{q_{nn}} X_1 - \frac{q_{2n}}{q_{nn}} X_2 - \cdots -$

$\frac{q_{n-1,n}}{q_{nn}} X_{n-1}$. In this case, the conditional expectation

$$E(\xi_n | \xi_1, \ldots, \xi_{n-1}) = \sum_{k=1}^{n-1} a_k \xi_k, \quad a_k = -\frac{q_{kn}}{q_{nn}} \tag{41}$$

is the unique linear function of $\xi_1, \ldots, \xi_{n-1}$ which makes the variable $\Pi = \xi_n - \sum_{k=1}^{n-1} a_k \xi_k$ independent of $\xi_1, \ldots, \xi_{n-1}$. The conditional variance equals the variance of Π: $D\Pi = \frac{1}{q_{nn}}$.

Now we proceed to the proof proper. Let us prove the necessity. Let the variable ξ have the structure $\Gamma(i), i \in I$. Consider an arbitrary Markov triple $\{i, A, j\}$. For it $P(X_i | X_A, X_j) = P(X_i | X_A)$ is satisfied. Hence, the equality for mathematical expectations

$$E(\xi_i | \xi_A, \xi_j) = E(\xi_i | \xi_A) \tag{42}$$

must also be satisfied. Particular densities $P(X_i, X_A, X_j)$ and $P(X_i, X_A)$ are also normal. By the above argument, the conditional mathematical expectations $E(\xi_i | \xi_A, \xi_j)$ and $E(\xi_i | \xi_A)$ are linear functions $\sum_{k \in A} a_k \xi_k + a_j \xi_j$ and $\sum_{k \in A} a'_k \xi_k$ such that the variables $\Pi = \xi_i - \sum_{k \in A} a_k \xi_k - a_j \xi_j$ and

$\Pi' = \sum_{k \in A} a'_k \xi_k$ do not depend on ξ_k, ξ_j, or $\xi_k (k \in A)$, respectively. Then for ξ_i, ξ_A, ξ_j there are no other similar linear functions. By the equality (42) $a_j = 0$ and $a'_k = a_k$.

196

Hence, $\Pi = \Pi^*$. By the independence property:

$$\text{COV}(\Pi, \xi_j) = 0$$
$$\text{COV}(\Pi, \xi_n) = 0 \ , \ k\epsilon A \tag{43}$$

Substituting in (43) for Π its equivalent expression we have:

$$\text{COV}(\xi_i, \xi_k) - \sum_{r\epsilon A} \text{COV}(\xi_r, \xi_k) a_r = 0, \qquad k\epsilon A$$

$$\text{COV}(\xi_1, \xi_j) - \sum_{r\epsilon A} \text{COV}(\xi_r, \xi_j) a_r = 0. \tag{44}$$

The first of the relations (44) uniquely defines a_r $(r\epsilon A)$ denoted later as a vector $a(i, A)$. Denoting by $C_{AA}, C_{iA}, C_{Aj},$ C_{ij} the corresponding covariance matrices, and replacing in the second of relations (44) $a(i, A)$ by its equivalent expression, we obtain the main formula:

$$C_{ij} = C_{Aj} \, C_{AA}^{-1} \, C_{iA} \tag{45}$$

For centered densities the last relation can be rewritten as:

$$\sigma_i \sigma_j \rho_{ij} = (\sigma_1 \sigma_j \rho_{1j}, \sigma_2 \sigma_j \rho_{2j}, \ldots, \sigma_\alpha \sigma_j \rho_{\alpha j}) \ \cdot$$

$$\cdot \begin{bmatrix} \sigma_1 \sigma_1 \rho_{11} & \sigma_1 \sigma_2 \rho_{12} \cdots \sigma_1 \sigma_\alpha \rho_{1\alpha} \\ \sigma_2 \sigma_1 \rho_{21} & \sigma_2 \sigma_2 \rho_{22} \cdots \sigma_2 \sigma_\alpha \rho_{2\alpha} \\ \cdot \ \cdot \ \cdot \ \cdot \ \cdot \ \cdot \ \cdot \ \cdot \ \cdot \ \cdot \\ \sigma_\alpha \sigma_1 \rho_{\alpha 1} & \sigma_\alpha \sigma_2 \rho_{\alpha 2} \cdots \sigma_\alpha \sigma_\alpha \rho_{\alpha\alpha} \end{bmatrix}^{-1} \begin{bmatrix} \sigma_i \sigma_1 \rho_{i1} \\ \sigma_i \sigma_2 \rho_{i2} \\ \cdot \ \cdot \ \cdot \ \cdot \\ \sigma_i \sigma_\alpha \rho_{ia} \end{bmatrix}$$

where ρ_{ij} denotes the correlation coefficients, and the elements of the set A have been enumerated from 1 to α. Reducing on the left and on the right by the value $\sigma_i \sigma_j$ and presenting the middle matrix and extreme vectors as the product of two vectors and one matrix, we have:

$$\rho_{ij} = (\rho_{1j}\rho_{2j}\cdots\rho_{\alpha j}) \begin{bmatrix} \sigma_1 & 0\ldots 0 \\ 0 & \sigma_2\ldots 0 \\ \cdot & \cdot\ \cdot\ \cdot\ \cdot \\ 0 & 0\ldots\sigma_\alpha \end{bmatrix} \cdot$$

$$\cdot \begin{bmatrix} \sigma_1 0 \ldots 0 \\ 0\ \sigma_2\ldots 0 \\ \cdot\ \cdot\ \cdot\ \cdot \\ 0\ 0\ \ldots\sigma_\alpha \end{bmatrix} \begin{bmatrix} \rho_{11}\rho_{12}\cdots\rho_{1\alpha} \\ \rho_{21}\rho_{22}\cdots\rho_{2\alpha} \\ \cdot\ \cdot\ \cdot\ \cdot\ \cdot\ \cdot \\ \rho_{\alpha 1}\rho_{\alpha 2}\cdots\rho_{\alpha\alpha} \end{bmatrix} \begin{bmatrix} \sigma_1 0\ \ldots 0 \\ 0\ \sigma_2\ldots 0 \\ \cdot\ \cdot\ \cdot\ \cdot \\ 0\ 0\ \ldots\sigma_\alpha \end{bmatrix}^{-1} \begin{bmatrix} \sigma_1 0\ldots 0 \\ 0\ \sigma_2\ldots 0 \\ \cdot\ \cdot\ \cdot\ \cdot \\ 0\ 0\ldots\sigma_\alpha \end{bmatrix} \begin{bmatrix} \rho_{i1} \\ \rho_{i2} \\ \cdot\ \cdot \\ \rho_{i\alpha} \end{bmatrix}$$

Since $AB = (B^{-1}A^{-1})^{-1}$, then by introducing converted matrices with σ's within the inverted matrix and then multiplying by the vectors, we obtain:

$$\rho_{ij} = (\rho_{1j}\rho_{2j}\cdots\rho_{\alpha j}) \begin{bmatrix} \rho_{11} & \rho_{12} & \cdots & \rho_{1\alpha} \\ \rho_{21} & \rho_{22} & \cdots & \rho_{2\alpha} \\ \cdot & \cdot & \cdot & \cdot\ \cdot\ \cdot \\ \rho_{\alpha 1} & \rho_{\alpha 2} & \cdots & \rho_{\alpha\alpha} \end{bmatrix}^{-1} \begin{bmatrix} \rho_{i1} \\ \rho_{i2} \\ \cdot \\ \rho_{ia} \end{bmatrix}$$

(46)

In the scalar form this equality has acquired the form of:

$$\rho_{ij} = \sum_{k,r\epsilon A} \rho_{ik}\rho_{rj}\rho^{kr} \tag{47}$$

where the ρ^{kr} are the coefficients in the matrix $[\rho^{kr}]$ = $[\rho_{kr}]^{-1}$, $k,r\epsilon A$. Necessity has thus been proved.

Now to prove sufficiency. For each Markov triple $\{i,A,B\}_\Gamma$ let the relation (47) hold. Equation (45) corresponds to it. Consider the particular normal densities $P(X_i,X_A,X_j)$ and $P(X_i,X_A)$. Obviously, the product $C_{AA}^{-1}C_{iA}$ may be regarded as a vector $a(i,A)$ obtained from the relation $C_{iA} - C_{AA}\cdot a(i,A) = 0$ which, in turn, means that $E(\xi_i|\xi_A) = \sum\limits_{k\in A} a_k\xi_k$ is the unique linear function making variables ξ_k ($k\in A$) independent of $\xi_i - \sum\limits_{k\in A} a_k\xi_k = \Pi$. Hence the the expression (45) can be rewritten as:

$$C_{ij} = C_{Aj}a(i,A)$$

or

$$C_{ij} = \sum\limits_{k\in A} C_{kj}a_k$$

where C_{ik} are covariances between ξ_i and ξ_k. The last equation means that the variable Π also does not depend on ξ_j. But there can be only one linear function, i.e. the mathematical expectation $E(\xi_i|\xi_A,\xi_j)$. Thus the equality

$$E(\xi_i|\xi_A,\xi_j) = E(\xi_i|\xi_A)$$

has been established. As for the equality of the conditional variances, this is satisfied since they equal the value $D(\Pi) = \dfrac{1}{q}$ where q is the diagonal element of the corresponding matrix of quadratic forms, similar to the value q_{nn} given at the beginning of the proof. Therefore, the conditional densities also coincide:

$$P(X_i|X_A,X_j) = P(X_i|X_A). \qquad Q.E.D.$$

As one can easily see, formula (47) is a generalization of the known formula for correlation coeficients of a normal Markov sequence $(Z_1,Z_2,\ldots,Z_t\ldots)$:

$$\rho_{ij} = \rho_{ik}\rho_{kj} \qquad i < k < j \tag{48}$$

But the main advantage of this formula is that it is possible, if the paired connection is known, to use it to find the structure of the random variable ξ. Indeed, if between the elements i and j there is no direct connection (i.e., on the graph Γ the edge between i and j is missing), then the triple

$$\{i, I - \{i,j\}, j\}_\Gamma$$

is Markov. Thus the equation

$$0 = \sum_{r,k\varepsilon I-\{i,j\}} \rho_{ik}\rho_{rj}\rho^{kr} \; \forall \; i,j \; : \; i \notin \Gamma(j) \tag{50}$$

must hold. Conversely, if the equality holds for some pair (i,j) , then $i \notin \Gamma(j)$. Therefore it is necessary to consider all conceivable pairs of differing indices i,j. Their number

equals $C_n^2 = \dfrac{n(n-1)}{2}$. For each such pair it is necessary to compute the inverse matrix $[\rho_{kr}]^{-1}_{k,r\varepsilon I-\{i,j\}}$ and to check to

see if equality (50) is satisfied. If it is satisfied, then there is no direct connection. Otherwise it is necessary to assume that i and j are connected by an edge $i\varepsilon\Gamma(j)$. Of course this equality only holds for true population correlation coefficients, and not for sample ones. Therefore, in fact, it will only be approximate, and additional statistical testing is needed to show that the correct graph has been found. As coefficients ρ^{kr} for all i, j are calculated on the basis of the same correlation matrices $[\rho_{ij}]_{n \times n}$, it seems possible to simplify the computing operation for inverting the matrices.

As was noted by M. A. Rodionov (1973), the absence of direct connection between components ξ_i and ξ_j of a gaussian variable is equivalent to the fact that in the matrix $[\varrho_{ij}] = [C_{ij}]^{-1}$ the element $\varrho_{ij} = 0$. Therefore in the case of a gaussian distribution it is necessary to calculate the inverse matrix (to the matrix of covariations) and to take out those of its elements which are zero. An estimation for this case was made by K. A. Karapetyan (1974).

As far as the existence of the structure is concerned, we can suppose, on the basis of general considerations of a methodological nature, that since the Markov property is a necessary condition for describing over time an interconnected system of causes and effects, therefore the structure is a necessary condition for the static model.

REFERENCES

Ashby, W. R. 1962. *Konstruktsia Mozga (Construction of the Brain)*, translated into Russian, Moscow.

Bellman, R. 1959. *Dynamic Programming*, Moscow.

Blalock, H. M., and A. B. Blalock (eds.). 1968. *Methodology in Social Research*. New York, McGraw-Hill.

Borodkin, F. M. 1968. "Statisticheskaia Otsenka Sviazei Ekonomicheskikh Pokazatelei" (Statistical Evaluation of the Connections Between Economic Indices). *Statistika* Moscow.

Feller, W. 1966. *Introduction to Probability Theory and Its Applications, Volume II.* New York: Wiley.

Gavrilets, Iu.N. 1969. "O Kolichestvennom Izuchenii Sotsial'Noekonomicheskikh Iavlenii" (On the Quantitative Study of Socio-economic Phenomena), *Economika i Matematicheskie Metodiss.*

Gavrilets, Iu.N. 1970a. "O Kolichestvennom Issledovanii Struktury Slozhnykh Sotsial'nykh Sistem" (On a Quantitative Study of the Structure of Complicated Social Systems) *Modelirovanie Socialnik Processor.* Moscow: Nauka

Gavrilets, Iu. N. 1970b. "Sluchainye Velichiny, Imeiushchie Strukturu i ikh Ispol' zovanie v Sotsiologii" (Random Variables Having a Structure and Their Utilization in Social Research) (mimeograph). Institute of Empirical Social Studies, Moscow.

Gavrilets, Iu.N. 1974. "Sotsialno-Ekonomitcheskoje Planirovanije. Sistemy i Modely (Social-Economic Planning: Systems and Models), *Economica.* Moscow.

Karapetian, K. A. 1974. "Ob Odnom Statistitchescom Kriterii Proverki Gipotezy (On a Statistical Method of Estimation of an Hypothesis.) *Utchenyje Zapiski po Statistike,* tom 26. Moscow, Nauka.

Rodionov, M. A. 1972. "Uslovia Sushchestvovania Zhostkoi Struktury Sluchainoi Velichiny" (Conditions for the Existence of a Random Variable Structure) (Mimeograph). Central Economic Mathematical Institute.

Rodionov, M. A. 1973. "O Structurnych Svojstvach
Raspredelenij" (On Structural Properties of Distribu-
tions), in "Voprosy Ekonomiko-Matematitcheskogo
Modelirovanija" (mimeograph). Moscow University.

Suppes, P. 1970. *A Probabilistic Theory of Causality*.
North-Holland Publishing Company, Amsterdam.

7

Structural Parameters of Graphs:

A Theoretical Investigation *

TORD HØIVIK AND NILS PETTER GLEDITSCH

International Peace Research Institute, Oslo

1. INTRODUCTION

The theory of graphs has found wide application in social science as a tool for representing group structures.
Concretely, a set of social units (e.g. individuals or
nations) is represented by a set of *vertices,* and relations
within pairs of units (e.g. friendship or exchange of ambassadors) by *edges* between the corresponding vertices.[1]

---

*
This is a revised version of a paper presented to the Second
Nordic Peace Research Conference, Örenäs, Sweden, 23rd May,
1968. It grew out of a chapter in the second author's thesis
on the international airline network (Oslo, 1968, unpublished). Tord Høivik is mainly responsible for sections 1-7 in
the present article and Nils Petter Gleditsch for section 8.
However, as a whole the article represents a joint effort in
the best sense of the word. We are grateful to Johan Galtung
for valuable comments and to the Norwegian Council for Peace
and Conflict Research (RKF) and the Norwegian Council for
Research in Science and the Humanities (NAVF) for financial
support. This article can be identified as publication M-5
from the International Peace Research Institute, Oslo (PRIO).

[1] The terminology follows Ore (1962).

We shall only treat the simplest type of graphs, where edges have neither direction, sign, value, nor multiplicity, and vertices are *labelled*. This means that we restrict our-selves to symmetrical relations which may only exist or not exist in any pair (exchange of ambassadors between countries) on the one hand, and on the other that we take vertices to be distinguishable. The two graphs below are thus distinct:

Fig. 1. Distinct Labelled Graphs.

Our task in this chapter is to systematize the use of graphs to study some important concepts in the theory of social structure: *integration, polarization,* and *centraliza-tion*. We first propose a set of parameters and discuss vari-ous ways of norming them. Some of the properties of the parameters are obvious, others are established as graph-theoretical theorems.

2. PRELIMINARIES

A graph is a set of points, *vertices,* some (or none) of which are connected by lines, *edges.*[2] The *distance* between two vertices is the smallest number of edges one must trav-erse to get from the one to the other. If it is impossible to get from one vertex to another the distance between them is taken to be infinite. The greatest distance in a graph is called its *diameter*. If this is finite the graph is *connec-ted,* otherwise *disconnected*.

Let (1,2, ..., n) be the vertices of a graph G. We shall represent G by its *incidence matrix* (e_{ij}), i, j=1, ..., n, or by its *distance matrix* (d_{ij}), i, j=1, ..., n, where

---

[2]The concept of a graph can be generalized in various ways. We may, e.g., allow edges to have direction *(digraphs),* value *(valued graphs)* or multiplicity--two or more in a single vertex pair--*(multiple graphs)*. The treatment in this paper can often be extended to these types of graphs, but no explicit notice will be taken of them.

$e_{ij}=0$ if there is no edge between i and j

$e_{ij}=1$ if there is an edge between i and j

and

$d_{ii}=0$

$d_{ij}=$distance between i and j.

3.   GRAPH PROPERTIES

Our main definitions are based on the distance matrix[3] and start with the properties of the single vertex.

A vertex i is characterized by its set of distances to other vertices $(d_{i1}, d_{i2}, ..., d_{in})$. Our interest is in whether it is centrally or peripherally located within the graph, and we define:

A vertex is *central* if its distances to other vertices on the whole are small. A centrality parameter for i should therefore be a measure of the central tendency in $(d_{i1}, ..., d_{in})$.

A graph is *integrated* if its vertices on the whole are centrally located. An integration parameter should therefore be a measure of the central tendency in the set of vertex centralities.

A graph is *unipolar* if there exists a very central vertex. A unipolarity parameter should therefore be the centrality of the most central vertex.[4]

A graph is *centralized* if there are great differences between the vertex centralities. A centralization parameter should therefore be a measure of the dispersion in the set of vertex centralities.

A simple set of parameters satisfying these definitions is given in Table 1.

---

[3] To cover the most widely used graph parameters, this approach was chosen. Others can be imagined, building on, e.g., the *number* of shortest paths between vertices, or on what *happens* to the graph when a vertex is removed.

[4] Sabidussi (1966) defines the center as the *set* of all vertices with minimal distance sums. For our purposes we need only one member of this set.

Name	Symbol		Definition
Centrality	s_i	$=$	$\Sigma_j d_{ij}$
Integration	S	$=$	$\frac{1}{2}\Sigma_{ij}d_{ij} = \frac{1}{2}\Sigma_i s_i$
Unipolarity	V	$=$	$\min_i s_i$
Centralization	H	$=$	$\Sigma_i (s_i - \min_i s_i)$
(Note that	H	$=$	$2S - nV)$.

Table 1. PARAMETERS BASED ON DISTANCE SUMS

Disconnected graphs create an obvious problem in that some distances become infinite. A common solution has been to work with inverse distances and we get, by analogy with Table 1.

Name	Symbol		Definition
Centrality	t_i	$=$	$\Sigma_{j \neq i}\ 1/d_{ij}$ (i fixed)
Integration	T	$=$	$\frac{1}{2}\Sigma\ i \neq j\, 1/d_{ij} = \frac{1}{2}\ \Sigma_i t_i$
Unipolarity	W	$=$	$\max_i t_i$
Centralization	L	$=$	$\Sigma_i (\max_i t_i - t_i)$
(Note that	L	$=$	$nW-2T)$.

Table 2. PARAMETERS BASED ON SUMS OF INVERSE DISTANCES

The inversion of distances is, however, a nonlinear transformation. Its consequence is that the parameter values will be influenced almost solely by the small distances in the distance matrix. Whether this is reasonable must depend on the underlying empirical situation and should not be taken for granted.

The inverted distance is a "nearness." We here propose a *linear* transformation of distance into "nearness" with distance value infinity corresponding to nearness value zero, viz.:

$$\text{nearness } n_{ij} = 1 - (d_{ij} - 1)/(n-1); \quad d_{ij} = 1, 2, \ldots, n-1$$

$$= 0 \qquad\qquad ; \quad d_{ij} \text{ infinite .}$$

The first transformation is generally valid when we have substituted n for infinite distance values in the distance matrix. Defining parameters by analogy with Table 2 we see that the resulting expressions are simply linear functions of the corresponding parameters in Table 1 when n has replaced infinity.

For the sake of completeness we include two other graph parameters current in social science literature,

Name	Symbol		Definition	Reference
Integration	B	$=$	$\Sigma_i 1/s_i$	Beauchamp (1965)
Centralization	F	$=$	$\frac{1}{2}\Sigma_{i \neq j} s_i/s_j$	Bavelas (1950)
(Note that	F	$=$	$SB - n/2)$.	

Table 3. THE BAVELAS AND BEAUCHAMP PARAMETERS

Finally, though we prefer to work with distances since they reflect the position of vertices in the graph as a whole, the same approach can be used in the incidence matrix, with the *degree*--the number of edges incident to a vertex-- fulfilling the function of the distance sum.

Name	Symbol	Definition
Centrality	r_i	$= \quad \Sigma_j e_{ij}$
Integration	R	$= \quad \frac{1}{2}\Sigma_i r_i$
Unipolarity	U	$= \quad \max_i r_i$
Centralization	J	$= \quad \Sigma_i (\max_i r_i - r_i)$

(Note that	J	$= \quad nU-2R)$.

Table 4. PARAMETERS BASED ON NUMBER OF EDGES

4. NORMING

Our parameters are numbers characterizing objects: single vertices or whole graphs. We use them to compare the objects: is this vertex more central than that one? If we change this graph by removing an edge, does it become more centralized? But comparison is not always immediate. If the two vertices belong to different graphs we may feel that direct comparison of their centrality values is meaningless. Large graphs will in general have greater row-sums of distances than small graphs--and *that* tendency is not what we usually take centrality of vertices to mean.

In general terms, we are willing to compare some objects directly with respect to the values of a certain parameter. Let us call such a set of objects a *comparability class*. We assume that the set of all objects (vertices or graphs) can be completely divided into disjunct comparability classes.

Norming then becomes an effort to achieve comparability between objects from different classes by applying a transformation to the parameter values. As a codification of practice the transformation should:

a) be of a conceptually simple type (e.g. linear);

b) have function parameters dependent on the comparability class, but;

c) have the same simple extreme values (e.g. O and 1) within each class.

When graphs are used to represent group structures the following five comparability classes seem particularly relevant:

a) the class of vertices within a given graph, G;

b) the class of graphs with n vertices, G(n);
c) the class of graphs with n vertices and k edges,
    G(n, k);
d) the class of connected n-vertex graphs, C(n);
e) the class of connected n-vertex, k-edge graphs,
    C(n, k).

(We shall use classes b-e for vertices as well as for
graphs.) In some applications other comparability classes,
e.g. that of graphs with a given diameter, might well be
relevant. (See Theorem IV below.)

As for transformation functions we shall limit ourselves
to 0 and 1 as extreme values and treat two main function
types:

a) linear functions;
b) cumulative distribution functions.

Case a is in principle very simple. If q is a parameter and
W a comparability class, let $m=\min_w q$ and $M=\max_w q$. The linearly normed parameter q* then is

$$q*=(q-m)/(M-m) \quad \text{or} \quad q*=(M-q)/M-m$$

according to the preferred direction of variation.

In Tables 5 to 7 we give m and M values for the parameters defined in section 3, as far as we were able to compute them.

In case b the basis for norming is a probability model
which for any class W establishes the graphs in W as a complete set of disjunct, random events. Any graph parameter q
then becomes a stochastic variable and the normed parameter
q*=F(q) where F is the cumulative distribution function.

We see from Figure 2 that q* may be interpreted as the
probability that our (un-normed) stochastic parameter will
fall in the interval $[m, q_{obs}]$.

5. GRAPHS WITH EXTREME VALUES IN TABLES 5 TO 7

We need some terms: the *null* graph has no edges; the
chain graph has all its vertices along a single "line"; the
star graph has one vertex directly linked with all other vertices and no additional edges; the *circle* graph defines itself; the *tree* graph is connected and has no circular subgraphs (*cycles*); the *regular* graph has a constant number of
edges incident to each vertex; the *complete* graph has edges
between all vertex pairs.

Basis	Name	Parameter	Min	Max	Max(inf=n)
Edge	Centrality	$r_i = \Sigma_j e_{ij}$	0	$n-1$	
	Integration	$R = \frac{1}{2}\Sigma_i r_i$	0	$\binom{n}{2}$	
	Unipolarity	$U = \max_i r_i$	0	$n-1$	
	Centralization	$J = nU - 2R$	0	$(n-1)(n-2)$	
Distance	Centrality	$s_i = \Sigma_j d_{ij}$	$n-1$	inf.	$n(n-1)$
	Integration	$S = \frac{1}{2}\Sigma_i s_i$	$\binom{n}{2}$	inf.	$n\binom{n}{2}$
	Unipolarity	$V = \min_i s_i$	$n-1$	inf.	$n(n-1)$
	Centralization	$H = 2S - nV$	0	undefined	
Inverse Distance	Centrality	$t_i = \Sigma_j 1/d_{ij}$	0	$n-1$	
	Integration	$T = \frac{1}{2}\Sigma_i t_i$	0	$\binom{n}{2}$	
	Unipolarity	$W = \max_i t_i$	0	$n-1$	
	Centralization	$L = nW - 2T$	0		
Beauchamp	Integration	$B = \Sigma_i 1/s_i$	0	$n/(n-1)$	
Bavelas	Centralization	$F = SB - n/2$	$\binom{n}{2}$	inf.	

Table 5. LINEAR NORMING IN $G(n)$

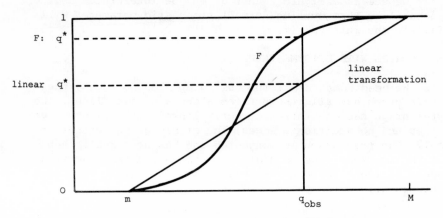

Fig. 2   Norming By Means Of A Distribution.

210

Table 6. LINEAR NORMING IN G(n,k) AND C(n,k)

Basis	Name	Parameter	C(n,k) Min	C(n,k) Max	G(n,k) Min	G(n,k) Max
Edge	Centrality	r_i	0	$n-1$	1	$n-1$
	Integration	R	k	k	k	k
	Unipolarity	U	0	$n-1$	1	$n-1$
Distance	Centrality	s_i	$n-1$	inf.	$n-1$	$\binom{n}{2} + (n-1) - k$
	Integration	S	$n(n-1)-k$	inf.	$n(n-1)-k$	
	Unipolarity	V	$n-1$	inf.		
Inverse Distance	Centrality	t_i	0	$n-1$		$n-1$
	Integration	T		$n(n-1)/4+k/2$		$n(n-1)/4+k/2$
	Unipolarity	W		$n-1$		$n-1$

Basis	Name	Parameter	Min	Max
	Centrality	r_i	1	$n-1$
Edge	Integration	R	$n-1$	$\binom{n}{2}$
	Unipolarity	U	2	$n-1$
	Centralization	J	O	$(n-1)(n-2)$
	Centrality	s_i	$n-1$	$\binom{n}{2}$
Distance	Integration	S	$\binom{n}{2}$	$\binom{n+1}{3}$
	Unipolarity	V	$n-1$	$(n^2-1)/4$ (n odd)
	Centralization	H	$n-1$ / O	$n^2/4$ (n even) / $\sim 5n^3/54$
Inverse Distance*	Centrality	t_i	$\sim \ln(n-1)+.58$	$n-1$
	Integration	T	$\sim \ln(n-1)^n-(n-1)+.58$	$\binom{n}{2}$
	Unipolarity	W	$\sim \ln((n-1)/2)^2 + 1.15$	$n-1$ (n odd)
	Centralization	L	$\sim(\ln(n/2)^2+2/n + 1.15$ / O	$n-1$ (n even)
Beauchamp	Integration	B	$\dfrac{1}{\Sigma_i\left[\binom{n+1-i}{2}+\binom{i}{2}\right]}$	$n/(n-1)$
Bavelas	Centralization	F	$\binom{n}{2}$	

*The well-known approximation to the harmonic series is used. .58 represents Euler's constant, 1.15 its doubled value.

Table 7. LINEAR NORMING IN C(n).

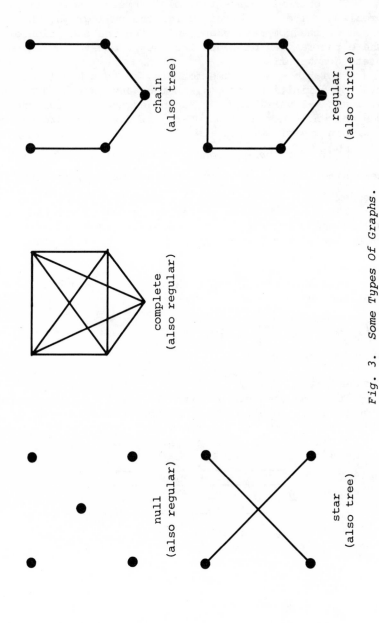

Fig. 3. Some Types Of Graphs.

chain
(also tree)

regular
(also circle)

complete
(also regular)

null
(also regular)

star
(also tree)

213

The extreme values in Table 5 present no particular problems. They are attained for the null graph, the star graph or the complete graph, with the one exception of max F where the removal of edges from, say, one vertex in the complete graph suffices.

In Table 6 we assume for G(n, k) that k≥n-1. This is true by definition for C(n,k) since any connected graph has at least n-1 vertices. By adding edges to a star graph we can evidently get a graph where all distances are either 1 or 2 within any of the classes G(n,k), C(n,k); k=n-1, n, n+1, ..., $\binom{n}{2}$. For these graphs S is minimal and T maximal. The remaining non-obvious value, that of $\max_i s_i$, is given as Theorem I.

In Table 7 extreme values are attained for the chain graph, the star graph or the complete graph, with the one exception of max H where the result is given as Theorem II.

Theorem I.

In a connected graph with n vertices and k edges the distance-sum for a single vertex has

$$(1) \qquad \binom{n}{2} + (n-1) - k$$

as its maximal value.[5]

Theorem II.

For connected graphs with n≥6 vertices, the centralization parameter H attains its maximal value for the, as near as possible, symmetrical tree with 3 branches.[6]

We give H-values for n=5,6,..., 10.

	Branches				
n	2	3	4	n-1
5	10	11	12	12
6	16	20	20	20
7	28	33	32	30
8	40	48	39	42
9	60	69	68	56
10	80	96	78	72

---

[5] The proof is in Høivik (1969), pp. 10-12.

[6] The proof is in Høivik (1969), pp. 13-15.

We note that F is minimal if and only if

$$s_1 = s_2 = \ldots = s_n.$$

As Sabidussi (1966) points out, the class of F-minimal graphs intersects the class of regular graphs, but there are non-regular graphs with all distance-sums equal, e.g., as in Figure 4.

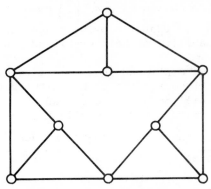

Fig. 4. A Non-Regular, F-Minimal Graph.

6. THE RELATION BETWEEN INTEGRATION AND UNIPOLARITY

If the number of edges k is given, how should they be placed to achieve maximal integration? If $k < n-1$ and infinite distances are normed to n, the answer is trivial: make a star over k+1 vertices, leaving the rest disconnected. Any other graph will be less integrated. If $k \geq n-1$ we have noted that we can always get maximal integration (minimal S) by adding edges to a star graph, which means that the graph will be maximally unipolar (minimal V). Theorem III shows that maximal integration can be attained with less than maximal unipolarity if and only if k is strictly greater than 2n-6 (and, trivially, less than or equal to $\binom{n-1}{2}$).

Theorem III.

If a graph has $n \geq 5$ vertices, $k \leq 2n-6$ edges and diameter 2, its most central vertex is directly linked with all the others.[7]

---
[7]The proof is in Høivik (1969), pp. 16-19.

7. PROBABILITY NORMING

The simplest model for generating stochastic graphs is probably the binomial one, where edges occur binomially, with probability p, say, in each of the $\binom{n}{2}$ vertex pairs of an n-vertex graph. The comparability class is then implicitly defined as G(n). To make comparisons with an empirical structure with k edges, a choice of $p=k/\binom{n}{2}$ seems reasonable.

It is easy to see that for p=.5, graphs in G(n) will have the same probability of being realized. We call this the *uniform* model.

In Section 4 we mentioned that the value of a normed parameter in case b) equals the probability that an (unnormed) parameter will be not larger than the one actually obtained. In the uniform model this is the same as

$$\frac{\text{no. of graphs with parameter values} \leq q}{\text{total no. of graphs in G(n)}} \cdot$$

Having defined a probability model, like the one above, its properties and the distribution properties of our parameters in particular may be studied, either by direct computation or by simulation. We have shown that:

Theorem IV.
In the binomial model

a) $P(d_{ij}=2)=q(1-(1-p^2)^{n-1})$ for any vertex pair (i, j);

b) $\lim_n P(D\leq 2)=1$

where the diameter D is defined as the maximal distance in the graph.[8] Taking the uniform model and applying IVb, we get the interesting corollary that

$$\lim_n P(D\leq 2)=\lim_n \frac{\text{no. of graphs with diameter} \leq 2}{\text{total no. of graphs in G(n)}} = 1.$$

For a large enough n, that is, almost all graphs have diameter 2. However, the direct computation of distribution functions of even the simplest parameters presents great difficulties, both when it comes to limit behavior (in n) and, even more, for fixed n. We must therefore resort to computer

---

[8] The proofs are in Høivik (1969), p. 21 and p. 28, where also stronger results—for non-constant p=p(n)—are given.

simulation of the model concerned. By well-known statistical theorems the empirical cumulative distribution function of our q will then approximate the theoretical distribution, and more closely, in general, the more graphs that are generated.

(Theoretically one could run through *all* graphs in a comparability class, computing their q-values and probabilities of occurring. In practice this can only be done for very small graphs. Even G(5) contains 1024 graphs and G(10) approximately 40 billion different graphs).[9]

Our first simulation, 150 runs with n=125 and p=.5, resulted in graphs with diameter 2 only. This unexpected finding led to the development of Theorem IVb. Gleditsch and Høivik (1971) deals with a variety of simulations and comparisons with empirical data.

8. RELEVANCE AND APPLICATION

In a series of well-known studies of communication patterns in small groups, Bavelas (1950), Leavitt (1951), Guetzkow and Simon (1955) and others used five graphs which since then have recurred in graph-oriented theory and experimentation, both in social psychology (e.g. Cohen *et al.*, 1961) and in inter-nation simulation games (Brody, 1963). These are the *chain*, the *star*, the *circle*, the Y (3-branched tree), and the *complete* ("all-channel") graph. Interestingly, all five graphs are extreme with regard to one or more of the parameters in Table 1.

	Graph:				
	Circle	Complete	Chain	Y	Star
Parameter:					
Integration	--	maximum	minimum in C(n)	--	--
Unipolarity	minimum in C(n)	maximum	minimum in C(n)	--	maximum
Centralization	minimum	minimum	--	maximum in C(n) (n>6)	

Table 9. EXTREME PROPERTIES OF EXPERIMENTAL GRAPHS

---

[9]The general formula is

$$G(n) = \Sigma_k G(n,k) = \Sigma_k \binom{\binom{n}{2}}{k} = 2^{\binom{n}{2}}$$

Thus, these five experimental graphs attain all maxima and minima in C(n) for these three parameters and provide a good basis for experimental comparisons of the effects of different properties of communication networks. Typically, these experiments have been carried out in 5-person networks. In our context this is somewhat regrettable since the centralization values for n=5 are atypical (Table 8).

For 7 or more vertices the maxima and minima set out in the Table would be unique to the graphs they are listed under, although there are other graphs, not among these five, which are extreme too.

How well do the particular operationalizations reflect important properties of group structure?

At the vertex level, the measure of *centrality* seems to be generally accepted as a good measure of the position of a unit in a network (see e.g. Flament, 1963; Harary *et al.*, 1965). Only our proposed norming is different, since the original measure (Bavelas, 1950) did not vary between 0 and 1 and did not belong to any of our four comparability classes.

At the graph level, the measure of *integration* is intended to capture the property of a social group variously referred to as cohesiveness, connectivity, connectedness, solidarity, "we-ness," or integration. We adopt the definition of cohesiveness advanced by Festinger *et al.* (1950) as "the total field of forces which act on members to stay within the group." If we assume that the edges represent a force of attraction (such as a friendship bond) and further assume that the force decreases with increasing step-distance between two members, S becomes a reasonable operationalization. A more commonly used measure is R, based on the number of edges. This we shall prefer to call the *density* of a network. It is not a very satisfactory measure since it takes account only of the direct links between two units. A nearly bipolar split in a group or a tendency to cliquishness in a subgroup is better reflected in S than in R. Coleman (1964, p. 454) suggests *connectivity*, the fraction of pairs with finite distances. But this presents a parallel problem: it takes account only of the relative number of finite and infinite distances. The distribution of high and low finite distances is not reflected in Coleman's measure, as it is in S. Finally, S is a direct parallel to s at the vertex level, whereas R would correspond to r (the number of edges incident to the vertex) and connectivity to the fraction of vertices at finite distances.

The concept of *polarization* is closely linked to conflict theory. It refers to the degree to which positive

relations are concentrated within subgroups, with negative
relations between them. For signed graphs a precise definition of polarization can be given. If we define a balanced
graph as a graph in which all cycles have an even number of
negative lines it follows from a theorem by Cartwright and
Harary (1956) that balance obtains if and only if the graph
may be partitioned into two subgraphs with all the negative
edges between the two subgraphs, and all the positive within.
The theorem is proved for digraphs, but applies to non-
directed graphs equally. It applies to complete, as well as
non-complete graphs. The index of the *degree of balance*
(measured as the number of balanced cycles over the total number of cycles, Harary *et al., op. cit.;* or as the number of
edges which must be changed to obtain balance, Flament, *op.
cit.)* can serve as an index of bi-polarity. Furthermore, the
Cartwright and Harary theorem has been extended by Davis
(1967), who defines a balanced graph in a looser sense as a
graph in which there are no cycles with exactly one negative
link. Using this definition of balance Davis proves that it
is equivalent to a graph with n subgraphs (poles, blocs),
where all positive edges are within the subgraphs, and all
the negative edges between them. The degree of balance can
now be defined, and can be used as a measure of n-polarity.

In unsigned graphs the concept of balance is trivial:
all cycles are balanced, hence all graphs are balanced. However, we can define bi-polarity or n-polarity in a parallel
way: an n-polar graph is a graph in which all edges are
within the n subgraphs, and no edges between them. The degree of n-polarity can, then, be measured as a function of
the difference between S within subgraphs and S between.

This measure is not included in our list of parameters.
The reason is that it introduces an idea which is extraneous
to the rest of the discussion, namely the idea of partitioning the graph into subgraphs. The application of this measure, then, depends on the existence of an independent criterion for partitioning the graph *or* the use of a clustering
method to group the vertices. As an example of the first
procedure, take the graph of European countries (the vertices) and their communication pattern (the edges). The set of
vertices can be divided into three on the basis of the criterion "affiliation to a military bloc": NATO countries,
Warsaw pact countries, and neutrals. We can then proceed to
measure bi-polarity (NATO vs. Warsaw pact) or three-polarity
in this graph. The whole exercise, however, depends on a
substantive interest in military blocs.

The idea here, however, is to define a measure of polarization without a reference to any particular number of subgraphs, and without the ad hoc introduction of outside criteria of grouping. The approach we have adopted follows Sabidussi (1966) in defining the most central vertex as the *center* of the graph. If the center is highly central to the graph, the graph is unipolar. If not, then it is multipolar. We therefore define unipolarity by V, and normed multipolarity as M=1-V. This index, then, measures "multi-centeredness" as opposed to "uni-centeredness," not as contrasted with "two-centeredness" as is often the issue when multipolarity is contrasted with bipolarity in contemporary international relations (See e.g. Waltz, 1967).

An alternative index of unipolarity would be the number of centers in a graph. This measure also has some attractive properties. However, its relationship to the other measures is less clear.

The idea of a parameter of *centralization* is to measure the disparity between the position of the central and the peripheral units. As we shall see below, a measure of centralization has figured prominently in experimental research under the name of "centrality." It has been found to be a good predictor to such characteristics of problem-solving activity as efficiency (positive correlation) and member satisfaction (negative correlation). The central member in a highly centralized communication network not only has better opportunities for direct communication with every other member in the net, he also has power over the communication process as a whole because many indirect communications have to pass through him. From the latter point of view it might be preferable to define a measure that would yield a maximum for the star (cf. in Table 4), and not for the three-branched tree. However, we prefer to retain a definition in terms of the dispersion of the distance sums.

Minimum centralization obtains both for the circle and the complete graph. This is as it should be, since in both groups the communication opportunities are identical for all members. In actual groups or networks, the structures may, of course, be used in different ways. Thus, there is evidence that the complete graph in fact usually *operates* as a chain or a star. But this is not an argument against the proposed measure of centralization. Rather, it is a warning against a facile assumption that the formal and informal structures are identical in communication networks.

A note must be included on the "centrality" of a graph, as distinct from the centrality of a vertex. The concept is

used a number of places in the empirical literature, but
there is no clarity at all with regard to what it is supposed
to mean. Thus Newcomb (1961, p. 181) writes: "By *centrality*
we refer to compactness, as opposed to extendedness, of the
network of high attraction bonds." His index of centrality
is (in our terminology) the maximum loss in connectivity
obtained by removing one vertex. The verbal definition
appears to refer to *integration*. The operational definition,
however, approximates *polarization*. Since polarized **struc-**
tures tend to be less integrated than one would expect *given
the number of links,* the measure can serve as an index of integration only in G(n,k) or C(n, k). Sabidussi (1966, p.
581) states that the index of centrality "purports to measure
the degree of centralization of a graph," and this explica-
tion appears to be in line with the original intentions
(Bavelas, *op. cit.,* Leavitt, *op. cit.).* Sabidussi goes on to
reject what he calls the Bavelas index, F. Along with
Flament (*op. cit.,* p. 51) he finds it counter-intuitive that
the complete graph and the circle should have the same "centrality." He goes on to comment on the proposed index by
Beauchamp, B, but ends up recommending what we have called
unipolarity, V! In his final paragraph he notes with regret
the fact, counter-intuitive again, that the star and the complete graph should have the same "centrality." Viewed in the
context of the discussion above Sabidussi appears to confuse
all our three basic aspects of group structure. The Bavelas/
Leavitt index, F, is one of *centralization,* the Beauchamp index, B, one of *integration,* and the measure proposed by
Sabidussi, V, one of *unipolarity.* Little appears to be gained by either subsuming all of these three under a master concept of "centrality" or by adding a fourth concept.

REFERENCES

Bavelas, A. 1950. "Communication Patterns in Task-Oriented
    Groups," *Journal of the Acoustical Society of America,*
    XXII, reprinted in Cartwright, D. and A. Zander (eds.),
    Group Dynamics, New York, Harper and Row, 1960.

Beauchamp, M. A. 1965. "An Improved Index of Centrality,"
    Behavioral Science, X, pp. 161-163.

Brody, R. A. 1963. "Some Systematic Effects of the Spread
    of Nuclear Weapons Technology: A Study through Simula-
    tion of a Multi-Nuclear Future, *Journal of Conflict
    Resolution,"* VII, pp. 663-753.

Cartwright, D. 1960. "The Nature of Group Cohesiveness," in Cartwright, D. and A. Zander, (eds.) *Group Dynamics*, New York, Harper and Row.

Cartwright, D. and F. Harary. 1956. "Structural Balance: A Generalization of Heider's Theory," *Psychological Review*, LXIII, pp. 277-293.

Cohen, A. *et al.* 1961. "The Effects of Continued Practice on the Behaviors of Problem-Solving Groups," *Sociometry*, XXIV, pp. 416-431.

Coleman, J. 1964. *Introduction to Mathematical Sociology*, New York, Free Press.

Davis, J. A. 1967. "Clustering and Structural Balance in Di-graphs," *Human Relations*, XX, (May).

Festinger, L., S. Schachter and K. Back. 1963. *Social Pressures in Informal Groups*, Stanford, Stanford University Press.

Flament, C. 1963. *Applications of Graph Theory to Group Structure*, Englewood Cliffs, Prentice Hall.

Gleditsch, N. P. and T. Høivik. 1971. "Simulating Structural Parameters of Graphs," *Quality and Quantity*," V, pp. 224-227.

Guetzkow, H. and H. Simon. 1955. "The Impact of Certain Communication Nets in Task Oriented Groups," *Management Science*, I, pp. 233-250.

Harary, F., et al. 1965. *Structural Models*, New York, Wiley.

Høivik, T. 1969. *Parameters of Graph Structure*, unpublished *cand. real. thesis*, Oslo.

Leavitt, H. 1951. "Some Effects of Certain Communication Patterns on Group Performance," *The Journal of Abnormal and Social Psychology*," XLVI, pp. 38-50.

Loomis, C. and C. Proctor. 1951. "Sociometric Methods," in Festinger, L., et al., *Research Methods in Social Relations*, New York, Dryden Press, Chap. 17.

Newcomb, T. M.   1961.   *The Acquaintance Process,* New York,
    Holt.

Ore, O.   1962.   *Theory of Graphs,* American Mathematical
    Society Colloquium Publications, XXXVIII.

Sabidussi, G.   1966.   "The Centrality Index of a Graph,"
    Psychometrika, XXXI (December), pp. 581-603.

Waltz, K.   1967.   "The Politics of Peace," *International
    Studies Quarterly,"* XI, pp. 199-211.

8

On the Theory of Social Dependence

FRANTIŠEK CHARVÁT AND JAROSLAV KUČERA
Institute for Philosophy and Sociology, Prague

INTRODUCTION

It is quite clear that the category of dependence is of
basic significance for science and that any sort of scientific cognizance would be impossible without using it. In
the natural sciences, dependences take on the forms chiefly
of different natural laws. As a rule, a method is sought as
to how phenomenon a or the set of phenomena A depend on
phenomenon b or on the set of phenomena B. In this regard
certain social sciences, in particular empirical sociology
where the dependence between social phenomena acquires the
form for instance of correlational or other statistical relations, have taken over the use of the term dependence. We,
however, shall not employ the category of dependence in this
usual, natural scientific sense, i.e. in the sense of
dependence in general. It turns out that the content of the
term "dependence" in social phenomena can be given a much
richer content than is the case in its reduced form, where
it is limited to a mere quantitative or verbal statement of
the dependence of social phenomena under given conditions.
Dependence in its second meaning is chiefly social
structure or what we call relations. An investigation of
social dependences from this viewpoint is an important part
of relational sociology. Likewise, even the use of dependence in this sense is quite customary in most social sciences
and in purely practical fields. This is true especially of
politics, including its continuation by other means. In
this regard, however, the category of dependence, perhaps
because of its apparent elementariness and general

dissemination, has not been as yet subjected to almost any thorough analysis by the social sciences. Giving a particular name to what has long been unknown or changing its name in some way does not yet mean knowing it. It certainly does not mean the factual use of the given category to increase the gnoseological effect of the particular discipline.

The problem of analyzing the category of dependence was first raised by Czeslaw Znamierowski (1930, p. 106; 1957, p. 366). Znamierowski also carried out its elementary analysis. However, he did not link dependence with the information character of inter-human interaction nor did he use it later on. This was attempted only by M. Halouzek (1967) but from the standpoint of the theory of management--and he also indicated several possibilities for using the category of dependence by the other social sciences. Apart from this, throughout sociology as a whole one finds here and there statements which in their implicit form approach C. Znamierowski's position in particular.

We have in mind such statements as "every interaction contains a moment of sanction just as it does a moment of performance ... In a certain sense, every activity is a reaction to the actions of others and contains a sanctional moment of rewards and punishments applied to individual units ..." and so forth.

In addition to its theoretical significance for relational sociology, the category of dependence is of importance mainly for political sociology and partially even for the sociology of management. It has been shown that it makes it possible to explain such categories as power, authority, political relations, to better define a political and social system. In addition to this, it is also advantageous from the standpoint of a quantitative cognizance of certain social phenomena, from the viewpoint of making them more precise and so on. Before attempting to indicate the possibilities of using the category of dependence in sociology we are unable to avoid some general theoretical considerations.

Derivation of Dependence

We shall not relate dependence only to Man but also to groups of people, their institutions, and so on--generally speaking, to a given system S. We shall understand by this system every structured social object defined as an ordered pair, its internal and external structure. We regard as the internal structure of the system the set of interests of the system and set of relations between them; we think of the external structure as the set of elements of behavior of the system together with the set of relations between the elements of this behavior. The relation between the internal and external structure will start from the assumption that every activity of system S fulfills some aspect of its interests.

It is obvious that circumscribing the category of dependence will relate to both structures of the given system and that the character, preciseness and totality of the circumscription of the given dependence will stem from the character, preciseness and totality of the circumscribed internal and external structure of the given system. Furthermore, it is clear that the concept of dependence of two or more systems will explicitly figure as a component of behavior of given systems. Therefore, in the future we shall act as though, at least from the beginning, we did not know the internal structure of the system, that is to say we shall judge it only from the standpoint of observed behavior, i.e. the external structure of the given system.

If we indicate the given object A and the totality of all its activities as $(a_i)_1^n$, then the pair $\{A; (a_i)_1^n\}$ represents the system S_1 in our concept, i.e.

$$S_1 = \{A; (a_i)_1^n\},$$

analogously   (1)

$$S_2 = \{B; (b_i)_1^m\}.$$

The assumption that every activity of a_i of system S_1 fulfills an aspect of its activities is not in conflict with reality. In practice it would be difficult, in the case of an individual, to find an activity which is not guided by the endeavor to fulfill one or some of his interests. This is obvious in particular with an activity leading to the attainment of some sort of palpable creation, for instance a product by means of which a particular interest is fulfilled. We shall call this creation the result of activity although it is clear that this result is a means of realizing one's interest. Other activities lead to the attainment of less obvious results that might be arrived at, for example, by relevant changes in the milieu of system S. Finally, there exist activities whose results are not evident at all. These are the so-called "aimless activities," for

instance throwing stones into the water, or "aimlessly"
wandering through a town or the country-side. Yet these
activities also fulfill some kind of interest which is to be
found in their very execution. The above-mentioned activities fulfill a given interest directly, i.e., without re-
course to any evident result of the activity, or change in
the environment of system S. Thus, intuitively, we have
confirmed the validity of the assumption that every activity
fulfills some aspect of interest of system S. But not just
this alone. From the above-mentioned remarks it follows that
activity is actually the only primary means of fulfilling the
interests of system S, since various products and changes in
the environment of system S are in fact the result of this
activity. This assertion at the very outset makes it possible for us to abstract from the above-mentioned results
which makes our work easier and increases the general approach to the derivation of dependence. Later, however, we
shall take these results into consideration.

The endeavor to fulfill a certain interest as an element
of the internal structure of system S is visible in the
effort to fulfill a certain activity. We shall term this
endeavor to fulfill a certain activity the need to fulfill
a given activity of system S. It is of course evident that
a mere listing of the activities of system S does not fully
determine its behavior. This behavior is not only determined
by the needs of realizing individual activities of system S,
as an expression of its internal interest structure, but also
by the possibilities of realizing these activities which are
set by the environment of a given system, i.e., for instance,
by a system--or better said by the interests of a system--
manifesting itself again in activities, in which the requisite system S is included, of which it is a part. In this
regard, therefore, the behavior of system S depends on the
behavior of the system in which system S is included.

To make things more graphic, we can present the whole
matter in the following manner: If it is true that "every
human activity is directed to the satisfaction of an interest," in the case of an activity with obvious results it
means that this activity is established from the very viewpoint of the possibilities of the emergence of this result,
which is at the same time the means of realization of the
interest. If something happens to reduce or to completely
remove this possibility, the course of the activity must be
changed so that this possibility is created once again.
In the opposite instance the activity would not lead to the
emergence of the result and, thereby, to the satisfaction of

the interest. The course of activities changes in a similar fashion even in the event that something happens which increases the possibility of the emergence of its results, or brings it closer in time, and so on. In such a case, the course of an activity--for instance--is shortened in time, its intensity is altered, several phases of the original activity disappear, and so on.

The above-mentioned remarks apply, basically, even to "activity for activity's sake." In the case where some influence in the environment prevents or disturbs the course of this activity, either a substitute activity arises or the course of the original activity is changed. The same applies to an influence which contributes to the success of this activity. The general rule holds that the course of human activity changes either by direct intervention from the environment of this activity or by the influence of this environment on its results.

The result of the effect of negative, outside influences in such activity or its change, which resists such influences, and in the event of favorable influences is activity or its change using these influences to strengthen endeavors tending to the satisfaction of interests.

Entropy of the Behavior of the System and its Quantitative Expression

The needs of activities of $(a_i)_1^n$ of system $S_1 = \{A;$ $(a_i)_1^n\}$ are an expression of the internal structure of the system in relation to its activities by which the system manifests itself in its environment. The needs of activities as relational categories of the internal structure of the system and its behavior express the rate of realization of individual activities of the given system S_1. The needs of activities are in themselves qualitative categories but, on the other hand, they possess characteristics which make it possible to arrange them according to a hierarchy, to scale and, finally, to quantify them.

It is intuitively evident if we say about a certain-- possible--activity of a system that it is more necessary for the given system than a different activity. There can be different reasons for such a decision: for instance, existential reasons of the system, the strategy of the system in the environment of a higher system, external influences of the given system in the environment of a higher system, and so forth.

The aim of an analysis of the needs of activities is the projection of these activities onto a certain numerical domain which has the quality of good order. An analysis of the needs of activities can be the projection of these activities onto a certain numerical domain which has the $(a_i)_1^n$ for which the following applies:

$$\sum_1^n p(a_i) = 1; \qquad p \geqslant 0;$$

where p is a given function. At the same time, for instance, it shall hold that if activity a_j is more necessary than activity a_k of system S_1, $p(a_j) > p(a_k)$ is applicable, and vice versa. In other words: that sought-for abstract function represents the normed measure on the set of activities of a given system. An analysis of the needs of activities of system S_1, therefore, leads to a quantification of the set of activities of the given system.

Let us note, for the sake of a better illustration of the given procedure, that it is possible to understand the given process on the basis of probability, i.e., to understand the quantities $p(a_i)$, i = 1, ..., n as the probabilities of the realization of activities a_i, i = 1, ..., n by system S_1. Thus the value $p(a_i)$ means the probability that system S_1 will realize activity a_i.

The quantification of the set of activities of system S_1 leads to the quantification of the differentiated complex of activities; therefore, it cannot be understood as a process of creation of overall characteristics of system S_1. For that purpose, it is necessary to express precisely the concept of the so-called entropy of behavior of system S_1.

By the entropy of behavior of system S_1 we mean the overall qualitative characteristics of this system, expressing the orderliness or disorderliness of a set of activities of a given system on the basis of an analysis of the needs of these activities.

For the sake of a concrete definition of the entropy of behavior, it is necessary to express precisely what is understood by the concept of orderliness or disorderliness of a set of activities of a given system.

By *orderliness,* in this case, we understand the homogeneity of these activities from the viewpoint of their needs.
If the needs of activities of a given system are the same, we
can speak of a high degree of orderliness; if the need of one
of the activities of the system greatly exceeds the other
needs of activities, we can speak of a low degree or orderliness, or better said of a high degree of disorderliness of a
set of activities of a given system.

In this sense it is also useful to mention the category
of *discernibility of behavior of a system,* or its *indiscernibility.*

If a set of activities of a given system is on a high
level of orderliness, i.e., the needs of individual activities of the system are loose or even equal, then it is very
difficult to predict a priori what activity will be realized
by the given system; in other words we say that its behavior
is difficult to discern. On the contrary, if a set of activities of a given system is very disorderly, i.e., if the need
of one of the activities of the system prevails over the needs
of other activities, or even if the situation is such that the
given system will be compelled to realize a certain activity
which prevails from the viewpoint of needs, it will be possible to predict its behavior, a priori, easily; in other
words we speak of an easy discernibility of its behavior. Thus
it is possible to record the possible relations of the above-
mentioned categories graphically:

$$\text{orderliness} \sim \text{indiscernibility}$$

$$\text{disorderliness} \sim \text{discernibility}$$

The concepts of orderliness and indiscernibility, which
is to say disorderliness and discernibility, are, however, not
the same; they only correspond to one another. They express
the same situation in this sense, but whereas the category of
orderliness is a characteristic of the system and its internal
structure, the concept of indiscernibility is a relational
category of the internal structure of the system and its
observer; therefore it stands outside the system. The same
applies to the respective polar categories of disorderliness
and discernibility.

Entropy, as a category of orderliness or disorderliness,
as a matter of fact can be understood as a category of indiscernibility, which is to say discernibility as well. In
the case of this twofold possible interpretation of defining
the entropy of behavior of a system it is, however, necessary
to bear in mind the qualitative difference between the intervening categories. This difference may be illustrated by
Figure 1.

The quantification of activities, already carried out, of a given system on the basis of an analysis of the needs of these activities will be used for a quantitative projection of entropy.

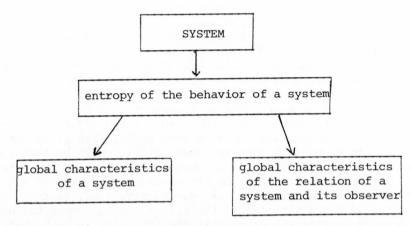

Figure 1

The *measure of entropy* which is also called inexact entropy, without running the risk of a misunderstanding, is defined as the so-called compound quantitative characteristics, i.e., the function of quantitative characteristics of activities of the given system. If we denote entropy, or the measure of entropy of behavior of a given system S_1, as $E(S_1)$, then the following applies:

$$E(S_1) = E(p(a_1), \ldots, p(a_n)), \text{ or in a simplified way:}$$

$$E(S_1) = E(p_1, \ldots, p_n), \text{ where } p(a_i) = p_i, \ i = 1, \ldots, n.$$

However, so that the measure of entropy of behavior of a given system can express the total properties of the internal structure of a system to a necessary and previously established extent, it is necessary to determine it axiomatically, so these axioms will express those required properties in an exact projection. These axioms are as follows:

1) $E(p_1, \ldots, p_n) \geqslant 0$, is connected in the domain

$$\sum_{i=1}^{n} p_i = 1, \ p_i \geqslant 0;$$

2) $E(1) = 0$, $E(\frac{1}{2}, \frac{1}{2}) = 1$;

3) $E(p_1, \ldots, p_{k-1}, 0, p_{k+1}, \ldots, p_n) =$

   $= E(p_1, \ldots, p_{k-1}, \ldots, p_{k+1}, \ldots, p_n)$;

4) $E(p_1, \ldots, q_{k1}, q_{k2}, \ldots, p_n) = E(p_1, \ldots, p_k, \ldots, p_n)$

$$+ p_k \cdot E \left(\frac{q_{k1}}{p_k}, \frac{q_{k2}}{p_k} \right),$$

where $q_{k1} + q_{k2} = p_k > 0$.

In this way we obtain the unitively defined measure of entropy of behavior of a given system:

$$E(S_1) = - \sum_{i=1}^{n} p(s_i) \log_2 p(a_i).$$

It has natural properties which follow from the axioms: the greater it is, the more indiscernible the behavior of the system from the viewpoint of the observer; and the more disorderly the set of activities of the system, the smaller it will be--in other words, the more discernible will be the behavior of the system from the viewpoint of the observer.

In our opinion, the concept of the entropy of behavior of social systems is an advantageous category not only for making precise the concept of dependence of two systems of a social totality of a given system. Due to the fact that it mirrors the internal structure of a system onto the behavior of this system, it is an important complementary characteristic explaining the given phenomenon in its totality. This fact can be illustrated by Figure 2.

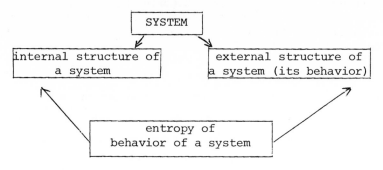

Figure 2

In our opinion, the introduction of the concept of the entropy of the behavior of systems of a social totality can be developed in many ways: for instance, it is certainly justified to consider the entropy of behavior of systems as the measure of freedom of its decision-making, as the measure of stability of its internal structure, and therefore to transfer this concept into the cognitive sphere of political science.

Relations of Dependence of the System on Its Environment

All our considerations have so far concerned the study of one system of social totality, both as its internal structure and its external structure. It is, however, evident from reality (and particularly from social reality) that every system is a part of another higher type of system. Every system that includes the system we have studied as its subsystem is called the *environment of the studied system*. It is the very fact that every system has its environment-- i.e., some principle of systemized permanence--that leads us directly to the definition of the category of dependence of the system on its environment, which is to say of dependences of two systems of a social totality.

It is necessary to make more precise the process of the so-called analysis of possibilities of activities of a given system in its environment to arrive at a concept of the dependence of a system.

The possibilities of activities of $(a_i)_1^n$ of system $S_1 = \{A; (a_i)_1^n\}$ are expressed in the internal structure of the system in relation to its activities, i.e., in relation to the behavior of the system, by which the system manifests itself in its environment. The possibilities of activities in themselves are qualitative categories but, on the other hand, they possess characteristics which enable the given activity, in relation to the environment of the system, to be hierarchized, scaled and, finally, quantified. Let us assume further, to illustrate this, that the environment of system S_1 is the creation of system S_2. By the possibilities of activities of $(a_i)_1^n$ of system S_1, in relation to its environment, i.e. in relation to system S_2, we understand the possibilities of fulfilling the activities of system S_1 by this system on the assumption of the fulfilment of each of the activities of system S_2 by this system. This means an analysis of the possibilities of activities of system S_1 with a view to system S_2 means an analysis of all the possibilities of activity of a_i on the assumption that the activities of b_k, $k = 1, \ldots, m$, $i = 1, \ldots, n$ occur (that they will be realized), which means an analysis of the entire $m \cdot n$ potentially possible situations.

Intuitively it is obvious that the realization of activities a_k by system S_1, assuming that the activities of b_v were fulfilled by system S_2, is more possible than the realization of activities a_p by system S_1, assuming that the activities of b_q were realized by system S_2.

There can be many reasons for this: for instance the situation in a higher system in which both these intervening systems find themselves, the political-strategic relations of systems S_1 and S_2, and so forth. The purpose of an analysis of the possibilities of activities is the projection of a Cartesian product of activities of systems S_1 and S_2 onto a given numerical domain that has the quality of a good order. One can understand the analysis of the possibilities as assigning an abstract function to sets

$$a_1/b_1; \ldots; a_1/b_m$$

$$a_2/b_1; \ldots; a_2/b_m$$

.
.
.

$$a_n/b_1; \ldots; a_n/b_m$$

for which the following applies:

$$\sum_{i=1}^{n} p(a_i|b_k) = 1 \qquad \text{for each } k = 1, \ldots, m; \; p \geqslant 0$$

where p is a given function.

At the same time, if for instance it is true that the realization of activities of a_k, on the assumption of the fulfillment of activities of b_v, is more likely than the realization of activities of a_p, on the assumption of the realization of activities of b_q, then $p(a_k|b_q) > p(a_p|b_q)$

and the reverse. For greater clarity of the given approach,
let it be said that it is possible to understand the given
process as one of probability and understand the quantity
$p(a_i|b_k)$ as a conditional probability of activities of a_i
assuming the realization of activities of b_k.

Now we can move on to the task of making more precise
the concept of dependence of system S_1 on system S_2, or
better said, on its environment.

We say that system S_1 is dependent on system S_2 if a
need for at least one activity of this system is different
from its possibilities, with a view to system S_2.

On the qualitative side, the dependence of system S_1 on
system S_2 means that at least one activity a_k, $k = 1, \ldots, n$
of system S_1 applies, that there exists at least one
activity b_v, $v = 1, \ldots, m$ so that the following applies:

$$p(a_k) \neq p(a_k|b_v). \qquad (2)$$

The fact that system S_1 is dependent on system S_2 is
indicated as follows

$$S_2 \to S_1 . \qquad (3)$$

The concept of dependence of system S_1 on system S_2 is therefore a relational category of the external structure of
system S_1 with a view to the external structure of system S_2.

The situation can be illustrated by Figure 3.

If $S_2 \to S_1$ is applicable to two social systems then
system S_1 is called a *hegemony system of dependence* $S_2 \to S_1$
and system S_2 is called a *dependent system of dependence*
$S_2 \to S_1$.

It is evident from this graph that the relation of
dependence can be separated from the entropy of
the hegemony system of dependence $S_2 \to S_1$, i.e. from the
internal structure of the hegemony system of dependence

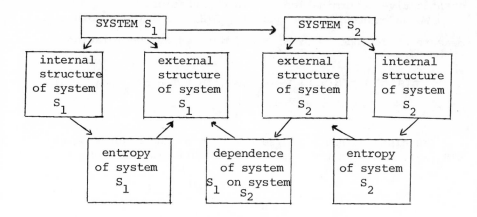

Figure 3

$S_2 \rightarrow S_1$ to a dependence of systems, or to the external structure of the dependent system. It is necessary to realize
this fact, since it will be important when constructing the
quantitative characteristics of dependence $S_2 \rightarrow S_1$. For the
dependence of $S_2 \rightarrow S_1$ an important creative component is the
entropy of the hegemony system of the given system of dependence, because it is natural to assume that the more the
behavior of the hegemony system is indiscernible, the greater
the given dependence will be, and vice versa.

In reality: for instance, if the behavior of the hegemony system is unambiguously predictable, then the situation
for the dependent system is much more favorable, its dependence on the behavior of the hegemony system is less than in
the case where the behavior of the hegemony system would be
more indiscernible. It is necessary therefore to assume that
for the quantitative characteristics of the dependence of
$S_2 \rightarrow S_1$, the function of the entropy of the hegemony system
of given dependence and further, of quantitative characteristics, will be acquired by an analysis of the possibilities
of activity of system S_1 with a view to system S_2, i.e. the
value of $p(a_i | b_k)$, where $i = 1, \ldots, n; k = 1, \ldots, m$. We
should now rightly go on to circumscribing the given quantitative characteristics axiomatically but, in view of the
length of this chapter, we shall limit ourselves only to their

quantitative determination and interpretation.

We understand by the quantity $D(S_2 \to S_1)$ the absolute measure of dependence of $S_2 \to S_1$, defined by the relation:

$$D(S_2 \to S_1) = E(S_2) + \sum_{i,k=1}^{n} p(b_k) \cdot p(a_i|b_k) \cdot \log_2 p(b_k|b_i). \quad (4)$$

We also designate the second term on the right side as $E(S_2|S_1)$, while at the same time the following applies:

$$p(b_k|a_i) = \frac{p(b_k) \cdot p(a_i|b_k)}{\sum_{e=1}^{n} p(b_e) \cdot p(a_i|b_e)}.$$

In abbreviated form, the measure of dependence of $S_2 \to S_1$ can be written in the form of:

$$D(S_2 \to S_1) = E(S_2) - E(S_2|S_1).$$

However, we introduce still further the so-called normal measure of dependence by the relation

$$D_n(S_2 \to S_1) = \frac{D(S_2 \to S_1)}{E(S_2)}). \quad (5)$$

The normed measure of dependence of $S_2 \to S_1$ will be the basic characteristic of the given dependence. It has the following properties:

a) It is equal to zero if system S_1 is not dependent on system S_2, which means relation (2) does not apply to any activity of a_k and b_k.

b) It is equal to 1 (maximum value) if the given dependence is maximal, i.e. any realization of the activity a_k of system S_1 is unambiguously determined by the behavior of system S_2, i.e., by the realization of a certain aspect of its activity.

c) Apart from these extreme types of values, the above-mentioned quantitative characteristic acquires values between 0 and 1 which, naturally, scale the degree of dependence of the systems.

We believe that the category of dependence of both systems or, better said, the theory of dependence of social systems can be further developed in many ways. For example, if we regard the intervening systems of dependence as components of the higher system, then we can regard their dependence as a means of describing the internal structure of this higher type of systems.

In other words, the bases of the dependence structures are the possibilities of influencing the satisfaction of interests. The possibilities of satisfying interests are created and changed by means of changes in their bearers which are the means of the realization of interests. The essence of dependence structures is manifested in the dependence of the behavior of mutually dependent systems. Dependent systems, by their very dependence, are forced to adopt a certain behavior.

All the behavior of a given social object, however, cannot exhaust dependence, and for the same reasons the established system cannot fully contain all the properties of the object. As we have already said, the character, preciseness and content of the given dependence is determined by the manner in which the system is introduced to the given social object. This system, as we know, is always introduced so that it meets the research interest of the solver. In practice, we are far from aware of all the dependences.

Just like an infant who gradually learns to respect the laws of gravity, without being able to describe them mathematically, a person can respect a given dependence without ever knowing or being able to describe it. Various systems and various individuals (for instance, workers in colonies and owners in metropolitan countries) are in mutual economic dependences without ever knowing each other or having seen one another. In view of the existence of the division of labor, dependences in society very often have many aspects and are complicated matters. Everyone, in some way, is dependent on others.

Dependent relations have the character of some sort of "information channel" through which information "flows." Its connection to the theory of information is very close. We regard as information every news item or signal that influences our decision-making; it goes without saying that we attribute information significance particularly to that news, to its parts and signals that apparently spread dependent relations. The soldier listens to the instructions of his superior because he is dependent on him. News (which only potentially contains information and does not yet influence our decision-making) becomes information influencing our decisions at the point when this news touches upon the satisfaction of our interests. "Attributing information significance" need not have a conscious character. A person reacts to a number of signals quite automatically.

From what has been said above it follows that influences affecting the means of realizing interests are one of the influences of basic dependences. In other words, changes in these cause changes in dependences, and changes in dependences in turn cause changes in people's behavior. In this regard, the movement of things causes the movement of people. This is, therefore, the explanation of K. Marx's well-known thesis.

Basically Szczepański calls the means of realizing needs "the platform of social relations" (viz J. S. "Základní sociologické pojmy," Czech ed.). Of course, Szczepański regards as the aforesaid platform also attitudes, interests, and so on. Szczepański obviously regards this "platform" as the subject of social relations. Without going further into the question of the platform, it can be said that, in the sense of our concept, we can regard it as:

 a) activity with an evident result,
 b) activity for activity's sake,
 c) the result of activity.

As has already been shown, changes in all these factors cause changes in the corresponding dependences and thereupon even in the behavior of dependent systems.

The factor that most often causes changes in the course of a given activity--whether this be in activity for activity's sake or in activity creating, for instance, a particular product--is information. The fact that information reduces the ambiguousness of activity causing changes in its course is also a factor of change in the quantity of dependence. At the same time, information can change dependence by acting directly on the criterial function of a person or institution or by the existence of more criterial functions causing changes in the order of their importance. In other words, it intensifies or weakens the intensity of interests or changes their order. The relevant relation is that with the growth in amount of information of a dependent system its dependence on the hegemony system is reduced.

2. DEPENDENCE AS A SOCIAL FORCE

Up until now we have approached dependence mainly be-
havioristically, i.e. as though we did not know the internal
interest structure of the social object under investigation.
Because we can judge this structure from the behavior of the
investigated object, or recognize it in a higher system
through the possibility of activities of the lower system--
which is a part of it--we sometimes know sufficiently well in
practice the internal interest structure of the investigated
object. In such an instance, we can modify our entire approach.
We can judge dependence, which is a relational category between behaviors, i.e., the external structure of any given
systems, directly from the internal interest structure because the external structure, i.e., behavior, is its form of
expression, because it realizes the internal interest structure. This approach is in fact only a special instance of an
approach which examines social dependence with the aid of the
conditional entropy of the hegemony system. In certain instances the forces of dependent structures, particularly in
management or political practice, are more suitable for practical experimentation and for empirical ascertainment.

From what has been said above it follows that from the
viewpoint of a certain relatively distant analogy we can regard dependence as some sort of "force" which compels a
dependent system to act in a certain way or to be changed. To
what will this force, acting on system S_1, be proportionate?

This force will obviously be proportionate chiefly to
the size of the possible sanction, i.e., activities contradictory to the hegemony system in the event that it becomes such
an activity of system S_1 which is directed against the interests of the hegemony system S_2 or against the instructions of

system S_2. This sanction might be, for example, brought on by

the loss of profit caused by an incorrect action in the poor
sale of the goods (for instance, a too high or too low price,
poor quality of the goods, the influence of competition, and
so on) or activities directed against stronger competition,
and so forth. Through this sanction, the offender might be
condemned to jail or morally condemned for a criminal act,
and so on.

A similar "reward" might be a profit on the market or
social recognition for a noble deed, an increase in pay, and
so forth, in the event that the activity of the dependent
system S_1 is in conformity with the interests and activities

of the hegemony system S_2. Dependence should therefore be in proportion to the "sanction" or "reward."

It turns out that this "force" should be proportionate to the likelihood that a sanction or a reward occurs in the above-mentioned instances. But, for example, in order to jail a criminal we must first catch him. Finally, this "force" should be in proportion to the value of the utility function of the relevant individual or system--some sort of "balance" of his interests.[1]

In the event of an individual's dependence, we would have to know his utility function and the subjective probability of sanctions or rewards. This is difficult to ascertain among individuals but less difficult, for instance, with economic institutions where these functions for the most part are measurable, for instance profit, rentability, and so forth. Naturally, not all utility functions can be expressed here in mathematical formulae, in financial units. Likewise, in such systems--as the State--it is easier to recognize, for instance, foreign policy, military, economic and power interests, and express them by utility functions better than for individuals. This is made possible by the circumstance that the foregoing systems, in contrast to individuals, can be observed "from the inside." Given sufficiently large systems and sufficiently long time intervals, we can count on objective probabilities and with a certain objective comparative utility function. Under certain conditions, the individual utility function in sufficiently long time intervals comes closer to certain "social" functions, just as subjective probability draws closer to objective probabilities.

For confirmation of the above-mentioned statement we can carry out the following experiment. Let us take for example ten independent economic units, say enterprises led by managing directors. At the head of these enterprises, let us say, is a board of management with a general manager. First we must determine among these ten managing directors the agenda of their working day over a longer period of time. We discover, for instance, that current operative matters (taking

---

[1]A subject of the so-called theory of utility is the problem of the creation of special quantitative characteristics which, in a certain way, would express the "utility" of elements of behavior of the object under investigation. The utility function basically is the projection of an ordered set of interests of a given object into a given mathematical space. It gives us the measure of utility or, in our instance, the measure of interest. In contemporary science, the theory of utility can be classified among the mathematical approaches to economics.

care of complaints, fulfilling operative orders from the managing director, and so on) takes up 20 per cent of the time, that meritorious activities (planning, work on the enterprise's future improving the organization of the enterprise, and so on) takes up 60 per cent,and 20 per cent is left for the training of subordinates. At the same time we must discover what the probabilities are of sanctions for non-fulfillment of operative orders (concerning, for example, certain minor matters) of the general manager and what sanctions are imposed on discovery of serious shortcomings, for instance in the organization of work, in the enterprise's future program, in the quality of the subordinates, and so on. At the same time we must, in both cases, find the relevant probabilities. Thus, for example, if we learn that the sanction for 30 unfulfilled operative orders of the general manager is the loss of job as managing director, the probability of non-fulfillment of an order is 0.95. The same sanction is imposed for discovering serious shortcomings in working out an enterprise's future program, but the fact that this could happen in the time interval covered by the time interval for discovering the non-fulfillment of 30 operative orders is hardly likely. The relevant probability is, let us say, equal to 0.01.

Then all we need is to multiply the number of operative orders,and we need a detailed control by the general manager. After a certain time we learn that the agenda of the working day of the managing director has changed. For instance, he devotes 60 per cent to operative matters, 30 per cent to meritorious activities and 10 per cent to training others. Why?

In both instances the sanction is approximately the same or at least close, given the same time interval, but in the event of operative orders there is a much greater probability of this sanction. In the event of operative orders there exists a much greater dependence which compels the managing director to act in a certain way.

Apart from the lesson we learn, consisting in the superior allowing his subordinate to "interfere" ("take a hand") in the work as little as possible, this example is further evidence that dependence really resembles a "force" impelling us to act in a certain way. Similar evidence of dependence as a force can be found even in spheres of international political and economic relations or in the field of property relations and elsewhere. The concept of the dependence of one country on another is, in this sense, absolutely classical. We know,in particular, of cases of the dependence of

developing countries on the delivery of foodstuffs from
countries which have an oversupply of these, we know of instances of dependence on the delivery of raw materials   or
military technique, and also of credits, technical aid, the
aid of experts,and so on. Curtailment or stopping these
deliveries and aid would mean a sanction, increasing and
making more effective the delivery of aid would mean a reward. Extreme instances of sanction or reward can be the
threat or aid of military force. The whole system of dependence stemming from the above-mentioned sanctions or rewards compels the dependent country to support the policy of
the hegemony countries (see,for instance,the relation of the
U.S.A. and the countries of Latin America in the United
Nations Organization), to adopt certain positions in the
solution of international disputes, and not only this. Very
often it even compels the adoption of disadvantageous economic programs,disadvantageous trade, disadvantageous prices,
and so forth. Economic dependence can be used to bring on
certain political talks, and,of course,political dependence
can be used to impel certain economic discussions.

All the above-mentioned dependences compel the dependent
State or coalition to behave in a certain way which,for the
above-mentioned reasons,is relatively easy to predict. The
behavior of a State in this case distantly recalls "the behavior of a body" whose size and direction is dependent on
the size and direction of the force.

As has already been pointed out, the dependent system
must react to the information of the hegemony system and
guide itself by this information. Its behavior must be in
conformity with the aforesaid dependence and can, with
certain probability, be anticipated. But what is "anticipated behavior" which is attuned to the behavior of other
persons or systems, which *depends* on the behavior of other
persons or systems? This is how sociology usually explains
a role. Thus, dependence is a relation which curtails the
set of possible roles of systems S_1 and S_2.

The size of this set is clearly in proportion to the
force of the dependence. At maximum dependence it contains
only one role. This sentence can also be understood as
dependence,as a force which compels us to enter into certain
roles or to leave them and to take on different roles and,
of course, to fulfill these roles. In other words, dependence curtails the variety of the dependent system.

For these reasons, dependence clearly enables us to predict, to a certain extent, human behavior. The example that
dependence compels us to take up a role, which enables the

prediction of our behavior, is the example of the managing directors who by a change in the dependence relations were compelled to change the order of their activities. This corresponds to the oft-repeated affirmation of sociologists that the "performance of every role contains within itself an element of sanction and an element of reward."

Together with the entry into a certain role, even the entropy of human action is reduced or the actions of a dependent system.

This behavior is predictable, describable, and is directed to the realization of a certain interest. But it should be added that, at the same time, the entropy of the hegemony system is also reduced since it, too, enters a role, that is the role of a hegemony system. And the interest to whose satisfaction a certain role is directed becomes more concrete, contains information about the means of its realization, becomes a less ambiguous state. This information which removes ambiguousness (information is even measured by the reduction of entropy of decision-making of a given society) transfers dependence structures which are, at the same time, informational structures.

The above-mentioned ideas satisfactorily correspond to the modern findings of social psychology included, in particular, under the theory of instincts. In connection with the well-known theory of R. E. Park that "man is born human but becomes human in the process of learning," we of course find the significance of dependence in that dependence compels a person to enter a role and to master it. Roles are basic elements in the processes of the socialization of man which are, in fact, a mechanism for the mastery of these roles.

Entering a role whose fulfillment is directed to the realization of a more concrete interest, containing the element of experience, means a reduction in the entropy of the internal and external structures (behavior) of the relevant individual or system. In the event of the internal structure of an individual this means that the process of mastering a certain role is, at the same time, a process during which we gain a certain experience as an important element of interest. Thus, mastering certain roles is likewise a process of the emergence of certain interests. The structure of mastering roles must, of course, correspond to the interest structure of the individual.

One of the examples, in this regard, is the existence of various social groups, including social classes. Classes and groups, in fact, are nothing but special subsystems of the role of the social system which the given individual was forced to enter by certain dependences, for instance by proprietary relations. In the case of social classes, the same character of dependence, particularly the proprietary dependences, compel various individuals to enter the roles of the same character, limit their place within the social system, and even curtail their class position. The mastering of these roles, which often lasts for whole generations, then leads to the emergence of certain interests, of a certain ideology which distinguishes the members of the class or social group from other classes or groups--in addition to their place in the social structure. The interests and ideology of certain classes and groups continue to exist even after a change in their place in the structure of the "social dependence field," as long as after the change occurs in their place in the social structure of society they do not yet master their new roles and therefore there has been no emergence of new interests and new ideologies. From this viewpoint, ideology appears as the projection of the interest area of a certain class into the area of phenomena of social reality. It is a certain optics by which a given social subject looks at social reality.

In this regard, the interest structure appears as the altered reflection of a structure of mastered roles in the consciousness of individuals. All the changes in this reflection relate back to the activities of the individual and not just to the individual because they are the basis of changes of the criterial utility functions of his decision-making processes. Ideology stems from interests which express, which decide on their order; it is a certain axiomatic apparatus of their order. It is the standpoint by which the social subject evaluates society, the world and his position in the world and in society. Interests which are the basis of ideology then stem from the real position of the social subject in society, which follow from the dependence that compelled him to occupy this position. Thus the central significance of dependence for the structure of all the above-mentioned phenomena is completely evident.

From the connections described above it follows that a person actually is "changed by the system of roles which he has mastered." This is only a somewhat different way of expressing Marx's idea: "The human substance is no abstract idea belonging to each individual. In its essence, it is the totality of social relations." (Marx and Engels, 1968, p. 419.)

This "changed or altered system of roles," or interest
structure of the individual (and not only the individual)
can, in the course of development, lag behind the development
of the external structure of roles which external dependence
compels individuals to enter. There can exist time incon-
formities and other contradictions between the development
of both structures. Although the external structure of dependences—and their corresponding roles with regard to the
individual—is decisive, we must assume a relative independence of its internal interest structure, its peripherally
relative independent changes and its relatively independent
"internal" development which need not correspond in all matters to the external one.

This relative independence of the internal interest
structure can be a source of anti-dependence discussion.

The above-mentioned discussion excludes the kind of discussion forced on us by dependence and is directed against
the relevant dependence. A further source of it might even
be conflicts in the external structure of dependence or, most
often, a combination of both reasons. Anti-dependence discussion is basically the same thing as sociology calls conflict. As G. Simmel, the author of the theory of conflict,
shows, even conflict is a form of socialization which is, at
the same time, the central idea of his main work "Conflict."

Apart from a certain correspondence between the internal
interest structure and the external structure of roles
"linked" to relevant dependences, there also exists a conflict or antagonism between both structures that keeps crop-
ping up. This antagonism is resolved by anti-dependence
discussions or by conflict. It is clear that the constant
solution of the afore-mentioned antagonism leads to direct
changes in the interest structure and in the structure of
dependences which relates to the internal interest structure.
This corresponds fully to Simmel's concept of conflict as a
"form of socialization."

Further Possibilities of Using the Category of Dependence

From what has been said before it follows that dependence is, in fact, the discrepancy between the possibilities
and needs of a certain activity of a given social object
which is solved by the fulfillment of its relevant role.
That is to say, dependence is a cause of human action. At
the same time, it is also its result. The deviation of a
possibility of a given action from its needs comes about,
in the final analysis, as the result of a given action and,

if this deviation occurs, then the dependence "happens," too. Through his conscious and unconscious actions, a human being continuously changes his possibility of realizing certain activities and thereby also the possibility of the realization of an interest and, finally, creates completely new possibilities and interests. Thus he changes the properties of a general dependence field or something that we might call "social space." The activity that most prominently encroaches upon the properties of a general dependent field and limits its basic property is, in the broadest sense of the word, production. Politics, too, encroaches on these properties in its endeavor to direct society by means of changes in dependences. In dependence changes, the actions and direction of social activities must also change. That is to say, dependence evokes action and action evokes dependence. Social movement cannot be explained in any other way except by social movement. Society can change and move thanks to the fact that, within it, there is a constant emergence and disappearance of deviations of needs from the possibilities of realization of given activities and thereby also of interests, that, within it, there is a constant renewal of antagonisms between possibilities and needs, that certain dependences are constantly coming into being and dying out. The history of mankind is actually the history of inter-human dependences.

Sociology, however, finds itself in the same or similar state as pre-Newton physics. This physics was able to describe an enormous amount of the most varied interactions but it lacked the principle to explain these interactions, to enable it to make a comparison between them, to measure them and thereby to transpose them into some sort of common denominator. Newton's principle of force became the common denominator along with, of course, other laws of Newton. The above-mentioned analogy is, however, quite remote and too different, qualitatively, for us to seek a comparison between it and the social sciences, at least at this stage. It should serve rather as an illustration. But the idea of a common denominator, at least for a certain fairly large area of social phenomena, is not entirely out of place. Certain properties of the category of dependence which we have tried to explain, particularly their universality and the possibilities of their all-around development, predestine them to this role, or so it would seem to date at least in certain social sciences—i.e., certainly in sociology and politology.

Sociology, however, often operates very freely with such concepts as "dimension" or "space" or "field," and so forth, which have their origin in mathematics or physics. Evidently, these concepts are not completely useless as far as sociology is concerned. The term "social space" which we have already mentioned, could really be of considerable significance for the future development of sociological theory. The category of dependence could then play a role, in defining this space, of some sort of "social distance," or, in the event of metrical social space, the role of a metrics of this space. It stands to reason that we need not define social space merely metrically but only as a given topological space.

Let us therefore assume that an element of social space is any possible role which, in this space, can be taken on by any social object. At the same time it is clear that the social object can, correspondingly or in the course of a short time interval, fulfill more than one role. We shall then define a role as a certain part of its resulting behavior which is determined by the mutual interaction of parts of the needs of its activities and the possibilities corresponding to it in the frame of the given social space. Thus, every role corresponds to a given dependence. Every behavior of a social object is then fixed by a set of roles which it occupies in social space, together with the set of dependent relations that are pertinent to it. This description, however, can never be complete as far as the social object is concerned, which is why we also contemplate a relevant social system that we introduce into a social object and project onto a relevant social space.

We introduce the social space in the following manner: Elements of this space form systems on objects of social reality (in this, however, we assume that one single system is fixed for every object of social reality, a system given by our gnostical intention or the frontier of our gnostical possibilities). Given certain meritorious sociological assumptions, we can equip this set of systems on objects of social reality with a structure of metric space or, in other words, introduce such a function on the Cartesian product of a given set of systems that fulfills certain conditions. Added to this, however, we must introduce certain--and in our opinion--justified assumptions about social dependence:

1. Let us assume that the given system is independent, that is "zero dependent" on the object of social reality, only on itself (two different systems are always dependent).

2. If system S_1 is dependent on system S_2, then system S_2 is equally dependent on system S_1 ("equally" = the same measure of dependence).

249

3. If system S_3 is dependent on system S_1, then the dependence of S_3 upon S_1 is not reduced by "inserting" system S_2 into the dependence relation between systems S_3 and S_1.[2]

Thus these assumptions can be written in the following manner:

$1'$: $D(S_2 \to S_1) = 0 \Longleftrightarrow S_2 = S_1$,

$2'$: $D(S_2 \to S_1) = D(S_1 \to S_2)$.

$3'$: $D(S_1 \to S_3) \not> D(S_1 \to S_2) + D(S_2 \to S_3)$

Under these conditions, the metrics can be introduced to the given set by the following formula:

$$\rho(S_1, S_2) = D(S_2 \to S_1) = D(S_1 \to S_2).$$

These metrics fulfill the pertinent properties, i.e.

$$\rho(S_1, S_2) = 0 \Longleftrightarrow S_1 = S_2,$$

$$\rho(S_1, S_2) = \rho(S_2, S_1),$$

$$\rho(S_1, S_2) + \rho(S_2^{g-}, S_3) \geqslant \rho(S_1, S_3)$$

(see definition of measure of dependence (4)).

We call the set of systems on the object of social reality, together with such metrics social space (special) social space with a dependent structure) and we designate it as (ϕ, ρ).

---

[2] The term "insertion of system S_2 into the dependence relation between systems S_1 and S_3" implies that the dependence of systems S_1 and S_3 is not analyzed directly (by confronting the activities of systems S_1 and S_3) but through the mediation of system S_2 (which is dependent on S_1 and hegemonic in relation to S_3).

Conceivably, the above-mentioned assumptions will not represent the real situation in each case: it is evidently necessary to consider even such types of social spaces where, e.g., the assumption 3) is not fulfilled (i.e., a particular case of a "curved" dependence social space). This is also why our account is to be regarded as one of the possible and apparently most simple types.[3]

Every social object A which we understand as system $S_1 = \{A; (a_i)_1^n\}$ is characterized by the needs for realization of individual activities which are the manifestation of its internal structure. Every role, as an element of social space, is then characterized by dependence with a view to other roles, or its "social distance." Then for every system S_1 the following applies:

a) The reason for the action of system S_1 is the difference between the needs for realization of its activities and their possibilities with a view to other systems appearing as the dependence of system S_1 on these systems. (6)

b) System S_1 has a tendency to continue in such roles or to enter such roles which minimize its dependence on other systems and maximize the dependence of these systems on system S_1. (7)

c) Dependence as a deviation of the needs of realization of activities of system S_1 from their possibilities (with a view to the environment) comes about: (i) if these possibilities change, as an expression of change in properties of social space, or (ii) with a view to the needs of activities of S_1, as an expression of the change of its internal interest structure; or (iii) if both change. (8)

Sentence (6) actually defines dependence once again and bares it as the reason of action from the viewpoint of system

---

[3]Let us point out that the "construction" of the given social space substantially depends on the selection of investigated activities of the system under consideration, i.e., elements of the given social space.

S_1. As we have already indicated, the dependence of system S_1 can at the same time be the result of action of another system. This is, in fact, something like a "principle of force." The first part of the sentence (7) which shows the general tendencies of movement of system S_1 towards a minimization of its dependence and is therefore something like a "principle of inertia," actually implies its second part. Under the set of roles of minimal dependence, the set of roles of social space is always smaller than the number of interested social objects. With the entry of certain objects into these roles, it follows that other objects do not enter. For instance, to prevent system S_1 from entering a role professing to be of minimal dependence as compared to other roles, it must--with the aid of dependence--be compelled, for instance, by system S_2 to enter another role, i.e., a role of greater dependence. This, of course, gives rise to conflict.

> From this point of view, conflict is nothing but an
> endeavor to transform the needs of the realization
> of activities of one system into the possibilities of
> realization of the activities of another system. (9)

For instance, the dependent system (but it need not necessarily be the dependent system) can work for a change in its needs to realize activities within the possibilities of the realization of activities of the hegemony system, i.e., transform the entire dependence situation. Conflict is therefore a kind of anti-dependence action. It is one of the paths of minimizing dependence or changing its meaning.

In such a connection one can counter that conflict action is also action, that it must be caused by dependences. How is it possible, one can ask, that it is anti-dependence action? This apparent discrepancy can be solved in several ways. In the first place, the relevant dependence against which the conflict is directed and which, for instance, has an institutionalized form, need not correspond in reality to the real possibility of the hegemony system to guide the behavior of the dependent system; on the contrary, in the dependent system there can arise new possibilities to begin to direct the behavior of the hegemony system.

> In other words, the cause of action against a given de-
> pendence can be either changes and differences within
> itself, or most often in some other dependence. (10)

252

Sentence (8) links the behavior of system S_1 with the properties of its social behavior. It is a kind of principle of social relativity. Dependence actually occurs only on the basis of the above-mentioned deviation of needs of the activity of system S_1 from their possibilities, with regard to the environment. At the same time, it makes no difference if the properties of the environment change, i.e., the social space, or if the properties of the relevant system change as a result of changes in its internal interest structure. Thus, so-called social change is nothing but every change of those components manifesting themselves in a change of size, structure, sense and character of the dependences, and thereby, naturally, in the relevant actions, in the relevant structure of the roles, and so forth.

Constant change of dependences is among the basic properties of social space. It is, in fact, space whose "distance" continuously changes, whose properties are subject to constant change; is is actually space in which, as a result of these changes, social laws are also subject to change. All these changes, very likely, are subject to or are guided by certain laws of a higher order. In many ways, social space resembles the so-called non-Euclidean space whose properties are determined, for instance, by the disintegration of matter in the universe. Just as light does not diffuse lineally in such space, so information in social space is also not diffused "lineally." Its currents are often crooked, deformed and often get lost somewhere. Streams of information follow the line of dependent structures and intersect in roles of a sort of minimal entropy. Various arrangements of these roles then represent kinds of "world lines" of social space which determine their basic properties, just as Einstein's world lines determine the properties of various spaces in the universe. Social objects have a tendency to minimize the distance of their roles from these "social world lines."

Authority, Power and the Political System

The *raison d'être* for the all-round use of the category of dependence is proved, inter alia, by the possibility of using it to define authority and power. It is clear, for instance, that if an officer wishes to direct the actions of a soldier then that soldier must follow the officer's instructions, which means he must be dependent on him. This is true of any manipulation with people, with their groups and institutions. If we agree that power rests in the possibilities of leading or manipulating people and their groups, then its base must be the dependence of the led on the one or ones who lead them. Nevertheless, dependence and power are not one and the same thing. In a general instance of dependence, neither the hegemony nor the dependent system may be aware of their mutual dependence relations. In the case of power, however, at least the dependent system must be aware of this dependence and guide its behavior accordingly.

The hegemony system, in the general instance, need not as yet register its relevant dependence and consciously gain something from it by directing the behavior of the dependent system. That is why, in the case of power, we speak of the possibility of leading, that is of the possibility which must not as yet be used. In practice, however, there are very few cases where the hegemony system is unaware of the dependence of the dependent system on itself. We shall probably not err very greatly if we define power in the following manner.

Power is the possibility that the hegemony system has to direct (or lead) the behavior of the dependent system (or more than one dependent system) on the basis of dependence of which, at least, the dependent system is aware.

In practice, as we have already pointed out, usually both systems are aware of this dependence. We can therefore say that the power of the hegemony system over the dependent system is recognized by the possibility the hegemony system has to guide the behavior of the dependent one on the basis of dependence of which the dependent system is aware. In practice, power is combined with the threat of sanctions in the event of not carrying out instructions given by the hegemony system. At the same time sanctions mean, in fact, a reduction if not a complete loss of the possibility of the dependent system realizing its own interests. It is, in fact, a real reduction of the possibility of realizing a certain activity of the dependent system (or its loss) below the level of needs of their realization. In the case of $S_2 \rightarrow S_1$, concretely, this means the realization of a situation where:

$$p(a_k) > p(a_k|b_v).$$

In the event of power, the deviation of realization of a given activity by the dependent system from its possibility—in view of the hegemony system—is negative and corresponds to sanctions.

In view of the fact that dependence is defined for the case where $p(a_k); \neq p(a_k|b_v)$, a situation can occur where $p(a_k) < p(a_k|b_v)$. Now the above-mentioned deviation is positive and represents the "reward" mentioned previously. Instead of the hegemony system using the possibility of directing the behavior of the dependent system through "sanctions," it directs it by "rewards," i.e., it actually offers it greater opportunities to realize its interests than the dependent system originally wanted, "it helps it"; it contributes to the satisfaction of its interests. This relationship is the basis of authority of the hegemony system with regard to the dependent system.

The authority of the hegemony system with regard to the dependent one is, once again, the possibility of leading the dependent system on the basis of dependence, based on a positive deviation from the needs of realization of a certain activity of system S_1 from the possibility of realizing this activity with a view to the hegemony system, which at least the dependent one is aware of and most often, in fact, both systems realize.[4]

Since authority and power are only opposite sides of one and the same dependence, one can be transformed into the other, one can generate the other. We shall therefore assume that authority is a form of power. As for quantification, measuring the size of authority and power, we can use the apparatus formed previously for the measure of dependence.

As we know, power is a basic logical category in political analysis. On the basis of our definition of power, we can define a political system which is a subsystem of a social system. We shall circumscribe the political system

---

[4] In both instances, i.e., the case of authority and power, we reckon the deviation from the viewpoint of the dependent system. This means that we choose as the basis the needs of realization of activities and, from this point, we decide as to the positive or negative deviation marks. This approach was chosen because it is more illustrative with regard to the intelligibility of the concept of sanction and reward which we apply to the dependent system. In the general instance of dependence of $S_2 \rightarrow S_1$, we, of course, choose as the basis the hegemony system, i.e., the possibility of realization of the activities of the dependent system with a view to the hegemony one.

as an ordered pair of an internal and external power structure of a given society.

We regard as an internal structure, for instance, the
legal pattern of a given society, particularly its constitution, which is nothing but a certain set of dependence relations. Additionally, the curtailment of certain real
mechanisms and elements of a given political system, the
relations between them--for instance, subjects of political
power, political parties, pressure groups, curtailing the
mechanisms for the choice of subjects of political power and
for the execution of this power.

We think of the external structure, for example, as the
legal-political pattern of a given society with a view to
its environment. This concerns, in particular, the system
of State agreements and obligations, demographic and geographic dependence, certain economic dependences, furthermore, the curtailment of the real mechanisms for the creation and realization of international dependences of the
most varied kinds.

Politics as the behavior of such a curtailed political
system of a given society can then be understood as the unity
of the process of creation and execution of power. This
curtailed political system and politics is, however, very
general, perhaps the most extensive that can be imagined.
It can be argued that the political structure of a given
society cannot be identified with its power structure,
just as you cannot identify political power with any kind of
power.

It will therefore be best to think of the term politics
in the narrow sense of the word. From this point of view,
we shall regard politics as purposive activity consisting in
the unity of dependent and anti-dependent action (conflict)
by the aid of which a given subject causes changes in dependent relations and thus directs the behavior of a given
social system or subsystem. All changes in dependences also
bring about, as we know, changes in the behavior of the
system that holds these dependences "together." Thus
politics consists in directing society by means of changes in
dependence relations carried out as an aid to the dependence,
as conflict or as anti-dependent action.

By what means can these changes be carried out?

a) By direct changes in the possibilities of realizing the activities of members of society. For instance,
through legal changes, by other curtailment of activities, by
banning or allowing them, by electoral victories or defeats,
by personnel policy, and so forth.

b) By changes in the means of realization of inter-
ests--i.e., indirectly. This can cover the realization of a
given investment or technical policy, and armaments policy,
in short,of all material and non-material factors that are
the bearers of the possibility of realization of interests
and,in their own way, also a platform of social relationships.

c) By affecting the internal interest structure,
for instance, the arrangement of the utility functions of
people, their ideology,and so forth. We would include in
this propaganda, ideological stress, education, and so on.
If the arrangement of human interests changes,then the dependence and, thereupon, the action must also change.

Insofar as these classical means of politics--which
basically are, in the main, the effect of the means of in-
formation--do not suffice to change or to retain the relevant dependence relations, then there is a resort to force
which is "the continuation of politics by other means." If
we are unable to change the dependence relations through
political means,we change them through war or revolution.
In other words, the continuation of politics by other means
does not mean only war but also revolution, counter-
revolution, armed coups d'état, and so on. If, for instance,
a certain class or group cannot attain changes in its
position in society, i.e., changes of dependence, through
classical political means, it continues its endeavors to
bring about a change of dependence with the aid of force and
violence. The same is true of a situation in which this
group cannot retain its position merely by classical political means. In a similar manner, if,for instance,a colonial
power cannot make a certain country economically and politi-
cally dependent on it through political means, if the conditions are favorable,it resorts to conquest through war.

In contrast to other types of power, political power is
a kind of power which makes possible a change in other dependence structures. The political system, in the narrow
sense of the word, is then curtailed this way by an ordered
pair of the internal and external structure of power. This
is true of power structures of a given society which make
it possible to change purposely other dependence structures in
the given society, or to work for the retention of other
dependence structures.

REFERENCES

Halouzek, M. 1967. "Funkční analýza clověka ve společnosti, in M. Halouzek (ed.), Věda a řízení společnosti. Praha: Svoboda.

Marx, K. and F. Engels. 1968. *Vybrané spisy*. Praha.

Znamierowski, Czeslaw. 1930. *Prolegomena do nauki o panstwie*. Poznán.

Znamierowski, Czeslaw. 1957. *Océny i normy*. Warszawa.

II

Design, Measurement, and Classification

9

Representation, Randomization, and Control [*]

LESLIE KISH

The University of Michigan

1. INTRODUCTION

Like the art of politics, statistical design always involves compromises of the desirable with the possible. Compromises are inevitable in the structure, scope and size of research. These compromises result in gaps between observed data and desired knowledge. Scientific inference is our attempt to bridge these gaps, and statistical inference is an important aspect of that attempt.

For an example consider designs for comparing the relative effectiveness of several techniques of instruction in classrooms. First, compromises are made in the choice of *realistic* explanatory variables: the predictor and the predictand variables. Defining and operationalizing the predictor variables, the several instructional treatments, will pose difficulties. We must operationalize and control teaching techniques; also assure satisfactory teachers, and appropriate materials and psychological situations. Even greater difficulties and compromises may be involved in choosing and operationalizing the predictand variables, the criteria of effectiveness. Must we accept simple tests, or opinions? Or attitudes of students? Or success in subsequent classrooms? Or can we undertake to measure eventual "real" lifetime achievement?

───────────

[*] Writing supported by grant GS-3191X from the National Science Foundation. Sections 1-4 are based in part on an earlier (1959) article by the author.

Second, the scientific rigor of designing and controlling the treatments involve further difficulties, and call for ingenuity and compromises. Can we undertake true *randomization* of individual students? Or, more likely, classes? Or entire schools? And can we obtain rigorous controls and uncontaminated measurements?

Third, choice of the target population, the *representative* selection of sampling units, and the inferences from sample to population also result in compromises. What ages and types of students shall we include? Shall we be satisfied with a city or a province? Or shall we aim for a national sample? Or even international comparisons?

This example exhibits the difficulties of satisfying the three criteria of research design discussed later: realism, randomization, and representation. Yet those difficulties are even greater in many other tasks now facing social research--such as evaluating the long-range effects of poverty, or of welfare policies. Severe compromises must usually be made within and between the three kinds of criteria and difficulties. Placing primary emphasis on the first, or second, or third kinds of problems tends to result respectively in controlled investigations, or in experiments, or in sample surveys, as defined and discussed in section 4.

2. FOUR CLASSES OF VARIABLES[1]

(E) *The explanatory variables,* sometimes called experimental variables, are the objects of the research design. They are the variables among which the researcher wishes to find and to measure some specified relationships. The potential relationships connect two sets of variables: the *predictand variables,* or "dependent" variables comprise the predicted effects; and the *predictor variables,* or "independent" variables are the sought causes of the relationships.

---

[1] "The statistician cannot evade the responsibility for understanding the processes he applies or recommends. My immediate point is that the questions involved can be disassociated from all that is strictly technical in the statistician's craft, and when so detached, are questions only of the right use of human reasoning powers, with which all intelligent people, who hope to be intelligible, are equally concerned, and on which the statistician, as such, speaks with no special authority. The statistician cannot excuse himself from the duty of getting his head clear on the principles of scientific inference, but equally no other thinking man can avoid a like obligation." (Fisher 1953, p. 1).

The researcher designates the explanatory variables that comprise the aims of the research on the basis of substantive scientific theories. He recognizes the existence of other sources of variation, and he needs to separate these extraneous variables from the explanatory variables. Sorting all extraneous sources of variation into three classes seems to me a useful simplification. Furthermore, no confusion need result from talking about sorting and treating "variables," instead of "sources of variation." The explanatory variables embody the aims of the research, and the other *three classes are extraneous to those aims.*

(C) *Controlled variables* consist of those extraneous variables that can be controlled by the research design. The control may be exercised in either the selection or the estimation procedures, or perhaps in both. The aims of controlling variables may be to decrease the effects of random error (Class R), or to decrease the biasing effects of disturbing variables (Class D), or both.

(D) *Disturbing variables* are uncontrolled extraneous variables which may be confounded with the explanatory variables (Class E). Failure to remove all of these into the Class C of controlled variables is the primary concern of non-experimental designs.

(R) *Randomized variables* are uncontrolled extraneous variables which are treated as random errors. In "ideal" experiments, discussed below, they are actually randomized, but in surveys and investigations they are only assumed to be randomized. Randomization may be regarded either as a form of experimental control or as a substitute for it.

The aim of efficient design is to place into Class C of controlled variables as much of the extraneous disturbing variables as appears feasible, practical and economical. However, it is not practical to control more than a few of the potentially disturbing extraneous variables. The aim of randomization in experiments is to place all of class D variables into class R. In the "ideal" experiment there are no variables left in class D; all extraneous variables have been either controlled in class C or randomized in class R. By placing disturbing variables into class C we eliminate the effects they would have in class R. Biases due to class D are eliminated, though random errors are left in class R.

In nonexperimental research (in surveys and investigations), controls must do double duty. They increase efficiency by reducing the errors from class R variables, as they would in true experiments. However, without randomization we cannot completely eliminate disturbing variables from class D. To the extent that we fail to control them in class

C, nor randomize them in class R, they remain confounded with unknown biasing effects on the explanatory variables of class E. Hence the crucial function of controls becomes the reduction of those biasing effects.

3. STATISTICAL TESTS

With this term I refer here briefly and collectively to statistical measures of random variability, whether tests of significance, or confidence intervals, or fiducial or credible intervals, or whatever. The function of statistical tests is to distinguish, at determined levels of probability, the effects of Class E variables from the random effects of Class R variables. In "ideal" experiments (discussed later) this separation is accomplished through randomization of all extraneous variables in Class R, except those controlled in Class C, and with no disturbing variables left in Class D.

However, in nonexperimental research the explanatory variables of Class E are confounded with disturbing variables of Class D. Thus statistical tests actually contrast the effects of the random errors of Class R against the explanatory variables of Class E confounded with unknown effects of Class D variables. For this reason the control and segregation of disturbing variables into Class C becomes doubly important in nonexperimental research. Control decreases random errors here also, but more importantly it decreases the possible biasing effects of disturbing variables on the explanatory variables.

Suppose, for example, that in a study of schools a criterion variable y appears to be related to predictor variable x. The criterion may define test abilities or later occupational success, or only student attitudes and satisfactions. The predictors may measure the nature of instruction, or class organization in the schools. Suppose for simplicity that when schools are sorted into types A and B according to the predictor x, type A schools have a higher average of the criterion of success y than type B schools have. The difference in success may be denoted as $(\bar{y}_a - \bar{y}_b)$.

But there also is variation in success between schools within the types, and a statistical test is conducted to measure the effect of that variability; it is often measured with the standard error, or [ste $(\bar{y}_a - \bar{y}_b)$]. A statistical test can show whether the difference $(\bar{y}_a - \bar{y}_b)$ between the two types of schools should be reasonably considered as a chance occurrence when compared against the measure of random variability

denoted by [ste $(\bar{y}_a - \bar{y}_b)$]. If the difference $(\bar{y}_a - \bar{y}_b)$ appears large ("significant"), we conclude that the difference
between the two types is not due to the random errors of
Class R variables.

If the assignment of schools to types A and B is randomized, a "significantly" large difference $(\bar{y}_a - \bar{y}_b)$ can be
reasonably attributed to the effects of the two types A and
B, of randomized treatments. However, in nonexperimental
research, in surveys and investigations, the treatment types
are not assigned at random. Hence, the difference $(\bar{y}_a - \bar{y}_b)$,
when found to be beyond random variability, cannot be clearly
and directly attributed to the difference between the two
types of treatments defined by predictor variables. Disturbing variables of Class D may be confounded with the defined treatments. For example, the salary of teachers and
the socio-economic level of students may also differ between
the two types; these differences may account for some or all
the difference $(\bar{y}_a - \bar{y}_b)$.

The researcher may try to remove the effects of disturbing variables with diverse methods of control (section
5). Those attempts at controlling for Class D variables can
be followed with further statistical tests. The separation
of Class E from Class D variables should be determined in
accord with the nature of hypotheses with which the researcher is concerned. But that separation is beyond the
functions and capacities of statistical tests. Their function is not explanation; they cannot point to causation.
Their function is to ask: "Is there anything in the data
that *needs* explaining? Is the difference (or relationship)
great enough to place confidence in the result? Or con-
trarily, may the latter be merely a chance happenstance of
the specific sample on which the test was made?"--and to
answer those questions with a designated probability.

It is incorrect to allege that "tests of statistical
significance are inapplicable to nonexperimental research."[2]

---

[2] This allegation was clearly expressed by Selvin (1957):
"The basic difficulty in design is that sociologists are unable to randomize their uncontrolled variables, so that the
difference between "experimental" and "control" groups (or
their analogs in nonexperimental situations) are a mixture
of the effects of the variables being studied and the uncontrolled variables or correlated biases. Since there is no
way of knowing, in general, the sizes of these correlated

It is true and inconvenient that Class E explanatory variables are confounded with Class D disturbing variables. Nevertheless statistical tests can be used to separate the effects of Class R random variables from them.

Statistical tests of significance have definite functions, and those functions are limited. Their limitations should be emphasized against their common misuse for measuring the strengths of relationships between explanatory variables. The results of tests of significance are functions not only of the magnitudes of relations but also of the numbers of sampling units used, and of the efficiency of design. In small samples meaningful results may fail to appear "statistically significant," whereas in large samples the most insignificant relationships can appear "statistically significant."

The word "significance" conveys a sense of importance, of meaning, in common parlance; its use in "statistical significance" amounts to a statistical pun whose effects are confusing.

Tests of significance are particularly ineffective as they are commonly used in social research: to test null hypotheses of zero difference, or null relationships. Such hypotheses are trivial reflections of the actual aims of social research. Independence between social variables hardly ever exists, and is seldom even approached. If we have a large sample or a complete census on our tapes, we can almost always find the relationship between any two variables to be greater than zero. This is a consequence of the highly multivariate and complex interrelationships of social

---

biases and their directions, there is no point asking for the probability that the observed differences could have been produced by random errors. The place for significance tests is after all relevant correlated biases have been controlled ...In design and in interpretation, in principle and in practice, tests of statistical significance are inapplicable in nonexperimental research."

In a criticism, McGinnis (1958) shows that the separation of explanatory from extraneous variables depends on the type of hypothesis at which the research is aimed. See also Kish (1959): "The control of all relevant variables is a goal seldom even approached in practice. To postpone to that distant goal all statistical tests illustrates that often the perfect is the enemy of the good"...*In this sense,* not only tests of significance, but any comparisons, any scientific inquiry other than the "ideal" experiment would be "inapplicable." Such defeatism is indeed advocated by enemies of the social sciences.

variables.[3]

4. EXPERIMENTS, SURVEYS, AND OTHER INVESTIGATIONS

Until now, the theory of sample surveys has been developed chiefly to provide descriptive statistics--especially estimates of means, proportions and totals. On the other hand, experimental designs have been used primarily to find explanatory variables in the analytical search of data. In many fields, however, including the social sciences, survey data must be used frequently as the analytical tools in the search for explanatory variables. Furthermore, in some research situations, neither experiments nor sample surveys are practical, and other investigations are utilized.

By "experiments" I mean here "ideal" experiments in which all the extraneous variables have been randomized. By "surveys" (or sample surveys), I mean probability samples in which all members of a defined population have a known positive probability of selection into the sample. By "investigations" (or "other investigations"), I mean the collection of data--with care, and often with considerable control-- without either the randomization of experiments or the probability sampling of surveys. The difference between experiments, surveys, and investigations are not the consequences of statistical analysis; they result from different methods for introducing the variables and for selecting the population elements (subjects).

---

[3] "Usually quantitive estimates and fiducial limits are required. Tests of significance are preliminary and ancillary. "The emphasis on tests of significance, and the consideration of the results of each experiment in isolation, have had the unfortunate consequence that scientific workers have often regarded the execution of a test of significance on an experiment as the ultimate objective. Results are significant or not significant and this is the end of it." (Yates, 1951)

"Null hypotheses of no difference are usually known to be false before the data are collected; when they are, their rejection or acceptance simply reflects the size of the sample and the power of the test, and is not a contribution to science." (Savage, 1957)

"For presenting research results statistical estimation is more frequently appropriate than tests of significance...Too much of social research is planned an presented in terms of the mere existence of some relationship." (Kish, 1959)

In considering the larger ends of any scientific research, only part of the total means required for inference
can be brought under objective and firm control; other parts
must be left to more or less vague and subjective--however
skillful--judgment. The scientist seeks to maximize the
first part, and thus to minimize the second. In assessing
the ends, the costs, and the feasible means, he makes a
strategic choice of methods. He is faced with three basic
problems of scientific research: control, representation,
and measurement.

Experiments are strong on control through randomization;
but they are weak on representation, and often on the realism, "naturalism" of measurements. Surveys are strong on
representation, but they are often weak on control. Investigations are weak on control and often on representation;
their use is due frequently to convenience or low cost, and
sometimes to the need for realism of measurements in "natural
settings." We are faced with conflict between randomization,
representation, and realism.

Experiments have three chief advantages: 1) Through
randomization of extraneous variables biases from disturbing
variables (Class D) are eliminated. 2) Control over the introduction and variation of the predictor variables clari-
fies the direction and nature of causation from predictor to
predictand variables. In contrast, for correlations found in
surveys that direction is not clear.[4] 3) The modern design
of experiments allows for great flexibility, efficiency, and
powerful statistical manipulation, whereas the analytical use
of survey data presents difficult statistical problems.

The advantages of the experiment method are so well
known that we need not dwell on them here. It is considered
the scientific method par excellence--when feasible. In many
situations experiments are not feasible, and this is often
the case in the social sciences. Yet it is a mistake to use
these situations to separate the social from the physical and
biological sciences. Such situations also occur frequently

---

[4] My earlier [1959] article gave several references dealing
with inferring causation from correlation, especially with
"path coefficients" in economics and genetics. Since then a
sizable literature on the topic has grown up in sociology,
especially by H. M. Blalock, R. Boudon, O. D. Duncan, D. R.
Heise, K. C. Land; see the collections in Blalock (1971) and
Goldberger and Duncan (1973).

in the physical sciences (in meteorology, astronomy, geology), the biological sciences, medicine, and elsewhere.

The experimental method also has some shortcomings. First, it is often difficult to choose the "control" variables so as to exclude all the disturbing extraneous variables; that is, it may be difficult or impossible to design an "ideal" experiment. Many of the initial successes reported about mental therapy, which later turn into vain hopes, may be due to the hopeful effects of any new treatment in contrast with the background of neglect. George Bernard Shaw, in the preface to "The Doctor's Dilemma," writes: "Not until attention has been effectually substituted for neglect as a general rule, will the statistics begin to show the merits of the particular methods of attention adopted."

Thus, the advantages of experiments over surveys in permitting better control of treatments, are only relative, not absolute. The design of proper experimental controls is not automatic; it is an art requiring scientific knowledge and foresight in planning the experiment, and hindsight in interpreting the results. Nevertheless, the distinction in control between experiments and surveys is real and considerable. To emphasize this distinction we refer here to "ideal" experiments in which the control of biases from disturbing variables is complete.[5]

Second, it is generally difficult to design experiments so as to represent a specified important population. In

---

[5] In actual experiments the "ideal" is not reached easily, hence the distinction between all experimental and nonexperimental research is not absolute. Troubles with experimental controls misled even the great Pavlov into believing temporarily that he had proof of the inheritance of an acquired ability to learn: "In an informal statement made at the time of the Thirteenth International Physiological Congress, Boston, August, 1929, Pavlov explained that in checking up these experiments it was found that the apparent improvement in the ability to learn on the part of successive generations of mice was really due to an improvement in the ability to teach on the part of the experimenter" (Greenberg 1929, p. 327). Nevertheless the distinction is real and worthwhile. Hence Sir Austin Bradford Hill overstates his good case by saying: "the difficulties of experiments are no less," when discussing the difficulties of observational studies (in Cochran, 1965).

fact, the questions of sampling, of the *representation* of specified populations in experimental results, have been largely ignored in experimental design. Both in theory and in practice, experimental research has often neglected the basic truth that causal systems, the distributions of rela-tions--like the distributions of characteristics--exists only within specified universes. The statistical inferences derived from the experimental testing of several treatments are restricted to the population(s) included in the experi-mental design.

Third, for many research aims, especially in the social sciences, contriving the desired *realism* of a "natural set-ting" for the measurements is not feasible in experimental designs. Hence, social experiments sometimes give answers to questions that have only vague meanings. That is, arti-ficially contrived experimental variables may have only a tenuous relationship to the variables the researcher would like to investigate.

The second and third weaknesses of experiments point to the advantages of surveys. Not only do probability samples permit clear statistical inferences to defined populations, but the measurements can often be made in the "natural set-tings" of actual populations. Thus in practical research situations the experimental method, like the survey method, has its distinct problems and drawbacks as well as its ad-vantages.

In social research, in preference in both surveys and experiments, frequently some design of controlled investiga-tion is chosen--for reasons of cost, or feasibility, or to preserve the desired realism of the measurements. Ingenious adaptations of experimental designs have been contrived for these controlled investigations. The statistical framework and analysis of experimental designs are used, but not the randomization of true experiments. Great ingenuity is often used in these designs to provide flexibility, efficiency, and especially some control over the extraneous variables.

Controlled investigations are of a great variety and have many names: observational studies, controlled observa-tions, quasi-experiments, natural experiments, and so on. I prefer not to borrow the prestige word "experiment" for studies where the predictors are not randomized. Controlled investigations and sample surveys are not merely second-class experiments; they have their own justifications.

In practice we usually lack the resources to overcome all difficulties, thus to achieve the simultaneous perfec-tion of realism of measurement, randomization to control treatments, and representation of the desired population.

If we cannot satisfy all these three criteria: Is one of them always more crucial that we must have above and before all other considerations? I disagree with those who prefer a hierarchy among these criteria--although the aggregate of their separate partisans could add to a majority. I believe that there is no supercriterion for a unique, overall, and ubiquitous selection among the three criteria. Rather, one must choose and compromise; we must choose a research strategy to fit our resources to the situation. In any specific situation one method may be better or more practical than the other; but there is no overall superiority in all situations for any of the three methods. Understanding the advantages and weaknesses of each should lead to better choices. Furthermore, some great research problems need to be attacked separately with two or all three methods.[6]

Each of the three kinds of design can be improved with efforts to overcome their specific weaknesses. Because the chief weakness of surveys is lack of control over treatments, survey researchers should improve their collection and use of auxiliary variables as controls against disturbing variables. They should become alert to social changes to measure the effects of "natural experiments." They should more often utilize efficient analytical techniques.

On the other hand, experiments and controlled investigations can often be improved with efforts to specify their populations more clearly, and to make their results more representative of the population. Often more can and should be done to broaden the base of statistical inference to wider and more significant populations. Researchers too often and too early commit themselves to small, convenient, or captive populations. Too often the researcher justifies those restrictions as attempts to make his subjects more "homogeneous"; if common sense will not dispel this error, reading Fisher may.[7] The researcher should view the population base

_____

[6] These anti-hierchical views on strategy are in partial disagreement with some of the best writing on controlling variables in social experiments and investigations by Campbell (1957), Campbell and Stanley (1963).

[7] "We have seen that the factorial arrangement possesses two advantages over experiments involving only single factors: (i) Greater *efficiency,* in that these factors are evaluated with the same precision by means of only a quarter of the number of observations that would otherwise be necessary; and (ii) Greater *comprehensiveness* in that, in addition to the 4 effects of single factors, their 11 possible interactions

in terms of cost factors and components of variation; then broaden the base of statistical inference as much as his resources allow.

5. CONTROL OF DISTURBING VARIABLES

Disturbing variables may be: a) controlled, or b) left uncontrolled, or c) subjected to tests to determine whether they should be controlled or left uncontrolled (Cochran, 1965, section 3).

Some potentially disturbing variables may be assumed so important--because of past experience, or because of *a priori* theoretical considerations--that their control is undertaken without preliminary tests of their effects on the actual research results. However, it is not practical to consider controlling for all possibly disturbing extraneous variables. On the contrary, anyone with the slightest ingenuity can conjure up, especially in nonexperimental situations, a long list of variables, which may conceivably have some disturbing effect on the explanatory variables. However, practical and economic considerations force the researcher to confine controls to a small number of variables. Choice of a few key variables become a crucial aspect of his research design. Rather than being satisfied with the first few that suggest themselves immediately, he should draw up a longer list, then choose those that appear most important.

---

are evaluated. There is a third advantage which while less obvious than the former two, has an important bearing upon the utility of the experimental results in their practical application. This is that any conclusion, such as that it is advantageous to increase the quantity of a given ingredient, has a wider inductive basis when inferred from an experiment in which the quantities of other ingredients have been varied, than it would have from any amount of experimentation, in which these had been kept strictly constant. The exact standardization of experimental conditions, which is often thoughtlessly advocated as a panacea, always carries with it the real disadvantage that a highly standardized experiment supplies direct information only in respect to the narrow range of conditions achieved by standardization. Standardization, therefore, weakens rather than strengthens our ground for inferring a like result, when, as is invariably the case in practice, these conditions are somewhat varied." (Fisher, 1953, p. 99.)

272

Part of the strategy consists of spreading the few choices widely among variables not highly related to each other. This strategy resembles the choice of predictor variables in regressions, and of stratifying variables in surveys. It is also related to philosophical ideas of Popper's "falsifiability" (Salmon, 1967).

Reasons for leaving potentially disturbing variables uncontrolled are of four kinds, often leaving us far from complete control of all relevant, potentially disturbing variables.

1. Some may be intentionally omitted for the strategic, practical, and economic reasons mentioned above.

2. There may be others the researcher would like to control, but for which data are unavailable and unobtainable. The costs of obtaining the necessary measurements are beyond the resources of the research project. They may be honestly and sorrowfully admitted as desirable controls for future research.

3. Many more are simply overlooked, ignored, unknown, because of our limited knowledge of the field. This obvious *caveat* about the limitations of controls for disturbing variables should not be forgotten from our list of reasons for omissions.

4. Some variables may be deliberately included with the predictor variables although their inclusion there is subject to doubt and explanation.

The last statement leads naturally to a brief consideration of the strategy of controls. Such discussions often arise in judging empirical research results. Suppose that we consider again our example of comparing techniques of classroom teaching. Should the qualifications, attitudes, and motivations of teachers be considered jointly with the techniques, as its necessary implementation? Or, on the contrary, are they to be considered as disturbing variables whose effects we want to control, separate and measure? What about classroom sizes and organization? Similar questions about predictor and disturbing variables arise in most actual situations. Variables in research seldom present themselves as obvious, pure, unidimensional variables--like mass and time in physics. They are more likely to be vectors, combinations of several variables that may be potentially separated--either actually (operationally) or conceptually. They may be treated jointly as single variables, due to the restrictions of the research situation. The definition of the predictor variables may include some variables which may in another context be considered disturbing variables.

273

Let us now discuss several methods for controlling disturbing variables. For simplicity we may think of the difference $(\bar{y}_a - \bar{y}_b)$ of the means for the predictand variable computed for two treatments (a and b), or two levels, or two categories of the predictor variable. This is a simple relationship of predictand and predictor; but the methods of control can also be used for more complex measures: comparisons of several pedictor means, ratios of means, regression lines, and other measures of relationships. The discussion here is concerned with nonexperimental research; it would be wasteful to include experimental research for which a vast literature exists.

   O. *Separate analysis in subclasses* is the most obvious method of control. The sample is separated in subclasses of the disturbing variable, and the relationship $(\bar{y}_{ai} - \bar{y}_{bi})$ is computed in each subclass (i). Studying these relations separately through *inspection* and *introspection* is perhaps the most common procedure. A degenerate case of the above is *control by restriction* to a single subclass: to avoid effects of a disturbing variable the researcher deliberately restricts his research to a single subclass of the variable. Such restrictions may be justified if imposed by stringent economic demands, and if it brings commensurate savings. But the penalty is often a drastic narrowing of the inferential scope of the research.[8]

   Control through separate subclass analysis is most common, and it leads to methods for uncovering more complex relationships.[9] However, such control evades the task of yielding a single combined estimate of the relationship $(\bar{y}_a - \bar{y}_b)$, which the following five methods yield. It should be clear that the formation of subclasses can be, and often is, done simultaneously with several disturbing

---

[8]See again the argument in footnote 7. Exceptions may be found: Physical and chemical constants specify highly standardized materials and conditions; then in applications allowance must be made for imperfect standardization. In social research such standardization is neither practicable nor desirable.

[9]A large literature exists for these methods, and is rapidly growing. See Moser and Kalton (1971), Hyman (1955) and Rosenberg (1968).

variables, leading to combined control of the effects of several disturbing variables, and of their interactions.

1. *Selection of matched units.* The two categories, *a* and *b*, of the predictor variables establish two subpopulations to be compared. Similar subclasses are formed in both subpopulations in accord with appropriate divisions of control variables. One unit is selected at random from each subclass for both categories. The difference $d_i = (y_{ai} - y_{bi})$ in the i-th subclass becomes the basis of the statistical test. The method can be extended to three or more subpopulations (a, b, c ...). The subclasses i usually follow several control variables. Matching becomes difficult when the reservoirs of units within subclasses is not great, and when the distributions of the two categories within subclasses differs greatly. Then judicious and parallel (a and b) combinations of subclasses may become necessary; this may be accompanied with parallel divisions of other subclasses to achieve the desired number of subclasses equal to the desired number of sample units. The procedure can become wasteful in numbers of units discarded, and in the required effort (Freedman & Hawley, 1949). It may be useful when one of the categories is rare (at the extreme, one in each subclass) and the other category is plentiful, and easy to classify and to subject to selection. The advantage of this method comes from the extreme amount of control it presumably provides.

2. *Selection of matched subclasses.* With this method the same number ($n_{ai} = n_{bi} = n_i$) of units is selected from the i-th subclass for both categories a and b (or for more categories). Thus matched units is the special case when $n_i = 1$ for all subclasses and for both categories. For a fixed number of sample units the second method requires fewer subclasses, hence less effort, but provides decreased control. A mixture of the two methods would match $n_{ai} = 1$ (or $n_{ai} = k' < k$) from the rarer, or more expensive class, and $n_{bi} = k$ from the other.

The n_i to be selected from the subclasses becomes a matter of design and strategy. With $n_i = k$, a constant, the analysis may be easier. On the other hand a varying and proportionate n_i may better approximate the distribution of a target population of our inference. Further, optimal allocation may be attempted when unit costs and variances vary greatly between subclasses. Nevertheless the convenience of

275

constant n_i = k may be restored, yet the target population approximated, with judicious splitting of subclasses to represent the target population. This may be accomplished often because there may be a great deal of arbitrariness in the formation of subclasses.

3. *Standardization or adjustment of subclasses.* In contrast to the above two methods of matching by selection, here all the n_{ai} and n_{bi} units are retained; instead we equalize the categories a and b within subclasses by using common weights W_i for both. Thus we compute $\Sigma W_i (\bar{y}_{ai} - \bar{y}_{bi})$ for the combined estimate of the difference, where $\Sigma W_i = 1$.

Matching by selection is wasteful of the reservoir of units and of the effort required for selection. Equalization by weighting requires more computation and more complex handling, but this difficulty becomes less awesome with advances in computer technology. Another disadvantage is that the weighted estimates tend to have higher variances than a similar number $n = \Sigma_i (n_{ai} + n_{bi})$ units would have from matched selections. This is often a serious loss; Table 5.1 gives estimates of the relative losses for different ranges 1 to W of relative sizes of weights. Here uniform distributions of frequencies are assumed; a fuller treatment of losses from weights is available elsewhere (Kish, 1974).

W_{max}	1.5	2	3	4	5	10	20	50	100
L continuous	.014	.04	.10	.16	.21	.41	.66	1.04	1.35
L discrete	.042	.12	.22	.30	.37	.61	.89	1.30	1.62

Table 5.1 – Relative Loss (L) for Different Ranges 1 to W_{max} from Uniform Distributions, Continuous and Discrete, of Relative Weights.
e.g. 5 classes, each of size 1/5, and weights 1, 2, 3, 4, 5, has variance 1.37 greater than equal weights (1,1,1,1,1), when these are optimal.

Neither disadvantage—increased variance per sample unit, and increased complexity of computation—is very serious in many situations. I believe that weighted combined results should be more often computed and presented in social research—as they have been in economics and demography. This would be a valuable addition to the usual presentation and reading of research results, with mere inspection of separate analyses in subclasses, as in method (0) above.

Now we come to the question of what should the weights W_i be. The answer is often not clear, and this a common psychological obstacle to its use. Fortunately it may not be a crucial aspect of the analysis. Begin with the separately weighted means $\bar{y}_a = \Sigma_i w_{ai} \bar{y}_{ai} = \Sigma n_{ai} \bar{y}_{ai} / \Sigma n_{ai}$ and $\bar{y}_b = \Sigma_i w_{bi} \bar{y}_{bi} = \Sigma n_{bi} \bar{y}_{bi} / \Sigma n_{bi}$. Often the weights of one category may appear as obvious weights, so that we compute $\Sigma w_{ai} (\bar{y}_{ai} - \bar{y}_{bi})$. Sometimes their average, $(w_{ai} + w_{bi})/2$ or $\sqrt{n_{ai} n_{bi}} / \Sigma \sqrt{n_{ai} n_{bi}}$ may seem more reasonable; but more often the weights W_i of a "standard" population seem better than either. The literature of index numbers in economics may provide clues (or see Kitagawa, 1964).

If we want to minimize the variance of $\Sigma W_i (\bar{y}_{ai} - \bar{y}_{bi})$, the weights W_i can be chosen to be inversely proportional to their variances: make W_i proportional to $1/(\sigma^2_{ai}/n_{ai} + \sigma^2_{bi}/n_{bi})$. When the unit variances are approximately equal, W_i is proportional to $n_{ai} n_{bi} / (n_{ai} + n_{bi})$ (Kalton, 1968; Keyfitz, 1953).

Fortunately, whether we use one set of weights or another usually makes for small, second order differences in the results, compared to the first order effects of using common weights at all. This may be seen from the decomposition of the effects of weighting on the difference of two means:

$$\Sigma w_{ai} \bar{y}_{ai} - \Sigma w_{bi} \bar{y}_{bi} = \Sigma w_{ai} (\bar{y}_{ai} - \bar{y}_{bi}) +$$

$$\Sigma \bar{y}_{ai} (w_{ai} - w_{bi}) - \Sigma (w_{ai} - w_{bi}) (\bar{y}_{ai} - \bar{y}_{bi}).$$

We may view the first term as a component for the difference of means that interests us; and the second term as a component due to the weight differences to be removed. The third term is an "interaction" term which is typically smaller than the others, due to the second order differences. But this term also equals the divergence between the two sets of weights applied to the differences:

$$\Sigma (w_{ai} - w_{bi}) (\bar{y}_{ai} - \bar{y}_{bi}) = \Sigma w_{ai} (\bar{y}_{ai} - \bar{y}_{bi}) - \Sigma w_{bi} (\bar{y}_{ai} - \bar{y}_{bi}).$$

4. *Adjustment by covariance or regression*. This method removes the effects of a disturbing variable x from the difference $(\bar{y}_a - \bar{y}_b)$ by computing the covariance of y with x and adjusting for its regression effects. This method can be more efficient than standardization with a few subclasses, and its theory is prominent in the statistical literature (Cochran 1957, 1969), but has severe limitations, which prevent widespread applications. 1) It requires somewhat complex computations; this minor handicap is disappearing in the shadows of large computers. 2) Its simple, common format is designed for linear regression on a single disturbing variable; however we may desire to remove simultaneously the effects of several disturbing variables and whose relationships are nonlinear. But multivariate covariance adjustments may be available, though more complex. 3) It requires continuous data for the disturbing variables, whereas these are commonly categorical. This is the most serious handicap in many research problems.

Advances in statistical methodology and computer technology are likely to overcome--perhaps partly and gradually-- the three limitations of covariance adjustments. Regression with dummy variables, and MCA (multiple classification analysis) are two nonparametric techniques with available computer programs for treating simultaneously multivariate relationships with several categorical variables.

5. *Analysis of residuals* is an extension of the regression method which allows greater flexibility. In essence the method proposes removing through regression some of the disturbing variables, computing residual values of the predictand adjusted for the removed variables, then analyzing the adjusted residuals by other methods. These methods can be separate analysis (0), or adjustment (3) in subclasses. The combination of regression with other methods allows great flexibility, and variety. A linear multivariate regression may be used to remove continuous disturbing variables for which linearity is assumed; then other variables are analyzed separately. Or a nonparametric method may be used to remove the disturbing variables, leaving the few critical variables for separate analysis. (Draper and Smith, 1966, Coleman 1964).

In all methods of control for disturbing variables, questions arise about their adequacy in the face of errors in measuring them. One problem concerns the loss of control due to grouping into few subclasses an underlying variable that is continuous, or approximately continuous with many potential classes. This common problem can arise because either the variable gets measured that way, or it is reduced

278

later to a few subclasses (with any of methods 0 to 3 above).
This problem receives its best treatment from Cochran (1968a)
for a wide range of distributions of the disturbing variable.
His results have broad meaning, with reassuring uniformity of
consequences for different distributions of the disturbing
variable; Table 5.2 presents a basic summary.

Numbers of subclasses	1	2	3	4	5	6	∞
Prop. of bias removed	0	.64	.80	.86	.90	.92	1.00

Table 5.2   Proportions of Constant Bias Removed with
Different Numbers of Subclasses.

Further, Cochran also deals with random error which introduces misclassification into the subclasses.   Such misclassifications reduce the above ratios of effectiveness.
The reduction is by the ratio (1+h), where h is the additional variance due to random errors of classification, computed as a ratio of the variance caused by an errorless disturbing variable in the predictor.

	Mean age	Number of subclasses			
		1: Unadjusted	2	3	11
Nonsmokers	57.0	13.5	13.5	13.5	13.5
Cigarettes only	53.2	13.5	16.4	17.7	21.2
Cigars and pipes	59.7	17.4	14.9	14.2	13.7

Table 5.3   Adjusted Death Rates per 1,000 U.S. Adult Males,
Using 2,3 and 11 Subclasses Compared to Unadjusted
(1) Rates.

Source: Cochran   (1968a) Tables 2 and 3, and originally by
Hammond for the American Cancer Society.

In Table 5.3 we borrow from Cochran (1968a) an example
to illustrate the use of controls to remove the effects of a
distrubing variable, age.   First we see that unadjusted
cigarette smokers seem to do as well as nonsmokers, whereas
cigar and pipe smokers live dangerously.   The differences in
mean ages, though not great, raise doubts, since age is
strongly related to death rates.   Adjusting for age

subclasses (of smokers to nonsmokers) brings out step by step
a more correct relationship of smoking habits to death rates:
cigarettes are deadly, cigars and pipes are not. Canadian
and British data of Cochran lead to similar conclusions.

Finally, this example also serves to make another point,
not strange to empirical researchers, about controls for disturbing variables. Commonly such controls serve to probe the
validity of differences found in the predictand variables,
and imposing controls often reduces those differences. In
this case, however, nonsmokers and cigarette smokers show no
difference at first, but imposing proper controls discovers
the differences, which were hidden by the disturbing variable
of different age subclasses with contradicting death rates.

6. DOMAIN AND UNITS OF RANDOMIZATION

The contrasting disadvantages of experiments and surveys
can both be viewed as problems of randomization. Experiments
have but surveys lack randomization of predictor treatments;
in surveys the predictor-predictand relationships are confounded with effects of disturbing variables. For example,
we may find that some teaching methods are strongly associated with high academic achievement. However, the schools
characterized by successful techniques also have higher
socio-economic status, teacher salaries, etc. than schools
with unsuccessful techniques. The predictor techniques were
not randomized, and they occur associated with disturbing
variables. To remove their effects is the aim of controls.

On the other hand, surveys have but experiments lack
randomization over population units. Effects of this failure
to randomize and represent responses are not widely appreci-
ated. This lack of understanding is due (I believe) to a
one-sided view of predictors as singular causal agents, instead of conceiving of predictands (responses) as due to interaction between predictor (treatment) and unit (subject)
in the population. Predictor-predictand relationships are
not absolute, but are functions of (conditional on) the
population units in which they occur. For example, the success of teaching methods may not be absolute, but depend on
the type of school, or student population, or social situa-
tion--or on all three. Teaching methods which prove successful in middle-class U.S. may fail in urban slums, and in
other countries. Results are "culture bound," we say. The
consequences of the unit-predictor-predictand triad on the
lack of randomized selection of units from the population
for experiments can be serious. Inferences to target population can be biased to the extent that the experimental

units diverge from it. To assume a lack of bias demands that
the selection of experimental units be unbiased and representative with regard to the mean predictor-predictand bias.
Randomized selection of experimental units can assure that
representativeness; but voluntary, judgmental, or haphazard
selection cannot. Units are not randomly distributed in the
population, hence a non-random selection method often fails
to obtain an unbiased representation of the triad of relations.

Overcoming the gaps between experimental units and target populations is difficult, but ignoring or hiding them
only confuses and hinders knowledge. Three kinds of verbal
screens are at times attempted to hide the gaps. First,
that the predictor-predictand relation is absolute, independent of the experimental unit. But such determinate relations are rare, and they do not need statistical treatment.
Second, that the predictor-predictand relation is randomly
distributed in the population of units; hence the selection
of units will be automatically randomized. This assumption
is thoroughly and widely ingrained, because it is convenient,
and because it remains unstated. In my view it is never
valid, though it is well enough approximated for some simple
physical and chemical relationships. In social research I
think, it is never a reasonable assumption. Third, that with
controls of disturbing variables, we can stabilize within
control classes the relationship of units to the predictor-
predictand relation; that within control classes we can make
the second assumption of random relation of units to the
predictand-predictor relation. Research design must rest on
that assumption when randomized selection of units from the
population is not feasible. It may or may not be a reasonable approximation; but we should not forget its tenuous, at
best approximate, nature.

The domain of randomization affects the bias of research
results, as argued above. For similar reasons the units of
randomization determine the sampling variability for the results of research, whether experiments or surveys. If entire
schools, or entire classes are selected for diverse teaching
methods, it is incorrect to compute sampling errors as if the
students were selected independently. The responses of students within selected units may, and probably will, be correlated. Positive correlation of responses tend to inflate
the variability of results. This remains obscured if the
variability (variance) is computed from students as if these
were selected independently. This kind of discrepancy, between the elements of computing and the actual units of
selection, results in underestimates of sampling variability.

These remain undiscovered, causing unknown inflations of the precision and significance of the research findings as presented. (Kish, 1957; Kish and Frankel, 1970, 1974.)

REFERENCES

Blalock, H. M. (ed.). 1971. *Causal Models in the Social Sciences,* Chicago: Aldine-Atherton.

Campbell, D. T. 1957. Factors relevant to the validity of experiments in social settings, *Psychological Bulletin,* 54, 297-312.

Campbell, D. T. and J. C. Stanley. 1963. *Experimental and Quasi-Experimental Designs,* Chicago: Rand McNally & Co.

Cochran, W. G. 1957. The analysis of covariance; its nature and uses, *Biometrics,* 13, 261-281.

Cochran, W. G. 1965. Planning of observational studies of human populations, *Journal of the Royal Statistical Society* (A), 128, 234-266.

Cochran, W. G. 1968a. The effectiveness of adjustment by subclassification in removing bias in observational studies, *Applied Statistics,* 18, 270-275.

Cochran, W. G. 1968b. Errors of measurement in statistics, *Technometrics,* 10, 637-666.

Cochran, W. G. 1969. The use of covariance in observational studies, *Applied Statistics,* 18, 270-275.

Coleman, J. S. 1964. *Introduction to Mathematical Sociology,* Glencoe, Ill.: Free Press. Ch. 15: The Method of residuals.

Draper, N. R. and H. Smith. 1966. *Applied Regression Analysis,* New York: John Wiley and Sons, Chapter 3: The Examination of Residuals.

Freedman, R. and A. H. Hawley. 1949. Unemployment and Migration in the depression, *Journal of the American Statistical Association,* 44, 260-272.

Goldberger, A. S. and O. D. Duncan, Eds. 1973. *Structural Equation Models in the Social Sciences,* New York: Seminar Press.

Greenberg, B. G. 1929. *The Story of Evolution,* New York: Garden City.

Hyman, H. H. 1955. *Survey Design and Analysis,* Glencoe, Ill.: Free Press.

Kalton, G. 1968. Standardization: a technique to control for extraneous variables, *Applied Statistics,* 17, 118-136.

Keyfitz, N. 1953. A factorial arrangement of comparisons of family size, *American Journal of Sociology,* 58, 470-480.

Kish, L. 1957. Confidence intervals for complex samples, *American Sociological Review,* 24, 328-338.

Kish, L. 1959. Some statistical problems in research design, *American Sociological Review,* 22, 154-165.

Kish, L. 1975. Optima and proxima in linear sample designs, *Journal of the Royal Statistical Society* (A).

Kish, L. and M. R. Frankel. 1970. Balanced repeated replications for standard errors, *Journal of the American Statistical Association,* 65, 1071-1094.

Kish, L. and R. M. Frankel. 1974. Inference from complex samples, *Journal of the Royal Statistical Society* (B), 1-37.
Kitagawa, E. M. 1964. Standardized comparisons in population research, *Demography,* 296-315.

McGinnis, R. 1958. "Randomization and inference in sociological research," *American Sociological Review,* 23, 408-414.

Moser, C. A. and G. Kalton. 1971. *Survey Methods in Social Investigations,* London: Heinemann, Ch. 17.

Rosenberg, M. 1968. *The Logic of Survey Analysis,* New York: Basic Books.

Salmon, W. C. 1967. *The Foundations of Scientific Inference,* Pittsburgh: The University of Pittsburgh Press.

Savage, R. I. 1957. Nonparametric statistics, *Journal of the American Statistical Association*, 52, 332-333.

Selvin, H. C. 1957. A critique of tests of significance in survey research, *American Sociological Review*, 22, 527.

Yates, F. 1951. The influence of Statistical Methods for Research Workers, *Journal of the American Statistical Association*, 46, 32-33.

10

Some Linear Models for Two-Wave, Two-Variable

Panel Analysis, with One-Way

*Causation and Measurement Error**

OTIS DUDLEY DUNCAN

The University of Arizona

Recent literature on panel analysis gives considerable attention to the question of whether one can, with 2W2V panel data, "decide the direction of causation" (Campbell, 1963), "detect causal priorities" (Pelz and Andrews, 1964), or "choose among [the] competing causal hypotheses" that A causes B or B causes A (Rozelle and Campbell, 1969). That this cannot be done under perfectly general conditions is implied by a previous paper (Duncan, 1969) wherein it is shown that no causal inference or estimate of a causal coefficient is possible in the absence of assumptions that render a model for 2W2V data identified. A further complication (treated only briefly in that paper by means of a single example, Figure 3, the numerical results in which were erroneous owing to use of an incorrect formula) is the possibility if not likelihood that measurements will be subject to more than negligible error. This possibility had been mentioned by Campbell (1963) and discussed at some length, though in somewhat obscure fashion, by Rozelle and Campbell (1969).

Actually, the panel design is one that calls attention to the importance of measurement error, since it involves measuring the same characteristic(s) repeatedly, whereas remeasurement (test-retest) is one of the techniques commonly used to detect and estimate the extent of measurement error.

---
*This chapter is a contribution from NSF project GS 2707, "Causal Models in Social Research." Programming was executed by J. Michael Coble and computation by Eugene Won.

But the assumptions of test-retest estimates of reliability
are that the repetitions are independent while no change in
true scores occurs between the occasions of measurement. In
panel analysis, on the contrary, we are interested in remeasurement precisely because we hope to detect true change
and to interpret its sources. Analysts of panel data have
also been aware for some time that measurement error can
masquerade as change, so that estimates of the amount of
"turnover" are particularly vulnerable. Even so, in relatively few substantive applications of panel analysis does
one find an explicit treatment of measurement error.

This chapter considers some seven models with exceedingly restrictive properties; they are more likely to be used
for didactic or heuristic purposes than they are to serve as
serious representations of actual social or behavioral processes. Such limited utility may well be inherent in the
2W2V design except under the most favorable circumstances.

1. SPECIFICATION OF MODELS

Let X_1 and X_3 be the measurements of Characteristic A
obtained on the first and second occasions of measurement,
respectively, and let X_2 and X_4 be the corresponding measurements of Characteristic B. Corresponding to each measured
X_i (i = 1, 2, 3, 4) is the "true" score, X_i^*. In the original
units of measurement, the obtained measurement is taken to
be the sum of the true score and a measurement error, E_i.
Throughout the paper, however, it will be assumed that
observed variables, true scores, and measurement errors are
all in standard form (zero mean, unit variance). Hence with
regard to errors of measurement all the models postulate
that

$$X_1 = \sqrt{q_1}\, X_i^* + \sqrt{1 - q_i}\, E_i \ , \ i = 1, 2, 3, 4, \quad (1)$$

where q_i is the reliability coefficient conceptually analogous to a test-retest correlation. In conformity with clas-
sic test theory it is assumed that $r_{E_i X_j^*} = 0$ (i, j = 1, 2, 3,
4), and with one exception, which will be explicitly noted,
that $r_{E_i E_j} = 0$ (i, j = 1, 2, 3, 4; i ≠ j).

The "causal" sector of all the models considered here is limited to the true variables. The general form of such a linear model is the same as that previously suggested (Duncan, 1969) and may be written

$$X_3^* = aX_1^* + cX_2^* + eX_4^* + uX_u^*$$

(2)

$$X_4^* = bX_2^* + dX_1^* + fX_3^* + vX_v^*$$

where the lower-case letters are path coefficients. In this model, X_3^* and X_4^* are the endogenous variables, X_1^* and X_2^* are the predetermined variables, and X_u^* and X_v^* are the disturbances. As is customary with this type of model, the disturbances are taken to be uncorrelated with the predetermined variables. Other assumptions are stated subsequently. Figure 1 provides a path diagram for the general form of the model; the particular models to be discussed are derived from the general model by setting certain paths and correlations in Figure 1 or coefficients in (2) equal to zero, by assumption. This will always be done in such a way that the causal relationship is either A $\rightarrow$ B or B $\rightarrow$ A, but not both. Each type of model, therefore, is considered to have two versions, e.g., 1A and 1B, according to which of the characteristics is taken to be causally prior.

It will be noted that the model as shown in Figure 1 makes explicit the possibility of non-zero values of $r_{E_1 E_2} = $ s and $r_{E_3 E_4} = $ t. In most of the particular models, however, it is assumed that s = t = 0. In all of them it is assumed that the disturbances are uncorrelated, i.e., $w = r_{X_u^* X_v^*} = 0$. This last assumption will not be mentioned again, but is nevertheless critical in securing identification of the parameters in all the models.

A synoptic presentation of all the particular models to be considered is afforded by the conjunction of equations (1) and (2) or Figure 1 and the specific assumptions noted below:

Model 1: e = f = s = t = 0; $q_1 = q_3$; $q_2 = q_4$.

    Model 1A: c = 0.

    Model 1B: d = 0.

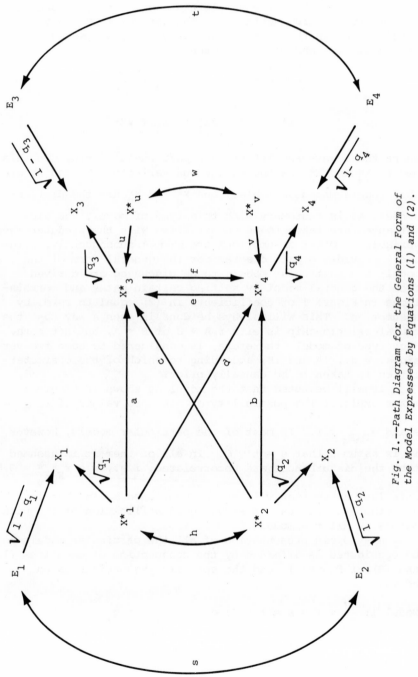

Fig. 1.--Path Diagram for the General Form of
the Model Expressed by Equations (1) and (2).

288

Model 2: $e = f = s = t \; 0;$ $q_3 = k^2 q_1;$

$\qquad q_4 = k^2 q_2;$ $r_{x_1^* x_2^*} = r_{x_3^* x_4^*}$

Model 2A: $c = 0.$

Model 2B: $d = 0.$

Model 3: $e = f = 0;$ $s = t \neq 0;$ $q_1 = q_3;$ $q_2 = q_4.$

Model 3A: $c = 0.$

Model 3B: $d = 0.$

Model 4: $c = d = s = t = 0;$ $q_1 = q_3;$ $q_2 = q_4.$

Model 4A: $e = 0.$

Model 4B: $f = 0.$

Model 5: $c = d = s = t = 0;$ $q_3 = k^2 q_1;$

$\qquad q_4 = k^2 q_2;$ $r_{x_1^* x_2^*} = r_{x_3^* x_4^*}.$

Model 5A: $e = 0.$

Model 5B. $f = 0.$

Model 6: $s = t = 0;$ $q_1 = q_3;$ $q_2 = q_4.$

Model 6A: $c = e = 0.$

Model 6B: $d = f = 0.$

Model 7: $s = t = 0;$ $q_3 = k^2 q_1;$ $q_4 = k^2 q_2;$ $r_{x_1^* x_2^*} = r_{x_3^* x_4^*}$

Model 7A: $c = e = 0.$

Model 7B: $d = f = 0.$

2. PROPERTIES AND SOLUTIONS OF MODELS

In order to study the properties of these models, it is expedient to use the theory of path coefficients (Wright, 1934; Duncan, 1966) to express each of the six observable correlations estimated by a set of 2W2V panel data in terms of the coefficients in each model. Inasmuch as the algebraic steps are the same in the two versions of each model, only version A will be treated explicitly.

For model 1A we have:

$$r_{12} = h \sqrt{q_1 q_2}$$

$$r_{23} = ah \sqrt{q_1 q_2}$$

$$r_{14} = (d + bh) \sqrt{q_1 q_2}$$

$$r_{34} = a(d + bh) \sqrt{q_1 q_2}$$

$$r_{13} = aq_1$$

$$r_{24} = (dh + b)q_2 .$$

The expressions for r_{12} and r_{23} imply that $a = r_{23}/r_{12}$ whereas those for r_{14} and r_{34} imply that $a = r_{34}/r_{14}$. For both implications to hold requires that $r_{14}r_{23} - r_{12}r_{34} = 0$.

Even if the model were completely valid, we would not expect this condition to be met exactly in a sample of finite size. Hence, this condition is an overidentifying restriction, one which might be used as a partial test of the model. The quantity $r_{14}r_{23} - r_{12}r_{34}$ will be recognized as one of the tetrad differences which are encountered in Spearman's general factor theory. Spearman and Holzinger (1924) proposed a formula for the sampling error of a tetrad difference, which may be applicable here. The exact form of their formula is cumbersome. A very rough approximation is

$$\text{S.E. (tetrad difference)} \cong 2\bar{r} (1 - \bar{r})/ \sqrt{N}$$

where $\bar{r}$ is the mean of six correlations for a set of four variables, and N is the number of sample observations.

Supposing that the analyst concludes that $r_{14}r_{23} - r_{12}r_{34}$ differs from zero by no more than he can reasonably attribute to sampling variation, he must still reconcile the two different estimates of a. On explicitly *ad hoc* and heuristic grounds, the following procedure is suggested. Let adjusted correlations (r') be defined as follows:

$$r'_{12} = r_{12} + m$$

$$r'_{34} = r_{34} + m$$

$$r'_{14} = r_{14} - m$$

$$r'_{23} = r_{23} - m$$

and let m be so chosen that

$$r'_{14}r'_{23} - r'_{12}r'_{34} = 0 .$$

It follows that

$$m = (r_{14}r_{23} - r_{12}r_{34})(r_{12} + r_{34} + r_{23} + r_{14})^{-1} .$$

The adjusted will replace the observed correlations in all numerical work, which begins with the computation of $a = r'_{23}/r'_{12} = r'_{34}/r'_{14}$, since both equalities now hold as a consequence of the adjustment.

We may proceed to solve for $q_1 = r_{13}/a$ and $h \sqrt{q_2} = r'_{23}/a \sqrt{q_1}$. It is now clear that the model is in part underidentified, since there is not enough information to solve for h and q_2 separately, nor for b and d. We may, however, obtain conditional solutions. If, for example, we assign an arbitrary numerical value to q_2 we obtain h immediately and the remaining two coefficients by solving the matrix equation

$$\begin{bmatrix} 1.0 & h \\ h & 1.0 \end{bmatrix} \begin{bmatrix} d \\ b \end{bmatrix} = \begin{bmatrix} r'_{14} & / & \sqrt{q_1 q_2} \\ r_{24} & / & q_2 \end{bmatrix}.$$

To facilitate numerical work a program was written to perform these computations for each value of $\sqrt{q_2}$ = .50, .51, .52, ..., .99.

It is important to note that the tetrad difference test mentioned earlier does not adjudicate the question of "which way the causal arrow runs," for exactly the same overidentifying restriction occurs in Model 1B that is encountered in 1A. Indeed, it also reappears in another model discussed subsequently, so that the test is not one that decides between these alternative models.

Turning to Model 2, we note that it resembles Model 1 in that the causal influence of A on B (or of B on A in the B-version of each model) operates with a lag, taken to be equal to the time interval between the two occasions of measurement. Whereas in Model 1 the reliability of measurement remains constant over time, in Model 2 it is assumed to improve or deteriorate by the same ratio for each characteristic. Thus Model 2 incorporates an additional parameter, k, which represents the changing reliability of measurement. Such a change might be plausible if we thought that interviewing a panel on one occasion, for example, made respondents more (or maybe less!) careful about their replies on a second occasion. While the measurement process, therefore, is assumed not necessarily to be in equilibrium, we do assume--contrary to Model 1--that the true causal process is in equilibrium in that $r_{X^*_3 X^*_4} = r_{X^*_1 X^*_2}$. This equilibrium assumption can be expressed $h = a(d + bh)$ or $h = ad/(1-ab)$. The observed correlations are expressed in terms of the coefficients in Model 2 as follows:

$$r_{12} = h \sqrt{q_1 q_2}$$

$$r_{23} = akh \sqrt{q_1 q_2}$$

$$r_{14} = k(d + bh) \sqrt{q_1 q_2}$$

$$r_{34} = ak^2(d + bh) \ \sqrt{q_1 q_2}$$

$$r_{13} = akq_1$$

$$r_{24} = k(dh + b)q_2 \ .$$

We encounter the same overidentifying restriction that appeared in Model 1, since $r_{23}/r_{12} = ka$ but also $r_{34}/r_{14} = ka$. Thus the test based on this restriction does not adjudicate the decision as between the two models. Assuming the test is passed, however, and that the analyst does prefer Model 2, the adjustment of four observed correlations may proceed as suggested for Model 1. Thus we compute $ka = r'_{23}/r'_{12} = r'_{34}/r'_{14}$. Invoking the equilibrium assumption we have $r'_{34} = k^2 h \ \sqrt{q_1 q_2}$ so that $k^2 = r'_{34}/r'_{12}$. We may also solve for $q_1 = r_{13}/ka$ and $h \ \sqrt{q_2} = r'_{23}/ka \ \sqrt{q_1}$. The remainder of the coefficients are underidentified, but we secure illustrative solutions, conditional on q_2, following the same strategy that was adopted with Model 1. The conditional solution for h is $r'_{23}/ka \ \sqrt{q_1 q_2}$; and the remaining coefficients are given by the solution of

$$\begin{bmatrix} 1.0 & h \\ h & 1.0 \end{bmatrix} \begin{bmatrix} d \\ b \end{bmatrix} = \begin{bmatrix} r'_{14}/k \ \sqrt{q_1 q_2} \\ r_{24} /kq_2 \end{bmatrix} .$$

Model 3 is the same as Model 1, except that the errors of measurement of the two variables are correlated within waves although not between waves. This correlation between errors, like the reliability of measurement itself, is assumed to be constant over time, so that t = s. Correlations among observed variables are given by the following functions of the parameters.

$$r_{12} = h \ \sqrt{q_1 q_2} + s \sqrt{1 - q_1} \ \sqrt{1 - q_2}$$

$$r_{13} = aq_1$$

$$r_{14} = (d + bh) \ \sqrt{q_1 q_2}$$

$$r_{23} = ah \sqrt{q_1 q_2}$$

$$r_{24} = (dh + b) \, q_2$$

$$r_{34} = a(d + bh) \sqrt{q_1 q_2} + s \sqrt{1 - q_1} \sqrt{1 - q_2}$$

$$= a \, r_{14} + s \sqrt{1 - q_1} \sqrt{1 - q_2}$$

Manipulation of the expressions for r_{12}, r_{23}, and r_{34} produces this quadratic in a:

$$a^2 r_{14} + a(r_{12} - r_{34}) - r_{23} = 0 \ .$$

Since a is a correlation as well as a path coefficient, and since it would be difficult to make substantive sense of the results if this correlation were negative, we accept either of the solutions from this quadratic only if $0 < a \le 1.0$. Given an acceptable value for a we obtain $q_1 = r_{13}/a$, and again accept the result only if $0 < q_1 \le 1.0$. The remaining coefficients in the model are underidentified. Solutions conditional upon arbitrary choices of q_2 are obtained from the following formulas, derived from the equations given above:

$$h = r_{23}/a \sqrt{q_1 q_2}$$

$$s = (r_{34} - ar_{14})/ \sqrt{1 - q_1} \sqrt{1 - q_2}$$

$$d = \left(\frac{r_{14}}{\sqrt{q_1 q_2}} - \frac{hr_{24}}{q_2} \right) / (1 - h^2)$$

$$b = \left(\frac{r_{24}}{q_2} - \frac{hr_{14}}{\sqrt{q_1 q_2}} \right) / (1 - h^2)$$

Model 4 alters an important assumption common to all the first three models. The causal influence of A on B (or B on A the B-version of the model) is simultaneous rather than lagged. Reliability of measurement is taken to be constant over waves. Observable correlations are related to the coefficients in the model as follows:

$$r_{12} = h \sqrt{q_1 q_2}$$

$$r_{23} = ah \sqrt{q_1 q_2}$$

$$r_{13} = aq_1$$

$$r_{14} = (af + bh) \sqrt{q_1 q_2}$$

$$r_{34} = (f + abh) \sqrt{q_1 q_2}$$

$$r_{24} = (b + afh) q_2 .$$

The solution for $a = r_{23}/r_{12}$ is obtained at once, whence $q_1 = r_{13}/a = r_{12}r_{13}/r_{23}$. Making appropriate substitutions, we may rewrite the expressions for r_{14} and r_{34} as

$$r_{14} = \sqrt{r_{13}r_{23}/r_{12}}f \sqrt{q_2} + r_{12}b$$

$$r_{34} = \sqrt{\frac{r_{12}r_{13}}{r_{23}}} f \sqrt{q_2} + r_{23}b .$$

This is a pair of linear equations in two unknowns, b and $f \sqrt{q_2}$, treating the latter as a single quantity for the moment. When we have solved for these two unknowns we may rewrite the expression for r_{24} to obtain

$$q_2 = [r_{24} - a(f \sqrt{q_2}) (h \sqrt{q_2})]/b$$

in which a, b, $f \sqrt{q_2}$, and $h \sqrt{q_2}$ all are now known, so that the expression provides the solution for q_2. Dividing $f \sqrt{q_2}$ and $h \sqrt{q_2}$ respectively by $\sqrt{q_2}$ yields, finally, the solutions for f and h. The entire model is just identified. However, it is quite possible for a set of data to give rise to impossible values for the estimated coefficients. Hence, we shall be disinclined to give much credence to the model if we obtain a solution for a, h, q_1, or q_2 which is not a possible value for a correlation coefficient. The solution must also be checked, for example, to see that it does not imply an impossible value for $r_{x^*_4 x^*_2}$.

   The causal structure of Model 5 is the same as that of Model 4, but the assumption of constant reliability is discarded in favor of the assumption that reliability of measurements changes by the same ratio for both characteristics, so that $q_3/q_1 = q_4/q_2 = k^2$. Whereas the measurement process is not necessarily in equilibrium (in this model), the causal process is assumed to be so; hence $r_{x^*_3 x^*_4} = r_{x^*_1 x^*_2}$ or $h = f$ + abh = f/(1 - ab)$. Expressing observable correlations in terms of coefficients in the model, we have

$$r_{12} = h \sqrt{q_1 q_2}$$

$$r_{23} = kah \sqrt{q_1 q_2}$$

$$r_{13} = kaq_1$$

$$r_{34} = (f + abh) k^2 \sqrt{q_1 q_2}$$

$$= hk^2 \sqrt{q_1 q_2}$$

$$r_{14} = (af + bh) k \sqrt{q_1 q_2}$$

$$r_{24} = (afh + b) kq_2 .$$

We obtain k^2 immediately as r_{34}/r_{12}. But $r_{23}/r_{12} = ka$, so that $a = r_{23}/ \sqrt{r_{12} r_{34}}$ and $q_1 = r_{13}/ka = r_{12}r_{13}/r_{23}$. We may compute $h \sqrt{q_2}$ as $r_{12}/ \sqrt{q_1} = \sqrt{r_{12}r_{23}/r_{13}}$. Substituting in the expressions for r_{14} and r_{34}, we obtain two equations in which there are two remaining unknowns, b and $f \sqrt{q_2}$:

$$r_{34}/k^2 \sqrt{q_1} = f \sqrt{q_2} + a(h\sqrt{q_2})b$$

$$r_{14}/k \sqrt{q_1} = af \sqrt{q_2} + (h\sqrt{q_2})b .$$

Having obtained b and f $\sqrt{q_2}$ we may write the expression for r_{24} as

$$q_2 = r_{24}/bk - a(h \sqrt{q_2})(f \sqrt{q_2})/b$$

and solve finally for f as f $\sqrt{q_2}/\sqrt{q_2}$.

Model 6 resembles Models 1 and 5, in that the causal influence of A on B (or vice versa in the B-version) is both lagged and simultaneous. There are seven coefficients in the model so that, with only six correlations available from a set of 2W2V data, it must obviously be underidentified at least in part. The observable correlations are expressed as functions of coefficients in the model as follows:

$$r_{12} = h \sqrt{q_1 q_2}$$

$$r_{23} = ah \sqrt{q_1 q_2}$$

$$r_{13} = aq_1$$

$$r_{14} = (af + d + bh) \sqrt{q_1 q_2}$$

$$r_{24} = (afh + dh + b) q_2$$

$$r_{34} = (f + ad + abh) \sqrt{q_1 q_2} .$$

The first two expressions imply that $a = r_{23}/r_{12}$ and, with the third, that $q_1 = r_{12} r_{13}/r_{23}$. We may now compute $h \sqrt{q_2} = \sqrt{r_{12} r_{23}/r_{13}}$ and note that, upon arbitrarily fixing q_2, conditional solutions for h and the remaining three coefficients are possible, for we obtain from the last three expressions the set of linear equations:

$$\begin{bmatrix} a & 1.0 & h \\ ah & h & 1.0 \\ 1.0 & a & ah \end{bmatrix} \begin{bmatrix} f \\ d \\ b \end{bmatrix} = \begin{bmatrix} r_{14}/\sqrt{q_1 q_2} \\ r_{24}/q_2 \\ r_{34}/\sqrt{q_1 q_2} \end{bmatrix}$$

which is solved by standard methods for f, d, and b.

Model 7 has the same causal paths as Model 6, but changes the assumption regarding reliability of measurement to that appearing in Models 2 and 5, i.e., $q_3/q_1 = q_4/q_2 = k^2$. The true causal process is assumed to be in equilibrium so that $r_{x_3^* x_4^*} = r_{x_1^* x_2^*}$. Hence $h = f + ad + abh = (f + ad)/(1-ab)$. Observable correlations can be expressed as the following functions of the coefficients in the model:

$$r_{12} = h \sqrt{q_1 q_2}$$

$$r_{34} = k^2(f + ad + abh) \sqrt{q_1 q_2}$$

$$= k^2 h \sqrt{q_1 q_2}$$

$$r_{13} = akq_1$$

$$r_{23} = ahk \sqrt{q_1 q_2}$$

$$r_{14} = k (af + d + bh) \sqrt{q_1 q_2}$$

$$r_{24} = k(afh + dh + b)q_2 .$$

Although the model as a whole is underidentified, we obtain unique solutions for three coefficients: $k^2 = r_{34}/r_{12}$; $a = r_{23}/kr_{12}$; and $q_1 = r_{13}/ak$. Moreover, since $h = r_{12}/\sqrt{q_1 q_2}$ we may solve for h conditionally upon an arbitrary choice of q_2 and then obtain the remaining coefficients via the solution of the matrix equation below:

$$\begin{bmatrix} a & 1.0 & h \\ ah & h & 1.0 \\ 1.0 & a & ah \end{bmatrix} \begin{bmatrix} f \\ d \\ b \end{bmatrix} = \begin{bmatrix} r_{14}/k \sqrt{q_1 q_2} \\ r_{24}/kq_2 \\ r_{34}/k^2 \sqrt{q_1 q_2} \end{bmatrix} .$$

It might be noted that Model 7 would be just identified if we added either the requirement that the two characteristics are measured with the same reliability, so that $q_2 = q_1$, or the constraint that f = -e.

3. NUMERICAL EXAMPLES

A dozen or so miscellaneous sets of 2W2V panel data were examined in a search for plausible empirical illustrations. The exercise does not encourage the expectation that models of the general form studied here will prove to be widely applicable. Some results are given, not because of any presumed substantive significance, but to bring out certain contingencies that may arise in applications.

One illustrative set of data concerns rates of school enrollment for 48 states and the District of Columbia (Duncan, 1965, Ch. 6). X_1 is the State's proportion of all 16-year-old boys enrolled in 1950, X_2 is the enrollment rate for seven-year-old boys in 1950, and X_3 and X_4 are the same variables as reported in the 1960 Census. The data are as follows:

$$r_{12} = .7107 \qquad\qquad r_{23} = .6762$$

$$r_{13} = .8507 \qquad\qquad r_{24} = .8103$$

$$r_{14} = .7295 \qquad\qquad r_{34} = .6691$$

We find $r_{14}r_{23} - r_{12}r_{34} = .017759$, a value which seems low enough to pass the tetrad test that arises in Models 1 and 2.

For Model 1A we find that a = .934, $\sqrt{q_1}$ = .954, and h $\sqrt{q_2}$ = .751 are the values that satisfy our equations. Thus in obtaining solutions conditional upon choices of $\sqrt{q_2}$ we shall avoid any value lower than .751, since this would require h > 1.0, an impossibility for a correlation coefficient. We discover, moreover, that choices of $\sqrt{q_2}$ in the range .76 - .90 yield values of h, b and d that are similarly impossible in regard to the values they imply for $r_{X_2^* X_4^*}$ and/or $R^2_{X_4^*(X_2^* X_1^*)}$. Hence, although we obtain a solution only upon an arbitrary choice of q_2, our choice is constrained within fairly narrow limits. Three illustrative sets of results are shown in Table 1. The middle set is perhaps most interesting since it is based on $\sqrt{q_2}$ = .950 while we found that these data imply $\sqrt{q_1}$ = .954. We have no information to indicate that the census obtains enrollment data more reliably at age 16 than at age 7, or vice versa. (Incidentally, if we included in the model the specification $q_1 = q_2$, then the model would no longer be underidentified.)

An interesting feature of this example is that the data lead to implausible estimates of parameters if we use Model 1B. Formulas of the type exhibited for Model 1A imply that the coefficient b in Model 1B is 1.008. But since in this model b is a correlation as well as a path coefficient, this estimate is not acceptable. Thus the data do, in a certain sense, lead us to choose the hypothesis A → B over B → A, both hypotheses being relative to a model of the particular form under study. Moreover, the results are unambiguous as to the sign of the causal coefficient, d, even though we are unable to deduce a unique value for its numerical magnitude.

The same data provide an example for Model 2A, illustrating the point that it may prove impossible to base a choice between the two models on the data alone.

We obtain k = .971 (indicating, if we take the result seriously, a somewhat lower reliability of census data in 1960 than in 1950), a = .962, and $\sqrt{q_1}$ = .954. Since h $\sqrt{q_2}$ = .751 we cannot consistently entertain estimates of $\sqrt{q_2}$ smaller than .751. Indeed, if we are not to violate the properties of certain other correlation coefficients, we are free to entertain only values of $\sqrt{q_2}$ > .91. A selection of illustrative solutions is in the second panel of Table 1. The results are not markedly different from those obtained with Model 1. As was true with that model, the data seem to contraindicate acceptance of Model 2B, for with that model we obtain b = 1.039, an impossible value for a path coefficient which is also a correlation coefficient.

The numerical example for Models 1A and 2A will serve as well for Model 3A. As before, although there are no unique solutions for h, s, d, and b, the range of acceptable solutions is fairly narrow, given that h $\sqrt{q_2}$ = .758. In fact, with a = .935 and $\sqrt{q_1}$ = .954, we find that choices of $\sqrt{q_2}$ ≤ .90 produce meaningless solutions for the

Model	a	b	d	f	h	s	$\sqrt{q_1}$	$\sqrt{q_2}$	R^2 for x_4^*
1A	.934	.914	.078	...	.826	...	.954	.910	.959
	.934	.713	.234	...	.791	...	.954	.950	.827
	.934	.580	.325	...	.759	...	.954	.990	.728
2A (k=.971)	.962	.881	.129	...	.817	...	.954	.920	.979
	.962	.735	.241	...	.791	...	.954	.950	.877
	.962	.597	.335	...	.759	...	.954	.990	.773
3A	.935	.911	.081	...	.833	-.103	.954	.910	.959
	.935	.704	.243	...	.798	-.136	.954	.950	.827
	.935	.569	.337	...	.766	-.302	.954	.990	.730
6A	.951	.876	.416	-.307	.826	...	.946	.910	.971
	.951	.683	.551	-.294	.791	...	.946	.950	.842
	.951	.555	.626	-.282	.759	...	.946	.990	.745
7A (k = .970)	.981	.792	.985	-.785	.808	...	.946	.930	.972
	.981	.666	1.052	-.760	.783	...	.946	.960	.880
	.981	.572	1.092	-.737	.759	...	.946	.990	.805

Table 1. ILLUSTRATIVE RESULTS FOR FIVE MODELS, COMPUTED FROM CENSUS DATA ON SCHOOL ENROLLMENT, 1950–1960

remaining coefficients. Three illustrative solutions within
the acceptable range are in the third panel of Table 1. The
causal coefficients are not greatly different from those
obtained with Models 1 and 2. Again, the data seem to com-
port with the assumption A → B rather than B → A, for when
Model 3B is run, we obtain 1.008 and -1.070 as solutions for
b, which values are not acceptable as estimates of a correlation coefficient. Interestingly, in Model 3A, we have a
negative value for the correlation between errors in measurement of the two characteristics. If the analyst finds it
difficult to think of a reason for such a result, he may report some skepticism as to the applicability of Model 3 to
the particular set of data.

Although we cannot choose between Models 1, 2, and 3 on
the basis of numerical results alone, it does appear to be
possible to reject some models upon inspecting the data. For
neither Model 4A nor 4B do we secure acceptable parameter
estimates. With Model 4A we obtain coefficients that imply
an impossible value for $r_{x_4^* x_2^*}$ (1.16). With Model 4B, wherein
the parameter b is also a correlation, we obtain the value
1.03, which is likewise impossible. Both versions of Model 5
likewise are rejected for these data, for exactly parallel
reasons.

Model 6, involving both lagged and simultaneous causation, can be fitted to the census enrollment data. The general result is much like that reported for Models 1, 2, and
3: version B of the model produces unacceptable estimates,
while a relatively narrow range of estimates is plausible
with Model 6A. We find a = .951, $\sqrt{q_1}$ = .946, and h $\sqrt{q_2}$
= .752. Illustrative solutions for the remaining coefficients are in Table 1. Thus, all conditional solutions not
only support the conclusion A → B, but they also agree that
the positive lagged effect outweighs the negative simultaneous effect. The two coefficients are equal only in a solution which implies impossible values for certain correlations.

Results for Model 7, which closely resembles Model 6,
are compatible with the supposition that it holds for the
enrollment data. Version B is not acceptable, while we find
again that $\sqrt{q_1}$ = .946. Solutions are unacceptable, because of impossible values of implied correlations, for
choices of $\sqrt{q_2}$ ≤ .92. Illustrative coefficient values
within the acceptable range appear in the bottom panel of
Table 1. Again, the positive lagged coefficient outweighs

the simultaneous coefficient. It is noteworthy that the hypothesis that the two are equal is not strongly supported, for this result only obtains in a context in which the coefficient of determination for X_4^* exceeds unity.

A second set of data will illustrate some other contingencies encountered in empirical work. These data pertain to 730 boys who repeatedly took achievement tests in mathematics and science. X_1 is the score on the mathematics examination in grade 9 and X_3 the mathematics score in grade 11; X_2 and X_4 are the corresponding scores on science tests. The correlations, given by Jöreskog (1973), are as follows:

$$r_{12} = .7364 \qquad r_{23} = .6211$$

$$r_{13} = .7350 \qquad r_{24} = .7213$$

$$r_{14} = .6595 \qquad r_{34} = .6381$$

The tetrad difference that arises in connection with Models 1 and 2 is -.060, a rather large value in view of the sample size. The applicability of these two models is, therefore, questionable. It also turns out that acceptable coefficient values cannot be obtained from these data for Model 5, using the estimation routine sketched earlier. However, it is possible to fit each of the other models considered here. Even more interesting is the fact that both the A- and B-versions of three of the models yield coefficient values that are at least conceivable, if not wholly plausible. This means that, contrary to the experience with the school enrollment data, with the achievement test data one cannot from the statistical results alone decide the issue as to the direction of causation, even if the specific form of the model is taken as given.

Neither set of data provides an acceptable fit for Model 5; indeed, no actual numerical example for that model is available. The achievement test data, for instance, yield the value 1.089 for $\sqrt{q_2}$ when one attempts to solve for Model 5A, while for Model 5B the data imply a value of 1.244 for h.

In the results with the census data we found no case where the range of permissible solutions included a change of sign of a path coefficient. As Table 2 shows, however, the achievement test data do present such ambiguities, in the

Model	a	b	c	d	e	f	h	s	$\sqrt{q_1}$	$\sqrt{q_2}$	R^2 for:	
											x_4^*	x_3^*
3A	.899	1.054	...	-.088	...	...	.889	.208	.904	.860	.953	...
	.899	.625	...	.274	...	...	.831	.271	.904	.920	.749	...
	.899	.414	...	.417	...	...	.772	.753	.904	.990	.612	...
3B	1.336	.954	-.400	...	...	...	.914	.186	.870	.869	...	.969
	.779	.954	.104	...	...	...	.864	.234	.920	.869	...	.757
	.480	.954	.336	...	...	...	.803	.651	.990	.869	...	.603
4A	.843	.571	...	...	...	.319	.827	...	.934	.954	.681	...
6A	.843	1.218	...	-.587	...	.349	.907	...	.934	.870	.959	...
	.843	.676	...	-.089	...	.327	.848	...	.934	.930	.736	...
	.843	.458	...	.090	...	.307	.797	...	.934	.990	.613	...
6B	1.223	.896	-.804	...	.512	...	.912	...	.900	.897	...	.895
	.545	.896	-.169	...	.465	...	.829	...	.990	.897	...	.624
7A	.906	.939	...	-.548	...	.628	.876	...	.934	.900	.986	...
	.906	.492	...	-.143	...	.571	.797	...	.934	.990	.735	...
7B	.854	.962	-1.403	...	1.505	...	.873	...	.940	.897	...	.968
(k=	.585	.962	-1.109	...	1.429	...	.829	...	.990	.897	...	.823
.931)												

Table 2. ILLUSTRATIVE RESULTS FOR SEVEN MODELS, COMPUTED FROM ACHIEVEMENT TEST DATA

solutions for Models 3A, 3B, and 6A. The situation is quite
striking with regard to Model 3. Not only can we not choose
between A → B and B → A for these data, but on either hypothesis it is uncertain whether the causal influence is positive or negative. The student is indeed well advised to
remember the old adage, "Correlation does not prove causation." The plausibility of Model 3 for these data is perhaps
enhanced by the positive sign of the correlation, s, which is
the correlation between errors of measurement in the two
variables upon the same occasion of measurement. Evaluation
of this result would require information as to whether the
tests were administered in such a way that a correlation between measurement errors is probable.

4. DISCUSSION

It is hoped that nothing in the foregoing presentation
will be taken to encourage the idea that study of a set of
2W2V correlations can be reduced to a mechanical procedure
which will yield a trustworthy induction as to the causal
structure producing the observations. On the contrary, it
appears that a substantial amount of "structure" must be assumed as part of the maintained hypothesis to allow any
causal inference. The requisite conditions for such an inference may seem excessively stringent, if one had held the
hope that panel analysis would provide a means of inference
clearly superior to and more flexible than cross-sectional
analysis.
It must be emphasized that the models considered here,
though often underidentified, are nonetheless highly specialized. None of them allows for the effect of causes common
to both Characteristic A and B, whether such causes be
thought of as observable or as latent common factors (in the
sense of factor analysis). Moreover, all the models exclude
the possibility of two-way causation or mutual influence of
the two characteristics, whether lagged or simultaneous. It
is, however, a virtue of such highly specialized models that
the data may, upon occasion, allow one to reject a particular
version of the model as being implausible in the light of the
data. For this reason, it may be hoped that these models
will have some heuristic, as well as purely didactic,
utility. For example, in taking up the analysis of the
census school enrollment data, it was considered reasonable
to entertain a model with lagged causation, B → A, because
the seven-year-old boys in one year are an approximate cohort
match to the sixteen-year-old boys a decade later and it was
thought that enrollment rates might be subject to cohort

effects. But the data tell us that we cannot simultaneously hold to this notion and to a model with the particular structure of any of Models 1-7. Of course, it can well be the structure and not the initial, vague hypothesis which is at fault; but the results at least signal that more work is to be done before a conclusion can be responsibly reported.

REFERENCES

Campbell, D. T. 1963. From Description to Experimentation: Interpreting Trends as Quasi-experiments. In C. W. Harris (Ed.), *Problems in Measuring Change*. Madison: University of Wisconsin Press.

Duncan, Beverly. 1965. *Family Factors and School Drop-out: 1920-1960*. U.S. Office of Education, Cooperative Research Project No. 2258. Ann Arbor: The University of Michigan.

Duncan, O. D. 1966. Path Analysis: Sociological Examples, *American Journal of Sociology*, 72: 1-16.

Duncan, O. D. 1969. Some Linear Models for Two-Wave, Two-Variable Panel Analysis, *Psychological Bulletin*, 72: 177-182.

Jöreskog, K. G. 1973. A General Method for Estimating a Linear Structural Equation System. In A. S. Goldberger and O. D. Duncan (Eds.), *Structural Equation Models in the Social Sciences*. New York: Seminar Press.

Pelz, D. C., and F. M. Andrews. 1964. Detecting Causal Priorities in Panel Study Data, *American Sociological Review*, 29: 836-854.

Rozelle, R. M., and D. T. Campbell. 1969. More Plausible Rival Hypotheses in the Cross-lagged Panel Correlation Technique, *Psychological Bulletin*, 71: 74-80.

Spearman, C., and K. Holzinger. 1924. The Sampling Error in the Theory of Two Factors, *British Journal of Psychology*, 15: 17-19.

Wright, S. 1934. The Method of Path Coefficients, *Annals of Mathematical Statistics*, 5: 161-215.

11

Path Models with Latent Variables:
The NIPALS Approach *

HERMAN WOLD
University of Göteborg

SUMMARY

The evolution of causal and predictive analysis by path
models is reviewed, with special regard to the merging of two
central avenues: the multirelational forecasting models of
econometrics, and the modelling in terms of latent variables
that is of old standing in psychology and education. The
emphasis is on the rationale and broad scope of the NIPALS
(Nonlinear Iterative PArtial Least Squares) approach to path
models with latent variables. Characteristic of NIPALS
modelling is the specification of causal and/or predictive
relations in terms of predictors (conditional expectations),
followed by least-squares estimation of the unknowns; namely,
estimation by OLS (Ordinary Least Squares) regression of predictors where all variables are directly observed, and by
iterative OLS when it comes to predictors that involve latent
variables. At the gateway of the problem area is Hauser's
pioneering model (1968, 1971). Various partings of the ways
are examined on the basis of six NIPALS models, all of which
are simple modifications of Hauser's model. The concluding
remarks focus on the similarities and differences between
NIPALS and ML (Maximum Likelihood) modelling.

1. INTRODUCTION

For a graphic ingress, Figures 1 a-b and 2 show path
models of three types, denoted L, L*, L** and coded as

---
*
NIPALS = Nonlinear Iterative PArtial Least Squares.

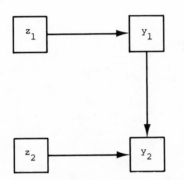

Fig. 1a. Path model of type L.

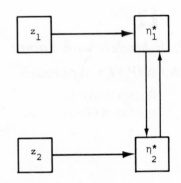

Fig. 1b. Path model of type L*.

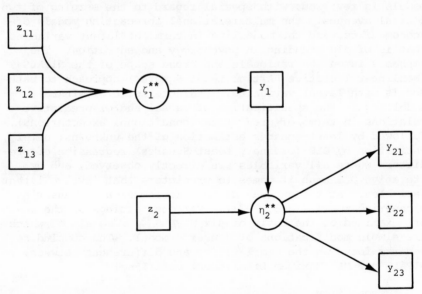

Fig. 2. Path model of type L**

follows:

Models L. All variables are directly observed (manifest).

Models L^* and L^{**} involve one or more latent (indirectly observed) variables. It is models L^{**} that are in focus in this chapter.

Models L^*. Each latent variable is the systematic part of a corresponding variable that is directly observed.

Models L^{**}. Each latent variable indicates or is indicated by several manifest variables (called indicators).

For the variables the notations are as follows. Note that in Models L^* the predetermined variables cannot contain latent variables, since the models define systematic parts only for the endogenous variables.[1]

	Notations	
	Symbols	Graphic[2]
Variables directly observed, Models L-L^{**}		☐
Endogenous	y	
Predetermined	x, z	◉
Latent variables in Models L^*		
Contained in an endogenous variable	η^*	
Contained in a predetermined variable	--	
Latent variables in Models L^{**}		◯
With endogenous indicators	η^{**}	
With predetermined indicators	ξ^{**}, ζ^{**}	

The arrows illustrate relations that the model assumes as a basis for causal and/or predictive inference, the arrows pointing from cause to effect and/or from a variable that serves as predictor to the variable that is predicted.

---

[1] Here and often in the following the terminology borrows from econometrics. For broad reviews of econometric modelling reference is made to Malinvaud (1964) for the classical methods and to Mosbaek, Wold *et al.* (1970) for the NIPALS approach.

[2] In the graphic notation we elaborate the usage of Jöreskog (1973).

Single arrows represent single causes and/or predictors; joint arrows indicate multiple causes and/or predictors.[3]

By the arrow schemes for the path models L and L*, Figures 1 a-b give simple illustrations of the two types of models that in econometrics are known as causal chain systems (introduced by Jan Tinbergen, 1935-1940) and interdependent systems (Trygve Haavelmo, 1943).[4] By the latent variables y_1^* , y_2^* , Figure 1b illustrates the new versions of interdependent (ID) systems, called REID (Reformulated ID) and GEID (General ID) systems, which were introduced by the author (1965). Figure 2 shows a corresponding model of type L**.

Continuing the graphic introduction, Figures 3 a-b and 4 a-f set forth an array of simple models as embryonic path models of type L**.

In Figures 3 a-b, the principal components (PC) and canonical correlations models (CC) are represented as simple cases of L** models.[5]

Introduced by Hauser (1968; 1971), the path model in Figure 4a has been further studied by Hauser-Goldberger (1971), Jöreskog-Goldberger (1973), and Wold (1973b). We have here used a notation ω for the latent variable that agrees with the subsequent notations. Note that in Figure 4a and later graphs the double stars have been dropped in the notations for the latent variables.

Figures 4 b-f show five modifications of Hauser's model obtained by

(a_1)   reversion of the direction of the inferential arrows, and/or

(a_2)   splitting up the latent variable in two parts.

---

[3] The joint arrows for multiple causes are an elaboration of the customary illustration of path models.

[4] For detailed references, see the monographs referred to in Note 1. For the general evolution of path models, and its beginnings in genetics and econometrics, see Blalock (1964) and Boudon (1965).

[5] The NIPALS modelling of the PC and CC methods belongs to the first applications of the NIPALS approach; see Wold (1966 b).

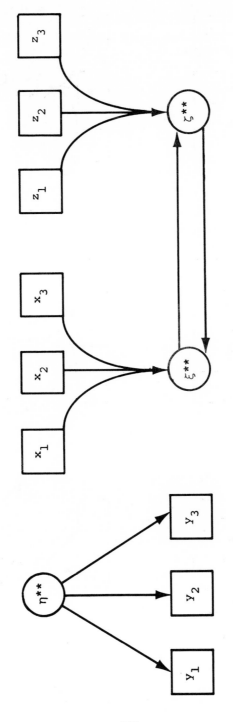

Fig. 3b. Canonical correlations (CC) model, interpreted as an L** model.

Fig. 3a. Principal components (PC) model, interpreted as an L** model.

311

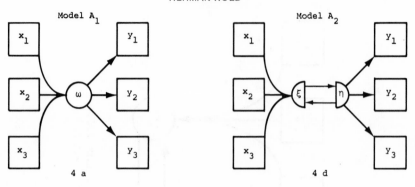

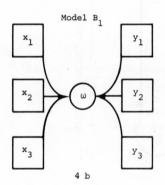

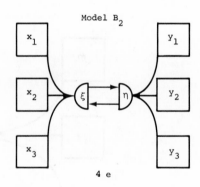

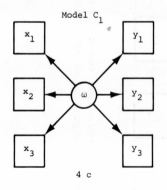

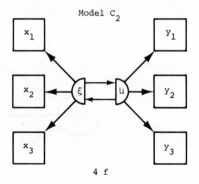

Fig. 4 a–f. Hauser's model (4a), which is graphically the same as NIPALS model A_1. Five related path models (4 b–f).

In Figure 4c we recognize the graph of a PC model (cf. Figure 3a) and in Figure 4e of a CC model (cf. Figure 3b). Referring to the latent variable(s) as the *kernel* of Hauser's model, the alternatives under $(a_1) - (a_2)$ will be called a "unit kernel" and a "twin kernel," respectively. (Another pair of names is "marble kernel" and "walnut kernel.")

Models of type L^{**} are of old standing in psychology and education, especially factor analysis and other well-known approaches such as principal components, canonical correlations, and test-retest models. In sociology and other social sciences the construction of causal models of types L and L^* has come to the fore since the late 1950's and is now in forceful development. In recent years, as emphasized by Blalock (ed.,1971a) and Costner (ed., 1971), causal models of type L^{**} are gaining momentum. By its simple structure, Hauser's model is of special interest and importance, a signpost at the beginning of the L^{**} avenue.

As is clear from Figure 2, path models L^{**} can be seen as a merger of models L and L^* on the one hand, and embryonic models L^{**} such as shown in Figures 3-4 on the other. This chapter sets out to explore the merger by the use of NIPALS (Nonlinear Iterative Partial Least Squares) modelling.

Section 2 serves background purposes, briefly reviewing the approach of predictor specification and OLS (Ordinary Least Squares) estimation; the general device of NIPALS modelling; and the OLS and NIPALS approaches as applied to linear models L and L^*.

Section 3 reports the results of NIPALS modelling as applied to Hauser's model (Figure 4a) and its five basic modifications in Figures 4 b-f. For the six models the exposition gives the NIPALS specifications; the iterative NIPALS procedures; the iterative procedures solved in algebraic form; numerical results of the NIPALS estimation as applied to Hauser-Goldberger's (1971) and other data; and some comments on the numerical results. Section 4 gives a broad discussion, with emphasis on the informational and operative aspects of NIPALS modelling as applied to models of type L^{**}, and in particular Hauser's model and its basic variations.

The limited purpose of this chapter must be emphasized. The aim is a brief orientation of the NIPALS approach to models of type L^* and L^{**}, with Hauser's model and its basic variations for illustration. Research is in progress for some of the many new problems that open up, in particular theoretical and applied studies, and comparative aspects of NIPALS vs. Maximum Likelihood modelling.

2. LINEAR MODELS L and L*: OLS AND THE NIPALS APPROACH.[6]

OLS (Ordinary Least Squares) Regression: Predictor Specification.

A linear regression is said to be specified as a *predictor* if the systematic part is the conditional expectation of the left-hand variable; in symbols,

$$y = \beta_0 + \beta_1 z_1 + \ldots + \beta_p z_p + \varepsilon \qquad (1a)$$

$$E(y|z_1, \ldots, z_p) = \beta_0 + \beta_1 z_1 + \ldots + \beta_p z_p \qquad (1b)$$

Further we write

$$y = b_0 + b_1 z_1 + \ldots + b_p z_p + e \qquad (2)$$

for the empirical regression obtained by applying OLS to data generated by the linear predictor (1). Then under general conditions of stochastic regularity the estimates for the coefficients β_i given by the OLS estimates b_i are consistent in the large-sample sense.[7] Subject to supplementary assumptions, asymptotic (large-sample) formulas are available for standard errors, confidence intervals, and small-sample bias.[8] It is well to note, however, that the OLS estimates b_i are not efficient, the standard errors not being the smallest possible in the class of general estimators.

NIPALS Modelling.[9] NIPALS is a general device for the linearization of nonlinear models. NIPALS is a two-pronged tool, which serves purposes of

---

[6]For more details in the argument and further references, see Mosbaek-Wold *et al.* (1970); see also Lyttkens (1973) and Wold (1973b).

[7]Wold (1963). To specify: in addition to (1b) it is assumed that all variables y, z_i have finite variances, and that the variables z_i are not linearly interdependent.

[8]Wold (1950), Lyttkens (1964).

[9]See Wold (1966b) and, for the recent developments, Wold (1973b).

(a_1)   model specification and

(a_2)   parameter estimation.

NIPALS specification works by a combination of two technical devices, namely

(b_1)   an *ad hoc* grouping of the unknowns of the model
        into two or more groups, so as to make the model
        linear if the unknowns in any fixed group remain
        free while they are kept constant in the other
        groups;

(b_2)   the relations of the model are specified as pre-
        dictors; see (1 a-b).

Known as *relaxation*, (b_1) is a standard device in numerical analysis.[10] It is the combination of relaxation with pre-dictor specification that makes NIPALS modelling a distinct approach.

NIPALS parameter estimation is an iterative procedure which supplements the NIPALS specification (b_1) ⟶ (b_2) and brings NIPALS modelling to full significance. As a rule it is a straightforward matter to make the formal and computa-tional design of the estimation procedure on the basis of the model specification.

We note two technical problems associated with NIPALS estimation procedures:

(c_1)   The Convergence of the Iterative Procedure.[11]
        The convergence problem being stochastic, refer-
        ence is made to Agren's convergence principle,
        which provides useful information by investigat-
        ing instead the convergence properties of the
        corresponding deterministic version of the itera-
        tive procedure. Set forth by Agren for the fix-
        point estimation of REID and GEID systems, his
        convergence principle is of general scope in
        NIPALS estimation;

---

[10]For this and other general aspects of iterative methods, see, e.g., Varga (1962).

[11]Agren (1972); Wold (1973 b).

(c$_2$) The Consistency of NIPALS Estimates. Under general conditions of stochastic regularity the consistency of OLS regression (1) - (2) carries over
to NIPALS estimates. The essential requirement is
that the observed means and product moments should
tend to the corresponding means and moments in the
population as the sample increases indefinitely.

To sum up briefly the experience of NIPALS applications,
the NIPALS approach works satisfactorily under a wide variety
of circumstances. The following features are of general
scope:

(d$_1$) NIPALS modelling is highly flexible in its adaptation to different types and varieties of cognitive models;

(d$_2$) NIPALS modelling is especially well suited for the
construction of models with causal and/or predictive aims, inasmuch as NIPALS specifies the
operative relations of the model as predictors;

(d$_3$) In comparison with other approaches, especially
the maximum likelihood method, NIPALS is often
more general, and typically so since it works with
less stringent assumptions about the correlation
properties of the residuals. Hence the NIPALS
approach makes for models that give a closer fit
to the given observations.

(d$_4$) Being an iterative sequence of OLS regressions, a
NIPALS procedure is easy to program and handle on
the computer.

Linear Models L and L*; Applications of OLS Regression
and NIPALS Modelling.[12] The models L and L* under consideration are linear multirelational systems. For the ith relation of systems of type L we shall use the general notation

$$y_i = \alpha_i + \sum_{j=1}^{p} \beta_{ij} y_j + \sum_{k=1}^{q} \gamma_{ik} z_k + \delta_i \qquad (3a)$$

with i = 1, ..., p and

$$\beta_{ii} = 0 \qquad (3b)$$

---

[12] Note 6 is repeated. For the conceptual aspects of causal
and predictive modelling, see also Wold (1966 a, 1973 a).

In econometric usage, (3) is the structural form of the model, and if we solve for y_i $(i = 1, \ldots, p)$ we obtain the reduced form. Writing in vector and matrix notation, the structural form is

$$Y = \alpha + \beta Y + \Gamma Z + \delta \tag{4}$$

and the reduced form (here we drop the constant terms)

$$Y = \Omega Z + \varepsilon \tag{5}$$

with

$$\Omega = [I - \beta]^{-1} \Gamma \; ; \quad \varepsilon = [I - \beta]^{-1} \delta \tag{6 a-b}$$

The subscript t $(= 1, \ldots, n)$ will indicate observed values for the variables. We spell out the observed version of the structural form (3),

$$y_{it} = \alpha_i + \sum_{j=1}^{p} \beta_{ij} y_{jt} + \sum_{k=1}^{q} \gamma_{ik} z_{kt} + \delta_{it} \tag{7}$$

or in the vector and matrix notation (4),

$$Y_t = \alpha + \beta Y_t + \Gamma Z_t + \delta_t \tag{8}$$

Until further notice we shall consider linear models L and L^* in which there are no identities.

Causal Chain Systems. These are models L of type (3 a -b) where matrix β is subdiagonal,

$$\beta_{ij} = o \text{ for } j > i \; , \; (i = 1, \ldots, p-1) \tag{9}$$

This implies that the transformation from the structural form (3) to the reduced form (5) can be performed by consecutive substitutions of the endogenous variables y_i in terms of the predetermined variables z_k.

(e₁) Under general conditions of stochastic regularity, the structural relations of causal chain systems can be specified as predictors,

$$E(\underset{\sim}{Y}|\underset{\sim}{Y}, \underset{\sim}{Z}) = \underset{\sim}{\beta}\, \underset{\sim}{Y} + \underset{\sim}{\Gamma}\, \underset{\sim}{Z} \tag{10}$$

Thanks to the substitution theorem just referred to, the relations of the reduced form will also make predictors, although in general with larger residuals than (6b);

(e_2)   Thanks to (e_1), OLS regression as applied to the structural relations provides consistent estimates for the parameters $\underset{\sim}{\beta}$, $\underset{\sim}{\Gamma}$. Formula (6a) then gives consistent estimates for the coefficients $\underset{\sim}{\Omega}$. OLS regression as applied to the reduced form in general will not give consistent estimates for the coefficients $\underset{\sim}{\Omega}$.

Interdependent (ID) Systems. These are models L of type (3 a-b) where the endogenous variables $\underset{\sim}{Y}$ cannot be arranged so as to make matrix $\underset{\sim}{\beta}$ subdiagonal in the sense of (9).

(f_1)   In general it is not possible to specify the structural relations of ID systems as predictors. This is the predictor aspect of Haavelmo's classical discovery (1943) that OLS regression in general will give inconsistent estimates if applied to the structural relations of ID systems;

(f_2)   Reference is made to FIML (Full Information Maximum Likelihood), LIML (Limited Information Maximum Likelihood), TSLS (Two Stage Least Squares) and other classical methods for the estimation of ID systems.[13] All of these methods start by estimating the reduced form by OLS regression. All of the same methods are based on the *assumptions of Classical ID systems:* Every residual δ_i (or, equivalently, ε_i) has zero correlation with every predetermined variable z_k; in symbols

$$r(\delta_i, z_k) = 0 \tag{11}$$

for $i = 1, \ldots, p$ and $k = 1, \ldots, q$;

---

[13]See Lyttkens (1973) for a comprehensive review from the present points of view.

(f_3) If the structural relations of Classical ID systems do not constitute predictors, what is their
operative use, if any?[14] This question--crucial
indeed since the structural relations contain the
behavioral relations, the conceptual basis of the
entire model--gave the author the incentive to a
reformulation of the Classical ID systems so as
to make the structural form accessible to a predictor specification. Making use of latent variables, an answer to the problem was found in the
REID (Reformulated ID) systems. This approach
led to the fix-point method of estimation, and
this in turn to the GEID (General ID) systems and
to the general device of NIPALS modelling.

REID (REformulated ID) Systems.[15] These are models of
type L^*, obtained by the following reformulation of the
structural form of Classical ID systems, without numerical
change of the parameters $\underset{\sim}{\beta}$, $\underset{\sim}{\Gamma}$.

Structural form of REID systems:

$$\underset{\sim}{Y} = \underset{\sim}{\beta}\, \underset{\sim}{Y}^* + \underset{\sim}{\Gamma}\, \underset{\sim}{Z} + \underset{\sim}{\varepsilon} \qquad (12)$$

where $\underset{\sim}{Y}^*$ is the systematic part of Y, which gives

$$\underset{\sim}{Y}^* = \underset{\sim}{\beta}\, \underset{\sim}{Y}^* + \underset{\sim}{\Gamma}\, \underset{\sim}{Z} \qquad (13a)$$

or equivalently,

$$\underset{\sim}{Y}^* = [I - \underset{\sim}{\beta}]^{-1}\, \underset{\sim}{\Gamma}\, \underset{\sim}{Z} \qquad (13b)$$

$$= \underset{\sim}{\Omega}\, \underset{\sim}{Z} \qquad (13c)$$

In words, Y^* is the systematic part of $\underset{\sim}{Y}$; that is, what is
left of $\underset{\sim}{Y}$ when the residual $\underset{\sim}{\varepsilon}$ is removed.

The reduced form of REID systems is obtained by solving
(12) for $\underset{\sim}{Y}$, taking into account (13 a-c). This gives the

---

[14] This was a key question in the prestigious symposium by
Christ *et al.* (1960).

[15] Note 12 is repeated.

same reduced form as for Classical ID systems, namely (5)
with (6 a-b). Note that in REID systems the residuals ε_i are
the same in the structural and reduced forms.

Given the coefficients $\underset{\sim}{\Omega}$ of the reduced form, the "identification problem" of ID systems is to retrieve the para-
meters $\underset{\sim}{\beta}$, $\underset{\sim}{\Gamma}$ of the structural form. In practice the typical
case is that an ID system is "overidentified"; then the iden-
tification problem cannot be solved by purely algebraic
methods. The identification problem has been deemphasized by
the advent of LIML, TSLS and other statistical techniques
that provide consistent estimates of the parameters β, Γ;
see (f_2). Otherwise stated, the identification problem is
an analytical, not a statistical problem.

(g_1) Under general conditions of stochastic regularity, the structural relations of REID systems can
be specified as predictors,

$$E(\underset{\sim}{Y}|\underset{\sim}{Y}^*, Z) = \underset{\sim}{\beta} \underset{\sim}{Y}^* + \underset{\sim}{\Gamma} \underset{\sim}{Z} \qquad (14)$$

and thanks to (13 a-c) the relations of the reduced form will also make predictors. Just as
for an ordinary regression (1)--(2) the
specification (14) provides the rationale for using any structural relation (12) for causal and/or
predictive aims. We see that (12) explains any
endogenous variable y_i in terms of observed predetermined variables z_k and *expected* values y_j^*
of other endogenous variables $(j \neq i)$. For example, if y_i is consumer demand for food, and y_j
is food price, y_i is assumed to depend, not upon
observed price y_j, but upon expected food price
y_j^* .

(g_2) The predictor specification (14) makes for OLS
regression, but Y^* is unknown and must be estimated as part of the estimation procedure. The
estimation problem as posed by (14) thus is nonlinear. The FP method is an iterative procedure
for solving this nonlinear problem.

(g_3) In the reduced form of ID systems each relation
as a rule involves all of the predetermined variables. A weakness in the classical estimation
methods (f_2) emerges in consequence of this
feature, for in large ID systems the predetermined variables are often more numerous than the
available observations, and in such case the
classical methods break down in their first
phase, the OLS estimation of the reduced form.
This difficulty gave the incentive for designing
an estimation method for REID systems that stays
in the structural form, and this is a key feature
of the FP method.

(g_4) The FP method belongs under the general class of
NIPALS estimation methods referred to in (a_2) and
(c_1)-(c_2). Under appropriate conditions, the FP
procedure is convergent, and the resulting parameter estimates are consistent.

$_*$ GEID (GEneral ID) Systems. These are models of type
L* and formally the same as REID systems, both in structural
form (12) with (13 a-c) and in reduced form (5) with (6 a-b),
but the classical assumptions (11) are generalized in accordance with the predictor specification (14). In the ith
structural relation the residual ε_i is assumed to be uncorrelated with the variables y_j^*, z_k that occur in the right-
hand member of that same relation, but not necessarily with
all predetermined variables Z.

(h_1) The generalization from REID to GEID systems
manifests itself in overidentified ID systems,
not in just-identified systems.

(h_2) The FP method carries over from REID to GEID
systems without any formal change. Again under
appropriate conditions, the FP procedure is convergent and consistent. On the other hand, the
classical estimation methods (f_2) for ID systems

in general give inconsistent estimates when applied to GEID systems.

(h_3) The FP method for the estimation of REID and
GEID systems has been extended and modified in
several ways. We note FFP (Fractional FP) by A.
Agren, RFP (Recursive FP) by L. Bodin, AFP

321

(Algebraic FP) by E. Lyttkens, and PFP (Parametric FP) by E. Lyttkens.[16] When the estimation procedure converges for any two of these methods, they give numerically the same estimates.

(h$_4$) The parity principle: the same numbers of non-correlation assumptions for the residuals as there are parameters to estimate. The parity principle is honored by GEID systems, but not by Classical ID systems or REID systems.[17]

(h$_5$) If the ID systems involve one or more identities, the parity principle cannot be maintained in GEID systems.[18]

3. THE NIPALS APPROACH TO SIX SIMPLE MODELS OF THE TYPE L**.

With reference to Figures 4 a-f for illustration we shall consider Hauser's model (Figure 4a) and the five models obtained by reversion of causal directions and by defining the latent variable(s) either as a unit kernel or as twin kernels. For a unified treatment of the six models by the NIPALS approach, we allow the models to have an arbitrary number of variables, say

$$x_1, \ldots, x_p ; \qquad y_1, \ldots, y_q \tag{15}$$

and use the same notation for the three unit kernels,

$$\omega = \gamma_o (\sum_{i=1}^{p} \alpha_i x_i + \sum_{k=1}^{q} \beta_k y_k) \tag{16}$$

and for the three pairs of twin kernels,

$$\xi = \gamma_1 \sum_{i=1}^{p} \alpha_i x_i ; \qquad \eta = \gamma_2 \sum_{k=1}^{q} \beta_k y_k \tag{17 a-b}$$

---

[16] See the contributions of the various authors in Wold-Lyttkens (eds., 1969), Mosbaek, Wold et al. (1970), and Lyttkens-Wold (eds., 1972).

[17] See the author's chapter in Wold-Lyttkens (eds., 1969).

[18] See, also for references to his earlier works, Lyttkens (1973).

although the parameters α_i, β_k in general differ from one model to another. Since it involves no restriction of generality, all variables x_i, y_k, ω, ξ, η are assumed to have zero mean,

$$E(x_i) = E(y_k) = E(\omega) = E(\xi) = 0 \qquad (18\ a\text{-}e)$$

and be normalized so as to have unit variance,

$$E(x_i^2) = E(y_k^2) = E(\omega^2) = E(\xi^2) = E(\eta^2) = 1 \qquad (18\ f\text{-}k)$$

The factors γ in (16) and γ_1, γ_2 in (17 a-b) are normalization constants in accordance with (18 f-k). This gives for γ_o

$$\gamma_o^2 [\Sigma \Sigma \alpha_i \alpha_j E(x_i x_j) + \Sigma \Sigma \beta_k \beta_m E(y_k y_m)$$
$$\qquad (19\ a)$$
$$+ 2 \Sigma \Sigma \alpha_i \beta_k E(x_i y_k)] = 1$$

and for γ_1 and γ_2

$$\gamma_1^2 \Sigma \Sigma \alpha_i \alpha_j E(x_i x_j) = 1 \ ; \quad \gamma_2^2 \Sigma \Sigma \beta_k \beta_m E(y_k y_m) = 1$$

$$(19\ b\text{-}c)$$

NIPALS Specification. The NIPALS modelling of the six models specifies linear predictors in accordance with the arrow schemes in Figures 4a - f.

Model A_1. Following Figure 4 a, the NIPALS specification of Hauser's model is as follows.

Having assumed the kernel ω to take the form (16), we shall further assume ω to be given by a linear predictor relation in terms of x_1, ..., x_p ; in symbols,

$$\omega = \alpha_1 x_1 + \ldots + \alpha_p x_p + \nu \qquad (20\ a)$$

$$E(\omega | x_1, \ldots, x_p) = \alpha_1 x_1 + \ldots + \alpha_p x_p \qquad (20\ b)$$

On the other hand, y_k is for each k assumed to be related to ω by a linear predictor; that is

$$y_k = \beta_k \, \omega + \nu_k \qquad \qquad \text{(21 a)}$$

with

$$E(y_k|\omega) = \beta_k \, \omega \qquad k = 1, \ldots, q \qquad \text{(21 b)}$$

<u>Model A$_2$</u>. With the twin kernels ξ, η in the form (17 a-b), the NIPALS specification interchanges the twins when forming predictors in accordance with the arrow scheme in Figure 4 d. Thus η is assumed to be given by a linear relation in terms of $x_1, \ldots, x_p$; that is

$$\eta = \alpha_1 \, x_1 + \ldots + \alpha_p \, x_p + \nu \qquad \qquad \text{(22 a)}$$

with

$$E(\eta|x_1, \ldots, x_p) = \alpha_1 \, x_1 + \cdots + \alpha_p \, x_p \qquad \text{(22 b)}$$

On the other hand, y_k is for each k assumed to be related to ξ by a linear predictor; this gives

$$y_k = \beta_k \, \xi + \nu_k \qquad \qquad \text{(23 a)}$$

with

$$E(y_k|\xi) = \beta_k \, \xi \qquad k = 1, \ldots, q \qquad \text{(23 b)}$$

<u>Models B$_1$, B$_2$, C$_1$ and C$_2$</u>. The NIPALS specifications are easily obtained by reshuffling formulas (20)-(23) in accordance with Figures 4 a-f. Thus for Model B$_1$ the specification involves two predictors of type (20 a-b), and for Model B$_2$ a predictor of type (22) for each twin kernel. For Model C$_1$ the NIPALS specification involves two sets of predictors of type (21), and for Model C$_2$ there is one set of predictors (23) for each of the twin kernels ξ, η .

Among the resulting NIPALS specifications we recognize two NIPALS models previously established, namely for Model C$_1$

the PC (principal components) model, and for Model B_2 the CC (canonical correlations) model.[19]

NIPALS Estimation. As always in NIPALS modelling, the estimation is an iterative procedure that involves a sequence of OLS regressions. For each step of round s in the iterative procedure ($s = 1, 2, \ldots$) proxies are computed for the unknowns, that is for the parameters and latent variables.

We shall use the same notations for the various procedures, as follows:

Unknowns	Notation	Proxy	NIPALS estimate
Parameter	α_i	$a_i^{(s)}$	$a_i = \lim\limits_{s \to \infty} a_i^{(s)}$
Latent variable	ω	$w^{(s)}$	$w = \lim\limits_{s \to \infty} w^{(s)}$
Normalization factor	γ_0	$g_0^{(s)}$	$g_0 = \lim\limits_{s \to \infty} g_0^{(s)}$

and similarly for the parameters β_k, the latent variables ξ, η and the normalization factors γ_1, γ_2.

As always in iterative procedures, the design of the procedure can be modulated in various ways; see e.g. Section 2 (h_3). For one thing, the order in which the unknowns are are proxied is flexible. In Models A_2, B_2, C_2 we shall calculate the proxies in the order

$$a_i^{(s)} , g_1^{(s)} , x^{(s)} , b_k^{(s)} , g_2^{(s)} , y^{(s)} \tag{24}$$

In Models A_1, B_1, C_1 we could follow the order

$$a_i^{(s)} , b_k^{(s)} , g_0^{(s)} , w^{(s)} \tag{25 a}$$

but to make for more speedy convergence we shall compute two kernel proxies in each round, in the following order,

$$a_i^{(s)} , g_1^{(s)} , w_1^{(s)} , b_k^{(s)} , g_0^{(s)} , w^{(s)} \tag{25 b}$$

---

[19] See Wold (1966 b), Sections 1-2. As shown by Lyttkens (1966, 1972), the NIPALS versions of the PC and CC models are numerically equivalent to the classical methods. The advantages of the NIPALS approach come beautifully to the fore in PC models; see Christoffersson (1970).

The data input in the estimation procedure may either consist of raw data (time-series or cross-section data), or of variance-covariance matrices. Assuming that all variables x_i, y_k are measured from their means, and are normalized to unit variance, we denote the raw data by

$$x_{it} \text{ , } y_{kt} \qquad (t = 1, \ldots, n) \qquad (26 \text{ a})$$

and the (correlation) matrix data by

$$\underset{\sim}{R}_{xx} = [r(x_i, x_j)]; \; \underset{\sim}{R}_{yy} = [r(y_k, y_m)]; \; \underset{\sim}{R}_{xy} = [r(x_i, y_k)]$$
$$(26 \text{ b})$$

The NIPALS procedure takes slightly different forms in the two cases, but is essentially the same. We shall describe both versions, assuming raw data input (26 a) for Model A_1 and matrix data (26 b) for Model A_2.

Model A_1. To describe this and other iterative procedures, we specify the start, s = 1, and the general round from s-1 to s. To repeat, raw data input (26 a) is assumed.

Start: s = 1. Making all $a_i^{(1)} = b_k^{(1)} = 1$, we form

$$w_t^{(1)} = g_o^{(1)} \; (\sum_i x_{it} + \sum_k y_{kt}) \qquad (27)$$

where t = 1, ..., n and where the normalization factor $g_o^{(1)}$ is computed so as to give $w_t^{(1)}$ unit variance. To spell out the normalization, we compute

$$w_t^{(1)} = \sum_i x_{it} + \sum_k y_{kt} \qquad (t = 1, \ldots, n) \qquad (28 \text{ a})$$

and

$$g_o^{(1)} = [\sum_{t=1}^{n} (w_t^{(1)})^2]^{-\frac{1}{2}} \qquad (28 \text{ b})$$

The round from s-1 to s: In words, the proxy $w^{(s-1)}$ obtained in the previous round is adjusted on the basis of OLS regressions formed in accordance with the predictor specifications (20 a-b) and (21 a-b). To spell out, the previous round has given the proxy

$$w_t^{(s-1)} = g_o^{(s-1)} [\sum_i a_i^{(s-1)} x_{it} + \sum_k b_k^{(s-1)} y_{kt}]; (t = 1, \ldots, n)$$

(29)

In the first phase of the sth round we follow (20 a-b), and form new proxies $a_i^{(s)}$ for the coefficients x_i by computing the multiple OLS regression

$$w_t^{(s-1)} = \sum_i a_i^{(s)} x_{it} + u_t^{(s)}$$

(30)

In the second phase we follow (16), and form the half-way proxy kernel $w_1^{(s)}$ in (25 b) by computing

$$w_{1t}^{(s)} = g_1^{(s)} [\sum_i a_i^{(s)} x_{it} + \sum_k b_k^{(s-1)} y_{kt}]$$

(31)

where the device for calculating the normalization factor carries over from (28 a-b).

In the third phase we follow (21 a-b), and compute new proxies $b_i^{(s)}$ for the coefficients β_k by calculating for each $k = 1, \ldots, q$ the simple OLS regression

$$y_{kt}^{(s)} = b_k^{(s)} w_{1t}^{(s)} + v_{kt}^{(s)}$$

(32)

In the fourth and last phase of the sth round we compute the proxy kernel

$$w_t^{(s)} = g_o^{(s)} [\sum_i a_i^{(s)} x_{it} + \sum_k b_k^{(s)} y_{kt}]$$

(33)

where the normalization factor is calculated in the same manner as in (28 a-b) and (31).

Model A_2. Data input in the form of correlation matrices (26 b) is assumed. As compared with raw data input (26 a) this brings the following two changes in the computatations:

(i) The normalization factors $g_1^{(s)}$ are computed from the formula

$$1 = r(x^{(s)}, x^{(s)}) = \frac{1}{n} \sum_t (x_t^{(s)})^2 \tag{34}$$

$$= (g_1^{(s)})^2 \sum_i \sum_j a_i^{(s)} a_j^{(s)} r(x_i, x_j)$$

for $s = 1, 2, \ldots$; and similarly for $g_2^{(s)}$.

(ii) For the OLS regressions based on (22a) and (23 a) we need the correlations $r(x_i, y^{(s)})$ and $r(y_k, x^{(s)})$. The first correlations are computed from

$$r(x_i, y^{(s)}) = g_2^{(s)} \sum_k b_k^{(s)} r(x_i, y_k) \tag{35}$$

for $s = 1, 2, \ldots$; and similarly for $r(y_k, x^{(s)})$.

Again we describe the NIPALS estimation procedure by the start $s = 1$ and the general round from s-1 to s. In each round we follow (17 a-b) to form new kernel proxies $x^{(s)}$ and $y^{(s)}$ on the basis of new proxy estimates $a_i^{(s)}$ and $b_k^{(s)}$ for the parameters. As in Model A_1 the proxies $a_i^{(s)}$ and $b_k^{(s)}$ are obtained by OLS regressions, now in accordance with the predictor specifications (22 a-b) and (23 a-b).

Start: $s = 1$. Making all $b_k^{(1)} = 1$, we form the first proxy of the second twin kernel,

$$y^{(1)} = g_2^{(1)} \sum_k b_k^{(1)} y_k \tag{36}$$

where a computation of type (34) gives the normalization factor $g_2^{(1)}$. Next, using formula (35) we compute the correlations $r(x_i, y^{(1)})$.

The round from s - 1 to s : The previous step has given the proxy

$$y^{(s-1)} = g_2^{(s-1)} \sum_k b_k^{(s-1)} y_k \tag{37}$$

and the correlations $r(x_i, y^{(s-1)})$.

In the first phase of sth round we form new proxies $a_i^{(s)}$ for the coefficients α_i by computing the multiple OLS regression

$$y^{(s-1)} = \sum_i a_i^{(s)} x_i + u^{(s)} \tag{38}$$

In the second phase we form the proxy kernel $x^{(s)}$ by computing

$$x^{(s)} = g_1^{(s)} \sum_i a_i^{(s)} x_i \tag{39}$$

where a calculation of type (34) is again used to obtain the normalization factor $g_1^{(s)}$. Next, again using a formula of type (35) we compute the correlations $r(y_k, x^{(s)})$.

In the third phase we compute new proxies $b_k^{(s)}$ for coefficients β_k by calculating for each $k = 1, \ldots, q$ the simple OLS regression

$$y_k = b_k^{(s)} x^{(s)} + v_k^{(s)} \tag{40}$$

In the fourth and last phase of the sth round we compute the proxy kernel

$$y^{(s)} = g_2^{(s)} \sum_k b_k^{(s)} y_k \tag{41}$$

where again a calculation of type (34) gives the normalization factor $g_2^{(s)}$. The sth round is concluded by calculating the correlations $r(x_i, y^{(s)})$, once more using formula (35).

Numerical Illustration

For numerical illustration of the iterative OLS procedures in the NIPALS remodelling of Hauser's model we shall use Data III as given by (63 c). As in (63 d) and Table 1 we specify $p = 0.6$, $q = 0.5$, $r = 0.4$. The numerical results come from the computer, and further we spell out the algebraic expression for unspecified p and r, in accordance with (63 e-f). We shall consider Model A .

Start: $s = 1$. We set $b_1^{(1)} = b_1^{(2)} = 1$, and obtain from (36)

$$y^{(1)} = g_2^{(1)} (\psi_3 + (1 + 2r) \psi_4 + \sqrt{2(1 - 2r^2)} \psi_5)/\sqrt{2}$$

with the normalization factor $g_2^{(1)} = 1/\sqrt{2(1+r)} = 0.5976$

For $s = 2$ the multiple regression (38) gives the normal equations

$$a_1^{(2)} + pa_2^{(2)} = E(x_1 y^{(1)}) = 0$$

$$pa_1^{(2)} + a_2^{(2)} = E(x_2 y^{(1)}) = 1/\sqrt{8(1+r)} = 0.2988$$

Hence

$$a_1^{(2)} = - p/(1-p^2) \sqrt{8(1+r)} = - 0.2801$$

$$a_2^{(2)} = 1/(1-p^2) \sqrt{8(1+r)} = 0.4669$$

which after substitution in (39) gives

$$g_1^{(2)} = \sqrt{8(1-p^2)(1+r)} = 2.677$$

and

$$x^{(2)} = (-p \sqrt{2(1 - 2p^2)} \psi_1 + (1 - 2p^2) \psi_2 + \psi_3)/\sqrt{2(1 - p^2)}$$

Next, the regressions (40) give

$$b_1^{(2)} = E(y_1 x^{(2)}) = 1/2 \sqrt{1-p^2} = 0.6250; \quad b_2^{(2)} = E(y_2 x^{(2)}) = 0$$

which by (41) gives

$$g_2^{(2)} = 2 \sqrt{1 - p^2} = 1.6$$

and

$$y^{(2)} = (\psi_3 + \psi_4)/\sqrt{2}$$

For the next step s = 3 we return to (38), and obtain the normal equations

$$a_1^{(3)} + pa_2^{(3)} = E(x_1 \, y^{(2)}) = 0$$

$$pa_1^{(3)} + a_2^{(3)} = E(x_2 \, y^{(2)}) = \frac{1}{2}$$

which give

$$a_1^{(3)} = -p/2(1 - p^2) = -0.4688 \; ; \; a_2^{(3)} = 1/2(1 - p^2) = 0.7812$$

Hence, again using (39),

$$g_1^{(3)} = 2 \sqrt{1 - p^2} = 1.6$$

and

$$x^{(3)} = (-p \sqrt{2(1 - 2 p^2)} \psi_1 + (1 - 2 p^2) \, \psi_2 + \psi_3)/\sqrt{2(1 - p^2)}$$

We see that $x^{(3)} = x^{(2)}$, as could be expected since $a_1^{(3)}$, $a_2^{(3)}$ are proportional to $a_1^{(2)}$, $a_2^{(2)}$. This implies that the iterative procedure has reached its limit in two steps. Hence the following NIPALS estimates are obtained for the latent variables,

$$x = x^{(3)} \; ; \quad y = y^{(3)} = y^{(2)}$$

while the corresponding parameter estimates are given by

$$a_i = a_i^{(3)} \; ; \; b_k = b_k^{(3)} = b_k^{(2)} \quad , \; (i, \, k = 1, \, 2)$$

This is in accordance with the numerical results given in Table I for Model A_2 with Data III, except for the normalization. For example, $a_1 = a_2 = 0.6$ in both cases.

Models B_1, B_2, C_1 and C_2. The NIPALS estimating procedures for raw data input (26a) and matrix input (26 b) are readily written down by reshuffling formulas (27) – (41) in accordance with the appropriate NIPALS specifications outlined in the beginning of Section 3. Thus for Model B_1 the estimation procedure with raw data input involves two multiple regressions of type (30), and Model B_2 with matrix data input two multiple regressions of type (38). For Model C_1 with raw data input the estimation procedure involves two sets of simple OLS regressions of type (32), and for Model C_2 with matrix data input there is one set of simple OLS regressions of type (40) for each proxy $x^{(s)}$, $y^{(s)}$ of the twin kernels.

Computer Programs. The NIPALS estimation procedures for Models A_i - C_i (i = 1,2) have been programmed by B. Areskoug, Statistics Department, University of Göteborg. The programs are available at request (nominal cost).

Algebraic Solutions of the NIPALS Estimations

The conceptual and theoretical definitions of the six models in Figures 4 a-f are given by their NIPALS specifications; for Models A_1 and A_2 see formulas (20 a-b) and (21 a-b). The parameters α_i, β_k, γ_a are defined, implicitly, by the predictor specifications and the corresponding normalizations. Hence in the technical sense of statistical theory, the normal equations that follow from the predictor relations and the normalization assumptions constitute the NIPALS estimators of the parameters α_i, β_k, γ_a.[20]

The present section gives algebraic solutions for the parameters, showing that the predictor relations lead to explicit equations of the eigenvalue type. The resulting equations are the natural tool for the analysis of an array of problems, including the algebraic calculation of the parameters when a model is applied to a multivariate empirical or theoretical distribution, or in making comparative theoretical studies between the six models.

For Model C_1 the resulting eigenvalue equation is the same as for principal components, confirming that Model C_1 is nothing else than a PC model. Similarly, Model B_2 reveals

---

[20] This last statement carries over from Agren's (1972) treatment of FP and FFP estimation.

itself as a canonical correlations model. It will be noted that neither Model A_1 nor Model A_2 give eigenvalue equations that are in line with the results that Hauser and Goldberger (1971) report on their version of Hauser's model.

Whereas Model A_1 in general is not equivalent to A_2, and Model C_1 not equivalent to C_2, it turns out that Model B_1 is always equivalent to B_2. Models B_1 and B_2 cannot be distinguished numerically. Hence Model B_1 provides a new interpretation of canonical correlations.

Model A_1. We consider relations (20)-(21) as applied to the theoretical distribution of the variables x_i, y_k. Spelling out the ith normal equation of the multiple regression (20 a-b) we obtain

$$\alpha_1 r(x_1,\ x_i) + \ldots + \alpha_p r(x_p,\ x_i) = E(\omega x_i)$$

$$= \gamma_o\ [\alpha_1\ r(x_1,\ x_i) + \ldots + \alpha_p r(x_p,\ x_i) + \beta_1 r(y_1,\ x_i) +$$

$$\ldots + \beta_q r(y_q,\ x_i)]\qquad\qquad (42a)$$

with $i = 1, \ldots, p$. Similarly, the kth regression (21 a-b) gives

$$\beta = r(\omega,\ y_k)$$

$$= \gamma_o\left[\alpha_1 r(x_1,\ y_k) + \ldots + \alpha_p r(x_p,\ y_k) + \beta_1 r(y_1,\ y_k)\qquad (42b)\right.$$

$$\left. + \ldots + \beta_q r(y_q,\ y_k)\right]$$

with $k = 1, \ldots, q$.

Writing (42 a-b) in matrix and vector notation (26 b),

$$\underset{\sim}{R}_{xx}\ \underset{\sim}{\alpha} = \gamma_o\ (\underset{\sim}{R}_{xx}\ \underset{\sim}{\alpha} + \underset{\sim}{R}_{xy}\ \underset{\sim}{\beta})\qquad\qquad (43\ a)$$

$$\underset{\sim}{\beta} = \gamma_o (\underset{\sim}{R}_{yx} \underset{\sim}{\alpha} + \underset{\sim}{R}_{yy} \underset{\sim}{\beta}) \tag{43 b}$$

Since this system is linear and homogeneous in α_i , β_k, it has non-zero solutions only for γ_o -values that satisfy the eigenvalue equation

$$\begin{vmatrix} (1 - \lambda) \underset{\sim}{R}_{xx} & \underset{\sim}{R}_{xy} \\ \\ \underset{\sim}{R}_{yx} & \underset{\sim}{R}_{yy} - \lambda \underset{\sim}{I} \end{vmatrix} = O \tag{44}$$

where we have written $\lambda = 1/\gamma_o$.

In (20)-(21) we want solutions that make for a large linear form in (16); that is, a large variance for the expression within brackets in (19a), giving a small value for γ_o. Hence we seek the largest root λ of equation (44), say

$$\lambda = \lambda_1 \tag{45}$$

It remains to substitute $\gamma_o = 1/\lambda_1$ in (43 a-b) and solve for α_i , β_k.

<u>Model A$_2$</u>. Turning to (22)-(23), we proceed in the same manner. For the ith and kth normal equations we obtain

$$\alpha_1 r(x_1, x_i) + \ldots + \alpha_p r(x_p, x_i) = E(\eta\, x_i)$$

$$= \gamma_2 \left[\beta_1 r(x_i, y_1) + \ldots + \beta_q r(x_i, y_q) \right] \tag{46 a}$$

$$\beta_k = r(\xi, y_k)$$

$$= \gamma_1 \left[\alpha_1 r(y_k, x_1) + \ldots + \alpha_p r(y_k, x_p) \right] \tag{46 b}$$

with i = 1, ..., p and k = 1, ..., q.

In matrix notation this gives

$$\underset{\sim}{R}_{xx}\,\underset{\sim}{\alpha} = \gamma_2\,\underset{\sim}{R}_{xy}\,\underset{\sim}{\beta} \qquad\qquad (47\ a)$$

$$\underset{\sim}{\beta} = \gamma_1\,\underset{\sim}{R}_{yx}\,\underset{\sim}{\alpha} \qquad\qquad (47\ b)$$

whence

$$\underset{\sim}{R}_{xx}\,\underset{\sim}{\alpha} = \gamma_1\,\gamma_2\,\underset{\sim}{R}_{xy}\,\underset{\sim}{R}_{yx}\,\underset{\sim}{\alpha}\ ; \qquad \underset{\sim}{\beta} = \gamma_1\,\gamma_2\,\underset{\sim}{R}_{yx}\,\underset{\sim}{R}_{xx}^{-1}\,\underset{\sim}{R}_{xy}\underset{\sim}{}$$

$$(48\ a\text{-}b)$$

While (43 a-b) makes a joint system for $\underset{\sim}{\alpha}$ and $\underset{\sim}{\beta}$, we have now obtained a linear homogeneous system for each of α and β. To obtain non-zero solutions, we shall first consider the parameters $\underset{\sim}{\alpha}$. Writing

$$\lambda = 1/\gamma_1\,\gamma_2$$

(48a) gives the eigenvalue equation

$$\underset{\sim}{R}_{xy}\,\underset{\sim}{R}_{yx} - \lambda\,\underset{\sim}{R}_{xx} = O \qquad\qquad (49\ a)$$

or, for direct comparison with (44),

$$\begin{vmatrix} \underset{\sim}{R}_{xx} & \underset{\sim}{R}_{xy} \\[2mm] \underset{\sim}{R}_{yx} & \lambda\,\underset{\sim}{I} \end{vmatrix} \qquad\qquad (49\ b)$$

Solving (49) for the largest root, say

$$\lambda = \lambda_2 \qquad\qquad (49\ c)$$

we substitute $\gamma_1\,\gamma_2 = 1/\lambda_2$ in (48 a) and solve for $\underset{\sim}{\alpha}$. To obtain $\underset{\sim}{\beta}$, we start from (48 b) and follow the same line of deductions, which gives for Model A_1 the eigenvalue equation

$$\underset{\sim}{R}_{yx}\,\underset{\sim}{R}_{xx}^{-1}\,\underset{\sim}{R}_{xy} - \lambda\,\underset{\sim}{I} = O \qquad\qquad (50)$$

Model B_1. In this case the same argument as used above gives two sets of normal equations of type (42) or (43 a) in matrix notation

$$R_{xx} \, \alpha = \gamma_o \, (R_{xx} \, \alpha + R_{xy} \, \beta) \qquad (51 \text{ a})$$

$$R_{yy} \, \beta = \gamma_o \, (R_{yx} \, \alpha + R_{yy} \, \beta) \qquad (51 \text{ b})$$

With $\lambda = 1/\gamma_o$ this gives the eigenvalue equation

$$\begin{vmatrix} (1 - \lambda) \, R_{xx} & R_{xy} \\ & \\ R_{yx} & (1-\lambda) \, R_{yy} \end{vmatrix} = 0 \qquad (52)$$

Solving for the largest λ , say $\lambda = \lambda_3$, we substitute $\gamma_o = 1/\lambda_3$ in (51 a-b) and solve for α , β.

Model B_2. Here the same type of argument gives two sets of normal equations of type (46b) or (47 b) in matrix notation

$$R_{xx} \, \alpha = \gamma_2 \, R_{xy} \, \beta \qquad (53 \text{ a})$$

$$R_{yy} \, \beta = \gamma_1 \, R_{yx} \, \alpha \qquad (53 \text{ b})$$

To obtain α we use (53 b) to express β in terms of α ,

$$\beta = \gamma_1 \, R_{yy}^{-1} \, R_{yx} \, \alpha \qquad (54 \text{ a})$$

which on substitution into (53a) gives

$$R_{xx} \, \alpha = \gamma_1 \, \gamma_2 \, R_{xy} \, R_{yy}^{-1} \, R_{yx} \, \alpha \qquad (54 \text{ b})$$

With $\lambda = 1/\gamma_1 \, \gamma_2$ this gives the eigenvalue equation

$$R_{xy} \, R_{yy}^{-1} \, R_{yx} - \lambda \, R_{xx} = 0 \qquad (55 \text{ a})$$

Again solving for the largest λ, say $\lambda = \lambda_4$, we substitute $\gamma_1 \, \gamma_2 = 1/\lambda_4$ in (54 b) and solve for α. The parameters β are obtained by similar deductions; we spell out the eigenvalue equation that corresponds to (55 a),

$$R_{yx} \, R_{xx}^{-1} \, R_{xy} - \lambda \, R_{yy} = 0 \qquad (55 \text{ b})$$

Remark. In (53) - (55) we recognize the classical eigenvalue solution for canonical correlations: Hotelling (1936). Hence the NIPALS approach to Model B_2 is numerically equivalent to the classical multivariate notion of canonical correlations. In complete accordance herewith, our iterative NIPALS estimation procedure to Model B_2 is nothing else than the NIPALS estimation procedure for canonical correlations given previously by the author; see Wold (1966 b), Section 2.

It will further be noted that Models B_1 and B_2 are numerically equivalent. First, if we modify system (53 a-b) by making

$$\gamma_1 = \gamma_2 = \gamma^* = \sqrt{\gamma_1 \, \gamma_2}$$

its solutions may be written α, β^*, with

$$\beta^* = \beta \, \sqrt{\gamma_2/\gamma_1}$$

showing that the parameter vectors β and β^* are proportional. Second, the modified system is equivalent to (51 a-b), subject to the substitution

$$\lambda = (1 + \gamma^*)/\gamma^*$$

Model C. Here the same argument that carries from (21 b) to (42 b) gives two sets of normal equations of the same simple type, in matrix notation

$$\alpha = \gamma_0 \, (R_{xx}\alpha + R_{xy} \, \beta)$$

$$\beta = \gamma_0 \, (R_{yx} \, \alpha + R_{yy} \, \beta) \qquad (56 \text{ a-b})$$

With $\lambda = 1/\gamma_0$ this gives the eigenvalue equation

$$
\begin{vmatrix}
R_{xx} - \lambda I & R_{xy} \\
R_{yx} & R_{yy} - \lambda I
\end{vmatrix} = 0 \qquad (57)
$$

We solve (57) or (59) for the largest λ, say $\lambda = \lambda_5$, substitute $\gamma_0 = 1/\lambda_5$ in (56 a-b), and solve for α and β.

Remark: If we write

$$
R = \begin{bmatrix}
R_{xx} & R_{xy} \\
R_{yx} & R_{yy}
\end{bmatrix} \qquad (58)
$$

for the correlation matrix of the joint set of variables x_i, y_k, we see that (57) is the same equation as

$$
\begin{vmatrix} R - \lambda I \end{vmatrix} = 0 \qquad (59)
$$

and this is nothing else than the classical eigenvalue equation for the principal components of the joint set x_i, y_k; see K. Pearson (1901). This is in complete agreement with the fact that our iterative NIPALS estimation procedure for Model C_1 is nothing else than the NIPALS estimation procedure for the first principal component of the joint set of variables x_i, y_k given previously by the author; see Wold (1966b), Section 1.

Model C_2. The same argument as in (21) and (47 b) now gives the following normal equations

$$
\alpha = \gamma_2 R_{xy} \beta
$$

$$
(60 \text{ a-b})
$$

$$
\beta = \gamma_1 R_{yx} \alpha
$$

Hence

$$\underset{\sim}{\alpha} = \gamma_1 \ \gamma_2 \ \underset{\sim}{R}_{xy} \ \underset{\sim}{R}_{yx} \ \underset{\sim}{\alpha} \tag{61}$$

which with $\lambda = 1/\gamma_1 \ \gamma_2$ gives the eigenvalue equation

$$\underset{\sim}{R}_{xy} \ \underset{\sim}{R}_{yx} - \lambda \ \underset{\sim}{I} = 0 \tag{62}$$

Again we solve for the largest λ, say $\lambda = \lambda_6$, substitute $\gamma_1 \gamma_2 = 1/\lambda_6$ in the system (61), which we then solve for $\underset{\sim}{\alpha}$, and finally (60 b) gives $\underset{\sim}{\beta}$.

Illustrations

We shall report applications of our six models to three sets of data. The numerical results are summarized in Table 1, and some first comments are adduced.

Data I. Here we use the data of Hauser and Goldberger (1971), briefly H-G, who have applied their version of Hauser's model to empirical data where the three variables x_i are indicators of social status, and the three variables y_k are indicators of social participation. Note that when Table 1 quotes H-G's results, their parameter estimates have been multiplied by a normalization constant q_0 in accordance with (16).

Data II. Here we shall use data in the form of a theoretical population, given as a multivariate distribution which is defined in terms of variables ψ, Δ_1, Δ_2 that are assumed to be mutually independent and to have zero mean and unit standard deviation.

$$x_1 = \psi \qquad\qquad y_1 = \psi$$

$$\tag{63 a}$$

$$x_2 = (\psi + \Delta_1)/\sqrt{2} \qquad\qquad y_2 = (\psi + \Delta_2)/\sqrt{2}$$

In (63 b) we give the correlation matrix (58) for Data II.

$$\underset{\sim}{R} = \begin{bmatrix} 1 & \frac{1}{2}\sqrt{2} & 1 & \frac{1}{2}\sqrt{2} \\ \frac{1}{2}\sqrt{2} & 1 & \frac{1}{2}\sqrt{2} & \frac{1}{2} \\ 1 & \frac{1}{2}\sqrt{2} & 1 & \frac{1}{2}\sqrt{2} \\ \frac{1}{2}\sqrt{2} & \frac{1}{2} & \frac{1}{2}\sqrt{2} & 1 \end{bmatrix} \; ; \; \underset{\sim}{R} = \begin{bmatrix} 1 & p & O & O \\ p & 1 & q & O \\ O & q & 1 & r \\ O & O & r & 1 \end{bmatrix}$$

$$(63\ b\text{-}c)$$

Data III. Here the multivariate distribution is de-fined by the correlation matrix given by (63 c). As illus-trated in Figure 5, Data III can be interpreted as belonging to a path model with three consecutive steps. The results for Data III in Table 1 refer to the special case

$$p = 0.6 \; ; \qquad q = 0.5 \; ; \qquad r = 0.4 \qquad (63\ d)$$

With $q = 0.5$ and unspecified p and r, a set of variables with correlation matrix (63 c) is given by

$$x_1 = \sqrt{1 - 2 p^2} \; \psi_1 + p \sqrt{2} \; \psi_2 \; ; \quad y_1 = (\psi_3 + \psi_4)/\sqrt{2}$$

$$(63\ e)$$

$$x_2 = (\psi_2 + \psi_3)/ \sqrt{2} \; ; \qquad y_2 = r \sqrt{2} \; \psi_4 + \sqrt{1 - 2 r^2} \; \psi_5$$

$$(63\ f)$$

where ψ_1 through ψ_5 are independent variables with zero mean and unit standard deviation.

Normalization of the paramater estimates for direct comparison between the models. For any model M in Table 1 we shall take the estimates a_i, b_k of parameters α_i, β_k to in-clude the normalization factor g according to formula (16) or (17). Let $a_i^*(M)$, $b_k^*(M)$ denote the normalized estimates given in Table 1. Further let

$$s_1(M) = s(\sum_i a_i x_i) \; ; \qquad s_2(M) = s(\sum_k b_k y_k)$$

denote the standard deviations of the two linear forms

I. Hauser-Goldberger's data, and (line H-G:) their parameter estimates.
II. Illustration (63 b). -- III. Illustration (63 c-d).

(1)	(2)	(3)	(4)	(5)	(6)	(7)	(8)	(9)	(10)
Data	Model	α_1	α_2	α_3	β_1	β_2	β_3	ρ	NOIT[c]
I	H-G	0.176	0.054	0.243	0.234	0.504	0.339	0.401	
	A_1	0.155	0.086	0.242	0.347	0.422	0.334	0.385	13
	B_1	0.287	0.088	0.395	0.34	0.473	0.234	0.412	35
	C_1	0.276	0.267	0.308	0.235	0.315	0.240	0.380	12
	A_2	0.163	0.073	0.242	0.239	0.501	0.337	0.401	4
	B_2	0.287	0.088	0.395	0.034	0.473	0.234	0.412	5
	C_2	0.278	0.223	0.341	0.179	0.357	0.240	0.395	4
II	A_1	0.372	0		0.372	0.325		0.934	7
	B_1	0.500	0		0.500	0		1.000	14
	C_1	0.304	0.255		0.304	0.255		0.878	7
	A_2	0.30	0		0.40	0.28		0.949	2
	B_2	0.500	0		0.500	0		1.000	2
	C_2	0.324	0.229		0.324	0.229		0.900	2
III	A_1	-0.338	0.564		0.536	0.289		0.476	17
	B_1	-0.409	0.682		0.595	-0.238		0.682	23
	C_1	0.354	0.489		0.385	0.186		0.254	23
	A_2	-0.324	0.539		0.672	0		0.625	2
	B_2	-0.409	0.682		0.595	-0.238		0.682	2
	C_2	0	0.696		0.450	0		0.500	2

[a]The computer calculations have been performed by B. Areskoug; see the previous section on Computer programs.

[b]For direct comparison of the models, the parameters are normalized; see formulas and explanation in the text.

[c]NOIT = Number of iterations in the NIPALS estimation procedure.

Table 1. NIPALS PARAMETERS IN MODELS A_i, B_i, C_i (i=1,2) FOR DATA I-III.[a,b]

$\Sigma \, a_i \, x_i$ and $\Sigma \, b_k \, y_k$. For Hauser-Goldberger's model and the NIPALS models A_1 and A_2 the normalized parameter estimates are calculated as

$$a_i^*(M) = a_i(M) \, \frac{s_1(A_1)}{s_1(M)} \; ; \; b_k^*(M) = b_k(M) \, \frac{s_2(A_1)}{s_2(M)}$$

which makes for direct comparison between these three models. Note that $a_i^*(A_1) = a_i(A_1)$ and $b_k^*(A_1) = b_k(A_1)$. For Models B_1 and B_2 the normalized parameter estimates are calculated by the same formulas after substituting A_1 by B_1 and M by B_2, and similarly for Models C_1 and C_2.

Hauser and Goldberger's Version of Hauser's Model versus the NIPALS Versions A_1 and A_2. Comparing H-G's model with the two models A_1-A_2, we see from Table 1 that the numerical results are somewhat different. This is as expected, since Hauser and Goldberger's design of their model is conceptually and formally different from the NIPALS approach.

Having specified the structural relations (20 a) and (21 a), which are formally the same as in the NIPALS approach, Hauser and Goldberger eliminate ω by substitution to obtain the reduced form, which we quote in the present notation system,

$$y_k = \pi_{k1} \, x_1 + \ldots + \pi_{kp} \, x_p + \delta_k \qquad \text{(64 a)}$$

where the substitution formally gives

$$\pi_{ki} = \alpha_i \beta_k \qquad \text{(64 b)}$$

Hauser and Goldberger estimate the parameters α_i and β_k on the basis of a criterion that makes for approximate fulfillment of the relations (64 b). The argument behind (64 b) and the ensuing criterion draw from the assumption of classical ID systems, namely that every residual ν_k in (21a) is uncorrelated with all variables x_i. We see that this makes pq non-correlation assumptions, while the NIPALS specification with the predictors (20 b) and (21 b) involves p+q

342

non-correlation assumptions. Hence the classical assumptions are more numerous if $p > 2$ and $q > 2$, and with a large number of variables they are much more numerous than in the NIPALS specification. This is a case where the NIPALS approach satisfies the parity principle (see Section 3 (h_4)), making the NIPALS model more general than a corresponding model that does not honor the same principle, in this case Hauser and Goldberger's model.

Equivalence of Models B_1 and B_2. Table 1 shows that for all Data I-III the results are numerically the same for Models B_1 and B_2. This is in full agreement with the theoretical analysis in (51)-(55), from which we have inferred that the algebraic equations for the parameters of the two models are equivalent. To repeat, while it is already known that Model B_2 gives a regression interpretation of the classical concept of canonical correlations, Model B_1 now gives a novel regression interpretation of the same concept.

While the "unit kernel" designs A_1, B_1, C_1 at first sight look rather different from the "twin kernel" designs A_2, B_2, C_2, the equivalence of Models B_1 and B_2 is an indication that the two modes of design have much in common. This last statement is supported by the numerical results, for although we know from the analysis in (51)-(55) that the equivalence does not carry over to Models A_1 and A_2, nor to Models C_1 and C_2, we see from Table 1 that the parameter estimates are rather similar. At the same time there are large differences between the parameter estimates for Models A_i and C_i.

The Intercorrelation ρ Between the Kernel Forms in x_i and y_k. For Models H-G and A_2-C_2 the last column in Table 1 gives the (product-moment) correlation between the twin kernels ξ and η as defined by (17 a-b),

$$\rho = r(\xi, \eta) \tag{65}$$

For Models A_1-C_1 the same column gives the correlation of the two linear forms in x_i and y_k that are obtained by splitting up the unit kernel (16).

Let $\rho(K)$ denote the correlation that the last column in Table 1 gives for the model K. To repeat, we know that $\rho(B_2)$ is the canonical correlation of the x_i's and y_k's, and further we know that this correlation is reproduced by Model B_1, whence $\rho(B_1) = \rho(B_2)$.

Owing to the maximum property of canonical correlations Models A_i and C_i give smaller correlations ρ than Models B_i; in symbols,

$$\rho(A_i) \leq \rho(B_i) \; ; \quad \rho(C_i) \leq \rho(B_i) \qquad (i = 1,2) \qquad (66 \text{ a-b})$$

We see from Table 1 that Models A_1 and C_1 give smaller correlations ρ than Models A_2 and C_2, and that the correlations ρ of Models A_i are intermediate between those of Models B_i and C_i,

$$\rho(A_1) \leq \rho(A_2) \; ; \; \rho(C_1) \leq \rho(C_2) \; ; \; \rho(C_i) \leq \rho(A_i), \; (i = 1,2)$$

$$(67 \text{ a-c})$$

This is as could be expected. As to (67 a-b), the twin kernels ξ and η of Models A_2 and C_2 involve one parameter more than the corresponding unit kernel ω of Models A_1 and C_1, and will therefore in general give a higher correlation ρ. As to (67c), Model A_i is formally a hybrid between Models B_i and C_i.

Data II and III give instructive examples of (66) - (67). Regarding (66) we note from Table 1 that with Data II and Models B_1-B_2 the (canonical) correlation ρ reaches its highest value, unity, and this is owing to the perfect correlation between x_1 and y_1 in (63 a). In Model C_2 the correlation ρ is smaller than unity, and this is due to the variables x_2 and y_2 which in this model enter into the kernels ξ and η, respectively, and thereby pull their correlation downwards.

344

4. DISCUSSION

Situations of Low versus High Degrees of Information.[21]
Models L, L*, L** mark an evolution in model building from
situations of high degrees to lower degrees of information.
In Models L the structural form specifies causal and/or predictive relations between directly observed variables, and
the ensuing residuals provide direct evidence about the
agreement or disagreement between actual observations and
forecasts generated from the model. Models L* involve
causal-predictive endogenous variables that are latent (being
indirectly observed as the systematic part of the corresponding directly observed variables), and latent variables provide less operative information than directly observed variables. In Models L**, as illustrated by the path model in
Figure 2, not only the endogenous causal but also the predetermined causal variables can be latent, and this makes
for further reduction in the operative information from the
model. Briefly expressed, in Models L the causal-predictive
relations give operative inference by way of directly observed variables, in Models L* and L** by way of latent variables, and latent variables are less informative than directly observed variables.

Incentives for Modelling with Latent Variables. Model
building with latent variables has a variety of incentives,
and takes several different forms. We note (1) the classical
models of variables and relations subject to observational
errors, where the latent variables represent the true variables and relations behind the manifest observations; (2)
the classical applications of factor analysis and principal
components, where the latent variables serve to represent the
unobservables of the human mind as subject to indirect
measurement by manifest indicators; (3) in REID and GEID
systems the systematic parts of the current endogenous variables are introduced as latent variables, to enable predict-
or specification of the structural form that constitutes the
behavioral basis of the model, and thereby make for operative use of the behavioral relations for predictive and/or
causal purposes; (4) in canonical correlations and more
clearly so in Hauser's model the model builder introduces
latent variables to represent groups of manifest variables,
and the relations are never designed to pass from one manifest variable to another; they always pass via a latent

---

[21]For a more elaborate discussion of this aspect, see Wold
(1973 b; 1974 a-b).

variable.

Our review of the evolution of path models L, L*, L** refers to simple models of type (4). The review here links up with the pioneering work on path models with latent variables in the last five or ten years in sociology and other social sciences.[22] We proceed to discuss some general aspects of the models under (4).

Aspiration Levels of Path Models: Consecutive Steps of Causal and/or Predictive Inference. Owing to its simplicity, Hauser's model is of fundamental relevance in the evolution of path models with latent variables. Hauser's model and Models A_1, A_2 push the aspiration level of causal-predictive inference one significant mark higher than Models B_1, C_1 (=PC), B_2 (=CC) and C_2, inasmuch as the inferential path of the former models has two consecutive steps, namely

$$x_i's \to \text{latent variable } \omega \text{ or } (\xi, \eta) \to y_k's$$

whereas the inferential paths in the latter models involve just one step, either from a manifest to a latent variable, or conversely.

Inward versus Outward Indicators. In modelling with latent variables the concept of *indicator* has been used for any manifest variable that is linked to a latent variable, irrespective of whether the causal-predictive inference goes from manifest to latent variable, as in Models B_1 and B_2, or from latent to manifest variable, as in Models C_1 and C_2. To remove this ambiguity, we shall speak of *inward indicators* in cases like Models B_1, B_2 or the variables x_i in Models A_1, A_2, and *outward indicators* in cases like Models C_1, C_2 or the variables y_k in Models A_1, A_2.[23]

We see that the NIPALS specification of Models A_i-C_i brings to surface the distinction between inward and outward indicators. In fact, the conceptual difference between the models A_1-C_1 lies in the direction of the indicators, and as illustrated by Table 1 the three models in general are

---

[22]See, also for further references, Blalock (ed. 1971 a) and Costner (ed. 1971).

[23]For the same distinction, Blalock (1971 b) uses the terms "cause indicator" and "effect indicator."

numerically different. The same holds true for the NIPALS models A_2, B_2 and C_2.

In NIPALS modelling with latent variables it is characteristic that the latent variables are explicitly defined in terms of directly observed variables. To emphasize this aspect, we shall sometimes speak of *generators versus indicators* instead of inward versus outward indicators.

Residual Aspects of Models A_i, B_i, C_i. Models B_1, B_2 involve one residual for each latent variable, models C_1, C_2 one residual for each manifest variable, whereas Models A_1, A_2 are intermediate in this respect. Thus with regard to the potential information contained in residuals, Models C_1, C_2 are more informative than A_1, A_2, and A_1, A_2 more informative than B_1, B_2.

Another important aspect is the difference between Models B_i and C_i as measures of intercorrelation between the x_i's and y_k's. Speaking broadly, and with reference to Table 1 for illustration, Models B_i measure the maximum correlation between two linear forms in x_i and y_k, whereas Models C_i serve as measures of the average correlation between the x_i's and y_k's.

Modelling with Latent Variables in Complex Situations

To repeat, and again with reference to Hauser's model for illustrations, Models L** have a bearing on situations of a lower degree of information than corresponding models of type L obtained when the latent variables are replaced by directly observed variables. More specifically, the scarcity of information is reflected in Hauser's model having no direct relations between the manifest variables. Over a wide range of more or less complex situations there is here a trade-off between the prior information and the device of latent variables in the model construction. On the one hand, the model may involve relatively few variables, whereas the available information does not suffice to specify direct relations between the observables. On the other hand, in models that have to cope with many variables and large masses of data, latent variables may serve as a simplifying approximation, being introduced as aggregates of entire groups of variables.

The potential scope and importance of path modelling with latent variables in complex situations can hardly be

exaggerated. NIPALS modelling has only recently entered
this problem area, a begining being made with the NIPALS
versions A_1 and A_2 of Hauser's model. While Models A_1 and
A_2 involve one and two latent variables, respectively, NIPALS
models with three or more variables are under construction
and will be reported elsewhere.[23a] In these new developments, the predictor specification remains the basic feature
of the NIPALS approach. As to the rationale of predictor
specification, we note three aspects (i)-(iii) of which the
two first are of general scope in NIPALS modelling (see
Section 2 (b_2)), while the third is specific to NIPALS
modelling with latent variables.

(i)   The predictor specification allows the model
      builder to design the model in accordance with
      its intended purposes of prediction and/or
      causal inference.

(ii) Predictor specification covers the approach of
      "errors in equations" as a special case. It suf-
      fices to consider the simple case of a linear re-
      gression. According to the customary interpreta-
      tion in terms of "errors in equations," (1a) is
      seen as an equation, namely

$$y = \beta_o + \beta_1 z_1 + \ldots + \beta_p z_p \qquad (69)$$

      while the residual ε is seen as errors that are
      superimposed on the equation (69). In the pre-
      dictor specification (1 b) of relation (1 a),
      the right-hand member is the same as in (69),
      whereas the left-hand member is not the variable
      y, but its conditional expectation $E(y|z_1, \ldots,$
      $z_p)$. As is well known, the *equation* (69) is a
      special case of the (stochastic) *relation* (1 b),
      and in theory and practice (1 b) is of much wider
      scope than (69). In path models the inferential
      directions of the predictors (1b) are indicated by
      prior information; hence in such models the time
      is long overdue to replace the errors-in-equations
      approach   (69) by predictor

[23a]Wold (1974 a-b).

specification (1 b).[24]

(iii) In NIPALS modelling, latent variables are explicitly specified in terms of directly observed
variables, usually a linear form of a set of
directly observed variables. The estimation of
the parameters of the latent variable is part of
of the NIPALS estimation problem.

NIPALS versus Maximum Likelihood (ML) Modelling

We are now in a position to make comparative comments on
NIPALS versus the ML approach. As is well known, ML modelling is highly flexible and of very general scope, and has
high aspiration levels with regard to exactness and efficiency in the statistical implementation.[25] NIPALS modelling
is somewhat differently oriented, being primarily intended
for purposes of predictive and/or causal inference, and with
predictor specification as the key feature in the model design. While the NIPALS approach thus is more specific, the
scope of predictive-causal modelling is still very wide.
Within its wide domain, NIPALS modelling is highly flexible,
and has distinct advantages relative to the ML approach. We
proceed to elaborate this last statement.

Predictor specification being the basic device of NIPALS
modelling, we note that this device in itself does not create
a parting of the ways relative to ML modelling. Thus if we
consider the regressions (1 a), we know from R. A. Fisher
(1925) that on the classical assumptions (nonrandom variables
z_i, residuals normally distributed and mutually independent
and independent of the variables z_i) the ML and OLS parameter
estimates are numerically the same. In multirelational models, however, NIPALS and ML modelling often are conceptually and numerically different.

A main difference between NIPALS and ML modelling lies
in the fact that for any causal-predictive relation of the
model the predictor specification primarily involves assumptions about the systematic part of the relation, whereas the

---

[24] For a more detailed discussion, see Wold (1969), Section
5.2, and Mosbaek, Wold *et al.* (1970), Ch. 1.3.

[25] Cramér (1945/46).

ML assumptions also involve the residual properties. This is
so because the systematic part is specified with regard to the
intended causal-predictive use of the model, whereas the ML
approach must specify the likelihood function, and this is
determined by the residual properties. In consequence, a
NIPALS model usually will be more general than the corresponding ML model. To specify, the predictor specification
of a relation implies that the residual is uncorrelated with
the explanatory variables of that same relation, whereas the
ML approach usually imposes more numerous assumptions about
zero intercorrelations between residuals and variables. A
case in point is Hauser's model, where the ML and NIPALS
approaches involve p x q and p + q zero intercorrelations,
respectively. Another case is the generalization from Classical ID (and REID) systems to GEID systems; see Section 3
$(h_4)-(h_5)$. We conclude that NIPALS modelling since the zero
intercorrelation assumptions are less numerous, will by and
large give better results when testing the goodness of fit
of the models.[26] For empirical support of this conclusion,
reference is made to FP estimation of ID systems as compared
with the classical methods referred to in Section 3 (f_2).[27]

In modelling with latent variables, NIPALS defines the
latent variables explicitly in terms of the directly observed
variables, whereas ML often does not specify the structure of
the latent variables. So much the more ML must impose assumptions on the residuals; in actual fact this is the situation in the cases referred to in the previous paragraph.

ML modelling with latent variables thus is conceptually
more general than the NIPALS approach, inasmuch as ML does
not specify the structure of the latent variables, but this
is a mixed blessing since there will be more assumptions on
the residuals. For another thing, and equally important, the
explicit structuring of the latent variables gives the advantage to NIPALS relative to ML modelling in that the sample
values of the latent variables can be numerically assessed.
Such information is valuable for exploring the possible connection between latent and manifest variables, for testing

---

[26]Note 17 is repeated.

[27]See the reports of Bergström (1969, 1974).

for outliers, and for further development of the model.[28]
Moreover, the assessment of sample values of the latent
variables makes it possible to assess sample values of the
residuals of the model's relations, and again this is valuable for testing and further development of the model.

To sum up, when comparing NIPALS with ML and other approaches of modelling, a balanced view of the various aims of
the model construction is appropriate. More specifically,
there is a trade-off in NIPALS modelling between operative inference and consistent estimation. The predictor specification which is characteristic of NIPALS models makes for high
degrees of information in the operative use of causal and/or
predictive inference, whereas the estimation is on the low
side of information relative to ML and other estimation
methods that aim not only at consistent but also at efficient
parameter estimates. Hence with regard to parameter estimation, as the author sees it, the NIPALS and ML approaches are
complementary rather than competitive. In particular, ML
needs or assumes specific information about the residuals and
their correlation and distributional properties, and NIPALS
comes to the fore in situations where such information is
scarce or dubious.

The Parity Principle. In deterministic models it is a
well known principle that, in general, the model builder can
impose just as many but not more assumptions or conditions as
he has degrees of freedom at his disposal, be it number of
relations, number of parameters, or other elements of the
model. Turning to stochastic models, this parity principle
carries over in a weaker sense. A case in point is the non-
correlation assumptions between residuals and explanatory
variables in OLS regression and NIPALS modelling. Disre-
garding singular cases, the model builder must impose as
many assumptions as he has free parameters at his disposal,
lest the parameters be underidentified. As to additional
assumptions, we remember that the systematic part of an OLS
regression is an orthogonal projection into a linear space.

---

[28] Principal components (PC) versus Factor analysis (FA) is
typical for the difference at issue between NIPALS and ML
approaches. Components are linear forms in the observables
and can accordingly be consistently estimated. In FA this
is not so; consistent estimates for the loadings will for
each sample item of the observables provide a consistent estimate not of the corresponding factor, but of its conditional expectation; cf Lyttkens (1966) and Wold (1966 c).
The situation is analogous in NIPALS versus ML modelling of
Hauser's model.

Clearly, additional assumptions that violate the parity principle can be imposed, but then the projection space will have fewer dimensions, and the regression residual will in general have a larger variance.

It is well to note that the goodness of fit of the model as reflected in the residual variances will not be impaired by additional assumptions that violate the parity principle, *provided the additional assumptions are in actual fact fulfilled*. This is in particular true in applications to simulated data that are generated in strict accord with the assumptions of the model under analysis. And in such cases there will be no point in using the NIPALS approach. To repeat from a recent discussion of FP estimation,[29] if NIPALS estimates give consistent estimates under conditions that are more general than for the estimation methods under comparison, the NIPALS estimators cannot be expected to compete in efficiency with the other estimation methods when applied to data that fulfill these more stringent assumptions.

Applications: Low-Information Situations. It sometimes happens that the model builder has little or no more prior information at disposal for the model construction than its intended operative use. The NIPALS models A_1 and A_2 are designed with particular view to applications in such low-information situations. When numerous variables x_i, y_k are observed by way of time-series or cross-sections, explanatory OLS regression analyses of the y_k's in terms of the x_i's are likely to give irregular or amorphous results unless there is prior information available to guide the assessment of relations that may exist between the variables. When such information is scarce or absent, the introduction of latent variables ω or (ξ, η) by the NIPALS models A_1 or A_2 may give more regular and stable relations. If this succeeds it amounts to genuine scientific progress, for establishment of new regularities is a push forward at the research frontier. On the other hand, when prior information is more plentiful, it is likely that the operative aspirations of the path models can be raised by making them more complex, with several inferential steps and/or several latent variables. As discussed in the beginning of this section, Models A_1 and A_2 are

---

[29] See the author's contribution to the oral discussion following Lyttken's recent presentation of the FP method (1973).

simple examples of modelling with latent variables in such
complex situations, using latent variables constructed as
aggregates of directly observed variables. Here Models A_1
and A_2 are at the gateway of a long avenue of model building
with gradually increasing complexity in the model design, a
line of evolution where modelling by NIPALS and other approaches is as yet only beginning.

Standard Errors in Low-Information Situations. To repeat, the parameter estimation in NIPALS modelling primarily
aims at obtaining estimates that are consistent. Beyond the
predictor specification, relatively mild assumptions will
suffice to establish the consistency; see Section 3, (e_2).
While this is fine in low-information situations, the
customary formulas for confidence intervals and other tools
for hypothesis testing are on the high-information side, requiring elaborate assumptions, especially about the residuals and their distributional and correlational properties.
This makes a headache if little or no prior experience about
the residuals is available. Hence in low-information situations "quick-and-dirty" methods for the assessment of standard errors come to the fore, such as John Tukey's jackknife.[30]

---

[30]
See Miller (1974) for a recent review of the jackknife.

REFERENCES

Agren, A. 1972. *Extensions of the Fix-Point Method. Theory and Applications*. Doctoral Thesis, University of Uppsala.

Bergström, R. 1969. Chapter 17 in Wold-Lyttkens (ed., 1969).

Bergström, R. 1974. *Studies of Iterative Methods for the Estimation of Interdependent Systems, especially the FP and IIV Methods*. Doctoral Thesis, University of Uppsala.

Blalock, H. M. 1964. *Causal Inferences in Nonexperimental Research*. Chapel Hill: University of North Carolina Press.

Blalock, Jr., H. M. ed. 1971a. *Causal Models in the Social Sciences*. Chicago: Aldine-Atherton.

Blalock, Jr., H. M. 1971b. "Causal Models Involving Unmeasured Variables in Stimulus-Response Situations," pp. 335-347 in Blalock (ed. 1971 a).

Bodin, L. 1974. *Recursive Fix-Point Estimation. Theory and Applications*. Doctoral Thesis, University of Uppsala.

Boudon, R. 1965. "A Method of Linear Causal Analysis: Dependence Analysis," *American Sociological Review*, 30: 365-374.

Christ, C. F., C. Hildreth, T.-Ch. Liu and L. R. Klein. 1960. "Any Verdict Yet? A symposium on Simultaneous Equation Estimation," *Econometrica*, 35: 835-871.

Christoffersson, A. 1970. *The One Component Model with Incomplete Data*. Doctoral Thesis, University of Uppsala.

Costner, H. L. ed. 1971. *Sociological Methodology 1971*. San Francisco: Jossey-Bass.

Cramér, H. 1945/46. *Mathematical Methods of Statistics*. Uppsala: Alqvist & Wiksells, 1945. Princeton: Princeton University Press, 1946.

Duncan, O. D. 1966. "Path Analysis: Sociological Examples," *American Journal of Sociology*, 72: 1-16. Also in Blalock (ed. 1971a): 115-151.

Fisher, R. A. 1925. *Statistical Methods for Research Workers*. Edinburgh: Oliver & Boyd.

Haavelmo, T. 1943. "The Statistical Implications of a System of Simultaneous Equations," *Econometrica*, 11: 1-12.

Hauser, R. M. 1968. *Family, School and Neighborhood Factors in Educational Performances in a Metropolitan School System*. University of Michigan (unpublished doctoral thesis).

Hauser, R. M. 1971. *Socioeconomic Background and Educational Performance*. Washington, D.C.: American Sociological Association.

Hauser, R. M. and A. S. Goldberger. 1971. "The Treatment of Unobservable Variables in Path Analysis," pp. 81-117 in Costner (ed. 1971).

Hotelling, H. 1936. "Relations Between Two Sets of Variates," *Biometrika*, 28: 321-377.

Jöreskog, K. G. 1970. "A General Method for Analysis of Covariance Structures," *Biometrika*, 57: 239-251.

Jöreskog, K. G. 1973. "Analysis of Covariance Structures," pp. 263-285 in *Multivariate Analysis, III;* ed. P. R. Krishnaiah. New York: Academic Press.

Jöreskog, K. G. and A. S. Goldberger. 1973. "Estimation of a Model with Multiple Indicators and Multiple Causes of a Single Latent Variable." Research Report 73-14, Department of Statistics, University of Uppsala.

Lyttkens, E. 1964. "Standard errors of regression coefficients by autocorrelated residuals," pp. 169-228 in *Econometric Model Building: The Causal Chain Approach,* ed. H. Wold; Amsterdam: North-Holland Publishing Co.

Lyttkens, E. 1966. "On the Fix-Point Property of Wold's Iterative Estimation Method for Principal Components," pp. 335-350 in *Multivariate Analysis;* ed. P. R. Krishnaiah. New York: Academic Press.

Lyttkens, E. 1972. "Regression Aspects of Canonical Correlations," *Journal of Multivariate Analysis,* 2: 418-439.

Lyttkens, E. 1973. "The Fix-Point Method for Estimating Interdependent Systems, with the Underlying Model Specification." *Journal of Royal Statistical Society,* B, 136: 353-394.

Lyttkens, E. and H. Wold eds. 1973. "FP (Fix-Point), IIV (Iterative Instrumental Variables) and Related Approaches to Interdependent (ID) Systems; Theory and Applications," European Meeting of the Econometric Society, 28-31 Aug. 1973, Oslo.

Malinvaud, E. 1964. *Méthodes Statistiques de l'Econometrie.* Paris: Dunod.

Miller, R. G. 1974. "The Jacknife--a Review," *Biometrika,* 61: 1-15.

Mosbaek, E. J. and H. Wold, with contributions by E. Lyttkens, A. Agren and L. Bodin. 1970. *Interdependent Systems. Structure and Estimation.* Amsterdam: North-Holland Publishing Co.

Pearson, K. 1901. "On Lines and Planes of Closest Fit to Systems of Points in Space," *Philosophical Magazine* (6) 2: 559-572.

Tinbergen, J. 1937. *An Econometric Approach to Business Cycle Problems.* Paris. Hermann.

Tinbergen, J. 1939. *Statistical Testing of Business Cycle Theories, II. Business Cycles in the United States of America 1919-32.* Geneva: League of Nations.

Turner, M. E. and C. D. Stevens. 1959. "The Regression Analysis of Causal Paths," *Biometrics,* 15: 236-258. Also in Blalock (ed. 1971); 75-99.

Varga, R. S. 1962. *Matrix Iterative Analysis.* Englewood Cliffs, N.J.: Prentice Hall.

Werts, C. E., R. L. Linn and K. G. Jöreskog. 1971. "Estimating the Parameters of Path Models Involving Unmeasured Variables," pp. 400-409 in Costner (ed. 1971).

Wold, H. 1950. "On Least Square Regression with Autocorrelated Variables and Residuals," *Bulletin of the International Statistical Institute,* 32; No. 2: 277-289.

Wold, H. 1963. "On the Consistency of Least Squares Regression," *Sankhyā,* A, 25 No. 2: 211-215.

Wold, H. 1965. "A Fix-Point Theorem with Econometric Background," *Arkiv for Matematik,* 6: 209-240.

Wold, H. 1966 a. "On the Definition and Meaning of Causal Concepts," pp. 265-295 in *La Technique des Modèles dans les Sciences Humaines.* Entretiens de Monaco en Sciences Humaines, Session 1964; eds. R. Peltier and H. Wold, Monaco: Union Européenne d'Editions.

Wold, H. 1966 b. "Nonlinear Estimation by Iterative Least Squares Procedures," pp. 411-444 in *Research Papers in Statistics. Festschrift for J. Neyman;* ed. F. David. New York: Wiley and Sons.

Wold, H. 1966 c. "Estimation of Principal Components and Related Models by Iterative Least Squares," pp. 391-420 in *Multivariate Analysis,* ed. P. R. Krishnaiah. New York: Academic Press.

Wold, H. 1969. "Nonexperimental Analysis from the General Point of View of Scientific Method," *Bulletin of the International Statistical Institute,* 42; No. 1: 391-424.

Wold, H. 1973 a. "Cause-Effect Relationships: Operative Aspects," pp. 789-801 in *Logic and Philosophy of Science, eds.* P. Suppes et al. Amsterdam: North-Holland Publishing Co.

Wold, H. 1973 b. "Nonlinear Iterative Partial Least Squares (NIPALS) Modelling: Some Current Developments," pp. 383-407 in *Multivariate Analysis III,* ed. P. R. Krishnaiah. New York: Academic Press.

Wold, H. 1974 a. "Causal Flows with Latent Variables. Partings of the Ways in the Light of NIPALS Modelling," European Economic Review, no. 5: 67-86.

Wold, H. 1974 b. "Soft Modelling by Latent Variables. The NIPALS Approach," Research Report 1974-6, Department of Statistics, University of Göteborg.

Wold, H. and E. Lyttkens, eds. 1969. "Nonlinear Iterative Partial Least Squares (NIPALS) Estimation Procedures," *Bulletin of the International Statistical Institute,* 43: 29-51.

Wright, S. 1934. "The Method of Path Coefficients," *Annals of Mathematical Statistics,* 5: 161-215.

12

Indirect Measurement in Social Science:

Some Nonadditive Models

H.M. BLALOCK
University of Washington

There seems to be no question but that measurement problems constitute one of the most important roadblocks to the
advancement of social science. Many of our ongoing debates
concerning the relative advantages of "hard" as compared with
"soft" approaches to data collection and analysis also seem
to involve as a core issue the question of how to measure and
conceptualize our most important variables. On the one hand,
there are those who rely primarily on objective indicators
such as environmental stimuli and behavioral responses as the
data that are most suitable to statistical manipulations and
controls. On the other hand, sociologists and social psychologists who emphasize the subjective or "meaning" aspects
of reality tend to reject objective behavioral kinds of
measures as being totally inadequate for many purposes.

Many readers of this volume will have comparative or
cross-cultural research interests. One of the most serious
problems we face in such comparative research is that of
finding comparable indicators that have the same meanings in
diverse cultures. We often can find objective measures, such
as the number of years of formal schooling, annual income,
occupation, or even religious denomination, which on the surface seem to make international comparisons possible. Yet
these may not be the variables that are of theoretical interest to the investigator, who instead may be concerned with
occupational prestige, class position, purchasing power, or
minority status. Theories that have been stated in such a
manner as to apply to a wide range of phenomena or to different cultures will, of necessity, contain many concepts and
variables that are very abstractly defined, with the linkages to operational indicators being highly indirect and

therefore subject to dispute. These points are of course obvious. Much less obvious, however, is the problem of finding a clearcut rationale for proceeding in a reasonably rigorous fashion without giving up a quantitative approach to measurement.

There is now a growing literature on the causal approach to measurement error showing that this approach seems flexible enough to permit the introduction of subjective variables that are only indirectly measurable, while at the same time permitting a quantitative method of data analysis.[1]

Of course unmeasured variables introduce additional unknowns into a causal system, but it can reasonably be claimed that such unknowns have always existed in our analyses, at least to the degree that objective indicators inadequately reflect the kinds of subjective and personality variables that are more likely to appear in our theories. In fact, most of us recognize that our "tests" of such theories are highly indirect, usually requiring one or more untestable assumptions that have often remained more implicit than explicit. The purpose of this chapter is to explore several important kinds of indirect measurement situations involving both subjective states and operational measures.

As long as measurement errors in a dependent variable are purely random, we produce no systematic distortions in regression coefficients, though of course we attenuate correlational measures of association. If there are also random measurement errors in independent variables, we attenuate slopes as well as correlations, and we must find ways of assessing the measurement error variance in relation to the variation in the true value of the independent variable X. Provided one has either multiple indicators or an *a priori*

---

[1]Most of this literature deals with multiple indicator approaches, where the indicators are taken as effects of the unmeasured variables, and where one can then allow for different kinds of nonrandom measurement errors. See especially Althauser and Heberlein (1970); Althauser, Heberlein, and Scott (1971); Blalock (1970); Bohrnstedt (1969); Costner (1969); Heise (1969); Siegal and Hodge (1968); Wiley and Wiley (1970); and Werts and Linn (1970). There has been much less discussion of situations where some indicators are causes and others effects of the unmeasured variables. See Blalock (1971); Costner (1971); Hauser and Goldberger (1971); and Land (1970).

theory linking his major variables to certain auxiliary or
"instrumental" variables, these problems involving purely
random measurement errors can be handled in a relatively
straightforward manner.[2] Also, certain simple kinds of non-
random measurement errors can be assessed if there are
available enough measures of each variable and if linear
additive models are assumed.

Many kinds of measurement situations involving linkages
between subjective states and objective indicators would
seem to require more complex models, however. In general,
the more complex the model the more unknowns relative to
knowns, and the less likely that a determinate solution can
be found. In particular, there seem to be a number of
measurement situations involving nonadditivity or statistical
interactions of the indicator with some extraneous factor
that also appears elsewhere in the theory. Rather than considering a single illustrative example in some depth, we
shall examine five distinct situations, all of which are
reasonably common in social research, in order to suggest the
generality of the problem. Our basic argument will be that
careful conceptualization of the causal relationship between
indicator and the unmeasured variable is a necessary step
prior to the collection of data that might shed additional
light on the true relationships.

All of the models to be discussed below involve multiplicative relationships as well as standard additive ones,
and therefore it seems advisable to ask at the outset why the
strictly additive relationships are not adequate, at least as
first approximations. Consider the very simple two-variable
linear equation $Y = \alpha + \beta X$. Whenever we apply this equation
to a population and attempt to estimate the parameters α and
β, we make the fundamental assumption that members of the
population are *homogeneous* in the sense that they are all
subject to the same causal law. That is, the *same* parameter
values apply to each individual. If the population contains
diverse elements for which different sets of parameter values
are appropriate, then we attempt to form subpopulations that
are internally homogeneous with respect to the parameter
values.

But this of course means that the "parameters" are
not constants across all individuals and therefore may be

---

[2] The instrumental-variables approach enables one to avoid the
use of multiple indicators but is relatively more sensitive
to specification errors in one's underlying theory. See
Blalock, Wells, and Carter (1970).

taken as variables in their own right. Thus we could replace the "parameter" β by a variable W, also replacing α
by a variable V, so that the equation becomes Y = V + WX,
where V, W, and X are all variables that may be linked to
other variables in the causal system. We now have multiplicative terms (e.g., WX) because of the added complexity of
the model. In the context of our introductory remarks,
diverse members of a very heterogeneous population may require different parameter values because they attach different meanings to objective factors in their environment.
Thus, the more broadly comparative one wants to make the
analysis the less realistic it will be to assume constant
coefficients in additive equations. Yet equation systems
cannot be made too complex, particularly in instances where
some of the variables will have to be taken as unmeasured
or as indirectly measured. Multiplicative terms seem to
represent a reasonable compromise between the need for simplicity, on the one hand, and the need for realism and
flexibility, on the other.

Mention should be made of an alternative strategy which
seems to enjoy greater usage, at least within the United
States. If a variable such as "education," as measured in
terms of years of formal schooling, is not a perfect measure
of "true education," then years of schooling might be treated as an ordinal rather than a ratio scale. A single year
of schooling will have a different "meaning" if it involves
the completion of a degree program (e.g., graduation from
high school or college), than if it does not. Therefore,
years of schooling might be best treated as an ordinal scale
and perhaps lumped into categories that reflected natural
groupings. If all variables in the system are likewise
treated as ordinal, it is then meaningless to distinguish between additive and multiplicative relationships because of
the fact that a simple logarithmic transformation will con-
vert a multiplicative relationship into an additive one without altering the orderings of any of the scores (Wilson,
1971).

This position is certainly defensible, and I would ad-
vocate that whenever an investigator is in doubt about the
level of measurement he or she should analyze the data in
several different ways, including the use of ordinal procedures. My own position, however, is that in falling back
on ordinal measurement in situations of this sort, one is
likely to give up too soon. That is, one is not forced to
think about the relationship between the indicator (here,
years of schooling) and the variable in which one is really
interested (here, "true education"). Converting variables

into ordinal scales because of imperfections in the objective measures does not really solve the problem, as it only obscures measurement error, while perhaps adding further error through the process of categorization and the creation of additional tied scores. My argument will be that it is fruitful to *think* in terms of interval and ratio scales, even though the ultimate *tests* of one's reasoning may have to be much more crude and indirect than one would like.

1. SUBJECTIVE MEANINGS VERSUS OBJECTIVE INDICATORS

One of the most frequently encountered situations in both experimental and nonexperimental social research involves instances where the measured variable is a situational factor that is thought to influence personal "definitions of the situation," and thereby to affect behavior. In experimental designs one often manipulates the setting, the instructions, the behavior of confederates, or the reward-punishment incentives in order to influence behavior. But the variable of more fundamental theoretical interest is likely to be some motivational or attitudinal variable such as degree of frustration, satisfaction, personal threat, expected gain, or conformity needs. Presumably, the experimental manipulations "activate" these motivational and attitudinal variables, but it is usually recognized that this will occur to varying degrees for different individuals. Similarly, naturally occurring events such as the influx of a large number of minority-group members into a community are expected to increase the perceived threat to dominant-group members, but again to varying degrees.

If one takes the objective manipulation or change as an indicator of a change in some subjective state, which in turn is assumed to affect the measured behavior, then there is slippage in the theoretical system whenever there is an imperfect correlation between the forcing event and the subjective state. Unfortunately, however, it is often extremely difficult and expensive to measure the intervening state, and therefore objectivists have tended to bypass such variables in their actual research, if not in their theoretical explanations. Such a procedure is ordinarily theoretically as well as practically justified if the errors involved are strictly random, but the essential argument of those who have criticized this simplistic approach boils down to the assumption that the errors produced are likely to be systematic rather than random. In effect, they have argued that "meanings" given to events, or definitions of situations, are likely to be associated with *other* variables in the

theoretical system. I have not seen the argument put in exactly these very general terms, but I believe this is the
essential nature of the controversy.

The basic strategy proposed in this chapter is to conceive of models with both kinds of variables, and to express
subjective variables as non-additive functions of objective
factors and other kinds of variables. As already noted, we
shall use very simple multiplicative models in order to keep
the number of unknowns down to reasonable proportions.[3] In
many instances it would seem warranted to express the degree
of motivational force (e.g., experienced frustration, perceived threat, expected gain) as a multiplicative function of
some objective factor and another (unmeasured) psychological
state. The latter state, in turn, may be a function of other
variables in the causal system, thus necessitating a relatively complex theoretical model. I believe this to be
merely a formalization of some of the criticisms that have
been leveled at extreme empiricists.

At this point it seems necessary to utilize a specific
example to illustrate the basic approach. Suppose one is investigating the relationship between the relative size of a
minority and discriminatory behavior against the minority.
The linkage between these two "objective" variables can be
made through notions such as perceived threats, fear of competition, fear of close interaction, and so forth. Clearly,
not all members of the majority group perceive the situation
in the same way. Some will be more threatened than others,
but it may be exceedingly difficult to obtain good measures
of such perceived threats. Hopefully, in the aggregate one
might rely on idiosyncratic individual factors cancelling
each other out. But if so, one had better make these assumptions explicit, for there are many conditions under which
this will not happen.

---

[3]These models will be of the form $Y = kWX$, where the exponents of W and X are assumed to be unity rather than unknown
parameters. Such simplifications seem absolutely essential
when one is dealing with unmeasured variables. The theory
can of course be refined in instances where one is willing
to assume that all variables have been well measured. Also,
it would be possible to introduce error terms into this
multiplicative model, but I shall treat them as exact since
we are dealing with unmeasured variables in all illustrative
examples.

Let us take the measured independent variable X' to be
the minority percentage in some well defined area (say a respondent's residential area). Our causal argument may be
that behavior Y should be a function of the *perceived* threat
X, plus additional factors that need not concern us. But
perceived threat X may be a function of the actual threat X'
(which is taken to be the measured variable, minority percentage) *and* some kind of threat coefficient W tapping the
relevancy of the minority to the specific individual. If so,
it would seem reasonable to take X as a *multiplicative* function of W and X', a simple version of which would be X =
kWX'. It is this W factor that is most likely to be ignored
when one thinks only in terms of "objective" measures, and it
is presumably this kind of variable that the subjectivist has
in mind as an instance of the "meaning" that the objective
threat has to the respondent.

If W, the relevancy factor, is completely unrelated to
other variables in the theoretical system or very nearly constant from one individual to the next, then it can safely be
neglected. But suppose W is a function of the respondent's
education, income, occupational level, or some other objective factor that we shall label Z. If we restrict values of
W to the range $0 \leq W \leq 1$ it might be most reasonable to take
W as a nonlinear function of Z, but we might use a linear
approximation with the understanding that this would hold
only for a specified range of Z. If so, then we would have
the following hypothetical (recursive) model:

$$X = kWX' \, ,$$

$$Y = \alpha + \beta X + \varepsilon_1 \, ,$$

$$W = \delta + \gamma Z + \varepsilon_2 \, ,$$

from which we derive the result

$$Y = \alpha + \beta(kWX') + \varepsilon_1 = \alpha + k\beta(\delta + \gamma Z + \varepsilon_2)X' + \varepsilon_1$$

which is of the form

$$Y = A + B_1 X' + B_2 ZX' + \varepsilon_3 \, .$$

Thus we would be led to infer that Z (say, income) in-
teracts with percent minority X' in affecting discriminatory
behavior. This is of course what the model implies and would

365

not be misleading *provided* that one does not slide back and
forth between the operational index minority percentage and
the social-psychological notion of perceived threat, in terms
of which one's original theory is more likely to have been
conceived. Unfortunately, we often find such tendencies to
substitute the indicator for the unmeasured variable in verbal discussions that follow the empirical analysis.

Of course it would be desirable to obtain more direct
measures of perceived threat and to use these as additional
(imperfect) indicators of X, thereby increasing the proportion of measured variables in the model. Along with this
strategy, however, one should attempt to take advantage of
any peculiarities in the model (in this case a multiplicative
relationship) so as to predict interactions and specific
kinds of nonlinearities in advance of data collection. If
such interactions and nonlinearities are then found, one will
have an additional form of indirect evidence in favor of the
theory since, presumably, there will be relatively few alternative theories that would also predict such specific patterns of interactions. This same basic strategy will be appropriate in all of the illustrations that follow.

2. TIME AS AN INDICATOR OF INFLUENCE OR QUALITY

One is often interested in variables such as the degree
of influence something has had, how much of a quality an individual has absorbed, or the quality of some learning experience. Such factors are extremely difficult to measure,
but there may be available a very simple measure of time or
other resources (e.g. money) that have been expended. For
example, one might measure the influence of T.V. on a child
by counting the number of hours he or she spends watching it,
or perhaps by refining the measure by counting the time spent
watching specific kinds of programs. The "influence" of a
leader may be measured in terms of the amount of money he or
she controls or expends, or by the number of times he or she
is agreed with by members at a meeting. Or an investigator
may attempt to measure degree of frustration by the length of
time food or sleep has been withheld. Let us consider in
somewhat greater detail another example of a measurement device that is extremely common in sociological research,namely
the measurement of "education" by the number of years of formal schooling that an individual reports. The very simple
model we shall use is basically identical to that of the previous section, so that our discussion can be reasonably
brief.

The variable "education" is often used without much

refinement in empirical research. There is almost a conspiracy of silence involved in the neglect of the quality aspect of education in stratification research, where years of schooling is related to occupational prestige, income, and various parental background factors. "Education" also appears as a standard control variable in survey research, again with little attention being paid to exactly what variable one has in mind. Often, it would seem, one is really interested in some measure of quality of education, either in some generic sense of total amount of learning absorbed or in a more specific sense of detailed knowledge appropriate to occupational skills or knowledge about foreign affairs or the causes of prejudice. The indicator "years of schooling" may stand as a surrogate for all such unmeasured variables. But obviously, not all schools are alike, nor do all students benefit equally from a year's exposure to formal education. Furthermore, amount learned may be a nonlinear function of years of schooling. For all of these reasons we recognize considerable measurement error in this very crude indicator. But our data analyses and theories normally do not take this into account.

Suppose we are interested in the conceptual variable "quality of general education" X and are willing to take this as a function of years of schooling and some unmeasured variable W that can be conceptualized as average amount learned per year. For the sake of simplicity let us rule out the factor of retention of knowledge in later years, which in more refined analyses might itself be taken as a function of W and years elapsed since formal education has been completed . Then if years of schooling X' is used as our measured indicator, we might again take X as a multiplicative function of W and X', i.e., $X = kWX'$. Once more, if we may assume that quality per year W is a constant across all individuals, or a factor that does not vary systematically with other variables in the theoretical system, then quality may safely be ignored. But obviously this is an unrealistic assumption.

Most likely, quality will be a function of family background factors, not only because higher-income parents may be able to send their children to better schools and universities, but also because the motivation of their children may be different from that of lower-income children. Hence quality W is likely to be a function of SES variables, say father's occupational status Z. Although we might again prefer a nonlinear relationship, we can confine our attention to the linear approximation $W = \delta + \gamma Z + \varepsilon_2$. Finally, if we are using "education" to explain some dependent variable Y, and if we are really interested in "true education" (however defined conceptually) rather than years of schooling, then we might use the equation $Y = \alpha + \beta X + \varepsilon_1$. We thus arrive at the identical model as used in the previous section and infer that Y will be a nonadditive function of years of schooling X' and father's occupation Z. Again, this would be a reasonable expectation *provided* we did not gloss over the distinction between true education and years of schooling.

The above reasoning would lead one to predict interactive models whenever years of schooling is combined with background factors to "explain" later occupational achievement. In particular, in comparing blacks and whites in the U.S., one would anticipate different slope estimates and correlations *if* years of schooling is substituted for quality of education, since there can be no doubt that the quality factor differs for the two groups. The model would lead us to predict that "education" (as measured by years of schooling) will be less important as a causal agent for blacks than for whites, as has in fact been found in numerous studies.[4] The important point is that careful conceptualization and even rudimentary distinctions between underlying variables and their imperfect indicators can help account for these findings, and to enable one to predict them in advance of data collection.

3. INCOMPLETE SAMPLING OF BEHAVIORAL ACTS

There are many instances in which one wishes to predict or explain behavior but where it is by no means certain that the behavior will be detected or properly recorded. Sometimes the behavior involves a single act, such as suicide or homicide, whereas the theoretical variable of interest is an internal state such as "propensity to suicide" or "suicidal tendencies." Unless suicide has been attempted more than once (and even here there may be doubts as to whether it was "really" intended), it will be necessary to infer propensity to suicide by relying on aggregated data for individuals

---

[4] The most systematic study that has found such racial differences is that of Blau and Duncan (1967). Whenever one finds such differences and wishes to attribute them to "discrimination" one must be cautious in linking them with discrimination by employers, who are supposedly not treating persons with "equal" educations in the same way. The essential point is that quality of education may *not* be equal, and therefore one may need to look elsewhere in the system in order to explain the discrimination.

assumed to be homogeneous with respect to such tendencies.
But as Douglas (1967) among others has convincingly argued,
reported suicide rates are likely to be biased in systematic
ways. In particular, not all true suicides will be recorded
as such, so that the investigator will have an incomplete
sampling of the suicidal acts within the population of interest. If the sampling procedure is systematically related to
other variables in the system, we are likely to make faulty
inferences.

Basically the same argument holds for repeated acts of
single individuals, particularly when these acts are either
secretive or so common that they are likely to go unrecorded
or be difficult to recall. Let us consider the important
example of crime or delinquency rates, confining our attention to the individual level of analysis. Let Y be the actual
number of times an act (or series of similar acts) is com-
mitted. But suppose Y' represents the number of times the
act has been detected, recorded, or recalled. Then ordinarily $Y' \leq Y$ unless we allow for exaggerated reporting, false
arrests, and so forth. If we let W be the proportion of
times the individual's behavior is actually recorded, assuming that $W \leq 1.0$, then we may write $Y' = WY$.

Now suppose we wish to study the relationship between
crime or deviance and some SES variable X. Furthermore, it
will be reasonable to suppose that W, the proportion of times
one is caught, will also be a function of X. If we simplify
the model so as to take both of these functions as linear,
then we will have the following set of equations:

$$Y = \alpha + \beta X + \varepsilon_1 ,$$

$$W = \delta + \gamma X + \varepsilon_2 .$$

Therefore

$$Y' = WY = (\alpha + \beta X + \varepsilon_1)(\delta + \gamma X + \varepsilon_2)$$

$$= \alpha\delta + (\alpha\gamma + \beta\delta + \varepsilon_1\gamma + \varepsilon_2\beta)X + \beta\gamma X^2 + (\delta\varepsilon_1 + \alpha\varepsilon_2 + \varepsilon_1\varepsilon_2)$$

$$= A + B_1 X + B_2 X^2 + \varepsilon_3 .$$

We see that the *measured* rate Y' is a second degree
function of X, whereas the function linking the true rate Y

369

to X has been assumed linear.[5] It can also be seen that if, in fact, there is no linear relationship between the actual rates and SES, so that $\beta = 0$, we will obtain a linear relationship between Y' and X because of the term $(\alpha\gamma + \varepsilon_1\gamma)X$.

This is a mere formalization of a very common argument that apparent class differences in deviancy may be spurious and due to biased measurement.

The most important question, of course, involves the issue of whether or not we could ever separate the measurement error component from the true relationship. Notice first that the above model permits a very crude kind of test, since it implies a specific kind of nonlinear relationship between Y' and X. If we impose the assumptions that $\alpha > |\beta x| > 0$ and $\beta < 0$, implying that deviancy rates decrease linearly with SES but that they can never be negative, and similarly assume that $\delta > 0$ and $\gamma < 0$, implying that the probability of being caught decreases toward zero as SES increases, then it can easily be verified that the equation linking Y' and X is a parabola that opens upward, that has a minimum beyond the permitted range of SES values, and that has the general form represented in Figure 1.[6] If this kind

---

[5]Notice that this set of equations differs from the previous two sets in that the measured value Y' is taken as a multiplicative function of W and the true value Y, whereas previously we took Y = kWY', implying that Y' is one of the causes of Y. Sometimes it is more reasonable to conceive of indicators as causes rather than effects of the unmeasured variables, and this difference can be an important distinction in considering the implications of multiple indicators. See Blalock (1971); Costner (1971); and Land (1970).

[6]This can be seen as follows. First let us assume that ε_1 and ε_2 are random variables with $E(\varepsilon_1) = E(\varepsilon_2) = 0$, so that we can neglect their influence in the case of large samples. The maximum or minimum point of the parabola $Y' = A + B_1 X + B_2 X^2$ is at $X = -B_1/2B_2$. To determine whether we have a minimum or maximum we take the second derivative, which is $2B_2 = 2\beta\gamma > 0$. Also, this minimum is to the right of the origin since for the minimum

$$X = -\frac{B_1}{2B_2} = -\frac{(\alpha\gamma + \beta\delta)}{2\beta\gamma} > 0 \qquad \text{since} \quad \begin{array}{ll} \alpha > 0 & \delta > 0 \\ \beta < 0 & \gamma < 0 \end{array}$$

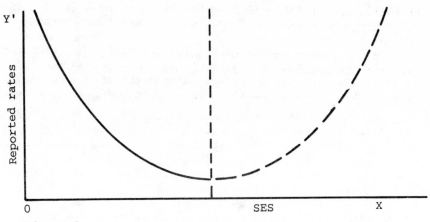

Figure 1.

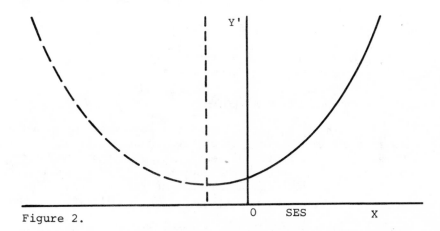

Figure 2.

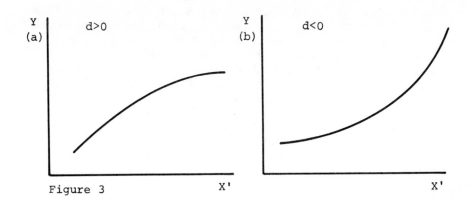

Figure 3

of nonlinear relationship were predicted in advance of data collection, then one would have an indirect test of the theory.

If the theory seemed plausible, one would then want to estimate the parameters involved. But the four parameters α, β, δ, and γ cannot be estimated from the three quantities A, B_1, and B_2. Furthermore, unless the non-linearity were very pronounced within the range of variation, problems of estimation would be serious because of the high (linear) correlation between X and X^2. The fact is that formalization of an argument, alone, will not make it possible to do the impossible. It merely makes it more clear what must be done. There would need to be some serious effort to measure W indirectly, perhaps utilizing multiple indicator techniques, and to study its relationships with other variables in the system. Once this has been done and replicated several times, one may feel more comfortable making specific *a priori* assumptions. For example, it may be found that W is not related to the specific independent variables in the model. Once we have reached a higher degree of standardization than we have at present, an investigator may even be willing to utilize slope estimates found in other studies.

4. SYSTEMATIC RESPONSE ERRORS

In this and the final section we shall be concerned with response errors that may be related to other variables in the system. In many instances we expect such errors to be related to factors such as the education of the respondent, the similarity between respondent and interviewer, the interviewer's skills, and the difficulty and sensitivity of the

---

We have been assuming linear approximations for the relationships of W and Y to SES X, restricting ourselves to SES levels which are such that neither W nor Y can be negative. If we solve the equations for W and Y for the points where the lines cross the X axis, this will give us the upper limits of X beyond which the approximation no longer holds. These values will be at $X = -\alpha/\beta$ (for the Y relationship) and $X = -\delta/\gamma$ (for the W relationship), both of which are positive by assumption. We also note that the minimum value of the parabola is at $X = (-1/2)(\alpha/\beta + \delta/\gamma)$ which is the arithmetic mean of these two upper limits for the SES variable. We therefore conclude that we are concerned with X values to the left of the minimum but to the right of the origin.

items being used. These notions are discussed in virtually all elementary texts on research methods, with the obvious objective of improving measurement at the data *collection* stage. Yet even though we recognize the existence of such possible errors in any particular study, we have not really taken them into consideration in the *analysis* stage of research. We have not built them into our theoretical conceptualization utilized to interpret our findings. Obviously, to the degree that such errors introduce systematic distortions, this practice can be highly misleading.

Let us consider a specific illustration. Suppose one is trying to tap a very controversial attitudinal dimension such as degree of favorableness of whites toward black militancy in the U.S. Or perhaps one is trying to estimate the degree to which respondents have engaged in homosexual practices. Suppose Y respresents the "true" score, with Y' again indicating the measured score. Since it is reasonable to assume that $Y' \leq Y$ for most individuals, and since the degree of underestimation is likely to be a function of both personality variables (e.g., insecurity, alienation, tolerance) and situational factors (e.g., attitudes of one's neighbors) we may again use an unmeasured variable W to summarize the effects of these variables. Thus W may indicate the respondent's degree of willingness (ranging from 0 to 1) to admit his or her true feelings or past behavior to the interviewer, and we might once more take Y' as a multiplicative function of W and Y, namely $Y' = WY$.

If we wish to study the relationship between Y and some independent variable X we again encounter the very real possibility that W is also related to X. If X is an SES variable, say "education," then willingness to respond accurately may also be a function of education, however defined. If we make use of linear approximations, using the equations

$$Y = \alpha + \beta X + \varepsilon_1$$

and $$W = \delta + \gamma X + \varepsilon_2$$

we once more obtain a second-degree equation linking Y' to X. In this particular illustration it is reasonable to assume that both favorableness and willingness to answer correctly are positively related to education X, and this will imply that the parabola opens up. Ordinarily, we will be concerned with the portion of the curve indicated in Figure 2, and this prediction can be used to provide an indirect test of the model.[7]

If we wish to use Y as an *independent* variable, then any variable that is a linear function of the true score Y will be a relatively complicated function of Y' and either W or factors that affect W. Once more, we are likely to find non-additive models appropriate. In one sense it can be claimed that many instances of interaction involving measured values are "mere artifacts" of the measurement process. It would seem more constructive, however, to develop theories about the measurement process so as to explain these interactions as well as we can.

5. RANDOM MEASUREMENT ERRORS WITH DIFFERENT VARIANCES

Even where we would expect response errors to be strictly random, as where a respondent tires of a questionnaire and begins to check items randomly, or where a respondent does not understand a question but feels he or she needs to give some answer, we recognize that the extent of random measurement error may vary. In particular, the tendency to give random responses may vary with education, motivation, the length of the interview, or skill of the interviewer. Or there may be random coding errors that are made more often by unskilled interviewers than well-trained ones. Such errors may also be biased in one or the other direction, as indicated in the previous section. But it is helpful to make the analytic distinction between random and nonrandom errors so that the implications of the former can be noted.

Random measurement errors in the independent variable X attenuate both correlations and slope estimates, the latter being our focus of attention. The approximate large-sample formula for the attenuation of the slope estimate for the regression equation $Y = \alpha + \beta X + \varepsilon$, where X is measured by $X' = X + e$, and where $E(e) = 0$ and $Cov(X,e) = 0$, is as follows:

---

[7] Here we are assuming that α, β, δ, and γ are all positive, since both favorableness and willingness to state one's true feelings are assumed to increase with SES. Therefore $2\beta\gamma > 0$, as before, and we are still dealing with a minimum and a parabola that opens upward. Since β and γ are both positive, however, the minimum falls to the left of the origin. Of course this kind of argument, strictly speaking, can only be applied to ratio scales, but it seems preferable to spell out implications that can be crudely tested, rather than to rely on models that require only ordinal scales and that imply only very weak assertions.

$$E(b_{YX'}) = \beta \frac{\sigma_X^2}{\sigma_{X'}^2} = \beta \frac{\sigma_X^2}{\sigma_X^2 + \sigma_e^2}$$

where $b_{YX'}$ represents the ordinary least-squares estimate applied to X' as the measure of X. We thus see that the degree of attenuation is a function of the size of σ_e^2 relative to σ_X^2.

Now suppose that the variance of the random measurement error is not a constant across all individuals, as is commonly assumed, but that it varies with X, with some cause of X, or with Y. There are numerous possibilities only a few of which can be illustrated. If

$$\sigma_e^2 = c + dX + u$$

where u is a strictly random component uncorrelated with X, and with E(u) = 0, then for large samples it will be approximately true that

$$E(b_{YX'}) = \beta \frac{\sigma_X^2}{\sigma_X^2 + c + dX}$$

If we restrict ourselves to nonnegative X values and assume $c \geq 0$ (since σ_e^2 cannot be negative), then the expected value of $b_{YX'}$ will vary with X, producing a nonlinear relationship between Y and X'. Considering the case where $\beta_{YX} > 0$, if $d > 0$ the expected value of the slope $b_{YX'}$ will be a decreasing function of X, as in Figure 3(a), whereas if $d < 0$ it will be an increasing function of X, as in Figure 3(b). Thus we would be led to infer a nonlinear relationship when the true relationship is actually linear, and this effect will be produced by strictly random measurement errors with differing error variances.

If σ_e^2 is a linear function of the dependent variable Y, with Y being a linear function of X, we will obtain basically the same results. If σ_e^2 is a function of W which causes X, then we may conceive of σ_e^2 as a variable that is spuriously

related to X via their common cause W. If we were able to
control for W this particular kind of distortion might be
eliminated, but we must remember that the true X scores will
be unmeasured, and therefore the application of such a control would require some rather strong linearity assumptions
about the remainder of the model. If it appears likely that
any of these kinds of random measurement error models are
appropriate across a variety of applications, then systematic
methodological study would seem necessary. As a prior crude
check, one can ascertain whether the dispersion of the measured X' scores is a function of X', with the recognition
that, since the true scores will be unknown, such a correla-
tion of $\sigma^2_{X'}$ with X' would not necessarily imply that σ^2_e is a
function of X.

6. CONCLUDING REMARKS

It is hoped that the above five illustrations involve
sufficient variety that they have convinced the reader of the
general advisability of constructing theories of measurement
that include both objective indicators and subjective psychological states and other kinds of unmeasured variables. My
own reading of the criticism of the subjectivists and others,
who have urged us to question the adequacy of many of our
indicator variables, is that these authors often imply that
objective and subjective factors interact to produce non-
additive relationships. The neglect of the subjective aspects merely because they are more difficult to measure
therefore may lead us to make incorrect inferences. However,
it would seem to be a grave mistake to reject quantitative
approaches to model building and data analysis for these
reasons alone. Instead, we should try to incorporate the
arguments of the subjectivists by constructing more complex
models that explicitly include unmeasured variables and that
involve alternative assumptions about the relationships of
these variables to the measured variables in the system.

Obviously, the process of including such variables in a
theoretical system does not, in itself, help to resolve data-
collection problems. It merely alerts us to additional difficulties and complications that we may have previously
neglected. But it does seem to be a necessary first step in
identifying the specific kinds of problems we face, the kinds
of supplementary data that need to be collected, and in
pointing to problems that are empirically hopeless in the
sense that there will be too many unknowns for solution. It
may also suggest indirect or weak tests of theories where
estimation of specific parameters is impossible.

The models dealt with in this chapter all have involved nonadditive and/or nonlinear models. Hopefully, this line of inquiry can be integrated with the multiple-indicator approach to causal models which, thus far, has been confined to linear additive models. It would appear that the more complex our models and the less sure we are of our *a priori* assumptions, the greater our reliance must be on multiple measures. Therefore, to the degree that we are modest about the adequacy of our theories and realistic about the complexity of our models, the more careful we must be about our measurement procedures and the more we must rely on the kind of insurance provided by multiple measures. Also, the more conscientious we need to be in reporting the results obtained using different measures and the more attention we must give to methodological studies of measurement errors.

In short, we need theories of measurement errors. These must be sufficiently general that they can be applied to diverse sets of variables, yet they must be specific enough to imply clearly stated models. Such theories of measurement errors will inevitably seem totally inadequate when first stated explicitly, but, like other theories, they can always be refined and improved if they do not adequately account for the data.

REFERENCES

Althauser, Robert P. and Thomas A. Heberlein. 1970. "A Causal Assessment of Validity and the Multitrait-Multimethod Matrix," in Edgar Borgatta (ed.), *Sociological Methodology 1970*. San Francisco, Jossey-Bass, Inc., Chap. 9.

Althauser, Robert P., Thomas A. Heberlein and Robert Scott. 1971. "A Causal Assessment of Validity: The Augmented Multitrait-Multimethod Matrix" in H. M. Blalock (ed.) *Causal Models in the Social Sciences,* Chicago, Aldine-Atherton, Chap. 22.

Blalock, Hubert M. 1968. "The Measurement Problem: A Gap Between the Languages of Theory and Research," in H. M. Blalock and Ann B. Blalock (eds.), *Methodology in Social Research,* New York, McGraw-Hill, Chap. 1.

Blalock, Hubert M. 1970. "Estimating Measurement Error Using Multiple Indicators and Several Points in Time," *American Sociological Review,* 35 (February) pp. 101-111.

Blalock, Hubert M. 1971. "Causal Models Involving Unmeasured Variables in Stimulus-Response Situations," in H. M. Blalock (ed.), *Causal Models in the Social Sciences*, Chicago, Aldine-Atherton, Chap. 19.

Blalock, Hubert M., Caryll S. Wells, and Lewis F. Carter. 1970. "Statistical Estimation in the Presence of Random Measurement Error," in Edgar Borgatta (ed.), *Sociological Methodology*, San Francisco, Jossey-Bass, Inc., Chap. 5.

Blau, Peter M. and Otis Dudley Duncan. 1967. *The American Occupational Structure*, New York, John Wiley.

Bohrnstedt, George W. 1969. "Observations on the Measurement of Change," in Edgar Borgatta (ed.), *Sociological Methodology 1969*, San Francisco, Jossey-Bass, Inc., Chap. 4.

Costner, Herbert L. 1971. "Utilizing Causal Models to Discover Flaws in Experiments," *Sociometry*, 34, 398-410.

Douglas, Jack D. 1967. *The Social Meanings of Suicide*. Princeton University Press.

Hauser, Robert M. and Arthur S. Goldberger. 1971. "The Treatment of Unobservable Variables in Path Analysis," in Herbert L. Costner (ed.) *Sociological Methodology, 1971*, San Francisco, Jossey Bass, Inc., Chap. 4

Heise, David R. 1969. "Separating Reliability and Stability in Test-Retest Correlation," *American Sociological Review*, 34 (February), 93-101.

Land, Kenneth. 1970. "On the Estimation of Path Coefficients for Unmeasured Variables from Correlations Among Observed Variables," *Social Forces*, 48 (June) pp. 506-511.

Siegel, Paul M. and Robert W. Hodge. 1968. "A Causal Approach to the Study of Measurement Error," in H. M. Blalock and Ann B. Blalock (eds.), *Methodology in Social Research*, New York, McGraw-Hill, Chap. 2.

Werts, Charles E. and Robert L. Linn. 1970. "Path Analysis: Psychological Examples," *Psychological Bulletin*, 74, pp. 193-212.

Wiley, David E. and James A. Wiley. 1970. "The Estimation of Measurement Error in Panel Data," *American Sociological Review,* 35 (February), pp. 112-117.

Wilson, Thomas P. 1971. "Critique of Ordinal Variables, *Social Forces,* 49 (March), pp. 432-444.

13

The Role of Entropy in Nominal Classification

FRANK MÖLLER
University of Milan
VITTORIO CAPECCHI
University of Bologna

1. INTRODUCTION

The importance of common or joint entropy as a dispersion measure for nominal scale variables has been largely
demonstrated in the last few years. Some confusion has
arisen because of the different names given by authors to the
same concept, such as "divergence" by Kullback (1959), "re-
partition" by Maccacaro (1958), "measure of information" by
McGill (1954), "mutual information" by Abramson (1963), "inaccuracy" by Kerridge and Nath (1968), "joint uncertainty" by
Garner (1962) and Entwisle (1970). The reason for the wide
use made of entropy can be found in what is now known as
Shannon's first theorem, Shannon (1948), in which a relation
between the length of a coded message and the entropy has
been formulated. It is true that Shannon himself thought
primarily about the transmission of information from one
source through a transmission channel, which may be distributed, to a receiver. But it was realized almost immediately that this information channel could be extended to most
statistical experiments, as pointed out by Kullback (1959).
The estimation of an unknown population parameter could be a
very simple example. This can be regarded as the message
emitted by the source, the sampling as the transmission channel and the sample function used to estimate the unknown parameter as the received message. The importance of Shannon's
theorem lies in the fact that if we know the entropy of the
transmission channel we can establish a lower limit of the
length of the code word and so be able, at any predetermined
confidence level, to get correct messages through that

channel. In our example it means that through the knowledge of the entropy it is possible to establish a sample size so that the estimation of the true population parameter can be expected to be correct.[1]

Now let us consider another example. Let there be two or more separate classes and an individual to be classified with the help of a battery of tests. How many tests must be chosen to be able to classify that individual correctly? Again the answer can be given by the knowledge of entropy.

Hence entropy is seen to be of fundamental importance for classifying problems. Now it is true that Shannon's theorem tells us that there exists a minimum code length and that this length depends on the entropy, but it does not tell us how to choose the code words, nor in our example, the tests.

The techniques which permit us to solve this last problem are generally known under the term "classification," but it must be pointed out, quoting Rescigno and Maccacaro (1960), "that, whatever the method adopted, one does not classify individuals but one's knowledge about individuals. This knowledge is obtained as answers to a battery of tests. Some tests can give more information than others, both of the individuals and of the tests."

The result of classification will either be an ordered set of classes, each one specified by a sequence of as many deductive propositions as possible, which we will call hereafter a typical sequence, or an ordered set of tests which minimize the number of disjunctive propositions, which we will call the discriminatory sequence necessary to single out a given class.

The first attempts at finding classification methods based on entropy were undertaken by Maccacaro (1958), Rescigno and Maccacaro (1960), Rogers and Tanimoto (1960) and we, the authors, separately in our papers; Möller (1962a), Capecchi (1964); and together (1968). The aim of this contribution, partly a review of our previous articles, is to show how the concept of entropy can be usefully employed, especially in social sciences, where a predominance of qualitative data is the rule, i.e. variables with nominal scales, to build classes with their typical sequences. It will be seen that by our method the discriminatory sequence is a subset of the typical sequence. This method will be applied to

---

[1] We will not discuss what is meant by "correct" estimation since it is not the aim of this chapter.

a survey to measure the political participation of 108 party
workers.

Then we propose a classification key by which, given any
set of classes, it will be possible, again by the use of
entropy, to establish the discriminatory sequence and further
a between-class distance. We have applied this method again
to the 108 party workers which were formerly classified by a
completely different grouping method. We have considered in
our example only strictly dichotomous variables but this is
not a necessary condition as long as the scale is truly
nominal.

2. A METHOD OF CLASS BUILDING

By this method we will try to arrive at homogeneous
classes with typical sequences as long as possible on the
basis of the smallest possible number of tests. This means
in effect choosing the tests with the largest discriminating
power. The process runs through the following steps:
   a) Identification of the test which has the largest
       information content with respect to all the others;
   b) Verification of the homogeneity of the classes
       obtained on the basis of the answers of the indi-
       viduals in this test.
If the classes are homogeneous the typical sequences are
established and the process ends. If not all classes are
homogeneous there are two possibilities for classification:
hierarchic and structural classification. The first considers all classes separately and repeats the operations
a) and b) on every class. The second is always based on all
individuals so that the same battery of tests will be used.

Therefore, if not all classes are homogeneous we continue our classification process by:
   c) The identification of the pair of tests which to-
       gether have the largest information content;
   d) Verification of the homogeneity of the classes
       obtained on the basis of the answers to these two
       tests. If the classes are homogeneous the typical
       sequences are established and the process ends.
       Otherwise we have to consider three, four, etc.
       tests until all classes are found to be homogeneous,
       a result which is always achieved when the classes
       are made up of only one individual.
For this kind of analysis it is necessary to state:
i) Criteria in order to arrive at one or more tests which
   have the largest information content;

ii) Criteria in order to establish whether a given regrouping of the individuals on the basis of the answers given to all tests is homogeneous or not.

As far as the first point is concerned the solution is found in considering the entropy as a dispersion measure. For data which are not at the nominal level it is possible to consider, as in the item analysis, the most correlated test, using some techniques related to the analysis of variance, e.g. Sonquist and Morgan (1964). As far as the second point is concerned it is possible to use the contributions of numerical taxonomy in terms of similarity matrices, but if the data are nominal, as we have supposed, even more rapid processes are possible.

We start by considering a test battery of m tests T_i, $(i = 1,\ldots,m)$ and a set of n individuals which are to be ordered in homogeneous classes. Since the responses to the tests are dichotomous, they can only be of two kinds, which we will conventionally indicate by + and -. For each test we will have a number of positive responses $n_i(+)$ and $n_i(-)$. Obviously $n_i(+) + n_i(-) = n$, for all i.

Now we put

$$p_i = \frac{n_i(+)}{n} \; , \; q_i = \frac{n_i(-)}{n} \; ,$$

with

$$p_i + q_i = 1 \text{ for all i.}$$

A dispersion measure of the response for each test is then known to be given by the entropy

$$H_i = - (p_i \log_2 p_i + q_i \log_2 q_i), \quad i = 1, \ldots m \qquad (1)$$

where $\log_2$ indicates the logarithm with base 2, the binary logarithm. The choice of the base is arbitrary anyway, but since our variables are dichotomous, base 2 works out to be quite useful.

For computational purposes the alternative form may be used

$$H_i = \frac{1}{n} n \log_2 n - n_i(+) \log_2 n_i(+) - n_i(-) \log_2 n_i(-) . \qquad (2)$$

In the binary case we have

$$0 \leqslant H_i \leqslant 1 ,$$

with $H_i = 0$ in the case of all identical responses, hence of no dispersion, and $H_i = 1$ in the case of the greatest dispersion or uncertainty among the responses achieved when $p_i = q_i = \frac{1}{2}$.

The next step is to measure the mutual influence between one test, say T_i, and the others T_j, $(j \neq i)$, taken one by one. For each of the $(m - 1)$ pairs of tests which can be formed with the test T_i, we get a two-dimensional nominal variable as follows:

Responses to test T_i	Responses to test T_j		Marginal distribution of T_i
	+	−	
+	$n_{ij}(++)$	$n_{ij}(+-)$	$n_i(+)$
−	$n_{ij}(-+)$	$n_{ij}(--)$	$n_i(-)$
Marginal distribution of T_j	$n_j(+)$	$n_j(-)$	n

We can now evaluate the entropy of the T_i marginal distribution, which is identical to H_i, and also for the entropy of the other marginal distribution, H_j. Further, the total entropy

$$H_{ij} = \frac{1}{n}[n \; \log_2 n - n(++)\log_2 n(++) - n(+-)\log_2 n(+-) -$$

$$n(-+)\log_2 n(-+) - n(--)\log_2 n(--)]. \tag{3}$$

It is immediately seen that H_{ij} can assume all values within the interval $(0,2)$, again the lowest value if there is no dispersion at all, and the highest value if all n_{ij} values are equal to $\frac{1}{4}$, which has a consequence that $H_i = H_j = 1$. In the case of perfect association between T_i and T_j, which is achieved either if $n_{ij}(++) = n_{ij}(--) = 0$,

or $n_{ij}(+-) = n_{ij}(-+) = 0$, we have

$$H_{ij} = H_i = H_j \; ; \tag{4}$$

in the case of no association, i.e. of statistical independence, we have instead

$$H_{ij} = H_i + H_j \; . \tag{5}$$

The difference

$$H_{ij} - H_i = H_{j;i} \tag{6}$$

thus indicates the part of entropy, and hence dispersion of T_j, which is left after having obtained knowledge of the responses to T_i. This difference is known as the conditional entropy of T_j. This entropy vanishes in the case of perfect association, i.e. if (4) is satisfied. In fact in this situation all the information about T_j lies within T_i.

In the case of independence, i.e. if (5) is satisfied, the conditional entropy equals the total entropy H_j of test T_j; hence the knowledge about the dispersion within one test remains unaffected by the knowledge of another one. It follows that the difference between the total entropy of T_j and the conditional entropy, defined by (6), gives that part of the entropy of test T_j which is explained by T_i. We put

$$H_j - H_{j;i} = H_i + H_j - H_{ij}$$

$$= H_i - H_{i;j} \tag{7}$$

$$= h_{ij}.$$

It is useful to represent the relationships between all different entropic values by a Venn diagram, as shown in Figure 1.

A relative partial index of the influence of T_i on T_j could then be defined as

$$\frac{h_{ij}}{H_i} . \tag{8}$$

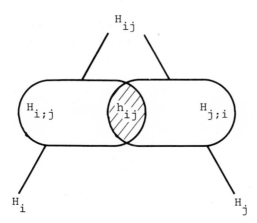

Fig. 1 - The Venn diagram showing the relationships between the entropic values of a two-dimensional nominal variable.

Analogously a partial index of the influence of T_j on T_i would then be

$$\frac{h_{ij}}{H_j} \ . \tag{9}$$

In our previous joint work, (1968), we had considered first the two mean values of (8) and (9) separately for all $j \neq i$, and then the mean of these resulting values. This index worked out to be a good measure of the reciprocal influence between the test T_i and those remaining. But considering the fact that h_{ij} is symmetrical in i and j, as can be seen in (7), and that the range of h_{ij} is

$$\left\{ \begin{array}{l} = 0, \text{ in the case of independence because of (5)} \\ = H_i = H_j = H_{ij} \text{ in the case of perfect association} \\ \quad \text{because of (4)} \end{array} \right.$$

a simpler and yet more effective way can be followed by proposing the joint index

$$\frac{h_{ij}}{H_{ij}} \tag{10}$$

which varies between zero in the case of independence and one in the case of perfect association. Taking the weighted mean for all $j \neq i$, we get

$$M \left\{ \frac{h_{ij}}{H_{ij}} \right\} = \frac{\sum\limits_{j \neq i} \frac{h_{ij}}{H_{ij}} H_{ij}}{\sum\limits_{j \neq i} H_{ij}} \tag{11}$$

$$= \frac{\sum\limits_{j \neq i} h_{ij}}{\sum\limits_{j \neq i} H_{ij}} = I_i$$

For computational purposes we can write, because of (7)

$$\sum\limits_{j \neq i} h_{ij} = (m-1)H_i + \sum\limits_{j \neq i} H_j - \sum\limits_{j \neq i} H_{ij}$$

$$= (m-2)H_i + \sum\limits_{j \neq i} H_j - \sum\limits_{j \neq i} H_{ij} \ .$$

The range of I_i is $(0,1)$ and the test with the highest I value is the one that has the greatest information content with respect to the others. It is possible, therefore, on the basis of this test, to subdivide the original set of individuals into two classes: the class of those individuals whose responses to the selected test are (+) and the class of those individuals whose responses to the selected test are (−).

It remains to establish whether these two classes are homogeneous on the basis of the most frequent responses to all other tests. We indicate by $r_j(k)$, $j = 1, \ldots m$, the number of the most frequent responses to the test T_j in the k-th class, where $k = 1$, if the responses to T_i are all negative, and $k = 2$, if they are all positive. Therefore it is possible to evaluate the probability of misclassification for each test given by

$$p_j(\varepsilon) = \frac{n - \Sigma_k r_j(k)}{n} \tag{12}$$

and hence the mean misclassification probability of the whole battery of tests,

$$p(\varepsilon) = \frac{\Sigma_j p_j(\varepsilon)}{m} = \frac{nm - \Sigma_j \Sigma_k r_j(k)}{nm} . \tag{13}$$

Since the homogeneity of a class is defined by $1 - p(\varepsilon)$, we only need to compare this value with an arbitrarily chosen homogeneity level, or what is the same: to compare the error probability (13) with an arbitrarily chosen error which we do not want to be exceeded.

In the case of the two classes not being homogeneous, it is necessary to proceed by establishing whether homogeneous classes could be found on the basis of the pair of tests, which taken together share the greatest information content. Thus it will be necessary to consider the part of entropy which two tests, T_i and T_j, have in common with a third test T_g. Straightforward generalization of (7) leads us to

$$h_{(ij)g} = H_{ij} + H_g - H_{ijg} \tag{14}$$

while the corresponding Venn diagram is shown in Figure 2.

The index corresponding to (11) capable of singling out the two tests with the highest information content with respect to the other m - 2 tests is given by

$$I_{ij} = \frac{\sum\limits_{g \neq i,j} h_{(ij)g}}{\sum\limits_{g \neq i,j} H_{ijg}}$$

(15)

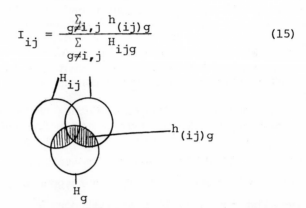

Figure 2. The Venn diagram showing the relationship between entropic values of a three-dimensional nominal variable.

For computational purposes it may be convenient to write

$$\sum\limits_{g \neq i,j} h_{(ij)g} = (m - 2)H_{ij} + \sum\limits_{g \neq i,j} H_g - \sum\limits_{g \neq i,j} H_{ijg}$$

The highest value of I_{ij} specifies the two tests T_i and T_j which have the highest information content in common with the other tests; hence they can be chosen to determine the four classes, characterized by the responses (++), (+−), (−+), and (−−) to the selected pair of tests.

The homogeneity will again be measured by formula (12) where k ranges from 1 to 4. If the homogeneity level is still not reached, formula (15) must be generalized to

$$I_{i_1 \dots i_s} = \frac{\sum\limits_{j \neq i_1 \dots i_s} h_{(i_1 \dots i_s)j}}{\sum\limits_{j \neq i_1 \dots i_s} h_{(i_1 \dots i_s j}}$$

$$h_{(i_1 \dots i_s)j} = H_{i_1 \dots i_s} + H_j - H_{i_1 \dots i_s j}$$

The classification comes to an end as soon as the desired homogeneity level is reached. At first sight this type of classification leads to monothetic classes, which means that there are some tests which are characterized for each class by exactly the same responses. This could be considered a disadvantage of the method. But it will be seen in the last section of this chapter how it will be possible by means of between-classes distance, if suitable conditions are satisfied, to get polythetic classes which can be still more homogeneous than the original monothetic classes.

3. AN APPLICATION OF THE CLASSIFICATION METHOD BASED ON ENTROPY

For an application of class formation based on entropy we shall make use of data obtained from a survey carried out by Francesco Alberoni (1968) for the Istituto Carlo Cattaneo to measure the political participation of 108 party-workers of two Italian parties (we may name them party A and party B).

Following a number of research analyses seven dichotomous items or tests have been finally considered:

T_1 attitude for (+) or against (-) a plurality of political currents;

T_2 intense (+) or non-appreciable (-) religious observance;

T_3 dichotomy attitude towards reality (i.e. division of reality into good-bad, Marxist-Catholic, exploited-exploiter, etc.) very intense (+) or mild (-);

T_4 culture preparation: high (+), very low (-);

T_5 age: up to 35 years old (-), over 35 (+);

T_6 search for personal advantages through political party work: very intense (+), slight (-);

T_7 admiration for party leaders or authority: very intense (+), slight (-).

In view of the fact that these tests make no distinction between party A and party B, two possibilities present themselves:

a) the difference between the two classes of party-workers are (on the basis of the above seven tests) really striking, and in that case the homogeneous classes obtained will coincide with the groups of party-workers belonging to either party; or

b) the difference between the two classes of party-
workers are not very striking and the homogeneous
classes will not coincide with the groups. We have
reported the response matrix (7 x 108) in Table 1.

Hence we immediately get

$H_1 = 0.908678$ $H_{12} = 1.702265$ $H_{14} = 1.783739$ $H_{27} = 1.775066$

$H_2 = 0.987775$ $H_{23} = 1.885524$ $H_{15} = 1.835680$ $H_{35} = 1.931708$

$H_3 = 0.999766$ $H_{34} = 1.837417$ $H_{16} = 1.664589$ $H_{36} = 1.759033$

$H_4 = 0.974898$ $H_{45} = 1.889944$ $H_{17} = 1.789951$ $H_{37} = 1.905072$

$H_5 = 0.958042$ $H_{56} = 1.715634$ $H_{24} = 1.927184$ $H_{46} = 1.738331$

$H_6 = 0.763803$ $H_{67} = 1.681309$ $H_{25} = 1.945665$ $H_{47} = 1.923105$

$H_7 = 0.964151$ $H_{13} = 1.766662$ $H_{26} = 1.748060$ $H_{57} = 1.912154$

On the basis of the values of H_i and H_{ij} we get, conforming
to formula (7):

$h_{12} = 0.194188$ $h_{14} = 0.099837$ $h_{27} = 0.176860$

$h_{23} = 0.102017$ $h_{15} = 0.031040$ $h_{35} = 0.026100$

$h_{34} = 0.137247$ $h_{16} = 0.007892$ $h_{36} = 0.004536$

$h_{45} = 0.042996$ $h_{17} = 0.082878$ $h_{37} = 0.058445$

$h_{56} = 0.006211$ $h_{24} = 0.035489$ $h_{46} = 0.000370$

$h_{67} = 0.046645$ $h_{25} = 0.000152$ $h_{47} = 0.015944$

$h_{13} = 0.141782$ $h_{26} = 0.003518$ $h_{57} = 0.010039$

Code number of party workers of Party A		T_1	T_2	T_3	T_4	T_5	T_6	T_7
A	10	−	−	−	−	+	−	+
	11	−	−	−	−	+	+	+
	12	−	−	+	+	+	−	+
	13	−	−	+	−	+	−	+
	14	−	−	+	−	−	−	+
	15	−	−	−	−	+	−	+
	16	−	−	−	+	−	−	+
	17	−	−	+	−	+	−	+
	18	−	−	−	+	−	−	+
B	10	−	−	−	+	+	−	+
	11	−	−	+	−	+	−	+
	12	−	−	+	−	+	−	+
	13	−	−	+	+	+	+	+
	14	−	−	+	−	+	−	+
	15	−	−	+	−	−	−	+
	16	−	−	+	−	+	−	+
	17	−	−	+	−	−	−	+
	18	−	−	+	−	−	−	+
C	10	−	−	+	−	+	−	+
	11	−	−	+	−	+	−	+
	12	−	−	+	−	+	−	+
	13	−	−	−	+	−	−	+
	14	−	−	−	−	−	−	+
	15	−	−	+	+	−	−	+
	16	−	−	−	+	−	−	−
	17	−	−	−	+	−	−	−
	18	−	−	−	+	−	−	+
D	10	−	−	+	−	+	−	+
	11	−	−	+	−	+	−	+
	12	−	−	−	−	+	−	+
	13	−	−	+	−	+	−	−
	14	−	−	−	−	+	−	+
	15	−	−	−	+	−	−	+
	16	−	−	−	−	−	−	+
	17	−	−	+	−	−	−	+
	18	−	−	+	−	−	−	+

Table 1: THE RESPONSE MATRIX OF 108 PARTY-WORKERS FOR THE SEVEN TESTS REPORTED IN THE TEXT

Table 1 (Continued)

		T₁	T₂	T₃	T₄	T₅	T₆	T₇
	10	−	−	+	+	+	−	+
	11	−	−	+	−	+	−	+
	12	−	−	+	−	+	−	+
	13	−	−	+	+	+	+	+
E	14	+	−	−	−	+	+	−
	15	−	−	+	−	+	+	+
	16	−	−	+	+	−	+	+
	17	−	−	+	+	−	+	+
	18	−	−	+	−	−	+	+
	10	−	−	+	−	+	−	+
	11	−	−	+	−	+	−	+
	12	−	−	+	−	+	−	−
	13	−	−	+	−	−	−	+
F	14	−	−	+	−	+	−	+
	15	−	−	+	−	−	−	+
	16	−	−	+	−	−	−	+
	17	−	−	+	−	+	−	+
	18	−	−	+	−	+	−	+

Code number of party workers of Party B T_j		T_1	T_2	T_3	T_4	T_5	T_6	T_7
	1	−	+	+	−	+	−	+
	2	−	+	−	+	+	−	−
	3	−	+	−	+	+	−	−
	4	+	+	−	−	+	−	+
A	5	+	+	−	+	+	−	+
	6	−	+	−	+	−	+	−
	7	+	+	−	+	−	−	+
	8	+	+	−	+	−	−	−
	9	+	+	−	+	−	−	−
	1	+	−	−	+	+	+	−
	2	−	+	+	−	+	+	−
	3	−	+	+	−	+	−	+
	4	−	+	−	−	+	+	−
B	5	+	+	−	−	+	−	−
	6	+	+	−	+	+	−	−
	7	+	+	−	+	−	−	−
	8	−	+	+	−	−	+	+
	9	−	+	−	−	−	−	+

Table 1 (Continued)

	1	+	+	−	+	+	−	+
	2	−	+	+	−	+	−	−
	3	−	+	+	+	+	−	−
	4	−	+	−	−	+	−	−
C	5	+	+	−	+	+	−	+
	6	+	+	−	−	+	−	−
	7	+	+	−	+	−	−	+
	8	−	−	−	−	+	−	−
	9	+	+	−	+	−	−	−
	1	+	+	−	+	+	−	+
	2	−	+	+	−	+	−	−
	3	+	+	+	−	+	−	+
	4	+	+	−	−	+	−	−
D	5	+	+	−	+	+	−	+
	6	−	+	−	+	−	−	−
	7	+	+	−	−	−	−	+
	8	+	+	−	+	−	−	−
	9	+	−	+	−	−	−	−
	1	+	−	+	+	+	−	−
	2	+	+	+	+	+	−	+
	3	+	−	−	+	+	+	+
	4	+	−	−	+	+	+	−
E	5	−	+	+	+	+	+	−
	6	+	+	−	−	+	−	−
	7	+	+	−	+	−	−	+
	8	+	+	−	+	+	+	−
	9	+	+	−	+	−	−	−
	1	−	+	+	−	+	+	−
	2	−	+	+	−	+	+	−
	3	+	+	+	−	+	+	−
	4	+	−	+	−	+	+	−
F	5	+	+	−	−	+	+	−
	6	+	+	+	−	−	+	−
	7	+	+	−	+	−	+	−
	8	−	+	−	−	−	−	−
	9	−	+	−	+	−	−	−
Sum of Responses		73(−) 35(+)	47(+) 61(−)	53(−) 55(+)	64(−) 44(+)	41(−) 67(+)	84(−) 24(+)	42(−) 66(+)

and from these, on the basis of formula (11) we obtain the values of the index I_i:

T_j:	T_1	T_7	T_2	T_3	T_4	T_5	T_6	$\sum_j \sum_k r_{kj}(k)$
Classes k	Favorable attitude towards a plurality of currents	Admiration of authority	Religious practice	Dichotomy attitude	Cultural preparation	Age	Search for personal advantage	
I	73(−)	53(+)	49(−)	48(+)	51(−)	45(+)	59(−)	
II	35(+)	22(−)	28(+)	28(−)	22(−)	22(+)	25(−)	
$\sum_k r_j(k)$	108	75	77	76	73	67	84	560

Table 2: THE MOST FREQUENT SIGNS IN THE TWO CLASSES OBTAINED BY A NEGATIVE RESPONSE TO TEST T_1 (CLASS I), AND BY A POSITIVE RESPONSE TO THE SAME TEST (CLASS II)

$$I_1 = \underline{0.05289} \qquad I_5 = 0.01037$$

$$I_2 = 0.04663 \qquad I_6 = 0.00671$$

$$I_3 = 0.04245 \qquad I_7 = 0.03561$$

$$I_4 = 0.02990 \qquad Sum = 0.22456$$

The values of this index demonstrate that the test with the greatest information content is the test T_1, which indicates the attitude towards plurality of currents. On the basis of this information it is possible to form two classes; one formed of those individuals who have a favorable attitude to plurality of political currents, the other of those who have an unfavorable attitude. Considering the most frequent answers Table 2 is obtained, indicating the values of $r_j(k)$. We now use formula (13) and obtain

$$p(\varepsilon) = \frac{756 - 560}{756} = 0.258$$

Since we would like a homogeneity level of 80%, i.e. an error probability of 0.2, we will not consider these classes as homogeneous. Therefore it is necessary to consider the pair of tests which share the highest information content. First we evaluate the H_{ijg} values:

$$H_{123} = 2.532663 \qquad H_{125} = 2.641350$$

$$H_{234} = 2.710389 \qquad H_{236} = 2.604318$$

$$H_{345} = 2.730562 \qquad H_{347} = 2.724058$$

$$H_{456} = 2.640674 \qquad H_{467} = 2.620828$$

$$H_{567} = 2.619021 \qquad H_{126} = 2.379089$$

$$H_{124} = 2.602694 \qquad H_{237} = 2.379089$$

$$H_{235} = 2.803787 \qquad H_{356} = 2.674873$$

$$H_{346} = 2.551496 \qquad H_{127} = 2.347823$$

$$H_{457} = 2.813896 \qquad H_{245} = 2.838602$$

$$H_{357} = 2.824318 \qquad H_{257} = 2.728053$$
$$H_{134} = 2.589842 \qquad H_{145} = 2.722040$$
$$H_{246} = 2.655833 \qquad H_{267} = 2.484382$$
$$H_{367} = 2.604413 \qquad H_{146} = 2.554533$$
$$H_{135} = 2.692453 \qquad H_{147} = 2.664708$$
$$H_{247} = 2.694962 \qquad H_{156} = 2.610581$$
$$H_{136} = 2.512394 \qquad H_{157} = 2.740439$$
$$H_{256} = 2.702123 \qquad H_{167} = 2.470680$$
$$H_{137} = 2.615337$$

Then with the H_i and H_{ij} values already obtained, we determine $h_{(ij)g}$:

$h_{(12)3} = 0.169368$	$h_{(14)2} = 0.168820$	$h_{(27)1} = 0.335921$
$h_{(12)4} = 0.074469$	$h_{(14)3} = 0.193663$	$h_{(27)3} = 0.120127$
$h_{(12)5} = 0.018957$	$h_{(14)5} = 0.019741$	$h_{(27)4} = 0.055002$
$h_{(12)6} = 0.086978$	$h_{(14)6} = 0.006991$	$h_{(27)5} = 0.005053$
$h_{(12)7} = \underline{0.318593}$	$h_{(14)7} = \underline{0.083182}$	$h_{(27)6} = \underline{0.054486}$
Sum $= 0.668365$	Sum $= 0.472397$	Sum $= 0.570589$
$h_{(23)1} = 0.261539$	$h_{(15)2} = 0.182105$	$h_{(35)1} = 0.147933$
$h_{(23)4} = 0.150033$	$h_{(15)3} = 0.142993$	$h_{(35)2} = 0.115696$
$h_{(23)5} = 0.039779$	$h_{(15)4} = 0.088538$	$h_{(35)4} = 0.176044$
$h_{(23)6} = 0.043008$	$h_{(15)6} = 0.011099$	$h_{(35)6} = 0.020638$
$h_{(23)7} = \underline{0.194970}$	$h_{(15)7} = \underline{0.059392}$	$h_{(35)7} = \underline{0.071511}$
Sum $= 0.691329$	Sum $= 0.484127$	Sum $= 0.531822$
$h_{(34)1} = 0.156253$	$h_{(16)2} = 0.273275$	$h_{(36)1} = 0.155317$
$h_{(34)2} = 0.114803$	$h_{(16)3} = 0.109822$	$h_{(36)2} = 0.142490$
$h_{(34)5} = 0.064897$	$h_{(16)4} = 0.028906$	$h_{(36)4} = 0.182435$
$h_{(34)6} = 0.049723$	$h_{(16)5} = 0.012050$	$h_{(36)5} = 0.039447$
$h_{(34)7} = \underline{0.077510}$	$h_{(16)7} = \underline{0.158060}$	$h_{(36)7} = \underline{0.118771}$
Sum $= 0.463186$	Sum $= 0.582113$	Sum $= 0.638460$

$h_{(45)1}$ = 0.076583

$h_{(45)2}$ = 0.039417

$h_{(45)3}$ = 0.159148

$h_{(45)6}$ = 0.013072

$h_{(45)7}$ = 0.040199

Sum = 0.328419

$h_{(17)2}$ = 0.429903

$h_{(17)3}$ = 0.174380

$h_{(17)4}$ = 0.100141

$h_{(17)5}$ = 0.007554

$h_{(17)6}$ = 0.083073

Sum = 0.795051

$h_{(37)1}$ = 0.198813

$h_{(37)2}$ = 0.238542

$h_{(37)4}$ = 0.156312

$h_{(37)5}$ = 0.039196

$h_{(37)6}$ = 0.064861

Sum = 0.697724

$h_{(56)1}$ = 0.013731

$h_{(56)2}$ = 0.001286

$h_{(56)3}$ = 0.037720

$h_{(56)4}$ = 0.049858

$h_{(56)7}$ = 0.060764

Sum = 0.163359

$h_{(24)1}$ = 0.233168

$h_{(24)3}$ = 0.206561

$h_{(24)5}$ = 0.046624

$h_{(24)6}$ = 0.035153

$h_{(24)7}$ = 0.196373

Sum = 0.717879

$h_{(46)1}$ = 0.092476

$h_{(46)2}$ = 0.070273

$h_{(46)3}$ = 0.186601

$h_{(46)5}$ = 0.055699

$h_{(46)7}$ = 0.081654

Sum = 0.486703

$h_{(67)1}$ = 0.119307

$h_{(67)2}$ = 0.184702

$h_{(67)3}$ = 0.076662

$h_{(67)4}$ = 0.035379

$h_{(67)5}$ = 0.020330

Sum = 0.436380

$h_{(25)1}$ = 0.212993

$h_{(25)3}$ = 0.141644

$h_{(25)4}$ = 0.081961

$h_{(25)6}$ = 0.007344

$h_{(25)7}$ = 0.181763

Sum = 0.625705

$h_{(47)1}$ = 0.167075

$h_{(47)2}$ = 0.215918

$h_{(47)3}$ = 0.198813

$h_{(47)5}$ = 0.067251

$h_{(47)6}$ = 0.066079

Sum = 0.715136

$h_{(13)2}$ = 0.221774

$h_{(13)4}$ = 0.151718

$h_{(13)5}$ = 0.032251

$h_{(13)6}$ = 0.018070

$h_{(13)7}$ = 0.115476

Sum = 0.539289

$h_{(26)1}$ = 0.277649

$h_{(26)3}$ = 0.143508

$h_{(26)4}$ = 0.067125

$h_{(26)5}$ = 0.003979

$h_{(26)7}$ = 0.227829

Sum = 0.720090

$h_{(57)1}$ = 0.080393

$h_{(57)2}$ = 0.171876

$h_{(57)3}$ = 0.087602

$h_{(57)4}$ = 0.073156

$h_{(57)6}$ = 0.056935

Sum = 0.469962

Finally, by use of (15) we get the information content of the test pairs:

$$I_{12} = 0.0535 \qquad I_{24} = 0.0532 \qquad I_{37} = 0.0531$$

$$I_{13} = 0.0417 \qquad I_{25} = 0.0456 \qquad I_{45} = 0.0239$$

$$I_{14} = 0.0360 \qquad I_{26} = 0.0561 \qquad I_{46} = 0.0374$$

$$I_{15} = 0.0361 \qquad I_{27} = 0.0452 \qquad I_{47} = 0.0529$$

$$I_{16} = 0.0465 \qquad I_{34} = 0.0348 \qquad I_{56} = 0.0123$$

$$I_{17} = \underline{0.0619} \qquad I_{35} = 0.0387 \qquad I_{57} = 0.0342$$

$$I_{23} = 0.0531 \qquad I_{36} = 0.0493 \qquad I_{67} = 0.0341$$

From the values indicated above it is possible to infer the two tests having the greatest information content are T_1 the favorable attitude to a plurality of political currents, and T_7 the admiration of the party leaders. It is therefore possible to form four classes:

Class I: subjects who are not favorable to a plurality of currents and who admire their own leaders.

Class II: subjects who are not favorable to a plurality of currents and who do not admire their leaders.

Class III: subjects who are favorable to a plurality of currents and who admire their leaders.

Class IV: subjects who are favorable to a plurality of currents and who do not admire their leaders.

To establish the homogeneity of these four classes it is necessary to know the frequency of the most repeated answer and for this end we get Table 3.

k \ T_j	T_1	T_7	T_2	T_3	T_4	T_5	T_6	$\Sigma_j r_k$ (k)
I	53(-)	53(+)	49(-)	39(+)	40(-)	31(+)	45(-)	
II	20(-)	20(-)	15(+)	11(-)	11(-)	14(+)	14(-)	
III	13(+)	13(+)	12(+)	11(-)	10(+)	9(+)	12(-)	
IV	22(+)	22(-)	6(-)	17(-)	12(+)	13(+)	13(-)	
$\Sigma_k r_j$(k)	108	108	92	78	73	67	84	610

Table 3:   THE MOST FREQUENT SIGNS WITHIN THE FOUR CLASSES k OBTAINED BY THE RESPONSES TO TESTS T_1 and T_7

Formula (13) now tells us the error probability $p(\varepsilon) = 0.193$ and hence lies below the desired value. Thus the classification process is stopped.

We now have to identify the four classes by their typical sequences.

4. THE IDENTIFICATION OF CLASSES BY MEANS OF THEIR TYPICAL SEQUENCES.

Any class obtained by any classification method whatsoever will have certain characteristics defined by the type of responses given to a particular selection of tests, i.e. the most informative tests. Some of the responses can be the same as those for other classes, and some will be an exclusive characteristic of the class under consideration.

In the introduction we have already defined a typical sequence as a sequence of as many deductive propositions as possible which best describe the characteristics of the individuals belonging to the class. So we are faced with the problem of defining the tests which enter into the typical sequence of each class.

The process of identification will be considered as a statistical experiment: the typical sequence of each class being considered the hypothesis of the experiment. This experiment will give us a set of responses (for the individuals) which under the null hypothesis would not be different from the typical sequence of the class to which those individuals belong. The typical sequence can then be viewed as a message sent after having been suitably coded, and the test battery as the transmission channel. The signals received, which are the responses, will be the result of the experiment. In other words we can consider the typical sequence as a "word" of the code.

Let us dwell further on some principles of the theory of communications. Consider a code alphabet A of the information source, a transmission channel, and the code alphabet B of the receiver. Let us suppose that the code of the receiver is the same as that of the source. It may then happen that a symbol sent by A reaches its destination just as it was sent, or it may reach it in a different form, in which case it is said to be wrong. It all depends on the kind of transmission channel. Noiseless channels are characterized by the fact that the symbol sent is identical to the symbol received, with probability one. This is an ideal case and beyond any practical interest.

Noisy channels thus imply a certain nonzero probability of receiving a wrong symbol. For a binary source alphabet

A (0,1) we get one binary channel defined by a probability for each symbol sent to arrive correctly and one for each symbol to arrive wrongly. In Figure 3 we have schematically shown a binary transmission channel. If all probabilities are known, the transmission channel is defined in all its aspects.

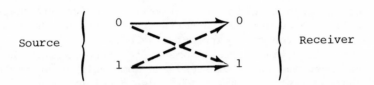

Figure 3. A binary transmission channel. The solid lines indicate a correct transmission, the dotted lines a wrong transmission, of the input symbols at the source.

The matrix connected to a binary transmission channel is defined by

$$
\begin{array}{c}
\quad \overbrace{\quad}^{B} \\
\quad\;\; 0 \qquad\qquad 1 \\
A \left\{ \begin{array}{c} 0 \\ \\ 1 \end{array} \right. \begin{bmatrix} P_{oo} & P_{o1} \\ \\ P_{1o} & P_{11} \end{bmatrix}
\end{array}
$$

If $P_{oo} = P_{11} = p$, and $P_{o1} = P_{1o} = q$, with $p + q = 1$, we have a binary symmetric transmission channel, defined by the matrix $\begin{vmatrix} p & q \\ q & p \end{vmatrix}$. If P_o and P_1 represent the probabilities of the symbols of A we have the probability of a wrong transmission determined by $p(\varepsilon) = P_o P_{o1} + P_1 P_{1o} = q$, which is independent of the input probabilities. This allows us to determine the capacity of the transmission channel, which is defined by the maximum value of the information transmitted, hence by the maximum value of the joint entropy h_{AB} in relation to the changes in the distribution of the symbols of A. Reconsidering formula (7) we have

$$h_{AB} = H_B - H_{B;A} = H_B - (H_{AB} - H_A)$$

$$= H_B - [- \Sigma_A \Sigma_B P(AB) \log_2 P(AB) + \Sigma_A P(A) \log_2 P(A)] .$$

Since $P(AB) = P(A)P(B|A)$ it follows that

$$h_{AB} = H_B + \Sigma_A P(A) \Sigma_B P(B|A) \log_2 P(B|A) . \qquad (16)$$

If the channels are noiseless $P(B|A) = 1$, and hence it is seen that there exists a perfect association between the input and output symbols, so that $h_{AB} = H_A = H_B$. The summation of the last term in (16) extended over B generally depends on the input symbols but in the case of a binary symmetric channel, or more generally speaking of a uniform transmission channel, the summation is independent of A, so we have

$$h_{AB} = H_B + \Sigma_B P(B|A) \log_2 P(B|A) .$$

To find the maximum value of h_{AB} it is sufficient to find the maximum value of H_B as long as the probability of the output symbols is equal to that of the input symbols, which occurs in uniform transmission channels. We have already seen that the maximum value of H_B in a binary alphabet is one, hence the capacity C is given by

$$C = 1 + \Sigma_B P(B|A) \log_2 P(B|A) .$$

But for uniform transmission channels the probability $P(B|A)$ is given by permutations of p and q, so that

$$C = 1 + p \log_2 p + q \log_2 q \qquad (17)$$

$$= 1 - H(p)$$

where $H(p)$ indicates the binary entropy function

$$H(p) = - [p \log_2 p + (1 - p) \log_2 (1 - p)]$$

For classification problems it must be admitted that the conditions of uniform transmission channels are not always satisfied, so that the conclusions might be distorted for one class or the other. With hopes for future refinements we shall accept the consequences of non-fulfillment of the initial conditions because it is the principle which we believe to be basically sound.

We were left at the end of the last section with the problem of finding the typical sequence for each class. We understand that the typical sequence is the message word A which has been sent, and that because of the non-identity of the responses of the individuals which have been classified in that class, the channel, i.e. the battery of tests, is not noiseless. Hence we determine the error for each test and each class. This error is given by the difference between the most frequent responses $r_j(k)$ and the number of individuals belonging to the class, divided by that same number. Indicating the number of individuals belonging to one class by $n_j(k)$ and the error probability by $p_j(k)$, we thus get:

the error probability of the j-th tests and the

kth class

$$p_j(k) = \frac{n_j(k) - r_j(k)}{n_j(k)} \qquad (18)$$

404

with the corresponding capacity

$$c_j(k) = 1 - H(p_j(k)) \quad ; \tag{19}$$

the error probability of the j-th test

$$p_j = \frac{n - \sum_k r_j(k)}{n} \tag{20}$$

with the corresponding capacity

$$c_j = 1 - H(p_j) \tag{21}$$

The error probability of the whole channel is defined by (13) and hence the corresponding capacity is

$$C = 1 - H(p(\varepsilon)) \quad . \tag{22}$$

The higher the value of the capacity, the more significant is the underlying sign. Hence tests with a low capacity can be eliminated. But what level must be chosen to decide if a capacity is small or large? In statistics it is known that these decisions are made by means of the distribution functions, but in information theory the problem is not that of knowing the confidence limit for any capacity value but rather that of knowing the capacity which will permit reliable messages to pass through unreliable transmission channels. Without entering into the details of Shannon's second theorem which is not easily understandable, transposing into classification problems, we can say that since our response pattern has shown a certain degree of variability which is also reflected within the classes, it is not reasonable to imagine a channel capacity higher than the capacity of the total channel for every single test and class.

Neither is it reasonable to stay below the total channel capacity, in which case the homogeneity of the whole channel would be higher than that of the single classes, which is evidently nonsense. So we decide that the total channel capacity (22) based on the error probability (13) will be taken as the decision level. Now if $C_j(k) \geqslant C$ we subsitute the most frequent sign for this value, which we indicate by $s_j(k)$. If $C_j(k) < C$ we substitute a zero. Thus for every class we have a succession of positive, negative and zero signs which we define as the typical sequence of that class.

5. THE EVALUATION OF THE TYPICAL SEQUENCE IN THE CLASSIFICA-
   TION OBTAINED FOR 108 PARTY WORKERS

Let us reconsider our example dealing with 108 party workers. We were left with Table 3 reporting the most frequent responses and characterized by an error probability of $p(\varepsilon) = 0.193$ to which corresponds a value of the binary entropy function of $H(p(\varepsilon)) = 0.707$ and hence a total channel capacity of $C = 0.293$. Now with the data of Table 3 we evaluate all channel capacities for each test/class using (19), thus obtaining Table 4.

k \ T_j	T_1	T_7	T_2	T_3	T_4	T_5	T_6
I	1	1	0.61	0.17	0.20	0.02	0.39
II	1	1	0.19	0.01	0.01	0.12	0.12
III	1	1	0.61	0.39	0.22	0.11	0.61
IV	1	1	0.16	0.23	0.01	0.03	0.03

TABLE 4: THE CHANNEL CAPACITIES $C_j(k)$ FOR EACH TEST AND
CLASS

It is seen that besides the tests which have defined the classes, 5 other channel capacities lie above the general capacity value of 0.293. We can thus build the matrix with the typical sequences of the four classes, where tests T_4 and T_5 have been omitted since they did not present for either class a significant channel capacity. For the other tests we have put the most frequent sign where the capacities lie above the value of 0.293 and a zero if they lie below that value. The matrix is reported in Table 5. The frequencies of A and B party workers have been shown in the last two columns.

T_j / k	T_1	T_7	T_2	T_3	T_6	Frequencies of party-workers in	
						Party A	Party B
I	−	+	−	o	−	0.91	0.07
II	−	−	o	o	o	0.07	0.30
III	+	+	+	−	−	0.00	0.24
IV	+	−	o	o	o	0.02	0.39
Total sum of frequencies						1.00	1.00

Table 5: THE TYPICAL SEQUENCE MATRIX

Considering the frequencies of the two different kinds of party workers it is possible to make the following observations:

1) The differences between the two groups of party workers are quite distinct and there are, in fact, only five party workers of party A who find themselves in those classes which are characterized by a greater proportion of party workers from party B, whereas there are only four party workers of party B who find themselves in the group characterized by party A.

2) The group of party A is more compact (identifying itself as a single homogeneous group) than the group of party B which subdivides itself into subsidiary groups which are only vaguely delineated in terms of predominant signs.

3) The group of A party workers is characterized by: the presence of an attitude of dichotomism, by the denial of currents, admiration for their own party leaders, and by the fact that they do not seek personal advantages. On the other hand, the party workers of the B party are the most favorable to a plurality of currents (that is accepting the party as it is actually made up) and can be more or less satisfied with their leaders. There does exist as well a group of party workers in party B who do not accept a plurality of currents and therefore have a consequent indifference toward their

leaders. In effect the party workers of party B indicate a lesser degree of compactness in the party, and the heterogeneous political currents facilitate the presence of contrasting attitudes.

We shall see that for points 2) and 3) the situation will remain unchanged even for the results of Tables 6 and 7 and also in the last tables.

6. A CLASSIFICATION BASED ON ENTROPY: THE DISCRIMINATING SEQUENCE

In this section we consider the problem of finding, with the help of some notions of information theory, an ordered set of tests which minimize the number of disjunctive propositions necessary to single out a class represented by its typical sequence. If the classes are obtained by the method shown in Section 2, where monothetic classes were obtained, this problem does not arise since the tests with the highest information content are themselves the tests with the highest discriminatory power. Thus such tests build in the discriminatory sequence.

But very often the researcher is faced with the problem of classes already existing and he has to find out some method, a diagnostic formula, which will permit him with the smallest number of questions (tests) to classify an individual into one of the classes. Necessarily some kind of information about the classes must be available. The result of such an analysis is generally called a classification key. The methodology of numerical classification keys at the nominal level has been illustrated by Maccacaro (1958), as far as monothetic classes are concerned, and by one of us, Möller (1962 b and c) generalizing this method to polythetic classes with the possibility of determining the probability of the classes being correctly identified. This method will be shown in the following in an improved version. For a general review of classification keys reference may be made to an article of Morse (1971).

We start with the typical sequence matrix which is composed only of the signs +, -, and o. For each test we evaluate the test capacity C_j defined by (21). The smaller the number of zeros found in a column the greater is the power of the test to divide the classes without overlap. For instance, consider following two tests with the typical responses of five classes:

$$
k \left\{
\begin{array}{lcc}
 & T_i & T_j \\
\text{I} & + & + \\
\text{II} & + & + \\
\text{III} & - & o \\
\text{IV} & - & - \\
\text{V} & - & -
\end{array}
\right.
$$

If we divided the classes using test T_i we would get classes (I, II) and (III, IV, V) separated from each other. But if we used test T_j we would be left with classes (I, II, III) on one hand and (III, IV, V) on the other. This means that the third class cannot be classified univocally by test T_j, and the two resulting classes are overlapping.

The test capacity gives us a precise measure concerning which test is to be preferred. Nevertheless the test capacity alone is not sufficient because a test having, for instance, a positive response for all classes, even with a capacity near to one, is completely useless as far as subdivision is concerned since it has no discriminatory power. Here entropy is very useful. Our method of constructing a classification key is based on the following steps:

1) determine the test capacity c_j for each test;
2) determine the number of positive and negative signs $N_j(+)$, $N_j(-)$ of each test in the typical sequence matrix;
3) evaluate the entropy value for this distribution of signs, for each test

$$
H_j(s) = \frac{1}{N_j(+) + N_j(-)} \left\{ \left[N_j(+) + N_j(-) \right] \log_2 \left[N_j(+) + N_j(-) \right] \right.
$$
$$
\left. - N_j(+) \log_2 N_j(+) - N_j(-) \log_2 N_j(-) \right\} \quad ; \quad (23)
$$

4) determine the product $D_j = C_j \times H_j(s)$ for each test. This is the discriminatory value of the test. The highest value will indicate the test which has the best discriminating property;
5) divide the set of all classes by the response to the first discriminatory test into two subsets of classes:

    i)   one subset comprising all classes which have the typical response (-,o) in correspondence to the discriminatory test;

    ii)   the other subset composed of all classes which have the typical responses (+,o) in correspondence to the discriminatory test.

This method can be performed in two ways:

    1)   by trying to find a second discriminatory test which divides both subsets simultaneously into further subsets;

    2)   by separately considering each subset we have found and applying to each subset the above listed points 1) to 4); in this case the key found is said to be hierarchic.

Following the first way has the advantage that all classes are identified by the same tests. The test capacities thus remain unvaried for the whole process. To determine the entropy values one first evaluates the entropy for every test of each subset, and then takes the weighted mean value where the weightings are the number of typical responses different from zero from which the subset entropies (23) have been calculated. Following the second way the test capacities of each subset have to be determined, and as a result generally more efficient keys can be expected, but a wider range of tests may also be required.

Once the classification key is found the probabilities of belonging can be evaluated (Möller 1962c). To do this it is only necessary to consider the matrix with the most frequent sign. Suppose that the first discriminating test is test T_1 and the next discriminating T_2, then our key indicates four possibilities, or four itineraries, namely (+) to T_1 and (+) to T_2, (+) to T_1 and (-) to T_2, etc. Suppose furthermore there is one given class k of 10 individuals which is characterized by 8 positive answers to T_1 and thus $r_1(k) = 8$ and $s_1(k) = +$, and 1 positive answer to T_2 so that $r_2(k) = 9$ and $s_2(k) = -$. Then it is easy to see that the probability of one individual in that class following the first itinerary (+,+) is given by $\frac{8}{10} \times \frac{1}{10}$.

At every terminal of the key we thus have for every class an itinerary probability. Dividing this by the sum of the itinerary probabilities for the same itinerary of all classes, we get a value which indicates the probability that one individual who has followed that itinerary will belong to the corresponding class. These probabilities are called the probabilities of belonging.

7. AN APPLICATION OF THE THEORY OF INFORMATION TO THE IDENTIFICATION OF CLASSES

For an example of the method we consider once more the same individuals as before, i.e. A and B party workers, characterized by their responses to the seven tests specified in Section 2. These individuals have been classified into 5 classes following the grouping method with mean linkage, by which the classes are characterized by their overall similarity. With this method, largely discussed in Sokal and Sneath (1963) and in Jardine and Sibson (1971), the most stable classification is composed of five groups which we shall continue to call classes. We have reported the result of this classification in Table 6 enumerating the individuals which belong to the five classes.

Classes k	Individuals	Individuals of Party A	Individuals of Party B
I	F6 F4 F3 E5 C3 B4 F2 F1 B2		9
II	E1 D9		2
III	E3 E4 B1 E14	1	3
IV	F8 D7 B9 F5 E8 C4 E6 D4 C6 B5 A4 E9 D8 C9 B7 A9 A8 E7 C7 A7 D5 D1 C5 C1 A5 F9 D6 B6 A3 A2 F7 A6 C17 C16	2	32
V	B8 E2 D3 D2 C2 B3 A1 C8 E18 F16 F15 F13 D18 D17 B18 B17 A18 B15 A14 F12 D13 F18 F17 F14 F11 F10 E12 E11 D11 D10 A16 C12 C11 C10 B16 B14 B12 B11 A17 A13 E10 A12 E15 A11 B13 B10 D14 D12 A15 A10 E17 E16 C15 E13 D16 C14 D15 C18 C13	51	8

Table 6: THE CLASSIFICATION OF PARTY WORKERS INTO FIVE CLASSES ACCORDING TO A GROUPING METHOD

411

Obviously each one of these classes is characterized by the positive or negative responses given to the seven considered tests. We can then pick out the responses which occur most frequently, this time without caring about their capacities. We thus get Table 7 where for each class the most frequent responses to the seven different tests are given.

Classes k	Number of Subjects	Most frequent responses to the seven tests							
		T_1	T_2	T_3	T_4	T_5	T_6	T_7	
I	9	6(-)	8(+)	8(+)	7(-)	8(+)	8(+)	9(-)	$\sum_j r_{kj}$ (k)
II	2	2(+)	2(-)	2(+)	1(±)	1(±)	2(-)	2(-)	
III	4	4(+)	4(-)	4(-)	3(+)	4(+)	4(+)	3(-)	
IV	34	24(+)	32(+)	34(-)	24(+)	18(-)	30(-)	23(-)	
V	59	57(-)	52(-)	45(+)	45(-)	38(+)	51(-)	54(+)	
k^r_j(K)	108	93	98	93	80	69	95	91	619

Table 7:   THE MOST FREQUENT RESPONSES TO THE SEVEN TESTS BY INDIVIDUALS BELONGING TO THE FIVE CLASSES

On the basis of this table it is possible to determine by the method shown in the preceding sections:

i)   the general channel capacity, first determining the error probability with

$$p(\varepsilon) = \frac{nm - 619}{nm} = 0.181$$

so that C = 0.318;

ii)   the capacities for each class and test, which are reported in Table 8.

iii)   the capacities C_j for the tests only. Those capacity values which exceed C = 0.318 have been underlined.

Classes K \ T_j	Capacity values $C_j(K)$ for each test T_j and class K						
	T_1	T_2	T_3	T_4	T_5	T_6	T_7
I	0.08	0.50	0.50	0.24	0.50	0.50	1.00
II	1.00	1.00	1.00	0.00	0.00	1.00	1.00
III	1.00	1.00	1.00	0.19	1.00	1.00	0.19
IV	0.13	0.68	1.00	0.13	0.00	0.48	0.09
V	0.79	0.48	0.21	0.21	0.06	0.43	0.58
C_j	0.42	0.56	0.42	0.18	0.06	0.47	0.37

Table 8: THE CAPACITY VALUES FOR EACH TEST AND CLASS, $C_j(K)$, AND FOR EACH TEST SOLELY C_j

Now we are able to determine the typical sequences of the five classes which we report in Table 9 by comparing the sample capacities with the overall value of 0.318. In the same table are further reported all quantities necessary to construct a classification key following the proposed method, i.e. utilizing the same test for the whole key. First the number of positive signs, $N_j(+)$, and negative signs, $N_j(-)$, of the typical sequence matrix have been counted, then the entropy (23), H'_j has been evaluated. Finally the product of C_j, determined from Table 8, and H'_j has been calculated producing the D'_j values. So we find that the second test is the best discriminatory test. This test divides the five classes into a subset of classes (I,IV) and another non-overlapping subset of classes (II,III,V).

Following the scheme of Table 9, we next evaluate for each test and subset the entropies H''_j (subset) and hence the weighted mean H''_j (with weights given by the sum of signs different from zero: $N_j(+) + N_j(-)$ which multiplied by C_j determines the second discriminatory test. Computations are reported in Table 10 for the second discriminatory test, and in Table 11 for the third one.

Classes K \ T_j	T_1	T_2	T_3	T_4	T_5	T_6	T_7
I	o	+	+	o	+	+	-
II	+	-	+	o	o	-	-
III	+	-	-	o	+	+	o
IV	o	+	-	o	o	-	o
V	-	-	o	o	o	-	+
$N_j(+)+N_j(-)$	3	5	4	0	2	5	3
H'_j	0.918	0.971	1	0	0	0.971	0.918
D'_j	0.386	0.544	0.420	0	0	0.456	0.340

Table 9: THE TYPICAL SEQUENCES OF THE FIVE CLASSES REPORTED IN TABLE 7 AND THE EVALUATION OF THE DISCRIMINATORY VALUES D_j OF THE TESTS

T_j	T_1	T_2	T_3	T_4	T_5	T_6	T_7
Classes I	o	+	+	o	+	+	-
IV	o	+	-	o	o	-	o
$N_j(+)+N_j(-)$	0	2	2	0	1	2	1
H''_j (subset)	0	0	1	0	0	1	0
Classes II	+	-	+	o	o	-	-
III	+	-	-	o	+	+	o
V	-	-	o	o	o	-	+
$N_j(+)+N_j(-)$	3	3	2	0	1	3	2
H''_j (subset)	0.918	0	1	0	0	0.918	1
H''_j (mean)	0.918	0	1	0	0	0.951	0.667
D''_j	0.386	0	0.420	0	0	0.450	0.025

Table 10: THE COMPUTATIONS NEEDED TO FIND THE SECOND DISCRIMINATION TESTS UTILIZING THE SAME TESTS

T_j	T_1	T_2	T_3	T_4	T_5	T_6	T_7
Class I	O	+	+	O	+	+	−
$N_j(+) + N_j(-)$	O	1	1	O	1	1	1
H_j''' (subset)	O	O	O	O	O	O	O
Class IV	O	+	−	O	O	−	O
$N_j(+) + N_j(-)$	O	1	1	O	O	1	O
H_j''' (subset)	O	O	O	O	O	O	O
Class III	+	−	−	O	+	+	O
$N_j(+) + N_j(-)$	1	1	1	O	1	1	O
H_j''' (subset)	O	O	O	O	O	O	O
Classes { II	+	−	+	O	O	−	−
V	−	−	O	O	O	−	+
$N_j(+) + N_j(-)$	2	2	1	O	O	2	2
H_j''' (subset)	1	O	O	O	O	O	1
H_j''' (mean)	0.667	O	O	O	O	O	0.667
D_j'''	0.28	O	O	O	O	O	0.247

Table 11:   THE COMPUTATIONS NEEDED TO FIND THE THIRD
DISCRIMINATORY TEST USING THE SAME TESTS

This method is continued until all entropic values are
zero. The resulting key is shown in Figure 4. Also indicated are the probabilities of belonging. For instance, the
probabilities of the first terminal defined by positive answers to tests T_2 and T_6, by reference to Table 7 are given as

$$\frac{8}{9} \times \frac{8}{9} = 0.7901 \text{ for the first class}$$

$$0 \times 0 = 0 \qquad " \quad " \quad \text{second} \quad "$$

$$0 \times 1 = 0 \qquad " \quad " \quad \text{third} \quad "$$

$$\frac{32}{34} \times \frac{4}{34} = 0.1107 \text{ for the fourth class}$$

$$\frac{7}{59} \times \frac{8}{59} = 0.0161 \quad " \quad " \quad \text{fifth} \quad "$$

Sum   0.9169

Dividing the itinerary values by the total we get the probabilities of belonging as reported in Figure 4. Hence it is seen that an individual classified in class I having answered positively to tests T_2 and T_6, independently of the answer to test T_1, has a probability of 0.121 of belonging to class I, which should be listed in the base of the key. The individual also has a probability of 12.1% of belonging to class IV and of 0.017 of belonging to class V.

Hence all individuals answering positively to tests T_2 and T_6 will be attributed to class I, which means that we will find in this new class I the following individuals who do not belong to it, namely:

F5 E8 A6 F7 from class IV and B8 from class V. Instead, two individuals who should be classified in class I are found in other classes, namely F4 in class III and C3 in class IV. Analogously we have the following other misclassifications:

C16 and C17 from class IV to class V,

E2 D3 D2 C2 B3 A1 from class V to class IV.
The total number of misclassifications is 15. It can be seen that the greatest number of misclassifications has been performed within Party B, while only two individuals of Party A have been misclassified, confirming our previous impression of the compactness of both parties.

Following the second method of key construction the computations shown in Table 9 remain exactly the same, but instead of Tables 10 and 11 we shall have the results of Table 12 since all subsets have been treated separately. For each subset we have to determine the new test capacities. The resulting key is shown in Figure 5 together with the probabilities of belonging. As may be seen in this caśe, the modal probabilities, which are most important since our decision is based on them, are with only one exception a little greater than with the previous key, confirming the higher efficiency of the hierarchic keys. In fact, only 11 shifts which were reported in Section 4 have now taken place. If still more efficient keys were desired, although at considerably higher costs, one could increase the general capacity value requested for establishing the typical sequence. In consequence a greater number of zeros will be necessary for a complete discrimination.

Figure 4 - The classification key obtained with the tests T_2, T_6, and T_1 and the probabilities of belonging for each itinerary.

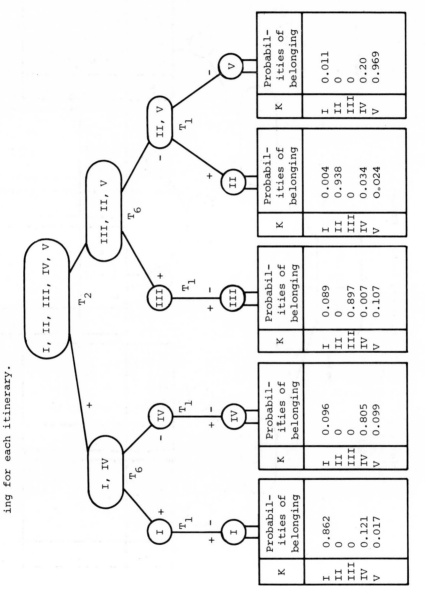

417

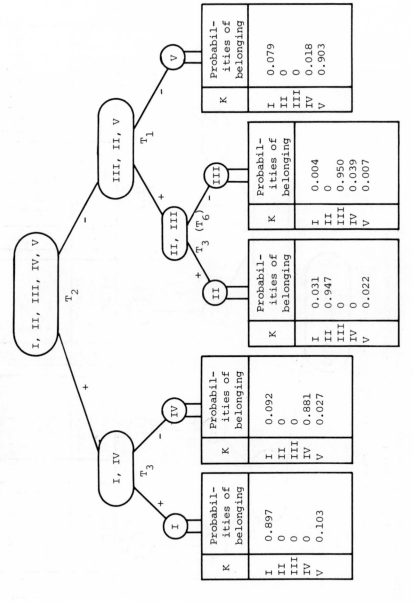

Figure 5 — The hierarchic classification key and the probabilities of belonging.

T_j	T_1	T_2	T_3	T_4	T_5	T_6	T_7
Classes { I	O	+	+	O	+	+	−
Classes { IV	O	+	−	O	O	−	O
H_j (subset)	O	O	1	O	O	1	O
C_j (subset)	O	O	0.84	O	O	0.48	O
D_j (subset)	O	O	0.84	O	O	0.48	O
Classes { II	+	−	+	O	O	−	−
Classes { III	+	−	−	O	+	+	O
Classes { V	−	−	O	O	O	−	+
H_j (subset	0.918	O	1	O	O	0.918	1
C_j (subset)	0.81	O	0.25	O	O	0.46	0.55
D_j (subset)	0.743	O	0.25	O	O	0.422	0.55
Classes { II	+	−	+	O	O	−	−
Classes { III	+	−	−	O	+	+	O
H_j (subset)	O	O	1	O	O	1	O
C_j (subset)	O	O	1	O	O	1	O
D_j (subset)	O	O	1	O	O	1	O

Table 12:   THE COMPUTATIONS NEEDED TO FIND FURTHER DISCRIMI-
NATORY TESTS FOR THE HIERARCHIC KEY

8.   A BETWEEN-CLASS DISTANCE FOR NOMINAL SCALE VARIABLES

The final result of any type of classification should
be a distance matrix in which distances between classes are
shown. For quantitative data this presents no difficulties,
but for qualitative data it is not so easy. Even in this
area information theory can make some useful contributions.
In fact, in information theory it is customary to resort to
the so-called Hamming distance to measure the distance between a message received and the one sent simply as the number of discordances divided by the total number of symbols
sent. This somewhat unsophisticated definition, known to

numerical taxonomists as the matching coefficient, is suitable for a very useful graphic representation, however. In fact, if we observe the messages OO and 11, it is evident that they are farther apart than OO and O1 or 1O and 11, etc. If we put these 4 messages at the edges of a square we have the following scheme:

In view of the fact that in our case there are never, or at least very seldom, tests presenting the same response for all subjects, it will be necessary to establish some coordinates of the classes in that hypercube made by as many dimensions as there are tests which form the typical sequence. The formula we suggest for the coordinates $x_j(k)$ for the k-th class and test T_j is given by

$$x_j(k) = \frac{1}{2} [1 + s_j(k) \times c_j(k)] \qquad (24)$$

We have seen from the above scheme of unitary length that an axis corresponds to each test. With formula (24) a class is then placed on this unitary axis as a function of the test/class capacity $C_j(k)$. The nearer the capacity is to one, the nearer are the coordinates of that class to the edges of the hypercube. For noiseless channels, where $C_j(k) = 1$, the class coordinates coincide with the messages sent and are hence on the edges.

Once the matrix of the coordinates $x_j(k)$ has been determined it will be easy to calculate the distances d_{ks} between all classes according to the usual formula

$$d_{ks} = \left[\Sigma_j (x_j(k) - x_j(s)) \right]^{\frac{1}{2}} , \text{ all } k,s . \qquad (25)$$

It is further possible to determine relative distances by dividing the above formula by $\sqrt{2}$ if only two tests are considered, by $\sqrt{3}$ if three, and by $\sqrt{s}$ if s tests are considered, these values being the length of the longest diagonal of the hypercube.

As we have seen, the individuals always fall at the corners of the unitary hypercube. If we now assign all individuals to the class which is nearest to the corner

we can first of all check the stability of the classification
and hence the significance of the typical sequence. Secondly, we can eliminate atypical individuals from some classes
so that the final result of this reclassification should be,
as far as the typical sequence is concerned, at a higher
homogeneity level. Furthermore, it must be pointed out that
if the typical sequence is sufficiently long even originally
monothetic classes can become polythetic so that this limitation can be eliminated from the method described in Section
2.

9. THE DISTANCES BETWEEN CLASSES OBTAINED FOR THE PARTY
   WORKERS

To determine the distances defined previously, we first
consider only those tests whose capacity is larger than the
total channel capacity. From Table 8 it is seen that tests
T_4 and T_5 can be disregarded. With the aid of Table 7 giving
us the most frequent sign, and Table 8 giving us the class/
test capacities it is easy to establish the coordinates of
the 5 classes, which we have reported in Table 13.

Classes \ Tests	T_1	T_2	T_3	T_6	T_7
I	0.46	0.75	0.75	0.75	0
II	1	0	1	0	0
III	1	0	0	1	0.41
IV	0.56	0.84	0	0.26	0.45
V	0.10	0.26	0.60	0.29	0.79

Table 13. COORDINATES $X_j(k)$ OF THE FIVE CLASSES ACCORDING
TO THE FIVE TESTS WHICH HAVE A SIGNIFICANT
CAPACITY.

Now we have evaluated the distances between the classes
by (25). We have evaluated them once considering all 5
tests, and once considering only 3 tests, namely those found
previously to have the highest hierarchic discriminatory
power. They were tests T_2, T_3, and T_1. The distances are

reported in Table 14 in matrix form. In the lower part of
the matrix are reported the distances with 5 tests and in the
upper part those based only on 3 tests.

Classes	I	II	III	IV	V
I		0.96	1.19	0.76	0.63
II	1.22		1.00	1.38	1.02
III	1.28	1.47		0.95	1.11
IV	1.01	1.47	1.20		0.94
V	1.11	1.32	1.37	1.01	

Table 14: THE BETWEEN-CLASS DISTANCE MATRIX BASED ON 5 TESTS
(LOWER PART OF MATRIX) AND ON 3 TESTS (UPPER PART
OF MATRIX)

By dividing the distances by their largest possible
value, which is $\sqrt{5}$ = 2.236 for the lower part of the matrix,
and $\sqrt{3}$ = 1.732 for the upper part, we get the matrix of the
relative distances, reported in Table 15. It can be seen
that the relative distances based on 5 tests do not differ
very much from those based on only 3 tests. In fact the mean
difference amounts to 0.063. Hence we can graphically represent the classes in 3 dimensions without distorting the
underlying situation too much. This we have done in Figure
6.

Classes	I	II	III	IV	V
I		0.55	0.69	0.44	0.36
II	0.55		0.58	0.80	0.59
III	0.57	0.66		0.55	0.64
IV	0.45	0.66	0.54		0.54
V	0.50	0.59	0.61	0.45	

Table 15: THE BETWEEN-CLASS RELATIVE DISTANCE MATRIX BASED
ON 5 TESTS (LOWER PART OF MATRIX) AND ON 3 TESTS
(UPPER PART OF MATRIX).

Figure 6 - The Hamming cube showing the distances between the five classes using the first three tests.

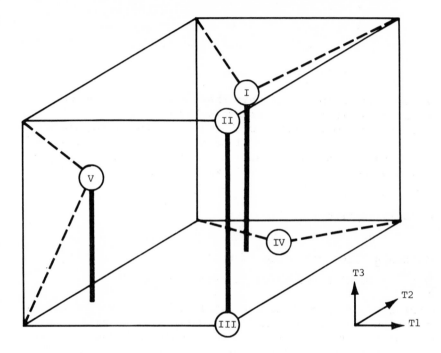

As far as this three-dimensional model is concerned, if the individuals falling on the 8 corners of the unitary cube are assigned to the five classes which are nearest to the corners then all individuals responding to the three tests as indicated will be assigned as follows:

$\pm$ + + will be assigned to class I

+ − + "   "   "   "   " II

+ − − "   "   "   "   " III

$\pm$ + − "   "   "   "   " IV

− − $\pm$ "   "   "   "   " V

We would like to point out that these are exactly the same itineraries shown in our hierarchic key of Figure 5.

If we now form classes with regard to the above signs or itineraries, the original classes will be slightly changed although remaining within the limits for the evaluated probabilities of belonging. The following 11 shifts will take place:

Individual F4 from I to II

"   B4 " I " IV

Individuals C16 C17 from IV to V

"   B8 E2 D3 D2 C2 B3 A1 from V to IV.

For the sake of completeness we will now also give the situation which would be obtained considering all 5 tests. In this case the error probability based only on these tests is as low as 0.124 and only the following shifts will take place:

Individuals A11 from V to III

"   E2 D3 " V " IV (as before)

"   D2 C2 " V " I

"   A6 " IV " I (as before)

"   C16 C17 " IV " V (as before) .

The distances shown in Table 15 are, of course, valid over a five-dimensional space. But in some cases they can be briefly diagrammed in a two-dimensional space if we consider some limiting condition. One such condition we can

accept is the so-called triangularity condition.   Given
three classes (I,II,III) placed so that:

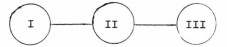

the triangularity condition is the condition in which the
distance between the two classes considered farthest (I and
III) with respect to an intermediate class (II) must be less
than or at least equal to the sum of the distances of the two
classes (I) and (III) from the intermediate class II.

$$d(I,III) \leqslant d(I,II) + d(II,III) .$$

The above condition can further be limited by the following

$$d(I,III) > d(I,II)$$

$$d(I,III) > d(II,III)$$

i.e. by the condition that the distance between the two
classes farther apart must not be less than or equal to the
distance between the two classes that are nearer to each
other.

On the basis of these conditions, using the values of
Table 14 (lower part of matrix), we therefore have the following two-dimensional scheme:

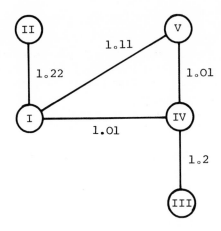

in which we see that the farthest distance is between class II and class III, so that the distance between class I and class III is greater than between I and V and I and IV.

In conclusion, we have tried to show the usefulness of entropy in classification, either for the formation of the classes of subjects, on the basis of tests having the greater contents of information, or as a possibility, once the classes are obtained, to individuate the typical sequence of subjects (with the smallest number of tests possible) in such a way as to arrive at the evaluation of between-class distance.

REFERENCES

Abramson, N. 1963. *Information Theory and Coding.* New York: McGraw-Hill.

Alberoni, F. (Ed.) 1968. *L'attivista di partito.* Bologna: Il Mulino.

Attneave, F. 1959. *Application of Information Theory to Psychology.* New York: Holt, Rinehart and Winston.

Capecchi, V. 1964. "Une Methode de Classification Fondee sur l'Entropie," *Revue Francaise de Sociologie,* V: 290-306.

Capecchi, V. and Möller, F. 1968. "Some Applications of Entropy to the Problems of Classification," *Quality and Quantity,* 2: 63-84.

Edwards, E. 1964. *Information Transmission.* London: Chapman and Hall.

Entwisle, D. R. and Knepp. 1970. "Uncertainty Analysis Applied to Sociological Data," pp. 200-216 in E. F. Borgatta and G. W. Bohrnstedt (eds.) *Sociological Methodology* 1970. San Francisco: Jossey-Bass.

Garner, W. R. 1962. *Uncertainty and Structure as Psychological Concepts.* New York: Wiley.

Jardine, N. and Sibson, R. 1971. *Mathematical Taxonomy.* New York: Wiley.

Kullback, S. 1959. *Information Theory and Statistics*. New York: Wiley.

Maccacaro, G. A. 1958. "The Information Content of Biological Classifications," *Annals Microbiol. Enzimol.*, 8: 231-239.

MacGill, W. J. 1954. "Multivariate Information Transmission," *Psychometrica*, 19: 97-116.

Möller, F. 1962a. "La formazione dei gruppi in base al contenuto di informazione dei criteri di classificazione," *Bollettino del Centro di R. O. dell'Universita Bocconi*, VI: 22-36.

Möller, F. 1962b. "Proposta di una chiave di classificazione," *Bollettino del Centro di R. O. dell' Universita Bocconi*, VI: 37-44.

Möller, F. 1962c. "Quantitative Methods in the Systematics of Actinomyceteles. IV. The Theory and Application of a Probabilistic Identification Key," *Giornale di Microbiologia*, 10: 29-47.

Morse, L. E. 1971. "Specimen Identification and Key Construction with Time-sharing Computers," *Taxon*, 20: 269-282.

Nath, P. 1968. "Inaccuracy and Coding Theory," *Metrika*, 13: 123-135.

Quastler, H. 1954. "The Specificity of Elementary Biological Functions," pp. 170-188 in *Information Theory in Biology*. Urbana, Ill.: University of Ill. Press.

Rescigno, A. and G. A. Maccacaro. 1960. "The Information Content of Biological Classifications," pp. 437-446 in *Information Theory--A Symposium Held at the Royal Institution*, London: Butterwood.

Rogers, D. J. and T. T. Tanimoto. 1960. "A Computer Program for Classifying Plants," *Science*, 132: 1115-1118.

Shannon, C. E. 1948. "A Mathematical Theory of Communication," *Bell System Tech. J.*, 27: 379-423, 623-656.

Sonquist, J. A. and J. N. Morgan. 1964. *The Detection of Interaction Effects*. Research Monograph no. 35, Survey Research Center, Ann Arbor: University of Michigan Press.

Sokal, R. E. and P. H. A. Sneath. 1963. *Principles of Numerical Taxonomy*. San Francisco: Freeman.

14

Pattern Recognition Methods in Sociological Research

N.G. ZAGORUIKO
State University of Novosibirsk
T.I. ZASLAVSKAIA
Institute of Economics and Industrial Engineering, Novosibirsk

1. INTRODUCTION

"Pattern recognition" is a field of cybernetics which
develops techniques for distinguishing significant common
properties of some phenomena, for determining on the basis
of these properties whether or not a phenomenon is a known
type, for clustering phenomena into a number of groups, and
so forth.

A *pattern* is a name of a set of objects or phenomena
distinguished according to a specific criterion, bearing
resemblance to each other and differing from the objects of
other sets. Depending on the specific objective of the research, one and the same pair of objects may be related to
one pattern or to different ones. According to this, a
tractor driver and a rural teacher in one case may be representatives of one pattern (S_o - "rural resident"), in an-
other--representatives of different patterns (S_1--"manual"
and S_2--"nonmanual"). Each object and phenomenon Z from the
set S_i is described by an X set of properties x_1, x_2, ...,
x_n and a point in the space of these properties. The points
of one pattern in the property space are a set with some
structure or another. Sometimes a structure is distinguished
in that the objects of the same pattern are mapped in the
property space into points which are close to each other or
into a "solid" cloud of points. In other cases the structure

of a set of points of one pattern may be of a more complex character.

The rule (D) by which an unknown ("check") realization is identified as some pattern or other is called a "decision rule" or a "decision function."

These elements (a list of k patterns $S = \{S_1, S_2 \ldots, S_k\}$ which are to be discriminated, the n-dimensional property-space $X = \{x_1, x_2, \ldots, x_n\}$, and the decision function D) are available in some form in any recognition problem.

Depending on which of these elements are given and which are to be found, the problems dealt with by the designer of recognition machines, or algorithms, may be classified into 3 major types of pattern recognition problems (Zagoruiko, 1972).

2. DECISION RULES

In a problem of the first type we are given the set of patterns to be recognized (S), the set of differentiating properties (X) for describing the set of objects and the learning set of objects (Z_ℓ) whose identity with some or other pattern is known. It is necessary to form a decision function (D) which would allow one to identify correctly not only the objects of Z_ℓ with their patterns but other objects of the set Z as well.

The cost of recognition errors and the cost of recognizing algorithms may be evaluated by some N value of costs. Admissible costs N_0 are also given. The decision function D must minimize these costs.

In forming the decision function (i.e., in the process of "learning") the machine has no information about a check sequence. According to some hypothesis (H) about the nature of regularity in the structure of the learning sample and about the relationship between the learning and the check samples, it must find in the set V of various decision rules such a rule D which would provide good recognition of the learning sample. If the hypothesis is correct, D_v minimizes recognition and checks realization errors. If V is the number of the decision function, the task of the first type is in the search for D_v for which the following condition is fulfilled:

$$v = \underset{v=1 \div V}{\text{argu min}} \ N(D_v) \,|\, S, X, Z_\ell, \ H, \ N_o.$$

Most available algorithms of D_v construction are oriented to the hypothesis of "Solidity" (Braverman, 1962). If
the points of one pattern are concentrated into a "solid"
cloud which is not overlapped by "solid" sets of the points
of other patterns, the decision function may be some hypersurface separating out a one-relation area into which are
mapped the points of one pattern, of both the learning and,
hopefully, the check samples. In the simplest case the
hypersurface will be a plane delimiting the space, or a
sphere circumscribed around the concentration of points of
the learning sequence. If the shape of these concentrations
is more complex, then the boundary will be a surface of
higher order. The methods used in these cases have been
borrowed from probability theory and mathematical statistics
(Anderson, 1963).

For algorithms for the recognition of patterns which are
distributed in a more complicated way, a method of "potential
functions" (Aizerman, *et al.*, 1964) and of "splintering stan-
dards" (Zagoruiko, 1966) may be noted. The complexity of a
distribution (bizarre boundaries) is an indication that either
the sample is not representative, or properties have been
chosen unsuccessfully.

The hypothesis of "the simplicity of structural regularities" (Zagoruiko and Samokhvalov, 1969; Gavrilko, *et al*,
1969) assumed the construction of a decision rule describing
special features in the structure of the set of points in the
given pattern. The points may lie by no means "solidly" be-
side each other, but if there is some regularity in their
array it should attract attention. In order to secure the
regularity against the influence of arbitrariness because of
choosing scales of devices which measure properties, an
isomorphism between the system's relations that are being
considered and the numerical model of this system is
required (Zagoruiko, *et al*, 1969). This means that whatever
symbols are used as scale markings, e.g. of weights, it is
necessary that between the symbols a, b and c denoting
weights 2, 3, 5 kg, respectively, the relation a+b=c should
be true.

Each system of properties X may be put into correspondence with the system of relations $\{R_1, R_2 \ldots, R_n\}$. Then the
properties of each element Z from the set S_i, i.e. its role
in the structure of this set in the property space X, are
entirely determined by a set of relations of type $\{R_1, \ldots, R_n\}$

between the element Z and all other elements of the set S_i. And the properties of the set S_i as a whole, i.e., the nature of its structure, are determined by the set of relations of the same type between all the elements from S_i. Those relations which are true for one set and which are wrong for others serve as invariant characteristics of this set. The more such characteristics the set has, the more meaningful and the simpler its structure.

The decision concerning the identification of the check realization is made in favor of that pattern for which, after the joining operation, the regularity found on the learning sample is retained to the highest degree or is even manifested still more clearly.

The more general aspect of a recognition problem is that of an empirical prediction (in our case it is a prediction to which pattern a check realization belongs). Criteria for universal algorithms of prediction are described in Vitiaev, et. al. (1972).

3. SELECTION OF PROPERTIES

The problem of the second type is the search for the test system of informative properties (X) which would allow correctly identifying the objects from Z with some or other given pattern (S) with the help of the decision function (D) of a given type. In problems of this type, in addition to D, S, and Z_ℓ, the knowns are (1) the permissible value of the costs N_o which is composed of the recognition error cost and the properties measurement cost, and (2) some hypothesis (H) about the nature of the relationship of the learning sample structure to the structure of the general population. If it is possible to try B different property systems, one should stop with that system X_β which satisfies the condition:

$$\beta = \underset{\beta = 1 \div B}{\text{argu min}} \; N(X_\beta) \, | S, D, H, Z_\ell, N_o \; .$$

The properties to be included in these β sets are determined by a practitioner in that field where the problem is being solved. Thus far, formal techniques for selecting an initial system do not yet exist. The mathematical apparatus only allows one to select from β initial systems a best, i.e. most informative, system of properties to test whether it is sufficient, and if so, whether all properties in it are

necessary. The method of random search with adaptation (RSA)
(Lbov, 1965; Sagoruiko and Zaslvaska, 1968) allows one to exclude from the system properties that are not very informative and to rank them according to their relative significance.

In the method involving tests intended for studying
binary properties, that property is considered most
significant which enters most of the deadlock discriminating
matrices or minimal disjunctive normal forms.

The method of RSA is based on the following idea. Let
it be necessary from q properties of the initial system X_q
to select $n \leq q$ of the most informative properties, i.e.
the best system X_n.

At first some (r) random trials are conducted, and each
selected X_n system is evaluated on the basis of some quality
criterion F. Then the properties which formerly entered the
best system X_n' of r systems are "encouraged," i.e., the
probability of their being selected on the subsequent steps
increases by some magnitude. And those properties which formerly entered the worst set X_n'' are "punished," i.e., the
probability that at subsequent random selections they will
get into the set X_n decreases. The procedure of random
selection, property evaluation, and adaptation continues
until the probability of selection of some properties increases so much that at further steps only this system X_n is
selected.

Tests have shown a high effectiveness of the RSA method.
For fixed machine time this algorithm would select more informative systems than other known algorithms.

The selection of one or another X_n system depends on the
quality criterion F, i.e., on the objective which we desire
to attain by the use of selected properties. Different
objectives may be stated, as for example: "to select an X_n
which would allow one to recognize the check sequence to a
given degree of accuracy"; "to select an X_n system which
would allow one to describe the structure of the general
population by using a most concise language"; or to select
an X_n system of properties which are the most highly correlated with some target function."

4. TAXONOMY

Often it is important to know an inner structure of some
set (Z), i.e. to know whether this set is a homogeneous

mass or whether its structure contains some local subsets of individuals or objects "similar" to each other or regularly related to each other. Finding ways for detecting such sub- sets ("taxons") is the objective in solving problems of the third type--the problem of "taxonomy." In this problem the knowns are: a property space X, the initial set of elements Z, a desirable number of taxons K, an hypothesis H about pos- sible regularities in the taxon structure and, preconditioned by this hypothesis, a type of decision function D by which the elements of one taxon might be distinguished from the elements of other taxons.

If there is a way to evaluate the quality of taxonomy F, then the larger F, the smaller the costs associated with the loss of information that is unavoidable as a result of the grouping procedure. At the expense of these losses we gain the possibility of describing in a simple way the structure of the set of investigated objects.

The smaller are the total costs N minimized in the task of taxonomy, the higher (on the one hand) the quality of taxonomy F, and the simpler (on the other) the description of the obtained result of the taxonomy.

Of Ω versions of the taxonomy it is necessary to select an S_w for which the following condition is satisfied:

$$w = \underset{w = 1 \div \Omega}{\text{argu min}} \ N(S_w) \,|\, X, D, H, Z, K, N_o$$

If the hypothesis of "solidity" serves as the assumption, then the more "solid" the subsets of elements of the taxon, the higher the quality of taxonomy F.

This hypothesis is the basis for the algorithms of the taxonomy of a "Forel" series. By means of the algorithm "Forel-1" the spherical taxons are distinguished. The center of the hypersphere of the given radius moves into the area of the largest concentration of points and stops at the global or local extremity of the distribution density of the points of the Z set. Then the second hypersphere which searches among another concentration of points is put in, and so forth, till all points of Z are inside the hyper- spheres. The longer the radius R of the sphere, the smaller the number of taxons distinguished by the algorithm. Con- sequently, by changing R it is possible to obtain the given number of taxons K. (Zagoriuko and Zaslavskaia, 1968).

More perfect is the algorithm of the taxonomy "Crab" (Elkina and Zagoriuko, 1969) giving a response to a more com- plex character of structural regularities. This makes it

possible to distinguish "chain-" "spiral-shaped" taxons, and
so forth. All points of the set Z are first connected in a
shortest unclosed way. Using an intermediate criterion one
evaluates the probability of the boundary passing between the
taxons on some or other part of this path. The parts having
the maximum probability are partitioned and the quality of
the taxonomy obtained in this partitioning is evaluated. Of
Ω versions, the one selected is such that the regularities of
the taxon structure will be most clear and distinctive. In
particular, if the set actually breaks down into isolated
"solid" concentrations, then such taxons as possessing the
simplest structure will be distinguished in the first place.

5. APPLICATIONS

In sociology all these types of tasks may be encountered.
Assume, for instance, that in studying rural population migration processes, the list of patterns recognized consists of
the following elements;

1. S_1 - a group of rural residents who are definitely
   oriented to remain in the countryside.

2. S_2 - a group of the "hesitating," i.e. the potential
   migrants.

3. S_3 - a group of inhabitants firmly determined to
   move from the countryside to the city.

Learning sample (Z_ℓ) is the information about some number of representatives of these three patterns. The information is usually contained in questionnaires having the
responses to n indirect questions X_1 -- "age," X_2-- "educational background," X_3--"satisfaction with work," and so
forth. This is the system X_n. We shall assume that people
of one pattern give approximately identical answers to the
same questions (the hypothesis of "solidity"). Here the
search for the decision function D consists in the construction of a surface (hyperplane or hypersphere) delimiting the
area of one pattern from the area of other patterns. Now to
predict on the basis of questionnaire replies whether this man
is going to stay in the country or to move to the city it is
sufficient to test concerning what pattern his questionnaire

(his point) is mapped into within the property space X_n. If
the hypothesis of "solidity" is true for this case and if the
learning sample was representative, then these check points
will be adequately identified.

Applying the same information, it is possible to solve
the second type of task as well. One may receive an answer
to such questions as: whether there is sufficient information in one questionnaire in order to identify an individual
with some or other pattern with the required reliability
(test for sufficiency); whether it is possible to exclude
some questions from the questionnaire (test for necessity);
what properties provide the most information about the investigated process or phenomenon (test for relative significance).

Now if all the questionnaires from the learning and
check samples are combined into a common set Z, with the help
of the algorithm of the taxonomy it is possible to know
whether the partitioning of the rural population into the
three aforementioned patterns was legitimate. Maybe the
structure of the set will become more evident and simple if
five patterns instead of three were considered.

Members of the Institute of Economics and the Institute
of Mathematics of the Siberian Division of the USSR Academy
of Sciences have solved some sociological tasks by applying
pattern recognition methods (Zagoruiko and Zaslavskaia, 1968).

The RSA algorithm was used for determining the most
significant properties by which it was possible to predict
with greatest accuracy the direction and intensity of labor
migration between towns and villages of the Russian Federa-
tion. All provinces, regions and autonomous republics of the
RSFSR (61 regions altogether) were considered. Into the
initial system of properties X_q, 50 properties were included
with regard to income level and employment of the population,
to housing and consumer services, climatic conditions of the
region, and so forth. Two methods were compared: regression
analysis (RA) and random search with adaptation (RSA).

The coefficient of multiple correlation between the intensity of migration and seven most significant properties
selected by the RSA method was 0.850 and for RA was 0.826.
The mean errors in prediction of migration by seven properties selected by RA and by RSA were 5.3 and 4.8 per cent
respectively.

With 12 variables used in prediction according to RSA
we managed to reduce the error down to 3.8 per cent. This
accuracy may be held acceptable for planning calculations.

Several tasks have been solved by taxonomic methods. One of them is associated with a social sampling research design. For subsequent study, the first stage required us to select some (approximately a half) of the districts of the Novosibirsk province, and then, the second stage, to select some (20 per cent) of local soviets of these districts. For this purpose "Forel-1" worked in the space of such properties as the size of the rural population in the district, the percentage of collective farm households, the distance from the center of the province, and so forth. At the first stage five properties were used, and at the second, six properties.

As a result, 14 districts of 29 were selected which were closest by their parameters to the centers of their taxons (typical districts). These districts have 185 local soviets of which 34 ("typical") have been selected on the basis of the algorithm of the taxonomy at the second stage. The inhabitants of these local soviets were then subjected to a thorough sociological survey.

The second task in the field of taxonomy deals with the blocking of occupations, i.e., separating groups in a rural population having identical social position. Here were used properties which were determined by major aspects of labor: skills (measured by training time), complexity of work according to assignments, and physical conditions, social significance, supervisory or operative functions, and so forth.

The blocking of occupations in this property space was made by the algorithm "Forel-1." As a result, groups of workers were distinguished with similar kinds of mobility and with similar patterns of stability, enterprise and occupations.

Algorithms for a solution to problems of a complex type, particularly those of simultaneous search for the best grouping (taxonomy) of objectives and for such a system of properties in whose space the structure of taxons would be the simplest, (algorithm "SX" (Zagoruiko, 1969)) are of great interest. Using the same notation as that above, this problem of combined types is formulated as follows:

$$w, \beta = \text{argu min } N(S_w, X_\beta) \,|\, D, H, Z, K, n, N_o.$$
$$\beta = 1 \div B$$
$$w = 1 \div \Omega$$

This is an algorithm described below. In the original space X_q, the best variant of taxonomy $S_w^{(1)}$, is selected. One then takes a system $X_n^{(1)}$ which is the best from the point of view of separating selected taxons. Then n properties of this system may be found with method RSA or with a unification into n factors with the help of the taxonomy algorithms. In this space $X_n^{(1)}$ taxons S_w are "punished," and individual (but new) properties of all Z realizations are renewed. Further, the search for a new taxonomy variant of a set Z into K taxons $S_w^{(2)}$ is carried out. By these taxons readings of all devices of a system X_q are "punished" (restored), producing a new variant of subsystem $X_n^{(2)}$, the best for taxons separating $S_w^{(3)}$. Such a procedure involving the formation and destruction of taxons on the property set is repeated until the table "taxons - factors" stops changing. In the general case the result depends on the beginning of a process, starting with a taxonomy of objects or a factorization of properties. Hence, two problems are solved in parallel: the first one begins with a grouping of objects, the second with that of properties. The best variant of a solution from these two is selected. A quality of grouping both objects and properties is estimated according to criterion F for the taxonomy quality used in the algorithm "crab." If the taxonomy quality of objects is F_s and that of the factors is F_x, then the quality of a table "taxon-factor" is estimated with the magnitude $F_s \cdot F_x$.

The initial data of one of the problems solved with this method were a table originally containing 50 variables and 193 units. The observation units were rural populated points of the Novosibirsk province. The objective of this study was to find characteristics influencing the urbanization of the villages and to classify the latter into groups by their degree of urbanization. According to this, the system X_q included variables which supposedly influenced urbanization, such as the number of inhabitants in a village, the age composition of the population, the level of medical attendance, the provision of shops and consumer services, the level of incomes from the public economy and from private households, and so forth.

The algorithm "Crab" was used for grouping both units and variables. The best "taxon-factor" table contained 21 taxons of 193 settlements and 11 factors extracted from 50 variables. The comparison of the variables of "typical" members from different taxons showed important distinctions, and the meaning of the factors conforms well with sociologists' concepts of the attributes determining the urbanization process in rural populated areas.

REFERENCES

Aizerman, M. A., E. M. Braverman and L. I. Rozonoer. 1964. "Theoretical Foundations of the Potential Functions Method in the Task of Learning Machines for Partitioning Situations into Classes." (Russian). *Avtomat. i. telem.* 25:6.

Anderson, T. W. 1963. *Introduction to Multivariate Statistical Analysis.* (Russian translation). Moscow: Fizmatgiz. (New York: John Wiley, 1958).

Braverman, E. M. 1962. "An Attempt with the Learning Machine at Visual Pattern Recognition." (Russian). *Avtomat. i telem.* 21: 349–364.

Elkina, V. N., and N. G. Zagoruiko. 1969 "Quantitative Criteria of Taxonomy Quality and their Utilization in the Process of Decision-making." (Russian). In *Vychislit. sistemy* 36. Novosibirsk: Nauka.

Gavrilko, B. P., N. G. Zagoruiko, and K. F. Samokhvalov "Simplicity Hypothesis Clarification." (Russian). In *Vychislit. sistemy* 37. Novosibirsk : Nauka.

Lbov, G. S. 1965. "Selection of an Effective System of Properties." (Russian). *Vychislit. sistemy* 19. Novosibirsk: Nauka.

Suppes, P., and J. Zinnes. 1967. "Psychological Measurements." In R. D. Luce (ed.) *Handbook of Mathematical Psychology.* (Russian translation). Moscow: Mir. (New York: Wiley, 1963).

Vitiaev, E. E., B. P. Gavrilko, N. G. Zagoruiko, and K. F. Samokhvalov. 1972. "Demands for Prediction Algorithms." *Vychislit. sistemy* 50. Novosibirsk: Nauka.

Zagoruiko, N. G.   1966.   *Auditory Pattern Recognition.*
    (Russian).   Novosibirsk: Nauka.

Zagoruiko, N. G. and T. I. Zaslavskaia (eds.)   1968.   *Pattern
    Recognition in Social Research.*   (Russian) Novosibirsk:
    Nauka.

Zagoruiko, N. G. and K. F. Samokhvalov.   1969.   "The Nature
    of the Pattern Recognition Problem."   (Russian)
    Vychislit.   *sistemy* 36.   Novosibirsk: Nauka.

Zagoruiko, N. G., K. F. Samokhvalov, and A. S. Nudelman.
    1969.   "Sketches in the General Theory of Pattern
    Recognition."   (Russian).   Paper submitted to the
    Second All-Union Conference on Computing Systems and
    Computing Media.   Moscow.

Zagoruiko, N. G.   1969.   "Simultaneous Search for an Effec-
    tive System of Properties and the Best Version of a
    Taxonomy."   (Russian).   *Vychislit.*   *sistemy* 36.
    Novosibirsk: Nauka.

Zagoruiko, N. G.   1972.   *Recognition Techniques and Their
    Application.*   (Russian).   Moscow: Sov. radio.

15

On the Problem of Reconciling Partitions *

B.G. MIRKIN

Institute of Economics and Industrial Engineering, Novosibirsk

1. INTRODUCTION

We consider the following problem. There is a set of objects A on which a number n of partitions R^i (i=1,...,n) are given.[1] It is necessary to find a partition R which would agree, in some natural sense, with all of them, being their "concentrated" representation.

Let us give examples of such situations.

1. <u>Group choice</u>. We may have n individuals who express their judgments about objects a_1, a_2, ..., a_N. It is required to find out the group judgment on the basis of individual ones. Let us confine our task to the simplest judgments which arise at the onset in studying the objects of A and consist of indications of their similarity or dissimilarity.[2]

---

*This is part of my paper (Mirkin, 1971. See also Mirkin, 1974). I am greatly indebted to F. Borodkin, Iu. Voronov, K. Szaniawsky and L. Chorny for their stimulating comments and criticisms.

[1]As usual the partition of a given set $A = \{a_1,...,a_N\}$ is a set of non-empty subsets (classes) $R_1,...,R_m$ such that each element aεA relates to one and only one of the $R_1,...,R_m$ classes.

[2]In the literature, usually preference judgments are considered (see Arrow, 1951).

Then the judgment of each individual is characterized by the partition of the set A into groups of similar objects, and the group judgment corresponds to the "agreed" partition.

2. <u>Finding a common basis in research classifications.</u> Very often social survey data on a single population are considered by various researchers from different aspects so that every researcher has a classification of his own for this population. Sometimes a question arises: is it possible to find a common classification underlying the individual ones? In our terminology, the question concerns the formation of "agreed" partitions.

3. <u>Factor analysis of nominal attributes.</u> Suppose we have n nominal attributes describing the surveyed human population. They are assumed to be external manifestations of some latent factor measured as a nominal scale. Since nominal attributes are determined by corresponding partitions into groups of persons with the same values, finding this "latent factor" actually means finding an "agreed" partition.

The principle of reconciling partitions is the rule for constructing an "agreed" partition R on the basis of arbitrary given partitions $R^1,\ldots,R^n$. Each principle of reconciling is characterized, therefore, by a function

$$R = F(R^1,\ldots,R^n) ,$$ whose arguments $R^1,\ldots,R^n$ and values R are the partitions of the set A.

In the case where n is small compared with the number of objects N, as an agreed partition an intersection (combination grouping) of given partitions is usually chosen:

$$R = F(R^1,\ldots,R^n) = R^1 \cap \ldots \cap R^n .$$

Under intersection $R^1 \cap \ldots \cap R^n$ a partition is meant whose classes are non-empty sets of the type $R^1_{i_1} \cap R^2_{i_2} \cap \ldots \cap \ldots \cap R^n_{i_n}$ where $R^1_{i_1},\ldots,R^n_{i_n}$ are classes of partitions $R^1,\ldots,R^n$.

A special case of an intersection is the so-called hierarchical classification obtained as a result of linear ordering in a set of given partitions which is just what determines the hierarchy. The hierarchical classification is often represented as a tree whose zero level (root) the set A itself corresponds to, and the k-th level of which is the intersection class of the first k (by hierarchy) partitions. The classes of the k-th level are connected by lines with the classes of the (k-1)-th level including them.

We shall impose, according to Arrow's (1951) approach, certain natural constraints on conceivable principles for the agreement of partitions. It will be shown that these constraints necessarily lead to taking an intersection of some of the initial partitions.

However, for the case where the number of classes in the agreed partition is to be limited beforehand (this situation is very common in practice), it is necessary to take as an agreed partition one of the initial partitions.

2. AXIOMS AND RESULTS

If R is a partition of the set A, then by xRy we shall denote the fact that $x, y \in A$ are in one class, and by $x\bar{R}y$ that x and y are in different classes. The relation xRy is obviously a relation of equivalence. For two partitions R and S we will say that R is contained in S (denoted by $R \subset S$) if and only if for any $x, y \in A$, xRy implies xSy. The inclusion $R \subset S$ means that the classes of the S partition are obtained as unions of the classes of the R partition, i.e. S is an "enlargement" of R.

We now state the requirements for the principle of agreement $R = F(R^1, \ldots, R^n)$.

__Axiom 1.__ Function $F(R^1, \ldots, R^n)$ is uniquely defined for any sets of partitions $R^1, \ldots, R^n$.

__Axiom 2.__ Let $R = F(R^1, \ldots, R^n)$ and $R' = F(R^{1'}, \ldots, R^{n'})$. If xRy, and if $R^{i'}$ is either equal to R^i or obtained from R^i by placing x in the same class as y, then $xR'y$. If $x\bar{R}y$, and if $R^{i'}$ is either equal to R^i or obtained from R^i by displacing x into a class not including y, then $x\bar{R'}y$ $(i=1, \ldots, n)$.

__Axiom 3.__ Let A' be an arbitrary subset of A and $R^{i'}$ a partition of A' obtained from R^i through eliminating all the elements from $A - A'$. Then $F(R^{1'}, \ldots, R^{n'})$ coincides with $R' = [F(R^1, \ldots, R^n)]'$.

__Axiom 4.__ For any $x, y \in A$ such sets $R^1, \ldots, R^n$ and $P^1, \ldots, P^n$ exist that xRy and $x\bar{P}y$ where $R = F(R^1, \ldots, R^n)$, $P = F(P^1, \ldots, P^n)$.

Axiom 1 demands that the agreement principle should be applicable to any sets of partitions. Axiom 2 states that a mutual arrangement of objects in an agreed partition will not change if some initial classifications are changed to its benefit (and the others remain the same).

Axiom 3 requires that no decision about a subset of objects should be connected with the decision about other objects so that, in this sense, all objects are independent. Axiom 4 guarantees that no a priori decision will be made prior to consideration of initial partitions.

Denote by M a set of indices $\{1, 2, \ldots, n\}$. We shall say that the set $I \subset M$ is *yes-decisive* for $x, y \in A$ if from that xR^iy (for all $i \in I$) it follows that xRy $(R = F(R^1, \ldots, R^n))$

443

irrespective of the relation of x and y in the remaining partitions $R^i (i \notin I)$. We shall call the subset $I \subset M$ *no-decisive* for x,y$\in$A if from $x\overline{R^i}y$ (for all i$\in$I) $x\overline{R}y$ follows. If the subset $I \subset M$ is at the same time both yes-decisive and no-decisive for the pair x,y$\in$A , then we shall call it *decisive* for x and y.

Note that if the subset $I \subset M$ is yes-decisive for any pair x,y$\in$A , this means that the agreed partition R satisfies the relation $\bigcap\limits_{i\in I} R^i \subset R$.

Similarly, if the subset $I \subset M$ is such that for any i$\in$I the set {i} is no-decisive for any pairs x,y$\in$A , this means that the agreed partition R satisfies the relation

$$R \subset \bigcap\limits_{i\in I} R^i.$$

These statements are direct corollaries of the definitions of the relation $\subset$ and the yes-(no-) decisive set.

The introduced terms permit one to prove a number of statements that follow from axioms 1-4 (for $n \geqslant 2$, $N \geqslant 3$).

Lemma 1. (Pareto's principle).

The agreed partition R is certain to be such that the set M is decisive for any pair x,y$\in$A.

Proof.

By axion 3 we can confine ourselves to a consideration of only two arbitrary objects x,y$\in$A. Let xR^iy for all i$\in$M , but $x\overline{R}y$. Then, in view of axiom 2, $x\overline{R}y$ for any arguments $R^1,\ldots, R^n$ since they differ from the initial ones only in that x and y may happen to appear in different classes. But by Axiom 4 this contradicts xRy if only for one set $R^1,\ldots,R^n$. The obtained inconsistency proves that M is yes-decisive for an arbitrary pair x,y$\in$A. In the same way it can be shown that M is a no-decisive set. Q.E.D.

From Lemma 1 it follows, in particular, that the set of yes-decisive sets is non-empty because it includes M.

Let V be the minimum yes-decisive set, i.e. V is a yes-decisive set if only for one pair x,y$\in$A , but any of its subsets is yes-decisive for no pair of objects. Obviously, V is non-empty since otherwise xRy would be satisfied at $x\overline{R^i}y$ for all i$\in$M , and this is inconsistent with Pareto's principle (by which M is a no-decisive set).

The two statements given below show that V uniquely defines the agreed partition.

Lemma 2.

Any yes-decisive set is yes-decisive for all pairs x,y$\in$A.

Proof.
Let I be yes-decisive for some $x,y \epsilon A$. We show that I is yes-decisive for all $w,z \epsilon A$. Let the set $R^1,\ldots,R^n$ be such that x,y,z are in one class for all R^i where $i \epsilon I$ and y,z are in one and x in another class R^i for $i \not\in I$. This can be represented by the following table:

I	$\overline{xyz}$	
$A-I=\overline{I}$	$\overline{x}$	$\overline{yz}$

Here the elements of one class are separated above by a line. According to axiom 3, the mutual arrangement x,y and z in the agreed partition R is determined only by this information, irrespective of the "behavior" of the remaining objects. Since I is yes-decisive for x and y then xRy. Moreover, yRz by Pareto's principle. But from xRy and yRz it follows that xRz. Hence, by axioms 2 and 3, I is yes-decisive for x and z (and therefore, by symmetry, for y and z) since xR^iz only for the indices $i \epsilon I$.

Now consider the set of partitions $R^1,\ldots,R^n$ in which the mutual arrangement x,z,w is described by the following table:

I	$\overline{xzw}$	
$\overline{I}$	$\overline{xw}$	$\overline{z}$

Since I is yes-decisive for x and z, then xRz. According to Pareto's principle, xRw. But then, in view of the transitivity of R, zRw. And this means that I is a yes-decisive set for z and w in view of axioms 2 and 3, Q.E.D.

From Lemma 2 it follows that if V is the minimum yes-decisive set, then $\bigcap\limits_{i \epsilon V} R^i \subset R$.

Lemma 3.
If V is a minimum yes-decisive set, then for any $j \epsilon V$ the set $\{j\}$ is no-decisive for any pair $x,y \epsilon A$.

Proof.
Since V is non-empty, denote its arbitrary element by j. Let $V - \{j\} = W$.

Let $x,y \epsilon A$ be arbitrary objects. It is necessary to prove that $\{j\}$ is a no-decisive set for x and y. Let $z \epsilon A$ be an arbitrary object, different from x and y.

Consider a set of partitions $R^1,\ldots,R^n$ such that in R^j x and z are in one class, and y in another; x,y,z are in one class of all partitions R^i ($i\varepsilon W$) ; x and y in one, and z in another class of all partitions R^i ($i\notin V$) which can be represented in the following table:

j	$\overline{x z}$	$\overline{y}$
V - {j}	$\overline{x y z}$	
$\overline{V}$	$\overline{x y}$ $\overline{z}$	

Since $V = W \cup \{j\}$ is yes-decisive for any pair of objects (by Lemma 2), then xRz. Moreover, $y\overline{R}z$ only for $i\varepsilon W$, where yR^iz, so that yRz would mean, according to Axiom 2, that W is a yes-decisive set for y and z. But this is inconsistent with the minimality of the set V. Therefore, y belongs in R to a class different from that containing z (and hence x also). Therefore $y\overline{R}x$. But y and x are in the same class for all indices, except j. So by Axiom 2, {j} is a no-decisive set for an arbitrary pair $x,y\varepsilon A$. Q.E.D.

Lemma 3 means that if V is a minimum yes-decisive set, then $R \subset \bigcap\limits_{i\varepsilon V} R^i$. Jointly with Statement 2 this leads to the equality $\bigcap\limits_{i\varepsilon V} R^i = R$. True, axioms 1-4 tell nothing about how the minimum yes-decisive set is formed (save that it is non-empty). Thus we have obtained the following description of all agreement principles satisfying axioms 1-4.

Theorem 1.

Axioms 1-4 are satisfied by those and only by those agreement principles which consist of a choice of a non-empty set of "significant" indices $V \subset M$ and in the definition of the agreed partition R as the intersection of those of initial partitions which have indices from V:

$$R = \bigcap_{i\varepsilon V} R^i \qquad (1)$$

Thus we see that axioms 1-4 lead to a common procedure. Some of the initial classifications are said to be significant, others insignificant, and an intersection of significant classifications is taken. For the choice of "significant" partitions it is possible to make use of the concept of distance between partitions (Mirkin and Chorny, 1970). It is natural to choose V in such a way as to minimize

$$f(V) = \sum_{k=1}^{n} d \left(\bigcap_{i \in V} R^i, R^k \right),$$

where $d(R,S)$ is the distance between partitions R and S.

But if the initial partitions are equivalent, then a set of conceivable agreed partitions degenerates into a single partition--the intersection of all the initial ones. To prove this, we state the condition for the equivalence of initial partitions.

Axiom 5. The initial partitions are equivalent, i.e. for any one-to-one mapping $f: M \to M$

$$F(R^1, \ldots, R^n) = F(R^{f(1)}, \ldots, R^{f(n)}) .$$

Theorem 2.
The intersection $\bigcap R^i$ is the only agreed partition satisfying axioms 1-5, $i \in M$ (at $n \geqslant 2$, $N \geqslant 3$).
In fact, the equality $\bigcap_{i \in V} R^i = \bigcap_{i \in V} R^{f(i)}$ holds for all f only if $V = M$.

But as is known, the principle of taking an intersection is not always acceptable, since it may lead to a very large number of classes in the agreed partition. It is natural to restrict our consideration to a case where the number of classes of partitions considered does not exceed the pre-fixed number k. A set of such partitions will be denoted by E_k. Axiom 1 may be relaxed in two ways.

Axiom 1.k. The function $F(R^1, \ldots, R^n)$ is uniquely defined for any $R^i \in E_k$, and its values also relate to E_k.
Axiom 1.^{k} The function $F(R^1, \ldots R^n)$ is uniquely defined for any sets of partitions, and its values relate to E_k.

Theorem 3.
If the function $R = F(R^1, \ldots, R^n)$ holds for axioms 1.k, 2-4, and the number of objects $N \geqslant k + 1$, then there is an index $j \in M$ such that

$$R = F(R^1, \ldots, R^n) = R^j.$$

Proof.
According to the natural modification of Lemma 3, there exists a $j \in M$ such that $\{j\}$ is a no-decisive set for any $x, y \in A$. We need to show that $\{j\}$ is a yes-decisive set for any $x, y \in A$. To this end, let us consider R^j consisting of k non-empty classes in which x and y belong to the same class.

Choose objects one-by-one in each remaining class and number them: $x_1, x_2, \ldots, x_{k-1}$. Since $\{j\}$ is a no-decisive set, all these objects must be in k-1 different classes of the agreed partition on R. For the same reason the objects x and y cannot be in any of these k-1 classes and, therefore, they belong to the only class left. Thus $\{j\}$ is a yes-decisive set for any x,yεA, i.e., xR^jy implies xRy, i.e. $R^j \subset R$. But in view of (1), $R \subset R^j$, which proves the statement.

Theorem 3 is similar to the Arrow theorem (1951). It states that any agreement principle satisfying axioms 1.k and 2-4 must consist in the choice of a "dictator-index" j, such that for any set $R^1, \ldots, R^n$, we take R^j as an agreed partition. Axiom $1.^k$ is even more rigid.

Theorem 4

If $N \geqslant k + 1$, then there is no function F satisfying axioms $1.^k$ and 2-4.

Indeed, repeating the proof of Theorem 3, we have $F(R^1, R^2, \ldots, R^n) = R^j$. But the choice as R^j of the partition with the number of classes greater than k leads to an inconsistency with axiom $1.^k$.

3. CONCLUSION

Thus, we have stated some axioms about principles of reconciling partitions and obtained some corollaries from them (Theorems 1 - 4). These axioms are fully analogous to Arrow's known axioms in the theory of collective choice (Luce and Raiffa, 1957), but they seem more obvious. In particular, the usual criticism of the independence axiom of irrelevant alternatives (the analogue of Axiom 3 about independence of objects) based on the fact that irrelevant alternatives can give essential information in cardinal treatment of preferences (Luce and Raiffa, 1957) is inapplicable in this context, since the cardinal treatment of partitions is meaningless.

We have shown that "good" principles of reconciling are in the choice of a system R^i($i\varepsilon$V) of "significant" partitions and in consideration of the simultaneous cross-classification by all R^i($i\varepsilon$V) as a reconciled one (Theorem 1). Some strengthening of Axiom 1 leads to a still more rigid inference: as a reconciled partition, one of the initial ones (Theorem 3) must be considered. These propositions therefore characterize standard procedures in the analysis of nominal attributes constantly applied in real data processing.

The obtained results cast some light on the meaning of Arrow's "impossibility theorem." In the context of the analysis of rank attributes it does not present itself as a paradox. Like the theorems proved by us, it characterizes a standard procedure in the analysis of objects, ordered by a system of rank attributes with the help of lexicographic ordering. This treatment of different forms of Arrow's "paradox" has been described in Mirkin (1974).

REFERENCES

Arrow, K. J. 1951. *Social Choice and Individual Values*. New York: John Wiley.

Luce, R. D. and H. Raiffa. 1957. *Games and Decisions*. New York: John Wiley.

Mirkin, B. G. and L. B. Chorny. 1970. "On Measuring Proximity Between Different Partitions of a Finite Set." (Russian). Avtomat. i telem. 5: 120-127.

Mirkin, B. G. 1971. "On Axiomatic Approaches to the Reconciliation of Classifications." Paper submitted at the Conference on Logic and Methodology, Wroclaw. Novosibirsk (mimeograph).

Mirkin, B. G. 1974. *The Group Choice Problem*. (Russian). Moscow: Nauka.

16

Theoretical Considerations and Simulation Models
*Related to the Method of Sonquist and Morgan**

ROBERT REICHARDT AND B. SCHMEIKAL
University of Vienna

The raw material for Sonquist and Morgan's (1964) data analysis method is a population of individuals i that are characterized each by a set of independent variables $(x_1^i, x_2^i, \ldots, x_n^i)$ and a dependent variable y^i. The tree-structure from the application of this method reveals some interactive properties of the independent variables related to their influence on the dependent variable.

The raw material--i.e. this distribution of values of the variables on the population--can itself be considered as the result of a process P. This paper shows: (1) that the same distribution can be generated by quite different processes P_1, P_2, $\ldots$, (2) that the method of Sonquist and Morgan succeeds in revealing some aspects of these processes; and (3) that, on the other hand, it is not possible on the grounds of this method to decide, from which process P_1, P_2, $\ldots$, the raw material originated.

In this paper, two different processes P_I and P_{II}, that generate raw material for a Sonquist and Morgan-type analysis, are described. Both processes can be considered as simulation procedures and are suited for computer application. Both processes also reflect some theoretical conceptions which are known from the literature on social science. In the following these theoretical considerations are inserted into the description of the procedures.

---

*The first P_I-model (eqns. 4 to 14) was developed by Bernd Schmeikal, the second P_I-model (eqns. 15 to 25) as well as the remaining parts were developed by Robert Reichardt. The writing and final reduction was done by Robert Reichardt.

1. NARROWING-DOWN-TREE, DEFINITION

We call the procedure P_1 the *narrowing-down-tree*; in this model, each individual is characterized by q dichotomous attributes A_1, A_2, ..., A_k, ..., A_q. This characterization can be written as a q-component-vector consisting of zeros and ones. Furthermore, each individual starts with an initial value y_o^i of the dependent variable.

Now, each individual goes through a process of modifications of his y-value, in which the attributes A_1, A_2, ..., A_q come into play in this order. In each step, the resulting y_k^i depends on the y-value of the preceding step y_{k-1}^i and the kth component of the i's characterization vector. For the latter we write Φ_k^i.

$$(\Phi_k^i = 0) \text{ and } (\Phi_k^i = 1) \text{ are disjunctive;} \qquad (1)$$

The negation of Φ_k^i is written $\bar{\Phi}_k^i$. It follows that

$$(\Phi_k^i = 0) \Leftrightarrow (\bar{\Phi}_k^i = 1) \text{ and} \qquad (2)$$

$$(\Phi_k^i = 1) \Leftrightarrow (\bar{\Phi}_k^i = 0)$$

We now define two real valued regressive functions g and h:

$$y_k^i = \Phi_k^i \, g(y_{k-1}^i) + \bar{\Phi}_k^i \, h(y_{k-1}^i) \qquad (3)$$

The modification process of the y^i-values can thus be imagined as a tree structure, in which at each level k, the same regressive functions are applied (see Figure 1). This tree describes the process P_1 which we called "the narrowing-down-tree." A simulation study related to P_1 would go as follows: First, each individual i goes through the tree-structure P_1 in which its y^i-values are modified. At the end, we have a new distribution of the dependent variable, namely y_q^i, which can be considered as a function of the vector $(\Phi_1^i, \Phi_2^i, ..., \Phi_q^i)$. Now this distribution $y_q^i(\Phi_1^i, \Phi_2^i, ..., \Phi_q^i)$ is the raw material for a Sonquist and Morgan type of analysis. We now ask:

What properties of the process P_I *have to be required, if we*

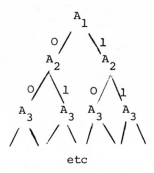

etc

Figure 1

demand that the second-run Sonquist and Morgan analysis leads to a tree-structure identical with that of the original process P_I?

The process P_I can be characterized by the number N of individuals, by the distribution of the individuals on the several types of vectors $(\Phi_1^i, \Phi_2^i, \ldots, \Phi_q^i)$, by the distribution of the initial values y_o^i as a function of this vector and by the two regressive functions g and h. Of course, only a fraction of all possible P_I's have the property of reflecting a Sonquist and Morgan type of tree.

We start with those P_I's in which the distribution of the several attributes A_k are statistically independent. Let a_k denote the fraction of the total number of individuals, for which $\Phi_k^i = 1$. The assumption of statistical independency allows one to multiply these fractions in order to get subsets characterized by several Φ's. Thus, for example, we can write

$$a_j \, a_k N$$

for the number of those for which $\Phi_j^i = \Phi_k^i = 1$ and

$$a_j (i - a_k) N$$

for the number of those for which $\Phi_j^i = 1$ and $\Phi_k^i = 0$.

2. NARROWING-DOWN TREE, SPECIAL CASE

Let us first look at the case where the several nodes of process P_I's tree reflect exactly the Sonquist and Morgan variance tree. Under this condition, the y-values that come up through the application of the functions g and h are identical with the mean values of y, at the same node, that will come up when we apply the Sonquist and Morgan analysis to the final distribution y_q^i.

In order to describe this case further, we have to use the following property of arithmetic means which is known from elementary statistics: We have a set S of N individuals, each having a value y^i. Let us consider any partition of S into S_1 and S_2 with $S_1 \cup S_2 = S$, $S_1 \cap S_2 = \emptyset$. Then the sum of the mean y-values over these subsets weighted with the relative number of individuals in these subsets equals the mean value over the whole set. This can easily be proved.

We call N_1, N_2 the number of elements in S_1 and S_2, and $\bar{y}_1$, $\bar{y}_2$ their mean values.

$$\frac{N_1}{N} \cdot \bar{y}_1 + \frac{N_2}{N} \cdot \bar{y}_2$$

$$= \frac{N_1}{N} \cdot \frac{1}{N_1} \cdot \sum_{i \varepsilon S_1} y_i + \frac{N_2}{N} \cdot \frac{1}{N_2} \sum_{i \varepsilon S_2} y_i$$

$$= \frac{1}{N} \left(\sum_{i \varepsilon S_1} y_i + \sum_{i \varepsilon S_2} y_i \right) = \bar{y} . \tag{4}$$

If we apply this condition to our process P_I, we get the following:

$$y_k = a_{k+1} g(y_k) + (1 - a_{k+1}) h(y_k) . \tag{5}$$

Considering the functions g and h as acting on the means, we write equation (5) without mean symbols and leaving out superscript i for the individuals.

We now have to recall the concept of the "between sum of squares" henceforth denoted by BSS--as used by Sonquist and Morgan. The program tries out splits into "left" and "right" groups at any node tree. We call n_1 the number of persons in the left group, n_2 the number of persons in the right group, n the total number at the node under consideration, $\bar{y}_1$ the mean value of the dependent variable for the left group, $\bar{y}_2$ the same for the right group, $\bar{y}$ the total mean value at the node under consideration. Then, having $n_1 + n_2$ = n, the BSS is defined as:

$$BSS = n_1 \cdot \bar{y}_1^2 + n_2 \cdot \bar{y}_2^2 - n \cdot \bar{y}^2 . \tag{6}$$

The program tries out at a given node any possible split according to the independent variables which were not yet used in the foregoing part of the tree. The split which yields a maximal value for BSS is chosen for the further branching of the tree.

Since we postulate $BSS(A_1) > BSS(A_i)$

$$\bigwedge_i a_1 N(g(y_o))^2 + (1 - a_1)N(h(y_o))^2 > a_i N(g(y_o))^2 +$$

$$+ (1 - a_i)N(h(y_o))^2 \tag{7}$$

where the symbol $\bigwedge_i$ means that the given formula holds for all possible values of i. (In our case $1 < i \leq q$.) Therefore

$$\bigwedge_i a_1 [(g(y_o))^2 - (h(y_o))^2] > a_i [(g(y_o))^2 - (h(y_o))^2] . \tag{8}$$

Let us now assume that $g(y_o) > h(y_o)$ which does not affect the validity of the proof. Remember that any linear transformation of the measured y's into the domain of positive reals does not change the variables and thus leaves the analysis unaltered. Then $(g(y_o))^2$ has to be greater than $(h(y_o))^2$ and we are allowed to divide the inequality by $g(y_o)^2 - h(y_o)^2$ and obtain:

$$\bigwedge_i a_1 > a_i \quad \text{as the necessary condition for } A_1 \text{ to maximize}$$

the BSS. $\tag{9}$

Let us now consider the second step in the variance tree:

Let L be the left group corresponding to the first node and A_2 the attribute which splits L optimally relative to the BSS. Let us henceforth use the notation:

n(0.)   ... the number of individuals with $\Phi_1 = 0$

n(1.)   ...   "   "   "   "   " $\Phi_1 = 1$

n(.0)   ...   "   "   "   "   " $\Phi_2 = 0$

n(.1)   ...   "   "   "   "   " $\Phi_2 = 1$

n(00)   ...   "   "   "   "   " $\Phi_1 = 0$ and $\Phi_2 = 0$

n(01)

n(10)

n(11)   ... defined analogously

Then the portion a_2 which equals the proportion of individuals in L for which $\Phi_2 = 0$ has to be $a_2 = n(00)/n(0.)$.

Since A_2 explained most of the variance in L:

$$\overset{\Lambda}{i}\ a_2 a_1 N(g^2(y_o))^2 + (1 - a_2)a_1 N(hg(y_o))^2 >$$

$$a_i a_1 N(g^2(y_o))^2 + (1 - a_i)a_1 N(hg(y_o))^2 \tag{10}$$

which immediately leads to the condition

$$\overset{\Lambda}{i}\ a_2\ [(g^2(y_o))^2 - (hg(y_o))^2] > a_i [g^2(y_o))^2 - (hg(y_o))^2] \cdot \tag{11}$$

We can always define the Φ_k's in such a way that $g(y_k) > h(y_k)$ holds. Therefore we find the condition for A_2 to split optimally

$$\underset{i>2}{\Lambda}\ a_2 > a_i \tag{12}$$

Now let us deal with the right group R. It has not yet been shown that A_2 guarantees an optimal splitting in R as well. It may happen that A_i is the one that fits in R. So let a_i be the proportion of individuals in R for which $\Phi_i = 0$ holds. If A_i would guarantee an optimal splitting in R, $\bigwedge_j a_i > a_j$, it should hold that j>1. However we prove that i = 2.

Suppose for a moment that we apply A_2 to both groups L and R. Since the covariances $s_{21} = 0$ and $s_{12} = 0$, we have n(00) = n(0.)n(.0) and n(10) = n(1.)n(.0). Together with the tautology n(0.)n(.0)n(1.) = n(1.)n(.0)n(0.) we can conclude

$$\frac{n(00)}{n(0.)} = \frac{n(10)}{n(1.)} . \tag{13}$$

This means that the proportion a_2 (for which $A_2 = 0$) in group L is the same in group R. Since a_2 was greater than a_j for all j in L it has to be greater than any a_j in R as well because all covariances are equal to zero. Therefore A_i has to be represented by A_2.

Generally the rank order of the proportions a_i in the original population determines the order of applications of the attributes. If $a_1 > a_2 > \ldots > a_n$ we have to apply $A_1, A_2, \ldots, A_n$ step by step until the variance is explained. If we now allow for negative (g.h.) the situation becomes a bit different.

For example the term $ghg(y_o)^2 - h^2 g(y_o)^2$ which arises in the third step may be negative. If we then divide the corresponding inequality in the BSS's by this difference the direction of the inequality changes. This means that we obtain equations like $\bigwedge_j a_i < a_j$ as necessary for an optimal split of A_i. Thus it is not the attribute with the greatest a_i but the one with the smallest a_i that maximizes BSS. This seems to be improbable since then we would obtain asymmetric trees in the case of independent attributes. If for example A_1, A_2, A_3 were three attributes operating on y and the corresponding a's were $a_1 = 3/5$, $a_2 = 3/4$, $a_3 = 2/3$, the variance-tree would look like the diagram in Figure 2.

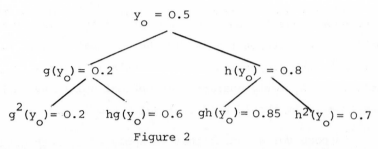

$$y_o = 0.5$$

$$g(y_o) = 0.2 \qquad h(y_o) = 0.8$$

$$g^2(y_o) = 0.2 \quad hg(y_o) = 0.6 \quad gh(y_o) = 0.85 \quad h^2(y_o) = 0.7$$

Figure 2

We would have to apply A_1 in the first step since $g(y_o) < h(y_o)$ and $a_1 < a_3 < a_2$ in the second step A_3 in the left group because $g^2(y_o) < hg(y_o)$ and $a_3 < a_2$ and A_2 in R because $gh(y_o) > h^2(y_o)$ and a_2 is the largest a.

However, it can easily be shown that this argument is meaningless. Let $g^2(y_o)$ be less than $hg(y_o)$ in L. Then we have to apply an A_i which is different from A_1 and has an a_i less than those of the other attributes; this is of course a_3 in our case. If then we had $gh(y_o) > h^2(y_o)$ in R let us exchange the value of the attribute in R, so that the value 1 changes into 0 and 0 into 1. Then $gh(y_o)$ and $h^2(y_o)$ exchange as well and we get $gh(y_o) < h^2(y_o)$.

This means we perform the transformation as is depicted in Figure 3. Since a_3 was the smallest $a_i \neq a_1$ in L and since $s_{31} = 0$ it has to be the smallest in R as well and therefore A_3 must be applied in R.

It is now possible to summarize the foregoing analysis of this specific type of P_I-process (in which the y_k-values at each node equal the mean values coming up at the second run through the Sonquist and Morgan method) by stating a necessary and sufficient condition: the functions

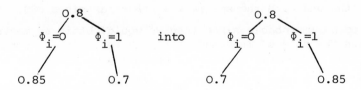

$$0.8 \qquad\qquad 0.8$$
$$\Phi_i = 0 \quad \Phi_i = 1 \qquad \text{into} \qquad \Phi_i = 0 \quad \Phi_i = 1$$
$$0.85 \qquad 0.7 \qquad\qquad 0.7 \qquad\qquad 0.85$$

Figure 3

g and h simulate a variance-tree with statistically independent distributions of the attributes if and only if:

$$\bigwedge_k \frac{y_k - h(y_k)}{g(y_k) - h(y_k)} > \frac{g(y_k) - hg(y_k)}{g^2(y_k) - hg(y_k)} = \frac{h(y_k) - h^2(y_k)}{gh(y_k) - h^2(y_k)} \qquad (14)$$

and

$$\bigwedge_{k,u,v} \frac{y_k^u - h(y_k^u)}{g(y_k^u) - h(y_k^u)} = \frac{y_k^v - h(y_k^v)}{g(y_k^v) - h(y_k^v)}$$

where the superscripts u and v denote different nodes in the kth level of the tree.

Inequality (7) can easily be interpreted. It suffices that $(g(y_o))^2 > (h(y_o))^2$. Then we split unity into a_i and $(1-a_i)$. The greater the weight a_i we attach to the greater factor $(g(y_o))^2$, the greater also the resulting sum of the two products. From this, inequality (9) can be understood immediately.

3. NARROWING-DOWN-TREE, MORE GENERAL CASE

We are now ready to start the analysis of more general types of process P_I. For this, the condition (5) can be deleted. That means that we are looking for processes P_I which yield a final distribution of the dependent variable, which after having been analyzed by the Sonquist and Morgan method lead to a tree in which the order of the splits and the number of elements within the resulting subgroups are identical with those of the original P_I-tree. However, the y_k-values on the several levels of the P_I-tree no longer reflect the subgroup mean-values in the Sonquist and Morgan tree. Therefore, in this case any computation of BSS-values has to be based on the y_q-values, i.e. the end-points of the P_I-tree. We confine ourselves to the case of identical sizes of the subgroups, i.e.

$$a_1 = a_2 = \ldots\ldots = a_q = \frac{1}{2} \qquad (15)$$

and of a constant initial value y_o for all individuals. In order to simplify the notation, we write only the functions,

e.g. ggh for ggh(y_o). These have to be read, of course, from
the right to the left. Thus a person having a characterizing
vector (1,1,0) will get a final y-value hgg. Furthermore,
we leave out the brackets, when we multiply final y-values,
but we separate the factors by the "multiplication-point."
Thus, ghg . ggh stands for (ghg(y_o)) . (ggh(y_o)). We
use exponents for repeated use of the same function in order
to bring out as clearly as possible the combinatorial properties of our next problem, that is, we write for the moment
ggh and not g^2h.

Let us look at the three-level tree (q = 3). Here, we
have the conditions:

$$BSS(A_1) > BSS(A_2) \tag{16a}$$

$$BSS(A_1) > BSS(A_3) \tag{16b}$$

$$BSS(A_2) > BSS(A_3) . \tag{16c}$$

From (16a) we get:

$$\frac{N}{32} [(ggg + hgg + ghg + hhg)^2 + (ggh + hgh + ghh + hhh)^2] +$$

$$\tag{17}$$

$$+ N\bar{y}_3^2 > \frac{N}{32} [(ggg + hgg + ggh + hgh)^2 +$$

$$+ (ghg + hhg + ghh + hhh)^2] + N\bar{y}_3^2$$

We can reduce this to the two squares of the brackets at each
side of the inequality sign. After multiplying out the
squares of the brackets we can delete all squares, as they
come up on both sides of the inequality. Dividing the remaining expression by two, we get:

ggg . ghg + ggg . hgg + ggg . hhg + ghg . hgg + ghg . hhg +

+ hgg . hhg + ggh . ghh + ggh . hgh + ggh . hhh + ghh . hgh +

+ ghh . hhh + hgh . hhh >   (18)

ggg . hgg + ggg . ggh + ggg . hgh + hgg . ggh + hgg . hgh +

+ ggh . hgh + ghg . hhg + ghg . ghh + ghg . hhh + hhg . ghh +

+ hhg . hhh + ghh . hhh

In condition (18) the 2nd, 5th, 8th and 11th terms of the left side of the inequality sign have their identical counterparts in the 1st, 6th, 7th and 12th terms of the right side. The remaining inequality can be transformed into:

$$(hhg + ghg - hgh - ggh)(ggg + hgg - ghh - hhh) > 0 \cdot$$
(19a)

By similar procedures, we can derive from (16b) the expression (19b) and from (16c) the expression (19c):

$$(ggg + ghg - hgh - hhh)(hgg + hhg - ggh - ghh) > 0$$
(19b)

$$(ggg + ggh - hhg - hhh)(hgg + hgh - ghg - ghh) > 0 \cdot$$
(19c)

It can easily be seen that in the inequalities (19) a symmetry property holds. In the brackets, from one term a corresponding expression is subtracted which results when we change g into h and h into g. In order to study the direction of the minus sign in these symmetric subtractions, we use the graphic representation as seen in Figure 4.

Here the term at the end of an arrow is subtracted from the term at the beginning of the same arrow. The subtractions symbolized by dotted lines are in the same brackets. The same is true for the uninterrupted lines. In the inequalities (19) the two brackets on the left side of the inequality have to be either both positive or both negative. A sufficient condition for this would be that the terms in Figure 4 are ordered according to the greater-sign in one of the directions from the top to the bottom or from the bottom to the top. Also the brackets in (19c) would be both positive or both negative, as from the above condition, and equation (20) results:

$$sign [(hgg - ghh) - (hgh - ghg)] = sign [(ggg - hhh) -$$

$$- (ggh - hhg)] \cdot$$
(20)

However, the conditions (16c) and (19c) are not necessary in this form, because the Sonquist and Morgan program splits after having verified conditions (16a) and (16b) according to variable A_1. Condition (16c) can be confined to the new left and right subgroup. Thus we find, for example, for the left subgroup:

$$(ggg - hhg)(hgg - ghg) > 0 \cdot$$
(21)

Also for these conditions it suffices that the final y-value follows a lexicographic order.

From the foregoing considerations, we advance the following conjecture: *Under equal distributions of the attributes (eq. 15), a sufficient condition for the functions g*

(19a) (19b) (19c)

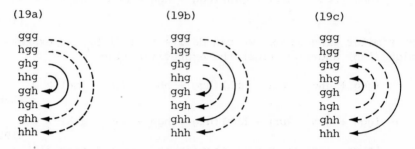

Figure 4.

and h to create a final distribution of the dependent variable, the Sonquist and Morgan type reanalysis of which yields the same order of the attributes A_k *as in the original process* P_I *is*

$$sign(y - g(y)) = - sign(y - h(y)) \text{ and the greater-sign} \quad (22)$$

constitutes on the final values of the dependent variables a complete order following the legicographic arrangements of the functional terms (read from the right to the left.)

This conjecture was proven for q = 3.

Let us give an algebraic example for functions which fulfill condition (22), namely

$$g(y) = 2y - 1, \ h(y) = 2y \quad (23)$$

The following values can easily be verified:

$$g^3 = 8y - 7, \quad hg^2 = 8y - 6$$

$$ghg = 8y - 5, \quad h^2g = 8y - 4 \quad (24)$$

$$g^2h = 8y - 3, \quad hgh = 8y - 2$$

$$gh^2 = 8y - 1, \quad h^3 = 8y$$

The lexicographic order is obvious. Given a characterization vector $\underset{\sim}{\Phi} = (\Phi_1, \Phi_2, \ldots, \Phi_q)$ the general case can easily be written:

$$y_q(\Phi) = y_o \cdot 2^q - B(\Phi) \qquad (25)$$

in which $B(\Phi)$ is defined as the number corresponding to the zero-one-vector $\underset{\sim}{\Phi}$, if interpreted as a symbol for binary numbers. As the binary numbers follow the lexicographic order, this is also secured for the possible values of $y_q(\Phi)$.

In general, condition (22) induces a principle of monotonic decreasing differences between the y_k values. This corresponds to the intuitive notion of the Sonquist and Morgan tree in which the greatest differences are explained in the first steps and the smaller differences in later steps.

From this the theoretical background for the specific notion of the P_I and for the name "narrowing-down" tree can be explained. In social life, we often observe processes in which a certain property (the dependent variable) undergoes a transformation in a sequence of decisions, in which the changes, however, are getting smaller and smaller. Examples are social status, prestige, and intensity of affiliation of a person with a given social unit. That is, we know that in a social context the early decisions about one person's prestige are more important than later ones, i.e. that the variation in prestige gets smaller. This can be expressed by the German saying: "Wer hat, dem wird gegeben." In such a process, it can be imagined that a person starts his life with a fixed set of dichotomous independent variables--as e.g. race ("white"--"non-white"), religion ("protestant"--"non-protestant"), place of birth ("urban-born"--"rural-born"). These independent variables come into effect during the person's life in this order. Race acts first and is responsible for the greatest part of variance within prestige. The next factor, religion, starts to act later and is responsible for somewhat less prestige-variance, and so on. Now, if a Sonquist and Morgan analysis yields a tree in which the independent variables follow such an order, it may well reflect the outcome of a dynamic process which is to some extent reconstructed by this method.

Another process of determination of prestige which takes place, however, in a much shorter period of time, is the so-called "grilling-process." Here the social status of a person is estimated from several cues. Characteristically, in

most cases, the first estimations are modified only slightly
during this procedure (Moore and Kleining, 1959).

A third phenomenon, that is relevant here, is the fact
that with increasing age people get more stable in their
political preferences and affiliations. This regularity was
shown by American and West German investigations (Zohlnhofer,
1965).

4. SOCIAL INTERACTION PROCESS GENERATING THE DATA

There is quite a different process P_{II} which can be reconstructed by a Sonquist and Morgan analysis. Let us call
P_{II} the *process of interaction among social categories*.
Here, as in P_I, each individual is characterized by a zero-
one-vector $\underline{\Phi}^i = (\Phi_1^i, \Phi_2^i, \ldots, \Phi_q^i)$ and the initial value of
the dependent variable y_o^i. We consider now two-person inter-
actions. The probability with which such an interaction
occurs depends on the type of Φ^i, Φ^j, to which the two persons belong. For this probability, we write $\pi(\Phi^i, \Phi^j)$. As
there are 2^q different Φ's, we have to use $2^{2q} - \binom{2^q}{2}$ different π's.

We suppose the following: the π's decrease with the
number of unequal components of the same position $(\Phi_k^i \neq \Phi_k^j)$.
Furthermore, the smaller the k's (the earlier unequal components occur), the smaller the resulting π.

Now, the y^i and y^j values of the two interacting partners
approach each other, i.e. the difference $|y^i - y^j|$ is smaller
after the interaction than it was before. If we allow the
population to have interactions according to these rules,
after a while we find a distribution of the y_q^i-values that
serves as raw material for a Sonquist and Morgan analysis.
This latter furnishes a tree structure, in which the split
follows the original Φ-vectors, i.e., the first split separ-
ates the individuals according to Φ_1^i being zero or one. The
second split within the two subgroups uses the two values of
Φ_2^i as the criterion for splitting. Thus the Sonquist and
Morgan analysis reconstructs the properties which determined
P_{II}. A mathematical treatment of this second model was given
by Dr. B. Schmeikal. It will be published in a separate
paper.

The theoretical notion behind the P_{II} model can easily
be grasped. From many investigations in social psychology,
and especially since Katz and Lazarsfeld's important contribution (1955, Ch. 4), we know that people who interact approach
each other in their opinions (the dependent variable y). Now
the frequency of interaction is different according to the
social categories to which the partners belong. The greatest
frequency of interaction is among people belonging to the
same category. Social categories are characterized by
several variables. Some of them (as was shown for "race")
have a greater influence on the interaction-frequency than
others (e.g., marital status). The order of the components
in $\underset{\sim}{\Phi}$ reflects these differences in influence.

5. CONCLUDING REMARKS

The data we observe in social research are the end-
products of processes. It was the purpose of this paper to
show that the Sonquist and Morgan method is able to bring out
some aspects of these processes. In other words, we can
hope, through this method to have a look beneath the surface
of data. However, it will not always be possible to decide
which of several plausible processes is responsible for the
data we have. For example in our two models the same personal characteristics came into play. But, whereas in P_I the
temporal order of these variables' acting was important, no
such consideration was necessary in model P_{II}.

Our conclusion is that much intellectual effort should
be put into working out the empirical and theoretical background which will enable us to have a better understanding of
what we do and can do with the mathematical and technical
tools for data analysis.

APPENDIX NOTE:

G. Bonelli
University of Vienna, Austria

TREE-ANALYSIS--THE METHOD BY SONQUIST AND MORGAN

A1. INTRODUCTION

The method by J. A. Sonquist and J. N. Morgan, also
called "Contrast-Group Analysis," is a special regression

method. One tries to obtain those combinations of categories
out of the independent variables entering into an analysis
which are typical or decisive for the position of a sample
unit in relation to the dependent variable, i.e., which best
"explain" this position for the greatest percentage of cases.
Besides this explaining aspect, the method enables us to predict (with a certain uncertainty) the value of a sample unit
relative to the dependent variable based on the information
about the independent variables.

A basic presupposition is the following: the dependent
variable has to be at least an interval scale (a dichotomy is
admitted as a special case of an interval scale); whereas the
independent variables can be of an arbitrary level of measurement, for interval scales can easily be transformed into
nominal or ordinal scales.

The characteristic feature of this method is an iterative splitting of the principal sample and of the resulting
subsamples. Thus, first of all, the totality of the individuals is divided into two groups by dichotomization of an
independent variable. Then these groups are divided after a
dichotomization of the remaining categories of the same or of
a different variable, and so on. The pair of subgroups resulting by splitting should have

    (i)   greater homogeneity within each subgroup than the
           initial group;

    (ii) maximum mutual heterogeneity.

As statistical tools, we use the arithmetic mean and variance
(total sum of squares, respectively).

The combinations of the categories of the final groups
can be interpreted as the typical ones for the certain position of the dependent variable.

A2.   STATISTICAL CONSIDERATIONS

For the splitting into subgroups we use the principle of
analysis of variance (analysis of sum of squares), for the
variance is a statistic for homogeneity or heterogeneity of a
sample.

$$s^2 = \frac{1}{n} \sum_{i=1}^{n} (y_i - \bar{y})^2 \tag{1}$$

and

$$\bar{y} = \frac{1}{n} \sum_{i=1}^{n} y_i. \tag{2}$$

The term

$$n \cdot s^2 = \sum_{i=1}^{n} (y_i - \bar{y})^2 \qquad (3)$$

is called "Total Sum of Squares" (TSS).

Splitting all data into two groups: (a) in each group there are n_j elements ($j = 1,2$), and

$$\sum_{j=1}^{2} n_j = n ; \qquad (4)$$

(b) the index number i is so defined that it runs in each group from 1 to n_j. Now the data have the shape y_{ij} ($i = 1, \ldots, n_j$; $j = 1,2$). Furthermore

$$\bar{y}_{.j} = \frac{1}{n_j} \sum_{i=1}^{n_j} y_{ij} . \qquad (5)$$

Now TSS can be transformed as follows:

$$n \cdot s^2 = \sum_{j=1}^{2} \sum_{i=1}^{n_j} (y_{ij} - \bar{y})^2 \qquad (6)$$

$$= \sum_{j=1}^{2} \sum_{i=1}^{n_j} ((y_{ij} - \bar{y}_{.j}) + (\bar{y}_{.j} - \bar{y}))^2$$

$$= \sum_{j=1}^{2} \sum_{j=1}^{n_j} ((y_{ij} - \bar{y}_{.j})^2 + (\bar{y}_{.j} - \bar{y})^2 + 2(y_{ij} - \bar{y}_{.j})(\bar{y}_{.j} - \bar{y}))$$

$$= \sum_{j=1}^{2} \sum_{i=1}^{n_j} (y_{ij} - \bar{y}_{.j})^2 + \sum_{j=1}^{2} n_j (\bar{y}_{.j} - \bar{y})^2 +$$

$$+ 2 \sum_{j=1}^{2} (\bar{y}_{.j} - \bar{y}) \cdot \sum_{i=1}^{n_j} (y_{ij} - \bar{y}_{.j}) .$$

Because of

$$\sum_{i=1}^{n_j} (y_{ij} - \bar{y}_{.j}) = \sum_{i=1}^{n_j} y_{ij} - n_j \cdot \bar{y}_{.j} = n_j \cdot \bar{y}_{.j} - n_j \cdot \bar{y}_{.j} = 0$$

it follows that

$$n \cdot s^2 = \sum_{j=1}^{2} \sum_{i=1}^{n_j} (y_{ij} - \bar{y}_{.j})^2 + \sum_{j=1}^{2} n_j (\bar{y}_{.j} - \bar{y}^2). \qquad (7)$$

The term

$$\sum_{j=1}^{2} \sum_{i=1}^{n_j} (y_{ij} - \bar{y}_{.j})^2 \qquad (8)$$

is called "Within Sum of Squares" (WSS). This is the TSS-sum of the subgroups and a statistic for their homogeneity.

The term

$$\sum_{j=1}^{2} n_j (\bar{y}_{.j} - \bar{y})^2 = n_1 \cdot \bar{y}_{.1}^2 + n_2 \cdot \bar{y}_{.2}^2 - n \cdot \bar{y}^2 \qquad (9)$$

is called "Between Sum of Squares" (BSS). It is constructed from the arithmetic mean of each subgroup and the arithmetic mean of the total group. This TSS-sum is weighted with the size of each subgroup. Therefore BSS is a statistic representing the mutual heterogeneity of these subgroups.

A3. THE MODEL

Given m independent variables X_i (i = 1, ..., m), each variable X_i with k_i categories C_{ij_i} (j_i = 1, ..., k_i); a variable Y dependent on those X_i, and a sample with size n. Each of these n cases belongs to exactly one of the $k_1, k_2, ..., k_m$ classes so that no class is empty. Consequently, we get an m-dimensional space of data. There exists a 1-1 relation between the classes and the m-tuples $(j_1, ..., j_m)$.

In each class there are $n_{j_1...j_m}$ data. Then

$$\sum_{(j_i)} n_{j_1...j_m} = n. \qquad (10)$$

Instead of the variety of values $_h y_{j_1 \ldots j_m}$ ($h = 1, \ldots,$ $n_{j_1 \ldots j_m}$) in a certain class we take their arithmetic mean:

$$\bar{y}_{j_1 \ldots j_m} = \frac{1}{n_{j_1 \ldots \circ j_m}} \sum_{h=1}^{n_{j_1 \ldots j_m}} {}_h y_{j_1 \ldots j_m}. \tag{11}$$

The arithmetic mean for all cases is:

$$\bar{y} = (1/n) \sum_{(j_1) \ldots (j_m)} n_{j_1 \ldots j_m} \cdot \bar{y}_{j_1 \ldots j_m}. \tag{12}$$

Having prepared the material, we now have to split. This means the division of the set of all categories belonging to an independent variable X_i (i arbitrarily chosen, but then fixed) and at the same time the division of the sample into two dichotomous subgroups. The next step is the calculation of WSS, BSS and, consequently, of TSS. Formally, this involves the following steps.

For arbitrarily chosen but then fixed i, in the following equations denoted by 1 without loss of generality, we get

$$\bigcup_{(j_1)} C_{1,j_1} = \{C_{1,I}\} \cup \{C_{1,II}\} \text{ and } \{C_{1,I}\} \cap \{C_{1,II}\} = \phi \tag{13}$$

with $I \subseteq \{j_1 | j_1 = 1, \ldots, k_1\} = I \cup II$. Furthermore

$$\sum_{(j_1 \in I)} \sum_{(j_i \neq j_1)} n_{j_1 \ldots j_m} = n_{C_{1,I}}, \tag{14}$$

and

$$\sum_{(j_1 \in II)} \sum_{(j_i \neq j_1)} n_{j_1 \ldots j_m} = n_{C_{1,II}}. \tag{15}$$

This leads to

$$\bar{y}_{C_{1,I}} = \frac{1}{n_{C_{1,I}}} \sum_{(j_1 \in I)} \sideset{}{'}\sum_{(j_i \neq j_1)} n_{j_1 \ldots j_m} \cdot \bar{y}_{j_1 \ldots j_m}$$

(16)

$\bar{y}_{C_{1,II}}$ is computed analogously. Then we form (cf. (9)):

$$BSS = n_{C_{1,I}} (\bar{y}_{C_{1,I}} - \bar{y})^2 + n_{C_{1,II}} (\bar{y}_{C_{1,II}} - \bar{y})^2 . \quad (17)$$

We call the quotient (BSS/TSS)·100 the "percentage of explained TSS" (often incorrectly called percentage of explained variance).

As mentioned, BSS ought to be maximal after each splitting. Thus, the point is to find the optimal combination of the $C_{i,j_i} \in C_{i,I}$ or $C_{i,II}$, respectively, out of all X_i. This is only possible by empirical testing. But the following consideration makes it easier. If we arrange the k_i categories C_{ij_i} of an independent variable X_i in such a way that the corresponding values $\bar{y}_{j_1 \ldots j_m}$ are ranked according to their size, then it can be easily proved that the optimal splitting is one of the following:

$I = \{1\}$ $II = \{2 \ldots, k_i\}$

$I = \{1,2\}$ $II = \{3, \ldots, k_i\}$

....

$I = \{1, \ldots, k_i - 1\}$ $II = \{k_1\}$

Instead of

$$\frac{1}{2} \sum_{j_i=1}^{k_i} \binom{k_1}{j_i} = 2^{k_i-1}$$

splittings we have to test only $k_i - 1$ ones for each variable X_i.

Having found the optimal splitting, we proceed with the remaining categories in the same way with respect to the splitting and stoppping rules. We can illustrate all optimal splittings in a tree-structure.

If there are p optimal splittings, then the quotient

470

$(1/TSS) \sum_{s=1}^{p} BSS_s$ represents the total percentage of ex-

plained TSS, and p runs from 1 to at most $\sum_{i=1}^{m} k_i - 1$. But

since the aim of this method is to get a certain selection of explaining categories we need some *splitting and stopping rules* which must be applied:

(i)   After splitting ş (s=1, ...,p) that subgroup with the greatest TSS_s should be analysed, since this is a necessary condition for a maximum BSS_s-value.

(ii) TSS_s/TSS should be greater than 1-2%, otherwise this subgroup is fairly homogeneous.

(iii) n_s should be greater than 10-20 entities (individuals), otherwise the standard error becomes too great.

(iv) $\dfrac{BSS_s}{TSS}$ should be greater than 1-2%, otherwise the splitting does not provide much additional explanation.

(v)   p should not be too great, otherwise difficulties of interpretation arise. (Note: After p splittings we get p+1 unsplit subgroups and a total of 2p+1 groups.)

REFERENCES

Katz, E., and P. F. Lazarsfeld. 1955. *Personal Influence. The Part Played by People in the Flow of Mass Communication.* Glencoe, Ill.: The Free Press.

Moore, H. and G. Gleining. 1959. "Das Bild der Sozialen Wirklichkeit. Analyse der Structur und der Bedeutung eines Images," *Koelner Zeitschrift für Soziologie und Sozialpsychologie,* Vol. XI, pp. 353-376.

Sonquist, J. A. and J. N. Morgan. 1964. *The Detection of Interaction Effects. A Report of a Computer Program for the Selection of Optimal Combinations of Explanatory Variables,* Monograph Nr. 35, Institute for Social Research, University of Michigan, Survey Research Center, Ann Arbor, Michigan.

Zohlnhoefer, W. 1965. "Parteiidentifizierung in der Bundesrepublik und den Vereinigten Staaten" in Scheuch, E. K., and Wildenmann, R., (eds.), Zur Soziologie der Wahl, *Sonderheft 9 der Koelner Zeitschrift für Soziologie und Sozialpsychologie*, pp. 126–168.

III

Social Models:
Some Applications

17

Comparative Statistics in Sociology:
Including a Mathematical Theory of Growth
and Differentiation in Organizations *

KENNETH C. LAND
University of Illinois at Urbana—Champaign

1. INTRODUCTION

For some time now sociologists have been becoming more
and more familiar with the potential uses of simultaneous-
equation linear functional equation models ("linear causal
models," "path analysis," "dependence analysis," "structural
models," etc.) in cross-sectional sociological research.
Most of the attention given to such models, however, has focused upon their *empirical evaluation* via identification of
the parameters, parameter estimation, and hypothesis testing
(see, e.g., Blalock, 1964, 1969; Duncan, 1966; Boudon, 1965,
1968; Heise, 1969; Land, 1969, 1971, 1973). In this process,
little or no attention has been given to the *theoretical uses*
and implications of the models. The purpose of this paper is
to illustrate how the method of comparative statics can be
used as a tool for the theoretical analysis of functional
equation sociological models. Comparative statics has been
widely applied in mathematical economics for many years (see,
Samuelson, 1947). The present discussion will proceed by going from relatively simple to more complex applications of
comparative statics. That is, we will exhibit the procedure
first for strictly linear models. As an application we will
analyze one of Duncan's (1968) models of the process of
social stratification. Then we will generalize the results
to the larger class of models which are linear in the parameters but non-linear in the variables. Finally we shall
show how comparative statics can be applied to models

---
* The research reported here was supported by a grant from
the Russell Sage Foundation.

consisting of general functions with no linearity restrictions. A mathematical theory of differentiation in organization which recasts Blau's (1970) research will be utilized as a particular substantive application of the method for this class of models.

2. COMPARATIVE-STATICS ANALYSIS OF LINEAR MODELS

Before proceeding, we must establish certain notation and terminology. First, we assume that the model to be specified involves a total set of H variables, denoted by $x_1, x_2, \ldots x_H$. We assume that this set can be partitioned into the following two mutually exclusive and exhaustive subsets: (1) a set of K *exogenous variables* (K < H), denoted by $z_1, z_2, \ldots, z_K$; and (2) a set of G *endogenous variables* (G < H), denoted by $y_1, y_2, \ldots, y_G$, and H = G + K. The distinction between these two sets of variables is that the endogenous variables ("originating from within") are those variables which the model is designed to explain, while the exogenous variables ("originating from without") are assumed to be determined by forces external to the model and whose magnitudes are only accepted as given data. More particularly, it must be impossible to write structural equations (i.e., causal equations or identities) for any of the exogenous variables as a function of the remaining variables. This stipulation is necessary for the application of comparative statics which requires that one take partial derivatives with respect to the exogenous variables. The latter operation assumes that the exogenous variables are independent of one another, so that each can vary by itself without directly affecting the others.

Given the distinction between exogenous and endogenous variables, we must clarify what we mean by the term model. First of all, by a *mathematical structure* (or structure, for short), we mean a set of functionally independent and consistent structural equations sufficient to determine the *numerical* values of the endogenous variables, given the values of the exogenous variables. Thus, a mathematical structure specifies a numerical value for each parameter of each structural equation; that is, for each mathematical coefficient of each equation. Then we can define a *mathematical model* (or model, for short) as a set of structures. Specifically, we call a set of structures a model if all the structures in the set are identical in these four respects: (1) the number of equations, (2) the lists of endogenous and and exogenous variables, (3) the list of variables that

476

appear in each equation, and (4) the range of values which it is possible for each parameter to assume.

In this section, we will deal with the class of static-exact linear simultaneous-equation sociological models. These terms need to be clarified. First of all, the term *static model* refers to the fact that all of the equations in the model relate the variables measured simultaneously at a single instant in time; and, in addition, the stated relationship among the variables is time-invariant so that time does not enter as an independent variable. Thus, the equations of the model are algebraic rather than differential. Second, there are varying degrees of linearity which must be distinguished. By *linear model* one denotes a model whose equations contain as terms only constants (parameters) and products of single variables by constants (parameters). More precisely, such a model can be said to be *linear in variables* (because no variable appears to a power other than the first, nor multiplied or divided by any other variable) and *linear in unknown parameters* as well (because no parameter appears as a power or in a product or quotient with another parameter). If such a model is unrealistic in a particular context, usually a model can be used instead that is *nonlinear in variables* but is still *linear in parameters*. Any term of such a model must consist either of only a constant (parameter) or of a product of a constant (parameter) by any function of the variables, provided only that the function does not itself have any unspecified parameters (otherwise, a nonlinearity in the parameters would occur). Models linear in parameters, but not in variables, sometimes are more difficult to manipulate than linear models, but they have the advantage of being able to describe curved graphs, by the use of logarithmic or quadratic or other nonlinear functions of the variables. We will outline the method of comparative statics for such models in the next section of the chapter.

Finally, for the sake of convenience, we will assume in this chapter that all models are *exact*. In other words, we assume that the structural equations of the model suffice to describe real phenomena without approximation or error. This is not too restrictive an assumption for purposes of theoretical analysis. Of course, for empirical analysis (parameter estimation and hypothesis testing), we add a stochastic disturbance (or error) term to each structural equation and the typical assumption is that the structural equations describe reality *on the average* so that the expectation of each disturbance is zero although it possesses a positive variance. Here, for theoretical analysis, we set that variance to zero.

The *general form* of a linear static-exact simultaneous-equation sociological model can now be written as follows:

$$\sum_{i=1}^{G} \beta_{1i}y_i + \sum_{k=1}^{K} \gamma_{1k}z_k = 0$$

$$\sum_{i=1}^{G} \beta_{2i}y_i + \sum_{k=1}^{K} \gamma_{2k}z_k = 0$$

$$\hspace{8cm} (1)$$

$$\vdots \qquad\qquad \vdots$$

$$\sum_{i=1}^{G} \beta_{Gi}y_i + \sum_{k=1}^{K} \gamma_{Gk}z_k = 0$$

or, in more compact form:

$$\sum_{i=1}^{G} \beta_{gi}y_i + \sum_{k=1}^{K} \gamma_{gk}z_k = 0 \quad (g = 1, \ldots, G) \hspace{2cm} (2)$$

where the β's are the parameters of the endogenous variables and the γ's are the parameters of the exogenous variables. By defining the following vectors and matrices (note, in particular, that it is not necessary for the model to be recursive, i.e., triangular $\tilde{\beta}$, in order to apply comparative statics):

$$\underset{\sim}{y} = \begin{bmatrix} y_1 \\ \cdot \\ \cdot \\ \cdot \\ y_G \end{bmatrix} \qquad \underset{\sim}{z} = \begin{bmatrix} z_1 \\ \cdot \\ \cdot \\ \cdot \\ z_K \end{bmatrix} \qquad \underset{\sim}{O} = \begin{bmatrix} 0_1 \\ \cdot \\ \cdot \\ \cdot \\ 0_G \end{bmatrix}$$

$$\beta = \begin{bmatrix} \beta_{11} & \beta_{12} & \cdots & \beta_{1G} \\ \beta_{21} & \beta_{22} & \cdots & \beta_{2G} \\ \cdot & & & \\ \cdot & & & \\ \cdot & & & \\ \beta_{G1} & \beta_{G2} & \cdots & \beta_{GG} \end{bmatrix} \qquad \Gamma = \begin{bmatrix} \gamma_{11} & \gamma_{12} & \cdots & \gamma_{1K} \\ \gamma_{21} & \gamma_{22} & \cdots & \gamma_{2K} \\ \cdot & & & \\ \cdot & & & \\ \cdot & & & \\ \gamma_{G1} & \gamma_{G2} & \cdots & \gamma_{GK} \end{bmatrix}$$

we can write equations (1) as the following matrix equation:

$$\beta y + \Gamma z = 0 \tag{3}$$

This is the general matrix form of an exact linear model; and by appropriate relabeling of variables and parameters and proper choice of G and K, any exact linear model can be made to look like equations (1), (2), or (3). This is a great advantage when we analyze properties that all linear models have in common. In most models, many of the parameters are equal to zero, which means that many of the variables do not appear in every equation.

A substantive example will help at this point. Consider Duncan's (1968) model of the process of social stratification. Here z_1 = father's education, z_2 = father's occupation, z_3 = number of siblings, z_4 = intelligence (c. age 12), y_1 = son's education, y_2 = son's 1964 occupation, y_3 = son's 1964 earnings, and G = 3, K = 4, H = 7. In typical path analysis notation, the structure can be written as follows:

$$y_1 = .16z_1 + .20z_2 - .15z_3 + .40z_4 + .76u_1$$

$$y_2 = .52y_1 + .04z_1 + .12z_2 - .04z_3 + .08z_4 + .75u_2$$

$$y_3 = .26y_2 + .11y_1 + .03z_1 \qquad\qquad + .10z_4 + .91u_3$$

$$\tag{4}$$

where u_1, u_2, and u_3 are mutually independent stochastic disturbance terms. The structural coefficients in these equations are standarized coefficients ("path coefficients") which were estimated for the cohort of

white men in the United States aged 25 to 34 in 1964. By a
suitable change of algebraic signs of the coefficients, and
by setting the disturbances equal to their expected values
(zero), equations (4) can be written in the following manner
which conforms to the general form as defined above and which
is more convenient for theoretical analysis:

$$-y_1 \qquad\qquad +.16z_1+.20z_2-.15z_3 + .40z_4 = o_1$$

$$+.52\ y_1\ -\quad y_2 \qquad +.04z_1+.12z_2-.04z_3 + .08z_4 = o_2$$

$$+.11\ y_1 + .26\ y_2 - y_3 \qquad +.03z_1 \qquad\qquad + .10z_4 = o_3$$

(5)

which can be written as

$$\beta_{DS}y\ +\ \Gamma_{DS}z\ =\ o \qquad\qquad (6)$$

if we define

$$y = \begin{bmatrix} y_1 \\ y_2 \\ y_3 \end{bmatrix} \qquad z = \begin{bmatrix} z_1 \\ z_2 \\ z_3 \\ z_4 \end{bmatrix} \qquad o = \begin{bmatrix} o_1 \\ o_2 \\ o_3 \end{bmatrix}$$

$$\beta_{DS} = \begin{bmatrix} -1 & o & o \\ +.52 & -1 & o \\ +.11 & +.26 & -1 \end{bmatrix} \qquad \Gamma_{DS} = \begin{bmatrix} +.16 & +.20 & -.15 & +.40 \\ +.04 & +.12 & -.04 & +.08 \\ +.03 & o & o & +.10 \end{bmatrix}$$

More generally, we could define the following β and Γ
matrices for the Duncan model:

$$\underset{\sim}{\beta}_{DM} = \begin{bmatrix} -1 & 0 & 0 \\ +\beta_{21} & -1 & 0 \\ +\beta_{31} & +\beta_{32} & -1 \end{bmatrix} \quad \underset{\sim}{\Gamma}_{DM} = \begin{bmatrix} +\gamma_{11} & +\gamma_{12} & -\gamma_{13} & +_{14} \\ +\gamma_{21} & +\gamma_{22} & -\gamma_{23} & +\gamma_{24} \\ +\gamma_{31} & 0 & 0 & +\gamma_{34} \end{bmatrix}$$

This allows us to write a general Duncan model of the process of social stratification which subsumes the Duncan structure in equation (6) as a particular instantiation of the model:

$$\underset{\sim DM}{\beta}\underset{\sim}{y} + \underset{\sim DM}{\Gamma}\underset{\sim}{z} = \underset{\sim}{0}. \tag{7}$$

With this, we can now inquire into the kinds of theoretical analysis which can be made on the general class of static-exact models whose general form is given in (3). One method which is generally applicable is *the method of comparative statics* which refers to "the investigation of changes in a static system from one position of equilibrium to another without regard to the transitional process involved in the change" (Samuelson, 1947: 8). In general, once the exogenous variables and the structural parameters of (3) have been given specific numerical values (i.e., once we have specified a structure such as equations (5) for the Duncan model), we can find the resulting numerical values of the endogenous variables. These latter values form an equilibrium set for the system. That is, they specify the values of the endogenous variables determined by a specific set of conditions. It is hardly theoretically sufficient, however, to show that under certain conditions we can define enough relations (equations) to determine the equilibrium values of the unknown endogenous variables. It is important that our theoretical analysis be developed in such a way that we are aided in determining how our variables change either qualitatively or quantitatively with changes in the parameters or the exogenous variables. Therefore, we change the values of the parameters or the exogenous variables, which, in turn, causes shifts in our functional relations and defines new equilibrium values for the endogenous variables. The utility of the method derives from the fact that by such an analysis we are often able to determine the nature of the changes in the endogenous variables resulting from a designated change in one or more parameters or exogenous variables.

In terms of specific operation procedures, *there are two steps in a comparative-statics analysis. First,* the model must be solved for the equilibrium values of the endogenous

variables as a function of the structural parameters and the
the exogenous variables. In order that the system of equations (3) be in equilibrium (not necessarily a stable equilibrium), it is sufficient for the exogenous variables and
the parameters of the system not to be changing with respect
to time (i.e., that the time-derivatives of the variables and
the parameters be identically zero). Then, one method for
finding the solution is to premultiply equation (3) by
β^{-1}, assuming that it exists:

$$\beta^{-1}\underset{\sim}{\beta}\underset{\sim}{y} \; + \; \beta^{-1}\underset{\sim}{\Gamma}\underset{\sim}{z} \; = \; \beta^{-1}\underset{\sim}{0} \tag{8}$$

or

$$\underset{\sim}{y}^{e} \; = \; -\beta^{-1}\underset{\sim}{\Gamma}\underset{\sim}{z}$$

$$= \; \underset{\sim}{\Pi}\,\underset{\sim}{z}, \tag{9}$$

where $\Pi = -\beta^{-1}\Gamma$, and y^{e} denotes the vector of equilibrium
values of the endogenous variables. By rewriting equation
(3) as

$$\underset{\sim}{\beta}\underset{\sim}{y} \; = \; -\underset{\sim}{\Gamma}\underset{\sim}{z},$$

one sees that premultiplying equation (3) by β^{-1} is nothing
more than an application of Cramer's rule for solving a system of nonhomogeneous linear equations since, by the definition of the exogenous variables as fixed numbers or data,
$-\underset{\sim}{\Gamma}\underset{\sim}{z}$ is simply a G x 1 vector of constant numbers.

Again, a specific example is helpful here. Consider the
Duncan structure of stratification which was given above in
(6). It is easily verified that β^{-1} is given by:

$$\underset{\sim}{B}_{DS}^{-1} = \begin{bmatrix} -\;1 & 0 & 0 \\ -.52 & -\;1 & 0 \\ -.25 & -.26 & -\;1 \end{bmatrix} \tag{10}$$

and that the solution of the model is given by:

$$\underset{\sim DS}{y}^e = -\underset{\sim DS}{B}^{-1} \underset{\sim DS}{\Gamma} \underset{\sim}{z}$$

$$= \underset{\sim DS}{\Pi} \underset{\sim}{z}$$

$$= \begin{bmatrix} .16 & .20 & -.15 & .40 \\ .12 & .22 & -.12 & .29 \\ .08 & .08 & -.05 & .12 \end{bmatrix} \begin{bmatrix} z_1 \\ z_2 \\ z_3 \\ z_4 \end{bmatrix} \tag{11}$$

or, in terms of individual equations:

$$y_1^e = \sum_{k=1}^{4} \pi_{1k} z_k = .16z_1 + .20z_2 - .15z_3 + .40z_4 \tag{12a}$$

$$y_2^e = \sum_{k=1}^{K} \pi_{2k} z_k = .12z_1 + .22z_2 - .12z_3 + .29z_4 \tag{12b}$$

$$y_3^e = \sum_{k=1}^{K} \pi_{3k} z_k = .08z_1 + .08z_2 - .05z_3 + .12z_4 \tag{12c}$$

The solution (11) is referred to as being in the reduced form. Specifically, the *reduced form* gives the equilibrium values of the endogenous variables as explicit expressions of only the structural parameters and the exogenous variables.

The *second step* in a comparative-statics analysis consists of posing and answering the following: What happens to the equilibrium values of the endogenous variables if the values of the structural parameters or of the exogenous variables are changed? At first glance, one might conceive of answering this question by taking the partial derivative of an endogenous variable with respect to an exogenous variable or structural parameter directly from the structural equation form of the model. However, because of the many interdependencies among the endogenous variables which may occur in a simultaneous-equation model (as opposed to a single-equation model), such a procedure would not in general be correct. This is illustrated in equation (14), which shows the composition of the total effect of father's education on son's occupation as a sum of direct and indirect effects. Rather, the answer to this question is found by taking the partial derivatives, called *comparative statics derivatives*, of each endogenous variable with respect to each structural parameter and each exogenous variable in the reduced form. For linear models, it is clear that the first partial derivatives will contain all of the information that it is possible to derive from the model. More specifically, we see that the comparative statics derivative for the i-th endogenous variable with respect to the j-th exogenous variable in (9) is given by

$$\frac{\partial y_i^e}{\partial z_j} = -\underset{\sim}{\beta}_i^{-1} \underset{\sim}{\Gamma}^j = \pi_{ij} \quad (i = 1, \ldots, G; \; j = 1, \ldots, K), \quad (13)$$

where $\underset{\sim}{\beta}_i^{-1}$ denotes the i-th row of $\underset{\sim}{\beta}^{-1}$, $\underset{\sim}{\Gamma}^j$ denotes the j-th column of $\underset{\sim}{\Gamma}$, and π_{ij} is the ij-th element of the matrix $\underset{\sim}{\Pi}$. This result means that, given an increment of z_j by one unit, we would expect a change in y_i by π_{ij} units. Because they multiply increments in the exogenous variables in this manner, comparative statics derivatives are also known as *multipliers*. Hence, for a linear model, the elements of the reduced form coefficient matrix, $-\underset{\sim}{\beta}^{-1} \underset{\sim}{\Gamma} = \underset{\sim}{\Pi}$, are the multipliers; that is, the π_{ij} are the numbers by which increments in the z's must be multiplied in order to find the corresponding increments in the y's. Of course, it is almost never possible to know the values of the elements of the matrix $\underset{\sim}{\Pi}$ from *a priori* sociological theory alone; that is, the numerical values of the reduced form coefficients are usually not known on the basis of theory alone. More generally, one rarely knows the structural parameters of the $\underset{\sim}{\beta}$ and $\underset{\sim}{\Gamma}$ matrices on an *a priori* basis. On the other hand, it is often possible to assert the algebraic signs of the elements of $\underset{\sim}{\beta}$, $\underset{\sim}{\Gamma}$, and $\underset{\sim}{\Pi}$ on the basis of theory. In such a case, one may be in a position to make *qualitative deductions* regarding comparative statics derivatives; that is, one may be able to assert whether their algebraic signs are positive or negative. In some cases, however, past empirical research on a model will have provided evidence regarding the numerical values of the π_{ij} (as in the Duncan model), in which case, one can use such values to make *quantitative deductions* concerning the amount of change of an endogenous variable given a change in a particular exogenous variable (as we do next for the Duncan model).

Continuing with our example, it is clear that one would find the following partial derivatives with respect to the exogenous variables for the endogenous variable y_2:

$$\frac{\partial y_2}{\partial z_1} = \pi_{21} = .12 \tag{14a}$$

$$\frac{\partial y_2}{\partial z_2} = \pi_{22} = .22 \tag{14b}$$

$$\frac{\partial y_2}{\partial z_3} = \pi_{23} = -.12 \tag{14c}$$

$$\frac{\partial y_2}{\partial z_4} = \pi_{24} = .29 \tag{14d}$$

The method of comparative statics is ordinarily applied to entities for which the exogenous variables can take on different values, in which case the interpretation of the comparative statics derivative applies to tell the direction of change for an endogenous variable on that particular entity given a change in its value on a particular exogenous variable. However, such an interpretation cannot apply in general to the Duncan model of stratification since the father's statuses are ordinarily thought of as fixed. Rather, its interpretation must be applied to the population governed by a particular stratification system, so that one would compute such a derivative to study the effect on the son's status variables, given a change in one of the father statuses, with all the others held constant. Empirically, this corresponds to estimating the difference in the particular status value of two sons whose fathers' statuses differ in the prescribed manner. Thus, for example, given a positive increase of one unit in father's education, one would expect (on the average) .12 units of change in the equilibrium value of son's occupation. Since this is a considerably different value than the direct effect reported in the structure (5), it is useful to examine its composition in order to gain insight into the mechanisms which compose it.

Thus, we note the following composition of the coefficient π_{21}:

$$
\begin{aligned}
\pi_{21} &= (-\beta^{21})(\gamma_{11}) + (-\beta^{22})(\gamma_{21}) + (-\beta^{23})(\gamma_{31}) \\
&= (.52)(.16) + (1)(.04) + (0)(.25) \qquad\qquad (15) \\
&= .12
\end{aligned}
$$

where $-\beta^{21}$, $-\beta^{22}$, and $-\beta^{23}$ are the corresponding elements of $-\beta_{\sim DS}^{-1}$. In brief, the reduced form coefficient relating fathers education to son's occupation is composed of the product of the effect of father's education on son's education from the structure (5), which is an *indirect* effect *plus* the *direct* effect of father's education on son's occupation.

One could analyze the remaining reduced form coefficients in a similar fashion. Furthermore, one could also find the comparative statics derivatives of each endogenous variable with respect to each of the structural parameters of the model. For example, sociologists would be interested in examining the effect of an increase in the parameter relating son's education to son's occupation. However, rather than examine such comparative statics derivatives here, we shall give a general treatment of the method in the next section.

3. COMPARATIVE-STATICS ANALYSIS OF NONLINEAR MODELS

We now shift the discussion to nonlinear static-exact simultaneous-equation sociological models. Two classes of nonlinear models can usefully be distinguished. First, we consider the class of nonlinear models which are linear in the parameters. Although these models include nonlinear functions of the variables, their essential identifying characteristic is that the parameters enter only in a linear manner. Thus, such models are only slightly less linear than those of the preceding section. The general form of a nonlinear model which is linear in the parameters is:

$$\sum_{i=1}^{G} \beta_{1i} y_i + \sum_{m=1}^{M} \beta_{1,G+m} f_m(y_1,\ldots,y_G) + \sum_{k=1}^{K} \gamma_{1k} z_k$$

$$+ \sum_{j=1}^{J} \gamma_{1,K+j} f_j(z_1,\ldots z_K) = 0 \qquad\qquad (16)$$

.
.
.

$$\sum_{i=1}^{G} \beta_{Gi} y_i + \sum_{m=1}^{M} \beta_{G,G+m} f_m(y_1,\ldots,y_G) + \sum_{k=1}^{K} \gamma_{Gk} z_k$$

$$+ \sum_{i=1}^{J} \gamma_{G,K+j} f_j(z_1,\ldots,z_K) = 0$$

or more compactly,

$$\sum_{i=1}^{G} \beta_{gi} y_i + \sum_{m=1}^{M} \beta_{g,G+m} f_m(y_1,\ldots,y_G) + \sum_{k=1}^{K} \gamma_{gk} z_k$$

$$+ \sum_{j=1}^{J} \gamma_{g,K+j} f_j(z_1,\ldots,z_K) = 0$$

$$(g = 1,\ldots,G) \qquad\qquad (17)$$

Here the β_{gi} are the parameters of the endogenous variables in their linear terms; the $f_m(y_1,\ldots,y_G)$ are functions of the endogenous variables having no unspecified parameters; the $\beta_{g,G+m}$ are the parameters of these functions. A similar interpretation holds for the terms in the exogenous variables. In most models many of the parameters are equal to zero, which means that many of the variables and functions do not appear in every equation. By letting β^* and Γ^* be the matrices of the parameters of the nonlinear functions of the endogenous and the exogenous variables, respectively, we can write equations (16) in the following matrix form:

$$\beta y + \beta^* f(y) + \Gamma z + \Gamma^* f(z) = 0 \qquad\qquad (18)$$

More generally, by defining the following vectors and matrices:

$$\underset{\sim}{y}^* = \begin{bmatrix} \underset{\sim}{y} \\ \underset{\sim}{f}(\underset{\sim}{y}) \end{bmatrix}, \qquad \underset{\sim}{z}^* = \begin{bmatrix} \underset{\sim}{z} \\ \underset{\sim}{f}(\underset{\sim}{z}) \end{bmatrix},$$

$$\underset{\sim}{B}^{**} = [\underset{\sim}{B} \quad \underset{\sim}{B}^*], \qquad \underset{\sim}{\Gamma}^{**} = [\underset{\sim}{\Gamma} \quad \underset{\sim}{\Gamma}^*],$$

we can write equation (18) as

$$\underset{\sim}{\beta}^{**} \underset{\sim}{y}^* + \underset{\sim}{\Gamma}^{**} \underset{\sim}{z}^* = \underset{\sim}{0}. \tag{19}$$

For this class of nonlinear models, the method of comparative statics involves the same procedures as in the preceding section. That is, one first solves the model for the equilibrium values of the endogenous variables as a function of the values of the exogenous variables and the parameters of the model. Then one takes various partial derivatives of the endogenous variables with respect to the parameters and the exogenous variables. This allows one to examine the effect on the endogenous variables of various changes in the parameters and the exogenous variables. In particular, one can study the direction of change of the system, that is, the direction of movement of the system towards new equilibrium values of the endogenous variables.

As a second class of nonlinear models, we consider models composed of equations upon which no linearity restrictions are placed. Thus, this class of models includes the preceding class as a special subset. In order to write the general form of this class of models, it is useful, first to combine and relabel all of the parameters and exogenous variables of the model as $(\alpha_1, \ldots \alpha_M)$, which we will henceforth call the parameters, and to let M denote the total number of different parameters. Second, the set of G equations which constitute the model may be written most generally in implicit function form:

$$f^1(y_1, \ldots, y_G, \ \alpha_1 \ldots, \alpha_M) = 0$$

$$f^2(y_1, \ldots, y_G, \ \alpha_1, \ldots, \alpha_M) = 0 \tag{20}$$

$$\vdots \qquad \qquad \vdots \qquad \qquad \vdots$$

$$f^G(y_1, \ldots, y_G, \ \alpha_1, \ldots, \alpha_M) = 0$$

or more concisely

$$f^g(y_1,\ldots,y_G,\ \alpha_1,\ldots,\alpha_M) \ = \ 0 \quad (g = 1,\ldots,G) \tag{21}$$

Here $f^1,\ldots,f^G$ represent G different functions, not necessarily all linear, each of which *formally* includes all of of the parameters $(\alpha_1,\ldots,\alpha_M)$. That is, we let the form of each function indicate whether a given parameter *effectively* enters it or not.

The reduced form of a nonlinear model will typically be nonlinear, and it may not even be single-valued for all the endogenous variables y_g. Nonetheless, if one or more solutions exist, we can write down the reduced form of (21) thus:

$$y_g^e \ = \ h^g(\alpha_1,\ldots\alpha_M) \quad (g = 1,\ldots,G) \tag{22}$$

Having solved for the reduced form we proceed to show how the rates of change of our endogenous variables with respect to any parameter, say α_1, may be computed from (2). Let

$$\frac{\partial y_g^e}{\partial \alpha_1} \ = \ \frac{\partial h^g(\alpha_1^e,\ldots,\alpha_M^e)}{\partial \alpha_1} \ = \ h_1^g(\alpha_1^e,\ldots,\alpha_M^e) \quad (g = 1,\ldots,G) \tag{23}$$

stand for the rate of change of the g-th variable with respect to the parameter α_1, with all other parameters held constant. Such partial derivatives must be evaluated as of a given initial value of the set of parameters $(\alpha_1^e,\ldots,\alpha_M^e)$, and, hence, as of a corresponding set of values of the endogenous variables $(y_1^e,\ldots,y_G^e)$. Next, we differentiate each equation of (20) with respect to α_1 under the condition that all other parameters are to be held constant while all of the endogenous variables vary. This amounts to an application of the implicit function theorem of the differential calculus:

489

$$f^1_{y_1} \frac{\partial y^e_1}{\partial \alpha_1} + f^1_{y_2} \frac{\partial y^e_2}{\partial \alpha_1} + \ldots + f^1_{y_G} \frac{\partial y^e_G}{\partial \alpha_1} = - f^1_{\alpha_1}$$

$$f^2_{y_1} \frac{\partial y^e_1}{\partial \alpha_1} + f^2_{y_2} \frac{\partial y^e_2}{\partial \alpha_1} + \ldots + f^2_{y_G} \frac{\partial y^e_G}{\partial \alpha_1} = - f^2_{\alpha_1} \quad (24)$$

$$\cdots \qquad \cdots \qquad \cdots \qquad \cdots$$

$$f^G_{y_1} \frac{\partial y^e_1}{\partial \alpha_1} + f^G_{y_2} \frac{\partial y^e_2}{\partial \alpha_1} + \ldots + f^G_{y_G} \frac{\partial y^e_G}{\partial \alpha_1} = - f^G_{\alpha_1}$$

where

$$f^g_{y_i} = \frac{\partial f^g(y^e_1, \ldots, y^e_G, \alpha^e_1, \ldots, \alpha^e_M)}{\partial y_i} \quad , \quad (25)$$

with *all* other variables held constant, and similarly

$$f^g_{\alpha_1} = \frac{\partial f^g(y^e_1, \ldots, y^e_G, \alpha^e_1, \ldots, \alpha^e_M)}{\partial \alpha_1} \quad , \quad (26)$$

In matrix terms, equations (24) can be written as

$$[f^g_{y_i}] \; [\partial y^e_i / \partial \alpha_1] = [-f^g_{\alpha_1}] \quad (27)$$

We note that the numerical values of the partial derivatives (25) and (26) are fully determined at the equilibrium point in question. Thus, we have in (27) a set of G linear equations with constant coefficients in G unknowns $[(\partial y^e_1/\partial \alpha_1), \ldots, (\partial y^e_G/\partial \alpha_1)]'$. The solution of the matrix equation (27) thus is:

$$\left[\frac{\partial y^e_i}{\partial \alpha_1} \right] = - [f^g_y]^{-1} [f^g_{\alpha_1}] \quad . \quad (28)$$

Observe that the application of comparative statics to linear models in the preceding section could be cast in this general framework in which case the matrices of equation (28) consist of the appropriate constants and exogenous variables of the model. In particular, the matrix $[f^g_{y_i}]$ reduces to the matrix $\underset{\sim}{\beta}$ in the case of a linear model, and, if α_1 corresponds to an exogenous variable, say z_j, then the vector $[f^g_{\alpha_1}]$ corresponds to the j-th column vector of the $\underset{\sim}{\Gamma}$ matrix in a linear model. Denoting the latter by $\underset{\sim}{\Gamma^j}$, we see that (28) reduces to

$$\left[\frac{\partial y^e_i}{\partial z_j}\right] = -\underset{\sim}{\beta}^{-1}\ \underset{\sim}{\Gamma^j} \tag{29}$$

which is the matrix form of equation (13) of the preceding section. In brief, we see that the comparative statics analysis of a linear model is indeed a particular case of the general comparative statics analysis.

In the absence of numerical values for each of the elements of the matrices in (29), we noted in the preceding section that one could sometimes make qualitative deductions regarding the signs of the elements of the left-hand side of (29). In the general case, such inferences regarding signs are facilitated either by assuming:(1) that the static system (20) is the solution of a stable dynamic system (see, e.g., Samuelson, 1947: 257-283, or Bonacich and Bailey, 1971, for a discussion);or (2) that the system (20) is the solution of an optimizing system (see Samuelson, 1947: 21-56, for a discussion). Also, Lancaster (1965; 1966) has derived gen-algorithms for incorporating these and other assumptions into a comparative statics analysis. All of these general methods are treated in Land (1975). For the present discussion, we shall illustrate the qualitative use of comparative statics for nonlinear models with an application to the theory of differentiation of organizations.

4. GROWTH AND DIFFERENTIATION OF ORGANIZATIONS

We now consider some topics concerning the structure of human work organizations. In this context, the term *work organization* refers to a complex structure of social relationships for coordinating the activities of many persons to achieve specified ends. Our discussion will illustrate

principles of construction and analysis (via comparative
statics) of nonlinear recursive models by reformulating a
theory of structural differentiation in work organizations
due primarily to Blau's recent research (see Blau, 1970; Blau
and Schoenherr, 1971; Blau, 1972). We use the term theory
here rather than the term model because of the generality of
some of the concepts utilized extends beyond particular
operational procedures. The range of applicability of the
theory is not yet known. Blau's empirical generalizations
were originally from research on government employment
security agencies (Blau, 1970; Blau and Schoenherr, 1971).
However, Blau (1972) has recently corroborated his findings
for samples of government finance departments at the city,
country, and state levels, department stores, universities
and colleges, and teaching hospitals. Therefore, we are led
to believe that the theory may have rather wide applicability
to work organizations. We shall return to the issue of generality at the end of the section.

The theory to be developed is primarily concerned with
three characteristics of work organizations: their *size,*
their *internal differentiation,* and their *administrative
apparatus.* Size is conceptualized as the scope of an
organization and its responsibilities. Because the theory is
concerned with the way people are organized for accomplishing
work, size is usually operationalized as the number of employees in the organization. This not only facilitates comparisons between different types of work organizations, but
the number of employees has a close empirical relationship
with other measures of an organization's volume of responsibilities such as number of clients, sales, and assets (Blau,
1972: 3). The internal differentiation of work organizations
is usually construed in several ways. Vertical differentiation is ordinarily tapped by the number of hierarchical
levels, whereas horizontal differentiation is measured in
terms of major divisions under top management (for the organization as a whole) and in terms of sections per division
(for each division), and geographical differentiation is indicated by the number of branches. Next, the differentiation
of work is measured by the subdivision of work into occupational specialties (e.g., job titles or positions). The administrative apparatus of work organization is operationalized as the proportion (of size) of managerial personnel
(managers and supervisors) at all levels. An alternative
operationalization of this variable would involve a decomposition of work-time of employees into administrative and
nonadministrative components, so that a ratio of the former
to the latter could be formed. This procedure seems

preferable for those organizations where "management and supervision" responsibilities constitute only a fraction of the total responsibilities of managers and supervisors. In brief, all of the pertinent variables in the theory are amenable to measurement by counting or other extensive procedures and thus possess absolute or ratio scale properties.

In developing a model of structural differentiation in work organizations, we shall proceed by first stating the postulates, laws, and identities of the model. We then prove several theorems which follow from these basic relations. Although there are differences in some of the theorems and proofs, Hummon (1971) arrived at a similar treatment to this part of the theory independently of the present author.

We begin our statement of the theory by defining notation for the following six variables:

S = size of the organization (number of members);

D = number of structural components in which the organization is differentiated, where a structural component is either distinct official status (e.g., payment of clerk or first-line supervisor), or a submit in the organization (e.g., a particular branch or division);

A = average size of the structural components;

P = proportionate size of the structural components;

R = ratio of administrative or supervisory to total personnel;

C = supervisory span of control.

Of these six variables, size usually is regarded as exogenously determined, and the remaining five are considered as endogenous variables whose values are to be solved for with the model. That is, for work organizations, size is thought of as fixed by some combination of the demand for the goods or services produced by the organization and the cost-budget faced by the organization. On the other hand, the remaining five variables denoted above are thought of as responding to the size of the organization, although they may also be influenced by other factors.[1]

---

[1] Although this is the standard division of the variables into exogenous and endogenous subsets, we should note that it is not required by the model developed here. Thus, some organizations may have additional divisions or jobs imposed on them by the external environment in which case D is exogenous. For example, an employment security agency may be forced to create a "job counselor" position by a change in the public laws governing the agency. The present model can handle this merely by the designation of D as exogenous.

With respect to these variables, we shall assume, for theoretical purposes, that the S and D variables can take on any
nonnegative real (in the algebraic sense) values. Empirically, since any measurement procedure must result in a termi-
nating decimal number, one must always compute with numbers
from a subset of the rational numbers. However, for the
theoretical analysis, it is useful to allow values in the
real domain. Thus, although one would find empirically that
organizations typically add whole (integral) members and
whole positions, it is theoretically possible to have part-
time (fractional) positions and employees. Finally, we note
that the variables may be indexed across many organizations
(as in a cross-sectional study such as Blau's), across time
units on a single organization (as in a time-series study),
or across time units on many organizations (as in a panel
study). Given this notation, we are now ready to state the
postulates of the theory.

Postulates for a Model of Organizational Growth and Differentiation.

In a model of organizational growth and differentiation,
we assume that:
(OGD1) Principle of Negative Allometric Growth. In the presence of structural differentiation, the average size
of the structural components of a work organization
grows at a *relative rate* that is proportional to, and
less than, the *relative rate* at which the total organization grows.
(OGD2) Principle of Cumulative Learning. With no change in
the nature of the roles, divisions, tasks, etc., to
be supervised (i.e., constant D), an increase in the
overall size of an organization causes an increase in
the volume of administrative work (ΔAW) to be performed which is less than proportional to the increase
in size (ΔS):
$$\Delta AW < b(\Delta S) \ ,$$

where b is a constant of proportionality.
Each of these postulates deserves some comment and elaboration. First, the so-called principle of allometric growth
has been used primarily with respect to the growth of animal
organisms (see, e.g., Rensch, 1959; 133-190), where it has
been observed that subparts of organisms grow at a relative
rate that is proportional to the relative rate at which the
total organism grows. Moreover, the relative growth rates
tend to be invariant throughout the growth period of the

organism. In organisms, an organ or structure can grow more
quickly during certain periods than the body as a whole
(positive allometry), more slowly (negative allometry), or
with the same speed (isometry). Our postulate asserts that
the average size of all structural components grows at a
negative allometric rate. The reasoning is as follows. In
the absence of differentiation, we have $\Delta A = [(S + \Delta S)/D] - [S/D] = \Delta S/D$ and

$$\frac{\Delta A/A}{\Delta S/S} = \frac{(\Delta S/D)/(S/D)}{\Delta S/S} = \frac{\Delta S/S}{\Delta S/S} = 1, \tag{30}$$

so that we get isometric growth. However, in the presence of
differentiation, we have $\Delta A = [(S + \Delta S)/(D + \Delta D)] - [S/D]$, a
quantity which is less than the ΔA found in the case of no
differentiation and which therefore leads to negative allometric growth. Similarly, in the case of an organization
decreasing in differentiation but growing in size, we would
observe positive allometry. Thus, it is the differentiation
of organizations which makes for negative allometric growth.

Two particular forms of this allometric growth principle
will be useful in the model to be developed below. The first
of these could be termed the *law of constant relative growth,*
and it specifies that the ratio of the relative growth rates
of the average size of subparts and the total size is a constant b:

$$\frac{dA/A}{dS/S} = \lim \frac{\Delta A/A}{\Delta S/S} = b, \tag{31}$$

where the postulate says that $b < 1$. This equation could be
rewritten as

$$dA/A = b(dS/S), \tag{32}$$

the antiderivative of which is

$$\log A = a + b \log S, \tag{33}$$

where a is a constant. By taking the antilogarithm of this
function:

$$A = aS^b, \tag{34}$$

we see that this form of the principle of negative allometric
growth leads to a power function specification of the organizational growth function. An alternative form of this principle could be called the *law of proportionately decreasing
relative growth,* and it specifies that the ratio of the relative growth rates is inversely proportional to the existing
average size of structural components:

$$\frac{dA/A}{dS/S} = \lim \frac{\Delta A/A}{\Delta S/S} = \frac{b}{A} , \qquad (35)$$

or

$$dA/A = (b/A)(dS/S) , \qquad (36)$$

which can be simplified to give

$$dA = b(dS/S) , \qquad (37)$$

the antiderivative of which is a logarithmic organizational growth function:

$$A = a + b \log S, \qquad (38)$$

for constant a. At present, there is no basis in our axioms for discarding one of these forms in favor of the other. They both embody the notion that the growth of subparts of work organizations is constrained by certain bounds of consistency. Only empirical investigation can decide whether one form or the other is more appropriate for a given organization or type of organization.

Next, consider our postulate of cumulative learning. It says that if an increase in S does not necessitate new learning time or work (D constant), then it follows that ΔAW is less than proportional to ΔS. Moreover, given fixed technology, the volume of work governs the number of persons needed to accomplish it (administrative size or AS), and, if AW is measured in time units, then this relationship should be of direct proportionality, so that:

$$\Delta AS = k(\Delta AW), \qquad (39)$$

where k is a constant of proportionality. From this, it follows that ΔAS grows slower than Δs:

$$\Delta AS < kb(\Delta S), \qquad (40)$$

so that the proportion of persons in administration (R) decreases with an increase in size. In fact, the impact of an increment in the size of an organization (in the absence of differentiation) on the administrative ratio varies inversely with the existing size, because the increment must be considered relative to the total administrative responsibility:

$$\Delta R = (c/S)(\Delta S), \qquad (41)$$

where c is a constant of proportionality. In order for this equation not to result in negative R and to be consistent with (40), we see that we must have $0 < c < 1$. Taking limits we get the differential form of the equation:

$$dR = c(dS/S), \qquad (42)$$

the antiderivative of which is:

$$R = a + c \log S. \tag{43}$$

Alternatively, we could incorporate this function together with the additional specification that the impact of an increment in the size of an organization on the administrative ratio depends also on the existing administrative ratio. Since such an effect can lower the administrative ratio more if the ratio is larger, it must be directly proportional to R:

$$\Delta R = c(R/S)\Delta S, \tag{44}$$

which implies the power function:

$$R = aS^c, \tag{45}$$

for relating a given level of S to R.

Consider next the direct dependence of R on D. Since an increase in D implies an increase in the complexity of the roles, divisions, tasks, etc. to be supervised within the organization, we can appeal to the cumulative learning postulate used in the preceding paragraph to deduce that the increase in the volume of administrative work must be proportional to the increase in differentiation.

$$\Delta AW = b(\Delta D), \tag{46}$$

where b is a positive constant of proportionality. By applying the same argument as before, we then find that the proportion of persons in administrative (R) increases proportionally with differentiation:

$$\Delta R = e(\Delta D), \tag{47}$$

where e is a positive constant of proportionality. Taking limits and anti-derivatives, this now leads to a linear function for the impact of D on R:

$$R = a + eD. \tag{48}$$

Thus, in these two paragraphs, we have an explanation of the administrative learning mechanisms underlying the relationship of R to D and S. In brief, an increase in size with differentiation held constant decreases the administrative ratio because the repetition of existing administrative tasks involves no new learning. On the other hand, an increase in

497

differentiation increases the administrative ratio, because the organizational heterogeneity associated with differentiation requires new learning. This explanation is consistent with that given by Blau (1972). Combining the power function formulation of the effect of S with the effect of D, we have:

$$R = a + bD - cS^e, \qquad (49)$$

with the constraints:

$$a > 0, \ b > 0, \ 0 < e < 1.$$

Since it implies a constant (partial) elasticity of R with respect to S, it could appropriately be called a *constant elasticity law of administrative learning* for work organizations. Similarly, combining the logarithmic function formulation of the effect of S with the effect of D, we have:

$$R = a + bD - c \log S, \qquad (50)$$

with the constraints:

$$a > 0, \ b > 0, \ c > 0. \qquad (51)$$

Since it implies a proportionally decreasing (partial) elasticity of R with respect to S, it could be labeled a *proportionally decreasing elasticity law of administrative learning* for organization. In brief, we now have deduced specific functional forms for the equations determining D and R from general theoretical principles of growth and learning.

On the basis of these postulates and laws, we can now specify the structural equation form of our model of organizational growth and differentiation. First, from our laws of growth, we have the following function relating the average size of structural components to total size:

$$A = f(S), \qquad (52)$$

with the constraints:

$$\partial f / \partial S > 0 ,$$

$$\partial^2 f / \partial^2 < 0,$$

where, for consistency, we use the partial derivative notation throughout this section even when the derivative may refer to a function on only one variable. We also use general notation for the function in order that the theorems deduced below may be applicable to both laws of growth derived above, each of which satisfies these constraints. Second, from our derivation of the laws of administrative learning, we have the structural equation:

$$R = g(D,S), \tag{53}$$

with the constraints

$$\partial g/\partial D > 0, \qquad \partial g/\partial S < 0,$$

$$\partial^2 g/\partial D^2 = 0, \qquad \partial^2 g/\partial S^2 > 0,$$

where these constraints on g are satified by the two forms of the law given above. This structural equation implies Blau's (1970: 213) empirical generalization that "structural differentiation in organizations enlarges the administrative component," and the empirical findings of Blau and others (e.g., Anderson and Warkov, 1961; Pondy, 1969) that the administrative ratio decreases with size. To complete our structural equation model, we also have certain definitional identities. First, by definition the average size of a structural component is the size of the organization divided by the number of components of that type:

$$A \equiv S/D \tag{54}$$

where $\equiv$ denotes definitional identity. Second, the proportionate size of the average structural component is defined as the average size divided by the organization's total size:

$$P \equiv A/S \tag{55}$$

Third, the supervisory span of control in an organization is defined as the inverse of the administrative ratio:

$$C \equiv 1/R. \tag{56}$$

All of these definitions should be familiar to the reader from the theory of organizations, and we will use them without further comment.

With all of this in hand, we can solve the model for the values of five endogenous variables, A, D, P, R, and C, in terms of the exogenous variable, S:

$$C = f(S), \tag{57}$$

$$D \equiv S/A = S/f(S) = h(S), \tag{58}$$

$$P \equiv A/S = f(S)/S = 1/D, \tag{59}$$

$$R = g(D,S) = g(S/f(S),S) = g(h(S),S), \tag{60}$$

$$C \equiv 1/R = 1/g(S/f(S),S) = 1/g(h(S),S). \tag{61}$$

From these equations, we can derive on additional constraint on the function g. This pertains to the value of the total derivative of g with respect to S which we claim must have the sign:

$$\frac{dg}{dS} = (\partial g/\partial D)(\partial h/\partial S) + (\partial g/\partial S) < 0. \tag{62}$$

Consider the application of this to the power function forms of $D = h(S) = S/f(s) = aS^{1-b}$, $0 < b < 1$, and $R = g(D,S) = c + dD - eS^q$ to obtain:

$$\frac{dg}{dS} = d[a(1-b)S^{-b}] - eqS^{q-1}$$

$$= \frac{da(1-b)}{S^b} - egs^{q-1} \tag{63}$$

For the permissible values of the coefficients, this derivative will be negative. Next, consider the application of
to the logarithmic forms of $D = h(S) = S/f(S) = S/(a + b \log S)$, $0 < b < 1$, and $R = g(D,S) = c +dD - e \log S$ to obtain:

$$\frac{dg}{dS} = d\left[\frac{(a + b \log S) - S(b/S)}{(a + b \log S)^2} - \frac{e}{S}\right]$$

$$= d[A-b/A^2] - e/S$$

$$\cong d/A - e/S, \tag{64}$$

where $\cong$ denotes approximately. It is not clear that this equation will be negative for all permissible values of the parameters. However, since (62) holds for the power function formulation (63), we shall assume that it also holds in (64). In brief, (62) constrains the effect of S on R through D to be less than its direct effect.

With this solution of the model we can proceed to find the comparative statics derivatives of the endogenous variables with respect to the exogenous variables, S. In this process, we will first demonstrate the versatility of the mathematical model by deriving all of Blau's (1970) empirical generalizations as fairly simple comparative statics derivatives. Then we will demonstrate the power of the mathematical theory by exhibiting additional theorems. Our procedure, therefore, will be to state each of Blau's propositions and then to give a mathematical proof of the proposition as the appropriate comparative statics derivative.

Theorem 1. As the size of an organization increases, its marginal influence on differentiation decreases (Blau, 1970: 207).

Proof: By taking the derivative of equation (57) with respect to S, we have

$$\frac{\partial D}{\partial S} = \frac{(1) f(S) - S[\partial f/\partial S]}{[f(S)]^2}$$

$$= \frac{A - S[\partial A/\partial S]}{A^2} > 0,$$

where the inequality holds only if the numerator is positive since the denominator is positive and $\partial f/\partial S > 0$ by our assumptions. But by our constraints on the power and logarithmic forms of f, it follows that the numerator must be positive. Moreover, without taking the second derivative, it is clear that the rate of change of this marginal function declines with S.

Theorem 2. The larger an organization is, the larger the average size of its structural components of all kinds (Blau, 1970: 207).

Proof: By direct application of the first-order constraint on the function f, we have (since f(S) = A):

$$\partial A/\partial S = \partial f/\partial S > 0.$$

Theorem 3. The proportionate size of the average structural component, as distinguished from its absolute size, decreases with increases in organizational size (Blau, 1970: 208).

Proof: According to our reduced form equations,

$$P = 1/D.$$

Thus, from Theorem 1, it follows that

$$\frac{\partial C}{\partial S} = \frac{\partial P}{\partial D} \cdot \frac{\partial D}{\partial S} = \frac{-1}{D^2} \cdot \frac{\partial D}{\partial S} < 0,$$

by the chain rule of differential calculus.

Theorem 4. The larger the organization is, the wider the supervisory span of control (Blau, 1970: 209).

Proof: The partial derivative of the reduced form equation for C with respect to S is:

$$\frac{\partial C}{\partial S} = \frac{\partial}{\partial S} \frac{1}{g(h(S),S)}$$

$$= \frac{- (dg/dS)}{[g(h(S),S)]^2} > 0,$$

where the inequality holds only if $\frac{dg}{dS} = \frac{\partial g}{\partial h} \cdot \frac{\partial h}{\partial S} + \frac{\partial g}{\partial S} < 0$, as we have assumed.

Theorem 5. Organizations exhibit an economy of scale in management (Blau, 1970: 210).

Proof: We have the following partial derivative of the reduced form equation for R with respect to S:

$$\frac{\partial R}{\partial S} = \frac{\partial}{\partial S} g(h(S),S)$$

$$= \frac{dg}{dS} < 0,$$

which holds under the constraint of equation (61).

Theorem 6. The economy of scale of organizations itself declines with increasing size (Blau, 1970: 210).

Proof: Taking the second partial derivative of the reduced form equation for R with respect to S, we have:

$$\frac{\partial^2 R}{\partial S^2} = \frac{\partial^2}{\partial S^2} (h(S),S)$$

$$= \frac{\partial^2 g}{\partial h^2} \cdot \frac{\partial^2 h}{\partial S^2} + \frac{\partial^2 g}{\partial S^2}$$

$$= \frac{d^2 g}{dS^2} > 0,$$

where the inequality holds only under certain constraints on the second derivatives of g with respect to S as have been specified. A set of constraints which suffices is $\partial^2 g/\partial S^2 > 0$, $\partial^2 g/\partial h^2 < 0$, and the constraint on the second derivative of h in Theorem 1. Under these constraints, the theorem follows:

Theorem 7. The large size of an organization indirectly raises the ratio of administrative personnel through the structural differentiation it generates (Blau, 1970: 213).

Proof: By a direct multiplication of the constraints on the first derivatives of the functions h and g, we have:

$$\frac{\partial g}{\partial D} \cdot \frac{\partial D}{\partial S} = \frac{\partial g}{\partial D} \cdot \frac{\partial h}{\partial S} > 0.$$

which proves the proposition.

This completes our derivation of Blau's propositions, but we hasten to point out that additional theorems not found in Blau's propositions can be derived from the present mathematical theory. Specifically, we cite the following three propositions.

Theorem 8. The larger an organization is, the slower the rate at which the average size of its structural components increases.

Proof: This assertion follows directly from the application of the second-order constraint on the function f to give (since f(S) = A):

$$\partial^2 A/\partial S^2 = \partial^2 f/\partial S^2 < 0.$$

Theorem 9. The larger an organization is, the faster the rate at which the proportionate size of the average structural component decreases.

Proof: Using the chain rule of differentiation, Theorem 1, and Theorem 3, we have

$$\frac{\partial^2 P}{\partial S^2} = \frac{2}{D^3} \cdot \frac{\partial^2 D}{\partial S^2} < 0.$$

Theorem 10. The larger an organization is, the faster the rate at which the supervisory span of control increases.

Proof: Taking the second partial derivative of the reduced form equation for C with respect to size, we have

$$\frac{\partial^2 C}{\partial S^2} = \frac{[g(S/f(S),S)]^2 [-d^2g/dS^2] - [-dg/dS][2g(Sf(S),S)][dg/dS]}{[g(S/f(S),S)]^4}$$

$$= \frac{-d^2g/dS^2}{R^2} + \frac{2[dg/dS]^2}{R^3} > 0,$$

We conclude this section with a number of observations regarding this model of organizational growth and differentiation. First, as an example of the application of comparative statics, the theory illustrates how definitional identities can be utilized advantageously in sociological models. That is, in contrast to most sociological models which specify a causal mechanism (represented by a structural equation) for determining each of the endogenous variables, this theory determines five endogenous variables from two mechanisms and three definitional identities. Second, as a theory, we note that our formulation has recast the original emphasis of Blau (1970) on the relationship of size to differentiation into a growth function framework within which the size-differentiation relationship can be derived.

With regard to the generality of the theory, we have cited above a number of studies which corroborate most of our theorems. Only Theorems 8, 9, and 10 are new derivations which have not been explicitly evaluated in the empirical literature. The most controversial of the propositions seems to be the size-administrative ratio relationship of Theorem 5. A number of studies have purported to show that this relationship is positive rather than negative as asserted in the theorem. The most frequently cited study reporting a positive relationship is Terrien and Mills (1955). However, they discarded more than four hundred small systems before performing one of their analyses and a lesser number of small systems before performing the other. Because the behavior of either the power or the logarithmic functional specifications of this relationship postulated above is such that large decreases in the administrative ratio occur only for relatively small organizational sizes, this practice casts considerable doubt on the meaningfulness of their findings. Put otherwise, the theory implies that economics of scale in administration occur, but that they become increasingly less apparent as size increases. Therefore, any study which does not include relatively small organizations is not very likely to corroborate Theorem 5.

Yet, study after study infers a positive size-administrative ratio relationship on the basis of samples of relatively large systems. For example, Holdaway and Blowers (1971) report data on the administrative ratios of 41 urban school systems in western Canada for the five-year period 1964-65 through 1968-69. Using their summary table of cross-sectional observations on the sizes of the schools and the corresponding administrative ratios, which they define as the ratio of central office administrative personnel plus school principals to the number of central office administrative and professional personnel plus school principals plus classroom teachers (rather than *all* personnel), one finds the following approximate least-squares fit for the logarithmic administrative ratio function:

$$R = 16.6 - 1.4 \log S, \tag{65}$$

where the logarithms are taken to the base e. This equation yields the following values of R for selected values of S:

S = 50,	R = 11.2;		S = 500,	R = 8.0;
S = 100,	R = 10.2;		S = 1000,	R = 7.0;
S = 200,	R = 9.3;		S = 2000,	R = 6.1;
S = 300,	R = 8.7;		S = 3000,	R = 5.5;
S = 400,	R = 8.3;		S = 4000,	R = 5.1

Assume first that these school systems are from the same population so that a function such as (65) estimated for the whole sample can be taken as describing the expected value of a particular school's administrative ratio if we are given its size. Second, suppose that equation (65) is a valid comparative statics approximation to the dynamic system which governs the S-R relationship for these schools; that is, suppose equation (65) is the equilibrium solution to the corresponding differential equation which governs the S-R relationship over time for the schools (which is a tenable assumption for school systems since major changes in school personnel are likely to occur only once a year). Then equation (65) gives the expected values of R as a function of S as S varies over the five time points for any one school system. Given this interpretation, we note, first of all, that R changes very slowly for S greater than, say, 500. But equation (65) gives only the expected values of R. By virtue of regression effects alone, we would further expect a school system which, at the beginning of the observation period, has

a higher than expected administrative ratio (on the basis of
its size and equation (65)) to exhibit greater changes in R
during the period than (65) predicts on the basis of changes
in its size alone. Similarly, if a school system has a
lower than expected administrative ratio (on the basis of
its initial size), then we would expect it to exhibit less
change in R than that corresponding to the changes in its S
value during the five-year period.

Holdaway and Blowers (1971: 284-285) exhibit plots of
the five pairs of S-R values observed for 15 of the 41
school systems. Most of them are relatively flat which is
to be expected from equation (65). Moreover, virtually all
of the deviations of these plots from the curve described by
(65) can be attributed to the aforementioned regression
effects. That is, those school systems which possess higher
than expected administrative ratios at the beginning of the
observation period exhibit greater yearly changes than predicted by (65). Likewise, those which possess lower than
expected administrative ratios at the outset exhibit nearly
flat plots for the five-year observation period and some of
them show a slight tendency to increase. But this could be
anticipated solely as a tendency to "regress towards the
mean" of the model, and it hardly constitutes a basis for
rejecting the assertion of Theorem 5. In brief, there is
little basis in these longitudinal data for rejecting the
negative size-administrative ratio relationship asserted in
Theorem 5, but this is the way in which the Holdaway-Blowers
study is usually interpreted.

Several other recent studies which have found a nonnegative size-administrative ratio relationship can be discounted on other grounds. For example, as with all scientific propositions, Theorem 5 could only be expected to hold
under ceteris *paribus* conditions. This implies that comparisons should probably be made only for samples of organizations using similar technologies and facing similar environmental constraints. This clearly is not the case for
Freeman's (1973) study of 41 diverse manufacturing organizations, and, thus, it is not surprising that he reports
significant technology and environmental effects but non-
significant size effects. Similarly, Kasarda's (1974) study
of samples of educational systems, communities, and societies shows that the negative size-administrative ratio relationship does not hold for total societies; in fact, the
relationship is positive. Again, societies which range from
under 500,000 to over 25 million in size undoubtedly employ
vastly different technologies and face very different
environmental constraints, and, consequently, this result is

not surprising. Kasarda's (1974) study also shows that one obtains a positive size-administrative intensity ratio if one defines administrative intensity (as did Pondy, 1969) to include managers, professionals, and clerical workers. The negative relationship of Theorem 5 holds only if one takes the managerial component as comprising the administrative ratio. This was Blau's (1970) operationalization, and Kasarda's (1974) results show how the inclusion of the other components may affect the empirical results.

5. CONCLUDING COMMENTS

In this paper, we have sketched some illustrative applications of the method of comparative statics to sociological models. For simultaneous-equation models, we have seen that the method rests upon the implicit function theorem of the differential calculus. As we have noted above, the method amounts to an investigation of changes in a static system from one equilibrium position to another, but it cannot tell us anything about the process of transition from one equilibrium position to another. Suppose, for example, that one constructs a model of a social system which is in a position of equilibrium under certain conditions. Then suppose that one does a comparative statics analysis to determine the effects on the endogenous variables of specified changes in the exogenous variables. Such an analysis will ideally be able to tell what the new equilibrium positions will be, but it will not be able to answer such questions as how long will it take the system to attain the new equilibrium or how fast will the variables approach their equilibria. It is not possible to answer such questions by the methods of comparative statics; rather, one must use a different modeling procedure which explicitly addresses itself to questions of time-dependent dynamics. Moreover, it should be emphasized that comparative statics is, in essence, nothing more than a mathematical version of the basic comparative method of science. That is, whether by experimental or naturalistic observation, scientific inquiry proceeds by a comparison of the configurations of systems which are identical in all but a small set of clearly defined parameters. The comparison may involve the same system at two different levels of an exogenous variable or parameter (and, thus, usually at two different time points); or it may pertain to two or more different systems at different levels of an exogenous variable or parameter (and, thus, usually at the same time point as in cross-sectional sociological research). Both types of comparison are also made in a comparative statics analysis.

However, in this case, the comparison does not involve empirically observed changes in a real system, but rather a comparison of inferred changes in the theoretician's model of real system. In this sense, comparative statics is the theoretician's analogue of the empiricist's observation of reactions to changes in a system. Even more, it is the theoretician's calculus for making deductions from his model of a system, which deductions can be verified by making the analogous empirical comparisons. Although we have illustrated comparative statics as an application of classical calculus to simultaneous-equation systems, there is no difficulty in applying the basic notions of the method to other types of models such as those based on combinatorial analysis. In any case, the method should provide a useful tool in the construction of deductive sociological theories.

REFERENCES

Anderson, T. R. and S. Warkov. 1961. "Organizational size and functional complexity." *American Sociological Review* 26: 23-28.

Blalock, H. M., Jr. 1964. *Causal Inferences in Nonexperimental Research*. Chapel Hill: University of North Carolina Press.

Blalock, H. M., Jr. 1969. *Theory Construction*. Englewood Cliffs, N.Y.: Prentice-Hall.

Blau, P. M. 1970. "A Formal theory of differentiation in organizations." *American Sociological Review* 35: 201-218.

Blau, P. M. 1972. "Interdependence and hierarchy in organizations." *Social Science Quarterly* 1: 1-24.

Blau, P. M. and R. A. Schoenherr. 1971. *The Structure of Organizations*. New York: Basic Books.

Bonacich, P. and K. D. Bailey. 1971. "Key variables," in H. L. Costner (ed.), *Sociological Methodology: 1971*. San Francisco: Jossey-Bass, Chap. 8.

Boudon, R. 1965. "A method of linear causal analysis." *American Sociological Review* 30: 365-374.

Boudon, R. 1968. "A new look at correlations analysis," in H. M. Blalock, Jr. and A. B. Blalock (eds.), *Methodology in Social Research*. New York: McGraw-Hill, Chap. 6.

Duncan, O. D. 1966. "Path analysis: sociological examples." *American Journal of Sociology* 72: 1-16.

Duncan, O. D. 1968. "Ability and achievement." *Eugenics Quarterly* 15: 1-11.

Freeman, J. H. 1973. "Environment, technology and the administrative intensity of manufacturing organizations." *American Sociological Review* 38: 750-763.

Heise, D. R. 1969. "Problems in path analysis and causal inference," in E. F. Borgatta (ed.), *Sociological Methodology: 1969*. San Francisco: Joseey-Bass, Chapter 2.

Holdaway, E. A. and T. A. Blowers. 1971. "Administrative ratios and organizational size; a longitudinal examination." *American Sociological Review* 36: 278-286.

Hummon, N. P. 1971. "A mathematical theory of differentiation in organizations." *American Sociological Review* 36: 297-303.

Kasarda, J. D. 1974. "The structural implications of social system size: a comparative analysis." *American Sociological Review* 39: 19-28.

Lancaster, K. J. 1965. "The theory of qualitative linear systems." *Econometrica* 33: 395-408.

Lancaster, K. J. 1966. "The solution of qualitative comparative statics problems." *Quarterly Journal of Economics* 80: 278-295.

Land, K. C. 1969. "Principles of path analysis," in E. F. Borgatta (ed.), *Sociological Methodology: 1969*. San Francisco: Joseey-Bass, Chap. 1.

Land, K. C. "Significant others, the self-reflexive act and the attitudinal formation process: a reinterpretation." *American Sociological Review* 36: 1085-1098.

Land, K. C. 1973. "Identification, parameter estimation, and hypothesis testing in recursive sociological models," in A. S. Goldberger and O. D. Duncan (eds.) *Structural Equation Models in the Social Sciences*. New York: Seminar Press, Chap. 2.

Land, K. C. 1975. Mathematical Sociology: Methods and models, Volume II: Analytical Foundations. Mimeographed.

Pondy, L. R. 1969. "Effects of size, complexity, and ownership in administrative intensity." *Administrative Science Quarterly* 14: 47-60.

Rensch, B. 1959. *Evolution Above the Species Level*. New York: Columbia University Press.

Samuelson, P. A. 1947. *Foundations of Economic Analysis*. Cambridge, Mass.: Harvard University Press.

Terrien, F. W. and D. L. Mills. 1955. "The effect of changing size upon the internal structure of organizations." *American Sociological Review* 20: 11-13.

18

*A Model for the Analysis of Mobility Tables**

RAYMOND BOUDON

The Sorbonne and Université René Descartes

A basic problem in intergenerational mobility analysis is the circular relationship between mobility and stratification: it is meaningless to compute mobility rates unless a valid set of stratification categories is previously defined, which cannot themselves be defined independently of mobility.

In the present paper a model will be presented which may be considered as an attempt to solve this problem. This model is a generalization of the intergenerational versions of the mover-stayer model. Thus, we shall present briefly, first, the original mover-stayer model, then the intergenerational adaptations which were proposed by Leo Goodman and Harrison White, before going to the generalization of these latter models.

1. THE ORIGINAL MOVER-STAYER MODEL

Blumen's original model (1955, 1956) deals with labor turnover, i.e. with intragenerational mobility. The model is derived basically from the empirical finding that job mobility always appears to be weaker than would be expected under the assumption of a Markov chain. Assume, in other words, that an observed transition matrix R describes the ways workers of a population move from one~occupational category to another from the beginning to the end of, say, a

---

*
With the collaboration of J. K. Lindsey.

quarter. Then we may try to predict the turnover between the initial quarter, say 0, and quarter t:

$$\underset{\sim}{p}_{(0)} \underset{\sim}{R}^t = \underset{\sim}{p}_{(t)} \ , \tag{1}$$

where $\underset{\sim}{p}_{(0)}$ and $\underset{\sim}{p}_{(t)}$ are the distributions respectively at time 0 and at time t, predicts the occupational structure at the t-th quarter. However, the diagonal elements of $\underset{\sim}{R}^t$ will generally be much smaller than the diagonal elements of the empirical matrix, say $\underset{\sim}{R}^{(t)}$, which gives the observed transition rates between quarter 0 and quarter t.

In order to account for this general empirical observation, Blumen and his colleagues proposed to consider the population as composed of two latent categories of people: the stayers and the movers. The movers are supposed to move according to a Markov chain. The stayers simply stay. In other words, they are supposed to stay with a probability equal to 1. Let us for instance consider r_{ii}, i.e. the proportion of people located in occupational category i at the beginning of quarter 0 who are still in category i at the beginning of quarter 1. This proportion will be considered as the sum of two latent components: s_i, the proportion of the stayers in category i, and $(1-s_i)m_{ii}$, where the proportion of movers is $(1-s_i)$ and these movers have a probability m_{ii} of moving from i to i, i.e. of staying, though they are movers. Then,

$$r_{ii} = s_i + (1 - s_i)m_{ii} \tag{2}$$

or, in matrix form,

$$\underset{\sim}{R} = \underset{\sim}{S} + (\underset{\sim}{I} - \underset{\sim}{S})\underset{\sim}{M} \ , \tag{3}$$

where $\underset{\sim}{R} = [r_{ij}]$ is the observed transition matrix, $\underset{\sim}{S}$ the diagonal matrix $[s_i]$, $\underset{\sim}{I}$ the identity matrix and $\underset{\sim}{M} = [m_{ij}]$ the transition matrix of the movers.

2. WHITE'S INTERGENERATIONAL MOVER-STAYER MODEL

We shall next present briefly some adaptations of this

model to intergenerational mobility. Obviously, this adaptation is possible: we may in the intergenerational case, as in the intragenerational, introduce the latent distinction between stayers and movers. If this distinction leads to consistent models, it may be used to solve the problem of measuring social mobility. Nonetheless, there is an important difference between intergenerational and intragenerational mobility: the size of the time unit. As a consequence, in the intragenerational case it may be possible, as in Blumen's example, to observe a sequence of mobility matrices. In the intergenerational case, a single or at most a very small number of matrices will be available. Thus, the model (3) clearly cannot be directly applied to intergenerational mobility. With a single matrix, the equations of this model cannot be solved. The models to be presented below are derived from the original mover-stayer model in the sense that, as with this latter model, they introduce a distinction between two latent sub-populations. However, their mathematical structure is very distinct from that of the original model.

One of the most interesting applications of the mover-stayer idea to intergenerational mobility is provided by Harrison White (1970). In fact, White proposed two models more or less directly inspired by the mover-stayer distinction. In this section, we shall present the most recent of these contributions.

The "modified inheritance model," as White himself calls it, assumes, like Blumen's model, that each social category i includes an unknown proportion of movers. Let us call s_i the number of stayers in i and m_{ii} the number of movers who happen to stay in i. (Note that to avoid the proliferation of symbols, these symbols have a slightly different meaning here than in the previous section). For the rest, let n_{ij} be the number of sons with father i who are themselves j; $n_{(0)i}$ the number of fathers in stratum i; $n_{(1)j}$ the number of sons in stratum j, etc. On the other hand, let us call m_{ij} the number of movers going from i to j, $m_{(0)i}$ the number of movers whose fathers belong to category i and $m_{(1)j}$ the number of movers among the sons currently belonging to social category j.

The first equation of the model is

$$n_{ii} = m_{ii} + (n_{(0)i} - m_{(0)i}) \qquad (4)$$

513

This equation states that the total observed number of families staying in i from one generation to the next is the sum of the number of movers who stay in i and of the number of stayers. Note that in the intergenerational case, the attributes "mover" and "stayer" apply to families and not to individuals.

A second equation states that all the families who moved from i to j belong to the class of the movers:

$$n_{ij} = m_{ij} \qquad (5)$$

Of course, the equations cannot be solved without further assumptions. In the case of Blumen's original model, the estimation of S, the diagonal matrix describing the proportions of stayers, was made possible because of the assumption that $\underset{\sim}{M}$ generates a Markov chain. Blumen and his colleagues then used $\underset{\sim}{M}^*$, the equilibrium matrix, for this estimation. Here, since we have at our disposal only one matrix, a functional substitute, so to speak, must be found. White derives this substitute by using the traditional assumption of perfect mobility.[1] This assumption is, of course, only applied to the movers.

Then

$$m_{ij} = m_{(0)i} \cdot m_{(1)j} /M , \qquad (6)$$

where M is the total number of movers.

We will not examine the problem of solving this model. This is merely a technical problem and we prefer to refer the reader to the White's original text on this point. The logical and substantive interest of the model proposed by White is more important for our purpose.

In one of the applications presented, White used his model for analyzing British and Danish trichotomous mobility tables. He found that the model applied in neither of the two cases: it was impossible to fit acceptable values for $m_{(0)1}, m_{(0)2}$ and $m_{(0)3}$ simultaneously. This negative result shows that the data to which the model was applied are incompatible with the assumptions described by (4) to (6)

---

[1]Mobility is perfect when destination (achievement) status is independent, in the statistical sense, of origin (ascriptive) status.

according to which the population could be divided into two latent subpopulations, i.e. a subpopulation of stayers and one of movers submitted to the rule of perfect mobility.

White then proceeded with further assumptions. He found a good fit for $m_{(0)1}$ and $m_{(0)3}$ when the supplementary assumption

$$m_{(0)2} = n_{(0)2} \qquad (7)$$

is introduced, i.e. when everybody is supposed to be a mover in social category 2. In another application, White used Blau and Duncan's data and found a good fit. He then computed what he calls the "inheritance fraction." Let us call this index I_W defined by:

$$I_{W(i)} = 1 - (m_{(0)i} / n_{(0)i}) \qquad (8)$$

The inheritance fraction is, in other words, the proportion of stayers in a given social category. In applying this index to Blau and Duncan's data, White found the rather small average value of .092. The index reaches a moderately large value only for the professionals (professional, self-employed: .156; professional, salaried: .240) and for the farmers (.153). However, the fit of the off-diagonal elements of the mobility matrix is, according to the author himself, rather poor.

3. A PARTICULAR VERSION OF THE WHITE'S MODEl: GOODMAN'S MODEL

L. Goodman (1965) has proposed in one of his papers a model which may be considered as a particular version of the White model, though the former predates the latter.

In White's model, while the stayers have a probability zero of moving, the movers have a non-zero probability of staying. In Goodman's model, the assumptions for the two latent subpopulations are symmetric: the stayers are not allowed to move and the movers are not allowed to stay. With this assumption, (4), reduces to

$$n_{ii} = n_{(0)i} - m_{(0)i} , \qquad (9)$$

since

$$m_{ii} = 0 \qquad\qquad (10)$$

The other assumptions of White's model, (5) and (6), are kept: the movers are, in other words, supposed to move according to the rule of perfect mobility.

The Goodman model, in contrast to White's, is very simple. While in White's model, the estimation of the number of stayers in each category is complicated, it becomes very simple in Goodman's model, since the stayers are those who are located in the main diagonal of a mobility matrix. Thus, the procedure for testing the adequacy of the model is very simple:

The first step consists of subtracting the diagonal figures from the corresponding row and column marginals and to blank out these diagonal figures. This will give the numbers $m_{(0)i}$ of movers in each row and the numbers $m_{(1)j}$ of movers in each column.

The next and final step is to verify that

$$m_{ij} = m_{(0)i} \cdot m_{(1)j} \; / \; M \qquad (i \neq j), \qquad (11)$$

where, as in White's model,

$$m_{ij} = n_{ij} \qquad (i \neq j) \qquad\qquad (12)$$

Goodman has proposed several variations of this simple model. Let us suppose, for instance, a trichotomous mobility table. In the version of the model which has just been described, the families located in the main diagonal are all considered as stayers: an inheritance phenomenon is assumed in each social category, and the degree of this inheritance is simply measured by the proportion of families belonging to the i-th row that are located in the i-th column.

An alternative assumption supposes that an inheritance phenomenon is at work in some social categories, say categories 1 and 3, but not in the other, category 2. Then, n_{11} and n_{33} are, as previously, considered to describe the numbers of stayers respectively in categories 1 and 3. The quantity n_{22} is considered to describe a sub-population of, so to speak, apparent stayers, i.e. of families that are movers but happen to stay. With this assumption, the test of the model would include the following steps:

1) subtract the diagonal figures from the corresponding row and column totals for the categories where a social

inheritance is assumed, i.e. in our example categories 1 and 3 and blank out these diagonal cells;

2) Keep the original row and column totals for the social categories where no social inheritance is assumed (in our example, for category 2); and

3) verify that

$$m_{ij} = m_{(0)i} \cdot m_{(1)j} / M \text{ (for all cells not blanked out)} \quad (13)$$

Thus, in our example, where social inheritance applies only to categories 1 and 3, we have to check that (13) holds for all cells except the blanked out diagonal cells corresponding to these categories.

Goodman's model has a great advantage in its simplicity. On the other hand, this advantage is the consequence of the rigidity of the assumptions. Either we assume the action of a social inheritance effect in a given social category, say i, and the families of row i located in column i are *all* considered as *stayers*. Or we do not assume this action and the same families are *all* considered as *movers,* even if they happen to stay. Even with a good fit, it is hard to accept, from a sociological point of view, that the effect of social inheritance could be zero in some social categories. White's assumption that the families located in the diagonal cells are of two kinds, i.e. a latent subpopulation of movers and a latent subpopulation of stayers, is undoubtedly more appealing for a sociologist, even it it leads to greater mathematical complications.

4. THREE TYPES OF MOVER-STAYER MODELS APPLIED TO INTERGENERATIONAL MOBILITY

Goodman's model is characterized by the assumption that the stayers are not allowed to move and the movers are not allowed to stay. More exactly, the stayers are never allowed to move and the movers are only allowed to stay when there are no stayers already in a given social category.

By contrast, White's model assumes that the movers are always allowed to stay. In other words, the diagonal cells of a mobility matrix will generally include stayers *and* movers, while in Goodman's model they include stayers *or* movers, but not both. On the other hand, White's model makes the same assumption as Goodman's for the stayers: they are never allowed to move.

Let us ignore for a moment the variations that Goodman has proposed in his model and consider its basic version described by the equations (9) to (11). Then we can summarize the fundamental difference between White's and Goodman's models as in Table 1. There we have called Goodman's model a type 1 model. White's model is called a type 2 model.

Type 1 model (Goodman's model)	stayers not allowed to move movers not allowed to stay
Type 2 model (White's model)	stayers not allowed to move movers allowed to stay
Type 3 model	stayers allowed to move movers allowed to stay

Table 1: Three types of mover-stayer models with their assumptions.

This presentation suggests a third type of model given at the bottom of the table. In this model, the stayers are allowed to move, exactly as the movers are allowed to stay in White's model.

We shall develop it in the next section. A general point is worth mentioning: while Table 1 shows that the type 3 model appears at the mathematical level as a natural extension of the type 2 model, it does raise a semantic problem. Indeed, in Goodman's or in White's model it is very easy to follow the stayers, since, by the assumptions of these models, they are always located in the diagonal. With the type 3 model, the symmetry of the assumptions with regard to the latent subpopulations has the consequence that the semantic interpretation of these subpopulations as stayers and movers will become questionable. Thus, the model we shall present belongs on the one hand to the mover-stayer family of models; but it has, on the other hand, a different interpretation and other uses.

5. A GENERAL MODEL FOR THE ANALYSIS OF MOBILITY TABLES

In the exposition of this model, we shall substitute a distinction between latent class 1 (LC 1) people and latent class 2 (LC 2) people to the distinction between movers and stayers. On the other hand, we shall retain the symbols m and s. The meaning of these classes will be examined later.

We shall suppose, as previously, that n_{ij} is the

observed number of families in cell (i,j) of the mobility matrix. For all i and all j, n_{ij} will be the sum of m_{ij}, the number of LC 1 people, and of s_{ij}, the number of LC 2 people located in the cell (i,j):

$$n_{ij} = m_{ij} + s_{ij} . \tag{14}$$

It is readily checked that if we suppose $s_{ij} = 0$ for $i \neq j$, we return to White's equations (4) and (5).

The second equation of the model is the same as equation (6) of White's model:

$$m_{ij} = m_{(0)i} \cdot m_{(1)j} / M . \tag{15}$$

This equation states that the LC 1 people move according to the rule of perfect mobility. M is the total number of these people.

An equivalent assumption will be made for the LC 2 people:

$$s_{ij} = s_{(0)i} \cdot s_{(1)j} / S , \tag{16}$$

where S is the total number of LC 2 people. Thus, s_{ij}, the number of stayers moving from i to j, is the product of the number of stayers who come from i times the proportion of stayers who go to j. In other words, within the latent sub-population of stayers, the destination of the moves is supposed to be independent of their origin. The same is true for the movers.

Equations (15) and (16) reveal why it is impossible to keep the semantic interpretation of the two classes that was used in the previous models: these two sub-populations must behave symmetrically and thus are interchangeable.

Let us, as an illustration, consider the fictitious matrix reproduced in Table 2. Applying the present model to this matrix, we find the following values for the parameters:

$$m_{(0)1} = 1800 \quad m_{(0)2} = 3600 \quad m_{(0)3} = 300 \quad m_{(0)4} = 300$$

$$m_{(1)1} = 3600 \quad m_{(1)2} = 1800 \quad m_{(1)3} = 300 \quad m_{(1)4} = 300$$

$$m_{(0)1} = 200 \quad s_{(0)2} = 200 \quad s_{(0)3} = 1600 \quad s_{(0)4} = 2000$$

$$s_{(1)1} = 200 \quad s_{(1)2} = 200 \quad s_{(1)3} = 1600 \quad s_{(1)4} = 2000$$

$$M = 6000 \qquad S = 4000$$

The interpretation of this solution is that underlying the four manifest social categories, we have two latent classes. The first one (LC 1) is characterized by the fact that its members are likely to come from social categories 1 and 2 or to go to categories 1 and 2. They are much less likely to come from categories 3 and 4 or to go to these categories. Reciprocally, the LC 2 people circulate between social categories 3 and 4, with few of them coming from or going to social categories 1 and 2.

		Son's social category				
		1	2	3	4	Total
	1	1090	550	170	190	2000
Father's	2	2170	1090	260	280	3800
Social	3	260	170	655	815	1900
Category	4	280	190	815	1015	2300
Total		3800	2000	1900	2300	10000

Table 2. A FICTITIOUS INTERGENERATIONAL MOBILITY MATRIX

This example illustrates the kind of uses the type 3 model may have. It also shows that the semantic distinction between stayers and movers has to be dropped.

While this model is an extension of White's model, the introduction of the possibility of any of the subpopulations moving or staying changes the interpretation of these subpopulations. In Goodman's model, the observed mobility matrix is split into a sum of two components. The first component is a diagonal matrix, the elements of which are either the corresponding elements of the observed mobility matrix or zero (for the categories where no inheritance effect is postulated. The second component is the difference matrix between the observed matrix and this diagonal matrix.

In White's model, the observed matrix is again split into two components: the diagonal matrix of stayers and the
difference matrix corresponding to the movers.

Here, in the type 3 model, the observed matrix is again
a sum of two components, both being non-diagonal matrices
following the same rule as the second component of Goodman's
or White's model, i.e. perfect mobility. Thus, finally, the
rationale for this model is *to decompose the circulation system described by a mobility matrix into a sum of sub-systems
characterized by freedom of circulation,* in the sense that
according to the concept of perfect mobility, the arrival
category is independent of the departure category. Of
course, the sum of two perfect mobility matrices will not
generally be a perfect mobility matrix.

Thus, in some cases, the model will make it possible to
isolate subsets of occupational categories *within* which a
large amount of free circulation may be observed, while the
amount of free circulation *between* these subsets is limited.
These subsets will in this case represent much more meaningful stratification categories than the original occupational
categories. In fact, they will be a step towards the transformation of these rough occupational categories into the
more valid stratification categories to which the concept of
"social class" is often associated.

Of course, in some other cases, the application of the
model will not lead to this simple interpretation. More
complicated patterns may appear when we solve for the parameters: the subsystems characterized by a free circulation
may not lead to a clearcut partition of the occupational
categories into stratification categories. Only repeated
application of the model to mobility tables could show which
types of structures are likely to occur empirically.

6. EXTENSION OF THE MODEL TO g COMPONENTS

Since the semantic distinction stayers-movers has to be
abandoned, nothing prevents us from supposing that an
observed non-perfect mobility matrix may be decomposable into more than just 2 perfect mobility components. We may for
instance wish to reproduce an observed matrix as the sum of
3 perfect mobility matrices. In this case, we speak of a
three-components model.

Of course, the number of components which may be introduced is dependent on the number of social categories which
appear in the observed mobility matrix. Let us suppose for
instance that the number of latent components, 2 in the

previous exposition of the model, is now g. This situation will introduce $2\sigma - 1$ independent parameters for each component except one or, for the g components, $(2\sigma - 1)$ $(g - 1)$ independent parameters, giving the proportion of families going to and coming from the σ social categories in each latent component.

Then, the number of independent empirical quantities is equal to $(\sigma - 1)^2$. Thus, for the model to be determinate, g must be chosen small enough so that the inequality

$$(2\sigma - 1) \ (g - 1) \leqslant (\sigma - 1)^2 \Rightarrow g \leqslant \sigma^2/(2\sigma - 1) \qquad (17)$$

holds. With $\sigma = 4$ or 5, g cannot be greater than 2. With $\sigma = 6$, g cannot be greater than 3, etc... This means that if a mobility matrix with 6 social categories cannot be decomposed into a sum of $g = 2$ latent perfect mobility matrices, we may try $g = 3$.

7. SOLUTION OF THE MODEL

For an individual in social stratum i, the probability of moving to stratum j is given by r_{ij}, with σ possible strata to which he may go. Then, each row of a turnover matrix defines a multinomial distribution. With n_{ij} being the number going from i to j:

$$\frac{(\sum_j n_{ij})!}{\prod_j n_{ij}!} \ \prod_j r_{ij}^{n_{ij}} \qquad (18)$$

Since the rows are observed independently, the overall distribution of the matrix $\underset{\sim}{N} = [n_{ij}]$ is given by:

$$\varrho(r_{ij}) = \prod_i \frac{(\sum_j n_{ij})!}{\prod_j n_{ij}!} \ \prod_j r_{ij}^{n_{ij}} \qquad (19)$$

After observing the mobility matrix, $\underset{\sim}{N}$, the corresponding likelihood function is

$$L(\underset{\sim}{R}) = \prod_i \prod_j r_{ij}^{n_{ij}} \qquad (20)$$

Indeed, since the coefficient in (19) does not contain r_{ij}, it will disappear in the equations $\partial \log Q(r_{ij})/\partial r_{ij} = 0$ which give the maximum value of $Q(r_{ij})$.

The probability distribution (19) is relatively uninformative about the mechanism producing the observed mobility matrix. Thus, we introduce a mathematical model specifying some relationship among the parameters r_{ij}. The first assumption, which is used in the model considered, is that the number of positions available in the social strata to which the individuals go is fixed, i.e. the column totals of $\underset{\sim}{N}$ are fixed at the observed values.

When a mathematical model of any kind is introduced, each r_{ij} may be defined as a function g_{ij} of the parameters, $\underset{\sim}{m}$, of the model:

$$r_{ij} = g_{ij}(\underset{\sim}{m}) \qquad (21)$$

These values may then be substituted into the likelihood function (20). The maximum likelihood estimate of $\underset{\sim}{m}$ is that value which makes the probability of observing the given data greatest. Hence, we maximize the likelihood function. In order to do this, consider the log likelihood function.

$$\log L(\underset{\sim}{m}) = \sum_i \sum_j n_{ij} \log g_{ij}(\underset{\sim}{m}) \qquad (22)$$

which is a monotone function of L (i.e. will be maximum for the same $\underset{\sim}{m}$) and take partial derivatives with respect to each parameter of the vector $\underset{\sim}{m}$. Setting these derivatives equal to zero gives the likelihood equations which must be solved to obtain the maximum likelihood estimates.

Unfortunately, the model considered in this paper yields nonlinear likelihood equations which must be solved by some iterative procedure. One general technique is Newton's method. Let $a(m)$ be the vector of first derivatives of the log likelihood function (the likelihood equations with a given value of $\underset{\sim}{m}$), $A(\underset{\sim}{m})$ be the corresponding matrix of second derivatives, and $\underset{\sim 0}{m}$ some initial estimate of the parameters. Then successive estimates are given by

$$\underset{\sim i+1}{m}' = \underset{\sim i}{m}' - a'(\underset{\sim i}{m}) A^{-1}(\underset{\sim i}{m}) \qquad (23)$$

until some convergence criterion is fulfilled.
If there are constraints on some of the parameters of m, e.g.
$m_1 + m_2 + m_3 = k$, then additional parameters (Lagrange multipliers) are included in the estimation by adding terms of
the form $\lambda (m_1+m_2+m_3-k)$ to the log likelihood function (22)
and considering the Lagrange multiplier, λ, as an additional
parameter to be estimated. These additional parameters are
only used to insure that the constraints are fulfilled, and
may be ignored once the iterative process has converged to
the maximum likelihood estimates.

Let us for the sake of illustration take the case of an
over-time process with a turnover matrix $\underset{\sim}{N}_t = [n_{(t)ij}]$ from
time $t - 1$ to time t and the corresponding transition matrix
$\underset{\sim}{R}_t = [r_{(t)ij}] = \prod_t R_t$.

Let us now consider the maximum likelihood estimates of
$\underset{\sim}{R}_t$ for given t without introducing any further assumptions.
With the Lagrange multipliers, the log likelihood function
becomes

$$\sum_i [\sum_j n_{(t)ij} \log(r_{(t)ij}) + \lambda_i (\sum_j r_{(t)ij} -1)] . \quad (24)$$

Then the likelihood equations are

$$\frac{\partial}{\partial r_{(t)ij}} : \frac{n_{(t)ij}}{\hat{r}_{(t)ij}} + \hat{\lambda}_i = 0 \quad (i = 1..., \sigma ; j = 1,...\sigma)$$

$$(25)$$

$$\frac{\partial}{\partial \lambda_i} : \sum_j \hat{r}_{(t)ij} - 1 = 0 \quad (i = 1,...,\sigma) .$$

These equations are linear and may easily be solved to give
$\hat{r}_{(t)ij} = n_{(t)ij}/n_{(t)i}$. Then the maximized log likelihood
function is

$$\log L (\underset{\sim}{\hat{R}}_t) = \sum_i \sum_j n_{(t)ij} \log(n_{(t)ij}/\sum_k n_{(t)ik}) . \quad (26)$$

When a mathematical model is introduced, the maximum value of
the likelihood function attainable is less than that given by
equation (26). Thus this equation provides a standard with
which any model may be compared to determine how good is the

fit of the model. The measure of fit is given by the relative likelihood

$$\log R(\underset{\sim}{R}_t) = \Sigma \; \Sigma \; n_{(t)ij} \left[\log \underset{\sim}{R}_t - \log \; (n_{(t)ij} / \underset{k}{\Sigma} n_{(t)ik}) \right] .$$

(27)

with R_t given by equation (21).

We shall now go back to the type 3 model and consider it in the case where $g > 2$ since this adds no further complications to the case $g = 2$. From equation (15) and (16) the relationship among the r_{ij}'s is given by

$$r_{ij} = \underset{k}{\Sigma} \; \frac{m_{(0)i}^k \; m_{(1)j}^k}{M_k \; n_{(0)i}}$$

(28)

and the log likelihood function by

$$\log L(\underset{\sim}{m}_{(0)}, \underset{\sim}{m}_{(1)}, \underset{\sim}{M}) = \Sigma \; \Sigma \; n_{ij} \; \log \left[\underset{k}{\Sigma} \; \frac{m_{(0)i}^k \; m_{(1)j}^k}{M_k \; n_{(0)i}} \right]$$

(29)

with the following constraints

$$\underset{k}{\Sigma} \; M_{(0)i}^k = n_{(0)i} \quad ,$$

$$\underset{k}{\Sigma} \; m_{(1)j}^k = n_{(1)j} \quad ,$$

$$\underset{k}{\Sigma} \; m_{(0)i}^k = M_k = \underset{j}{\Sigma} \; m_{(1)j}^k \quad ,$$

$$\underset{k}{\Sigma} \; M_k = N \; .$$

Theoretically, all of the constraints may be substituted into the likelihood function but this complicates greatly the first and second derivatives required.

Thus some of the constraints will be substituted directly into the likelihood function while others will require Lagrange multipliers. Then the likelihood equations are

$$\frac{\sum_j n_{ij} \left(\frac{\hat{m}_{(1)j}^{\ell}}{\hat{M}_{\ell}} - \frac{\hat{m}_{(1)j}^{g}}{\hat{M}_{g}} \right)}{\sum_k \left(\frac{\hat{m}_{(0)i}^{k} \hat{m}_{(1)j}^{k}}{\hat{M}_{k}} \right)} + \hat{\beta}_{\ell} = 0 \qquad \begin{array}{l} i = 1, \ldots, \sigma; \\ \ell = 1, \ldots, (g-1) \end{array}$$

$$\sum_i \frac{n_{ij} \left(\frac{\hat{m}_{(0)i}^{\ell}}{\hat{M}_{\ell}} - \frac{\hat{m}_{(0)i}^{g}}{\hat{M}_{g}} \right)}{\sum_k \left(\frac{\hat{m}_{(0)i}^{k} \hat{m}_{(i)j}^{k}}{\hat{M}_{k}} \right)} -$$

$$- \sum_s \frac{n_{is} \left(\frac{\hat{m}_{(0)i}^{\ell} \hat{m}_{(1)s}^{\ell}}{\hat{M}_{\ell}^2} - \frac{\hat{m}_{(0)i}^{g} \hat{m}_{(1)s}^{g}}{\hat{M}_{g}^2} \right)}{\sum_k \left(\frac{\hat{m}_{(0)i}^{k} \hat{m}_{(1)s}^{k}}{\hat{M}_{k}} \right)} - \beta_{\ell} = 0$$

$$\begin{array}{l} j = 1, \ldots, \sigma \\ \ell = 1, \ldots, (g-1) \end{array} \qquad (30)$$

where
$$\hat{M}_{\ell} = \sum_j \hat{m}_{(i)j}^{k} \; ; \quad \hat{m}_{(0)i}^{g} = n_{(0)i} - \sum_{\ell=1}^{(g-1)} \hat{m}_{(0)j}^{\ell} \; ;$$

and $$\hat{m}_{(1)j}^{g} = n_{(1)j} - \sum_{i=1}^{(g-1)} \hat{m}_{(1)j}^{\ell}$$

$$\sum_i (\hat{m}_{(0)i}^{\ell} - \hat{m}_{(i)j}^{\ell}) = 0 \qquad \ell = 1, \ldots, (g-1)$$

with Lagrange multipliers $\underset{\sim}{\lambda}$, $\underset{\sim}{\gamma}$, and β. The $\hat{m}_{(0)}$ σ^k are given by the relationship $\hat{m}(0)$ $\sigma^k = \hat{\underset{\sim}{M}}_k - \sum_{i=1}^{g-1} \hat{m}_{(0)i}{}^k$. After solving these non-linear likelihood equations for the maximum likelihood estimates of $\underset{\sim}{m}_{(0)}$, $\underset{\sim}{m}_{(1)}$, and $\underset{\sim}{M}$, we use the same procedure as above to determine goodness of fit and for comparison with other models.

8. CONCLUSION

Our hope is that the present model could be useful in the analysis of intergenerational mobility tables and that it could contribute to solving the problem raised by the circle between stratification and mobility. However, much further theoretical research and empirical application is needed before a definitive evaluation of the model may be reached.

REFERENCES

Blumen, I., M. Kogan and P. J. McCarthy. 1955. "The Industrial Mobility of Labor as a Probability Process," *Cornell Studies in Industrial and Labor Relations*, VI, Ithaca, New York.

Blumen, I. 1966. "Probability Models for Mobility," in Lazarsfeld, P. and Henry, N.(eds.), *Readings in Mathematical Social Sciences*, Science Research Associates, Chicago, pp. 318-334.

Goodman, L. 1965. "On the Statistical Analysis of Mobility Tables," *American Journal of Sociology*, 70, pp. 564-585.

White, H. 1970. "Stayers and Movers," *American Journal of Sociology*, 76 (2), Sept., pp. 307-324.

19

Systems of Social Exchange[*]

JAMES S. COLEMAN
University of Chicago

In this chapter, I want to present a theoretical framework appropriate for behavior in informal groups, but with
extensions to more formalized structures of collective action. The basic structure will turn out to be equally appropriate for representing the structure of action in an
economic market of private goods, while the extensions involve action structures that violate the simplicity of private goods markets. I will first outline the conceptual
framework, then show its application to simple informal situations, and finally show its extension to structures that are
less simple, involving collective decisions and collective
action.

1. EVENTS, ACTORS, CONTROL, INTEREST

A useful point from which to initiate any examination of
behavior in informal groups is the idea of "power." Power is
a very ambiguous term in social organization, ambiguous in
several respects. First, it is sometimes used to refer to a
relation between two individuals ("A has power over B"), and
sometimes used to refer to a relation between an individual
and a certain activity ("A has power over activity X"). For
example, in the Encyclopedia of the Social Sciences, Dahl
defines power as a relation between individuals, while most
of the work on community power structures (by Hunter,

[*]
This chapter has been published in *Journal of Mathematical
Sociology,* Vol. 2, 1972, pp. 145-163, and is reprinted with
permission of the publisher.

Freeman, and others) implicitly or explicitly defines power
as a relation between an individual and an activity.

Second, power sometimes refers to a dimension or ordering created by transitivity of the power relation, so that if
A has power over B, he also has power over those persons C,
D, E, ..., which B has power over. In such a case, we could
speak of more and less power, and know that if A has more
power than B, he can always get his way in any struggle with
B. In other work, however, power is not treated as necessarily transitive, but is a private relation between A and
B that does not have any implication for the power of A over
any other person.

These confusions arise, I believe, from the absence of
an internally consistent conceptual framework within which
power is embedded. In the framework I will present, the
fundamental relation is a relation between individuals and
activities (or "events" as I shall usually call them), with
the result that power between individuals is a derivative
quantity. It will turn out to have the following properties:

1. In a system with perfect social exchange, power is
transitive, and also contains a metric, such that if the
power of A plus the power of C exceeds that of B, then A and
C can determine the outcome of the event if they both favor
one outcome, and B favors the other--assuming that A, B, and
C all have equal interests in the event's outcome.

2. In a system without perfect exchange, power is not
always transitive, the amount of intransitivity depending on
the imperfections in exchange. (Demonstrations of this must
be reserved to a later paper, for this chapter considers only
perfect exchange systems.)

3. When control over an event is divided, as a result
of the physical or constitutional constraints under which
action takes place, the outcome of the event depends not only
upon the power of the actors and their interests in the outcome, but also upon the particular decision rule that the
physical environment or constitution imposes.

These points give some idea of the kind of conceptual
system to be developed. I will outline it in more detail below. A complete exposition may be found in two publications
(Coleman, 1973, forthcoming).

We first consider a system of action composed of two
kinds of elements, actors and events. Actors have an acting
self and an object self, the acting self taking actions to
affect the outcomes of events, and the object of self being
affected by the outcomes of events. There are, then, two
properties linking actors and events: control of events by
actors (i.e., by the acting self), and consequences of events

for actors, or as I will describe it, interests of actors in events (i.e., consequences of events for the object self). There is, in addition, one behavioral postulate: each actor will act so as to best satisfy his interests, given his re- sources.

The simplest system of action to be considered is one in which the events have two properties that I will call *divisi- bility* and *internality*. A divisible event is one in which a fraction of control over the event represents full control of a fraction of the consequences; and an internal event is one in which exercise of control gives consequences only to that actor who exercises control, and no others. The best ex- amples of divisible and internal events are finely divisible private goods whose consumption creates no externalities for others. Fractions of control over a quantity of a private good can be realized through division of that quantity into appropriate fractions fully controlled by each actor. Con- sumption of that quantity of the good has consequences only for the consumer, if the good has no externalities. An event which is divisible but not internal is exemplified by what economists term a private good with consumption externali- ties. It can be divided into quantities (i.e., sub-events), with independent outcomes, but consumption of each of these quantities produces some consequences for persons other than the consumer. An event which is not divisible is an event which cannot be divided into sub-events with independent out- comes, but has a single outcome. A fraction of control can mean only a fraction of the power to determine the event's outcome (through voting or some other means). An example of an indivisible but internal event is a private good which cannot be divided, but whose use has consequences only for the user. A house or other large indivisible commodity is an example. Often, such indivisible goods are jointly owned, with rights of usage divided among the owners. In poor countries, an automobile may be owned by several persons; in all countries, many goods are in effect owned by a household consisting of several members, all of whom have rights of usage. Table 1 shows the types of events deriving from the two dimensions of divisibility and internality.

Although systems of action involving divisible and in- ternal events are exemplified by economic markets of private goods, there are also non-economic activities that fit these definitions. In a social group in which each person is in- terested in gaining the attention or time of particular others, each person's attention or time can be conceived as a divisible event to be distributed among other persons. So long as the group is not engaged in any collective action to

TABLE 1

Types of Events Distinguished by Divisibility
and Internality

Internal

	Yes	No
Yes	private goods or actions that affect no one else	events or actions with externalities
No	goods or events too large be individually controlled. collective decisions required	events requiring collective decisions

be participated in jointly by all or by some subset, but all activities involve pairwise interactions, then a system of divisible internal events can mirror this action.[1] Thus we can think of a model for divisible internal events as appropriate for a group in which there is interaction but no joint or common action, no joint or collective decisions which entail joint or collective action.

In a system with divisible internal events, there is one state of the system, one distribution of control over events, in which each actor has no reason for interaction with others, because his distribution of control over events is the one most satisfactory to him, given his resources. But if the system is in any state other than this, some actors will find that they can best realize their interests by exchanging control over one event for control over another.

Such a system of activities can be modelled by a linear systems with the following characteristics:

1. There are m events and n actors

2. The amount of initial control over event i by actor j is represented by c_{ij}, where $0 \leqslant c_{ij} \leqslant 1$, and $\sum_{j} c_{ij} = 1$. Since events are divisible, c_{ij} represents the fraction of i that actor j has full control over.

---

[1] A complication is produced when outcomes of the events are not independent. For example, if j spends time with k, this means that k must spend that same amount of time with j. For this chapter, I will ignore such complications.

3. Each actor has an interest in event i, x_{ji}, with the following properties:

a) $0 \leqslant x_{ji} \leqslant 1$

b) $\sum_{i} x_{ji} = 1$

c) x_{ji} represents the fraction of this resources that he allocates in a perfect exchange system toward control of event i, independent of the total size of his resources and independent of the cost of gaining control of event i. This independence of allocation from cost and resources represent two behavioral assumptions. They can also be expressed in economists' terms as assumptions that the price elasticity and resource (or income) elasticity for all events equal - 1 and 1 respectively.[2] In the appendix, these two properties (independence of cost and independence of total resources) are derived from the Weber-Fechner law, in conjunction with the behavioral postulate of maximization of satisfaction.

The quantities x_{ji} and c_{ij} are the fundamental properties relating actors and events.

If we let v_i be the value of full control over event i, and c^*_{ij} be the amount of control over event i that actor j controls at equilibrium, then $v_i c^*_{ij}$ is the amount of resources he must devote to event i to control the amount c^*_{ij}. If we let r_j be defined as the actor's total amount of resources, then according to (c) above, the amount of resources he devotes to i also equals $x_{ji} r_j$. Thus by definition of x_{ji}, we have in a perfect exchange system the equation

$$v_i c^*_{ij} = x_{ji} r_j , \tag{1}$$

---

[2] Price and income elasticities of -1 and 1 are ordinarily considered by economists to be the "normal" elasticities in private goods consumption, from which certain goods may deviate. They imply declining marginal utility of a good, or more particularly, that the marginal utility of a good is inversely proportional to the amount of the good already held.

where, following the two assumptions under (c) above, x_{ji} is a constant for actor j and event i, independent of r_j and v_i.

The derived quantities v_i and r_j can be defined in terms of the matrix of x_{ji}'s and the matrix of c_{ij}'s by summing eq. (1) over i and over j. First summing over i gives:

$$\sum_{i=1}^{m} v_i c^*_{ij} = r_j \sum_{i=1}^{m} x_{ji} ,$$

and since $\sum_i x_{ji} = 1$,

$$r_j = \sum_{i=1}^{m} v_i c^*_{ij} . \tag{2}$$

Because in a perfect exchange system the value of an actor's total resources does not change, r_j is also equal to the value of his initial control,

$$r_j = \sum_{i=1}^{m} v_i c_{ij} . \tag{3}$$

Summing eq. (1) over j gives

$$v_i \sum_{j=1}^{n} c^*_{ij} = \sum_{j=1}^{n} r_j x_{ji} ,$$

and since $\sum_j c^*_{ij} = 1$,

$$v_i = \sum_{j=1}^{n} r_j x_{ji} . \tag{4}$$

Equations (2) and (4) provide intuitively appealing defini-tions for the resources held by each actor and the value of each event in a system of perfect exchange. Stated in words, these definitions are, from eq. (2) and eq. (4):

The resources held by actor j consist of the sum
of the initial control he has over all events,
each event weighted by its value; and
The value of an event is the sum of interests in
the event, each actor's interests weighted by his

total resources.

These definitions constitute the framework of the simple system of divisible events. The initially given quantities are the matrix of control, C, with elements c_{ij}, and the matrix of interests X, with elements x_{ji}. From these may be calculated the value of each event, and the resources of each actor in a system of perfect exchange, through eq. (3) and eq. (4), and the final equilibrium control that will be held by each actor, through eq. (1). The solutions for resources and value may be found from joint use of eq. (3) and (4). Substituting for v_i in eq. (3) its value from eq. (4) gives

$$r_j = \sum_{i=1}^{m} \sum_{k=1}^{n} r_k x_{ki} c_{ij} . \qquad (5)$$

Solution of this set of simultaneous equations for $r_1, \ldots, r_n$ (using also the fact that $\sum_j r_j = 1$) allows calculation of resources. Similarly, substituting for r_j in eq. (4) its value from eq. (3) gives

$$v_i = \sum_{j=1}^{n} \sum_{k=1}^{m} v_k c_{kj} x_{ji} . \qquad (6)$$

Solution of this set of simultaneous equations, using the fact that $\sum_i v_i = 1$, allows calculation of values of events.

This framework, though it contains no elements of conflict (since events are divisible with internal consequences), begins to give an idea of the way power will be treated in this system. Power in this system is merely another name for what I have called resources. It is derived from control over events, and is a quantity with a metric, showing just how much of the value of the system is held by actor j. Like money in an economic system of private goods, it is not a relation between two actors, but something which can be used in exchange to increase satisfaction, subject to quantity that one begins with. It is not, however, limited to economic systems, as the example of its application in informal groups in the next section will show.

2. EXAMPLE OF APPLICABILITY TO INFORMAL GROUPS

Because data are ordinarily not collected in ways that allow the applicability of this theory to real group, the examples in this and other sections are hypothetical. Assume there are three people together in a ski resort. There are two men and one girl. One man knows how to ski, and the other two people have some interest in learning (which can only be from him). The man who does not ski has the most money, the girl has only half as much, and the skier only a sixth as much. The two men each have an interest in money equal to their interest in the girl's attention. She has an equal interest in attention from each of them, and an interest in money equal to her interest in attention from the men. The structure of interests and control is given by the following matrices:

Interest Matrix (X)
Events

Actors	1 Skier's atten-tion	2 Moneyed man's atten-tion	3 Girl's atten-tion	4 Money	5 Learn-ing to ski
Skier	O	O	.5	.5	O
Moneyed Man	O	O	.4	.4	.2
Girl	.2	.2	O	.4	.2

Control Matrix (C)

Actors

Events		1	2	3
	1	1	O	O
	2	O	1	O
	3	O	O	1
	4	.1	.6	.3
	5	1	O	O

These matrices of interest and control can be used, with eq. (5), to calculate the resources of the skier, the moneyed man, and the girl. Use of eq. (5) and $\Sigma\, r_j = 1$ gives

$$r_1 = .05r_1 + .34r_2 + .44r_3,$$

$$r_2 = .3 \ r_1 + .24r_2 + .44r_3,$$

$$r_3 = .65r_1 + .52r_2 + .124_3,$$

and $1 = r_1 + r_2 + r_3$.

Solutions are:

$$r_1 = .269, \ r_2 = .335, \ r_3 = .396$$

Thus the three persons have unequal resources in the situation with which to realize their interests. The skier has least, the girl has most, and the moneyed man is between the two. Use of eq. (4) and eq. (1) allow calculation of the distribution of control after exchange, at equilibrium:

		1	2	3
C* =	1	0	0	1
	2	0	0	1
	3	.5	.5	0
	4	.315	.315	.370
	5	0	.459	.541

The girl has all the attention of both men, the skier has half and the moneyed man half of the girl's attention, the skier now has 31.5% of the money and the girl somewhat more than she started with, and both the moneyed man and the girl get ski instruction, though the girl gets more.

This is a trivial example, but it illustrates how the conceptual framework operates to characterize a system of action in a group. If the moneyed man had had a greater proportion of the money at the start, he would have ended both with more of the girl's attention and with more of the ski instruction. If the girl and the moneyed man had had more interest in learning to ski, the skier would have gained both more of the girl's attention and more of the money; if the skier were uninterested in money, he would have had more of the girl's attention, and she more instruction; and so on for other variations.

3. EXTENSION TO SYSTEMS WITH INDIVISIBLE EVENTS

In a system of action with divisible events, a fraction of final control over event i by actor j, c^*_{ij}, is well-defined. It means full control of a fraction of the event or good. But with indivisible events, the quantity c^*_{ij} is not well-defined unless it is 0 or 1, or unless it has been given a definition by introduction of a decision rule. For example, if the decision rule is a majority rule with a coin flip when control is equally divided, then $c^*_{ij} > .5$ represents full control, while $c^*_{ij} < .5$ represents no control, and $c^*_{ij} = 0.5$ represents full control with probability 1/2 and no control with probability 1/2.

In addition to the problem of divided control that is posed by indivisible events, there is also the question of what is meant by "interest" when there is no continuously-divisible quantity. For with an indivisible event, interest cannot be expressed in terms of the increment of satisfaction per increment of control. If it is a good, and truly indivisible, one experiences (or consumes) it either completely or not at all. If it is some more general state of the world, it either comes to pass or does not. Thus with truly indivisible events, we can think of only two outcomes, each giving some level of satisfaction or utility. It is possible, with such events, to design a procedure which could assign quantitative measures to these utility levels, which are specified up to an arbitrary scale coefficient and an arbitrary zero point.[3] The utility diference between outcomes is then specified up to a scale constant (since the constants for the zero point cancel). This arbitrary constant is specified by the criterion that $\sum_i x_{ji} = 1$. Thus it

---

[3] One procedure for doing this has been described by Von Neumann and Morgenstern (1947). This procedure involves choice between risky situations involving event outcomes, and involves the assumption that subjectively perceived probabilities correspond to objective probabilities. Another procedure, involving partial control of the event through vote trading in a collective decision, is described in the Appendix. It is the latter procedure that should be taken as defining interests in the present model, because the procedure involves observation of behavior that is intrinsic to the theory--an important criterion in arriving at measures of concepts in a theory.

is possible to think of the interests in indivisible events as the *relative utility differences* between the positive and negative outcomes of an event. Mathematically, if u^+_{ji} and u^-_{ji} are respectively the utilities of positive and negative outcomes of event i to actor j, then

$$x_{ji} = \frac{|u^+_{ji} - u^-_{ji}|}{\sum\limits_{k=1}^{m} |u^+_{jk} - u^-_{jk}|} . \tag{7}$$

As indicated above, any other measures of utility w_{ji} which are related to u_{ji} such that $w_{ji} = a+bu_{ji}$ are valid. This can be seen by substituting $a+bu_{ji}$ for u_{ji} in eq. (7), giving an equation which reduces back to eq. (1). (For another reason, which can be seen from discussion in the appendix, the sign of b must be positive.)

Thus interest must be defined differently for indivisible events, since they cannot be experienced or consumed in partial quantities. The definition of interest, however, as relative utility difference between positive and negative outcomes, is both compatible with the definition for divisible events and inutitively appealing.

It appears reasonable to apply the theory to indivisible internal events, for certain circumstances in which there is no conflict over the desired outcome. Examples of this are as indicated earlier, private goods that cannot be finely divided, such as a country club, or a pleasure boat. The fineness of division necessary is relative to the resources of the actors; a good example is automobiles, which are indivisible, but individually owned in rich countries, while they are often jointly owned because of their indivisibility in poor countries.

The formal analysis for indivisible internal events is like that for divisible ones, up to a certain point. But once the analysis is carried out, showing the final control, then further questions arise, if the matrix of final control shows divided control of indivisible events. For example, in the ski resort example, suppose a constraint existed, that ski instruction must be given to the two learners together, rather than individually. Then the matter becomes more complicated, because any of several conditions might exist. First, the ski instruction may have the nonconservative property of a public good, so that the total possible amount of instruction available now is twice what it was before, with the constraint that either learner can come to control a maximum of 1. That would imply one kind of analysis, in which ski instruction is split into two events which are tied together, in the sense that control of them either passes to the two learners or remains in the hands of the skier. If control does pass to the two learners, then there arises the problem between them of how costs are allocated between them. This is the usual problem of paying the cost of a public good, which arises quite generally with indivisible events. If the instruction does not have this nonconservative property, but the consumption remains tied together and must be equal, then the final control cannot vary between the two learners, as in the preceding example, but must be divided 0.5 and 0.5. Some indivisible events have this property, while others do not. As an example of indivisible events that do not have fixed ratios of final control, joint purchase of a yacht by two persons may be through unequal shares, leading to unequal rights of usage by the two persons. In this case of variable rights of usage, the mathematical analysis remains the same as the simple divisible internal event analysis, so long as all the person who, in the analysis, end up with some final control are able to divide usage according to their degree of control. This requires some organization (which the model assumes), but does not involve the problem of paying the cost of a public good, since each actor gives up resources in proportion to his rights of usage.

For the other variations discussed above, however, the present mathematical system is not sufficient, and it will be necessary in future work to introduce appropriate modifications to allow these variations to be mirrored.

There are other kinds of situations in informal groups in which events may be thought of as indivisible, but in which the question of final control does not arise, allowing them to be studied as if they were divisible events. When all actors favor the same outcomes for all events, then the question of what a fraction of control represents behaviorally need not be resolved in order to calculate the power of each actor and the value of each event. This can be illustrated by use of an example.

Suppose in a group each member is asked his interest in each other member's participation in the group. Although participation vs. nonparticipation is an indivisible event, interests could be elicited from group members as if it were divisible: "Suppose you knew that altogether there would be 100 hours of the presence of all other members of the group in the next 100 hours of its activities. If you had your preference, what would be the distribution of amounts of time present among the other members, summing to 100 hours altogether?"

Such a question posed to all members would give data that could be directly interpreted as an interest matrix. Since initially each person has control of his own presence, the control matrix C would have 1's in the main diagonal and zeros elsewhere. If actor 1 were quite popular with some of the group members, and 2 with others, interest and control matrices for a group of 5 members might look like this, where event i is the presence of actor i in the group.

	Events							Actors				
X	1	2	3	4	5		C	1	2	3	4	5
1	0	.25	.25	.25	.25		1	1	0	0	0	0
Actors 2	.4	0	.2	.1	.3	Events	2	0	1	0	0	0
3	.5	0	0	.2	.3		3	0	0	1	0	0
4	.3	.6	.1	0	0		4	0	0	0	1	0
5	.3	.7	0	0	0		5	0	0	0	0	1

Calculation of the power of each actor in this group would show power as follows:

$$R = .273, .276, .136, .123, .192$$

Value of events 1-5 has the same distribution as power of actors.

Thus the power of members 1 and 2 is about equal, the power of 3 and 4 is about equal, and the power of 5 is intermediate between these two levels. This means that 1 and 2 could get their ways more often than 3 or 4, using the threat of nonparticipation. It means that if there were a formal constitution to the group and votes were allocated among the members, then the distribution of votes that would preserve the interests of each in the others' participation is a distribution which gives actor 1 a power of .273 of the whole, and so on for the others. (This is not the same as .273 of the total votes, because the discontinuous character of most voting rules makes power nonlinearly related to number of votes. However, if the voting rule were probabilistic, with a chance mechanism giving a positive outcome with probability equal to the proportion of votes cast in favor, then power to control the outcome is equal to the proportion of votes held.)

This example suggests a rational basis for the allocation of power to group members in establishing a constitution. The power that each member has, in a constitution created in this way, is merely the embedded interests of all
other members in his participation in the group. Thus his
withdrawal from the group would reduce the others' interests
in the group by that amount. Giving him the power indicated
is giving power toward the direct satisfaction of his interests in future activities, but also toward the indirect
satisfaction of others' interests.

4. DIVISIBLE EVENTS WITH EXTERNALITIES

There are some divisible events which nevertheless retain, even after having been divided, interest of more than
one actor in events controlled by that actor. Private goods
that exhibit externalities exemplify this kind of event. Use
of water from a stream by an upstream actor, a town, a firm,
or a family, changes the quality of the water for the downstream user. The situation can be mirrored by a very simple
application of the theory, which is like that for divisible
internal events except that now each actor's use or consumption of a good must be designated as a distinct event. This
means that divisible events, such as private goods, are re-
defined in such a way that they become indivisible events, by
being broken down into each actor's consumption or use. In
this example, there are two actors and three events:

    Actor 1: The upstream water user
    Actor 2: The downstream water user
    Event 1: Use of water by the upstream user
    Event 2: Use of water by the downstream user
    Event 3: A generalized resource (money) divided in some
              ratio between them

The upstream user has control over his water use and
some fraction of the total money; the downstream user has
control over his water use and some fraction of the total
money. The upstream user has interest only in his water use
and in money; the downstream user has interests opposed to
the upstream user's water use, and interests in his own use
and in money. Interest and control matrices might be:

	X	Actor 1's use	Actor 2's use	Money
Upstream user	1	.5	O	.5
Downstream user	2	(-).2	.3	.5

C	Upstream user	Downstream user
Actor 1's use	1	O
Actor 2's use	O	1
Money	.3	.7

The negative sign in parentheses indicates that outcome 2 of event 1 (non-use of water by actor 1) is the outcome desired by actor 2. (Formally, this could be introduced by a third matrix S with +1, -1, and O, showing the sign of the directed interest of each actor in each event. In this case, the S matrix has a -1 only in s_{21}.)

The question in cases like this is what will happen: will the upstream user continue to pollute, or will the downstream user be able to induce him to stop his use? Note that in this application of the model, there is no mechanism other than use of the generalized resource, money, by which the downstream user can induce the upstream user to stop. If a political process had been included in the model, then depending on actor 2's control over other political events in which 1 was interested, he might be able to gain passage of a bill to prevent actor 1 from polluting. The general means by which this would be done would be political exchange, mirrored by this theory in much the same way as here, except with an expanded set of events and actors.

The application of the model in this case is somewhat different than for events with no externalities. Since we want to see whether the action will be carried out, we consider two sets of event outcomes, two possible "regimes": +++ and -++. It is only these outcomes which are desired, the first set more desired by actor 1 and the second set more desired by actor 2. The model is applied twice, first by excluding the interests of actor 2 opposed to 1's water use, and then by excluding the interests of actor 1 favoring his water use. Then it is possible to see whether actor 1's power (under the first regime) that he is willing to devote to his water use (as measured by x_{11} times his power) is greater than actor 2's power (under the second regime) that he is willing to devote to opposing 1's water use (measured by x_{21} times his power). Calculations are as follows:

Regime A: Outcome +++

The interest matrix is revised so that the second row is 0, .375, .625.
The equation $R_a = R_a X_a C$ gives:

$$r_{1a} = .65r_{1a} + .1875r_{2a}$$

$$r_{2a} = .35r_{1a} + .8125r_{2a}$$

Solving gives $r_{1a} = .35$, $r_{2a} = .65$

The ability of actor 1 to implement this outcome is $r_{1a}x_{11}$, or .35(.5) = .175.

Regime B: Outcome -++

The interest matrix is revised so that the first row is 0 0 1; the second row is as in X.

The equation $R_b = R_b X_b C$ gives:

$$r_{1b} = .3r_{1b} + .35r_{2b}$$

$$r_{2b} = .7r_{1b} + .65r_{2b}$$

Solving gives $r_{1b} = .333$, $r_{2b} = .667$.

The ability of actor 2 to implement this outcome is $r_{2b}x_{21}$, or .667(.2) = .133.

Comparison of $r_{1a}x_{11}$ with $r_{2b}x_{21}$ shows that the former is larger, so that outcome +++ can be successfully implemented by actor 1, in opposition to outcome -++. Thus the

pollution will continue, with actor 2's resources not quite
great enough to overcome the greater interest that actor 1
has in his use of the water than actor 2 has in its being
stopped. Thus the correct interest matrix to use for assessing final control is the one in which the downstream user's
interests opposed to the upstream user are deleted. He cannot gain control of that event, and thus must allocate his
resources elsewhere. The matrix is

$$.5 \qquad 0 \qquad .5$$

$$0 \qquad .375 \qquad .625$$

If actor 2's proportion of the generalized resource were
even greater than it is here, he could have enough power to
successfully oppose actor 1, paying him to stop polluting the
water--and paying a price high enough that actor 1 would find
it to his interest to stop. In that case, the appropriate
interest matrix to use would be

$$0 \qquad 0 \qquad 1$$

$$.2 \qquad .3 \qquad .5$$

and since the upstream user began with control over the e-
vent, the downstream user's interests would be realized only
through purchasing that control by use of event 3, his generalized resource. In that case, actor 1 would end up with .5
of the money, rather than .3, in return for his loss of control of his water usage.

In informal groups, there are many types of divisible
events with externalities. Some of these may be treated by
the above kind of analysis; others require some modification
of this analysis. One such modification involves conflict
processes, as discussed below.

5. CONFLICT

All the analysis to this point has assumed that one or
the other interest in the event with externalities will be
pursued, and the other interest will be withdrawn by the
actors who hold it, in return for compensation if they initially hold the rights to the action. Such withdrawal in
the presence of an opposition that can mobilize more powerful
resources is a rational action, while expenditure of resources that are either less than those of the opponent, or
that are excessive, constituting a diversion of resources

from other events that would bring greater gain, is not rational. That is, if for actor 2, $r_{2b}x_{21}$ is less than

$\sum\limits_{j=2}^{n} r_{1a}x_{11}$, it is not rational to expend resources $r_{2b}x_{21}$ on the event, because his opponent will spend more, and win. Neither is it rational to spend more than $r_{2b}x_{21}$, say enough to exceed $\Sigma r_{1a}x_{11}$, because the extra resources spent in that way will bring less satisfaction, even if they are sufficient to gain control of the event, than if they are employed to gain control of other events in proportion to his interests.

However, it may well be that $r_{1a}x_{11}$ and $\Sigma r_{2b}x_{21}$ are close enough that both sides estimate that they will be able to gain control of event 1. If control is gained merely through a market process in which the losing side can recover his offered resources, then the system will operate as described earlier, and those resources will be deployed in alternative ways. But if employment of these resources constitutes a struggle for control over the event, as is often the case in noneconomic transactions in society, the resources, or some large part of them, are lost and constitute a waste. We can, in effect, specify three levels of social functioning in a system where $v_{1a} > v_{1b}$. The first level is for the action to take place without employment of any opposing resources by the aggrieved parties--who would be compensated if they initially held rights to the action, but in all cases would use the resources $\Sigma r_{2b}x_{21}$ in other ways. The second level is for the action *not* to take place, and for actor 1 to employ the resources that he would have used for event 1, that is resources $r_{1a}x_{11}$, in other ways. In this case, the magnitude of the loss is a function of $v_{1a} - v_{1b}$ (or $r_{1a}x_{11} - \Sigma r_{2b}x_{21}$), for it is this extra amount of resources that is being redirected to events that produce lesser utility.

The third level of social functioning occurs when *both* sides employ their resources for control of the event, in a struggle for control in which the resources of the losing side are used up in the struggle. In this case, the loss is not merely the deployment of resources on events that bring lesser utility, as in the second level of functioning; it is a total loss of the resources.

546

The resources lost in this case cannot be calculated under regime a or regime b, because both of those regimes assume a redeployment of resources of the losing side, to give a set of values v_{ai} or v_{bi} for events i which sum to 1.0, the total set of resources in the system. What is necessary is to assume a regime c, in which the event with externalities is represented by *two* events, one in which a positive outcome is carrying out the offending action, and the other in which a positive outcome is not carrying out the offending action. Each of these events is fully controlled by each of two new hypothetical actors, actor n+1 for event 1, and actor n+2 for event k. These actors have exactly the same interest distribution as the real actor that initially controls action i; but one of these actors, whose event is of lower value, will withdraw his resources from the system, representing a resource loss. The other, whose event is of higher value, will combine his resources with the real actor who initially controls rights to event i, to give his final power.

The winning side is actor 1 if $v_{ic} > v_{kc}$, and actor 2 if $v_{ic} < v_{kc}$. This will ordinarily, but necessarily, be the same side that will win when there is non-destructive use of resources to gain control of the event, as in regime a or regime b. The lack of complete correspondence arises because under this different resource deployment, other events will have different values, and thus those who control them different resources.

The functioning of such a system in which there is a struggle for control with destruction of the resources of the losing side can be illustrated by use of the earlier example, under which regimes a and b were compared.

6. EXAMPLE WITH CONFLICT: REGIME C

In this example, the interest and control matrices are like those in the preceding example, except that event 1 (actor 1's use of water) becomes two events, 1 and 4. In addition, there are now two hypothetical actors, 3 and 4, whose interest distribution is identical to that of actor 1, and who control respectively events 1 and 4. The revised interest and control matrices are:

X	E_1	E_2	E_3	E_4
A_1	.5	0	.5	0
A_2	0	.3	.5	.2
A_3	.5	0	.5	0
A_4	.5	0	.5	0

Actors (left table), Events (right table)

C	A_1	A_2	A_3	A_4
E_1	0	0	1	0
E_2	1	0	0	0
E_3	.3	.7	0	0
E_4	0	0	0	1

Calculation of resources of the five actors, using eq. (5), gives

$$r_{1c} = .15 \qquad r_{3c} = .25$$

$$r_{2c} = .5 \qquad r_{4c} = .1$$

Resources devoted to event 1 by actor 1 (which includes resources of hypothetical actors 3 and 4) and to event 4 by actor 2 are:

$$v_{1c} = (r_{1c} + r_{3c} + r_{4c})x_{11} = .5(.5) = .25$$

$$v_{4c} = r_{2c}x_{21} = .5(.2) = .10$$

Since $v_{1c} > v_{4c}$, event 1 has a positive outcome (the upstream user uses the water), and event 4, which is logically incompatible with it (non-use of the water) has a negative outcome. This means that resources of value .10 are lost through conflict between actors 1 and 2. Hypothetical actor 4 withdraws his resources from the system, and the power of actor 1 is augmented by that of actor 3, whose resources remain in. Thus the power of actor 1 is $r_{1c} + r_{3c}$, or .40.

The total power in the system is now .40, .50, summing to .90 rather than 1.00; and the total value in the system is identical. The greater power of actor 1 derives from his control of events 1 and 4 (through hypothetical actors 3 and 4), which have, in this case, more interest concentrated on them than in the case where one side invested no resources in the event.

It is not in fact necessary to introduce explicitly the two new actors into the system, for they behave just like the actor who initially controls the event. They serve merely as a conceptually clarifying device, showing how resources are subtracted from the system, being withdrawn both from the value of events and from the power held by the actor who controls the event in question.

The introduction of conflict over divisible events with externalities is the opening wedge of a much broader investigation of collective decisions and conflict, involving many actors on both sides and many issues. This section has given an indication of how some aspects of such conflicts may be treated within the present framework of ideas. But this broader examination of conflict must be deferred to a subsequent work. Here the principal point is that when there are events with external effects opposite to the effects of the event for the actor himself, two kinds of social processes might occur: market valuation of the two outcomes of the event, with only one side devoting resources to gaining or keeping control of the event; or conflict, in which both sides devote resources to the event, and those of the losing side are wasted resources. In the latter case, the level of social efficiency of the system is below that in which the same side won, but with a redeployment of the potentially opposing resources by the losing side.

7. EXTENSIONS

Extension to collective decisions, with or without explicit decision rules, is possible, and some work has been carried out on those extensions, without, however, solving certain of the central problems. An initial statement is found in Coleman (1964, 1966), and further work is reported in Coleman (1973). Other extensions, in particular to imperfect exchange processes, have not been carried out. Work in both these directions is important to further development of the theory.

REFERENCES

Coleman, James S. 1964. "Collective Decisions," *Sociological Inquiry*, Spring, 166-181.

Coleman, James S. 1966. "Foundations for a Theory of Collective Decisions," *American Journal of Sociology*, 71, (May).

Coleman, James S. 1973. *Mathematics of Collective Action*. (London: Heinemann).

Coleman, James S. *A General Theory of Action* (tentative title, forthcoming).

Von Neumann, J., and O. Morgenstern. 1947. *The Theory of Games and Economic Behavior*. Princeton: Princeton University Press, 2nd edition.

APPENDIX

A.1 INTEREST IN DIVISIBLE EVENTS

In a system of action involving divisible events, it was assumed that the fraction of an actor's total resources allocated to gaining control of event i was independent of the cost of control of event i and independent of the actor's total resources. This can be derived from the Weber-Fechner law in conjunction with the behavioral postulate that the actor will act so as to maximize his satisfaction given his resources.

The Weber-Fechner law states that the increment of subjective state experienced by a given increment of objective stimulus is inversely proportional to the existing level of the objective stimulus. If the subjective state is taken as actor j's satisfaction with event i, denoted by s_{ij}, and the existing level of the objective stimulus is taken as the amount of i over which he has control, c_{ij}, then the Weber-Fechner law states that

$$\frac{\Delta s_{ij}}{\Delta c_{ij}} = k_{ji} \frac{1}{c_{ij}} . \tag{A.1}$$

where k_{ij} is a nonnegative constant for actor j associated with event i showing the amount of satisfaction derived from a 100% increase in the amount of event i controlled. The amount of resources required to gain an increment of control Δc_{ij} over event i is that increment times the value of i in the system, v_i, or $v_i \Delta c_{ij}$. Thus the increment of satisfaction per increment of resources expended is $\Delta s_{ij}/(v_i \Delta c_{ij})$, or

$$\frac{\Delta s_{ij}}{v_i \Delta c_{ij}} = \frac{k_{ji}}{v_i c_{ij}} . \tag{A.2}$$

The behavioral postulate of maximization of satisfaction given resources implies that the individual will gain control of each event to the point that the marginal satisfaction from expenditures of a given amount of resources is equal for all, or

$$\frac{\Delta s_{ij}}{v_i \Delta c_{ij}} = \frac{\Delta s_{hj}}{v_h \Delta c_{hj}} \quad \text{for all events } i, h. \quad (A.3)$$

Thus for all i and h, he will gain control of events i and h to the point that the final or equilibrium control, c^*_{ij}, which he has over each event is such that the following equation holds for all events i and h:

$$\frac{k_{ji}}{v_i c^*_{ij}} = \frac{k_{jh}}{V_h c^*_{hj}} \quad . \quad (A.4)$$

Expressed in terms of c^*_{ij}, this becomes

$$c^*_{ij} = \frac{k_{ji}}{v_i} \frac{v_h c^*_{hj}}{k_{jh}} , \quad (A.5)$$

where h is any other event in the system.

Since the quantity $v_h c^*_{hj}/k_{jh}$ is independent of event h, it may be replaced by a single constant for actor j, K_j, so that eq. (A.5) becomes

$$c^*_{ij} = \frac{k_{ji}}{v_i} K_j \quad (A.6)$$

Eq. (A.6) gives the proportion of control over event i that actor j will control after exchange. It is necessary now to show that this fraction of control, c^*_{ij}, is such that the fraction of his total resources allocated to i is independent of the unit cost of i, v_i, and of his total resources, r_j. Multiplying eq. (A.6) through by v_i gives the amount of resources, $v_i c^*_{ij}$, devoted to event i, and summing over all events gives his total resources:

$$\sum_{i=1}^{m} v_i c^*_{ij} = K_j \sum_{i=1}^{m} k_{ji} . \qquad (A.7)$$

The quantity on the left of the equation is equal to his total resources r_j, so that if we impose a scale on k_{ji} such that $\sum_{i=1}^{m} k_{ji} = 1$ (which eq. (A.1) shows can be done without loss of generality, since the scale on s_{ij} is arbitrary), then $K_j = r_j$. This also means that k_{ji} represents a fraction of resources devoted to event i, as is evident by multiplying eq. (A.6) through by v_i and substituting r_j for K_j:

$$v_i c^*_{ij} = k_{ji} r_j . \qquad (A.8)$$

As eq. (A.8) shows, since k_{ji} is a constant, independent of v_i or r_j, this means that the fraction of resources devoted to event i is independent of the cost or price, v_i, and of the total amount of resources held, r_j. Thus k_{ji}, when scaled so that $\sum_i k_{ji} = 1$, has all the properties attributed in the text to x_{ji}, j's interest in event i. Thus $x_{ji} = k_{ji}$, and its fundamental definition can be regarded as given by eq. (A.1) together with the definition of scale,

$$\sum_i x_{ji} = 1.$$

A.2. INTEREST IN INDIVISIBLE EVENTS

Interest in indivisible events cannot be assessed in the same way as divisible events. The indivisibility makes impossible a quantitative division of consequences through a division of control, and thus impossible a quantitative measure of the subjective impact of those consequences, such as shown in eq. (A.1). Thus it is necessary to attach discrete levels of satisfaction or utility to their discrete outcomes. If their outcomes are described as a positive outcome and a negative outcome, then we may think of two utility levels, or for the event a utility difference between positive and negative outcomes.

Although I have described "utility differences" as if a number can be associated with such a difference, the possibility of doing so depends on the existence of a measurement procedure to do so, which allows assignment of a unique number, or a number unique within a certain set of transformation, to the utility difference. The measurement procedure, to be valid for the theory at hand, must contain operations that are intrinsic to the theory itself, not imported from outside. There are two questions in such measurement: first, is it possible within the framework of the theory (or equivalently, does it have operational meaning within the theory) to specify a set of operations that will give a particular level of measurement? And, second, does the empirical use of these operations result in measurement which in fact has the properties of numbers specified in the level of measurement? Only the first is at question here; the second depends upon empirical examination.

Three levels of measurement, corresponding to three conditions that can exist in the theory, will be examined. These imply, for their verification, increasingly strong assumptions about behavior. The quantity being measured is the *directed interest* of actor j in event i, which will be denoted y_{ji}. This is intended to be actor j's interest in seeing outcome 1 occur rather than outcome 2. It may be thought of as deriving from the difference in utilities between positive and negative outcomes, but need not be.

We assume that actors act so as to maximize, subject to their initial resources, their realized interest, where interest is realized through attaining the outcome in which the actor has a positive interest (or equivalently, the outcome for which his utility is greater).

Level 1: Sign of y_{ji}

Assume a set of actors indexed j = 1,...,n, and a set of events indexed i = 1,...,m. An actor's behavior is constrained to that of casting a vote, when he does not know the votes of other actors. A vote for a given outcome has a normal meaning, i.e., an outcome will be achieved if the proportion of votes favoring it exceeds a certain minimum, or the probability of that outcome is increased as the proportion of votes for it increases.

If the events are separable, i.e., independent in their consequences, then the actor may consider each event separately.

The first level of measurement is achieved by giving y_{ji}

a number with a sign depending on whether he voted for a positive outcome, a negative one, or did not vote. Rational behavior dictates that he vote for that outcome which he prefers (i.e., in which he has positive interest or for which he has higher utility), because given lack of knowledge of others' votes, his subjective probability of achieving an outcome is increased by voting for it. The result of this level of measurement is assignment of positive or negative numbers or zero to y_{ji} (which may be +1, -1, 0, without loss of information, since any positive or negative numbers are equally valid).

Validation of this level of measurement occurs if there is consistency in his voting, independent of the order of events or other variations. The principal source of non-validation would probably be non-separability of events.

Level 2: Order relation among the absolute values of y_{ji}

The assumptions of level 1 measurement are continued here, but one constraint on behavior is removed. Actors are free to give up a vote on any event in exchange for a single vote on another event. The second level of measurement is achieved by assigning numbers to $|y_{ji}|$ such that $|y_{ji}| > |y_{jk}|$ if and only if the actor is willing to give up a vote on event k in return for a vote on event i, and $|y_{ji}| = |y_{jk}|$ if he is not willing to make a trade in either direction. His absence of knowledge about others' vote intentions makes his estimate of the probability that an additional vote will change the outcome the same for all events. Thus his implicit comparison in the trade is a loss of expected utility due to giving up a vote on k, $\Delta p_k |y_{jk}|$, where Δp_k is the subjective probability that this vote will change the outcome of k in the non-desired direction, versus a gain in expected utility due to gaining a vote on i, $\Delta p_i |y_{ji}|$, where Δp_i is the probability that this vote will change the outcome of i in the desired direction. Since nothing is known about others' votes, $\Delta p_k = \Delta p_i$, and the expected utility of the trade is positive if and only if $|y_{ji}| > |y_{jk}|$.

Validation of this level of measurement occurs if there is consistency in his exchanges, so that there are some numbers that can be assigned such that the relation " > " has the properties of an order relation, including transitivity.[4]

Level 3: A metric on y_{ji}

    The assumptions of level 2 measurement are continued here, but another constraint on behavior is removed. Actors are free to give up any number of votes on one or more events in exchange for any number of votes on one or more other events. This provides a "combination" operation analogous to that in classical physical measurement of combining weights, assigning numbers to $\left|y_{ji}\right|$, $\left|y_{jk}\right|$, and $\left|y_{jh}\right|$ such that the properties of addition are preserved. For example, he will give up one vote on h for one on k and one on i if and only if $\left|y_{ji}\right| + \left|y_{jk}\right| > \left|y_{jh}\right|$. It is assumed that his control of any event is so small that even with the proposed exchanges, the probability of an outcome change due to gain or loss of a vote is the same for all events.

    Validation of this level of measurement occurs if the actor's behavior in agreeing to combined exchanges is like that for simple one-vote exchanges, but with $\Delta p_i \left|y_{ji}\right| + \Delta p_k \left|y_{jk}\right|$ replacing $\Delta p_i \left|y_{ji}\right|$ in expected utility calculations when votes on i and k are offered together. This is in effect a validation that the combination operation in behavior (votes on two or more events) has the same properties as addition.

    The metric resulting from the above operation will be unique up to a positive scale constant. That is, there is nothing in observed behavior to distinguish between measures that have different (positive) scale constants. Thus an arbitrary positive scale constant can be applied, such that, over all events in a given system, $\sum_i \left|y_{ji}\right| = 1.0$. With this scaling, $\left|y_{ji}\right|$ can be thought of as relative utility differences between positive and negative outcomes. They have the properties of interest in indivisible events as described in the text and denoted by x_{ji}. Thus y_{ji} is a directed interest, with a sign depending upon the more desired outcome (and deriving from level one of measurement) and an absolute value

---

[4]The niceties of measurement, involving for example the possibilities of intransitivity due to the cumulation of small differences, will not be treated here. These are the same as in any calibration with an insensitive instrument in physical sciences.

equal to x_{ji}, which is nonnegative, and is the size of his relative interest in event i.

20

The Conceptual Representation of Choice Behavior and Social Interaction

KULLERVO RAINIO
Helsinki University

1. INTRODUCTION

In the behavioral sciences the gap between those who try
to use generally solvable mathematical models in describing
the problems and those who try somehow to understand behavioral processes by simulating them--using some exact
rules, usually computer programs--is getting wider and wider.
It is easy to criticize the "model-makers" for the lack of
any large application field for their constructs and for the
oversimplifications they have made in order to get the mathematical problem solvable in practical terms, oversimplifications which often raise the question whether there are any
interesting applications at all from the point of view of the
serious researcher in the special science concerned. The
enthusiasm for the models has been primarily based, I suppose, on their mathematical beauty. The simulation hobby is
usually as easy to criticize, although from a different point
of view. If one has tried to make the picture realistic, one
has troubles with too many parameters, the values of which
are impossible to estimate exactly. If the simulation gives
results which do not significantly differ from the empirical
data, the question arises whether it could happen as well
with a quite different set of parameter values or perhaps
also if some structural feature in the simulation model were
changed. If the simulation does not succeed, we do not know
whether this is a consequence of a wrong set of parameter
values or of a mistake in constructing the simulation model
itself. Very often it is as difficult to understand the
simulation process as the process simulated.

In the case of both mathematical models and simulation
programs the most essential criticism is, however, based on
the question, how our work organizes our scientific knowledge
and to what extent it generates new research. Organizing
knowledge is primarily the same as seeing old facts in a new
light, seeing new connections--or at least possibilities for
new connections. From this point of view, we need, particularly in the study of behavior, a coherent and exact system
of concepts, a formalized language abstract enough to throw
such a "new light," to show the connections between phenomena
which now seem to be isolated from each other in a way that
each of them is "explained" by a particular "model" of its
own.

This study is an attempt to show one possible way of
constructing a theory in social psychology based on as few
concepts and as few assumptions as possible, while still trying to cover equally the different problem areas. One must
make a tremendous number of risky decisions between different alternatives in forming such a system on this level of
knowledge. Many of them may be wrong. However, for getting
through the labyrinth, somebody must take the ungrateful
role of the first rat. In our situation, it might even be
enough to show that there is a labyrinth.

There are, indeed, intelligent analyses of social interaction done by, e.g., Heider, Thibaut and Kelley, and
Homans. One should never undervalue them. However, these
attempts are not strictly formalized. They create ideas,
give new insights in observing phenomena, but they cannot
combine together the results of different pieces of research in as deep a sense as a strictly formalized theory
does, as for example in physics.

The formalization now presented is based on a stochastic
theory of choice behavior of individuals (see, e.g.,
Galanter, 1966). After presenting the basic system, we shall
be concerned mainly with showing, in the frames of the
system, what kind of simplifications seem to be necessary in
deriving hypotheses for various situations of social interaction.

Some of the leading ideas have been already presented in
earlier studies (Rainio, 1961) but in a rather unsystematic
form. Some empirical research work has also been carried
through, particularly in testing basic ideas, and this has
already helped in making decisions in constructing the present system (Rainio, 1962 and 1965).

2. BASIC CONCEPTS

The basic concepts we shall use in building our formal description of social interaction are presented in the following list.[1]

Symbol: Verbal Description:

Be(i, a, t)   Behavior: *i* behaves (or acts) in
                                 the way *a* at the moment *t*.

Be´(i, a, t)   Cognitive behavior (or cognition):
                                 i imagines a way *a* (or more pre-
                                 cisely: *i* makes a cognitive choice
                                 a) at the moment t.

tr(i, b, t)   Behavioral trial: *i* tries to be-
                                 have (or act) in way *b* at the
                                 moment *t*.

tr´(i, b, t)   Cognitive trial: *i* tries to make
                                 a cognitive choice *b* at the moment
                                 t. *Note:* Instead of writing
                                 separately *i*'s behavior and trial,
                                 we shall use a shortened expression:

$$Tr(i, a, b, t)$$

which is thus defined in the following way

$$Tr(i, a, b, t) \equiv Be(i, a, t) \ \& \ Tr(i, b, t).$$

Correspondingly, we shall use the
shortened expression:

$$Tr´(i, a, b, t).$$

---

[1] The concepts are presented in the form of truth functions. Thus, the following "Be(i, a, t)" should be read: "The statement that the individual (*i*) behaves in the way *a* at the moment (*t*) assumes the value *true*." It is a shortened expression of the notation "Be(i, a, t)≡true" as well as "B̄e (i, a, t)" should be a shortened expression of the notation "Be(i, a,t)≡false." An alternative way to express the behavior of the individual *i* at the moment *t* could be to use a mathematical formula "Be(i, t)≡a." From our point of view the form of truth functions seem to be more convenient, although the expressions of mathematical formulae might be more familiar for many readers.

Succ(Tr(i, a, b, t))	Success of a trial: *i* succeeds in his trial to behave in the way *b* at the moment *t* after having behaved in the way *a*.
Succ(Tr´(i, a, b, t))	Success of a cognitive trial, correspondingly.
ECh(a, b, t)	Environmental change: the behavioral alternative *b* is substituted for *a* at the moment *t* and at any other following moment.

Note: ECh is applied to all behavioral descriptions of all individuals if the corresponding behavior alternative is *a*. Thus, in the case of ECh, the behavior of an individual is changed *without* any trial by him.--ECh is not the only possible environmental change--also changes in the conditions for Succ (Tr()) must be taken into account.

Pr(F(t))	Probability of an event: the probability of an event *F* at the moment *t*.

Note: The probabilities of events Tr´(i, a, b, t_o), Succ(Tr´(i, a, b, t)), and Succ(Tr(i, a, b, t)) shall be assumed to be given--as we shall see later--the others shall be derived from these.

*Outc (Pr)F(t)))	Outcome of a random choice where the probability vector Pr(F(t)) is used and which determines whether F will be true or false at the moment *t*.

Note: The probability vectors we shall denote Tr(i, a, t), Tr(i, t), Tr´(i, a, t), Tr´(i, t), etc. (but Succ(Tr(i, a, b, t))). Correspondingly, we shall write Outc (Tr(i, a, t)) etc.

---

*Editor's Note; Symbols in Letter Gothic type in the present chapter represent **vectors** or matrices.

Cor(i, a´, a, t)   Correspondence between cognitive
and real behavioral spaces: in i's
cognition, the cognitive alternative
$a´$ corresponds to the behavior
alternative a at the moment t.

Note: The correspondence between
real behavioral space (reality) and
each individual's cognition shall be
given by a probability matrix Pr
(Cor(i, a_c, a_r, t)), a_c meaning the
the cognitive alternatives and a_r
the behavior alternatives. Thus, no
particular correspondence is *a
priori* assumed.

Note: The time variable is a discrete one.

3. BASIC ASSUMPTIONS

The choice process of the individual is--in a stochastic
way--determined by the following basic assumptions:

$$(\forall i)(\forall t)(\exists a) \ Be´(i, a, t) \ . \tag{1}$$

Every individual behaves in some way in his cognition at
every moment.

Note: A passive state is assumed to be a way of behavior,
too, in this general sense.
It is necessary to assume an a for an individual at the moment t_o. Later the behavior is determined by the rules given
in the following.

$$(\forall i)(\forall a)(\forall t)(\exists b) \ Outc(Tr´(i, a, t))=b. \tag{2}$$

For every individual there exists at every moment some outcome of a random choice where the probability vector of
making a cognitive trial is used--in other words: every individual makes at every moment a cognitive trial and the outcome of this is determined by a random choice.

Note: The assumption implies that the $Tr´$ vector is a
stochastic one.

$$Tr´(i, a, b, t) \rightarrow (\exists x) \ Outc(Succ(Tr´(i, a, b, t)))=x. \tag{3}$$

If i makes a cognitive trial at the moment t an outcome of
its success is determined by a random choice.

$$Outc(Succ(Tr´(i, a, b, t))) \equiv Succ(Tr(i, a, b, t))a \tag{4}$$

$$\overline{Succ}(Tr´(i, a, b, t)).$$

There are two and only two possible outcomes of the random choice in the determination of the success of a cognitive trial, namely success or non-success (failure), which exclude each other.

$$Succ(Tr'(i, a, b, t)) \rightarrow Be'(i, b, t+1) . \qquad (5)$$

If a cognitive trial by i, directed to the alternative b at the moment t, then i's cognitive behavior is b at the following moment t+1.

$$\overline{Succ}(Tr'(i, a, b, t)) \rightarrow Be'(i, a, t+1). \qquad (6)$$

If a cognitive trial by i fails at the moment t then i continues his earlier cognitive behavior at the following moment t+1.

$$(\forall i)(\forall t)(Be'(i, a', t) \rightarrow (\exists a)(Outc(Cor(i, a', t))=a). \qquad (7)$$

For every individual there exists at every moment some outcome--a behavior alternative--which corresponds to the cognitive alternative in the individual's cognitive behavior at the same moment.

Note: We shall call $Outc(Cor(i, a', t))$ shortly a CRC-outcome (cognition-reality-correspondence-outcome).

$$(\forall i)(\forall t) (Outc(Cor(i, a', t))=a \rightarrow tr(i, a, t)) . \qquad (8)$$

For every individual and at every moment, if the CRC-outcome of the individual is a he makes a behavioral trial directed toward a at that moment.

Note: Assumptions (6), (7) and (8) clearly have the consequence that there exists also a behavioral trial for each individual at every moment.

$$(\forall i)(\forall t)(\exists a) \ Be(i, a, t_o) . \qquad (9)$$

Every individual behaves at the first moment in some way.

Note: For all moments other than t_o the behavior follows from the other assumptions.

$$Tr(i, a, b, t) \rightarrow (\exists x) \ Outc(Succ(Tr(i, a, b, t)))=x \qquad (10)$$

If i makes a trial at the moment t a random choice is made at the same moment for determining whether the trial succeeds or not.

$$\text{Outc}(\text{Succ}(\text{Tr}(i, a, b, t)))\equiv\text{Succ}(\text{Tr}(i, a, b, t))\, a \qquad (11)$$

See (4). $\qquad \overline{\text{Succ}}(\text{Tr}(i, a, b, t)).$

$$(\forall a)((\exists b)\ \text{ECh}(a, b, t) \rightarrow (c)(c\neq b \rightarrow \overline{\text{ECh}}(a, c, t))). \qquad (12)$$

If a behavior alternative is substituted for another through an environmental change there is no other behavior alternative substituting for it at the same moment.

$$\text{Succ}(\text{Tr}(i, a, b, t))\ \&\ (\forall x)\ \overline{\text{ECh}}\,(b, x, t) \rightarrow \text{Be}(i, b, t+1).$$
$$(13)$$

If i who behaves at the moment t in the way a succeeds in his trial to behave in the way b and if no environmental change is applied to the behavior b at the same moment t then i behaves in the way b at the next moment $t+1$.

Note: This is true independent of the fact whether an environmental change is applied to the behavior alternative a or not.

$$\overline{\text{Succ}}(\text{Tr}(i, a, b, t))\ \&\ (\forall x)\ \overline{\text{ECh}}(a, x, t) \rightarrow \text{Be}(i, a, t+1).$$
$$(14)$$

If i who behaves at the moment t in the way a fails in his trial and if no environmental change is applied to the behavior a at the same moment t then i continues his behavior in the way a at the next moment $t + 1$.

Note: This is true independent of the fact whether an environmental change is applied to the behavior alternative b or not.

$$\text{Succ}(\text{Tr}(i, a, b, t))\ \&\ (\exists c)\ \text{ECh}(b, c, t) \rightarrow \text{Be}(i, c, t+1).$$
$$(15)$$

If i succeeds in his trial to behave in the way b at the moment t and if some behavior alternative c is substituted for b at the same moment t then i behaves in the way c at the next moment. $\qquad (16)$

$$\overline{\text{Succ}}(\text{Tr}(i, a, b, t))\ \&\ (\exists c)(\text{ECh}(a, c, t) \rightarrow \text{Be}(i, c, t+1).$$

If *i* behaves in the way *a* and fails in his trial at the moment *t*, and if some behavior alternative *c* is substituted for *a* through an environmental change at the same moment then *i* behaves in the way *c* at the next moment *t*+1.

We leave open the question of the rules which determine the probability vectors and their changes as a function of time, because we have been dealing with the basic assumptions only. Actually, the assumptions needed for giving those rules form the real content of the theory. Much scientific work, however, seems to be necessary for fixing those rules, step by step. We shall argue some possibilities later in the discussion of the simplifications needed in scientific practice.

As a summary of the assumptions given above a description of the choice process of the individual is presented in Figure 1 which shows it in the often useful form of a program scheme.

4. STOCHASTIC VARIABLES

According to our assumptions, there are four instances where a random choice was made for determining the outcomes:

1) the choice of a cognitive alternative,

2) the determination of the success of a cognitive trial,

3) the determination of a behavioral alternative according to the cognitive alternative chosen, and

4) the determination of the success of the behavioral trial.

In addition, we could assume some environmental changes to be determined by some stochastic variables and use random choices for determining them.

Now we turn to the two questions, what determines the values of the above mentioned stochastic variables--probabilities of events--and what are the rules according to which they change.

The easiest answer to these questions is, apparently, to assume all probability values random and independent of each other at different points in time. This corresponds to full uncertainty and allows all kinds of outcome distributions. The lack of dependence between the time points actually means the same as continuously assuming all components in a probability vector to equal each other, i.e., the vector to be symmetric.

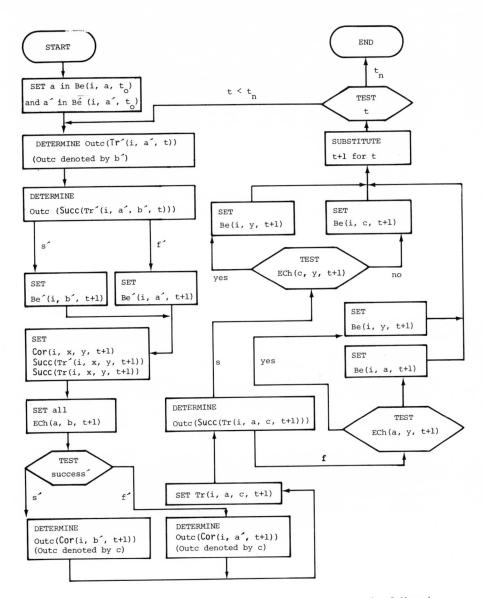

FIGURE 1.   A SCHEME OF THE INDIVIDUAL CHOICE PROCESS.   (s = success, f = failure.)

It is realistic to assume that an organism which has no information about its environment actually behaves according to a symmetric response probability vector, but it is thoroughly unrealistic to assume this situation to continue over time. Obviously, if such a world existed, we would have no knowledge of it. A thoroughly "random" world is an extreme, opposite to the other extreme, a thoroughly determined world.

Actually we already have a lot of information about the general processes we are dealing with--too much to take the position of full uncertainty. At least we can--from the beginning--limit our interest in relatively invariant phenomena, and still have much of interest to study.

It seems to me reasonable to assume that everywhere in the real world the stable, highly determined, invariant phenomena and the unstable, hardly predictable, "random" phenomena mix with each other.

Obviously we have to make some radical simplifications here. In our role of behavioral scientists we find quite uninteresting the laws of changes in the environment per se. We can control it sufficiently to keep it stable in some instances or make some changes in it voluntarily at certain points in time. Therefore, in the following we shall usually assume the environment to be constant, at least for a certain period in time. Formally stated:

Constant Environment Assumption:

$$(\forall t)(\forall a)(\forall b)((\overline{ECh}(a, b, t)) \quad \& \qquad (17)$$

$$(\forall t')\ Pr(Succ(Tr(i, a, b, t')))=Pr(Succ(Tr(i, a, b, t))))) \ .$$

We cannot maintain this assumption for example in dealing with a process which includes a series of different tasks in problem-solving. The change of problem is just such a change of the environment (ECh and/or a change in Succ probabilities). It is essential in making this assumption that we try to manage the problems as far as possible without assuming the environmental changes and the choice process to be mutually dependent.

In dealing with changes in the other stochastic variables we shall take as a starting-point the assumption that they follow the learning laws.

When we then try to develop the theory to make it applicable, we are forced to make some assumptions about the mathematical laws the changes of these probabilities follow, i.e., to select some simplified mathematical model for our use. As far as I can see, the problem of which model to select is a question of secondary importance compared with the decisions we have to make in developing assumptions about the reward and punishment effects of the outcomes. These decisions are necessary in using any mathematical learning model.

The most general and least risky way of manipulating the rewards and punishments in our system is to take them as given in the form of a utility matrix, the utility value of every outcome expressing the amount of reward or punishment. However, because the learning models are constructed in such a way that the relative amount of a change in the response probability vector always follows the same rule, it is technically better to express the differences in the utility values as probabilities of the reward (or punishment). (The consequences are not exactly the same in both cases—looked at from the point of view of one choice event—but approximately the same in the course of a process sufficiently long).

Further, we can easily assume that generally the probability of punishment is equal to 1 - the probability of reward if we remember that the size of both effects need not be the same (two-operator models).

We denote the reward probability of an outcome with the symbol Pr(Rew(Outc())) and the punishment probability with the symbol Pr(Pun(Outc())) and assume—as has been already discussed:

$$Pr(Pun(Outc()))=1 - Pr(Rew(Outc())) \cdot \qquad (18)$$

Thus, in the following we need to examine only one of these probabilities, the reward probability.

We apply the reinforcement event to the following probabilities which determine the trial made by an individual: Pr(Tr´ (i, a, b, t))), Pr(Succ(Tr´(i, a, b, t)))), and Pr(Cor(i, a´, a, t)), and, thus, we need the following vectors of reward probabilities in our system:

Rew(Tr´(i, a, b, t))

Rew(Succ(Tr´(i, a, b, t)))

Rew(Cor(i, a´, a, t)).

It is important to notice that these vectors are not probability vectors in the sense that the row sums must equal 1 (cf. Kemeny, Snell, and Thompson, 1956, p. 218). Each component can vary freely between 0 and 1.

In the following approach we shall apply a two-operator learning model (see, e.g., Bush and Mosteller, 1955) and denote the operators by Q_1 and Q_2, the former indicating the operator used in the case of reward, the latter indicating the operator used in the case of punishment. As Vilkkumaa has shown (Vilkkumaa, 1967), the operators can be taken as square matrices which have as many columns (and rows) as there are rows in the probability vector to be transformed, the sums in each column equalling 1. Multiplying the vector by this matrix we get the transformed vector needed. The laws of learning--whatever they are--can be expressed as characteristics of that transformation matrix. As examples we present here the transformation matrices corresponding to the Bush-Mosteller's Two Operator Learning Model (Bush and Mosteller, 1955):

Let us have n choice alternatives a_1, a_2, ..., a_k, ..., a_n.

Let us denote the probability of a_k by p_k. If a_k has been chosen and the outcome has been rewarding, the new choice probability is, according to the Bush-Mosteller Model:

$$p_{k,t+1} = p_{k,t} + \alpha(1 - p_{k,t})$$

where the coefficient α is between the limits $0 \leq \alpha \leq 1$.

Because p_k increases, the probability of other alteratives being chosen tends necessarily to decrease correspondingly since the sum of all components in the vector is always 1. According to Vilkkumaa, the vector shall be simply transformed by multiplying it by the following matrix which we denote by $Q_{1,k}$:

$$Q_{1,k} = \begin{array}{c|ccccccc} & 1 & 2 & 3 & \cdots & k-1 & k & k+1 \cdots n \\ \hline 1 & 1-\alpha & 0 & 0 & \cdots & 0 & 0 & 0 \cdots 0 \\ 2 & 0 & 1-\alpha & 0 & \cdots & 0 & 0 & 0 \cdots 0 \\ 3 & 0 & 0 & 1-\alpha & \cdots & 0 & 0 & 0 \cdots 0 \\ \cdots & \cdots & & & & & & \\ k-1 & 0 & 0 & 0 & \cdots & 1-\alpha & 0 & 0 \cdots 0 \\ k & \alpha & \alpha & \alpha & \cdots & \alpha & 1 & \alpha \cdots \alpha \\ k+1 & 0 & 0 & 0 & \cdots & 0 & 0 & 1-\alpha \cdots 0 \\ \cdots & \cdots & & & & & & \\ n & 0 & 0 & 0 & \cdots & 0 & 0 & 0 \cdots 1-\alpha \end{array}$$

Correspondingly, if a_k has been chosen and the outcome is punishing, the new choice probability of a_k is according to Bush-Mosteller's Model:

$$p_{k,t+1} = p_{k,t} - \beta p_{k,t}.$$

Because the probability p_k decreases, the other components of the vector have to increase correspondingly, the sum being always 1. The transformation of the whole vector is now easily arrived at according to Vilkkumaa by multiplying the vector by the following matrix which we denote by $Q_{2,k}$

$$Q_{2,k} = \begin{array}{c c} & \begin{array}{c c c c c c c c c} 1 & 2 & 3 & \cdots & k-1 & k & k+1 & \cdots & n \end{array} \\ \begin{array}{c} 1 \\ 2 \\ 3 \\ \cdots \\ k-1 \\ k \\ k+1 \\ \cdots \\ n \end{array} & \left[\begin{array}{c c c c c c c c c} 1 & 0 & 0 & \cdots & 0 & \frac{\beta}{n-1} & 0 & \cdots & 0 \\ 0 & 1 & 0 & \cdots & 0 & \frac{\beta}{n-1} & 0 & \cdots & 0 \\ 0 & 0 & 1 & \cdots & 0 & \frac{\beta}{n-1} & 0 & \cdots & 0 \\ & & & & & \frac{\beta}{n-1} & & & \\ 0 & 0 & 0 & \cdots & 1 & \frac{\beta}{n-1} & 0 & \cdots & 0 \\ 0 & 0 & 0 & \cdots & 0 & 1-\beta & 0 & \cdots & 0 \\ 0 & 0 & 0 & \cdots & 0 & \frac{\beta}{n-1} & 1 & \cdots & 0 \\ & & & & & \frac{\beta}{n-1} & & & \\ 0 & 0 & 0 & \cdots & 0 & \frac{\beta}{n-1} & 0 & \cdots & 1 \end{array} \right] \end{array}$$

The matrix operators above are only examples. By changing the elements in the matrix according to certain rules, it is easy to manipulate for example different types of transfer phenomena in learning. (Vilkkumaa presents in his paper also the manipulation of some dependence-of-path learning models using the matrix operators). In the following, thus, one has to give to the operators a general interpretation and leave open the question as to what special matrix has to be used in each particular case.

As said above, we shall take as a starting-point the principle that whenever an individual makes a behavioral or cognitive trial it is followed by a reward or punishment, and we shall use the corresponding matrix operators transforming the choice probability vectors. We assume that behavior according to a certain alternative produces in itself a

certain reward or punishment with a certain probability
associated with it, but, in addition, we shall assume that,
independent of that, the success or the failure of a trial
has in itself another rewarding or, correspondingly, punishing effect.

In detail, the rules of reward and of punishment are the
following:

$$\text{Be}(i, a, t) \rightarrow (\exists x) \text{ Outc}(\text{Rew}(\text{Be}(i, a, t)))=x, \qquad (19)$$

where $x \equiv \text{Rew a Pun}$.

If i behaves in a way a at the moment t then there exists a
reward or a punishment as the outcome of the random choice
where the corresponding probability vector is used.

$$\text{Be}'(i, a', t) \& \text{Be}(i, a, t) \&$$

$$\text{Outc}(\text{Rew}(\text{Be}(i, a, t)))=\text{Rew} \rightarrow \text{Cor}(i, a', x, t+1)=$$

$$Q_{1,a;\text{Cor}(1)} \quad \text{Cor}(i, a', x, t) \qquad (20)$$

If i has chosen in his cognition at the moment t the alternative a' and behaves in the way a at the moment t and if this
behavior is rewarding then the CRC-probability vector is
changed using the learning operator matrix $Q_{1,a;\text{Cor}(1)}$.

Note: Cor(1) is used to differentiate this operator from the
later one, Cor(2). We could make Q dependent on time and
provide it with the index t, but it seems reasonable to
simplify in such a way as to keep the learning operators constant during time. We will not discuss the realism of such
an assumption here.

Formula (20) where Pun is substituted for Rew and $Q_{2,a;\text{Cor}(1)}$
is substituted for $Q_{1,a;\text{Cor}(1)}$. $\qquad (21)$

Note: This assumption that the punishment following a behavioral trial has an effect on the correspondence between
the alternatives of the cognitive behavior and of the action
may seem curious, but it should be observed that the changes
may also be assumed to be very small.

$$\text{Be}'(i, a', t) \& \text{Be}(i, a, t) \&$$

$$\text{Outc}(\text{Rew}(\text{Be}(i, a, t)))=\text{Rew} \rightarrow (\forall y) \text{ Tr}'(i, y, x, t+1) =$$

$$=Q_{1,a';\text{Tr}'(1)} \quad \text{Tr}'(i, y, x, t). \qquad (22)$$

If i has chosen in his cognition the alternative a' and behaves in the way a at the moment t and if this behavior is
rewarding, then all the row vectors in the matrix indicating
the choice of cognitive alternative are changed using the
learning operator matrix $Q_{1a';Tr'(1)}$.

Note: The application of the operator to *all* the row vectors
of the matrix $Tr'(i, y, x, t)$ is an essential feature of the
theory presented here. It seems to be analogous to the
notion that the alternative a' has a *positive valence* for the
individual i--or, more precisely, that this positive valence
increases. In order to keep the system more general, it
would be possible to think also that the changes in the row
vectors were different, quantitatively or even qualitatively,
and that that row vector which corresponds to the latest cognitive trial of the individual would be in a special position. Thus our assumption is a simplification, but it is
naturally not a formal problem to substitute many operators
for one.

Formula (22) where Pun is substituted for Rew and
$Q_{2,a';Tr'(1)}$ is substituted for $Q_{1,a';Tr'(1)}$.   (23)

Note: Analogous to the case in which the *negative valence* of
the cognitive alternative a' is increasing.

We turn now to the reinforcements caused by the success
or failure of the trial. First we shall analyze the case of
the behavioral trial, then the case of the cognitive trial.

$$Succ(Tr(i,a,b,t)) \rightarrow (\exists x) \; Outc(Rew(Succ(Tr(i,a,b,t)))) = x,$$

where $x \equiv Rew \; a \; Pun$.   (24)

$$\overline{Succ(Tr(i,a,b,t))} \rightarrow (\exists x) \; Outc(Rew(\overline{Succ(Tr(i,a,b,t))})) = x,$$

where $x \equiv Rew \; a \; Pun$.   (25)

If i succeeds in his behavioral trial, there exits a reward
or a punishment as the outcome of a random choice where the
corresponding reward probability vector of the success (or
failure) of the trial is used.

It is realistic to assume that success means primarily
a reward and failure a punishment. Thus, we make the following specific assumptions:

$$Pr(Rew(Succ())) \geq 0.5 \ \& \ Pr(Rew(\overline{Succ}())) \leq 0.5. \tag{26}$$

Concerning the effect of success or failure of the behavioral trial, we make the following assumptions:

$$Be^{\checkmark}(i, \ b^{\checkmark}, t) \& \ Outc(Rew(Succ(Tr(i, \ a, \ b, \ t)))) = Rew$$

$$\rightarrow Cor \ (i, \ b^{\checkmark}, \ x, \ t+1) = Q_{1,b;Cor(2)} Cor(i, \ b^{\checkmark}, \ x, \ t). \tag{27}$$

If i has chosen the cognitive alternative $b^{\checkmark}$ at the moment t and his successful trial toward b at the moment t is rewarding then the CRC probability vector is changed using the learning operator matrix $Q_{1,b;Cor(2)}$.

Formula (27) where Pun is substituted for Rew and $Q_{2,b;Cor(2)}$ is substituted for the operator $Q_{1,b;Cor(2)}$.

$$\tag{28}$$

$$Be^{\checkmark} \ (i, \ b^{\checkmark}, \ t) \& Outc \ (Rew(Succ \ Tr(i, \ a, \ b, \ t)))) = Rew$$

$$\rightarrow (\forall y) \ Tr^{\checkmark} \ (i, \ y, \ x, \ t+1) = Q_{1,b^{\checkmark};Tr^{\checkmark}(2)} Tr(i, \ y, \ x, \ t). \tag{29}$$

See the note under (22).

Formula (29) where Pun is substituted for Rew and $Q_{2,b^{\checkmark};Tr^{\checkmark}(2)}$ is substituted for $Q_{1,b^{\checkmark};Tr^{\checkmark}(2)}$.

$$\tag{30}$$

We assume the reward of the behavioral trial to have an effect on the probability of success of the cognitive trials, too:

$$Tr^{\checkmark}(i, \ a^{\checkmark}, \ b^{\checkmark}, t) \ \& \ Outc(Rew(Succ(Tr(i, \ a, \ b, \ t))))) = Rew$$

$$\rightarrow Succ(Tr^{\checkmark}(i, \ a^{\checkmark}, \ b^{\checkmark}, \ t+1)$$

$$= Q_{1; \ Succ^{\checkmark}} Succ \ (Tr^{\checkmark}(i, \ a^{\checkmark}, \ b^{\checkmark}, \ t)). \tag{31}$$

Formula (31) where Pun is substituted for Rew and $Q_{2;Succ^{\checkmark}}$ is substituted for $Q_{1;Succ^{\checkmark}}$.

$$\tag{32}$$

If the behavioral trial does not succeed we cannot assume any effect on the CRC probabilities, since the individual has no experience of the correspondence between reality and his cognition.

Formula (31) where $\overline{\text{Succ}}$ is substituted for Succ and $Q_{1;\text{non-Succ}'}$ substituted for $Q_{1;\text{Succ}'}$. (33)

Formula (31) where $\overline{\text{Succ}}$ is substituted for Succ, Pun for Rew, and $Q_{1;\text{non-Succ}'}$ for $Q_{1;\text{Succ}'}$. (34)

There remains still an essential question: the question whether the success or the failure of a cognitive trial has any reinforcement effect or not. Would it be reasonable to assume that the cognition in itself, without any comparison with reality, has any reinforcement effect on the subsequent cognitive processes? What has been said about cognitive consonance (Festinger, Heider, etc.) indicates that this effect should be taken into account if we want to make the theory realistic. We set the following assumptions:

$$\text{Be}'(i, b', t) \ \& \ \text{Outc}(\text{Rew}(\text{Be}'(i, b', t))) = \text{Rew}$$

$$\to (\forall y) \ \text{Tr}'(i, y, x, t+1) = Q_{1,b';\text{Tr}'(3)} \text{Tr}'(i, y, x, t).$$

(35)

Formula (35), Pun substituted for Rew and $Q_{2,b';\text{Tr}'(3)}$ for $Q_{1,b';\text{Tr}'(3)}$. (36)

$$\text{Tr}'(i, a', b', t) \ \& \ \text{Outc}(\text{Rew}(\text{Succ}(\text{Tr}'(i, a', b', t))$$

$$= \text{Rew} \to (\forall y) \ \text{Tr}'(i, y, x, t+1) = Q_{1,b';\text{Tr}'(4)} \text{Tr}' \ (i,y,x,t).$$

(37)

Formula (37), Pun substituted for Rew and $Q_{2,b';\text{Tr}(4)}$ for $Q_{1,b';\text{Tr}'(4)}$. (38)

The picture of the rules governing the cognitive processes will become sharper later when we deal with communication.

5. DEPENDENCE OF BEHAVIOR

We are seeking to construct a formal analysis of social interaction, but before we can start to examine the phenomena of social influence we have to make formally clear the concept of dependence which is essential to it. In our system,

dependence upon something always means in principle the fact
that the probability variables which govern the process become conditional. Thus, dependence of behavior can be
defined in the following way:

$$\text{Dep}(i,\ a,\ b,\ t,\ E) \equiv \text{Pr}(\text{Be}(i,b,t+1);\ E) \tag{39}$$

$$\neq \text{Pr}(\text{Be}(i,\ b,\ t+1)).$$

Individual i, behaving in the way a at moment t is, at the
same moment, dependent according to the behavioral alternative b upon the event E if the probability of his behaving
in the way b at the next moment under condition E is different from the corresponding unconditional probability.

   If there exists a dependence of the behavior of an individual i then--since Pr(Be()) is a function of some ECh,
Tr, and Succ(Tr()) probabilities according to our basic
assumptions--at least some of these have to be conditional.
We shall, however, maintain the assumption of the constancy
of the environment and examine here only the other two cases
of dependence:

   1) When the individual i is dependent upon E for the
reason that Pr(Succ(Tr())) is conditional we shall call the
dependence an *environmental* one and write:

$$\text{Dep}_{\text{Env}}(i,\ a,\ b,\ t,\ E) \equiv \text{Pr}(\text{Succ}(\text{Tr}(i,\ a,\ b,\ t));\ E)$$

$$\neq \text{Pr}(\text{Succ}(\text{Tr}(i,\ a,\ b,\ t))) \tag{40}$$

   2) The probability of a behavioral trial is a function
of the CRC probabilities and the cognitive behavior probabilities (see Basic Assumptions (8) and (7)) and the latter is
a function of the cognitive trial probabilities and the
probability of success of the cognitive trial; thus there are
three possible types of "*cognitive* dependence:"

$$\text{Dep}'_{1}(i,\ b',\ b,\ t,\ E) \equiv \text{Pr}(\text{Cor}(i,\ b',\ b,t);\ E)$$

$$\neq \text{Pr}(\text{Cor}(i,\ b',\ b,\ t). \tag{41}$$

$$\text{Dep}'_{2}(i,\ b',\ b,\ t,\ E) \equiv \text{Pr}(\text{Tr}'(i,\ a',\ b',\ E)$$

$$\neq \text{Pr}(\text{Tr}'(i,\ a',\ b',\ t)). \tag{42}$$

$$Dep'_3(i, b', b, t, E) \equiv Pr(Succ(Tr'(i, a', b', t)); E)$$

$$\neq Pr(Succ(Tr'(i, a', b', t))). \tag{43}$$

When we deal with the sending and receiving of information we shall come back to these dependencies.

Measure of Dependence. The definition of dependence given above makes it possible to construct a scale for the dependence in a certain choice-situation simply by measuring the absolute difference of the conditional probability and the unconditional probability:

$$dep(i, a, b, t, E) = |Pr(Be(i, b, t+1); E)$$

$$-Pr(Be(i, b, t+1)|. \tag{44}$$

We can also measure the total environment dependence $dep_{Env,tot}(i, a, t, E)$ in the situation $Be(i, a, t)$ by computing the weighted sum:

$$dep_{Env,tot}(i, a, t, E) \tag{45}$$

$$= \sum_b Pr(Tr(i, a, b, t)) \, dep_{Env}(i, a, b, t, E).$$

Above we have shown the principle by which dependence measures are constructed. We leave open here the question of the details of other, more general measures of dependence, although these are essential in the analysis of social interaction. We could describe, for example, the life space of an individual in terms of total environmental dependencies at each point of it, thus getting the "dependence field of an individual:"

$$dep_{Env,tot}(i, a_1, t, E), \, dep_{Env,tot}(i, a_2, t, E), \, \ldots$$

In our system, dependence of behavior is taken into account by using conditional probabilities in determining the outcomes of the cognitive trial, of the success of the cognitive trials, of the success of the behavioral trial and of CRC, the event upon which the behavior is dependent being the condition. Adopting the conditional probabilities to the system makes the theory more complicated. Thus, in practice, rather rough simplifications concerning the dependence assumptions seem to be necessary.

6. SENDING AND RECEIVING INFORMATION

It seems rational to define the reception of information using the concept of dependence, since from the point of view of choice-behavior it is an essential part of the receiving of information that the individual "utilize it," i.e., being informed he makes his choices in another way than being un-informed. The information thus makes the cognitive behavior dependent upon the content of the information. In the fol-lowing definition this is expressed formally more clearly showing directly the conditions of the probabilities.

$$Be(i, Rec(E), t) \;\&\; Be'(i, a, t) \equiv$$

$$Outc(Tr'(i, x, t+1); E) \;\&$$

$$Outc(Succ(Tr'(i, a, x, t+1)); E) \;\&$$

$$Outc(Cor(i, a, t+1); E).$$

(46)

The event of individual *i*, who behaves in the way *a* in his cognition at the moment *t*, receiving information about E at the same moment means that--in determining his outcomes in the following cognitive trials--the vector of conditional probabilities should be used, E being the condition.

Note 1: We may assume that the process of receiving information about E takes time, e.g., occurs during a period $t+\tau$. Thus, at every moment from $t+1$ to $t+\tau+1$, the condi-tional probabilities should be applied. However, we can con-sider the probability of receiving information different at different points in time. (In an extreme case, the proba-bility may be constantly O.)

Note 2: The probability of receiving certain informa-tion may be assumed to be a decreasing function of time (the phenomenon of forgetting).

Note 3: The dependence of the path in the learning pro-cess might be handled now as a process of receiving informa-tion about the earlier behavior of oneself (memory):
$Be(i, Rec(Be(i, x, t-\tau)), t)$.

Note 4: Receiving information creates cognitive depend-ence--to what extent may depend on many factors, e.g., on the source of information (the status of the information sender, etc.).

Sending Information. All the actual behavior of an in-dividual may be taken, in principle, as information sending. However, as *active* sending of information we might call only the behavior which in some way raises the probability of some individual receiving certain information, e.g., through a verbal message which may raise the probability from 0 to 1. From the formal point of view, this is, however, rather uninteresting.

Perception a Special Case of Information-Receiving. Perception, as far as I can see, has to be taken as a special case of the whole process of information-reception, an extreme case in which certain conditional probabilities are very near 1 and where the path-dependence is high, too (because we are usually dealing with an extremely late level of learning).

In terms of our formalization the perception process may look like the following, in the case of perceiving a very familiar object:

$$Be'(i, a, t) \cdot$$

$$Outc(Tr'(i, a, t)) = Rec(E_1)'.$$

$$Outc(Succ(Tr'(i, a, Rec(E_1)', t))) = s, \text{ s meaning}$$
$$\text{success.}$$

$$Outc(Cor(i, Rec(E_1)', t)) = Rec(E_1) \cdot$$

$$Be(i, Rec(E_1), t+1) \cdot$$

$$Outc(Tr'(i, Rec(E_1)', t+1)) = Rec(E_2)'.$$

$$Outc(Succ(Tr'(i, Rec(E_1)', Rec(E_2)', t+1))) = s \circ$$

$$Outc(Cor(i, Rec(E_2)', t+1)) = Rec(E_2) \cdot$$

$$Be(i, Rec(E_2), t+2).$$
$$\text{etc.}$$

Note: Essential to our schema is the rapid sequence of continuously and successfully choosing the behavior which leads to the successful receiving of more and more information. This is of course a consequence of the fact that we assumed learning to be complete in our example so that the probabilities determining the choices and outcomes do not essentially differ from the value 1. As far as I can see, the scheme does not become really interesting until it is applied to such curious phenomena of perception as reversible figures etc. Since we are primarily interested in the analysis of social interaction we shall bypass here this problem area. (Cf., Galanter's fine modern analysis in Galanter, 1966).

7. SOCIAL DEPENDENCE. DEFINITION OF GROUP

We shall call dependence *social* (Dep_s) if the condition E is the behavior of an individual or some combination of behavior of many individuals. Thus:

$$Dep_s(i, a, b, t, E) \equiv (Dep(i, a, b, t, E) \vee Dep'(i, a, b, t, E))$$

$$\& \ (\exists j)(\exists c)(\exists x) \ E = Be(j, c, t_x). \tag{47}$$

A dependence relation is a social one if there exists at least one individual and one behavior alternative for him and one point in time such that the dependence condition is the behavior of this individual.

Note 1: According to the nature of the dependence relation we can talk of environmental social dependence-- $Dep_{s,Env}$ --or of cognitive social dependence--Dep'_s. (The Lewinian concept of "social induction" corresponds in some ways to some characteristics of our "cognitive social dependence").

Note 2: In particular, if

$$Pr(Succ(Tr(i, a, b, t)); Be(j, c, t)) > Pr(Succ(Tr(i,a,b,t)))$$

then we are dealing with *two alternatives of cooperative behavior,* *b* for *i* and *c* for *j,* in the opposite case with two alternatives of *competitive behavior.*

The concept of social dependence and the measure of dependence make it possible to define a social-psychological group in these terms:

$$S = \{i, j, \ldots, n\} \& (\forall i)(i \varepsilon S \rightarrow (\exists j)(j \varepsilon S \ \& \ j \neq i \ \&$$

$$(\exists b_i)(\exists b_j) \ dep_s(i, a_i, b_i, t, Be(j, b_j, t)) > 0))$$

$$\equiv G_t(i, j, \ldots, n) \tag{48}$$

If there exists a set S of individuals such that for each individual in it it is true that there exists at least one other individual upon whom he is dependent according to at least one behavior alternative at a given moment *t*, then these individuals form a social-psychological group at the moment *t*.

8. SOCIAL AND PHYSICAL ENVIRONMENT COMPARED

By making some special assumptions we can enlarge the concept of behavior so that the class of behaving objects (i) can include physical things, too.

The necessary assumptions are the following:

There exists no cognition in the case of "behavior" of a physical thing. This does not necessarily mean that we could not formally speak of cognition where the behaving subject is a physical thing (we use the notation $Be´(N, a, t)$ for such cognition, N denoting the "natural world," or "nature") but merely certain rules determining the outcomes so that the "cognition" has no effect. For this purpose we assume:

$$Be´(N, a´, t) \rightarrow Outc(Tr´(N, a´, t))=a´. \qquad (49)$$

If we maintain the axiom of the constancy of environment, it follows from basic assumptions (5) and (6) and from the assumption above (49) that

$$Be´(N, a´, t) \rightarrow Be´(N, a´, t+1). \qquad (50)$$

Further we assume:

$$(\forall a´)(\forall t)(\exists a) \ (Outc(Cor(N, a´, t))=a). \qquad (51)$$

For every cognitive alternative, there exists one and only one behavior alternative.

From this assumption (51), from the constancy of environment axiom, and from the basic assumptions (8), (13), and (14) we can derive:

$$Be(N, a, t) \rightarrow Be(N, a, t+1). \qquad (52)$$

Thus, every change of the "behavior" of a physical object is, according to the assumptions made above, dependent only upon the change of the environment (ECh). This is realistic. Formally, we do not need any new formulations for including physical objects in our theory-construction.

Note. In making the assumptions above, we have implicitly assumed the "learning coefficients" of the physical subjects to equal zero.

Perhaps the concept of "behavior" of physical objects sounds strange. However, the psychology of mental development makes it clear that the difference between social and physical environment has to be learned. More exactly, one has to learn

not to assume everything to be social--in our terms: one has
to learn in order to find out that there are things, all
learning operators of which are identity matrices. Who could
be a *priori* sure of this?

9. THE DYNAMICS OF THE WHOLE AND ITS PARTS

We have been dealing with the behavior of one subject
only in our analysis. Would it be meaningful to talk of the
behavior of a whole set of behaving subjects, $Be(S, a, t)$
where $S=\{i_1, i_2, \ldots, i_n\}$?

In social psychology this is the classical problem of
the description of group behavior--i.e, the problem of the
conditions under which it is allowable to think of a group as
a behaving subject without any "group mind" mysticism. An
assumption of a "group mind" actually means in our system the
same as allowing the behaving subject to be a group as well
as an individual, without giving any rules for reducing these
propositions to the form of a description of individual behavior. However, from one point of view, our assumption that
an individual is capable of making a choice, and thus allowed
to be the behaving subject, contains a lot of mysticism, too,
a kind of "personality" mysticism. Why should we allow an
individual to have a "mind" (to behave as a subject in
choice-behavior)?

We shall here examine the possibility of assuming the
subject of choice behavior to be set and the rules by which
one subject can be substituted for this set.

Let us examine the simultaneous trials of n individuals:

$$Tr(i_1, a_1, b_1, t) \ \& \ Tr(i_2, a_2, b_2, t) \ \& \ \ldots \ \& \ Tr(i_n, a_n, b_n, t).$$

We must note that there does not exist any *a* common to
two or more individuals, because each behavior alternative is
given in the life space of *one* individual. In graph form
this is expressed by *n* isolated subgraphs, each of them
describing the alternatives available to one and only one
individual:

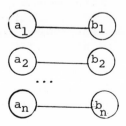

To express the concept of an aggregate of n individuals making trials by the notation $Tr(S, a, b, t)$ can be taken as a shortened expression of the conjunction given above, but the application of the basic assumptions forces us to make a very strong assumption that all elements of the set must always simultaneously succeed or fail in their trials, if we want to handle the process without reducing it to the behavior of the individual elements of the set. It would mean necessarily that the probabilities of the individual level equal 1 or 0--not only the sucess-of-trial probability but also the probability of making the trial. Otherwise the behavior at the moment t+1 could also take the form of some third alternative, not a or b.

This leads us to examine more exactly the formal construction of a "life space" of an aggregate of individuals (or of a set of elements, more generally speaking). As far as I can see, this has been a crucial problem in the construction of the Lewinian system--a problem which has not been satisfactorily solved there and which seems to be a basic weakness in the formalization attempts of several problems by group dynamists).

We shall describe the "life space" of an aggregate in terms of "states" (points, in a graph form) which include all possible combinations of the behavior alternatives available to the elements. After that we shall examine the possibility of applying the basic assumptions to the description which considers sets as behaving subjects.

If we use the notations A_1, A_2, ..., A_m for the states of the set and $a_{1,1}$, $a_{1,2}$, ..., a_{1,r_1} for the alternatives of the element 1 etc., then we can define the A's as the following sets:

$$A_1 = \{a_{1,1}, a_{2,1}, ..., a_{n-1,1}, a_{n,1}\}.$$

$$A_2 = \{a_{1,1}, a_{2,1}, ..., a_{n-1,1}, a_{n,2}\}.$$

$$...$$

$$A_{r_n} = \{a_{1,1}, a_{2,1}, ..., a_{n-1,1}, a_{n,r_n}\}.$$

$$A_{r_n + 1} = \{a_{1,1}, a_{2,1}, ..., a_{n-1,2}, a_{n,1}\}.$$

$$A_{r_n + 2} = \{a_{1,1}, a_{2,1}, ..., a_{n-1,2}, a_{n,2}\}.$$

$$...$$

$$A_{2r_n} = \{a_{1,1} , a_{2,1} , \ldots, a_{n-1,2} , a_{n,r_n}\}.$$

$$\ldots$$

$$A_{r_{n-1} r_n} = \{a_{1,1}, a_{2,1} , \ldots, a_{n-1,r_{n-1}}, a_{n,r_n}\}.$$

$$A_{\prod_{\nu=1}^{n} r_\nu} = \{a_{1,r_1} , a_{2,r_2} , \ldots, a_{n-1,r_{n-1}}, a_{n,r_n}\}.$$

$$(53)$$

If r_ν is the number of alternatives available to the element ν then the number of states of the set is $\prod_{\nu=1}^{n} r_\nu$ where n is the number of elements in the set.

Now it is possible to show the relation between the trial of the set and the trials of its elements by defining:

$$Tr(S, A_x, A_y, t) \equiv Tr(i_1, a_{1,x_1}, a_{1,y_1}, t) \ \&$$

$$Tr(i_2, a_{2,x_2}, a_{2,y_2}, t) \ \& \ \ldots$$

$$(54)$$

$$Tr(i_n, a_{n,x_n}, a_{n,y_n}, t)$$

where x_1 is the second index of i_1's alternative in the set A_x , y_1 the second index of i_1's alternative in the set A_y etc. (These indices are easily calculated from A's x and y indices if r_ν's are known).

We could, correspondingly, define Tr', Be', and Be by S. It is easy to see that $Pr(Tr(S, A_x, A_y, t))$ can be derived from $Pr(Tr(i, \ldots))$ values (in the case of independence):

$$Pr(Tr(S, A_x , A_y , t)) = \prod_{\nu=1}^{n} Pr(Tr(i_\nu , a_{\nu,x_\nu} , a_{\nu,y_\nu} , t).$$

$$(55)$$

This gives us the possibility of deriving the matrices $Q_{1,s;Tr}$ and $Q_{2,s;Tr}$ which will be used to transform the probabilities between the moment t and the moment $t+1$ after a reinforcement, from the corresponding individual

582

transformation matrices. (In doing this, however, we have to know to which individuals the outcome was rewarding and to which punishing--or make some general assumption of these effects).

In the application of the basic assumptions (14) and (16) there arises a problem:

If a set succeeds or fails in its behavior it is necessary to assume all elements in it simultaneously to succeed or to fail. If this limitation is not set, the basic assumptions (14) and (16) cannot be applied, because, e.g., in the case of failure the behavior of the set does not continue in the earlier state.

Another way, and as we shall see a more justifiable one, to solve the problem is to give up assumptions (14) and (16) in the case of a set. Instead of having only two possible states as the outcome of a trial we can determine the outcome through a random choice by using a vector which includes the probabilities of all possible changes of behavior of the set after a trial. We shall call these probabilities "state probabilities" and denote them by $Pr(St(A_z); Tr(S, A_x, A_y, t))$ and their stochastic vector by $St; Tr(S, A_x, A_y, t)$--the sum of the elements of this vector being equal to 1.

Now we shall substitute the following statements (56) and (57) for the basic assumptions (14) and (16) in the case of a set as subject:

$$(\forall t)(\exists A_z) \; \text{Outc}(St; \; Tr(S, A_x, A_y, t))=A_z . \tag{56}$$

$$\text{Outc}(St; \; Tr(S, A_x, A_y, t))=A_z \; \& \; \overline{ECh} \rightarrow Be(S, A_z, t+1) \tag{57}$$

where $\overline{ECh}$ is an abbreviation for the expression

$$(\forall X)(\overline{ECh}(A_x, X, t) \; \& \; \overline{ECh}(A_y, X, t) \; \& \; \overline{ECh}(A_z, X \; t)).$$

According to these new assumptions the behaving subject can after a trial assume a third state--not only the state of the earlier behavior or the state tried.

Note: If $Pr(St(A_y); \; Tr(S, A_x, A_y, t) + Pr(St(A_x); \; Tr(S, A_x,$

$A_y, t))=1$

then, naturally, assumptions (14) and (16) are valid. Thus, assumptions (14) and (16) are special cases of statements

(56) and (57) and the analysis of the set subject leads us to an interesting generalization.

If the elements of the St matrix are products of corresponding individual success probabilities then we are dealing with a case where nothing in the environment forces the individuals in the set into dependent behavior. If this is not the case there exists a "group problem," i.e., the structure of the St matrix regulates the learning of individuals toward some kind of coordination.

We have taken above the elements in S constantly given. However, in the course of the process S may also change, i.e., we may assume S to lose elements or to have new ones added to it. Actually, if an element is in its behavior completely independent of the behavior of other elements we can leave it out of our consideration if we are interested only in the behavior of the set. Correspondingly, if the elements in a set come to behave dependently upon some new behaving subjects these must be included in the set.

It would be particularly interesting to examine in this way the behavior of some sets of non-learning elements ("nature") to find out whether the set as a whole comes to have some of the characteristics of a learning subject. This is a special problem which would take us too far from our present topic, which is the presentation of the main features of our conceptual system, but--in carrying out this analysis--it might be possible, as far as I can see, to find a new interesting "explanation" of the learning phenomenon.

10. THE APPLICABILITY OF THE SYSTEM

The formal description of individual choice behavior and of social interaction is made above in a very generalized form; to test it would be a trial to test "everything." Our main purpose has been to show a way to link together problems of social interaction, to build a formalized system which helps us to see what kind of control is necessary--and justified--in the scientific manipulation of some special problems.

However, to verify the applicability of the conceptual framework we would need some concrete examples. Making certain simplifications, usually rather rough ones, it is actually possible to derive from the system models for certain types of social interaction. This work has already been done in principle, and some results are reported (e.g., Rainio 1962 and 1972). To include the details of such applications in this report would certainly have made it too lengthy.

REFERENCES

Berger, J., Zelditch, M. Jr. and B. Anderson. 1966. *Socio-logical Theories in Progress*. Boston: Houghton-Mifflin.

Bush, R. R., and F. Mosteller. 1955. *Stochastic Models for Learning*. New York: Wiley.

Galanter, E. 1966. *Textbook of Elementary Psychology*. San Francisco: Holden-Day.

Kemeny, J. G., Snell, J. L., and G. L. Thompson. 1956. *Introduction to Finite Mathematics*. Englewood Cliffs: Prentice-Hall.

Rainio, K. 1961. "A Stochastic Model of Social Interaction," *Transactions of the Westermarck Society,* Vol. VII, Copenhagen: Munksgaard.

Rainio, K. 1962. "A Stochastic Theory of Social Contact; A Laboratory Study and an Application to Sociometry," *Transactions of the Westermarck Society,* Vol. VIII, Copenhagen: Munksgaard.

Rainio, K. 1965. "Social Interaction as a Stochastic Learning Process," *Archives Européennes de Sociologie,* n. 6, pp. 68-88.

Rainio, K., 1972. "Group Maze Experiments and Simulations in Problem-Solving by Groups," *Commentationes Scientiarum Socialium,* Vol. 3. Helsinki: Societas Scientiarum Fennica.

Vilkkumaa, I. 1967. "A General Scheme for Probability Transformations in Choice Behavior," *Reports from the Institute of Social Psychology* at *Helsinki University,* n. 1. Helsinki.

21

Reproductive Value: With Applications
to Migration, Contraception, and Zero Population Growth*

NATHAN KEYFITZ

Harvard University

When a woman is sterilized and so has no further children, the community's expected births at all older ages for the calendar years to the end of her reproductive life are affected. When a woman dies or otherwise leaves the community, again all subsequent ages are affected. Our formal argument need make no distinction between emigration and death, between leaving the country permanently and leaving this world altogether. A single theory answers questions about the numerical effect of sterilization, of emigration, and of mortality, all supposed taking place at a particular age x. By means of the theory we will be able to compare the demographic effects of eradicating a disease that affects the death rate at young ages, say malaria, as against another that affects the death rate at older ages, say heart disease.

A seemingly different question is what would happen to a rapidly increasing population if its couples reduced their childbearing to replacement immediately. The period Net Reproduction Rate R_0, the number of girl children expected to be born to a girl child just born, would equal 1 from now on, and ultimately the population would be stationary. But the stationary total would be much higher than the total at the time when the birth rate dropped to bare replacement. The amount by which it will be higher is calculable, and by the same function--reproductive value--as handles problems of migration and changed mortality.

---

*I am grateful to Leo A. Goodman and James Frauenthal for several useful suggestions.

587

1. THEORY OF REPRODUCTIVE VALUE

Without having these problems in mind, R. A. Fisher (1929, p. 27) developed a fanciful image of population dynamics that turns out to provide solutions to them. He regarded the birth of a child as the loaning to him of a life, and the birth of his offspring as the subsequent repayment of the debt. Applying this to the female part of the population, suppose the chance of a girl living to age a is $\ell(a)$, the chance of her having a girl child between age a and a + da is $m(a)\,da$, so the expected number of children in this small interval of age is $\ell(a)m(a)\,da$. This quantity added through the whole of life is the Net Reproduction Rate R_O, defined as

$$R_O = \int_\alpha^\beta \ell(a)m(a)\,da \; ,$$

where $\underline{\alpha}$ is the youngest age of childbearing and $\underline{\beta}$ the oldest. The quantity R_O is the expected number of girl children by which the girl child will be replaced; for the population it is the ratio of the number in one generation to the number in the preceding generation, according to the current $\ell(a)$ and $m(a)$.

The value of one dollar, or one child, discounted back through $\underline{a}$ years at annual rate $\underline{r}$ compounded momently is e^{-ra}, so the value of $\ell(a)m(a)\,da$ children is $e^{-ra}\ell(a)m(a)\,da$. The present value of the repayment of the debt is the integral of this last quantity through the ages to the end of reproduction. Thus the debt that the girl incurs at birth is 1, and the discounted repayment is the integral $\int_\alpha^\beta e^{-ra}\ell(a)m(a)\,da$. If loan and discounted repayment are to be equal we must have

$$1 = \int_\alpha^\beta e^{-ra}\ell(a)m(a)\,da \; ,$$

and this is the same as the characteristic equation (Lotka, 1939, p. 65) from which the $\underline{r}$ implied by a net maternity function $\ell(a)m(a)$ is calculated. The equation can now be seen in a new light: the equating of loan and discounted repayment is what determines $\underline{r}$, $\underline{r}$ being interpretable either as the rate of interest of an average loan or as Lotka's intrinsic rate of natural increase.

The loan-and-repayment interpretation of the characteristic equation suggests asking how much of the debt is outstanding by the time the girl has reached age $\underline{x}$. The answer is the expected number of subsequent children discounted back to age $\underline{x}$:

$$v(x) = \frac{1}{e^{-rx}\ell(x)} \int_x^\beta e^{-ra}\ell(a)m(a)\,da , \qquad (1)$$

and $v(x)$ will be called reproductive value at age $\underline{x}$, normed to $v(0) = 1$.

For his studies in genetics Fisher needed an answer to the question, "To what extent will person of this age [say $\underline{x}$], on the average, contribute to the births of future generations?" This seemingly different question is answered by a function proportional to $v(x)$; Leo A. Goodman (1969) establishes its value at $v(x)/\kappa$, where

$$\kappa = \int_\alpha^\beta ae^{-ra}\ell(a)m(a)\,da , \qquad (2)$$

i.e., $\underline{\kappa}$ is the mean age of childbearing in the stable population. This enables us to say that the addition of a girl or woman aged $\underline{x}$ to the population at time zero adds $v(x)e^{rt}$ births at time $\underline{t}$, always supposing the continuance of the same regime of fertility and mortality.

From the fact that $v(x)$ according to (1) is the expected number of girl children to be born to a female aged $\underline{x}$, discounted at the rate $\underline{r}$, it is by no means obvious that the effect of a girl aged $\underline{x}$ on the subsequent birth trajectory is $v(x)e^{rt}/\kappa$, but Goodman (1969) proves this. Once we know the effect on the birth trajectory and assume a fixed birth rate $\underline{b}$, we have the effect on the population trajectory by dividing by $\underline{b}$. This is obvious, for since the birth rate b is B/P, births divided by population, then P = B/b, births divided by the birth rate. Hence the effect on the ultimate population of adding a girl or woman aged $\underline{x}$ is to add $v(x)e^{rt}/\kappa$ to ultimate births and $v(x)e^{rt}/\kappa b$ to ultimate population.

The average $v(x)$ for the age group 20-24 at last birthday will be written $_5V_{20}$. For Mauritius 1966, with an intrinsic rate $\underline{r}$ according to vital statistics of 0.0305 (Keyfitz and Flieger, 1971, p. 80), the values of $_5V_x$ for five-year age intervals are shown in Table 1.

Thus emigration or sterilization of a woman aged 20-24 at last birthday makes nearly 20 times as much difference to the ultimate population curve as emigration or sterilization of a woman aged 40-44. Reproductive value $v(x)$ is unity when $x = 0$; it rises to a peak of 1.78 at age 15-19, when childbearing is imminent, and falls towards zero by age 50 or so. Departure or sterilization of women past childbearing makes no difference to subsequent population growth.

In order to provide some intuitive feeling for the reason why the effect of one child just born on the ultimate birth trajectory is $v(0)e^{rt}/\kappa = e^{rt}/\kappa$, rather than just e^{rt} or some other value, suppose that all children are born at same age of mother and that this age is $\underline{\kappa}$. Then the birth of an additional girl child now will result in R_0 girl children in $\underline{\kappa}$ years, R_0^2 children in 2κ years, and similarly over later generations. That is to say, the child born now outlines a curve rising in the ratio of R_0 every $\underline{\kappa}$ years, where R_0 is the Net Reproduction Rate. But R_0 is equal to $\exp(r\kappa)$, since if all births occur at age $\underline{\kappa}$ of mother $\underline{\kappa}$ is the length of generation (Fig. 1). To fill in the curve suppose such a birth every year for $\underline{\kappa}$ years. Those $\underline{\kappa}$ births

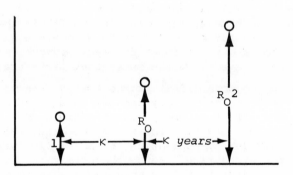

Fig. 1. Effect of one birth if all children are born at age κ of mother.

would raise the birth curve by e^{rt}, so one birth would raise it by e^{rt}/κ This argument is at best heuristic; the result applies much more generally than to the primitive model in which all births occur at the same age of mother.

To sum up this section, reproductive value considered as the fraction yet to be repaid of a life borrowed at birth is normed with $v(0) = 1$, following Fisher and Leslie (1945). Reproductive value considered as the contribution to the ultimate *birth* trajectory provided by a person aged x is $v(x)/\kappa$, normed with $v(0)/\kappa = 1/\kappa$ at age zero, and Goodman (1967) takes this as the definition of reproductive value. Since the population is equal to $1/b$ times the annual births, if reproductive value were defined as the contribution to the ultimate *population* trajectory made by a person aged x, then the function would be normed with a value at age zero equal to $1/b\kappa$.

The norming $v(0)/\kappa = 1/\kappa$ produces, as we saw, the ultimate birth curve $v(0)e^{rt}/\kappa$ resulting from one girl at age 0 and the ultimate birth curve $v(x)e^{rt}/\kappa$ resulting from one girl at age x. On our deterministic model it produces therefore $P(x)v(x)e^{rt}dx/\kappa$ female births if there are $P(x)dx$ females initially at age x to $x + dx$. Moreover these quantities are additive, so that the sum or integral

$$\int_0^\beta P(x)v(x)\,dxe^{rt}/\kappa$$ would give the ultimate birth trajectory

for an arbitrary initial age distribution $P(x)$.

This last statement is exact, but it requires that t be large. Suppose we make the calculation one year later, now with the age distribution $P_1(x)$ that has resulted from projection under the same fixed regime of mortality and fertility. From this new position at time 1 we would have for the

total at time t, $\int_0^\beta P_1(x)v(x)\,dxe^{r(t-1)}/\kappa$, and if this is to be the same as the value at time t calculated from time 0 we must have

$$\int_0^\beta P_1(x)v(x)\,dx = e^r \int_0^\beta P(x)v(x)\,dx .$$

It suggests that the total reproductive value of a population of arbitrary age distribution acted on by a fixed regime increases at the rate r in the short as well as the long run. Such a statement is conspicuously not true for the total population, whose increase in the short run depends very much on its age distribution. Both births and population acted on by a fixed regime *ultimately* go into an exponential trajectory with parameter $\underline{r}$; reproductive value *immediately* follows an exponential trajectory.

The above extended theoretical account is justified only by its ability to answer demographic questions. The following section deals with the first of a series of such questions.

2. ULTIMATE EFFECT OF SMALL OUT-MIGRATION OCCURRING IN A GIVEN YEAR

When people leave a crowded island like Barbados or Java they make life somewhat easier for those who remain behind, assuming that the rates of mortality and fertility do not change as a result of their departure.

The age at which they leave determines the effect. Departures of persons who are already past the ages of re-production cannot influence the ultimate population trajec-tory. Any one-time departure, moreover, can lower the trajectory, but cannot change its rate of climb as long as the age-specific rates of birth and death remain unchanged. In symbols, if the trajectory is Qe^{rt}, then a one-time de-parture of an individual or a group can lower $\underline{Q}$ but will not alter $\underline{r}$. It follows from the theory of Section 1 that a female of age x leaving reduces the female births at time $\underline{t}$ by $v(x)e^{rt}/K$, and the female population at time $\underline{t}$ by $\overline{v}(x)e^{rt}/Kb$, where we take $\underline{t}$ to be large Thus the change in $\underline{Q}$ on the departure of one female aged x is $\Delta Q = -v(x)/Kb$.

We are still on the one-sex model and suppose female dominance, which is to say that births are determined by the number of females at the several ages and not by the number of males. If births are determined by the number of males (as can happen if males are a small minority) then the de-parture of females would have little effect on the ultimate population. The extension of these notions to a genuine two-sex model is not easy, and we will stay with female dominance.

Table 1 shows for Mauritius, 1966, the quantities $v(x)/Kb$ grouped in five-year ages. These have been expressed as averages over five years, so the entries opposite 15-19 would be designated $_5V_{15}/Kb$, for example. A girl of 15-19

leaving is 1.679 times as helpful as the departure of a female of random age at the rates of Mauritius. Information on many other populations is given in Keyfitz and Flieger (1968). The curves of reproductive value for increasing populations have the same general shape from country to

Age	$_5V_x$	$_5V_x / (b\kappa)$
0-4	1.159	1.092
5-9	1.381	1.301
10-14	1.618	1.524
15-19	1.783	1.679
20-24	1.611	1.517
25-29	1.151	1.084
30-34	0.690	0.650
35-39	0.312	0.294
40-44	0.083	0.078
45-49	0.009	0.008

$v(0) = 1$

$$\frac{v(0)}{b\kappa} = \frac{1}{(0.03889)(27.30)} = 0.942$$

Table 1.   Values of $_5V_x$, the Fisher Reproductive Value of Females Aged $\underline{x}$ to x + 4 at Last Birthday, and $_5V_x/b\kappa$, the Amount by Which Population at Time $\underline{t}$ is Raised by One Added Person Aged $\underline{x}$ to x + 4 at Time Zero, Mauritius, 1966.

Source: Keyfitz and Flieger, 1971, p. 315.

country.

A female of an age selected at random out of the stable age distribution is a natural unit. Her expected reproductive value must be $b\kappa$, because an initial distribution $be^{-rx}\ell(x)$ under the given regime generates a population at time $\underline{t}$ equal to e^{rt}.

The effect of a one-time bulge in births is easily stated. With ΔB extra births in a given year the birth trajectory would be raised $v(0)e^{rt}\Delta B = e^{rt}\Delta B/\kappa$, and the population trajectory would be raised this amount divided by the birth rate $\underline{b}$. A female of a random age at time zero raises the population at time $\underline{t}$ an expected e^{rt}; a baby at time zero raises it by $e^{rt}/b\kappa$. Each girl baby aged zero is thought of as generating a population equal to $e^{rt}/b\kappa$. The mean age of childbearing $\underline{\kappa}$ is never very far from 27, and the reciprocal of 27 is 0.037. For low fertility populations $\underline{b}$ is considerably less than $1/K$, so the baby has somewhat more expected effect than a female between O and $\underline{\omega}$ randomly chosen from the stable age distribution. With high fertility populations on the other hand b is greater than $1/K$ and the baby has less expected effect than a randomly selected female.

The technique can be used to find a variety of equivalents. By what amount, for example, would births have to drop in a particular year to offset an immigration of 1000 women aged 15-19 in that year? The population at distant time $\underline{t}$ resulting from 1000 women aged 15-19 is

$1000 {}_5V_{15} e^{rt}/(bK)$. The population from $\underline{B}$ births at time $\underline{t}$ is $Bv(0) e^{rt}/(bK)$. Equating these two expressions we obtain

$$B = \frac{1000 {}_5V_{15}}{v(0)}$$

as the required equivalent number of births. From the Mauritius information in Table 1 we have, since ${}_5V_x$ is normed to $v(0) = 1$

$$B = 1000 {}_5V_{15} = 1783 .$$

In any one year a drop of 1783 female births would be required to offset immigration of 1000 women aged 15-19 at last birthday.

3. EFFECT OF CONTINUING BIRTH CONTROL AND STERILIZATION

Suppose a few women each year resort to birth control as they reach age a, and this occurs year after year, so that the birth rate m(a) is permanently lowered for year $\underline{a}$, but all other age-specific birth rates remain unaltered. If the change in the age-specific birth rate in the single year of age $\underline{a}$ was $\Delta m(a)$, a quantity that would carry a minus sign for decrease in m(a), then the change in the intrinsic rate of the population is given by finding the derivative $dr/dm(a)$ from

$\int_\alpha^\beta e^{-rx} \ell(x) m(x) dx = 1$. If the integral is called $\psi(r)$ we can easily find $\dfrac{dr}{dm(a)}$ as $-\dfrac{d\psi(r)}{dm(a)} \bigg/ \dfrac{d\psi(r)}{dr}$, and it turns out to be $e^{-ra} \ell(a)/K$. Thus for finite increments Δr and $\Delta m(a)$ we have approximately

$$\Delta r \doteq \frac{e^{-ra}\ell(a)\Delta m(a)}{K} \; ,$$

where the symbol $\doteq$ is used to designate approximate equality. As is to be expected, the change in r is in the same direction as the change in $m(a)$. The formula depends on $\Delta m(a)$ being small enough that e^{-ra} as well as K are unaffected. Subject to this same condition we can find the combined effect of small increments at two different ages, say a and $a + 1$. The effect on r would be approximately the sum of the Δr for $\Delta m(a)$ and for $\Delta m(a + 1)$.

Now suppose a change in $m(a)$ for all a from age x onwards, so that the new birth function is $m(a)$, $a < x$, and $(1 - f)m(a)$, $a \geq x$, f being a small positive or negative fraction. This could be the result of sterilization, or of the decision of the fraction f of women at age x and older to use conventional birth control methods in order to avoid all further children. If f is small enough not to drop r appreciably, we can enter $-fm(\varepsilon)$ for $\Delta m(a)$ in the preceding display, and find the total effect Δr by adding the Δr for several ages:

$$\Delta r = -\frac{f\int_{x}^{\beta} e^{-ra}\ell(a)m(a)\,da}{K} \; .$$

The integral here will be recognized as the same that turned up in $v(x)$ of (1). Entering $v(x)$ makes this

$$\Delta r = -fe^{-rx}\ell(x)v(x)/K \; . \tag{3}$$

In words, the decrease by the fraction f of fertility rates for all ages above x decreases the intrinsic rate by $v(x)$ multiplied by $fe^{-rx}\ell(x)/K$. Remembering that $be^{-rx}\ell(x)$ is the fraction of the population at age x, where at this point it is convenient to make x integral and have it mean exact ages $x - \frac{1}{2}$ to $x + \frac{1}{2}$, we can say that the decrease in r is $f/(bK)$ times the fraction of the population aged x, times the reproductive value at age x. Expression (3), based on stable population theory, shows the effect of sterilization of the small fraction f of women attaining age x, supposing the sterilization to be repeated year after year as successive cohorts of women reach age x.

An alternative way of expressing Δr of (3) is in terms of b_x, the fraction of births occurring to mothers aged $\underline{x}$ and over. On this definition we have

$$\Delta r = -fb_x/\kappa \ .$$

In words: when through birth control, sterilization, or other means births to women over age $\underline{x}$ are lowered by a small fraction $\underline{f}$, the rate of increase is lowered by $\underline{f}$ times the fraction of children born to women aged $\underline{x}$ and older, divided by the mean age of childbearing (Goodman, 1971).

Small fall of the birth rate at arbitrary ages

As the birth rate falls, in the United States or any other country, it falls more rapidly at some ages than at others. For modernizing populations the initial fall has been greatest at the oldest ages of childbearing, as has been noted alike for the United States and for Taiwan. The ages that drop are partly related to the means used; sterilization applies mostly to the older ages of childbearing, the pill to younger ages (at least while it is a novelty); abortion is used at all ages. The IUD is most commonly used after the birth of the first child, and so its impact must on the whole be on ages intermediate between the pill and sterilization (Fig. 2).

To deal with all cases consider deductions from m(a) equal to kg(a), which is to say that kg(a) is a bite of arbitrary shape taken out of the fertility m(a). For purposes of this section $\underline{k}$ is small enough that we can neglect second-order terms like $(\Delta r)^2$ and $k\Delta r$, where Δr is the difference that the deductions of kg(a) from m(a) will make to $\underline{r}$. Our question is what value of Δr corresponds to kg(a). The answer is obtainable from the equation

$$\int_\alpha^\beta e^{-(r+\Delta r)a} \ell(a) \, [m(a) - kg(a)] \, da = 1 \ ,$$

where $\underline{r}$ is defined by the same equation but omitting Δr and kg(a). Expanding the exponential $\exp(-\Delta ra) = 1 - (\Delta r)a$ and using the definition of $\underline{r}$ gives

$$\Delta r \doteq - \frac{\int_\alpha^\beta e^{-ra} \ell(a) g(a) \, da}{\kappa} \, k \ ,$$

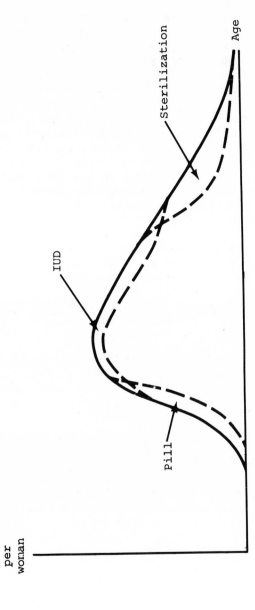

Fig. 2. Area g(a) removed from net maternity function by the several methods of birth control.

where $\underline{\kappa}$ is again the mean age of childbearing in the stable population.

This general expression can be specialized down to show the effect of birth control at a certain age or above a certain age. It gives the effect on $\underline{r}$ of any particular enduring change in the regime of fertility and mortality.

Large change in regime

So far only small changes have been discussed. We now ask the same questions in reference to an arbitrary, possibly large, change: if birth control is applied by women aged $\underline{x}$ and above, what fraction of births must they avoid in order to change the rate of increase from $\underline{r}$ to $r + \Delta r$? (For this statement of the problem $\Delta r < 0$, but we will solve for $\underline{f}$ positive or negative and Δr as any change in $\underline{r}$.)

Suppose that women aged $\underline{x}$ and higher apply birth control to the point where they reduce their age-specific rates by the fraction $\underline{f}$ of what they were before; $\underline{f}$ of the women reaching age $\underline{x}$ being sterilized would have this effect. The original intrinsic rate of increase was found by solving for $\underline{r}$ in the characteristic equation. The integral for the new rate of increase $r + \Delta r$ breaks down into two parts:

$$\int_{\alpha}^{\beta} \exp[-(r+\Delta r)a]\,\ell(a)m(a)\,da -$$

$$f \int_{x}^{\beta} \exp[-(r+\Delta r)a]\,\ell(a)m(a)\,da = 1, \tag{4}$$

where we suppose $\alpha \leq x \leq \beta$. The equation (4) could be solved for $\underline{x}$ if $\underline{f}$ and $\underline{r} + \Delta r$ were given, or for $r + \Delta r$ if $\underline{x}$ and $\underline{f}$ were given. A simple explicit solution is available for $\underline{f}$, the fraction of decrease above the given age $\underline{x}$ that will suffice to change the intrinsic rate from $\underline{r}$ to $r + \Delta r$:

$$f = \frac{\int_{\alpha}^{\beta} \exp[-(r + \Delta r)a]\,\ell(a)m(a)\,da - 1}{\int_{x}^{\beta} \exp[-(r + \Delta r)a]\,\ell(a)m(a)\,da}. \tag{5}$$

The result (5) depends in no way on Δr being small.

Note that the numerator of (5) is bound to be positive for $\Delta r < 0$, corresponding to the birth control formulation in which $\underline{f}$ is defined as positive and birth rates go from $m(a)$ to $(1 - f)m(a)$. In the special case where the desired $r + \Delta r = 0$ we would have the simpler form

$$f = \frac{\int_{\alpha}^{\beta} \ell(a)m(a)\,da - 1}{\int_{x}^{\beta} \ell(a)m(a)\,da} = \frac{R_O - 1}{\int_{x}^{\beta} \ell(a)m(a)\,da} . \qquad (6)$$

The $\underline{f}$ of (6) is the fraction by which women aged $\underline{x}$ and over must reduce fertility to bring the rate of increase $\underline{r}$ down to zero. The age $\underline{x}$ is arbitrary, but is required to stay within certain limits if $0 < f < 1$. On data for Colombia 1965 one observes that no reduction of fertility to women 30 and over can bring stationarity if ages under 30 retain existing rates. For we have $R_O = 2.267$ and $\int_{30}^{50} \ell(a)m(a)\,da = 1.001$; hence the drop to $R_O = 1$ would not occur even if all fertility above age 30 disappeared.

One would have thought that a girl child would contribute the same amount to the ultimate trajectory irrespective of the age of her mother; all babies start at age zero, after all. The expression $\Delta r = e^{-ra}\ell(a)\Delta m(a)/\kappa$ is consistent with this, for it says that the effect of a small change $\Delta m(a)$ in the age-specific birth rate is proportional to $e^{-ra}\ell(a)$, i.e., proportional to the number of women at that age in the stable population; this has to be right, in that a given change in the birth *rate* will have more or less effect in proportion to the number of women to whom that change is applied. The expression for Δr in the preceding sentence supposes that $\Delta m(a)$ is small enough not to affect $\underline{\kappa}$ the mean age of childbearing.

But when we consider the ultimate effect of a large change that takes place generation after generation, it does make a difference whether women have their children young or old. Expressions (5) and (6) take due account of the fact (among others) that avoiding a birth at age 40 is not as effective as avoiding one at age 20 because of the more rapid turnover of a population in which births occur to younger mothers.

The preceding covers also the consequences of a fall in

the death rate. Suppose that the rate at age $x - \frac{1}{2}$ to $x + \frac{1}{2}$ goes from $\mu(x)$ to $\mu(x) + \Delta\mu(x)$ and remains at that level, or what is practically the same, that $\Delta\mu(x)/\delta$ is permanently added to the density $\mu(x)$ over a narrow age interval $\underline{\delta}$. Then all the results of this section apply. The outcome for the deaths problem corresponding to (3) is

$$\Delta r = -e^{-rx} \ell(x) v(x) \Delta\mu(x) / \kappa , \qquad (7)$$

as demonstrated by an alternative method in Keyfitz (1971, p. 277). Again we can write this in terms of b_x, the fraction of births taking place to women aged $\underline{x}$ and older. It is then

$$\Delta r = -b_x \Delta\mu(x) / \kappa$$

Modification of (4) to allow for a large change in deaths is straightforward.

For a birth change over arbitrary ages, $kg(a)$, where now $\underline{k}$ may be large, a similar technique may be used. Consider the problem of finding $\underline{k}$, given the shape $g(a)$ representing the age impact of birth control, in order to attain ultimate stationarity. For bare replacement, the Net Reproduction Rate, the expected number of girl children by which a girl child born now will be replaced, must be unity. On the age-specific birth rates $m(a) - kg(a)$, R_O falling to unity means that

$$\int_\alpha^\beta \ell(a) [m(a) - kg(a)] da = 1.$$

where we are to solve for $\underline{k}$ to find the amount of the change $g(a)$ required to bring replacement. The answer is

$$k = \frac{R_O - 1}{\int_\alpha^\beta \ell(a) g(a) da} .$$

For $g(a) = m(a)$ this is $k = (R_O - 1)/R_O$. Special cases include (3), (6), and other formulas of the present chapter.

4. EMIGRATION AS A POLICY APPLIED YEAR AFTER YEAR

We turn now to a situation unlike either one-time emigration or a permanent change in the birth rate at any one age, though similar to a permanent change in a death rate (Keyftiz, 1971a). This is migration that takes place year after year. An example is that each year some inhabitants of Java go to Sumatra under an official transmigration program that has been government policy for two thirds of a century. The authorities have always recognized that the amount of relief provided to Java depends on the age of the migrants at the time of their outmigration, and that young couples are the ideal, but they have tended to exaggerate the effect. Widjojo (1970) shows realistic population projections under alternative assumptions about the rate of movement, from which the consequences of different policies can be seen. In the following we will examine one aspect of policy only: the effect of the age of the migrants on the ultimate rate of increase of the population, and we will derive the effect on somewhat different considerations from those applied earlier.

Suppose that migration in the number of $E(x)$ persons of age $\underline{x}$ occurs year after year. First consider only two years, say $\underline{t}$ and $t + 1$, and suppose that the trajectory of total population without emigration is given by AB of Fig. 3. Suppose that $E(x)$ individuals leave in year O, and that the trajectory is then CD. If $\underline{t}$ is large and the initial population is stable, then the point $\underline{A}$ is given by Pe^{rt}, and the point $\underline{D}$ by $Pe^{r(t+1)} - E(x)v(x)e^{rt}/(bK)$. To find the effective rate of increase between time $\underline{t}$ and time $t + 1$ allowing for the emigration we subtract the level at $\underline{A}$ from the level at $\underline{D}$, and then divide by the level at $\underline{A}$:

$$\text{Effective rate of increase at time } t = \frac{Pe^{r(t+1)} - E(x)v(x)e^{rt}/(bK) - Pe^{rt}}{Pe^{rt}}$$

$$= e^{r} - \frac{E(x)}{PbK} v(x) - 1 .$$

But if the initially stable population totals $\underline{P}$ then it contains $Pbe^{-rx}\ell(x)$ persons in the year O of age $\underline{x}$. Suppose the $E(x)$, who are $E(x)/P$ of the population of all ages, are $\underline{f}$ of the population of age $\underline{x}$: $E(x) = fPbe^{-rx}\ell(x)$. Entering this in the last display and putting $e^{r} - 1 = r$ gives approximately

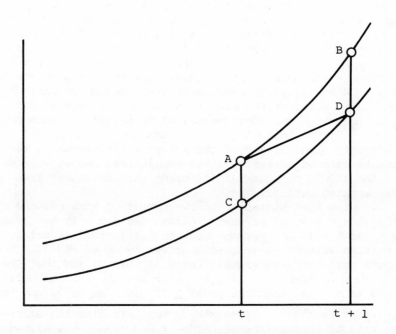

Fig. 3. Trajectory AB of population starting
with P persons at time zero; also CD, if by
time 1 E(x) persons aged x are lost by emigration.

effective rate of increase

$$\text{at time } t \doteq r - fe^{-rx}\ell(x)v(x)/\kappa , \qquad (8)$$

where $\doteq$ again signifies approximate equality.

But we could perform the same calculation for any pair of years, and hence (8) gives the effect on r of a fraction f of individuals aged x leaving. It shows r to be reduced $fe^{-rx}\ell(x)v(x)/\kappa$, a result that agrees with the earlier (3).

Aside from their effects on r, and therefore on the *angle* of the birth trajectory, the annual migrants also change its *level*. The E(x) persons who leave in year zero lower the births at time t by $E(x)v(x)e^{rt}/\kappa$; those who leave in year 1 lower the births time t by $E(x)v(x)e^{r(t-1)}/\kappa$, etc. The total lowering is

$$E(x)v(x)(e^{rt} + e^{r(t-1)} + e^{r(t-2)} + \ldots + e^{r})/\kappa$$

$$= E(x)v(x)e^{rt}(1 + e^{-r} + e^{-2r} + \ldots + e^{-(t-1)r})/\kappa$$

$$= \frac{E(x)v(x)(e^{rt} - 1)}{(1 - e^{-r})/\kappa} \doteq \frac{E(x)v(x)e^{rt}}{r\kappa} .$$

The approximate equality depends on t being large and the E(x) emigrants moving out uniformly through the year. This is the effect on population at time t of an emigration of E(x) persons aged x year after year starting at time zero.

It may not be superfluous to emphasize that the results of this chapter are to be regarded either as very long-run effects in a given population or else as the differences be-tween two populations alike in all respects except the one under analysis. The method is similar to that known in economics as comparative statics. We really compare two models, say one with fertility m(x) at age x and the other identical in all respects except that its fertility rate is $m(x) + \Delta m(x)$ at age x; the difference between the intrinsic rates of the two models is Δr as shown by our formulas. If we wish to think of the change $\Delta m(x)$ as actually taking place in the population, so that r was the rate of increase up to the moment of change, then $r + \Delta r$ would be the rate of increase only after many years when the new $m(x) + \Delta m(x)$ had worked its way through the age distribution. What the method does not provide is the trajectory of short-term change. In general this requires further roots of the characteristic equation and will not be discussed in this article.

5. SUMMARY OF PERTURBATION THEORY

Table 2 summarizes the effects of small changes. Its three main rows distinguish changes at age x only (say defined as exact ages $x - \frac{1}{2}$ to $x + \frac{1}{2}$), those affecting all ages from x onwards to the end of reproduction or the end of life, and arbitrary age distributions. Its two columns cover one-time changes (after which the schedule of mortality and fertility returns to its original values) and changes repeated year after year. We have seen that one-time changes cannot affect the intrinsic rate r, but they do raise the entire trajectory Qe^{rt}, and the quantity ΔQ measures the amount by which they raise it. On the other hand, a permanent change in the regime of fertility does change r, which is in effect the angle of climb of the trajectory Qe^{rt}, and the rise in r is given in the second column.

Table 2, derived by algebraic manipulation of the defined quantities, is a summary of the main formulas of the paper. It tells us for example that an added female aged x raises the birth curve by $\Delta Q = v(x)/\kappa$; this quantity is zero for $x > \beta$; no number of persons past the age of reproduction can have an effect on the trajectory beyond the time they themselves live. The addition of a female of random age raises the population curve by e^{rt}, and hence Q for births by b. The addition of P females distributed as the stable age distribution adds P to the trajectory. That the addition of a girl just born adds $1/b\kappa$ is less obvious; we may rationalize it by saying that the addition of one baby would add $e^{r\kappa}$ babies in κ years, a further $e^{2r\kappa}$ babies in 2κ years, etc., if all were born at the mean age κ of childbearing; it would take κ babies, one per year over κ years, to make a similar addition in every year of the trajectory; to a trajectory of e^{rt} births from the κ babies would correspond a population trajectory of e^{rt}/b. Hence we have an average population trajectory of $e^{rt}/b\kappa$ per baby added. (Such an argument is at best a crude way of understanding a proposition proved by the relatively tight algebra of Appendix I.)

The formulas of the table are related to one another. For example the change in Q due to the one-time small change in births becomes a change in r when the new birth rate is

	One-time small change; effect on level of births Q	Small change repeated year after year; effect on angle of climb r
Age x only		
One added female aged x	$\Delta Q = v(x)/\kappa$	
$x = 0$	$\Delta Q = \dfrac{1}{\kappa}$	
One female of random age drawn from stable population	$\Delta Q = b$ $b_x = \int_x^\beta e^{-ra}\ell(a)m(a)\,da$	
Change $\Delta m(x)$		$\Delta r = \dfrac{e^{-rx}\ell(x)}{\kappa}\,\Delta m(x)$ $= \dfrac{c(x)}{b\kappa}\,\Delta m(x)$
		$c(x)\,dx = be^{-rx}\ell(x)\,dx$ is the fraction of the population between ages x and $x + dx$
	is the fraction of births to mothers over age x	
Ages x and over		
Change $-fm(a)$, $a \geq x$ Sterilization of fraction f of those aged x Emigration of fraction f of those aged x		$\Delta r = -f\int_x^\beta e^{-ra}\ell(a)m(a)\,da/\kappa$ $= -fe^{-rx}\ell(x)v(x)/\kappa = -f\dfrac{b_x}{\kappa}$
Arbitrary age distribution		
Change $-kg(a)$ in birth function $m(a)$		$\Delta r = -\dfrac{k}{\kappa}\int_\alpha^\beta e^{ra}\ell(a)g(a)\,da$ $= -\dfrac{k}{b\kappa}\int_\alpha^\beta c(a)g(a)\,da$

Table 2: Effect of Small Population Changes on Level Q and on Rate of Increase r in Birth Trajectory Qe^{rt}.

repeated year after year.

6. THE MOMENTUM OF POPULATION GROWTH

The authorities of some underdeveloped countries fear
that once birth control is introduced their population will
immediately stop increasing. Such fears are misplaced partly
because people will take a long time to make use of birth
control. But leave aside this behavioral aspect, and consider only the momentum of population growth that arises because the age distribution of a rapidly increasing population
is favorable to increase. Suppose that all couples adopt
birth control immediately and drop their births to a level
that permits bare replacement. With modern mortality couples
that are fertile need average fewer than 2.3 children to give
a Net Reproduction Rate R_O of unity. The average of 2.3
children covers children dying before maturity, the
fact that not everyone finds a mate, and some sterility among
couples.

We saw that without any change in birth rates the ultimate birth trajectory due to $P(x) dx$ persons at age x to
$x + dx$ would be $e^{rt} P(x) v(x) dx/K$, and for the whole population
distributed as $P(x)$ would be $e^{rt} \int_O^\beta P(x) v(x) dx/K$. For calculating the effect of the fall to bare replacement we want the
trajectory based on the existing age distribution $P(x)$, but
with a function $v^*(x)$, corresponding to an intrinsic rate
$r = 0$. We can arrange this without changing any other feature of the age-incidence of childbearing by replacing $m(x)$
by $m^*(x) = m(a)/R_O$, which will ensure that $R_O^* = 1$ and
$r^* = 0$. Then the ultimate stationary number of births must
be

$$\int_O^\beta P(x) v^*(x) dx/K \text{ where } v^*(x)/K = \frac{1}{\mu \ell(x)} \int_x^\beta \frac{\ell(a) m(a) da}{R_O} , \quad (9)$$

where $\underline{\mu}$ is the mean age of childbearing in the stationary
population. The ultimate stationary total population will be
divided by $\underline{b}$, the stationary birth rate, which is the same as
being multiplied by e_O^o, the expectation of life at zero.

Expression (9) is readily usable. If we have a table of
the net maternity function in five-year age intervals up to
age 49, and the initial age distribution, then by cumulating

the net maternity function to obtain $_5V^*_x$ and multiplying ten pairs of $_5P_x$ and $_5V^*_x$ we have the ultimate stationary popula-

$$\overset{o}{e}_O \sum_{O}^{\beta-5} {}_5P_x \, {}_5V^*_x/\mu, \text{ where}$$

$$_5V^*_x = \frac{5}{_5L_x}\left(\frac{1}{2} \, {}_5L_x {}_F_x + {}_5L_{x+5}{}_F_{x+5} + \dots \right)/R_O . \qquad (10)$$

This calculation would give the same result as a full population projection with the new $m^*(x)$.

If the initial age distribution $P(x)$ can be taken as stable, then we have an even simpler form. Entering $P(x) = be^{-rx}\ell(x)$ in (9), where $\underline{r}$ is the intrinsic rate before the drop to zero increase, cancelling out $\ell(x)$, and multiplying by $\overset{o}{e}_O$ to produce the stationary population rather than stationary births, we obtain

$$\frac{\overset{o}{e}_O}{\mu} \int_O^\beta P(x) v^*(x) \, dx = \frac{b\overset{o}{e}_O}{\mu} \int_O^\beta \int_x^\beta e^{-rx}\ell(a) \frac{m(a)}{R_O} \, da\,dx \qquad (11)$$

as the ratio of the ultimate stationary population to the population at the time when the fall occurs.

The double integral is evaluated by writing b_x for $\int_x^\beta \ell(a)m(a)\,da/R_O$, and integrating by parts in (11) to obtain

$$\frac{b\overset{o}{e}_O}{\mu} \int_O^\beta e^{-rx} b_x \, dx = \frac{b\overset{o}{e}_O}{\mu}\left(\frac{e^{-rx}}{-r} b_x \Big|_O^\beta - \frac{1}{r} \int_O^\beta e^{-rx} \frac{\ell(x)m(x)}{R_O} \, dx \right) ;$$

the right-hand side reduces to

$$\frac{b\overset{o}{e}_O}{r\mu}\left(b_O - \frac{1}{R_O} \right) = \frac{b\overset{o}{e}_O}{r\mu}\left(\frac{R_O - 1}{R_O} \right) , \qquad (12)$$

on applying the fact that $b_O = 1$.

Expression (12) gives the ratio of ultimate population to population just before the fall, and is the main result of this section.

For Ecuador, 1965, we are given $1000b = 44.82$; $\overset{\circ}{e}_O = 60.16$; $1000r = 33.31$; $\mu = 29.41$; and $R_O = 2.59$. These make the expression (12) equal to 1.69. By simple projection, or by (10) which does not depend on the stable assumption, we would have a ratio of the ultimate stationary to the present population of 1.67. This and other experiments show that the degree of stability in many underdeveloped countries makes (12) realistic.

James Frauenthal points out to me that $(b\overset{\circ}{e}_O/r\mu)[(R_O - 1)/R_O]$ of (12) is very nearly $b\overset{\circ}{e}/\sqrt{R_O}$. For R_O is approximately $e^{r\mu}$, and hence

$$\frac{b\overset{\circ}{e}_O}{r\mu}\left(\frac{R_O - 1}{R_O}\right) = \frac{b\overset{\circ}{e}_O}{\sqrt{R_O}}\left(\frac{e^{(r\mu)/2} - e^{-(r\mu)/2}}{r\mu}\right)$$

$$= \frac{b\overset{\circ}{e}_O}{\sqrt{R_O}}\left(1 + \frac{r^2\mu^2}{24}\right),$$

on expanding the exponentials up to terms in $r^4\mu^4$. The product $r\mu$ can hardly be as large as unity, so that $r^2\mu^2/24$ must be less than 0.05. The example of Ecuador, 1965, gives $b\overset{\circ}{e}_O/\sqrt{R_O} = 1.68$ against 1.69 for (12).

To obtain an intuitive meaning of this, note that the absolute number of births just after the fall must be $1/R_O$ times the births just before the fall. Births will subsequently rise and then drop in waves of diminishing amplitude, and it seems likely that the oscillations will be about the mean of the absolute numbers before and after the fall. If the geometric mean of 1 and $1/R_O$ applies, then the ultimate number of births will be $1/\sqrt{R_O}$ times the births before the fall. In that case the ultimate population will be $\overset{\circ}{e}_O/\sqrt{R_O}$ times the births before the fall, or $b\overset{\circ}{e}_O/\sqrt{R_O}$ times the population before the fall.

The conclusion is that with an immediate fall of fertility to bare replacement Ecuador and demographically similar countries would increase by about two thirds before attaining stationarity. Note that (12), or $b\overset{\circ}{e}_O/\sqrt{R_O}$, is a good approximation in the degree in which the age distribution before the fall is stable.

7. MOMENTUM UNDER A LESS DRASTIC FALL OF FERTILITY

The long-term stationary level, if the age-specific birth rates of an arbitrary or observed population drop to bare replacement, is given by the simple expression (9), whose reproductive value $v^*(x)$ is calculated for a reduced schedule of birth rates $m^*(a) = m(a)/R_O$.

The technique is more general than here indicated. Suppose we require the population at time $\underline{t}$ if the age-specific birth rates drop not to bare replacement but to something short of this, say a Net Reproduction Rate R^*_O , where $1 < R^*_O < R_O$. Such an R^*_O would correspond to about r^* = $r \log R^*_O/\log R_O$, since for given length of generation $\underline{T}$ the annual rate $\underline{r}$ is proportional to $\log R_O$. Then all we need is to evaluate $v^*(x)$ with an intrinsic rate r^* rather than with $\underline{r}$ or with O. In fact, the same formula (9) would apply if we replace $\ell(a)$ wherever it appears by $e^{-r^*a}\ell(a)$, because the discount factor enters the expression for reproductive value in exactly the same way as does the survival factor. Hence we have for the population at time $\underline{t}$

$$\frac{1}{b^*} \int_0^\beta P(a)v^*(a)da\ e^{r^*t}/\kappa, \text{ the} \tag{13}$$

$$b^* = 1/\int_0^\omega e^{-r^*a}\ell(a)da \text{ and } v^* = \int_x^\beta e^{-r^*a}\ell(a)m^*(a)da/[e^{-r^*x}\ell(x)\kappa]$$

being calculated with r^* and with $m^*(a) = m(a)R^*_O/R_O$.

Similarly we could find the ultimate effect of women marrying later and so substituting illegitimate for legitimate births, the illegitimate presumably being at a lower rate. In no such case is a detailed projection required, though if computing expense is not of importance and a numerical result only is required, that can be found by projection.

8. ELIMINATING HEART DISEASE WOULD MAKE VERY LITTLE DIFFER-
ENCE TO POPULATION INCREASE, WHILE ERADICATION OF MALARIA
MAKES A GREAT DEAL OF DIFFERENCE

Age distributions of deaths from malaria and heart disease are shown in Table 3 for the Philippines, 1959. Evidently malaria affects the young ages, while heart disease is
negligible before middle life. Though the two causes are responsible for about equal numbers of deaths, malaria has a
much greater effect on the chance that a child survives to
reproductive age and on the number of women living through
reproduction.

To see the effect on the population trajectory of eliminating deaths in any one year requires that each death at age
x be evaluated as $v(x)$, which is to say, we need the sum

$\int_0^\beta P(x)v(x)dx$, where now $P(x)dx$ is the population removed by

death at age x to $x + dx$. (The constants b and k will not
affect the relative positions of the two causes.) The broad
age groups and lumping of the two sexes in Table 3 prevent
us from gaining high accuracy. Table 3 shows unweighted

Age x to x+n	Malaria Cause B-16 1959	Degenerative heart disease Cause B-26 1959	Reproductive value for females Philippines 1960 n^v_x
All ages	913	918	
-5	251	12	1.21
5-14	156	7	1.64
15-24	133	37	2.00
25-44	186	198	0.76
45-64	138	322	0
65+	45	333	0
Unknown	4	9	
Total reproductive value for deaths of stated age	967	250	

Table 3: Deaths from Malaria and Heart Disease, Philippines
1959 and Reproductive Value 1960.
Source: *United Nations Demographic Yearbook*, 1961, p. 498.
Keyfitz and Flieger, 1971, p. 411.

610

arithmetic averages of the v(x) for the age groups required.
The value of the malaria deaths, if they were female, would
be (251)(1.21) + (156)(1.64) + (133)(2.00) + (186)(0.76) =
967; that of the heart disease deaths similarly calculated
would be 250. The number of men influences births as much
as the number of women in a regime of rigid monogamy. Departures from such a regime probably make the number of men
less important for births; under conditions of promiscuity
births would depend almost wholly on the number of women, or
more precisely on their reproductive value.

But the complexities that a two-sex model would introduce would not greatly affect the present conclusion, that
though absolute numbers of deaths from heart disease are
about equal to those from malaria, malaria has nearly four
times the effect on subsequent population.

REFERENCES

Fisher, R. A.   1929.   *The Genetical Theory of Natural Selection*.   2nd rev. ed., New York: Dover Publications,
1958.

Goodman, L. A.   1967.   "On the Reconciliation of Mathematical Theories of Population Growth," *Journal of the Royal
Statistical Society,* Series A, 130: 541-553.

Goodman, L. A.   1969.   "The Analysis of Population Growth
When the Birth and Death Rates Depend Upon Several Factors," *Biometrics,* 25: 659-681.

Keyfitz, N.   1971a.   "On the Momentum of Population Growth,"
Demography, 8: 71-80.

Keyfitz, N.   1971b.   "Linkages of Intrinsic to Age-Specific
Rates," *Journal of the American Statistical Association,*
66: 275-281.

Keyfitz, N.   1971c.   "Migration as a Means of Population Control." *Population Studies,* 25: 63-72.

Keyfitz, N.   and W. Flieger.   1971.   *Population: Facts and
Methods of Demography*.   San Francisco: W. H. Freeman
and Company.

Leslie, P. H.   1945.   "On the Use of Matrices in Certain
Population Mathematics," *Biometrika,* 33: 183-212.

Lotka, A. J. 1939. *Théórie analytique des associations biologiques*. Part II. Analyse démographique avec application particulière à l'espèce humaine. (Actualités Scientifiques et Industrielles, No. 780) Paris: Hermann & Cie.

United Nations, *Demographic Yearbook*. 1961. New York: United Nations International Publications Service.

Widjojo Nitisastro. 1970. *Population Trends in Indonesia*. Ithaca, N.Y.: Cornell University Press.

22

Toward a Simulation of Urban Sprawl

ROGER MALM
University of Göteborg

GUNNAR OLSSON
University of Michigan

OLOF WÄRNERYD
University of Lund

1. INTRODUCTION

Like all social science disciplines, Geography is currently changing into an exact discipline making extensive use of mathematics, statistics and other quantitative tools. As in related fields, the formulation of general theories is particularly emphasized. To a large extent, these theories have been based on traditional geographic knowledge, but their further development has been facilitated by use of interdisciplinary quantitative techniques. In this way, statistics, operations research, regional science and economics have played an important role for modern geography. It is only rarely, however, that the adopted techniques have been applicable to spatial problems without considerable modification of the original formulations (Isard and Reiner, 1965).

The recognition of a minimum number of basic variables, by which any spatial system can be fully described, has been crucial in this development. It has led to a general agreement that spatial descriptions can be accomplished by specifying distances, angles, and connectivity within a set of spatially distributed points or locations (Nystuen, 1963, Bunge, 1962.) Out of these concepts, distance is probably most important. But it is also a very complex notion, quantifiable in physical, economical, time and a variety of sociological units of measurement (Deutsch and Isard, 1961). Generally, these units can be projected into each other and much work has been put into the search for correct transformation functions (Tobler, 1963). Having found these

613

functions, though, the analysis of angles between individual locations gets far more complicated and only non-Euclidean geometry seems applicable.

In some quantitative techniques, for example the transportation variant of the linear programming problem (Hadley, 1962, Dantzig, 1963, and Henderson, 1958), or the solutions of the travelling salesman problem (Dacey, 1960, Pollack and Wiebenson, 1960, Boye, 1965), the distance variable has been explicitly included. In most instances, though, the spatial variables have been regrettably neglected. Bearing this in mind, the present chapter will demonstrate how traditional Monte Carlo techniques can be employed in simulations of spatial patterns (Hammersley and Handscomb, 1964). More specifically, the general features of spatial simulation models will be noted and a simple model of urban sprawl will be sketched. The discussion will close with a few comments on the evaluation of simulated patterns.

2. THE DISTANCE VARIABLE

Spatial theorists usually assume the intensity of flows or interactions between points or locations to decrease with increases in intervening distance. The general agreement between reality and related parts of the theories has been overwhelmingly demonstrated (Isard, 1956, Olsson, 1965, Zipf, 1949). Therefore, if a spatial simulation model will be successful, this fact must be explicitly considered. Consequently, the derivation of feasible distance functions will be discussed in some detail.

Thus far, the majority of spatial simulation models have treated phenomena like diffusion of innovations (Hägerstrand, 1965, Bowden, 1965), migrations and the growth of urban systems (Morrill, 1963, Lund, 1965, Garrison, 1962), general interaction patterns (Taaffe, Garner and Yeates, 1963), cities' inner differentiation (Lowry, 1964, Steger, 1965, Morrill, 1965), etc. For all of these phenomena, the intensity of personal face-to-face communication has been assumed to determine the evolution of related spatial patterns. But data on face-to-face communication are rarely available and distance functions have generally been derived via surrogate data like migrations, telephone calls, and marriages. From the theoretical point of view, this is advantageous, since it reduces the risk for circular reasoning.

The distance decay function has often been determined via the social gravity formulation (Carrothers, 1956, Isard, 1960, Lukermann and Porter, 1960 and Olsson, 1965).

614

$$I_{ij} = G \frac{(w_i P_i)^{a_i} (w_j P_j)^{a_j}}{D_{ij}^b} \tag{1}$$

where I_{ij} = interaction between places i and j

P_i = number of inhabitants in place i

P_j = number of inhabitants in place j

D_{ij} = distance between places i and j

w_i = weight attached to P_i

w_j = weight attached to P_j

G = empirically derived constant

$a_i : a_j : b$ = empirically derived exponents

To facilitate computations: $w_i : w_j : a_i :$ and $a_j :$ have usually been set equal to 1 and expression (1) becomes

$$\log \frac{I_{ij}}{P_i P_j} = \log k - b \log D_{ij} \tag{2}$$

If expression (2) is treated as a regression line, simple correlation coefficients will indicate the goodness of fit (Olsson, 1965).

The value of b indicates, of course, how rapidly interaction intensity decreases with increases in intervening distance.

But expressions (1) and (2) consider only interactions between two points at a time. Hence they do not automatically account for the fact that these points belong to a whole system of places, offering alternatives for the interacting individuals. Although a special type of expression (2) might take these complications into account (Olsson, 1965), it seems more straightforward to employ the formulation (Reilly, 1931, Lakshmanan and Hansen, 1965)

$$I_{ij} = k \frac{\sum\limits_{h} \frac{P_j}{D_{ih}^b}}{\frac{P_h}{D_{ij}^b}} \qquad (3)$$

However, expressions (1), (2), and, to a lesser extent, (3) are basically deterministic formulations and before they can be used in simulation models, they must be transformed into non-deterministic ones. Via such formulations, the statistical probability for interaction over a given distance can then be derived. For example, expression (2), usually termed the gravity regression or the Pareto model, can be changed to read

$$\log p(d) = c - b \log d \qquad (4)$$

or

$$p(d) = c/d^b \qquad (5)$$

where $p(d)$ stands for the probability of interaction between two points separated by the distance d, while c and b are empirically derived parameters.

But many writers have found generations based on probabilities from (5) to over-estimate the amount of short-distance interactions (Morrill and Pitts, 1963, Morrill, 1963). On the other hand, generations based either on the lognormal function

$$p(d) = ce^{-b}(\log d)^2 \qquad (6)$$

where e stands for the base of the natural logarithms, or on the exponential function

$$p(d) = ce^{-bd} \qquad (7)$$

generally under-estimate the close-in contacts (Morrill and Pitts, 1963, Morrill, 1963). New generations have therefore been based on a combination of the Pareto and the exponential function (Johnsson, 1952, Tanner, 1961), specified as

$$p(d) = cd^{-1}e^{-bd} \qquad (8)$$

This expression, often characterized as an analogue to the physical law of absorption, has resulted in fairly good simulation results. The same applies to recent experiments (Claeson, 1964) with expression

$$\log p(d) = c_1 - c_2 \log d - c_3 (\log d)^2 \qquad (9)$$

All functions discussed thus far are reasonably easy to handle and the mathematics involved are simple. But the use of other, more complicated functions, has also been discussed, and attention should be drawn to the general gamma function (Järhult, 1958, Cavalli-Sforza, 1962), the truncated incomplete gamma function (Dacey, 1965), which are both special cases of the chi-square function (Morrill, 1963), the Gaussian function (Bateman, 1962), and to different types of Fourrier functions (Ajo, 1955, Curry, 1964). On the other extreme, the use of very simple distance functions is sometimes sufficient, and one example will be offered later in this chapter.

Although derivation of correct distance functions is the most important step in the formulation of spatial simulation models, the function cannot be fed into the model in its strict mathematical form. Instead, it is used for determining a spatial probability matrix, specifying for each part of the study area the probability that it is "it" (i.e. the probability of receiving an immigrant, being settled, etc.). In models where face-to-face communication is a decisive element, this probability matrix is usually termed as a *Mean Information Field* (Marble and Nystuen, 1963, Morrill, 1965). A hypothetical example of such a field is given in Figure 1.

	a	b	c	d	e
A	.022	.028	.032	.028	.022
B	.028	.045	.063	.045	.028
C	.032	.063	.127	.063	.032
D	.028	.045	.063	.045	.029
E	.022	.028	.032	.028	.022

Fig. 1. *Hypothetical Probability Matrix*

In this particular example it is assumed that a person lives in the center of the field, i.e. in cell Cc. The numbers in the matrix specify his probability of establishing face-to-face contact with someone else living in his own or in any other cell. In Figure 1, the probability of contacting a person in one's own cell was arbitrarily set equal to .127, while the other probabilities were derived via expression (5) above, i.e.

$$p(d) = c/d^b$$

where d was set equal to the length of one side in a cell, and c and b to 1. Integrations were now performed and each cell was centered at its geometric midpoint. The grid in Figure 1 is floating, indicating that it is successively inserted with Cc over the individual whose interaction pattern one is interested in at the moment.

To facilitate the use of Monte Carlo techniques, the Mean Information Field is generally translated into a matrix of random numbers. If these are allowed to vary between 000-999, where each random number represents a probability of .001, the Mean Information Field in Figure I can then be translated into the random number matrix in Figure 2.

A	000-021	022-049	050-081	082-109	110-131
B	132-159	160-204	205-267	268-312	313-340
C	341-372	373-435	436-563	564-626	627-658
D	659-686	687-731	732-794	795-839	840-867
E	868-889	890-917	918-949	950-977	978-999

Fig. 2. *Matrix of Random Numbers*

For a very simplified case, Figures 1 and 2 specify the rules by which individuals living in cell Cc are assumed to establish face-to-face contacts with other individuals. These rules are then given motive power by the drawing of random numbers. Suppose for example that one wants to simulate the face-to-face communication pattern of five individuals living in cell Cc. Suppose further, that the five random numbers 363, 678, 250, 400 and 630 are drawn. From Figure 2 it can then be determined that the first individual establishes contact with cell Ca, the second with Da, the third with Bc, the fourth with Cb and the last one with cell Ce. In the figure, these contacts have been shown by arrows.

In some simulation models, for example the one to be sketched later in this chapter, the assumption of face-to-face contact is irrelevant and the equivalent of the Mean Information Field should be termed something else. However, this would not change the principles already outlined and the example of a Mean Information Field was chosen for illustrative purposes only.

3. SPACE PREFERENCES

In Figure 1, the probability of being contacted by an individual in cell Cc decreases symmetrically as intervening distance increases. In reality, however, this is only rarely the case and most interaction patterns are in fact distinctly asymmetric. It is well verified, for instance, that the distance decay function varies both with the hierarchical order of the interacting places (Claeson, 1969, Olsson, 1965, Wärneryd, 1965), and with the demographical and socioeconomic characteristics of the interactors (Carroll, 1957, Hägerstrand, 1957, Dahl, 1957, Murdie, 1965). Further, contacts tend to follow traditional, well-established channels (Hägerstrand, 1956, Bergsten, 1951), which sometimes can be explained by the existence of physical obstacles like swamps, lakes, mountains etc. Generally, such deviations from symmetrical patterns are termed "space preferences."

As a rule, space preferences are very complex and it is difficult to force them into exact mathematical expressions. Sometimes, however, they can be included within the distance function. Thus, w_i, w_j, a_i, a_j, in the general gravity formulation, i.e. expression (1) above, might be allowed to vary according to demographical and socio-economic characteristics of the interactors (Taaffe, Garner and Yeates, 1963). If b in the same expression is made a function of the hierarchical order of the interacting places i and j, another type of space preference might be considered. The directional bias, that is the tendency that recent interactions follow traditional channels, can sometimes be studied via sector analyses (Kant, 1951). The results from these can then be fed into the model by assigning different b-values to different sectors.

However, the techniques mentioned in the previous paragraph are all related to the problem of physical versus functional distance, more specifically to the derivation of mathematical functions by which different distance concepts can be projected into each other. The mere recognition of space preferences might in fact indicate the researcher's confinement to physical distance and his mental inability of replacing this concept by a more functional one. Rephrased, this means that one has not yet been able to transform a non-homogeneous area into an isotropic, theoretical plain. However, recent work on map transformations and projections are well advanced and the mathematical treatment of space preferences might soon be solved by application of this technique (Tobler, 1961). It is doubtful, though, whether these transformations, generally performed in n-dimensional space, should be re-transformed into a two-dimensional map.

However, awaiting the further development of this technique, simulation models must consider space preferences in less sophisticated ways. One of these is to assign different "resistance values" to different individuals or cells in the probability matrix. Technically, this is accomplished by the inclusion of a rule stating how many times a cell has to be hit by a random number before it is settled, an innovation is accepted, an immigration performed, etc. The assignment of resistance values is, of course, based on empirical investigations, but it is still a very delicate and unprecise task.

It was previously mentioned that the persistency of traditional interaction routes is sometimes caused by physical barriers like lakes and mountain chains. Other barriers can be of a social or economic nature, for instance ghettos in large cities or political boundaries (Mackay, 1958). Several computer programs have already been worked out for the treatment of such barriers (Yuill, 1965). Although these programs have often been formulated as simple analogues to the passing of physical waves through various media, they are basically making use of the "resistance value technique" already outlined. When these models are viewed as physical analogues, it is tempting, of course, to automatically apply standard formulas from Physics. At closer examination, however, this approach seems very dangerous and it might be better to employ steplike distance functions.

4. A REVIEW OF URBAN MODELS

Urban structure has usually been viewed as the result of three partly counteracting forces: agglomeration or centripetal forces, deglomeration or centrifugal forces, and the force of specialization or inner differentiation (Dickinson and Olsson, 1965). Early models treated these factors in a

verbal way, while recent writers have managed to express them
in mathematical terms generally borrowed from the classical
theory of economic equilibrium (Isard, 1956, Alonso, 1960,
1964). Related ideas have also been inherent in many models
of the spatial distribution of urban populations (Clark, 1951,
Stewart, 1958, Wingo, 1961, Muth, 1961a, Berry, Simmons and
Tennant, 1963).

It is generally agreed that most urban models can be
rather easily related to von Thünen's well-known agricultural
theory (von Thünen, 1826) in which land use patterns were assumed to be generated by the maximization of rent at every
site. The intensity in land use was further supposed to be
inversely proportional to transportation cost or distance
from the market. On an isotropic plain, this leads to concentric land use pattern with the least intensive land use
located farthest away from the metropolis.

In an early study Haig applied von Thünen's ideas to internal city structure (Haig, 1928), assuming that any site
within the city was used in such a way that profit from the
land was maximized. More specifically, he assumed sales
volumes to vary inversely with distance from the city center,
while costs for each firm were determined as a function of
its sales volume. As in agriculture, these factors were supposed to generate a concentric zone pattern with the most
specialized activities concentrated to the city center. Provided every site was occupied by a firm paying maximum land
rent and minimizing distance to its customers, an optimal
city structure was thought to develop.

Similar ideas were also basic in Burgess' classical
model of urban growth (Burgess, 1925). Thus, he assumed that
most cities had a concentric differentiation of land use, but
also that this pattern had developed by successive expansion
starting at the city center and pushing each concentric zone
outwards. However, factors like topography or transportation
networks can cause disturbances in the ideal pattern. Therefore, Hoyt suggested that the Burgess model be modified so
that homogeneous sectors with the apex at the city center,
and not concentric zones were developed (Hoyt, 1939). As a
rule, these sectors were assumed to run along traffic routes.
This means that Haig and Burgess concentrated on the distance
and connectivity concepts, while Hoyt also included the
notion of direction. However, all the three writers have had
a great influence on subsequent theorists (Wright, 1936,
Colby, 1933, Olsson, 1937, 1940, Ratcliff, 1955) and it was
recently suggested that Burgess gave a good account of urban
growth, while Hoyt offered a better description of the
spatial distribution of population groups (Anderson and
Egeland, 1961).

This suggests that the zone and sector theories should be unified, possibly in the way proposed by Harris and Ullman (Harris and Ullman, 1945). According to these writers, cities are not centered around one single central business district but around several minor nuclei. The growth of the system was further supposed to be caused by a large number of factors. Thus, some activities always tend to be located in the vicinity of each other, others repell each other, while some cannot afford the high rents demanded for the best sites. The theory is supported by the fact that land values do not decrease with the same rapidity in all directions from the city core (Seyfried, 1963). This indicates that the very simple schemes discussed thus far can be applicable only if distance is measured in non-physical, preferably accessibility, terms (Watson, 1955, Olsson, 1965).

It should finally be mentioned that strict probability models have been formulated both for the spatial distribution of cities on a large scale (Curry, 1964), and for the inner differentiation of these places (Curry, 1962). In the latter model, Poisson distributions with varying parameter were used to portray the spatial variations in purchases of single goods. Via these patterns of distributions, spatial specializations were then generated. In the simulations, shopping goods tended to be purchased in downtown areas, while firms selling convenience goods were distributed more ubiquitously over the whole city. More specialized shops were located closer to the city center.

In conclusion, the probabilistic approach to location seems appealing. However, little work has yet been done and definite judgments must await empirical tests. Meanwhile, Berry and his associates have produced a large number of books and articles in which the non-probabilistic approach has been refined and employed with considerable success (Berry, 1963, 1964, Berry and Garrison, 1958). These workers have certainly demonstrated the complexity of the problem, but they have also verified very strong relationships between a number of well-defined variables.

As earlier theorists, they have noted how variations in land use generally can be explained by variations in distance from the city center. But they have also pointed out that details in many city patterns do not actually conform with the simple models. Instead, greater attention has been drawn to the modifying influence of demographic, social, economic and other space preferences. Some students have focused on the influence by domain structure or the partition of land between different owners (Bernouili, 1946, Sund, 1947, Hartke, 1953, Ruppert, 1955, Möller, 1959, Conzen, 1958, Lassau, 1962, Ward, 1962, Dethier, 1962).

Among these studies, a recent Swedish one treated the area sprawl of towns, considering it a function not only of land ownership but also of administrative boundaries (Améen, 1964). The results were summarized in three verbal "models," one for the preindustrial era, one for the industrialization period and one for the period after 1930. The latter model was the most dynamic one, partly because this period was characterized by a growing interest in physical city planning.

However, relatively few studies have been devoted to the physical growth of cities. As a consequence, the present knowledge about underlying processes is limited. Further, the random element in these processes is probably considerable, suggesting that city growth might be successfully analyzed via simulation models. In passing, some simulations of urban growth have already been mentioned, but the studies of American towns by Chapin and his associates should also be noted (Chapin and Weiss, 1962, Donelly, Chapin and Weiss, 1964). Thus, these writers started by mapping the individual factors judged to be most relevant for city growth. The derivation of probability matrices was then based on these maps. For example, it was verified that topography and ground conditions sometimes leave areas completely unsuitable for exploitation, while, in other cases, the probabilities are highly influenced by the configuration of a city's transportation system (Lathrop and Hamburg, 1965).

In closing this section, attention should finally be drawn to several handbook and research volumes offering good summaries of present knowledge (Mayer and Kohn, 1959, Norborg, 1962, Beaujeu-Garnier and Chabot, 1963, Friedmann and Alonso, 1964).

5. AN OUTLINE OF A SIMULATION OF URBAN SPRAWL

The previous discussion may serve as a general background for a simulation of physical sprawl of urban areas. Input data have been collected from the northern part of Gothenburg, Sweden, and the development between 1920 and 1940 will be simulated. Following the theory proposed by Harris and Ullman (Harris and Ullmann, 1945, Malm and Wäarneryd, 1965), cities were assumed to be centered around more than one nucleus, while the spatial expansion from these nuclei was supposed to conform with the general distance law. But

other types of space preferences must also be considered.
Thus, the influence of political decisions was allowed to
confine the growth to areas within the administrative city
limits. Further, the probability of erecting a new building
was made a function of local terrain and ground conditions.
More specifically, the proximity bias was quantified via a
chorologic matrix specifying the cost of extending roads,
water mains, sewerage, etc. Other space preferences were
determined via a matrix of construction costs per apartment,
with slopes of 1 to 8.75, while, for other areas, it increased or decreased at the same rate as changes in the angle
of inclination. This caused the production costs to vary
according to slope and ground conditions. Each cell in the
matrix was arbitrarily chosen as a square with the sides
equal to 400 meters.

For the investigated area, the cost of production had a
mean of 65,000 Swedish Kroner per apartment. This figure
applied to squares with a mean slope of 1 to 8.75, while, for
other areas, it increased or decreased at the same rate as
changes in the angle of inclination. This made the production
cost vary between 35,750 and 94,250 Sw. kr. per apartment.
Further, cost for extending roads, water mains, sewerage,
electricity, etc. was equal to 2,340 Sw. kr. per meter and
total extension cost consequently a function of distance from
the nearest built-up square. However, this cost must be
equally paid by all apartments in the cell. Since it was
normal to construct 80 rooms per hectar and 3.5 rooms per
apartment, this resulted in an average of 22.86 apartments
per hectar. As distance between two adjacent cells equalled
400 meters, the total cost for extending the "service network" to an adjacent square was 400(2,340)/22.86 x, where x
denotes net area suitable for construction. Total cost of
construction was finally obtained for each square by summing
production and extension costs.

Since the probability of erecting new buildings in a
cell is inversely proportional to the projected costs of construction, the cost matrix cannot be used for simulation purposes unless it has been inverted. This has been achieved by
calculating for every cell its difference from the average
construction cost. Retaining the signs, these differences
have then been multiplied by 2 and added to the calculated
production cost in each cell. These new values were finally
transformed via cumulative numbers to the matrix of random
numbers shown in Figure 3. Crossed squares mark areas that
were already built-up in 1920. This matrix will serve the
same purposes as the hypothetical one in Figure 2.

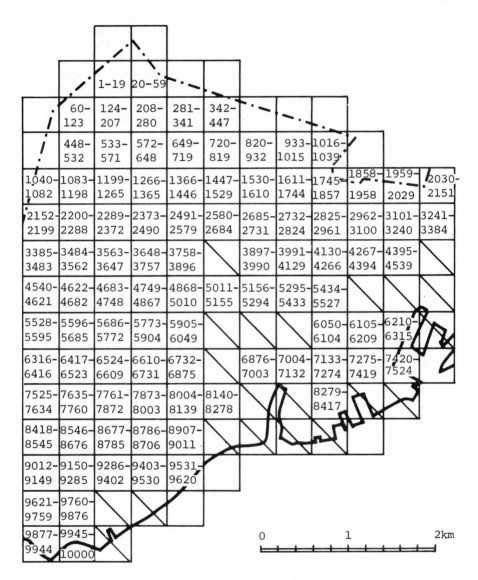

FIG. 3. PROBABILITY MATRIX

To summarize, the random number matrix in Figure 3 represents the probabilities for construction when proximity and "slope" preferences have been taken into account. As the investigated area lies entirely within the city limits, the influence of domain structure has been accounted for in an implicit way. However, the probabilities were derived without attention to ground conditions. This factor has therefore been considered by assigning to each cell a resistance value ranging from 1 to 3 (Bjurström, 1963). Squares with morain, gravel and sand, were assigned the value 1, indicating that they will be built up immediately as they are "hit" by a random number. Squares with a resistance value equal 2 consist of bedrock and must be hit twice, while the value 3 represents squares with clay, which must be hit three times before construction works are supposed to start. Since the built-up area increased from 250 to 600 hectars between 1920 and 1940 the building up of 22 squares, each one with an area of 16 hectars, was to be simulated. The location of simulated areas is shown by Figure 4, while the actual map of built-up areas in 1940 is reproduced in Figure 5.

Since this is only a first attempt at simulating urban sprawl, several simplifications have been made. After each generation or acceptance, for example, extension costs should have been adjusted to the new conditions and a new random number matrix calculated. However, such recalculations have not been performed. Further, the many simplifications made it meaningless to subject the model to a sophisticated and powerful test. Instead, the next section will be devoted to a general discussion of test techniques, and provided the model had been more detailed, one or several of these should have been applied.

In spite of the simplifications already mentioned, visual inspection of Figures 4 and 5 indicates a fair agreement between simulated and real-world patterns. The main differences can probably be explained by the exclusion of several general factors, particularly the price elasticity of total production cost. Furthermore, domain structure should have been included in the model in a more direct way and detailed rules for political goals, etc., should have been specified. From the technical point of view, the influence of the size of the cells should have been studied and new probability matrices should have been derived via recursion formulas.

6. EVALUATION OF SIMULATION MODELS

The evaluation of a spatial simulation model--i.e. the comparison between simulated and real-world patterns--

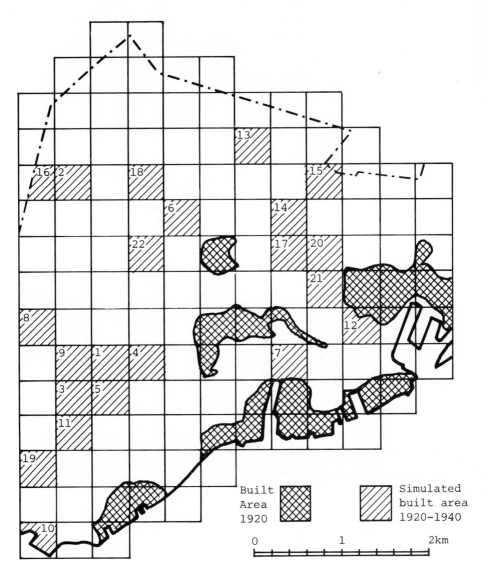

Built Area 1920

Simulated built area 1920-1940

0   1   2km

FIG. 4.   SIMULATED BUILT AREA FOR A PART OF HISINGEN,
          GOTHENBURG IN THE YEAR 1940.

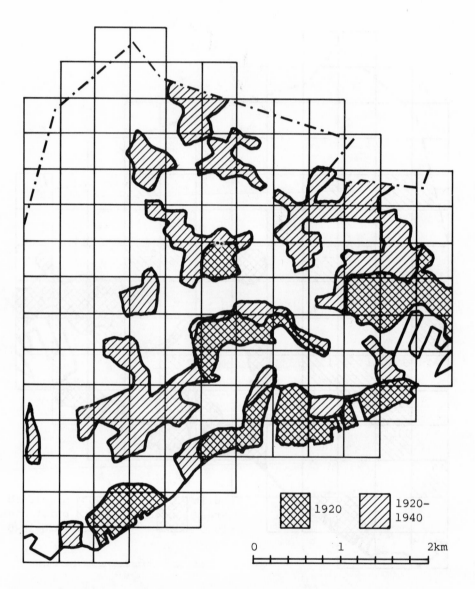

FIG. 5.   BUILT AREA FOR A PART OF HISINGEN, GOTHENBURG IN THE
YEARS 1920 AND 1940.

presents the researcher with a number of difficult problems.
These are in fact so intricate that they have been used as
arguments against the entire simulation technique, stating
that a model is rather meaningless unless it can be subjected
to an objective test.

One difficulty with testing of simulation models is, of
course, that only one or a mean of a limited number of simulated patterns, each one different in detail, is compared
with the unique real-world pattern. On the other hand, simulation models are not designed to portray *the* real world, but
rather to sketch some of its more general features. Therefore, the performance of a test might be characterized as an
objective description of and comparison between two or several spatial patterns, paying particular attention to their
evolution over time. By stressing the word "objective" in
the previous sentence, one has emphasized that visual tests
are not sufficient. This might sound trivial, but lacking
more exact techniques, most spatial simulation models have
hitherto been evaluated in this manner. In the light of
recent studies on individuals' perception of spatial patterns, this is of course regrettable indeed (Dacey and
Karaska, 1963, Shepard, 1962). On the other hand, present
techniques for description and analysis of patterns are underdeveloped. In addition, most methods emanate from
studies by plant ecologists, who naturally have designed
them to fit their own research questions (Greig-Smith, 1964).
Notwithstanding, evaluations of spatial simulation models
must rely on these techniques. By combining several of them,
it might be possible to first concentrate on the development
of patterns over time, and then on some more specific spatial
aspects.

Provided the time aspect is particularly emphasized, the
technique of quadrat counting could be used (Greig-Smith,
1964). In this type of analysis, a grid is placed over a map
on which the distribution of the study object has been represented by dots. The number of dots in each cell is then
observed and a theoretical statistical function is fitted to
the data. After that, the agreement between generated and
observed distributions can be analyzed by standard techniques
like chi-square, Kolmogorov-Smirnov or other tests. However,
both size and shape of the cells complicate the tests. This
means that even if a statistical analysis has shown no significant difference between an observed and a theoretical
distribution, this fact cannot be used as a formal *proof* of
a theory, only as an indication of its relevance (Curtis and
McIntosh, 1950).

In comments on quadrat count, it has been argued that observed and theoretical distributions always can be brought into closer agreement simply by the use of more complex functions. Although this is probably true, the technique can be extremely valuable, particularly since almost any theoretical function can be connected with at least one physical urn model. Via these, the student might then draw inductive conclusions about generating processes (Skellam, 1952). Thus, an urn model specifies how a particular distribution can be generated by drawing off differently colored balls from different urns (Feller, 1964). Only as an example, attention should be drawn to Pólya's famous scheme in which an urn contains black and red balls. One of these is then drawn at random and immediately replaced together with one or several balls of the same color. This means, of course, that the number of balls of the drawn color increases, while the number of balls of the opposite color remains unchanged. In mathematical terms, this implies that the drawing of either color increases the probability of obtaining the same color in the next drawing. Because of this, the Pólya urn model can be characterized as a very rough model of phenomena like the spread of a disease or the diffusion of an innovation. The technique is particularly valuable in the inductive stages of theory formulation and it has been used by many plant ecologists to scrutinize problems of process. Recently, the geographer Dacey has studied it (Dacey, 1963, 1964c, 1964d), while Harvey excellently applied the same idea in his analysis of diffusion of spatial innovations (Harvey, 1965). The technique must be employed with greatest care, however, since several fundamentally different models may give rise to the same probability distribution (Skellam, 1952).

The first step in a quadrat analysis is generally to test whether the pattern is random or not. An observed distribution is said to be random if it can be reasonably fitted to the Poisson function, i.e.

$$p(x) = \frac{e^{-\bar{x}} \bar{x}^x}{x!} \tag{10}$$

where $p(x)$ equals the probability of obtaining x number of points in any cell, $\bar{x}$ equals the mean number of points and e the base of the Naperian logarithms.

However, most spatial patterns are non-random. Thus, the proximity bias has already been discussed at some length, while other types of space preferences have been considered more briefly. It should be expected, therefore, that many

630

observed distributions cannot be successfully fitted to the Poisson function. In spatial diffusion studies, for instance, it must be explicitly assumed that the location of, say, the second and third acceptors are not independent of the location of the first one. In such cases, the data can often be fitted to some compound distribution generated via variants of the Pólya model already described. Generally speaking, a compound distribution arises when two or several distributions are added to each other, batches of eggs can be laid at random or in a Poisson fashion, while the larvae hatched from these batches are found very close to them, distributed in a clustered or contagious fashion (Neyman, 1939, Anscombe, 1950). Many compound distributions have been derived, but in this chapter, particular attention will be drawn only to the Pólya-Aeppli (Pólya, 1930, Evans, 1953, Anscombe, 1950, Skellam, 1952, Harvey, 1965), and the Pascal or negative binomial ones (Anscombe, 1954, Harvey, 1965).

The former can be specified as

$$\left\{ \begin{array}{l} p(0) = e^{-m} \\[2em] p(x) = e^{-m} p^x \sum_{j=1}^{x} \binom{x-1}{j-1} \frac{1}{j!} \left[\frac{m(1-p)}{p} \right]^{j} \end{array} \right\} \quad x \geq 1 \tag{11}$$

where the parameters are estimated as

$$p = \frac{(s^2 - \bar{x})}{(2\bar{x} + s^2)} \tag{12}$$

and

$$m = \bar{x}(1 - p) \tag{13}$$

with $\bar{x}$ equal to the mean of the distribution and s^2 to its variance. In plant ecology, the Pólya-Aeppli function is applicable when the parent generation is distributed over the study area randomly and all at one time, while the number of off-springs increases in a geometric fashion.

The Pascal or negative binomial function, on the other hand, specifies the probability of finding a cell with x dots as

$$p(x) = \binom{k + x - 1}{x} p^k q^x \tag{14}$$

with parameters

$$p = \frac{\bar{x}}{s^2} \tag{15}$$

$$q = 1 - p \tag{16}$$

and

$$k = \frac{\bar{x}p}{q} \tag{17}$$

This function is applicable when a set of events (dots) is randomly distributed over an area, not necessarily all at the same time, and has another set of events attached to it. The number of attached events increases logarithmically over time.

But the technique of quadrat counting considers only a limited number of spatial characteristics in a distribution of points. Therefore, the technique must be supplemented by others, in which features like direction and connectivity have been explicitly analyzed. Out of these, nearest neighbor analyses should be particularly mentioned (Greig-Smith, 1964, Clark and Evans, 1954, Morisita, 1954, 1957, Thompson, 1956, Dacey, 1962a, 1962b, 1964a). This technique can be employed for computing indices of non-randomness based on distance measures from a point to its nearest neighbor or neighbors located in one or several sectors radiating from the point. Estimates of density can thus be computed as

$$d_1 = \frac{1}{\pi} \cdot \frac{n-1}{N} \sum \frac{1}{r^2} \tag{18}$$

$$d_2 = \frac{1}{\pi} \cdot \frac{nk-1}{N} \sum_{i=1}^{N} \frac{k}{\sum_{j=1}^{k} r^2_{ij}} \tag{19}$$

where r denotes distance to the nth nearest neighbor in each of k sectors containing a total of N points (Morisita, 1954, 1957). If $d_1 < d_2$ the best estimate of density is $(d_1 + d_2)/2$, while in case $d_1 > d_2$, d_1 is the best estimate. In evaluations of simulation models, a density value might be computed for the model pattern and another one for the real-world pattern. In a test of the model, the two indices can then be compared.

Finally, it has been mentioned that quadrat counts are highly influenced by the size of the cells. But, provided the patterns are on a larger scale than the size of the cells, the dots will tend to occur in adjacent quadrats. This problem can be handled by applying so called contiguity analyses (Jones, 1955, Iyer, 1950, Dacey, 1964b), whereby observed connections between neighboring areas are compared with expected random occurrences. As before, simulation models can be evaluated by comparing indices computed for simulated and real-world patterns.

REFERENCES

Ajo, R. 1955. "An Analysis of Automobile Frequencies in a Human Geographic Continuum," in *Lund Studies in Geography*, Ser. B, No. 15.

Ajo, R. 1962. "An Approach to Demographical System Analysis," *Economic Geography*, XXXVIII.

Ajo, R. 1964. "London's Field Response, I and II," *Acta Geographica*, XVIII.

Alonso, W. 1964. *Location and Land Use: Toward a General Theory of Land Rent*. Cambridge: Harvard University Press.

Améen, L. 1964. "Stadsbebyggelse och Domänstruktur." *Meddelande från Lunds Universitets Geografiska Institution*, Avhandlingar, No. 46.

Anderson, T. R., and J. A. Egeland. 1961. "Spatial Aspects of Social Area Analysis." *American Sociological Review*, XXVI.

Anscombe, F. J. 1950. "A Sampling Theory of the Negative Binomial and Logarithmic Series Distributions." *Biometrika*, XXXVII.

Bateman, A. J. 1962. "Data from Plants and Animals," in J. Sutter (ed.), *Les Déplacements Humaines*. Entretiens de Monaco en Sciences Humaines, Prémière session.

Beaujeu-Garnier, J., and G. Chabot. 1963. *Traité de Géographie Urbaine*. Paris: Librairie Armand Colin.

Bergsten, K. 1951. "Sydsvenska Födelseortsfält," in *Meddelanden från Lunds Universitets Geografiska Institution*. Avhandlingar, No. 20.

Bernouili, H. 1946. *Die Stadt und ihr Boden*. Zürich.

Berry, B. J. L. 1963. "Commercial Structure and Commercial Blight." Department of Geography, University of Chicago.

Berry, B. J. L. 1964. "Cities as Systems within Systems of Cities," in J. Friedmann and W. Alonso (eds.) *Regional Development and Planning*. Cambridge: M.I.T. Press.

Berry, B. J. L., and W. L. Garrison. 1958. "Recent Developments of Central Place Theory." *Papers and Proceedings of the Regional Science Association*, IV.

Berry, B. J. L., J. W. Simmons and R. J. Tennant. 1963. "Urban Population Densities: Structure and Change." *Geographical Review*, LIII.

Bjurström, G. 1963. "Grundundersökningar vid Översiktlig Planering." *Vägoch Vattenbyggaren*, 2.

Bowden, L. W. 1965. "Diffusion of the Decision to Irrigate." Department of Geography, University of Chicago.

Boye, Y. 1965. "Routing Methods: Principles for Handling Multiple Travelling Salesman Problems." *Lund Studies in Geography*, Ser. C., No. 5.

Bunge, W. 1962. "Theoretical Geography." In *Lund Studies in Geography*, Ser. C., no. 1.

Burgess, E. W. 1925. "The Growth of the City" in R. E. Park, *et al.* (eds.), *The City*. Chicago: University of Chicago Press.

Carroll, J., J. Douglas, and H. W. Bevis. 1957. "Predicting Local Travel in Urban Regions," *Papers and Proceedings of the Regional Science Association* III.

Carrothers, G. A. P. 1956. "An Historical Review of the Gravity and Potential Concepts of Human Interaction." *Journal of the American Institute of Planners*, XXII.

Cavalli-Sforza, L. 1962. "The Distribution of Migration Distances: Models and Applications to Genetics," in J. Sutter (ed.), *Les Déplacements Humaines*. Entretiens de Monaco en Sciences Humaines, Prémière session.

Chapin, F. S., and S. F. Weiss. 1962. *Factors Influencing Land Development*. Chapel Hill, North Carolina: Center for Urban and Region Studies.

Claeson, C. 1964. "En Korologisk Publikanalys," *Geografiska Annaler*, XLVI.

Clark, C. 1951. "Urban Population Densities." *Journal of the Royal Statistical Society*. Ser. A., Vol. 114.

Clark, P. J., and F. C. Evans. 1954. "Distance to Nearest Neighbour as a Measure of Spatial Relationships in Populations." *Ecology*, XXXV.

Colby, C. C. 1933. "Centrifugal and Centripetal Forces in Urban Geography." Annals of the Association of American Geographers, XXIII.

Conzen, M. R. G. 1958. "The Growth and Character of Whitby," in G. H. J. Daysh (ed.), *A Survey of Whitby and the Surrounding Area*.

Curry, L. 1962. "The Geography of Service Centers within Towns," in *Lund Studies in Geography*, Ser. B, No. 24.

Curry, L. 1964. "The Random Spatial Economy: An Exploration in Settlement Theory," *Annals of the Association of American Geographers*, LIV.

Curtis, J. T., and R. P. McIntosh. 1950. "The Interrelation of Certain Analytic and Synthetic Phytosociological Characters." *Ecology*, XXXI.

Dacey, M. F. 1960. "Selection of an Initial Solution for the Travelling Salesman Problem." *Journal of Operations Research*, VIII.

Dacey, M. F. 1962a. "Analysis of Central Place and Point Patterns by a Nearest Neighbor Method." *Proceedings of the IGU Symposium in Urban Geography, Lund Studies in Geography,* Ser. B., No. 24.

Dacey, M. F. 1962b. "A Note on the Derivation of Nearest Neighbor Distances." *Journal of Regional Science,* II.

Dacey, M. F. 1963. "Order Neighbor Statistics for a Class of Random Patterns in Multidimensional Space." *Annals of the Association of American Geographers,* LIII.

Dacey, M. F. 1964a. "Description of Point Pattern by Two Classes of Near Neighbor Statistics," Department of Regional Science, University of Pennsylvania.

Dacey, M. F. 1964 b. "Measures of Contiguity for Two-Color Maps." Department of Geography, Northwestern University.

Dacey, M. F. 1964c. "Modified Probability Law for Point Pattern More Regular Than Random." *Annals of the Association of American Geographers,* LIV.

Dacey, M. F. 1964d. "Two Dimensional Random Point Patterns." Department of Geography, Northwestern University.

Dacey, M. F. 1965. "A Review on Measures of Contiguity for Two and k-Color Maps," Department of Geography, Northwestern University.

Dacey, M. F., and G. Karaska. 1963. "Some Experimental Evidence on the Perception of Dot Patterns and Two Dimensional Shapes." *Regional Science Research Institute,* Discussion Paper, No. 2.

Dahl, S. 1957. "The Contacts of Västerås with the Rest of Sweden," in D. Hannerberg, et. al. (eds.), *Migration in Sweden.* Lund.

Dantzig, G. B. 1963. *Linear Programming and Extensions.* Princeton: Princeton University Press.

Dethier, L. 1962. "L'Influence de la Structure Foncière et du Dessin Parcellaire sur le Développement Urbain." *Bulletin de la Société Belge d'Études Géographiques,* Tome 31.

Deutsch, K. and W. Isard, 1961. "A Note on a Generalized Concept of Effective Distance." *Behavioral Science.*

Dickinson, R. E. 1965. *City and Region: A Geographical Interpretation.* London: Routledge & Kegan Paul.

Donelly, T. G., F. S. Chapin, and S. F. Weiss. 1964. *A Probabilistic Model for Residential Growth.* Chapel Hill, N.C.: Center for Urban and Regional Studies.

Evans, D. A. 1953. "Experimental Evidence Concerning Contagious Distributions." *Biometrika,* XL.

Feller, W. 1964. *An Introduction to Probability Theory and its Applications,* Vol. I. New York: Wiley.

Friedman, J., and W. Alonso (eds.) 1964. *Regional Development and Planning.* Cambridge: M.I.T. Press.

Garrison, W. L. 1962. "Toward Simulation Models of Urban Growth and Development." *Lund Studies in Geography,* Ser. B., No. 24.

Greig-Smith, P. 1964. *Quantitative Plant Ecology.* London: Butterworths.

Hadley, G. 1962. *Linear Programming.* Reading, Mass: Addison-Wesley.

Hägerstrand, T. 1953. *"Innovations-förloppet ur Korologisk Synpunkt."* Lund: Gleerups Förlag.

Hägerstrand, T. 1965. "A Monte Carlo Approach to Diffusion," *Archives Européenes de Sociologie,* VI.

Haig, R. M. 1928. *Major Economic Factors in Metropolitan Growth and Arrangement.* New York.

Hammersley, J. M., and D. C. Handscomb. 1964. *Monte Carlo Methods.* London: Methuen.

Harris, C. D., and E. L. Ullman. 1945. "The Nature of Cities." *Annals of the American Academy of Political and Social Science,* CCXLII.

Hartke, W. 1953. "Die Soziale Differenzierung der Agrar-Landschaft im Rhein-Main-Gebiet. *Erdkunde,* 1953, Band 7.

Harvey, D. 1965. "Geographic Processes and the Analyses of Point Patterns." Department of Geography, University of Bristol and Pennsylvania State University.

Henderson, J. M. 1958. *The Efficiency of the Coal Industry.* Cambridge: Harvard University Press.

Hoyt, H. 1939. *The Structure and Growth of Residential Neighborhoods in American Cities.* Washington: U.S. Government.

Isard, W. 1956. *Location and Space Economy.* Cambridge: M.I.T. Press.

Isard, W. 1960. *Methods of Regional Analysis.* Cambridge: M.I.T. Press.

Isard, W. and T. A. Reiner. 1965. "Regional Science." Paper presented at the fifth European Congress of the Regional Science Association, Krakow.

Iyer, P. V. K. 1950. "The Theory of Probability Distributions of Points on a Lattice." *Annals of Mathematical Statistics,* XXI.

Järhult, D. 1958. "Arbetskraftsrekryteringen vid Norrbottens Järnverk AB: En Migrationsundersökning," in *Meddelande från Geografiska Institutet vid Stockholms Högskola,* No. 113.

Johnsson, H. 1952. "En Stads Flyttnings- och Födelseortsfält," in *Svensk Geografisk Årsbok, Årg.* 28.

Jones, E. W. 1955. "Ecological Studies on the Rain Forest of Southern Nigeria." *Journal of Ecology,* XLIII.

Kant, E. 1951. "Omlandsforskning och Sektoranalys," in G. Enequist (ed.), *Tätorter och Omland.* Uppsala: Lundequistska Bokhandeln.

Lakshmanan, T. R., and W. G. Hansen. 1965. "A Retail Market Potential Model." *Journal of the American Institute of Planners,* XXXI.

Lassau, C. 1962. *Annexation of Unincorporated Territory.* Evanston: Northwestern University Press.

Lathrop, G. T., and J. R. Hamburg. 1965. "An Opportunity-Accessibility Model for Allocating Regional Growth." *Journal of the American Institute of Planners*, XXXI.

Lövgren, E. 1956. "The Geographical Mobility of Labor," *Geografiska Annaler*, XXXVIII.

Lowry, I. S. 1964. "A Model of Metropolis." Memo RM-4035-RC. Santa Monica: Rand Corporation.

Lukermann, F., and P. W. Porter. 1960. "Gravity and Potential Models in Economic Geography." *Annals of the Association of Economic Geographers*, I.

MacKay, W. R. 1958. "The Interactance Hypothesis and Boundaries in Canada: A Preliminary Study," *Canadian Geographer*, XI.

Malm, R., and O. Wärneryd. 1965. "Urban Growth and Barrier Effects." *Proceedings from the First Scandinavian-Polish Regional Science Seminar*. Szcecin, Poland.

Marble, D. F., and J.D. Nystuen. 1963. "An Approach to the Direct Measurement of Community Mean Information Fields," *Papers of the Regional Science Association*, XI.

Mayer, H. M., and C. F. Kohn (eds.) 1959. *Readings in Urban Geography*. Chicago: University of Chicago Press.

Micklander, A. 1965. "Gravitation och Regression," in G. Olsson and O. Wärneryd (eds.), *Meddelande från ett Symposium i Teoretisk Samhällsgeografi*. Uppsala Universitet.

Möller, I. 1959. *Die Entwicklung eines Hamburger Gebietes von der Agrarzur*. Hamburg: Geogr. Stud., H. 10.

Morisita, M. 1954. "Estimation of Population Density by Spacing Method," in *Memoirs of the Faculty of Science*. Kyushu University, Ser. E, Vol. 1.

Morisita, M. 1957. "A New Method for the Estimation of Density by the Spacing Method Applicable to Non-Randomly Distributed Populations." *Psychology and Ecology*, VII.

Morrill, R. L. 1963(a). "The Distribution of Migration Distances," in *Papers of the Regional Science Association,* Vol. 11.

Morrill, R. L. 1963(b)· "The Development of Spatial Distributions of Towns in Sweden." *Annals of the Association of American Geographers,* LIII.

Morrill, R. L. 1965(a)· "Migration and Spread and Growth of Urban Settlement." *Lund Studies in Geography,* Ser. B., Human Geography, No. 26.

Morrill, R. L. 1965(b)· "The Negro Ghetto: Problems and Alternatives." *Geographical Review,* LV.

Morrill, R. L. and F. R. Pitts. 1963. "Marriage, Migration and the Mean Information Field: A Study in Uniqueness and Centrality" (unpublished manuscript).

Murdie, R. A. 1965. Cultural Differences in Consumer Travel," *Economic Geography,* XL1.

Muth, R. F. 1961a. "The Spatial Structure of the Housing Market. *Papers and Proceedings of the Regional Science Association,* VII.

Muth, R. F. 1961b. "Economic Change and Rural-Urban Land-Use Conversions." *Econometrica* XXIX.

Neyman, J. 1939. "A New Class of 'Contagious' Distributions Applicable in Entomology and Bacteriology." *Annals of Mathematical Statistics,* X.

Norberg, K. (ed.) 1962. *Proceedings of the IGU Symposium in Urban Geography, Lund Studies in Geography,* Ser. B., No. 24.

Nystuen, J. D. 1963. "Identification of Some Fundamental Spatial Concepts." *Papers of the Michigan Academy of Science, Arts, and Letters,* Vol. 48.

Olsson, G. 1965a. "Distance and Human Interaction: A Migration Study." *Geografiska Annaler,* XLVII, Ser. B .

Olsson, G. 1865b. *Distance and Human Interaction.* Philadelphia: Regional Science Research Institute.

Olsson, G. 1965c. "Inductive and Deductive Approaches to Model Formulation." *Proceedings from the First Scandinavian-Polish Regional Science Seminar.* Szeecin, Poland.

Olsson, W. 1937. "Huvuddragen av Stockholms Geografiska Utveckling 1850-1930," in *Meddelande från Geografiska Institutet vid Stockholms Högskola,* No. 37.

Olsson, W. 1940. "Stockholm: Its Structure and Development." *Geographical Review,* XXX.

Pollack, M., and W. Wiebenson. 1960. "Solutions of the Shortest Route Problem: A Review." *Journal of Operations Research,* VIII.

Pólya, G. 1930. "Sur Quelques Points de la Théorie des Probabilités. *Annales de l'Institut Henri Poincaré,* I.

Ratcliff, R. U. 1955. "Efficiency in the Location of Urban Activities," in R. M. Fisher (ed.), *The Metropolis in Modern Life.* New York: Doubleday.

Reilly, W. J. 1931. *The Law of Retail Gravitation.* New York: Knickerbocker Press.

Robinson, P. 1954. "The Distribution of Plant Populations." *Annals of Botany,* XVIII.

Ruppert, K. 1955. "Der Wandel der Sozialgeographischen Struktur im Bilde der Landschaft." *Die Erde,* Band 7.

Seyfried, W. R. 1963. "The Centrality of Urban Land Values." *Land Economics,* XXXIX.

Shepard, R. N. 1962. "The Analysis of Proximities: Multidimensional Scaling with an Unknown Distance Function, I and II." *Psychometrika,* XXVII.

Skellam, J. G. 1952. "Studies in Statistical Ecology: I. Spatial Pattern." *Biometrika,* XXXIX.

Steger, W. A. 1965. "The Pittsburgh Urban Renewal Simulation Model." *Journal of the American Institute of Planners,* XXXI.

Stewart, J. Q., and W. Warntz. 1958. "Physics of Population Distribution," *Journal of Regional Science,* I.

Sund, T. 1947. "Bergens Byområde og dets Geografiske Utvikling 1900-1940." *Skrifter fra Norges Handelshøyskole,* No. 2.

Taaffe, E. J., B. J. Garner, and M. H. Yeates. 1963. *The Peripheral Journey to Work.* Evanston, Ill.: North-western University Press.

Tanner, J. C. 1961. "Factors Affecting the Amount of Travel," *Road Research Paper* 51. Middlesex, England.

Thompson, H. R. 1956. "Distribution of Distance to nth Neighbour in a Population of Randomly Distributed Individuals." *Ecology,* XXXVII.

von Thünen, J. H. 1826. *Der Isolierte Staat in Beziehung auf Landwirtschaft und Nationalökonomi.* Hamburg.

Tobler, W. R. 1961. "Map Transformations of Geographic Space." Unpublished Ph.D. Dissertation, University of Washington.

Tobler, W. R. 1963. "Geographic Area and Map Projections." *Geographical Review,* LIII.

Ward, D. 1962. "The Pre-Urban Cadastre and the Urban Pattern of Leeds." *Annals of the Association of American Geographers,* LII.

Wärneryd, O. 1965. *Interaktion Mellan Urbaniserade Regioner.* Unpublished FL-thesis, Göteborgs Universitet.

Watson, J. W. 1955." Geography: A Discipline in Distance." *Scottish Geographical Magazine,* LXXI.

Wingo, L. 1961a. "An Economic Model of the Utilization of Urban Land for Residential Purposes," in *Paper and Proceedings of the Regional Science Association,"* VII.

Wingo, L. 1961b. *Transportation and Urban Land.* Washington, D.C.: Resources for the Future.

Wright, J. K. 1936. "The Diversity of New York City."
    Geographic Review, XXVI.

Yuill, R. S. 1965. "A Simulation Study of Barrier Effects
    in Spatial Diffusion Problems," in *Michigan Inter-
    University Community of Mathematical Geographers*,
    Discussion Paper, #5.

Zipf, G. K. 1949. *Human Behavior and the Principle of Least
    Effort*. Reading, Mass.: Addision-Wesley.

A 5
B 6
C 7
D 8
E 9
F 0
G 1
H 2
I 3
J 4